BEHIND THE MYTHS

THE FOUNDATIONS OF JUDAISM, CHRISTIANITY AND ISLAM

JOHN PICKARD

authorHOUSE®

AuthorHouse™
1663 Liberty Drive
Bloomington, IN 47403
www.authorhouse.com
Phone: 1-800-839-8640

Published by AuthorHouse   02/21/2013

ISBN: 978-1-4817-8362-0 (sc)
ISBN: 978-1-4817-8363-7 (e)

Contents

Introduction

As the twenty first century progresses, there has been an increasing interest and not a small amount of debate on the role of religion in society, on the rise of secularisation and on the role of religion in politics. The neo-liberal right wing in the United States is overwhelmingly supported by fundamentalist Christian organisations whose support for the billionaire-class is dressed up in the language of piety and self-righteousness. Internationally, many of the key political issues of war, revolution and social upheaval are brought into sharp focus by what appear, on the surface, to be issues of religious faith.

In the UK, Richard Dawkins' book, *The God Delusion*, was a best-seller and novels like *The Good Man Jesus and the Scoundrel Christ* by Richard Pullman touched raw nerves in church hierarchies. Against what they see as a growing tide of secularism, spokespersons for the Church have denounced the 'intolerance' of atheism and have fought a vigorous rearguard action to defend the special *public* position for faith, woven into the fabric of everyday life. Faith, they have argued, is more than a 'private' matter and must feature as part of wider, civil society. Alongside it and as part of the debate, there has been an on-going argument about Science education and the role that must be assigned to the story of the 'Creation' now propagated in its new guise of 'Intelligent Design'. In the United States especially, the extreme neo-conservative Right allies itself openly and unashamedly to what they see as Christian principles and draws its inspiration from the Bible as the unerring Word of God.

But if there is a significant weakness in the arguments of many modern atheists and secularists, it is that their case is presented as if the whole question of religion is purely an *ideological* struggle, an intellectual debate in which the followers of religion are charged with harbouring inferior and inconsistent ideas. This may indeed be the case, but it is important to see the historic foundation of these religions—and their continuation within society up to the present day—as being rooted in *material social conditions* and not due to intellectual stubbornness or obtuseness. Religions have not arisen in the past simply because their new *ideas* were superior and therefore supplanted the older, inferior *ideas*. The fundamental aim of this book is to demonstrate that the origins of Judaism, Christianity and Islam, were each rooted in a specific set of social and economic conditions at given moments in history. These material conditions were expressed ideologically—in political, but above all in religion movements. The new faiths *reflected* changes in society and politics rather than being their *cause*.

This is not to suggest that ideas have no place in historical development. Far from it; as Marx himself pointed out, when an *idea* gains mass support in society, it becomes a powerful *material* force. There is no doubt that in the history of religious movements—and still today—there have been many, many examples of individuals who have felt themselves inspired and motivated by religious fervour. Nor would we doubt that millions take daily comfort from the pressing problems of everyday life in God or in a spiritual world. But the sincerity and the passion of their beliefs does not explain for an atheist why ideas can gain a foothold at particular times in history and not others. School history books have traditionally focused on kings, queens and rulers and the majority of historical works today still explain historical developments, including religious movements, purely within the framework of ideas and charismatic individuals. This work seeks to redress the balance and focuses instead on real social forces as the *fundamental* drivers of history; it argues that the origins of new religious movements owe more to the national and class conflicts of the day than to theological clashes or debates about the nature of God. Likewise, in the future, it will not be 'defeat' in debates or ridicule by atheists that will lead to the decline of religion. It will be from the clashes of social contradictions and class forces that *a new social order* will be created within which religion faith and observance are no longer deemed necessary and after which they will wither away.

Marx and Engels

The economic crash of 2008 has ushered in a new age of permanent austerity and social conflict and in parallel with this there has been a renewed interest in the ideas of Karl Marx and his collaborator, Friedrich Engels. In economics, politics and philosophy, there have been a re-examination of the ideas of the old 'masters' and a re-appraisal of their relevance to the problems of today's society. It is in the spirit of their ideas and their basic philosophy that this book is presented. It aims to describe the historical roots of Judaism, Christianity and Islam—the so-called 'Abramic' faiths—using the method of historical materialism as it was developed by Marx and Engels. The two great founders of scientific socialism based their outlook on a consistently materialist view, moreover one which they applied to society and not just to the natural world. "Marx and I", Engels wrote, "were pretty well the only people to rescue conscious dialectics from German idealist philosophy and apply it in the materialist conception of nature and history".[1] In *The German Ideology*, the fundamental theme of historical materialism was elaborated by Marx:

> "The first premise of all human history is, of course, the existence of living human individuals. Thus the first fact to be established is the physical organisation of these individuals and their consequent relation to the rest of nature . . . . Men can be distinguished from animals by consciousness, by religion or anything else you like. They themselves begin to distinguish themselves from animals as soon as they begin to produce their means of subsistence, a step which is conditioned by their physical organisation. By producing their means of subsistence men are indirectly producing their actual material life"[2]

---

[1]   Preface to *Anti-Duhring*, Friedrich Engels, 1878,
[2]   Marx and Engels, *The German Ideology*, p 42

In *The Introduction to Contribution To The Critique Of Hegel's Philosophy Of Right*, Marx made specific comments on the role and origin of religion in society. "*Man makes religion*", he wrote, "Religion does not make man".

"Religion is the self-consciousness and self-esteem of man who has either not yet found himself or has already lost himself again. But *man* is no abstract being encamped outside the world. Man is *the world of man*, the state, society. This state, this society, produce religion, an *inverted world-consciousness*, because they are an *inverted world*. Religion is the general theory of that world, its encyclopaedic compendium, its logic in a popular form, its spiritualistic *point d'honneur*, its enthusiasm, its moral sanction, its solemn complement, its universal source of consolation and justification. It is the *fantastic realisation* of the human essence because the *human essence* has no true reality. The struggle against religion is therefore indirectly a fight against *the other world* of which religion is the spiritual *aroma*. *Religious* distress is at the same time the *expression* of real distress and also the *protest* against real distress. Religion is the sigh of the oppressed creature, the heart of a heartless world, just as it is the spirit of a spiritless situation. It is the *opium* of the people."[3]

In *Anti-Duhring*, Engels wrote:

"The materialist conception of history starts from the proposition that the production and, next to production, the exchange of things produced, is the basis of all social structure; that in every society that has appeared in history, the manner in which wealth is distributed and society divided into classes or estates is dependent upon what is produced, how it is produced, and how the products are exchanged. From this point of view the final causes of all social changes and political revolutions are to be sought, not in men's brains, not in man's better insight into eternal truth and justice, but in changes in the modes of production and exchange. They are to be sought, not in the *philosophy*, but in the *economics* of each particular epoch. The growing perception that existing social institutions are unreasonable and unjust, that reason has become unreason, and right wrong, is only proof that in the modes of production and exchange changes have silently taken place with which the social order, adapted to earlier economic conditions, is no longer in keeping. From this it also follows that the means of getting rid of the incongruities that have been brought to light must also be present, in a more or less developed condition, within the changed modes of production themselves. These

---

[3] Marx, *Introduction to Contribution To The Critique Of Hegel's Philosophy Of Right*.

means are not to be ***invented***, spun out of the head, but ***discovered*** with the aid of the head in the existing material facts of production."[4]

But while Marx and Engels argued for the importance of economic developments as the *fundamental* drivers of historical change, they bridled at what they saw as a crude and simplistic view of historical change, in which ideas, programmes and political theories were simply a mechanical reflection of underlying material processes. The interactions, they insisted, were far more complex. Engels, in a letter to the German social democrat, Bloch, explained his view and that of Marx:

> "According to the materialist conception of history, the *ultimately* determining element in history is the production and reproduction of real life. More than that, neither Marx nor I have ever asserted. Hence if somebody twists this into saying that the economic element is the *only* determining one, he transforms that proposition into a meaningless, abstract, senseless phrase.

> The economic situation is the basis, but the various elements of the superstructure—political forms of the class struggle and its results, to wit: constitutions established by victorious classes after a successful battle, etc., juridical forms and even the reflexes of these actual struggles in the brains of the participants, political, juristic, philosophical theories, religious views and their further development into systems of dogmas—also exercise their influence upon the course of the historical struggles and in many cases preponderate in determining their form . . .

There is an interaction of all these elements in which, amid all the endless host of accidents, the economic element finally asserts itself as necessary."[5]

This book makes no claims to be a *history* of Judaism, Christianity and Islam: it looks only at their *origins*. By using the methods of historical materialism, it is attempting to make a contribution to explaining the historical foundations of these three faiths. The fundamental outlook of this work is that while what might be called the *theological* considerations may have been important, they were *entirely secondary* to the general political, social and economic movements of the ancient world and it is these latter factors that we have tried to draw out. It may be that priests, bishops and imams concern themselves with theological matters; after all, they need to justify their existence. But for the overwhelming majority of people, the adoption of a religious mantle is above all a social, political and an economic decision. It remains the case to this day that a person's religion, in ninety-nine per cent of cases, is a matter of the national, ethnic, cultural and family identity into which they were born.

---

[4]   *Anti-Duhring, p 316*
[5]   Engels: letter to Bloch, of 21/22 September 1890 (italics added)

This book makes no apology for taking as a starting point a *materialist* view. Even where there are elements of history that are lost in the mists of time—and there are many—no credence whatsoever has been given to *supernatural* explanations, whether through God, his angels, prophetic visions, miracles, or magic. Historical change may have different interpretations and explanations—and there may be better ones than those put forward here—but in the last analysis it is based on real and not imaginary events. At this point, readers of one faith or another should put the book down and read no further. This book is not for them: it is written, to paraphrase the words of Patricia Crone, ". . . by an infidel, for infidels." This book is intended to be neither an insult nor a comfort to the faithful: it is an unashamed guide for unbelievers, part of a discussion among atheists and secularists.

Karl Kautsky

2008 marked the centenary of the publication by the German socialist Karl Kautsky of his book, *The Foundations of Christianity*, which was the first attempt to describe the rise of Christianity from the standpoint of class forces and the material developments of society using the method of historical materialism, in contrast to the official histories of the Church and the alleged history of the New Testament. Kautsky rejected the metaphysical myths behind Christianity—the miracles, supernatural events, and so on—and attempted to describe a history based on the social conditions that existed in the Roman Empire in the first three centuries of the modern era. Karl Kautsky's book was deficient in some respects, but his key arguments still stand scrutiny today.

I was a typical young socialist in the early 1970s in that I came from a working class background, the son of a sheet-metal worker and an auxiliary nurse. Like the majority of my comrades, I had a thirst for political theory and for an explanation for all the social and political processes going on around me, including religion. Having been alienated for several years from the Church I had attended in an earlier period, I was already looking for explanations for where Christianity came from, when I was introduced to Kautsky's *Foundations*. This book was not an easy read, but it had a great effect on me, as no doubt it had on hundreds of thousands or even millions of young socialists and activists since its original publication. It provided a solid base to my maturing atheist ideas. It is the aim of this book to play the same role today as was played by Kautsky's *Foundations* in the past. Just as Karl Kautsky's book helped to educate many generations of young activists, this book is aimed, with all due modesty, to make a similar contribution, not only by updating the *Foundation* study on Christianity, but by broadening it out to include its two related religions, Judaism and Islam.

This book is aimed at underpinning the beliefs of those atheists, agnostics and secularists who are opposed to, or who are just coming into opposition to the philosophies of these established religions. It is the culmination of decades of personal research and enquiry, a process that was started with a genuinely open mind about the historicity of figures like Moses, Jesus and Mohammed. It draws heavily from the work of renowned archaeologists and scholars in the fields of ancient Hebrew, Aramaic, Greek, Arabic and so on: historians whose skills and abilities have allowed them to surpass the modest efforts of the author of this book. In many instances a sentence or paragraph of theirs has been used to convey an idea far more lucidly than I could have done. The only *a priori* condition attached to the research was an unshakeable belief in a materialist world outlook. That means that whatever the directions pointed to by the work of great scholars of the past, the truth of 'what really happened' necessarily ruled out miracles, visions, angels, divine intervention and all things 'godly'. The published works of scholars, therefore, have been used as authoritative resources to lay bare the *real* history, in contrast to the *mythical* histories, of these three faiths.

Acknowledgements

I am extremely grateful for the help and support given by a number of friends and comrades in discussing drafts of sections of this book and in making some useful suggestions for changes. I am indebted to Terry Moston in Germany and Bill Hopwood in Canada for readings and suggestions and to Ed Collingwood for help with the graphics. I am especially grateful for the many discussions I have had with Brian Ingham and Roger Silverman in London and with Peter Doyle in Cumbria. Peter is a life-long friend and comrade from my days in Tyneside and he has been especially encouraging as this project has developed over the months and years.

Thanks are also due to Tracey Howton, Lee Singh Gill and Beverley Turner for proof-reading the final manuscript and to Rob Sewell for advice in the final phases of publication.

Last but not least, I am grateful for the encouragement, support and patience of my family who have suffered for the hundreds of 'Jesus' and 'Mohammed' books that have fallen onto the mat behind the front door and have no doubt wondered what it has done to the family budget.

John Pickard
January 2013

Comments to: Behindthemyths@live.com

Technical notes

<u>Dates</u>
Throughout the book, CE (Common Era) is used to indicate years rather than the somewhat tendentious AD (*Anno Domini*, 'Year of the Lord'), except in occasional quotations and where there is a particular reason for using the Islamic calendar designation (AH). The Islamic calendar begins at 622 CE and is based on a lunar cycle so it is therefore at least this number of years 'behind' the 'common' calendar. Correspondingly, BCE is used for 'Before the Common Era'.

<u>Names</u>
There are a variety of spellings of most of the names used, particularly those taken from Arabic (for example: Umar or Omar, Uthman or Outhman), but in most cases the simplest transliteration into English has been used, with some attempt to be consistent throughout. For example, we have used Mohammed (not Muhammad), Caliph (not Kaliph) and Koran (not Q'ran or Qur'an). Words borrowed from the Arabic but commonly used in English are not italicised, but words used less commonly in English have been italicised throughout, thus: *fatwa, hadith, mawali* and *sunna*.

<u>Squared Brackets</u>
Squared brackets inserted in cited text are short comments or clarifications by the author.

<u>Biblical and Koranic quotes</u>
Quotes from the Bible are in the normal format, thus *Exodus 12, 14* for chapter 12, verse 14. Where there are two books with a similar name, the number of the book is written first, as in 1 Kings, ie the first book of Kings.

Quotes from the Koran use a similar system, citing the number of the *sura* first and the *verse* afterwards, as in 12, 34.

Glossary

(Most readers will have been educated in the Judeo-Christian cultural tradition, so it is not surprising that most of the items in the glossary are Arabic words)

Abbasids—The Arab dynasty succeeding the Umayyads after the revolution of 750, named descent from an Arab notable, Abbas. The dynasty lasted until 940 CE.

Abd—servant or slave of, as in *Abd Allah*, servant of God.

Ali—according to tradition, the fourth Caliph after Mohammed, being the cousin and son-in-law of the Prophet. Tradition has it that he was defeated by Mu'awiya' and his sons and grandsons murdered in Iraq. Support for the Alid Imams and recognition of their martyrdom form the basis of the Shi'ite sect of Islam.

Alids—the descendents of the fourth Caliph after Mohammed, and those who supported this political movement.

Apocrypha—documents and esoteric scripture that is not considered 'canonical' or 'official', often of questionable or spurious authenticity.

Byzantines—the 'Roman' empire in the eastern Mediterranean its capital city being Constantinople, formerly Byzantium. Prior to the Arab empire, Syria (modern-day Syria, Lebanon, Jordan, Palestine and Israel) and Egypt were part of the Byzantine empire.

Caliph (Khalif)—most often described as 'successor', as in *Khalifat Rasul Allah* (successor of the Messenger of God). However, 'representative' was a more common understanding, since the early caliphs described themselves as *Khalifat Allah*, which could hardly have meant 'successors' of God.

Day'a—forms of land grants given by the caliph to family and favourites.

Dhimmis—non-Muslims, usually taken to be local peasants and workers.

Dihqans—local Iranian notables and big landowners who often established local dynasties of their own. After the Arab conquest these became the intermediaries between the Arab rulers and the local peasantry in relation to tax collection.

Fatwa—a 'ruling' by Islamic scholars.

Fitnah—civil wars between Muslims.

Gerousia—a committee of elders

Ghassanids—Arabs and the rulers in pre-Islamic Syria and parts of western Iraq, forming a client state of the Byzantine Empire

Hadith—the written tradition surrounding the life and teachings of Mohammed and his Companions.

Hajj—the pilgrimage to Mecca.

Hejaz—the desert hinterland of the Arabian Peninsula.

Hijra—the emigration of Mohammed and his followers from Mecca to Medina.

Ibn—often shortened to simple b, meaning 'son of'

Isnad—a chain of oral transmission of a tradition, usually from the Prophet onwards, with the names of the transmitters up to the time of their being written.

Jahiliyya—according to Islamic tradition, the period before Islam, one of idolatry, polytheism and paganism.

Ka'ba—the ancient shrine at Mecca and the focus of Muslim pilgrimage.

Kharajites—described in Islamic tradition as pious tribesmen, the murderers of Ali. The term is more likely a collective description for a wide variety of different insurrectionary opponents of the Umayyads, sometimes tribally-based bandits or revolutionary peasants and probably Muslim or Christian.

Lakhmids—Arab and the rulers who were clients of the Sassanid empire in eastern and southern Iraq and the Gulf, in similar position as the Ghassanids within the Byzantine empire, although with a longer tradition and, with Hira, the first Arabic-speaking capital city.

Mawali—converts to Islam from the conquered peoples, adopted as 'clients' by Arab tribes or notables.

Mohammed—The Prophet of Islam, as a *proper noun*, but with lower case 'm', meaning 'praiseworthy' or 'he who is praised'.

Pentateuch—the Greek translation of the **Torah**

Ptolemies—Hellenic rulers of Egypt following the death of Alexander the Great. (see also *Seleucids*)

Rasul—messenger, as in *Khalifat Rasul Allah* (successor of the Messenger of God)

Qata'i—forms of land grants given by the caliph to family and favourites.

Qibla—the direction of prayer for Muslims ie towards the Grand Mosque in Mecca. The direction of Mecca therefore dictates the architectural design of mosques, with the exception of the Dome of the Rock in Jerusalem, the first 'grand' mosque ever built.

Sassanids—the dynasty ruling the Persian empire prior to the Arab conquest. The Persian empire stretched from modern-day Iraq to Afghanistan in the east.

Seleucids—Hellenic rulers of Persia following the death of Alexander the Great. (see also *Ptolemies*)

Septuagint—the Greek translation of the early Hebrew Bible. This formed the basis of the later Christian Old Testament and differs in its composition from the later canonised Hebrew Bible the Tanakh.

Shia—originally supporters of the 'Party of Ali', *Shiat Ali*. Now the second main branch of Islam after Sunni Islam. (Also '*Shi'ite*')

Sira—the definitive description specifically of Mohammed's life and good works.

Sunna—the 'correct' interpretation of the life and works of Mohammed—hence, also, 'Sunni' Muslims, therefore the mainstream tradition describing the life and revelations of the Mohammed.

Sura—a section of the Koran, roughly equivalent to 'books' or 'chapters' in the Bible. The suras are named and numbered and sub-divided into verses.

Syncretism—the fusion of two or more different religious traditions, views or practices.

Tafsir—a commentary or commentaries on the meaning of a section of the Koran

Tanakh—the Hebrew Bible, equivalent to the Old Testament for Christians

Terminus a quo—the *earliest* possible date for an event or period

Terminus ad quem—the *latest* possible date for an event or period

Torah—the first five books of the Hebrew Bible

Tradents—a person responsible for preserving or handing on oral tradition.

Ulema—Muslim clerics.

Umayyads—the Arab Caliphal dynasty ruling after the first four Caliphs, named from an Arab notable, Umayi.

Umma—traditionally, the *community* of Muslims founded by Mohammed in Medina. The word pre-dates Islam but it has come to mean exclusively the *Islamic* community.

PART I

THE FOUNDATIONS OF JUDAISM

Chapter 1

Early myths: Creation, Exodus and Conquest

In this first chapter, we will look at the narrative of Jewish history as it is appears in the Bible and we will show that the Bible is a collection of books written by specific people, for specific reasons, at specific times. We will argue that the stories of the Creation and the Flood are legends common to all the ancient cultures of the Near East and that the books are an accumulation of writings, each with a real history rooted in the material conditions of ancient Israel/Palestine. Although the Bible, as a collection of books, has a real history, nearly all of the 'historical' narrative written in the first five books of the Old Testament is mythical.

. . . .

The first part of the Bible comprises the collection of books known to Christians as the "Old Testament" and to Jews as the "Tanakh" or simply the Hebrew Bible. It is a huge book; a mixture of myth, ritual laws, short stories, wisdom sayings, proverbs, poetry, songs and narrative descriptions of events. For biblical literalists, these narratives are a history of the Jewish people over the best part of four millennia, starting with the creation of the world in 4004 BCE, as dated by Archbishop Ussher in the seventeenth century. Modern day fundamentalists still use the writings in the Old Testament to argue against gay rights, women's rights or other democratic norms. It might seem incredible to rational people but in twenty-first century Israel it is the three thousand year-old stories of the Hebrew patriarchs and the biblical "covenant" between God and the Hebrew people which are used as justification for the ethnic cleansing of Jerusalem and for the Israeli settlement policy on Palestinian land. Biblical tradition is so deeply embedded in western culture and literature that arguably the majority of people—including many who are not even religious—still think that most of the narrative history of the Hebrew Bible is a more or less factual description of real events.

The first five books of the Bible are known to Jews as the Torah, also referred to as the Pentateuch from the Greek translation. With the addition of another nineteen books, it makes up the Tanakh which has been further supplemented over many centuries by rabbinical interpretations, explanations and commentaries to create a huge compilation of writings many times bigger than the original works. It is the Torah, however, which forms the core of Jewish scripture: the Books of Genesis, Exodus, Leviticus, Numbers and Deuteronomy, sometimes also referred to as the Books of Moses, from their supposed author. The Torah in use today originates from a manuscript dated around 900 CE and is known as the Masoretic Text. The discovery of books from the Torah among the Dead Sea Scrolls, dated

3

from the first century BCE, show that the Masoretic Text of the tenth century had not significantly changed for over a thousand years.

But for all its elevation to Holy Scripture, the large majority of modern biblical scholars believe that the Bible is a collection of books written by a variety of authors at different times and for different reasons. It is a literary accumulation with a real history rooted in the material conditions of ancient Israel/Palestine, including all the economic, political and social contradictions of the time. Prior to their 'canonisation', that is to say, their recognition as 'official' religious works, the books of the Bible were copied many times over and that inevitably caused additions, revisions and amendments to the text. Large passages, including sometimes whole chapters, can be seen to be repeated word for word in different books of the Bible, showing that sections of one were at one time copied into another by a later scribe. Large parts of the Second Book of Kings, chapter 19, for example, are identical to parts of the Book of Isaiah, chapters 36 and 37. The same historical events are sometimes described in different books in alternative ways, often one in contradiction to the other.

There are also occasional references in the text to other, books that may once have existed and have since been lost. In the accounts of the lives and work of the various kings of Judea and Israel, for example, there are frequent references to the "book of the chronicles of the kings of Judea" or the "chronicles of the kings of Israel". Elsewhere, there is reference to the "Book of Jasher". Without new archaeological discoveries, we have no way of knowing one way or the other if these books really existed.

In addition to the books within the canon, there are others that were not given the official seal of approval. These are known as the 'pseudepigrapha' ("false writings"). It is now thought, from the discovery of a lot of fragments of these texts among the Dead Sea Scrolls, that some of the books described as pseudepigrapha, like the Book of Enoch, were in fact much older than others within the official canon and it now appears that they circulated widely in Jewish communities in the first two or three centuries BCE.

Unfortunately, many historians of Judaism, have taken the Bible on face value as the foundation of their historical accounts. To take one tiny example, Max Margolis and Alexander Marx, in their *History of the Jewish People*, wrote: "After the death of Moses, the leadership of the nation fell to Joshua, an Ephraimite, trained in the arts of warfare and in statecraft."[6] In fact there is no historical evidence, other than the biblical story, that Moses or Joshua ever existed and the 'history' written by these two authors is no more than the biblical account reworked and rendered into modern prose. Another historian of the same period, Simon Dubnov, who we shall quote from time to time, wrote the classic ten-volume *History of the Jews*, based on what he called a "shift to a broader scientific conception of Jewish history,

---

[6]   Max L Margolis and Alexander Marx, *A History of the Jewish People*, 1927

to a *sociological* method"[7]. Dubnov's "sociological method" has not stopped him including, without questioning it, a great deal of historical detail which is also taken directly from the Bible, again with no confirmation from any other source. We have mentioned only two here, but thousands of books have been written on the history of Judaism, and are still being written, which are based fundamentally on the unreliable narratives collected into the Hebrew Bible. Every day, in hundreds of thousands of schools around the world, a rehash of the Old Testament is served up to children as the "history" of the Jewish people, when it is nothing of the sort. As it has been put by Norman Gottwald, one of the scholars we shall quote at length,

> ". . . the Hebrew Bible is an abiding legacy that has insinuated itself so pervasively into all historical inquiry about ancient Israel that we remain under the spell of a sacred aura surrounding the very subject of biblical Israel."[8]

We shall argue that an "Israelite" or "proto-Israelite" culture only developed in Canaan[9] from the fourteenth to the thirteenth century BCE and that this formed the basis of the only two "Jewish"[10] states attested by non-biblical evidence: *Israel* in the north of Canaan, and *Judah* in the south. The first of these lasted from approximately the ninth to the eighth century BCE and the second, from the eighth to the sixth. Moreover, the entire formative period of Judaism was dominated by the impact of the great empires around Canaan: in rough chronological order, the Egyptian, Assyrian, Babylonian, Persian, Greek and Roman. In common with most biblical historians, we shall argue that the earliest possible date for the writing of the first biblical text,

---

[7]   Simon Dubnov, *The History of the Jews, volume 1: from the beginning to the early Christian era"*(italics in the original)

[8]   Gottwald, *The Politics of Ancient Israel*, p 3

[9]   Even the place-name *Canaan* is probably a biblical literary construct: there is no archaeological evidence for its use as a place-name as it is in the Bible. However, for convenience, we will use it in its biblical meaning, to describe the region approximating to modern-day Israel/Palestine.

[10]   The names *Jews, Hebrews* and *Israelites* are often used interchangeably in literature, especially when looking backwards from a modern vantage point. However, the terms arose at different times. The earliest recorded use of the word *Israel* to describe some of the people living in Canaan is Egyptian and dates from the end of the thirteenth century BCE. There is no evidence whatsoever that "Israelite" was the name these people of Canaan used to call themselves, at least before the compilation of the Torah between the seventh and sixth centuries. However, for convenience and for the lack of an alternative, this is the name we will use. The word *Hebrew* was used by outsiders in reference to the same people and its origin may date back to the mid fourteenth century. (See later section on the Amarna Letters). That term also came to be the used for the local language, one of a group of Western Semitic languages. We will from this point use the words in their appropriate historical setting so that, for example, the much later word, *Jew* is not used until the approximate time when the term came into common use, from a Persian derivative of *Judah*, from the sixth century BCE onwards.

in something like the form that would be recognisable to us, *is the seventh century BC*, and that this took place *in Judah*, as a reflection of the material interests of the Judahite monarchy. Refinement and editing of the texts continued for at least another two centuries and later books, like Maccabees and the Book of Daniel, were written much later, around the middle of the second century BCE.

Even in scholarly and academic circles, the powerful cultural pull of the Bible should not be underestimated. Thus, the Catholic archaeologist and scholar, Roland de Vaux, known for his association with the early investigations of the Dead Sea Scrolls, commented at one point that "if the historical faith of Israel is not founded in history, such faith is erroneous, and therefore our faith is also."[11] Similarly the American William Albright, another great scholar in biblical archaeology, argued that, as a whole, the picture in Genesis is historical, and that therefore there is no reason to doubt its general accuracy.

Judaism, of course, does have a *real* history. As we shall see, it is a history steeped in class struggle, revolution and war and it was this which resulted, *as a bye-product,* in the development of the corresponding theology. It is not just that the socio-economic conditions *influenced* developing Judaism, but that these material factors *engendered* and *shaped* Judaism. This real history is not confirmed by biblical narrative, although it finds an echo in scripture, but by solid archaeological evidence that still remains to this day.

The great empires of the Near East all left their imprint on the history of Canaan and fortunately for us they also left much behind for historians to mull over many centuries later. Fragments of buildings, tombs, monuments, inscriptions, steles (stone tablets), papyri and parchments have survived in their tens of thousands. Even ancient Canaan itself has left a lot of archaeological evidence in the remains of buildings and settlements, upon which we will comment later. This real history, one underpinned by surviving artefacts and evidence, stands in sharp contrast to the myths and legends which accumulated over the centuries and which eventually found their way into the biblical canon.

The later narratives in the Bible, from the kings of Israel and Judah onwards, are broadly in agreement with the non-biblical evidence that survives today. Thus, the names associated in the Bible with Assyrian, Babylonia, Persian and Greek kings correspond to our knowledge of them from surviving evidence, as do the names of places, battles and some other events. But even where the biblical narratives correspond *broadly* to real history, the *detail* is often unverifiable and sometimes plain wrong.

Different biblical sources

Even as early as the nineteenth century, by their detailed analysis of the text of the Bible, scholars had come to the conclusion that the first five books of the Bible could not have been written by a single person. It became clear that the Torah is an *edited* construct made by splicing together different stories or different versions of the same story derived from different sources.

The two oldest sources to be identified were abbreviated as "E" and "J". Source E is based on the northern kingdom of Israel and is so-called for the word used there for God, *Elohim* or *El*. Many names, including personal names like *Elisha*, *Elijah* and place names like *Beth-el* (whence *Bethlehem*), *Peni-el* and even *Isra-el* contain a relic of this root. The J source, based in the southern kingdom of Judah, is so called from the word *Yahweh* (written in Hebrew, without vowels, as *Ywh* or *Yhwh*), also meaning God. Here too, names with the prefix Jo—or Ja—are an indication of the root. The word 'Jehovah' is a modern version of the name. As we shall see, the seventh century BCE authors of the first Bible gave more prominence to Yahweh—for particular reasons—and we will refer to early "Yahwist" traditions in Canaan.

In his book, *Who wrote the Bible?*, Richard Friedman goes into some detail to describe these E and J traditions which, although very similar, show a bias corresponding to the different interests of the priesthood and ruling classes of the northern and southern kingdoms, for example, by different degrees of emphasis on the roles of heroic figures like Moses, Aaron and Joshua. Friedman suggests that E and J represent the tradition that accumulated during the first tribal stage of development of the early Israelites. As such they would represent an accumulation of *oral* tradition and *folklore* that would eventually be written down by scribes or priests and be finally fused into a single document.

Another source identified early on in biblical textual analysis is the 'priestly' source, or "P", and this has been taken to represent the priesthood, especially of the northern kingdom. The main preoccupation of these authors was ritual, liturgy, purity, dietary laws, sacrifice and, of course, the privileges and status of the priests themselves. The priestly material was modified and clarified over many centuries. The first four books of the Torah, therefore, are in the first instance a skilful assemblage of stories and myths from these three early sources, E, J and P, written, amended and rewritten many times before the final version was settled.

But it also became clear to scholars that the fifth part of the Torah, the book of Deuteronomy, stood apart from the first four. It repeats many of the stories from Genesis and Exodus, although with some variations, and it is written in a style more in keeping with the later 'historical' books. It is therefore designated as a source in its own right, the "D" source. Deuteronomy and the later books that follow it, Joshua, Judges, Samuel 1 and 2 and Kings 1 and 2, are collectively referred to by scholars as the 'Deuteronomic History'. Although its written composition actually began in seventh century Judah, it is seen as representing a compromise between the Israelite and Judahite oral traditions, with a strong bias towards the latter.

There is an overwhelming consensus among scholars, therefore, that the first five books of the Hebrew Bible, taken as a whole, is a compilation of works from several different sources. It is a patchwork of books and parts of books, each written under different social and historical circumstances and expressing different political and religious interests.

"These first books of the Bible had as extraordinary a manner of composition as any book on earth. Imagine assigning four different people to write a book on the same subject, then taking their four different versions and cutting them up and combining them into one long, continuous account, then claiming that the account was all by one person . . ."[12]

It is important to note that in referring to authors E, J, P and D, we are not talking about four *individual* authors, E, J, P and D, so much as four *traditions*. Individuals may have played key roles in major editing and writing projects from time to time (Friedman proposes the prophet Ezra, in the middle of the sixth century, as the main editor of the Deuteronomic History), but we also need to bear in mind that perhaps dozens of later scribes or editors will have added, subtracted or otherwise amended the books before the final versions were reached.

The Torah is essentially a narrative 'history' from Creation to the settlement of the Israelites in Canaan, the land which had been promised to them by God. The book of Genesis describes the Creation and the first generations of humankind, starting with Adam and Eve, their 'fall' in the Garden of Eden and the generations that came after them. Most people are familiar with the story of the Creation, an episode that lasted six days, with the seventh day as a 'day of rest'. These early chapters of Genesis, leading up to the Flood and the life of Noah, have no particular bearing on the Jewish people; they are offered as a 'history' of all mankind.

These biblical Creation and Flood myths are in fact a rehash of myths that were very common among all peoples in the Near East, not least the Assyrians and Babylonians, the dominant cultures during the first period of setting oral tradition down in literary form. The epic Babylonian story of Gilgamesh has come down to us in the form of preserved cuneiform tablets[13] which predate Homer's *Iliad* by perhaps a thousand years and the writing of the biblical stories by nearly half as much again. In his *History*, Dubnov,[14] tabulates some of the Babylonian Creation myths alongside those of the Biblical narrative to show the remarkable similarity between the two.

---

12 Richard E Friedman, *Who wrote the Bible*, p 53
13 Cuneiform documents were written on clay tablets using a wedge-shaped stylus to create pictographic symbols. Once fired and hardened, thousands of such tablets have been preserved, to be discovered and translated in modern times
14 Simon Dubnov *The History of the Jews*, p 245

Genesis	The Babylonian narrative
Now the earth was unformed and the void and darkness was upon the face of the deep . . .	When on high the heavens had not been named, firm ground below had not been called by name . . .
And God made the firmament and divided the waters which were under the firmament . . .	The god Marduk killed Tiamat, the goddess of chaos and cut her body into two parts, out of which he
Let there be lights in the firmament of the heavens to divide the day from the night; and let them be for signs, and for seasons and for days and years . . .	made the sky and the surface of the waters, separating the heavens from the earth . . . The firmament was adorned with figures of the gods, the stars, so as to set the limits of time in years and months . . .
Then the Lord God formed man of the dust of the ground . . . He created woman out of the rib of Adam . . .	"Thou Aruru didst create Gilgamesh; create now his double . . ." When Aruru heard this, a doubler of Anu she conceived within her . . .

The commonality of creation myths from one culture to another and their overarching supernatural content does not deter some 'scholars' from taking Genesis literally and attempting to shoe-horn it somehow into modern science, even in the twenty-first century. A book by Andrew Parker, *The Genesis Enigma*, puts forward the idea that the story in Genesis can be considered to be broadly correct in the sense that, in the light of modern scientific understanding, the sequence in Genesis is accurate. (See Appendix I) The only 'enigma' that one can attach to this book is the mystery of how it ever came to be on bookshelves under 'popular science' in the first place.

Like the story of the Creation, the equally famous story of Noah and the Flood has its origins in Babylonian myth. Dubnov again tabulates the story in Genesis and sets it alongside the story from the Babylonian Gilgamesh epic:

9

Genesis	**The Gilgamesh Epic**
And God said unto Noah: "Make thee an ark . . . thou shalt come into the ark, thou, and thy sons, and thy wife, and thy sons' wives . . . and of every living thing of all flesh, two of every sort . . .	. . . Ea, the water god says to him, "build a ship! . . . aboard the ship take thou the seed of all living things . . . ten dozen cubits in length and width; he admitted his family and kin, along with the cattle . . .
. . . and the ark rested upon the mountain of Ararat . . . and he [Noah] stayed yet another seven days and again he sent forth a dove . . .	On Mount Nisir the ship came to rest . . . when the seventh day arrived, I sent forth and set free a dove . . .

As Dubnov writes:

> "These parallels, as well as a whole series of other ancient versions of the story of the Flood, testify to the unity, not only of the general contents, but also of the various details of the legend among Near Eastern peoples; even in the later religious and ethical interpretations of this cosmic legend in the Hebrew version, the traces of its origin are not obliterated."[15]

In the myth of the Flood, the two separate P and J sources are clearly identified in his book by Richard Friedman[16] who has carefully teased out the two accounts, as shown in Appendix II. The two versions of the same story can still be read separately, although each is recounted in a slightly different way.

The patriarchs

The stories of the Creation, the Flood and others like the Tower of Babel (as the legendary origin of different languages and nations) are common to all the societies of the Near East. These popular stories and fables have been given a particular 'Yahwist' flavour in the Torah. Like all 'creation myths' they were a rationalisation of human existence and they mostly originated in the second millennium BCE, to form a body of *oral* culture which was passed on for centuries, as songs, poems and folklore, before being committed to written form at a much later stage.

Within this Near East melting pot of oral traditions, there would have been stories specific to each of the regions and the 'nations' that were in the process of formation. The stories of the early Israelite patriarchs are of the latter kind;

---

[15]   Dubnov, p 249.

[16]   Friedman, p 54

although, again, not without borrowed ideas. They were intended to rationalise a 'history' and an identity that stood in contrast to the other nations around them.

The specific history of the Hebrew people only begins in the Bible with the story of Abram, re-named *Abraham* at a later point. According to Genesis, God established a 'covenant', an agreement, with Abraham in which God promised the whole of the land of Canaan to him and his descendents, in return for Abraham's people worshipping God to the exclusion of all others. The latter part of Genesis recounts the actions of Abraham, his son *Isaac* and his grandsons, especially *Jacob*. Jacob is renamed '*Israel*' and it is his twelve sons, including the best known, *Joseph*, who provide the genealogical origin of the twelve tribes of Israel. Abraham, Isaac and Jacob/Israel, therefore, are acknowledged as the three great patriarchs of the Jewish faith. Islamic tradition also traces its roots right back to Abraham, hence the description of Judaism, Christianity and Islam as the 'Abramic' religions.

One of the reasons we know that the stories were first codified much later, from the seventh century BCE, is that several of the nations mentioned in the stories of the patriarchs, such as the Arameans, Moabites, Edomites and Kedarites *didn't exist at the time the stories were set*.[17] Archaeological records of their presence date only from around the time of the writing of the stories.

The biblical authors, projecting their stories back in time, naturally wrote the most unflattering origins for their *contemporary* neighbours by giving them lines of descent from the least favoured sons of the house of Abraham. Thus the Moabites and Ammonites were said to have descended from the two daughters of Lot, both impregnated incestuously by their father. Similarly, it was *Ishmael*, Abraham's son by his concubine (as opposed to Isaac, a son by his wife) who founded the *Arab* nation. Likwise, The founder of the *Edomites* was said to have been *Esau*, who was compared unfavourably in the Bible to his brother *Jacob*, the founder of the nation of *Israel*. We now know from archaeological studies that the states of Edom, Moab and Ammon only came into existence around the eighth century BCE, long after the supposed lifetime of the patriarchs and this explains why this date corresponds to the earliest possible date for the story to have been written down.

Israel Finkelstein and Neil Asher Silberman are, respectively, the director of the Sonia and Marco Nadler Institute of Archaeology at Tel Aviv University and director of historical interpretation for the Ename Centre for Public Archaeology and Heritage Presentation in Belgium. They have pointed to several other obvious anachronisms in the biblical accounts. The stories of the patriarchs are full of incidences and events about camels, for instance. Yet, archaeological evidence shows quite clearly that camels were not widely domesticated as beasts of burden before 1000 BCE, the best part of a millennium after Abraham, Isaac and Jacob.

The *Philistines* also feature significantly in the stories of the patriarchs. For example in Genesis 26, 1, we read that "Isaac went unto Abimelech, king of the Philistines unto

---

[17]   Biblical' historians locate the period of the Patriarchs at 2000 to 1700 BCE. For this and other instances of 'biblical' dating (and in tables) *The Archaeology of Israel*, by James K Hoffmeier, is used.

Gerer." But in fact the Philistines, migrants from somewhere in the Mediterranean, were not established in the region until after 1200 BCE. Archaeological digs have shown that the city of Gerer, identified at a site north of Beersheba in modern-day Israel, was at that earlier time an insignificant village and only became a sizeable walled city by the late eighth and early seventh century BCE—again corresponding to the time and circumstances of the real authorship of the story.

According to the biblical account, it was during a period of famine in Canaan that Joseph was taken to Egypt, where he achieved great fame and a high position in the Pharaoh's court. He was followed by his father, Jacob, and his eleven brothers, who also established themselves in their adopted country. In the succeeding generations, we are told, the Hebrews multiplied, although retaining the tribal identities based on Jacob's sons and at some point they became estranged from the ruling Pharaohs, after which they were enslaved and mistreated. Eventually, as the Book of Exodus describes, the Hebrews were liberated under the leadership of Moses, God having assisted with miraculous plagues sent to afflict the people of Egypt. After fleeing across the Red (or Reed) Sea, the Hebrews wandered in the wilderness for forty years, during which time God also revealed the Ten Commandments (known later as the Mosaic Law) to his chosen people.

The importance of this story of 'deliverance' from Egypt should not be underestimated: it is a key component in the entire mythology of modern-day Judaism and runs as a vital thread through all the political motifs of Israeli politics today. It is celebrated by Jews worldwide as the festival of Passover. However, we are again indebted to Dubnov for pointing out that parts of the story of Moses are also borrowed from *Babylonian* tradition. He notes that even the biblical story of the rescue of Moses as a baby (from a crib floating among the bulrushes of the Nile) is a copy of a Babylonian fable. Dubnov compares the image of Moses in the Bible to that of the Babylonian king Hammurabi on inscriptions excavated in modern times:

> "Hammurabi is portrayed on a monument in the act of receiving the tables of the law from the sun god, Shamash. Moses is represented as carrying the Decalogue from the summit of Mount Sinai . . . Moreover, a consideration of the striking resemblance between the Code of Hammurabi, discovered in 1902, and the oldest portion of the biblical code—the *Sefer Ha'brith*, "Book of the Covenant," in Exodus 21-22—discloses a cultural milieu within which the germ of the Mosaic Law could have developed without any miracle."[18]

Dubnov again tabulates sections of the Code of Hammurabi and the Book of the Covenant side by side[19] and there are indeed many similarities, some word for word. Only the name "Moses" belongs elsewhere. Like a lot of Egyptian words that found

---

[18]   Dubnov, P 67.
[19]   See Dubnov pp 96-98

their way into Hebrew literature, it is borrowed from an Egyptian root. *Moses*, as in the Pharaonic names like Ra*mesis*, Ah*mose*, Thut*mose*, appears to be a *generic* name for 'son of' adopted for use in the Exodus legend.

According to the Bible, after a forty year period in the wilderness, mostly in Sinai, the Hebrews at last returned to Canaan, the 'promised land'. Although by the end of his life he had reached the age of one hundred and twenty years, the Bible relates that Moses did not live to see the conquest of Canaan[20]. This was left to *Joshua*, who took the land for the Israelites. Here the Old Testament presents two very different and somewhat contradictory descriptions of the conquest of Canaan. In the Book of Joshua there is a description of a lightning campaign in which "one and thirty kings" are slain and one city after another falls to the Israelites. The most famous, of course, is the city of Jericho, the fall of which has been the subject of hymns and songs:

"So the people shouted when the priests blew with the trumpets; and it came to pass, when the people heard the sound of the trumpet, and the people shouted with a great shout, that the wall fell down flat, so that the people went up into the city, every man straight before him, and they took the city".[21]

In the conquest scenario, the indigenous Canaanites were quickly and effectively subdued and were *driven out*, often with the murder of the entire population of a town or city, an ancient version of ethnic cleansing, or genocide. The land was then divided between the twelve tribes, according to allotments dictated previously by Moses. In contrast to this description of a more or less rapid conquest, the later Book of Judges gives an account in which the process is spread over a protracted period of time, during which the indigenous Canaanites were *not all* driven out. The first chapter of the Book of Judges in fact lists twenty cities which were not taken by the Israelites and in which the former residents still remained "to this day" (a clue, repeated many times in the Bible, of an authorship much later than the events described).

Whichever variation of conquest is favoured, the core of Jewish faith to the present day relies heavily on this biblical idea that those who became the Jewish people were *ethnically distinct* from the indigenous Canaanites and that after the Exodus and Conquest they became the sole inhabitants of Canaan. "Judaism is an ethnic religion", one author writes, ". . . a religious heritage tied to a specific ethnic or national identity . . ."[22] However, it is now clear from modern archaeological discoveries and a huge corpus of extra-biblical evidence that *nearly all of the historical narrative written in the Torah is myth.*

Even after nearly two hundred years of archaeological exploration of Sinai, there is not a shred of evidence anywhere of the transit of hundreds of thousands of

---

[20]   The Conquest of Canaan would be dated 'biblically' to the years running up to 1400 BCE. (Hoffmeier)

[21]   Joshua: 6, 20

[22]   Robert Goldenberg, *The origins of Judaism.* p 3

Hebrews on their way from Egypt to Canaan, despite the dry and sandy conditions that would have favoured the preservation of remains. It is possible to compare the place-names mentioned in the biblical forty-year sojourn in the wilderness with the names of those places that archaeologists know really did exist in the seventh century. The fact that places mentioned in the great 'Wandering' were based on *seventh century reality* is emphasised by the fact that some of these sites were occupied *only* at that particular time and most certainly did not exist six centuries earlier. The authors or editors of the Torah narrative used *contemporary* cities and place-names, projecting them back in time. They mixed up place-names they knew with traditional and half-remembered folk stories, without realising that the cities contemporary to them had not even existed a few centuries earlier. As for Jericho, where, in the words of the song, "the walls came tumbling down", there is no archaeological trace of any settlement at all during the thirteenth century.

The origins of Israel

The territory from which the Israelites originated, that is, the hill country of Canaan, was always subject to the economy and politics of the much greater empires to the north and Egypt to the west. In terms of its own economic, political and military development, it was always on the "fringe" of bigger events. Nevertheless, it was at the nexus of important coastal and overland routes, through which a lot of trade and marching armies needed to pass. It was because of their occasional strategic significance for the great powers around it that today we have evidence of the politics of Canaan and the states of Israel and Judah which came after it. Taking 2000 BCE as an approximate starting point, it is known from the nine hundred or so early Bronze Age[23] settlements that have been excavated, each no larger than a small walled town, that the indigenous population of Canaan had close similarities to the peoples to the north (modern-day Syria and Lebanon).

In the centuries following the turn of that millennium, a people from this region attained such a degree of military strength that they were able to invade northern Egypt and occupy it for a century. These invaders, or 'Hyksos', as they became known, ruled northern Egypt, from around 1650 to 1550 BCE, based in their own capital, Avaris, in the Nile delta. They are referred to in later Egyptian records as barbarians and 'Asiatics' although they may in fact have brought with them many technical innovations in the working of bronze and in the manufacture of weaponry and chariots. It is clear from the hints in the surviving Egyptian records that it was the superior productive technique of the Hyksos that allowed them to overrun the old Empire, at least until the latter caught up technologically. After a century of Hyksos rule in the north, native Egyptian rulers based in Upper Egypt eventually drove them out.

---

[23] The dates are very approximate, but we can take the Bronze Age in the Near East as lasting roughly from 3000 to 1200 BCE, overlapping with the later Iron Age which began around 1300 BCE

This relatively short episode in Canaanite/Egyptian history is worth noting because it may have provided some of the material for oral histories and folklore that persisted in later centuries. Inscriptions show that the name "Jacob" was shared by at least one Hyksos king. Thus, the archaeological evidence shows that large numbers of Canaanites, or similar people, were at one point *forcibly expelled* from Egypt, although clearly it is not the same as *Hebrews escaping* the Egyptians, as it is related in the Book of Exodus.

Following the Hyksos expulsion, from about 1550 until about 1120 BCE, Canaan was part of the Egyptian empire and their rule during this period is attested by a wealth of evidence that survives to this day in the form of thousands of inscriptions, tablets and papyri. We know for certain that during the entire period of the supposed biblical flight from Egypt and the Conquest, *Canaan was part of the Egyptian empire.*

> "A detailed comparison of this [biblical] version of the takeover of Palestine with the extra-biblical evidence totally discredits the former. Not only is there a complete absence . . . in the records of the Egyptian empire of any mention or allusion to such a whirlwind of annihilation, but also Egyptian control over Canaan and the very cities Joshua is supposed to have taken scarcely wavered during the entire period of the Late Bronze Age."[24]

The initial result of the Egyptian conquest of Canaan was the destruction of many Canaanite towns and settlements, creating considerable disruption and depopulation. According to surviving inscriptions, the Pharaoh Thutmose III (1479-1425 BCE) took over seven thousand captives, while his son Amenophis II took nearly ninety thousand. The boasts of these Pharaohs are exaggerated, as was usually the case on their inscriptions, but it was the normal practice for conquering armies to take captives as slaves and to plunder the conquered land for slaves long afterwards. Existing papyri attest to the existence of 'Asiatic' slaves in Egypt as late as the thirteenth and twelfth centuries BCE. So here, again, we have non-biblical evidence of events that may have added to the melting pot of oral history that was passed down for generations afterwards among the Canaanites and eventually found an echo in the story of Exodus written hundreds of years later.

Bearing in mind the irrefutable archaeological evidence we have today, it is notable that there is no mention in the Bible of this long period of Egyptian hegemony in Canaan and that the archaeology has only turned up one single Egyptian mention of an "Israel", on a stone tablet from the very end of the thirteenth century BCE.

> "There is no mention [in the Bible] of an Egyptian empire encompassing the eastern Mediterranean, no marching Egyptian armies bent on punitive

---

[24]   Donald B Redford, *Egypt, Canaan and Israel in Ancient Times*, p 264

campaigns, no countermarching Hittite[25] forces, no resident governors, no Egyptian kinglets ruling Canaanite cities, no burdensome tribute or cultural exchange . . . we cannot help but conclude that biblical writers of the seventh to sixth centuries BCE lacked precise knowledge of Egypt as recent as a few generations before their own time"[26]

There are, therefore, many insurmountable contradictions between the story in the Bible and the real, evidence-based, history of the area. At more or less the same time that Canaan was supposedly being conquered by Joshua, Pharaoh Thutmose III was taking home thousands of slaves after a victorious military campaign. There is silence on both sides: there is no Egyptian record of the patriarchs, a mass uprising of Hebrew slaves or Joshua's military campaign in Canaan. On the other hand, neither does the Bible say anything about the Egyptian empire or its military governance of Canaan.

Chapter 1 Time-line		
Dates (BCE)	*Biblical* dating (from Hoffmeier)[1]	Dating from a*rchaeological* evidence
2000	Abraham, Isaac and Jacob Arameans, Edomites, Moabites and Kedarites mentioned.	(No evidence for the patriarchs) Gilgamesh legends on cuneiform tablets
1500	Exodus from Egypt with Moses Conquest of Canaan by Joshua (1400 or 1230)	Hyksos conquest then expulsion from Egypt (1650-1550) Canaan part of the Egyptian Empire, (1550-1120) taking slaves from Canaan
1000		True dates of the foundation of states like Moab, Edom, Kedar and Aramea. First written version of Bible legends.

---

[25] The Hittites were a people from the area of modern-day Turkey and at one point their imperial ambitions challenged the Egyptians in the coastal area running north-south through Canaan.

[26] Donald B Redford, *Egypt, Canaan and Israel in Ancient Times*, pp 257-8

With justification, Donald Redford mocks those historians who are so bewitched by the all-pervading cultural traditions of the Bible that they base their studies on it:

"Scholars expended substantial effort on questions that they had failed to prove were valid questions at all. Under what dynasty did Joseph rise to power? Who was the Pharaoh of the Oppression? Of the Exodus? Can we identify the princess who drew Moses out of the river? Where did the Israelites make their exit from Egypt? . . . One can appreciate the pointlessness of the questions if one poses similar questions of the Arthurian stories, without first submitting the text to a critical evaluation. Who were consuls of Rome when Arthur drew the sword from the stone? Where was Merlin born? Where is Avalon?"[27]

In their book, *The Bible Unearthed*[28] Finkelstein and Silberman have come to the same conclusion as Redford:

". . . it is now evident that many events of biblical history did not take place in either the particular era or the manner described. Some of the most famous events in the Bible clearly never happened at all . . . we now know that the early books of the Bible were first codified (and in key respects composed) at an identifiable place and time: Jerusalem in the seventh century BCE."[29]

Chapter summary:

- The Bible is a collection of books written by specific people, for specific reasons, at specific times, an accumulation with a real history rooted in the material conditions of ancient Israel/Palestine.

- The stories of the Creation and the Flood are legends common to all the ancient cultures of the Near East. Nearly all of the historical narrative written in the first five books of the Old Testament is myth.

- There is no record, in all the numerous remains of Egyptian inscriptions and papyri, of the mass flight of Hebrew slaves under the leadership of Moses. Neither is there any archaeological evidence, despite centuries of searching, for the forty-year travels of the Hebrews in the wildernesses of Sinai.

- The archaeological record shows that at the time when Canaan was supposed to have been conquered by the armies of Joshua, it was in fact an Egyptian province.

---

[27] Donald B Redford, *Egypt, Canaan and Israel in Ancient Times*, p 261
[28] *The Bible Unearthed*, Finkelstein and Silberman. Touchstone books, 2001.
[29] Finkelstein and Silberman, *The Bible Unearthed*, p 5

Chapter 2

The first Israelites

We will argue in this chapter that long after its supposed 'conquest' by Joshua's Israelite armies, ancient Canaan was still an Egyptian province and we will cite well-known evidence to that effect. The biblical story of the Exile from Egypt and the subsequent Conquest of Canaan, which is such a prominent part of even modern Jewish culture, is a myth. We shall show that the physical evidence shows that in all likelihood, the early Israelites *were not ethnically distinct from the Canaanites*. Far from emanating from the great patriarch Abraham, we will argue that the cult of 'Yahweh' was associated with a revolutionary people known as the *Apiru* who were opposed to the rulers of the Canaanite city states and who formed independent hill settlements and it was these which became the nucleus of an 'Israelite' culture.

. . . .

If the "people of Israel" did not come out of Egypt, then where did they come from? The first evidence of an 'Israel' is that of the Merneptah Stele[30], dated to approximately 1207 BCE, which boasts of a victory of Egyptian forces over Canaanite people of that name:

> "Canaan has been plundered into every sort of woe
> Ashkelon has been overcome
> Gezer has been captured
> Yanoam was made nonexistent
> Israel is laid waste, his seed is not." [31]

This, then, is the first confirmed historical date for the use of the word "Israel". For these Canaanites to be able to field an army and to be significant enough for the Pharaoh to boast about defeating them in battle, must have meant that for at least decades prior to this date the 'Israelites' had been in the process of coalescing into an identifiable people. This "Israelite" population was living *in Canaan*, but there is no other evidence in the form of temple inscriptions, tablets, papyri or tomb inscriptions of a nation of Israel, either as an enemy or as an enslaved people.

---

[30]   Discovered in 1896 and now in the Egyptian Museum, Cairo
[31]   Taken from Hershel Shanks' translation, *The Rise of Ancient Israel* p 17

Other than the Merneptah Stele, Israel is completely absent from the huge legacy of Egyptian archaeological remains.

Yet the 'exodus' (usually with a capitalised 'E') and subsequent 'deliverance' ('D') from Egypt is perhaps the single most important component in the theoretical tradition of Zionism today. Leon Uris's novel about the Jewish refugees from Nazism and the establishment of the modern state of Israel in 1948 was not named *Exodus* by accident. However, notwithstanding this deeply held belief, *there is not a single serious archaeologist today in Europe or America and few even in Israel, who supports the 'Exodus' story or its sequel, the 'Conquest' story of the origin of the Israelites.* As we shall see, the early Israelites did not come 'down from Egypt'; their roots were in the indigenous people of Canaan. It is with a hint of outrage that Alan Perlman, an atheist from a Jewish tradition, writes, "It is rabbinical spin, and rabbinical spin alone, that gives the Torah its contemporary relevance."[32] The nearest any modern archaeologists come to accepting the biblical model is the concession that *perhaps* a *minority* of Israelites may have come from Egypt and mixed with Canaanites and others to create the Israelite people. But even this concession *has no evidential basis whatsoever outside of the biblical text* and is arguably no more than a reflection of the pressure of biblical tradition, even in the world of modern scholarship.

Across the Near East as a whole, archaeological investigations have shown a pattern of decline and collapse of Bronze Age states and cities from the thirteenth century BCE onwards, to be replaced at a later date with Iron Age cultures and cities. Once again the *material conditions and the productivity of labour* have been seen to assert their fundamental influence on historical developments. It is clear that it was the superior *iron-based* technology of the invading peoples—the Hittites from the north and a variety of 'Sea Peoples' from the Aegean—that led to the collapse of the older Bronze-based cultures. Canaan was not excluded from this generalised pattern of decline.

> "Digs in Greece, Turkey, Syria and Egypt reveal a stunning story of upheaval, war and widespread social breakdown. In the last years of the thirteenth century BCE and the beginning of the twelfth, the entire ancient world went through a dramatic transformation . . ."[33]

This period also saw the beginning of new settlements of Mediterranean peoples; for example in the southern coastal strip of Canaan, in the area of what is now southern Israel and Gaza. These people were the Philistines, migrants from elsewhere in the Mediterranean, who produced a characteristic culture that would feature significantly in biblical stories and which would last for a number of centuries. The settlement of the Philistines near the coast and the crystallisation of an Israelite people in the hill country of Canaan provide the real historical setting for the fables of the Bible, albeit long after the times recorded in the biblical narrative.

---

[32]   Alan M Perlman, *An Atheist reads the Torah,* p 39.
[33]   Finkelstein and Silberman, *The Bible Unearthed,* p 83

The decrepit and decaying city-states of Bronze Age Canaan were characterised by extreme class stratification. Dominated by a privileged core of aristocrats, bureaucrats, temple priests and soldiers, the majority of the population lived an unstable and insecure existence. Chronic indebtedness forced many peasants off the land, to become landless labourers, tenant farmers, serfs or slaves. A large proportion of the surplus produced within the system was consumed in warfare, which generated a supply of slaves, and in the provision of an excessive and luxurious lifestyle for the ruling elite. In addition to the local Canaanite ruling class having their share, there was also the tribute paid to the Egyptian empire.

> "A small minority of government-favoured people (1-5 per cent of the total population) controlled most of the economic surplus. "Surplus" here refers to what is produced over and above the minimum requirement to keep the 95-99 per cent of farmers, herders, and labourers alive and working. Professional soldiers formed the backbone of state armies."[34]

Egyptian Canaan was part of a large province, covering what is now modern-day Israel, Palestine, Lebanon and most of Syria. It had an Egyptian governor supported by a network of garrisons.

The governors ruled the city states, which in turn governed the rural hinterlands surrounding them, including farms, villages, towns and satellite cities. The native rulers of the city states were often referred to as "mayors" or "princes". They would have been responsible for the collection and payment of tribute tax to the Egyptians, the provisioning of garrisons and troops in transit, and the supply of forced labour ("corvée") to work on the crown-lands of the Pharaoh and on public work schemes.

The beginning of the twelfth century BCE saw a gradual weakening of Egyptian control over Canaan, following repeated challenges from the Hittite empire to the north. After an indecisive battle at Kadesh, generally dated to 1274 BCE, and following a further fifteen years of fighting, there was, in effect, a stalemate. The weakening of the Egyptian grip was not lost on the Canaanite leaders:

> "Headmen of Canaanite towns, vassals of Egypt, were impressed by what they divined as inherent weaknesses in Pharaoh's forces . . . rebellion was possible; Egypt could be beaten . . . in the wake of the retreating

---

[34] Gottwald, *The Hebrew Bible*, p 40. Gottwald, who describes himself as a "democratic socialist" and a "free church Christian", has been described by his contemporaries as a 'Marxist' historian. In his own words, he uses the method of "Historical Materialism" in his analysis of evidence and in the development of his ideas on ancient Israel—so he is something of an exception in modern historical scholarship. He dedicated his book, *The Tribes of Yahweh* to the people of Vietnam "in their common resistance to imperialist domination."

Egyptians, all Canaan flared into open revolt. For the first time in over two hundred years Egypt could scarcely lay claim to any territory beyond Sinai."[35]

The Amarna correspondence and the *Apiru*

Part of the evidence for the existence of Egyptian-governed Bronze Age city-states has come down to us in the form of correspondence to the Pharaoh from the rulers of some of these cities. The archive of cuneiform tablets, more than 350 of which were discovered in Egypt around 1887, are believed to have been written during a fifteen year period some time between 1380 and 1330 BCE. This collection of correspondence is called the "Amarna Letters" (or Amarna Tablets) after one of the city states.

The social crisis in Bronze Age Canaan is evident in the many references in the Amarna correspondence to *the gulf between the social classes*. Alongside the many references to taxes, tributes and upheavals recorded in the letters, there are other surviving indicators of the wealth and opulent life-style of the ruling class, like the remains of huge palaces, including some from which the Amarna letters were sent. Whereas some burial sites are relatively simple, others were found to have been filled with jewellery and luxury items from as far away as Greece.

> "At the bottom of the class structure in Canaanite society was the caste of farmers the *hupsu*, or "rural host" . . . Effectually tied to the land in perpetuity, the *hupsu* provided the local militia that fought wars or engaged in construction projects for the state . . .
> "A separate group called the *Apiru* lay slightly beyond the fringe of "polite" Canaanite society . . . a collection of antisocial renegades; castoffs from society who maintained a semi-independent community . . . the *Apiru* display a gypsy-like quality, and proved difficult for the state authorities to bring under effective control. Their heterogeneous nature is vividly illustrated by census lists from Alalakh, wherein an *Apiru* band includes an armed thief, two charioteers, two beggars and even a priest of Ishtar."[36]

The Amarna correspondence records the shifting military alliances between Egypt and the other power to the north, the Hittites. But they also show the jealousies, rivalries and unstable alliances between the native rulers of the city-states themselves. One of the most important threads running through many of the letters is the *revolt* of the *Apiru* against these native rulers and the incessant and somewhat pathetic appeals of the latter to the Pharaoh or one of his governors for military assistance.

---

[35]   Redford p 185
[36]   Donald B Redford, *Egypt, Canaan and Israel in Ancient Times*, p 195

These are some extracts from the letters (not always from the same correspondent)[37], translated by William Moran.

My merchants . . . were detained in Canaan for business matters . . . Sum-Adda, the son of Balumme, and Stuatna, the son of Saratum of Akka, having sent *their men, killed my merchants and took away their money* . . . *Canaan is your country*, and its kings are your servants. In your country I have been despoiled.

The war, however, of the Apiru against me is extremely severe, and so may the king, my lord, not neglect Sumur lest everyone be joined to the Apiru forces.

They have all agreed amongst themselves against me . . . they have now attacked day and night in the war against me.

What is Abdi-Asirta, servant and dog, that he takes the land of the king for himself? . . . Through the Apiru his auxiliary force is strong. So send me 50 pairs of horses and 200 infantry that I may resist him in Sigata until the coming forth of the archers. *Let him not gather together all the Apiru* . . .

Abdi-Asirta . . . *sent a message to the men of Ammiya, "Kill your lord and join the Apiru".* Accordingly, the mayors say, "He will do the same thing to us, and all the lands will be joined to the Apiru"

All my villages that are in the mountains or along the sea have been joined to the Apiru. Left to me are Gubla and two towns. After taking Sigata for himself, *Abdi-Asirta said to the men of Ammiya, "Kill your leader and then you will be like us and at peace." They were won over, following his message, and they are like Apiru* . . . Abdi-Asirta has written to the troops: "Then *let us drive out the mayors from the country that the entire country be joined to the Apiru* . . . Then will our sons and daughters be at peace forever" . . . they have made an alliance among themselves and accordingly, I am very, very afraid . . . like a bird in a trap.

The Apiru killed Aduna, the king of Irqata but there was no-one who said anything to Abdi-Asirta and so *they go on taking territory for themselves.*

---

37   All these extracts are from *The Amarna Letters,* edited and translated by William L Moran. The translation has been simplified by removing some accents marks and squared brackets (showing where missing elements have been inserted). The italic emphasis is added throughout.

Miya, the ruler of Arasni, seized Ardata and *just now the men of Ammiya have killed their lord. I am afraid.*

The war of Abdi-Asirta against me is severe . . . *he has just gathered together all the Apiru against Sigata and Ampi and he himself has taken these two cities* . . . now that the land of the king and Sumur your garrison-city, have been joined to the Apiru, you have done nothing . . . you are a great lord. You must not neglect this message.

If this year no archers come out, then all the lands will be joined to the Apiru . . . *I am afraid the peasantry will strike me down.*

Abdi-Asirta . . . said to the men of Gubla, "Kill your lord and be joined to the Apiru like Ammiya". And so they became traitors to me . . . I am unable to go out into the countryside . . . I fear for my life . . . *What am I to say to the peasantry?*

. . . *all the lands of the king, as far as Egypt, will be joined to the Apiru* . . .

Tyre . . . they have, I assure you, killed their mayor, together with my sister and her sons. My sister's daughters I had sent to Tyre away from Abdi-Asirta . . .

You have been negligent of your cities so that *the Apiru dog takes them* . . . moreover all the mayors are at peace with Abdi-Asirta

Why have you sat idly by and done nothing so that *the Apiru dog takes your cities?* . . . he has attacked me and my orchards, and *my own men have become hostile. I have been plundered of my grain.* May you pay a thousand shekels of silver and 100 shekels of gold so he will go away from me.

. . . *my peasantry long only to desert* . . .

There was an attack on our garrison and the sons of Abdi-Asirta seized it . . . *all my towns have been joined to the Apiru and all of them are extremely hostile to me* . . .

When previously Abdi-Astratu used to come up against me, *I was strong, but now there has been a controversy among my men and it is different. I am being hard-pressed.*

What am I, who live among the Apiru, to do? *If now there are no provisions from the king for me, my peasantry is going to fight against me.* All lands are at war against me.

They have attacked commissioners: counsellors of the king . . . I myself am afraid I will be killed.

Half of the city is on the side of the sons of Abdi-Asirti, and half of it is on the side of my lord . . . let not the troops of the sons of Abdi-Asrati take it for themselves and *its people revolt . . .* he took away the treasures and then drove me away . . .

May the king, my lord, know that *the mayors that were in the major cities of my lord are gone* and the entire land of the king, my lord, has deserted to the Apiru . . .

All the lands of the king, my lord, have deserted . . . Lost are all the mayors, *there is not a mayor remaining to the king . . .* The king has no lands. That Apiru has plundered all the lands of the king.

. . . *the Apiru have taken the very cities of the king. Not a single mayor remains to the king,* my lord . . . Behold, servants who were joined to the Apiru smote Zimredda of Kakisu, and Yaptih-Hadda was slain in the city gate of Silu . . .

And now as for Jerusalem . . . the entire land of the king has deserted.

. . . *only I am furnishing corvée workers.* But consider the mayors that are near me. They do not act as I do. They do not cultivate in Sunama and *they do not furnish corvée workers . . .*

Donald Redford also quotes a message received by the Pharaoh, Sety, soon after his accession around 1290 BCE, in which the local Egyptian representatives in Canaan still complained, somewhat prejudicially, about social ferment:

"Their chiefs are gathered together in one place, taking their stand on the hills . . . They have begun to go wild, every one of them slaying his fellow. They do not give a thought to the laws of the palace."[38]

This is clearly a chronicle of *enormous revolutionary upheaval*; not a minor skirmish in one town or another, but a mighty movement, reaching from modern-day Lebanon in the north to the Egyptian border in the south, involving perhaps tens of thousands of participants, and stretching over many decades. In 1848, Karl Marx and Freidrich Engels made the point in the Communist Manifesto that "all of hitherto written history is a history of *class struggle*". The Amarna correspondence is precisely that—one of the earliest *recorded* examples of a revolutionary movement,

---

[38]   Donald B Redford, *Egypt, Canaan and Israel in Ancient Times*, p 180

one that drew in principally rural workers and peasants, but also villages, towns, the "people of the city", brigands and "runaways" (possibly former slaves). Besides the Amarna letters, other Egyptian texts refer to the *Apiru* as vinters, stone-cutters, haulers, temple servants and auxiliary infantry; some *Apiru* were reported as having been captured in military campaigns in Syria/Palestine[39]. It is clear that they came from a very wide variety of economic and social backgrounds.

The term *Apiru* may have originally been a term of abuse, as Donald Redford implies. They are looked down upon by the authors of the letters, as "runaways", "dogs", "servants" and "traitors" and it has been suggested that the term is best translated as "refugee". Whatever may have been its origins, many scholars now believe that the word *Apiru* was transformed over the years into the word *Hebrew*. In fact, if Moran's translations are anything to go by, the spellings of place and personal names vary from one letter to another and sometimes the *Apiru* are referred to as *Hapiru*.

What is clear is that in the Amarna letters the word *Apiru* came to represent a whole class of revolutionaries and dissidents determined enough to have killed representatives of the local Canaanite ruling class (and their families) and even the representatives of imperial Egypt. That the leaders of the revolution were appealing for support to establish "peace" for their "sons and daughters" and that they requisitioned grain and produce from the local rulers are indications of the social and economic motives behind the revolution—unbearable taxation, tribute, indebtedness and unpaid forced labour. It is noteworthy that by the end of the revolutionary period described in this series of letters, none of the cities is providing levy for the Egyptians.

The correspondence reads in many respects like a classical peasant war: the local rulers are afraid to go out into the countryside then one by one the cities fall to the revolution until eventually the remaining cities are forced to come to agreements with the revolutionary forces. However, the total picture was probably extremely complex and contradictory. Gottwald and others have emphasised the heterogeneous character of the anti-state movement in Canaan at the time. As the Amarna correspondence suggests, many of the *Apiru* appear to be mercenary bands or outlaws who were prepared to hire themselves out, even to the rulers of city-states in their conflicts with rival cities. Others among the *Apiru* were peasant revolutionaries, who may occasionally have come into conflict with *Apiru* mercenaries hired by the rulers against whom they were rebelling.

Yet another additional factor in the overall *Apiru* movement was the incursion of groups of former pastoralists, particularly in the southernmost part of Canaan, in the area bordering on the Arabian steppe and which later became the land of Edom. Egyptian texts refer to the people from this region as *Shasu* and their participation in the struggles against the Canaanite city-states (they are mentioned also in the Amarna letters, although not as often as the *Apiru*) was disproportionally skewed towards these southern areas. As we shall suggest later, the *Shasu* element within the

---

[39]   Gottwald, *The Tribes of Yahweh* p 402

25

overall *Apiru* movement was significant as the originator of the specifically *Yahwist* cult which was its religious expression.

Consolidation of a revolutionary 'Israelite' culture

Although the process would not have been even and uniform, Gottwald has suggested that over a period of time there was a gradual consolidation of the *Apiru*. As the power of the Egyptian-controlled cities waned, the rebellious Apiru were able to find more opportunity to organise what Gottwald has described as an "*organised social egalitarian movement*" in the more remote hill areas, well away from the cities. There would not have been a clear and distinct boundary between the period of brigandage and the conversion of the *Apiru* into a settled community of pastoralists and agriculturalists, but at some point the settlements became permanent, until they formed a distinct community largely separated from their erstwhile 'lords'. Over time, more and more settlers established farmsteads. Deprived of any other means of living and encouraged by the example of the pioneers, more families arrived, more 'bandits', outlaws and dispossessed came to settle down on virgin land.

> "In order to succeed, the renegades needed to gather enough people, well enough fed and housed, skilled enough in the new methods required by upland agriculture (including the construction of terraces and water systems), to be able to extend mutual aid to one another, to absorb and encourage newcomers, and finally to defend themselves collectively against the constant efforts of the politically declining Canaanite city-states to reassert their control over the upstarts and over that portion of the means of production which the rebels had "stolen" from them."[40]

The Amarna tablets, still sitting today in museums around the world, provide the material evidence that leads us to two undeniable conclusions. The first is that long after the period of the alleged biblical Exodus and Conquest, Canaan was still subject to Egyptian rule. The second is that from the mid-fourteenth century BCE onwards, this part of the Near East was subject to enormous revolutionary upheavals. This was not myth, but *real* historical drama logged in the frantic appeals of local governors. The oral tradition of the *Apiru* 'wars' will have added important raw materials to the mix of folklore and legends of "deliverance" from Egypt and the "Conquest" of Canaan. Indeed, it would have been *more* surprising if these revolutionary upheavals *did not* leave an imprint on folk memory and the oral history of the surviving people of the region.

The detailed narrative of events may be irretrievably lost, but what we can say for sure is that for more than a century there was a period of unprecedented revolution and social turmoil, evidenced by the Amarna correspondence, and that this coincided with the military weakening of Egypt. The conclusion we would

---

[40]   Gottwald, *The Tribes of Yahweh*, p 662

26

draw is that it was out of this social maelstrom that there arose a well-defined community, a 'people', and it was these who came to call themselves *Israelites* and were perhaps referred to by others as *Hapiru*, or Hebrew.

As an aside, those sceptics who can not or will not see the imprint of class struggle and revolution in the movement of history should also note that Egypt recorded the first ever know *strike* in history, in the early twelfth century BCE. Through the records of minor scribes and officials, the details have been left for us:

". . . regnal year 29, 2ⁿᵈ month of *poyet*, day 10—on this day the workers crossed the 5 checkpoints of the necropolis and said 'we are hungry! Sixteen days have gone by in the month!' and they sat down (ie refused to work)" [41]

The most important point about the *Apiru* is that they were not an *ethnic* group, but one characterised by their socio-political status. During a protracted period of revolution, a new social order came into being in Canaan. By the middle or perhaps the late twelfth century BCE, the "Israel" mentioned in the Merneptah stele, was largely consolidated.

In October 1991, a symposium was held in the Smithsonian Institution, USA, on "The Rise of Ancient Israel" and attended by some the world's leading archaeologists. The consensus among these eminent scientists confirmed that the evidence we have simply cannot support the "conquest model" of the establishment of Israel, as it is outlined in the Bible. Some of the sites mentioned in the Bible, like Jericho, Ai and Gibeon were not even inhabited at the time of their supposed capture by Joshua. Some archaeologists supported a second theory, known as the "peaceful infiltration" model, according to which the Israelites were settlers, mostly from the north and east, who arrived in the hill country of southern Canaan over a period of time.

More significantly, the historical model that is now finding increasing support among archaeologists is one based on essentially a dissident population of Canaanites. According to this "peasant revolt" model:

". . . the Israelites emerged not from outside Canaan, but from inside. In short, the Exodus from Egypt, if there was one, was miniscule. According to this theory, the people who came to be known as Israelites were really peasants who revolted against their overlords in the late Bronze Age cities of Canaan. These peasants then fled to the hills, where under the ideological guidance of a deity called Yahweh they developed and expanded into a people called Israel." [42]

---

[41]   Quoted in Donald B Redford, *Egypt, Canaan and Israel in Ancient Times*, p 285.

[42]   Hershel Shanks, *The Rise of Ancient Israel* p 12

There is a growing body of evidence that supports this theory, particularly because it has become clear in recent years that *the Israelite settlements in the hill country are a continuation of the culture of the Canaanite settlements* that existed before them. Based, for example, on the evidence of pottery, which is always characteristic of particular cultures:

> "we would not even suspect that the people living in these hill-country sites were newcomers at all . . . they had been living alongside the Canaanite city states for some time, perhaps for several generations, probably for centuries . . . [The pottery] comes out of the local Canaanite repertoire."[43]

From the few inscriptions that have been found on jars and pottery, we know that the language is also Canaanite:

> "So again, these early Israelites, whoever they were, were writing in Canaanite script and probably speaking a dialect that was still a sub-dialect of Canaanite. Hebrew has not yet emerged as a national language and script, a development that only came with the monarchy in the tenth century."[44]

> ". . . since the birth of modern linguistics it has been clear that biblical Hebrew is a Canaanite dialect. And many scholars have recently argued that even Israelite religion derives many of its supposedly unique features from Canaanite religion (which was what the prophets were complaining about)."[45]

Hill settlements

What is characteristic of the new Israelite hill settlements is that they were not based on the ruins of previous Canaanite cities, but were founded, from new, well away from the cities. It supports the theory of a revolt from the hegemony of the city states and the establishment of 'pioneering' settlements and 'homesteads' in previously unoccupied frontier areas of central Canaan.

> "In the formerly sparsely populated highlands from the Judean hills in the south to the hills of Samaria in the north, far from the Canaanite cities that were in the process of collapse and disintegration, about two-hundred and fifty hilltop communities suddenly sprang up . . ."[46]

---

43 William Dever, *The Rise of Ancient Israel* p39
44 William Dever, *The Rise of Ancient Israel* p 48
45 William Dever, *Who were the Israelites?* p 168.
46 Finkelstein and Silberman, *The Bible Unearthed* p 107

Many of these hill-country settlements have now been excavated and the large majority of them were small, less than a single acre in size and supporting a population of around fifty. Not one of the settlements excavated so far has anything like an "urban" character. They were self-sufficient farmsteads, deliberately settled well away from the urban centres. "In my judgement" Dever writes, ". . . the early Israelites were a motley lot—urban refugees, people from the countryside, what might call "social bandits", brigands of various kinds, malcontents, dropouts from society . . . there does appear to be a kind of primitive democracy reflected in the settlements and the remains of their material culture."[47]

It was not a "conquest" that left its mark on the traditions handed down in the Hebrew Bible, but a revolutionary struggle to create a territory independent and free from the control of the Canaanite ruling class.

> "There was a common element in all the actions recounted both in the [conquest] sagas and in the annals: a socially and politically insurgent people had carved out a living space in a broad movement of insurgency against the Canaanite city-states."[48]

The Israelites, therefore, did not descend on Canaan and take it by force, after a "deliverance from Egypt". *They were mostly Canaanites themselves*, although a newly settled section of society that had been alienated from the government of the decaying city-states and who were revolutionary in their lifestyle and outlook.

> ". . . composed of a majority of tribally-organised peasants (80 per cent or more of the populace), along with lesser numbers of pastoral nomads, mercenaries and freebooters, assorted craftsmen, and renegade priests. These sectors of the indigenous populace joined in a combined socio-political and religious revolution against the imperial and hierarchic tribute-imposing structures of Egyptian-dominated Canaan."[49]

Starting in the mid fourteenth century and extending over a century or more, a wide variety of oppositionists, dissidents and revolutionaries, sometimes in conflict with one another, more often in cooperation with each other, slowly developed a new and viable economic and political order in the hill areas of southern Canaan. The decline of the larger city-states enabled this community to defend itself and survive in such a way as to put an egalitarian tribal and clan structure at the focus of its social organisation.

> "Israel is most appropriately conceived as an eclectic composite in which various underclass and outlaw elements of society joined their diffused

---

47   Dever, *The Rise of Ancient Israel* p 54
48   Gottwald, *The Hebrew Bible...* p 248
49   Gottwald, *The Hebrew Bible* p 284.

anti-feudal experiences, sentiments and interests; thereby forming a single movement that, through trial and error, became an effective autonomous social system."[50]

Settling in the hill country, far from the reach of the city-states, in self-sufficient farmsteads, the *Apiru*, in all their various forms and manifestations, thrived and developed a successful economy.[51] Whereas their previous relationship with the land had been as peasants, forced labourers, serfs or even slaves, these Israelites, or "proto-Israelites" as Dever calls them, were now free farmers, able to dispose of the fruits of their labour as they saw fit. They were not the offspring of Jacob's twelve sons, but the sons and daughters of dissidents, revolutionary peasants, artisans, renegade priests, city poor, brigands, bandits and runaway slaves.

The tribal federation and the Yahwist cult

What was the economic and social character of the first Israelite culture? What was it that marked out the early Israelite people as a separate and identifiable group in the decades that followed their settlement in the Canaanite hill-country? Some scholars have suggested that what made them unique was their adherence to the cult of Yahweh, but this is to turn reality on its head. The primary factors that welded the early Israelites together as a national grouping, as a 'people', *were their common revolutionary experiences, the common means of production and their shared social and political structures,* in other words, *the material conditions of life.* Theirs was a mode of production, with corresponding social relations, that were distinctly different from those of the Bronze Age city-states or the rural hinterlands adjacent to those cities. As Dever points out, ". . . the Iron I[52] country villages do exhibit a remarkable homogeneity of material culture and evidence for family and clan solidarity."[53]

Upland Canaan was not a land given to easy agricultural production like the regions adjacent to the Nile or the coastal plains. It was a rugged, hilly region with hills criss-crossed by valleys, making the area difficult to cultivate, especially in the south. The difficulty is seen in the cycle of settlement and abandonment evidenced from excavations of the earliest Bronze Age period more than a thousand years before.

There is a lot of archaeological evidence of intensive hillside terracing, without which it would have been impossible to farm the steep hillsides, during

---

50 Gottwald, *The Hebrew Bible* p 491
51 The origins of the Israelite people lie essentially in the land-locked hilly areas of Canaan, but it was not hermetically sealed off from the coastal strip which retained its importance as a major north-south route for trade and for armies advancing in both directions. The coastal plain, however, features only peripherally in the biblical history of Israel.
52 Iron I is the accepted term for the first 'phase' of the Iron Age
53 Dever, *Who were the Early Israelites...*p 185.

the formative period of the early Israelites. The period is also characterised by the introduction of *iron* farming tools, extensive waterproof cisterns and small-scale irrigation systems. Both Dever and Gottwald have suggested that these innovations were important to the economic development of *permanently* settled communities which could, as a result, develop a degree of social cohesion and eventually lead to a sense regional identity among the settlers. It is also clear from excavations that the nomadic pastoralist tradition which is very pronounced in the stories of the early biblical patriarchs did not accord with the reality. Almost certainly some of the settlers would have *formerly* been nomadic pastoralists, but such a lifestyle was only an occasional and peripheral adjunct to what became essentially a settled economy of intensive terrace farming and animal husbandry.

As well as the improvement and rapid expansion of terraced agriculture, the development of the farmstead economy has been associated in the archaeological evidence with the widespread production of olives and grapevines on scale a hitherto unprecedented. The agricultural produce—grain, olives, grapes, vegetables, fruit and animal products—was mainly for the consumption of the extended family in the homestead; jars that have been unearthed by archaeologists were for storage rather than for transport and trade. Likewise, there is evidence of the remains of storage silos. The economy of the settlements started as subsistence farming, mixed with some animal husbandry, and in time it grew increasingly productive and successful, eventually providing enough scope for barter and the trade of surpluses. The high agricultural productivity led to a big increase in the population, which, most archaeologists suggest, doubled or trebled in a little over a hundred years.

In this form of settlement, tribal, clan and family relationships were predominant and society would have been infused with a simple 'democracy' based upon mutual economic support and military combination when it was required. There would have been a relationship of approximate equality between tribes and family groups. Archaeological examination of these small upland hamlets has shown that they were self-contained and highly efficient production units, with structures that have no precedent in earlier periods of Canaanite history prior to the early twelfth century BCE. There were no 'public' buildings that are markers for the existence of state administration and bureaucracy. What was revolutionary about these settlements is that the farmers were free to use, store or trade their surplus production, and they were no longer obliged to pay taxes and tributes to rich landlords as their forebears had done, under the hegemony of the Canaanite city-states. The consolidation of the Israelites as a people was the result of a major shift in the mode of production with its attendant social and political relations.

> ". . . we may safely infer several qualities of the resultant lifestyle: "simple";
> "self-sufficient"; perhaps "egalitarian", or better, "communitarian" . . .
> I shall argue that early Israel was indeed such a tribal society, but that

both the later biblical memory and certain archaeological views of pastoral-nomadic origins . . . are not supported by the evidence." [54]

The social relations within this new culture were egalitarian in the sense that the majority of the population had equal access to, and opportunity of developing, agricultural production. Their economy was underpinned by strong mutual support within families and tribes. Describing this primitive egalitarianism, Gottwald writes:

> ". . . this communitarianism—however much aided by city-state decline—was an insurgent movement recruited among a coalition of peasants, pastoralists, mercenaries, bandits and disaffected state and temple functionaries who simultaneously worked to oppose city-state control over them and to develop a counter-society . . . there was social conflict in ancient societies and [this] conflict is not something Marxist method invents but rather uncovers and clarifies . . . the conflict of class interests in ancient Canaan is the most important key to understanding how Israel arose and took the shape it did"[55]

What role, then, did the cult of Yahwism play in the organisation of primitive Israelite society? We would argue that this cult was the *ideological expression* of the socio-economic revolution of the *Apiru* as they developed into 'proto-Israelites' and later Israelites. Norman Gottwald is the only scholar we have encountered who, in dealing with ancient Israel, explicitly develops a position based on the Marxist method of historical materialism. He has pointed out that the 'revolution' in religious outlook was closely associated with, but was *essentially secondary,* to the socio-economic revolution that took place in Canaan.

> "Israel's quarrel was with 'Canaanite' ruling classes and its resistance to rulers and bureaucrats was in reality a movement of socially and politically marginalised 'Canaanites'. It could be plausibly claimed that Israel was the socio-religious consequence of an inner-Canaanite movement which revolved around control of political economy rather than around ethnic religious claims *per se.*"[56]

How does this historical narrative square with what appears in the biblical history? We would argue that the real history of the Israelites' tribal society (and the two later kingdoms of Israel and Judah) is only *imperfectly preserved* as remnants in the Hebrew Bible. As we have seen, the majority of biblical scholars believe that the first draft of the Deuteronomic History was written no earlier than the late seventh

---

54   Dever, *Who were the Early Israelites* p 110
55   Norman Gottwald, *The Rise of the Ancient Israel* p 72-4
56   Gottwald, *The Tribes of Yahweh* p xxxiii

century BCE, in the kingdom of Judah. A considerable body of opinion further believes that the History was only perfected finally by a Judahite Yahwist priesthood in Babylonian exile and in the years immediately following. But the questions that have to be asked are why did these much later authors come to elevate Yahweh to such a prominent position as the "ancient" god of the Israelites and where does this fit in with what evidence we have of the real history of Israelite cultic practices?

The account that the biblical authors wrote presents the Israelites as essentially a monotheistic people from as far back as the time of the covenant between God and Abraham, notwithstanding the fact that the people and their kings frequently 'strayed' and were duly punished for it. Indeed, the Assyrians and the Babylonians were written into the story as the instruments chosen by God to punish Israel and Judah for their wickedness. The continuity of monotheism, lasting for three and a half thousand years up to the present day, is part of the halo of mythology that surrounds the theology of the Abramic religions today.

In fact, as most serious scholars nowadays agree, the Israelites and their descendents, right up to the third or fourth century BCE, were not at all monotheists in the sense that it is understood today. A little reference to Jewish polytheism even crept into Psalm 86: "Among the gods, there is none like unto thee, oh Lord". As we shall argue, the cult of Yahweh, which was originally only one of many similar cults in the Near East, was to eventually prosper in something like its modern form only *as the political expression of the re-established ruling elite in Persian Judah*, and even then, it was after a long struggle against other traditional forms of cultic practice.

Going back to the beginnings of the Israelites as an identifiable group, the first Yahwist cult is thought to have originated with the *Shasu* people who are referred to in Egyptian records that date from about 1550 BCE onwards. Lists in these texts associate the "land of the Shasu" with an area in the south and east of Canaan, including the region that later became Edom. One of the texts mentions "*Yhw* (in) the land of the Shasu". The Amarna correspondence also refers to them, like the *Apiru*, as being outside the control of the Canaanite Bronze Age city-states. Their semi-nomadic and pastoral life-style would have brought them into contact with the early settlements in the Canaanite hill-country and a part of their population may have settled alongside the indigenous people. Since, as we have described, the *Apiru* were a widely disparate group of dissidents, it is highly likely that some *Shasu* would have been incorporated and contributed to the developing Israelite culture. Redford directly links the *Shasu* with the aboriginal Israelite culture:

"in the sixty-year period, from about 1320 to 1260 BCE, the Shasu are chronicled as continuing to foment trouble in their native habitat of the steppe, and as pressing westward through the Negev towards major towns . . . It is not, in my opinion, an unrelated phenomenon that a generation later, under Merneptah an entity called "Israel" with all the character of a Shasu enclave makes its appearance . . ."[57]

Another scholar, P Kyle McCarter, takes a very similar position:

". . . some scholars long ago concluded that somehow the worship of Yahweh, the God of Israel, had its origin south and east of Israel and Judah in the region which today includes the northern part of Saudi Arabia, southern Jordan and Israel . . . primary devotion to a chief national god was the characteristic pattern of the religions that developed in Iron Age Palestine. This suggests that Yahwism and Israel arose at the same time as part of the same process."[58]

It is impossible to verify the cultic practices of the early Israelites because there is hardly any evidence at all in terms of preserved artefacts. The only item of any note to have been found is a bull figurine, similar to the Canaanite deity, El. The alternative view, therefore, is that Yahwism was a product of a later period. But if the cult of Yahweh was, or was becoming, a feature of Israelite culture at this time, it must have been so because it corresponded to the social and political traditions of the egalitarian and settled *Apiru/Shasu* culture. Some archaeologists have suggested evidence of some *class content* in the adoption of Yahweh, as against other Canaanite gods. Referring to the views of a fellow archaeologist (Chaney), Dever writes:

"Chaney asserts that the persistent rhetoric against the Canaanites in the Hebrew Bible, early and late, is less a rejection of their gods (who were sometimes adapted) as it is a radical critique and rejection of Canaanite "agrarian monarchy and its concomitants". I would say it is particularly a protest against a corrupt landed aristocracy that disenfranchised the peasant class."[59]

Effectively, the hypothesis advanced by Gottwald, brings together all these different elements into a single, coherent whole and provides what for us appears to be the most consistent and realistic model of historical development. He argues that the Yahwist cult was part and parcel of the *Apiru/Shasu* movement, in fact an essential part, in that it provided the ideological binding that held together the disparate groups within the anti-state movement. In the only political language of the time, the language of gods and cultic observance, Yahwism was the *ideological expression* of the egalitarian, anti-Canaanite, anti-city culture of the new movement. Against other scholars who adopt an idealistic standpoint by putting Yahwism at the core of the development of the new Israel, Gottwald, adopts a *materialist* viewpoint

---

[57]   Redford, *Egypt, Canaan and Israel in Ancient Times*, p 275
[58]   P Kyle McCarter Jnr, *The Rise of Ancient Israel* p 128
[59]   Dever, *Who were the Ancient Israelites...* p 186

by posing the socio-political and economic forces as the real drivers of historic change. Yahwism, he argues, may have been "innovative", but that was only in its status "as the religion of an egalitarian social revolution." As such it provided the religious, organisational and 'national' framework for the formation of a system of free peasants, loosely organised on tribal lines, but free of the taxation, tributes and power structures of the Canaanite city-states. "The religion of Yahweh," Gottwald argues, "appeared from the start exclusively as the religion of socially egalitarian peoples. It is not known to have any other kind of social base prior to its adoption or innovation by Israel."[60]

It may well have been the *Shasu* component within the revolutionary movement that brought the specifically Yahwist tradition, and that may explain its greater significance in the southern hill country (later the kingdom of Judah) in contrast to the north (later the kingdom of Israel), but in the final analysis, its origin is secondary. What is important is *the role the cult played* in cementing together a socio-political movement.

> ". . . a reservoir of social restiveness was available for mobilisation on explicitly anti-feudal lines, provided that a viable organisational and ideological model could be found . . ."[61]

Yahwism as an 'egalitarian' cult

In the classic manner described by Marx, an "idea" gained mass support, to become a powerful material force. In *The German Ideology*, he described what he saw as the proper relationship between ideology, the realms of 'ideas', and the real, material world.

> "The production of ideas, of conceptions, of consciousness, is at first directly interwoven with the material activity and the material intercourse of men, the language of real life. Conceiving, thinking, the mental intercourse of men, appear at this stage as the direct efflux of their material behaviour. The same applies to mental production as expressed in the language of politics, laws, morality, religion, metaphysics, etc., of a people. Men are the producers of their conceptions, ideas, etc.—real active men, as they are conditioned by a definite development of their productive forces and of the intercourse corresponding to these, up to its furthest forms. Consciousness can never be anything else than conscious existence, and the existence of men is their actual life-process. If in all ideology men and their circumstances appear upside-down as in a *camera obscura*, this

---

[60] Gottwald, *The Tribes of Yahweh*, p 643.
[61] Gottwald, *The Tribes of Yahweh*, p 399.

phenomenon arises just as much from their historical life-process as the inversion of objects on the retina does from their physic life-process."[62]

Engels, too, explained that in every historical epoch, ". . . the prevailing mode of economic production and exchange, and the social organisation necessarily following from it, form the basis upon which is built up, and from which alone can be explained, the political and intellectual history of that epoch".[63] It doesn't matter what the early Israelites themselves thought were their motives or their driving ideology. The point in question is that their ideology reflected a material social force. The main lines of the evidence, as Gottwald suggests,

". . . point conclusively to earliest Israel as eclectically composed of various social groups (and survivors of groups) with differentiated prior histories, socio-political fortunes, and religious affiliation. The point of conjunction for these groups was not the introduction of a new religion *per se* as an alternative to other religions, The point of conjunction was rather a *new set of social relations* with appropriate religious counterparts as an aspect of the new special relations or *as a symbolic phrasing of the new social relations.*"[64]

It was not Yahwism that 'created' the Israelites as a nation, but, in so far as Yahwism developed in this period (and the degree of development is debatable), it was as a result of, and on the basis of, the *material conditions that pertained*, that is, the economic, social and political organisation of the Israelites. Not unexpectedly, as Gottwald suggests, this status of Yahwism as "the ideology and cult of a social revolution" has tended to be deliberately suppressed or overlooked in histories of Israel.

Gottwald puts a date for the consolidation of the *Apiru* into a more or less unified movement, consciously based on the cult of Yahweh, at around 1325-1250 BCE, several decades before its appearance on the Merneptah Stele. However, as has already been suggested, the development of the Israelites as an identifiable people, in opposition to the feudal city-states of late Bronze Age Canaan, was not a simple and uniform process. As well as the hill settlements, the Amarna letters suggest that there were associated 'client' cities, allied by treaty to the *Apiru*. Inevitably, even within the broader *Apiru* culture, there would also have been some families, tribes or even large areas which were less enthusiastic for the communalistic ideology of the majority of the hill settlers. There would have been a tendency in every area, but especially the cities to be drawn into new cycles of trade, as the new Iron Age culture developed on the ruins of the Bronze Age cities—in Egypt, in the newly developing Philistine cities and in Phoenicia. It is more likely that it would be in these urban areas and 'less egalitarian' areas that the traditional cultic practices of Canaan would have continued.

---

62   Marx, *The German Ideology,* p 47. (italics added)

63   Engels *Preface to the English edition of the Communist Manifesto, 1888*

64   Gottwald, *The Tribes of Yahweh*, p 644

The Yahwist movement, whilst establishing itself as a major component, would not have consolidated itself completely and uniformly in all parts of the hill country, much less in Canaan as a whole. The cities, moreover, where the more traditional cultic practices remained, would also have been the main centres for the seeding of a new ruling class in Israel. *From the beginning*, therefore, the Yahwist cult would have had strong competition from the traditional cults and religious practices of the Canaanites.

Although the Hebrew Bible was, in the main, written centuries later, through folk tradition and oral lore, these later accounts may be giving us an echo of the antagonism between the Yahwist cult and the Canaanite cults which it had partially displaced. This explains the character of the biblical accounts of the period—as one long and unremitting polemic against the false "Canaanite" gods, with their idols, shrines and "high places". Even the name "Canaanite" is associated throughout the Bible with ruthless kings, wicked priests and false deities. It became a by-word for everything that was rotten in the former society—a pejorative term for the old order and the old gods that had been overthrown. In reality, as is suggested by the two main biblical sources, 'E' and 'J', it is more than likely that Yahwism happily co-existed with the traditional cults, so that the original chief Canaanite god, *El*, still lingered in the name Isra*el* and became absorbed into the *persona* of Yahweh, alongside other gods.

In his classic book, *The Tribes of Yahweh*, Gottwald develops a suggested history of early Israelite tribal society in great depth. Whether or not there were specifically *twelve* tribes, as is suggested in the Bible, is open to doubt. We shall never know. Some stories in the Bible even suggest different numbers of tribes. In the literary style of the Bible, both the Old Testament and the New, "twelve", like the number "forty", is one of those round numbers that are used for an *indeterminate* quantity, much like "several", "dozens" or "a few" are used in modern language. It is impossible to say if the names and precise locations of the tribes correspond to those outlined in the Bible, although some of the names existed in later centuries and were probably injected retrospectively into the histories. In any case, the precise number is not as important as the principle. The main point, to paraphrase Gottwald, is that the function of the tribal system was practically and theoretically a *political* one.

The biblical narrative of this period is described in the Books of Judges and Samuel. According to these accounts, the Israelites, following the conquest of Canaan by Joshua, formed a loose confederation of tribes—the names based on Jacob's sons—who were governed by community and religious leaders, variously called "prophets", "princes", "leaders", "captains", or, most often, "judges". Samson, who was fabled for his enormous strength, is one of the better known of these biblical judges. Like the first books of the Torah, these books too contain a lot of historical anachronisms that expose a much later compilation. Redford lists a number of them from the Books of Samuel and Kings:

". . . coined money (1 Sam 13:21), late armour (1 Sam 17: 4-7, 38-39; 25:13), the use of camels (1 Sam 30:17) and cavalry (distinct from chariotry) (1 Sam 13:5; 2 Sam 1:6), iron picks and axes (as though they were common: 2 Sam 12:13), and sophisticated siege techniques (2 Sam 20:15). Nor is the core of the "Succession Document" (2 Sam 13 to 1 Kings 2) free from clear indication of a date long after the events described. The author has his characters wear archaic clothing (2 Sam 13:18), talk of coined money (2 Sam 18:11), call up a troop of Gargantuan size for an immediate pursuit (2 Sam 17:1), engage in a battle with twenty thousand casualties (2 Sam 18: 7), and use cavalry (1 Kings 1:5). Moreover, one of the army runners is described by the generic "Kushite", a term that points to a period after the last quarter of the eighth century BCE . . ." [65]

Chapter 2 Time-line. The consolidation of 'Israel'		
Dates (BCE)	*Biblical* dating (from Hoffmeier)[2]	Dating from *archaeological* and other evidence
1500 ↓ 1000	Deliverance from Egypt Conquest of Canaan by Joshua (1400 or 1230)	Canaan is part of Egyptian empire Amarna letters 1380 to 1330 *Apiru* Yahwist cult develops Bronze Age cities in crisis replaced by Iron-Age cultures ↓ Merneptah Stele 1207 identifies 'Israel' 'Israel' is consolidated as a tribal federation. Settlement of Philistines

However, leaving aside the inaccuracies and fanciful narratives in these sagas, most scholars agree that these accounts of a tribal structure are a genuine, albeit faint, echo of a barely-remembered former society. They argue that the Bible contains an authentic residue, probably preserved in oral history and folklore, of a society much more egalitarian than the later monarchic periods when the stories were first set down in written form, centuries later. Referring to the design of the earliest hill settlements, Dever comments that they reflect just the kind of social and

---

[65] Redford, *Egypt, Canaan and Israel in Ancient Times*, p 305

economic structure that is presented in the narratives of the Book of Judges. The archaeological remains, he points out, show a notable degree of homogeneity which is indicative of an absence of any specialised elite.

The isolation of the hill settlements, however, could not last for ever. It would be inevitable that at some point they would feel social and military pressure from the reinvigorated Iron Age cities. In response to military threats from the new city-states and from Philistine cities in the coastal areas to the south-west, the tribal groups would have organised themselves in loose, temporary military alliances to defend their way of life. They became, in the words of Gottwald, "an agrarian people at arms". It is also possible, as Gottwald suggests, that the origin of the biblical "covenant" lies in a military treaty binding the tribes together—a *political* alliance dressed in the clothing of a holy covenant, in keeping with the political language of the times. As Gottwald suggests, some episodes related in the Bible, like a gathering of the tribes described in the Book of Joshua, would make sense in the context of a military-political treaty:

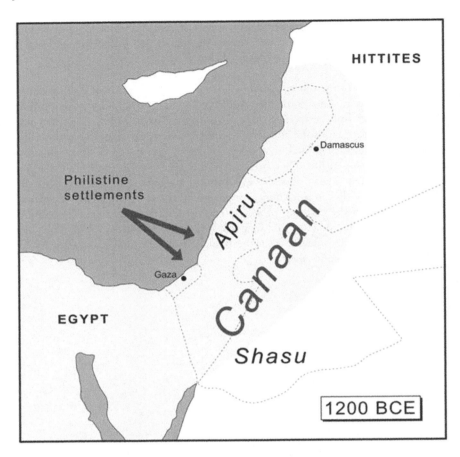

**Map 1: The region of ancient Canaan around 1200 BCE,
superimposed on modern borders**

"And Joshua gathered all the tribes of Israel to Shechem, and called for
the elders of Israel, and for their heads, and for their judges, and for their
officers, and they presented themselves before God."[66]

Archaeological evidence would suggest a Canaanite population of 75,000, or less,
in the twelfth century BCE, but by the eleventh century that figure had doubled,
a very significant indicator of increased agricultural productivity.[67] Whatever the

---

[66] *Joshua* 24, 1
[67] The exact figures are debated, but there is a general consensus that the population grew
considerably

precise figures, once established, the founding population shows evidence of rapid increase. Archaeologists know of about twenty-five sites in the thirteenth century BCE but more than two hundred and fifty by the twelfth, mostly as a result of economic growth and partly from new waves of settlement in the area.

Chapter summary:

- The first 'Israelites' are attested by archaeological evidence around 1207 BCE.

- The early Israelites were not ethnically distinct from the Canaanites, but were mostly Canaanites themselves. Their egalitarian Yahwist cult is associated with revolutionary *Apiru* and *Shasu* peoples who were opposed to the rulers of the Canaanite city states and who formed independent hill settlements.

- The hill settlements of the early Israelites formed a pattern of economic production and social organisation completely distinct to that of the Canaanite cities from which they had rebelled.

- The political structures of the hill settlement culture were based on loose federations of tribal and clan alliances.

Chapter 3

Class differences in the Israelite state

In this section we will comment on the archaeological evidence that points to the existence of the two separate kingdoms of Israel and Judah and we shall argue that the text of the Bible includes echoes of the class struggle in these early kingdoms in the same way that the references to the tribes of Israel reflects an earlier stage of Hebrew culture when there was a more egalitarian society. However, as we shall explain, there is no archaeological evidence for the existence of a single 'united' kingdom—the great biblical state of David and Solomon. Nor is there evidence for the temple built by the latter in Jerusalem. We shall argue that while the Bible includes an approximately correct historical description of the conquest of Israel by the Assyrian Empire and the later conquest of Judah by the Babylonian Empire, the relative strengths of these two 'Jewish' states are distorted in the biblical narrative to the advantage of the latter, where the first version of the Bible was produced. We shall also suggest that during the period of existence of these two kingdoms, most of the population could not be described as monotheists in the accepted sense.

. . . .

Within the general picture of a rural revolutionary society based on egalitarian structures, it is inevitable that there would have been *discontinuities* across Canaan taken as whole. As the Amarna letters imply, some of the cities of Canaan were spared by the *Apiru* and in effect became client cities. Moreover, it is inevitable that over a period of time the creation of an agricultural *surplus* would have led, not only to population growth and an increase in the size and number of settlements, but also to *disparities in wealth and power*. For a variety of chance reasons some farmers, clans or tribes would be more successful than others at producing crops. The surplus might then be traded on, and by the acquisition of greater reserves of wealth, opportunities would arise for some for the acquisition of larger tracts of farming land. Production of greater agricultural surpluses, for example olive oil, would have led to increased trade and the growth of artisanship in larger villages and towns. Alongside subsistence-farming, larger scale agri-business, trade and commerce would have developed. The very success of the Israelite economy would have led to *growing class differences* between different sections of society, not through ill-will or an ideological shift, but through *the material development of the means of production*.

With greater economic wealth for a minority of the population, came greater political power. As class relations became more sharply defined what inexorably followed was the establishment of a *state* with a corresponding apparatus of bureaucrats, scribes, priests, soldiers and kings. In his book *The Origin of the Family,*

Private Property and the State, Friedrich Engels described an analogous process in the rise of the Athenian state from a system that was also previously based on the tribe or clan, the *gens.*

> ". . . we also see the beginnings of its disintegration: father-right, with transmission of the property to the children, by which accumulation of wealth within the family was favoured and the family itself became a power as against the *gens*; reaction of the inequality of wealth on the constitution by the formation of the first rudiments of hereditary nobility and monarchy; slavery, at first only of prisoners of war, but already preparing the way for the enslavement of fellow-members of the tribe and even of the gens; the old wars between tribe and tribe already degenerating into systematic pillage by land and sea for the acquisition of cattle, slaves and treasure, and becoming a regular source of wealth; in short, riches praised and respected as the highest good and the old gentile order misused to justify the violent seizure of riches.
>
> Only one thing was wanting: an institution which not only secured the newly acquired riches of individuals against the communistic traditions of the gentile order, which not only sanctified the private property formerly so little valued, and declared this sanctification to be the highest purpose of all human society; but an institution which set the seal of general social recognition on each new method of acquiring property and thus amassing wealth at continually increasing speed; an institution which perpetuated, not only this growing cleavage of society into classes, but also the right of the possessing class to exploit the non-possessing, and the rule of the former over the latter. And this institution came. The state was invented."[68]

What had started as an egalitarian society in ancient Canaan, established by the early Israelites through a revolutionary tradition, was inevitably transformed in the hill-country into a petty state typical of others in the Near East.

> ". . . with all the usual trappings: dynastic succession, often disputed; overweening bureaucracy; highly stratified society; centralised economy; international ambitions. But here too, the biblical writers enter a vigorous critique, undoubtedly rooted in the pre-Monarchic tradition. Ironically, but not surprisingly, history repeats itself: Monarchic Israel becomes precisely the kind of oppressive, elitist state that the early Israel came into being to protest, complete with Canaanite-style overlords who usurp the land"[69].

---

[68]   Friedrich Engels, *The Origin of the Family, Private Property and the State*, p 127
[69]   Dever, *Who were the Ancient Israelites* p 198

The explanation given in the first Book of Samuel for the rise of the monarchy is that the Israelites were threatened by their neighbouring states, most notably the Philistines. According to the Bible, the Israelites came to the conclusion that they needed a single leader and so they asked the prophet Samuel to anoint a "worthy king" over them. As a result, we read, Samuel anointed Saul as the first king of the Israelites. Even in the biblical account there is a reflection of the class differentiation in the monarchic period, as Samuel issued a warning to the Israelites:

> "This will be the manner of the king that shall reign over you: He will take your sons, and appoint them for himself, for his chariots, and to be his horsemen; and some shall run before his chariots.
> And he will appoint him captains over thousands, and captains over fifties; and will set them to ear his ground, and reap his harvest and to make his instruments of war, and instruments of his chariots.
> And he will take your daughters to be confectionaries, and to be cooks, and to be bakers.
> And he will take your fields and your vineyards, and your olive-yards, even the best of them, and give them to his servants.
> And he will take a tenth of your seed, and of your vineyards, and give them to his officers, and to his servants.
> And he will take your menservants, and your maidservants, and our goodliest young men, and your asses, and put them to his work.
> He will take a tenth of your sheep and ye shall be his servants." [70]

Samuel reminds the people that his own reputation is sound, as the people address him, saying, "Thou has not defrauded us, nor oppressed us, neither hast thou taken ought of any man's hand." But he goes on to warn that the Israelites may come to regret the decision to seek a monarch: ". . . ye may perceive and see that your wickedness is great, which ye have done in the sight of the Lord, in asking you a king." [71] The Bible account echoes the nepotism that had already reached high places. Thus, the sons of the priest Eli are described as "the sons of Belial"[72] [The Devil] and even the sons of Samuel himself "took bribes and perverted judgement"[73]

The Book of Leviticus, although chiefly a vehicle for delineating the rights and powers of the priesthood, also includes laws and regulations that clearly express discontent with land ownership being concentrated in the hands of a few wealthy landowners. It raises the idea of a "Sabbath" of the land every seven years, so that land, vineyards or trees should not be cultivated or harvested in that so-called "Jubilee" year: "it is a year of rest unto the land." After forty-nine years (ie seven

---

[70]   1 Samuel: 8, 11-17.
[71]   1 Samuel 12, 4 and 17
[72]   1 Samuel 2, 12
[73]   1 Samuel 8, 3

times seven Jubilee years) there is deemed to be a special Jubilee when all debts are to be forgiven and all land returned to the original owners, and farmers remitted from bondage slavery.

> "And ye shall hallow the fiftieth year, and proclaim liberty throughout all the land unto all the inhabitants thereof; it shall be a jubilee unto you; and ye shall return every man unto his possession, and ye shall return every man unto his family . . .
>
> And if thou sell ought unto thy neighbour, or buyest ought of thy neighbour's hand, ye shall not possess one another . . .
>
> The land shall not be sold forever: for the land is mine [ie God's]; for ye are strangers and sojourners with me.
>
> And in all the land of your possession ye shall grant a redemption for the land.
>
> If thy brother be waxen poor, and hath sold away some of his possession, and if any of his kin come to redeem it, then shall he redeem that which his brother sold . . .
>
> And if thy brother that dwelleth by thee be waxen poor, and be sold unto thee; thou shalt not compel him to serve as a bondsman;
>
> But as a hired servant, and as a sojourner, he shall be with thee, and shall serve thee unto the year of the jubilee:
>
> And then shall he depart from thee, both he and his children with him, and shall return unto his own family, and unto the possession of his fathers shall he return."[74]

It is noticeable that the rule about remission of bondsmen or slaves did not apply to non-Israelites—"them shall ye buy . . . and they shall be your possession. And ye shall take them as an inheritance for your children after you . . ."[75] There is no proof at all that these laws were ever observed but they clearly represent an *aspiration* for an equitable arrangement of land ownership and opportunity. It is evident that the idea of a Jubilee as an *aspiration of economic and social emancipation* was preserved for many centuries. It makes a frequent appearance among the writings of the Dead Sea Scrolls and is associated with messianic literature in general in the first centuries BCE and later, in early Christian writings.

The Book of Psalms is generally thought to include some of the earliest elements of Hebrew scripture, handed down as songs and poems for many generations as oral tradition before being written down. Some of the psalms became the inspiration for Christians homilies about the "meek" and the "poor" but in their original form they are undoubtedly echoes of real anger and frustrations felt by the most down-trodden sections of society. Psalm 72, for example, describes the judgement of God:

---

[74]   From Leviticus, chapter 25
[75]   Leviticus, 25, 46-46

"He shall judge thy people with righteousness, and thy poor with judgement . . . he shall judge the poor of the people, he shall save the children of the needy and shall break in pieces the oppressor . . . the kings shall fall down before him: all nations shall serve him. For he shall deliver the needy when he crieth; the poor also, and him that hath no helper. He shall spare the poor and needy, and shall save the souls of the needy. He shall redeem their souls from deceit and violence."

The deliverance offered to the poor stands in sharp contrast to the fate that awaits the ruling elites, as it is outlined in the following psalm, number 73:

"They are not in trouble like other men; neither are they plagued like other men.
Therefore, pride compasseth them about as a chain; violence covereth them as a garment.
Their eyes stand out with fatness: they have more than heart could wish.
They are corrupt, and speak wickedly concerning oppression: they speak loftily. They set their mouth against the heavens, and their tongue walketh through the earth . . .
Behold, these are the ungodly, who prosper in the world; they increase in riches . . ."

As *history*, the narrative of events described in the Bible is insecure, to say the least. We have already seen that the stories of the Exodus and Conquest are fables. Likewise, we shall argue, the biblical history of the early kings is extremely doubtful, including the story about the anointment of the first king, Saul. But as *social commentary* these stories are undoubtedly lingering echoes of the very real class contradictions that accompanied the eclipse of the early tribal, communitarian society and the rise of the monarchy, notwithstanding that the class contradictions were usually expressed in the language of religious denunciation.

It would be wrong to imagine that the *whole* of Canaan was based on one single economic and social structure and that this gave way uniformly to another over the whole of Canaan. As we have said, from the very beginning, dotted here and there within the revolutionary society established by the *Apiru*, there were client cities and inevitably some of the rural areas would have been more and others less egalitarian than the average. Farmsteads may have been largely self-sufficient, but elements of barter and trade would have been present from the beginning, and indeed trade would have been the main basis of the economy of the client cities. From the outset, in other words, there would have been contradictions and tensions built into the tribal society of the early Israelites. These elements of 'anti-egalitarianism' would have been the seeds around which new class structures would have begun to crystallise. As Marx would have put it, the germ of the new society was present in the body of the old.

The establishment of a stable monarchic state, therefore, would not have been one single event, but a *process* that took place over an extended period of time, with tribal egalitarian tendencies competing with the growing power of wealthy chieftains and petty kings, perhaps for many decades or generations. It is not the detailed narrative, but the echo of that long period of class struggle and social upheaval that has reverberated down the ages and found its way into the written scripture.

The early prophets, Hosea and Amos, are said to have been active around the mid-eighth century BCE, at a time when the monarchy was established in the northern state of Samaria/Israel. Whether their words were written down at the time or (more likely) handed down in oral tradition and edited or written later, is not known. But their writing is also a clear reflection of the indignation and anger felt by the "poor of the land" at the growing inequalities and the class differences between them and the relatively new elites. Hosea refers to "swearing, lying, and stealing", "They have set up kings, but not by me: they have made princes and I knew it not: of their silver and gold have they made them idols", "They have deeply corrupted themselves", "He is a merchant, the balances of deceit are in his hand".[76] Amos, likewise, makes references to corrupt merchants who rob the poor and use "balances by deceit."

> "Woe unto them that are at ease in Zion, and trust in the mountains of Samaria, which are named chief of the nations, to whom the house of Israel came . . .
> That lie upon beds of ivory, and stretch themselves upon their couches, and eat the lambs out of the flock, and the calves out of the midst of the stall;
> That chant to the sound of the viol, and invent themselves instruments of musick, like David;
> That drink wine in bowls, and anoint themselves with the chief ointments . . .
> Hear this, O ye that swallow up the needy, even to make the poor of the land to fail . . ."[77]

In the only political language of the day, Amos and Hosea were railing against the monstrous greed and corruption of the wealthy and the impoverishment of the mass of the population. This is also true of the later prophets of the southern kingdom of Judah. Once again, these works, if they were written at the time at all, were later amended and added to, hundreds of years later[78]. The Book of Isaiah, particularly, is acknowledged by scholars as a product of much writing and editing spread over hundreds of years. But the *social content* of the Books of Isaiah and Micah reflect

---

[76] Hosea, 8,4; 9,9; 12,7

[77] From the Book of Amos, ch 6 to 8

[78] Many sections of the Books of Isaiah and Micah are similar and a section comprising two long verses (including the famous beating swords into ploughshares) is word for word identical

the bitter class antagonisms of the early Judahite state. Micah condemns the rich and powerful in very forthright language:

"... they covet fields, and take them by violence; and houses, and take them away; so they oppress a man and his house; even a man and his heritage ...
Are there yet the treasures of wickedness in the house of the wicked, and the scant measure that is abominable?
Shall I count them pure with the wicked balances, and with the bag of deceitful weights?
For the rich men thereof are full of violence, and the inhabitants thereof have spoken lies, and their tongue is deceitful in their mouth."[79]

Neither is there any respite for the poor from their judges and priests. As Micah, points out, they too, are corrupt:

"They build up Zion with blood, and Jerusalem with iniquity
The heads thereof judge for reward, and the priests thereof teach for hire, and the prophets thereof divine for money[80]

If anything, the Book of Isaiah is even more vitriolic in its condemnation of the opulence and wealth of the ruling elite of Judah, such as in this passage where he rails against the be-jewelled women of the ruling class:

"... the spoil of the poor is in your houses ...
What mean ye that ye beat my people to pieces and grind the faces of the poor? Saith the Lord God of hosts.
Moreover, the Lord saith, Because the daughters of Zion are haughty and walk with stretched forth necks and wanton eyes, walking and mincing as they go, and making a tinkling with their feet ...
... In that day the Lord will take away the bravery of their tinkling ornaments about their feet and their cauls, and their round tires like the moon,
The chains, and the bracelets, and the mufflers,
The bonnets, and the ornaments of the legs, and the headbands, and the tablets and the earrings,
The rings and nose jewels,
The changeable suits of apparel, and the mantles, and the wimples, and the crisping pins,
The glasses and the fine linen, and the hoots and the vails ..."[81]

---

[79] Micah, ch 2 to 6
[80] Micah 3 10-11
[81] Isaiah ch 3

Isaiah condemns the enlargement of farms at the expense of the poor: "Woe unto them that join house to house, that lay field to field . . ."[82] and again, "Woe unto them that decree unrighteous decrees, and that write grievousness which they have proscribed; to turn aside the needy from judgement, and to take away the right from the poor of my people, that widows may be their prey, and that they may rob the fatherless!"[83]

The state bureaucracy and the priesthood

In the Books of Samuel and Kings we read about the fortunes of the first three kings, Saul, David and Solomon. Leaving aside the doubtful historicity of the events described (which we shall deal with later), they are a useful commentary, again, on the rise of the *state*. Even the biblical story of David, which describes his rise to power as a *rural bandit*, may be a reflection of half-remembered rebellions against the growing power and influence of the monarchy.

> "And every one that was in distress, and every one that was in debt, and every one that was discontented, gathered themselves unto him; and he became a captain over them; and there were with him about four hundred men . . . Then David and his men, which were about six hundred, arose and departed out of Keilah . . . And Saul sought him every day, but God delivered him not into his hand . . . Doth not David hide himself with us in strong holds in the wood, in the hill of Hachilah . . ."[84]

There is another story of David in the first Book of Samuel, which hints at a raid by David and "six hundred" of his supporters on the farmhouse of a man called Nabal, ". . . the man was very great, and he had three thousand sheep, and a thousand goats."[85] Many of the stories contained in the Book of Judges reflect tensions and rivalries between groups and include instances of rape, kidnapping, serious disputes and open warfare between tribes. The story of David's rise to power could thus be interpreted as the reflection of a long process of *rural civil war* during which chieftains and petty kings were vying with one other before the final establishment of a single all-powerful ruler. Even in the biblical account there is no seamless transition between the reigns of Saul and David, indeed "there was a long war between the house of David and the house of Saul".[86]

Gottwald[87] outlines four major changes that took place in social and political structures in the establishment of the monarchy. There was an *increasingly*

---

[82]   Isaiah 5, 8

[83]   Isaiah: 10, 1-2

[84]   1 Samuel: 22, 2, and 23, 13-19

[85]   Samuel 25, 2

[86]   2 Samuel, 3,1

[87]   Gottwald, *The Hebrew Bible*, p 323

centralised state, which instituted taxation, the development of a state bureaucracy and a standing army in place of the voluntary tribal levies. There was *increased social stratification*, because the state was based on the richer tribes and families who were further favoured by the state. There were *shifts in land tenure* so that a system that had been based overwhelmingly on free farmsteads increasingly gave way to tenant farming, indebtedness and eventually landlessness. Finally, there were the beginnings of *trade and interaction with foreign states*, like Egypt and the Philistine cities to the south, Syria to the north and Transjordan. All four of these conditions are manifest in the archaeological records of Canaan, and are reflected as shadowy literary fossils in the biblical accounts. Despite the development of kingdoms and the collection and biased editing of the Bible at a much later date, the earlier *tribal* traditions have echoed down the ages in the literature and tradition that was passed down.

With the development of a state, came the rise of a state bureaucracy, with all the paraphernalia of government. Whereas the biblical description of King Saul shows him as little more than a clan chieftain, albeit a powerful one, by the time of Solomon, the impression is given, even in the Bible, of a growing bureaucracy. The first Book of Kings gives a glimpse of a royal court that would have sat at the top of a complex state bureaucracy:

> "So King Solomon was king over all Israel.
> And these were the princes which he had; Azariah the son of Zadok the priest,
> Elihoreph and Ahaiah, the sons of Shisah, scribes; Johoshaphat the son of Ahilud, the recorder.
> And Benaiah the son of Johoiada was over the host; and Zadok and Abiathar were the priests;
> And Azariah the son of Nathan was over the officers; and Zabud the son of Nathan was principal officer, and the king's friend:
> And Ahishar was over the household: and Adoniram the son of Abda was over the tribute.
> And Solomon had twelve officers over all Israel, which provided victuals for the king and his household; each man his month in a year provision.[88]

This book also refers to Solomon raising a levy of forced labour—the same kind of unpaid labour levied by the Canaanite cities, against which the *Apiru* had revolted. A later account has Solomon's son, Rehoboam, insisting that he will add even greater burdens to the poverty of the people: ". . . whereas my father did lay you with a heavy yoke, I will add to your yoke: my father hath chastised you with whips, but I will chastise you with scorpions."[89]

---

[88] 1 Kings: 4, 1-7.
[89] 1 Kings: 12, 11

The new state bureaucracy would have included tax (tribute) collectors, recorders and scribes. For the first time, it would have also had a growing caste of full-time priests to serve the interests of the ruling elite by legitimising the new state structures while at the same time the new professional priesthood would be nurturing and protecting its own material interests. Whereas pre-state religious practices did not require written records or any administrative or ceremonial centres, the establishment of a state religion necessarily promoted them. Although traces of the egalitarianism of the original cult remained in folk memory, sayings and some written documents, the Yahwism of the state was more concerned with ritual, sacrifice and the status of the priesthood and temple.

In the earlier period, with the exception of the patriarchs and great leaders, sacrifice to God or gods was conducted by *lay* officials. The Book of Judges describes how, ". . . In those days there was no king in Israel but every man did that which was right in his own eyes."[90] It is only towards the end of the Book of Judges that a full-time priest appears. The Book of Judges relates how a community leader by the name of Micah (who had "a house of gods"—note the plural) took a visiting Levite (one of the tribe of Levi) as his priest. "I will give thee ten shekels of silver by the year," Micah told him, "and a suit of apparel and thy victuals . . . and Micah consecrated the Levite; and the young man became his priest . . ."[91] The story clearly alludes to the idea of *social status* being attached to a household that can boast the exclusive services of a priest, with a fixed stipend and priestly vestments. It certainly would not be a poor household that could afford its own priest. By the second chapter of 1 Samuel there is already a story of a corrupt priest fleecing the worshippers for more than their fair share of sacrificial meat, a theft, moreover, not conducted by the priest himself, but by his "servant", most probably his slave.

As we have already pointed out, the interests of the full-time priesthood are reflected in the very considerable "priestly source" (P) that became a major component of the Bible. The biblical insertions by the priesthood were composed, reviewed and revised over hundreds of years, (especially in the post-exilic period which we deal with later) but their specific caste interests began with the rise of the state and in the final version of the scripture they clearly stand out. By hundreds of insertions and amendments, the priestly authors overlaid the entire traditional narrative and oral history with their own interpretation of Scriptural Law. By means of speeches put in the mouths of prophets or in the words of God and by putting their own slant on historical episodes and legends, they reinforced their privileged social position and at the same time authenticated it in ancient law. Thus, in the Book of Exodus, Moses is enjoined to create a new Israel with the words, "And ye shall be unto me a kingdom of priests, and a holy nation"[92]. The privileges of the priests are spelled out, over and over again, and in the greatest detail. After Moses is instructed to number the children of Israel:

---

[90]   Judges: 17, 7
[91]   Judges, 17, 10-12
[92]   Exodus: 19, 6

"This they shall give, every one that passeth among them that are numbered, half a shekel after the shekel of the sanctuary . . . an half shekel shall be the offering of the Lord.

Every one that passeth among them that are numbered, from twenty years old and above, shall give an offering unto the Lord,

The sinful are asked to make atonement for their sins, once again by a payment to the priesthood.

The rich shall not give more, and the poor shall not give less than a shekel, when they give an offering unto the Lord, to make an atonement for your souls."

"And thou shalt take the atonement money of the children of Israel, and shall appoint it for the service of the tabernacle of the congregation"[93]

The third book of the Torah, the Book of Leviticus is particularly concerned with the priesthood. It deals mostly with liturgy—that is, the conduct of religious observance and sacrifices—and personal conduct in the matter of food laws, adherence to the Sabbath, and so on. Repeatedly, the book lists the special privileges that belong to the priesthood as of right. As a sample:

"And the remnant of the meat offering shall be Aaron's and his sons' (2, 3)
And the remainder thereof shall Aaron and his sons eat . . . (6, 16)
All the males among the children of Aaron shall eat of it. It shall be a statute forever in your generations concerning the offerings of the Lord made by fire . . . (6, 18) all the meat offering that is baken in the oven, and all that is dressed in the frying pan, and in the pan, shall be the priest's that offereth it . . . (7, 9)
For the wave breast and the heave shoulder have I taken off the children of Israel from off the sacrifices of their peace offerings, and have given them unto Aaron the priest and unto his sons by a statute for ever from among the children of Israel . . . (7, 34)
And all the tithe of the land, whether of the seed of the land, or of the fruit of the tree, is the Lord's: it is hold unto the Lord . . . (27, 30)
And concerning the tithe of the herd, or of the flock, even of whatsoever passeth under the rod, the tenth shall be holy unto the Lord . . ."(27, 32)

Long sections of the Book of Numbers also repeat the guarantees to the priesthood:

"This shall be thine of the most holy things, reserved from the fire: every oblation of theirs, every meat offering of theirs, and every sin offering of

---

[93]   All from Exodus, ch 30

theirs, and every trespass offering of theirs, which they shall render unto me, shall be the most holy for thee and for they sons.

In the most holy place shalt thou eat it; every male shall eat it: it shall be holy unto thee.

All the best of the oil, and all best of the wine, and of the wheat, the first—fruits of them which they shall offer unto the Lord, them have I given thee.

And whatsoever is first ripe in the land, which they shall bring unto the Lord, shall be thine; every one that is clean in thine house shall eat of it.

The tithes of the children of Israel, which they offer as an heave offering unto the Lord, I have given to the Levites to inherit.[94]

---

[94]   Numbers, ch 8.

The myth of the united kingdom

The biblical kings of Israel	The biblical kings of Judah
Jeroboam 930-909	Reoboam 930-913
	Abijam 913-910
Nadab 909-908	Asa 910-869
Baasha 908-886	
Elah 886-885	
Zimri 885-882	
[Tibni 885-880]	
Omri 885-874	
Ahab 874-853	Jehosophat 872-848
Ahaziah 853-852	Joram 853-841
Jehoram 852-841	Ahaziah 841
Jehu 841-814	Athalia [queen] 841-835
Jehoahaz 814-798	Joash 835-796
Jehoash 798-782	Amaziah 796-767
Jeroboam II 793-753	Azariah 797-740
Zachariah 753	
Shallum 752	
Menahem 752-742	Jotham 750-735
Pekahiah 742-732	Ahaz 735-715
Pekah 740-732	
Hoshea 732-723	
	Hezekiah 715-686
	Manasseh 697-642
	Amon 642-640
	Josiah 640-609
	Jehoahaz II 609
	Jehoiakim 609-598
	Jehoiachin 598-597
	Zekekiah 597-586

Table showing the biblical kings of Israel and Judah, with dates
(Only those in bold are attested by non-biblical evidence)

According to the biblical account, Saul was the first king anointed by Samuel. He was succeeded by David, the well-known slayer of the Philistine champion Goliath. It was King David who also moved his capital from the city of Hebron to Jerusalem. He was then succeeded by his son, Solomon. It was in the days of David and Solomon that the kingdom of the Israelites, as described in the Bible, was at its greatest height. The wealth and power of the house of David was known and feared throughout the whole Near East and the borders of the territory expanded considerably by conquest. Solomon, we are told, "exceeded all the kings of the earth for riches and for wisdom."[95] The Book of Chronicles has Solomon ruling over "all the kings from the river (Euphrates) even unto the land of the Philistines, and to the borders of Egypt."[96] Moreover, this period was characterised by the establishment of great cities and by magnificent buildings and monuments. The most important of these was the great Temple—referred to by Jews and historians today as the 'First Temple'—built by Solomon in Jerusalem.

The Bible describes how, despite his reputation for wisdom, it was in fact due to the great folly of Solomon that that the previously *united* kingdom of the Israelites became *divided* and there began a long historical period of two separate kingdoms—Israel[97] to the north, and Judah to the south.

As we have explained, it is unfortunate that so many so-called scholars, have taken as their starting point the *assumption* that the Bible is more or less factually correct and they have therefore built their research and investigations around that assumption. What is worse is that there are even some archaeologists who have assumed the historicity of the Bible and have tried to shoe-horn findings from digs and excavations into a picture that matches the Old Testament narrative. The work of these scholars is an indication of the very powerful *cultural pull* of the Old Testament.

James K Hoffmeier, for example, is Professor of Old Testament and Ancient Near Eastern History and Archaeology at Trinity International University Divinity School, USA. Having the science of Archaeology in his job-title gives him some authority to speak on ancient history, one would presume. But it is clear from his book, *The Archaeology of the Bible*[98] that he appears to bring as much faith into his analysis as science. This is hardly surprising, when one sees that his academic institution describes itself on its website as a "community of people committed to one passion: that of serving God through his church".

Hoffmeier's entire method is based on a supposition that the biblical account of the history of the Jewish people is factually correct, at least in broad outlines, and the archaeological 'evidence' is wheeled out to support it. He describes, for example, "David's Empire" in some detail, without mentioning the fact that *there is no archaeological evidence for it whatsoever*. The reign of King Solomon, he says, ". . . is characterised by an era of peace, prosperity and stability. He maintained the kingdom largely by building a defensive network and diplomatic marriages

---

[95] 1 Kings: 10, 23

[96] 2 Chronicles: 9, 26

[97] The northern state had its capital in the city of Samaria and the state itself is often described in the Bible as Samaria, or, occasionally, after the largest tribes making up the northern kingdom, as Ephraim. Even in modern times, the northern and southern parts of the occupied Palestinian West Bank are referred to in Israel as "Samaria and Judea".

[98] James, K Hoffmeier, *The Archaeology of the Bible*

with surrounding nations . . ."[99], quoting, of course, the Book of Kings. One of Solomon's diplomatic marriages was to an Egyptian princess. Strange it is, therefore, that *none* of the surrounding states—particularly Egypt, with its thousands of inscriptions, stones and papyri—leaves any trace or mention of a nearby and powerful King Solomon who was fond of marrying local princesses.

In *The Archaeology of the Bible*, the biblical description of Solomon's Temple is taken from 1 Kings and 2 Chronicles and placed alongside a description of a *real* temple that has been excavated at Ain Dara in Syria. Hoffmeier even includes a plan of the Ain Dara Temple, inviting readers to note the similarity with the biblical description. There is a clear implication here that readers should take the plan from the Ain Dara remains as the *likely* plan of Solomon's Temple. From the biblical description, he goes on to list the features of the Jerusalem Temple, with its stone walls, bronze pillars, "carved basalt blocks (which) included lions and cherubs, ie winged sphinxes"[100] and so on. He mentions that the Temple was sacked by the Babylonians in 586 BCE, and "so thoroughly was the Temple destroyed that nothing remains of it."

What he does not say is that if this were true, *it would be an archaeological first!* There is no other instance of such a magnificent construction made, let us recall, of stone, bronze and basalt . . . to be completely and utterly obliterated. Reduced to dust. Without leaving any trace. Hoffmeier thus glosses over the fact that despite the most painstaking searches by biblical scholars and archaeologists for centuries, *no trace of Solomon's Temple in Jerusalem has ever been found.*

> "Over a century of excavations in the City of David have produced surprisingly meager remains from the late sixteenth to mid-eighth centuries BCE. They amount to no more than a few walls and a modest quantity of pottery sherds, mostly found in erosion debris. The situation has been found to be the same at every excavated site in Jerusalem. The suggestion that substantial tenth-century BCE building remains *did* exist in Jerusalem but were obliterated by erosion or massive building activity in later generations is simply untenable, since impressive structures from both the earlier Middle Bronze Age (c 2000-1550 BCE) and the later Iron Age II (c 750-586 BCE) *have* survived."[101]

Of course, as archaeologists and historians are fond of saying, "absence of evidence is not evidence of absence". Nevertheless, this particular "absence of evidence" is highly significant. A temple there may have been, but it is doubtful that it existed on the monumental scale described in the Bible. What is far more probable is that the description that was written into Jewish scripture (much later) was borrowed

---

[99] Hoffmeier, p 94.
[100] Hoffmeier p 96.
[101] Finkelstein and Silberman, *David and Solomon*, p 95.

from a real temple outside of Jerusalem, like Ain Dara, and projected back in time to the legendary King Solomon.

To take another example, Hoffmeier accepts without question the myth that many of the psalms in the Bible were actually written by King David and not collected by scribes from written and oral traditions over many centuries. "As a musician," Hoffmeier says, "David's name is associated with more than seventy songs in the Book of Psalms. Whether or not he composed them all is uncertain—it may be that some were composed for him, but *a musician he surely was*, as suggested by later tradition."[102] (My emphasis). And what is the evidence for this statement?—that the (eighth century BCE) prophet Amos refers to the Davidic tradition, as does a sixth century CE synagogue mosaic . . . and there are some Egyptian references to ancient lyres! In other words, because the evidence says it *could have* happened, therefore it *did* happen . . . because it says so in the Bible.

Much the same logic is used to support the story of Joseph who, in the Bible, took his eleven brothers and father Jacob into Egypt. Because the biblical story has elements that *plausibly* match the economic and social conditions in Canaan and Egypt in the Bronze Age (like famine in Canaan, trade with Egypt, etc), the story is *assumed* to be historically true. By much the same logic historians could also render the stories of King Arthur and Robin Hood to be true historical events.

In fact, despite the supposed richness, size and wealth of the united kingdom of the Israelites, *neither of the names "David" or "Solomon" appear anywhere in Egyptian inscriptions*. It is clear that the stories of the kings of the united monarchy, like the rest of the Deuteronomic History, were compiled many years later. When the 'Table of Nations' that appears in the Book of Genesis (chapters 10 and 11) is compared to the archaeological evidence for the existence of those states, it becomes clear that the earliest possible date for the list having been written is the last half of the seventh century BCE, long after the supposed unified kingdoms of David and Solomon. For his part, Gottwald appears ambivalent, at best, on the question of whether or not there ever was a unified kingdom. Comparing the Bible story to the hard evidence for it, he describes the matter as one "hovering in uncertainty".[103] But where Gottwald hovers in uncertainty, Finkelstein and Silberman are much more convinced. The *separate* northern and southern kingdoms may be well attested in the archaeological evidence and in non-biblical sources, they argue, but *there is no archaeological evidence at all for a united kingdom prior to the existence of these two states*.

---

[102] Hoffmeier, p 86.
[103] Gottwald, *GThe Politics of Ancient Israel*, p 198

Chapter 3 Time-line: the kingdoms of Israel and Judah		
Dates (BCE)	***Biblical*** dating (from Hoffmeier)[3]	Dating from a***rchaeological*** evidence
1000	Unified Israelite kingdom under Saul, David and then Solomon.	**No evidence of a united kingdom, or kings Saul, David or Solomon**
900		Monarchy is founded in **Israel/Samaria.** (Jerusalem is not much bigger than a village)
800	Kingdom is split due to the folly of Solomon.	(Amos and Hosea express discontent of poor and marginalised. Other northern prophets were Elijah and Elisha)
700		733 Israel conquered by Assyrian empire
		Kingdom of **Judah** rises to prominence as a vassal of Assyria
		(Judahite prophets Isaiah and Micah)
		The Biblical History is written down for the first time, under Judahite influence.
600		(Early works of the prophet Jeremiah)
		586 Judah conquered by Babylonian successors of Assyria and Jerusalem sacked.

Rather than a real history based on a real kingdom, the only unifying tradition common to both may have been the cult of Yahweh, even if the worship north and south was associated with different practices and differing oral history and folklore. What was no more than a broad cultural affinity between north and south, based fundamentally on a common settlement pattern, modes of production and social values, was conflated in later generations into a combined and fabulous history to be eventually woven into what we now have as the Books of Samuel, Kings and Chronicles.

The books of the Bible recount the histories of the two separate kingdoms, although with a peculiar structure. Instead of a narrative thread, linking the two kingdoms simultaneously and highlighting, for example, the frequent wars and occasional alliances between them, it jumps backwards and forwards between the north and south. The result is a staggered series of separate narratives, overlapping and repeating events from time to time, lacking coherence and any sense of flow. Over the period of the northern kingdom, (ca 930-722 BCE), just over 208 years, twenty kings are recorded in the Bible. Over the much longer period of the southern kingdom, (ca 930-586 BCE), over 344 years, there are also twenty, their average reign being much longer. Whereas the northern kingdom is ruled by several dynasties, Judah is ruled only by one, the so-called House of David.

The overriding preoccupation in these accounts, bearing in mind its much later compilation, near the end of the seventh century BCE, was whether or not the various kings were "righteous" in the eyes of God. These 'histories' and accompanying 'prophecies' were written long afterwards to 'explain' the fate of each kingdom, notably the conquest of Israel by Assyria and the later conquest of Judah by Babylon. To the authors of the biblical accounts, these catastrophes came about as punishments from God for the fact that so many of these kings "did evil in the sight of the Lord". Given special mention as setting the standard as evil kings were Ahab in the north and, later, Manasseh in the south. (See table for list of northern and southern kings). Because so many scholars have clung unswervingly to the biblical account, without looking at any extra-biblical evidence, a new affliction has arisen among these academics, described amusingly by one historian as *goodkingitis*. This is "an intellectual disability which affects predominantly biblical scholars trying to do history and results in heaping attributions of great achievements of 'good kings' to the detriment of 'bad' kings".[104] As we shall argue, much of the accounts in the Bible are actually constructs of a much later period, although with important elements of social history inevitably remaining within them.

The kingdom of Israel

The first of the kings to be attested by any non-biblical source is the northern king, Omri (885-874 BCE). Although the biblical narrative mentions that he had predecessors, they are completely unproven to archaeology. During the reign of Omri and his son, Ahab (874-853 BCE), the territory of Israel stretched from the Arabian steppe in the south as far as Damascus in the north, with a newly-built capital at Samaria. Israel in this period was a fully developed state, one of the most powerful in the region, trading or making war with other states. A stele written in the Moabite language, discovered in 1868, makes a significant reference to Omri. The writer of the stele complains about Israelite oppression of the Moab, a neighbouring kingdom to the south east. The stele relates that Omri was king of Israel and that he oppressed Moab for a long time, because Kemosh [the Moabite god] was "angry" with his people. It describes how Omri was replaced by his son and he to threatened to oppress Moab.

In 853 BCE, the Assyrian empire to the north-east launched its first invasion of the region of former Canaan and this is recorded in a cuneiform inscription which

---

[104]   Knauf, *Good Kings and Bad Kings*, p 169

describes the full range of the forces arrayed against the army of the Assyrian king Shalmaneser III. The inscription includes "2,000 chariots, 10,000 foot soldiers of Ahab, the Israelites", one of the strongest elements of the anti-Assyrian alliance.

Ironically, it may have been the grandeur and scale of this Omrid dynasty that provided the folk memory and inspiration for the legendary kingdom of David and Solomon. Be that as it may, while the Bible devotes a huge amount of words and space to the lives of Saul, David and Solomon, the three great kings of the 'unified' Israel, who are unsupported by any archaeological evidence, Omri, who *is* well attested in the archaeological record, gets little more than a mention, in fact only seven short verses. His successor, on the other hand, King Ahab, gets the full treatment, along with his wicked consort, Jezebel. "There was none like unto Ahab," the Bible tells us, "which did sell himself to work wickedness in the sight of the Lord".[105]

> "The court tragedy of the House of Omri is a literary classic, filled with vivid characters and theatrical scenes, in which a royal family's crimes against their own people are paid back with a bloody demise. The memory of the reigns of Ahab and Jezebel obviously remained vivid for centuries, as we can see from their inclusion in such a prominent way in the Deuteronomic History—compiled over two hundred years after their deaths. Nonetheless, the biblical narrative is so thoroughly filled with inconsistencies and anachronisms, and so obviously influenced by the theology of the seventh century BCE writers, that it must be considered more of a historical novel than an accurate historical chronicle."[106]

During the period of the rise of the kingdom of Israel, the southern hill country remained relatively undeveloped and sparsely populated. Although the bible narrative sets the two kingdoms as contemporary with one another, there is little archaeological evidence of a strong centralised state in Judah on anything like the scale of development in Samaria. Excavations show that most southern hill villages were tiny and there was not a single fortified town. Although it would have still comprised a small part of the overall economy, a pastoral, semi-nomadic life-style might have been more significant here than was the case in the north, perhaps with lingering contacts with the *Shasu* people further south.

Finkelstein and Silberman have speculated that around this time, there may indeed have been a local southern chieftain with the name of David. They have likened the description of David in the Book of Samuel to an *Apiru* chieftain, noting that the town of Keilah is mentioned both in the Amarna letters and in the biblical account of David's band of "six hundred" (see above). The only single piece of evidence for the existence of a David does come from this period. A stele was carved, around 835 BCE, and rediscovered in 1993, in which the king of Aram (an

---

[105]   1 Kings, 21, 25
[106]   Finkelstein and Silberman *The Bible Unearthed* p 175

area to the north, centred on Damascus in modern-day Syria) boasted of victories he had achieved over local kings. Among the vanquished, the stele mentions the killing of the king of Israel and his ally, an unknown king "of the House of David". The stele does not give any other clues but it does appear to suggest a line of kings tracing their heritage back to a David. Some scholars, however, doubt that the stele is referring to a king at all, and that it may be a reference to a place-name. The Aram stele is still a long way removed from the mighty kingdom covering the whole of Israel, Judah and much else besides, as it is described in the Bible, and other than this dubious source, there is no reference in any non-biblical sources for a David, much less a King David.

But whatever the truth of the hypothesis put forward by Finkelstein and Silberman, the archaeological evidence is clear about the stage of economic and social development of Judah in this period. Surveys of the region show that the population of the northern kingdom in the century after the Omrid dynasty was about 350,000, three or four time larger than that of the south. In fact, it would have been the presence of the much richer and more powerful state to the north that influenced the economic development of Judah. During its formative period, it is doubtful that a 'Davidic' Judah would have had the resources to raise an army large enough to conquer any substantial territory, much less a great kingdom. As for Jerusalem, although it is mentioned as long ago as the Amarna letters, in the mid-fourteenth century BCE, excavations show that the city, written into biblical scripture as the capital of a grand and unified kingdom, *was little more than a rural village in the ninth century BCE.*

The decline of the kingdom of Israel coincided with the rise of the great Assyrian empire to the north and from the mid ninth century BCE onwards, the kings of Israel were forced to pay tribute to their powerful neighbour. This is reflected in the Bible:

> "And Pul the king of Assyria came against the land; and [king] Menahem gave Pul a thousand talents of silver, that his hand might be with him to confirm the kingdom in his hand.
> And Menahem exacted the money of Israel, even of all the mighty men of wealth, of each man fifty shekels of silver, to give to the king of Assyria"[107]

Despite the biblical references to the wealthy, the extra burden, of course, would not have been borne by the ruling elite, but by the least politically empowered part of the population, the rural and urban poor. The writings of the northern prophets, Amos and Hosea, as we have already cited, may have reflected the growing social contradictions in society. This was a period of war, social turmoil, revolution and counter-revolution. It is significant that of the last six recorded kings of Israel, their average reign was *four years*. One reigned for six months and another for one month. Three of the six were killed in coups and the last deported to Assyria. The

---

[107]   2 Kings: 15, 19-20

authors of the biblical history, seeing all things through the lens of theology, seldom drew attention to class struggle and social issues, but the instability of the ruling regime during this period is clearly an indication of enormous class struggle and political convulsions.

> "The rumblings of discontent among the masses helped to undermine the existing social order, particularly in Northern Israel with its constant revolts and assassinations of ruling monarchs. Of its ten ruling dynasties in the relatively short period of 931-721 BCE, all but two were replaced after the reign of one or two kings."[108]

The Book of Isaiah (written, of course, after the event) reads like a prophesy of the Assyrian conquest that was *about to* happen and, naturally, as a punishment from God for the misdeeds of the Samarians. Warning the people and especially the kings against their sinful ways, Isaiah sees God's punishment in the form of the mighty and unstoppable Assyrian army:

> "Therefore the anger of the Lord kindled against his people . . .
> And he will lift up an ensign to the nations from far, and will hiss unto them from the end of the earth; and, behold, they shall come with speed swiftly;
> None shall be weary nor stumble among them; none shall slumber nor sleep; neither shall the girdle of their loins be loosed, nor the latchet of their shoes be broken;
> Whose arrows are sharp, and all their bows bent, their horses hoofs shall be counted like flint, and their wheels like a whirlwind;
> Their roaring shall be like a lion, they shall roar like young lions; yea they shall roar, and lay hold of the prey, and shall carry it away safe, and none shall deliver it,
> And in that day they shall roar against them like the roaring of the sea . . ."[109]

In 722 BCE, Israel was finally swallowed up by the great Assyrian Empire.[110] Most of the ruling elite of Israel were deported to Assyria and new population groups were brought in to Samaria as settlers. Some cuneiform texts with Assyrian names have been found in the area, attesting to these foreign settlements. There were several waves of deportations—king Tilgath-Pileser deported Israelites from the north (Galilee) and his successor Sargon II from Samaria proper. According to Assyrian

---

[108] Nachum Gross (ed) *Economic History of the Jews*, p 8
[109] Isaiah: 5, 25-29
[110] Assyria was based approximately on the area of modern-day state of Iraq, with its empire spread across Syria, Lebanon, parts of Iran and Turkey, and now Israel. Its capital was Nineveh.

texts the total for these deportations amounted to about forty thousand people. This was probably an exaggeration, like most of the numbers in ancient inscriptions, but would have still been less than twenty per cent of the original Samarian population. Most of those deported would have been from the ruling class and the urban areas, including artisans and possibly soldiers for use as mercenaries. It would not have been in the best interests of the Assyrian ruling class to have devastated the rural economy from which it would be expecting to squeeze tribute in subsequent years.

It is worth noting that from a reading of the biblical account—and, following that, the accounts of many historians—one would come to the conclusion that the history of Israel/Samaria comes to a dead stop at this point. This is because the overall shape and bias of the Bible was based on the priesthood and ruling elite of Judah to the south and from this point on it is *their* interests and the history *they* wished to present that has dominated. The destruction of old Israel may have been an important *theological* event, but that was not the sum of its real history.

The kingdom of Judah

According to Finkelstein and Silberman, it was only with the collapse of Israel in the grip of Assyrian power that the southern kingdom of Judah grew into a fully developed state with an elaborate structure of professional scribes, bureaucrats and priests. There is almost no archaeological trace of royal construction anywhere in Judah prior to the conquest of Israel. Lester Grabbe, in *Good King and Bad Kings*, also argues:

> "It looks as if the Northern Kingdom, for which there is archaeological evidence for the ninth and eighth centuries, was then replaced by the Southern Kingdom in the late eighth and seventh. The seventh century was not the 'high point' of the Kingdom of Judah but its entire history . . . We are left with the picture of a Northern Kingdom which began in the Iron Age and looks very much like its neighbours: worshipping a plethora of gods, a language more like those to the north, the presence of pig bones. When it was destroyed, Judah was created as an insignificant entity by Assyria on the inhospitable margin of the major Philistine cites which dominated the region in the seventh century."[111]

According to the Bible Judah was nominally independent, but this account plays down its status as a vassal of Assyria.

> "As the Assyrians advanced into foreign territories and forced their political regime to capitulate, the conquered king or an appropriate native replacement was accorded vassal status involving mutual pledges of loyalty and the payment of annual tribute . . . at the height of empire, virtually

---

[111]   Grabbe, *Good Kings and Bad Kings* p 23.

the entire Assyrian domain had been given provincial status, with only a few peripheral regions exempted, Judah being one."[112]

There is an admission in the Bible, however, that Judah not only paid tribute, but may have actively colluded with Assyria in its conquest of the north. The devastation in the region around Jerusalem is also missed out of the biblical account. Of more than 350 Judahite settlements that were known to have existed prior to the Assyrian devastation of the north, the archaeological records show that less than forty of them were rebuilt. The rise of the Judahite state was a direct result of Judah being drawn into the economic orbits, first of Israel and then, more significantly, of the giant Assyrian empire. Many of the cities and nations around Judah were conquered by Assyria and whereas Jerusalem was spared, its the chief economic rival, the city of Lachish, was destroyed and never rebuilt.

From this point on, there is evidence that Judah's population dramatically increased, possibly including an influx of refugees from Israel in the north. The Bible makes reference to Israelites fleeing south, and northern Yahwist priests for the first time would have begun to have a significant influence in the south. Many refugees appear to have fled to the area around the Yahwist shrine at Bethel, which, although it lay in the southern part of Samaria, was not far north of Jerusalem. The archaeological record shows that in the countryside there was an increase in the number of settlements and the existing villages and towns increased in size. As the population of Judah grew, so also did the capital. Excavations show that in the space of only a few decades, Jerusalem grew from a small hill town of ten to fifteen acres to a sizeable city of almost 150 acres.

> "Judah's population swelled to unprecedented levels. Its capital city became a national religious centre and a bustling metropolis for the first time. Intensive trade began with surrounding nations. Finally, a major religious reform movement—focused on the exclusive worship of YHWH in the Jerusalem Temple—started cultivating a revolutionary new understanding of the God of Israel."[113]

Excavations of large numbers of elaborate tombs from this time show a sudden increase in wealth in Judah and an *increased differentiation* between social classes. The Judahite king Hezekiah (715-686 BCE) is described in biblical tradition as a leader of revolts against the Assyrians but many scholars have raised doubts about this. The Assyrian king Sennacherib (705-681 BCE) invaded and gained control of large parts of the countryside around Jerusalem. The account in the Bible does not deal with this, except to mention that Hezekiah was a reformer who destroyed the non-Yahwist places of worship. On the other hand, a huge amount of

---

[112] Gottwald, *The Politics of Ancient Israel* p 135

[113] Finkelstein and Silberman, *The Bible Unearthed*, p 230.

disapproval is heaped on his successor, Manasseh (697-642 BCE), apparently for his re-establishment of the same pagan shrines:

> "And he did that which was evil in the sight of the Lord, after the abomination of the heathen, whom the Lord cast out before the children of Israel.
> For he built up again the high places which Hezekiah his father had destroyed; and he reared up altars for Ba'al, and made a grove, as did Ahab king of Israel; and worshipped all the host of heaven, and served them.
> And he built altars in the house of the Lord, of which the Lord said, In Jerusalem will I put my name.
> And he built altars for all the host of heaven in the two courts of the house of the Lord . . .
> Manasseh seduced them to do more evil than did the nations whom the Lord destroyed before the children of Israel"[114]

In fact, the period of Manasseh's rule was one of economic recovery and growth and his reign of nearly sixty years was the longest in the history of either Israel or Judah. Notwithstanding the story of the kings frequently 'straying', the period of the development of the state of Judah appears to coincide with the development of Yahwism as a something like a state religion for the first time. In the decades after the fall of Israel, though they were still in the shadow of Assyria, the Judahite kings gave vent to new political ambitions, aspiring to the political leadership of the whole region, including their conquered 'cousins' in the north. What we eventually came to know as Judaism many centuries later was launched for the first time as a *state* religion, as the ideological expression of the political interests and ambitions of these seventh century Judahite kings.

> ". . . after the fall of Samaria, with the increasing centralisation of the kingdom of Judah a new, more focused attitude toward religious law and practice began to catch hold. Jerusalem's influence—demographic, economic, and political—was now enormous and it was linked to a new political and territorial agenda: the unification of all Israel. And the determination of its priestly and prophetic establishment to define the "proper" methods of worship for all the people of Judah—and indeed for those Israelites living under Assyrian rule in the north—rose accordingly . . . the monotheistic tradition of Judeo-Christian civilisation was born."[115]

Coincident with this new movement archaeologists have noted the rapid development of indications of literacy in the seventh century, so that Judah became

---

[114] 2 Kings: 21, 2-9
[115] Finkelstein and Silberman, *The Bible Unearthed*, p 247.

a more 'literate' society than even the more powerful state of Israel had been. The development of alphabetic writing, particularly evident in the development of western Semitic languages, provided the starting point for a greater spread of literacy in the whole of the eastern Mediterranean basin. Alphabetical writing is quicker, easier, cheaper and far more accessible to wider layers of the population than the older hieroglyphic or cuneiform styles of writing and by itself represents an important landmark in social development. Excavation of Judahite sites show a rapid increase at his time in the number of signed seals, inscriptions and signets bearing personal, as opposed to royal, names, showing the spread of alphabetical writing.

Literacy in this context almost certainly would not have meant an increase in *generalised* literacy among the mass of the population where it would have remained extremely low, but it appears to have become far more common within the urban elite and even this expansion in literacy will have had a significant impact in condensing onto paper what had previously been more ephemeral and variable oral lore. With the development of alphabetic script and the increased social value of literacy, the value of a *written* tradition and with it an official history multiplies a thousand-fold. It becomes something that can achieve a significant social impact. It cannot be a coincidence that it was at this time that the oral history, stories, folklore and traditions of the Judahite and Israelite people were set down on a significant scale for the first time. The written texts thus produced would have provided an invaluable underpinning, by what were perceived to be solid and sacred links to ancient tradition, of the special position of kings, scribes and priests.

Class struggle in Judah

The biblical account of the kingdom of Judah was written after the fall of that kingdom and it looks at the history entirely through the prism of religious struggle—there is an alternating cycle of "righteous" kings who destroyed the "high places" and "unrighteous" kings who left the shrines of the false gods to flourish. Despite the pious overlay, the biblical history still contains remnants of a very real struggle, one part of which may have been due to the ruling elite attempting to promote a state religion, based exclusively in Jerusalem, at the expense of traditional religious practices of the majority of the Judahite population.

The scale of the social upheaval is almost hidden in the text, but is unmistakeable. In the story related in the second Book of Kings, it was said that King Manasseh "shed innocent blood very much, till he filled Jerusalem from one end to another"[116]. Later, following the assassination of King Amon by his "servants", "the people of the land slew all them that conspired against Amon."[117] These are clearly lingering echoes of the revolutionary and counter-revolutionary

---

[116] 2 Kings: 21, 16
[117] 2 Kings: 21, 24

upheavals which have been, for the most part, air-brushed out of the biblical narrative.

> "For at least some of Manasseh's subjects, settled in new development towns and subject to royal regulation and taxation, his long reign must have been a source of misfortune and far-reaching social dislocation. We have seen the abundant evidence in the archaeological record of the emergence of a wealthy, literate, and influential ruling class in Jerusalem, but no evidence of great prosperity beyond that."[118]

According to Ernst Knauf, the economic development during the reign of Manasseh led to a population increase and an increase in stability and the standard of life for ordinary people. But in this same period, there was a great increase in the *inequality* between the social classes. Knauf uses the distribution of the sizes of excavated settlements and the distribution of wealth within these settlements to measure inequality. The "coefficient of inequality" (q) was calculated from the ratio of the maximum size to the minimum size. In early Iron Age Judah, the value for q was about 10, whereas by the time of Manasseh, it had risen to 100.

> "The growing social inequality results, of course, not from the decadence and moral corruption as the united social romantics of all ages would have it, but from the population growth: Manasseh's Judah had about 100,000 inhabitants, tenth-century Judah less than 10,000"[119]

Under Assyrian tutelage, the agricultural produce of Judah was oriented towards the production of cash-crops like olive oil, linked to the now excavated factories in the Assyrian-controlled city of Ekron. The shift to cash crops would inevitably have led to the growth of large landholdings and the marginalisation of tens of thousands of agricultural workers and peasants.

There is even a strange episode related in the Book of Jeremiah, about the mass release of slaves when Jerusalem was threatened at an early stage of a Babylonian invasion, by King Nebuchadnezzar (634-562 BCE). Having released the slaves, the owners promptly took them back into captivity again, for which they were punished by God.

> "When the king of Babylon's army fought against Jerusalem . . . This is the word that came unto Jeremiah from the Lord, after that the king Zedekiah had made a covenant of all the people which were at Jerusalem, to proclaim liberty unto them; That every man should let his manservant, and every man his maidservant, being an Hebrew or an Hebrewess, go free; that none should serve himself of them, to wit, of a Jew his brother.

---

[118] Finkelstein and Silberman, *David and Solomon*, p 181
[119] Finkelstein and Silberman, *David and Solomon* p 167.

Now when all the princes, and all the people, which had entered into the covenant, heard that every one should let his manservant and every one his maidservant, go free, that none should serve themselves of them any more, then they obeyed and let them go. But afterwards they turned and caused the servants and the handmaids whom they had let go free, to return and brought them into subjection for servants and for handmaids."[120]

It is impossible, nearly three millennia later, to find the roots of this fabulous story, but it clearly speaks of large numbers of household slaves and servants and great political pressure both towards their enslavement and for their liberation. It speaks, in other words, of a huge divide between the social classes.

Judah's claim for political leadership

With the demise of the northern state, what had remained of the population of the north had been bereft of religious and political leadership. Moreover, the Samarian population was now mixed with a sizeable percentage of settlers from other parts of the Assyrian empire, bringing their own languages, traditions and religious practices. For many remaining Samarian Yahwists the focus of their aspirations therefore shifted to the weaker, but relatively independent kingdom to the south and a number of priests moved there. The Judahite priests and scribes were therefore in a position to absorb many northern traditions, while retaining their essentially southern bias. More than that, the priesthood in Judah was now ready to assume the mantle of religious leadership of the Israelite people as a whole.

It was at this point historically that the threads were drawn together to form the first versions of the Hebrew Bible. Part of the programme of the official priesthood involved setting down what became known as the Deuteronomic History, including the first books of the Hebrew Bible, at least in their first draft. The different sources and traditions of north and south ("E" and "J") were incorporated, but with a strong leaning in favour of the south. It is likely that the scribes who compiled the early version of Genesis and Exodus would have used sources now lost to us: scrolls and written fragments as well as oral history, folk-tales, songs and ballads. Gottwald[121] in *The Hebrew Bible* suggests that probably many of the first written texts in Israel had been orally composed and recited before being committed to writing—especially songs, psalms, laments, priestly sayings and regulations. Long after oral forms ceased to be used widely they would be compiled, committed to written form, further revised and edited. The books of Samuel and Kings cite three secondary sources which, if they existed in written form, have since been lost: The Acts of Solomon, The Chronicles of the Kings and Israel and The Chronicles of the Kings of Judah.

---

120 Jeremiah: ch 34
121 Gottwald, *The Hebrew Bible* p 96

As we have already mentioned, a large part of the early myth was composed with considerable Assyrian/Babylonian influence. The myth of the Conquest and the creation of a once-mighty "unitary" kingdom, with a Davidic (ie Judahite) tradition, was a religious-political attempt to lionise the *current* kings of Judah, by associating them with the imaginary glories of the past. This new written history was at best a "nostalgic construct"[122] of favourable folk tales. Thus the tradition of the very real and once great northern state was subsumed into the glorified tradition of Solomon's kingdom, to which the Judahite kings claimed to be heirs. A clear *selection* took place, one that played down or disguised northern traditions, while emphasising or exaggerating southern traditions. Gottwald gives a flavour of the selection process:

> "In the biblical accounts, kings are depicted as exercising ultimate oversight of the state religion. They build and renovate temples, supervise temple worship, introduce and suppress cults, launch reform initiatives, officiate on important religious occasions, and appoint priests to carry out routine cultic duties . . . Little is said about northern kings as temple builders and sustainers. Jeroboam's sanctuaries at Dan and Bethel[123] are noted as illegitimate alternatives to Jerusalem, and Ahab builds a Ba'al sanctuary that Jehu "reforms" by obliterating it. The erection of a Yahweh temple at Samaria is omitted, leaving the impression that the sole sanctuary in the capital was Ahab's Ba'al temple."[124]

It has been suggested that the main aim of the reforms of the Judahite King Josiah was to centralise the Yahwist cult around the temple in Jerusalem—by the destruction of other centres of worship, like local shrines—associated with the increased domination of the city state over the surrounding countryside. Jerusalem's hold over its rural hinterland allowed it to structure taxation so that tribute flowed more directly to the city priesthood, rather than to local rural priests. In addition to this, the commerce and income associated with thousands of pilgrims going to the Temple served to swell the income of Jerusalem.

Although it was not to reach its final form for a long time, *political Yahwism* had at last arrived, as a creation of the ruling class and its priesthood in seventh century BCE Judah. Nowadays, *the majority of serious biblical scholars, date the first draft of the Deuteronomic History to the reign of King Josiah, at the end of the seventh century BCE,* linking it to the reforms of King Josiah that are mentioned in the Bible.

---

[122]   Gottwald
[123]   Jeroboam was first king of Israel/Samaria, according to the Bible. Dan and Bethel were shrines in his kingdom.
[124]   Gottwald, *The Politics of Ancient Israel*, p 78

"The great cultural saga woven together during the reign of Josiah, which told the story of Israel from God's promise to the patriarchs, through Exodus, conquest, united monarchy, the divided states . . . was a brilliant and passionate composition. It aimed at explaining why past events suggested future triumphs, at justifying the need for the religious reforms of Deuteronomy, and most practically, at backing the territorial ambitions of the Davidic dynasty."[125]

The great epic of Joshua's conquest of Canaan, although not a part of the first five books of the Jewish scripture, was written, in effect, as part of what scholars refer to as the Deuteronomic history. The heroic figure of Joshua was invoked in support of an aspiring 'new' Joshua—king Josiah of Judah—to further his claims to the leadership of the whole community of the Israelites, in Israel to the north and in Judah to the south. Whereas the great emperors of Egypt and Assyria glorified their reigns by magnificent monuments and inscriptions, the King of Judah justified his right to rule through written texts and a 'proven' association with the glories of past Israelite tradition.

"These are not simply conventional parallels between righteous biblical characters, but direct parallels in phraseology and ideology—not to mention Joshua's and Josiah's identical territorial goals. Of course, Josiah's expansion, or desire for annexation of the territories of the northern kingdom in the highlands, raised great hopes, but at the same time posed severe practical difficulties." [126]

The conclusion that most modern scholars have come to, therefore, is that the five books that make up the Torah were first drafted during the reign of King Josiah of the southern kingdom of Judah around 620 BCE or soon after, as a means of furthering his territorial and political ambitions. There were a lot of further editorial alterations in later periods of crisis, particularly during and after the Babylonian conquest but the essential elements of the epic were composed in the late seventh century.

The first compilation reflected the religious world view of the writers of that era and was shaped by the political, social and economic conditions of late seventh century Judah. It was those writers who projected their world view back in time, using the majesty of an invented historical tradition to give added authority to their view. These stories and 'history' they created have no more historical validity than Arthurian legend.

"The landscape of the patriarchal stories is a dreamlike romantic version of the pastoral past, especially appropriate to the pastoral background of a

---

[125]   Finkelstein and Silberman, *The Bible Unearthed*, p 301
[126]   Finkelstein and Silberman, *The Bible Unearthed*, p 95

large proportion of the Judahite population. It was stitched together from memory, snatches of ancient customs, legends of the birth of peoples and the concerns aroused by contemporary conflicts . . ."[127]

"The ambitions of mighty Egypt to expand its empire and of tiny Judah to annex territories of the former kingdom of Israel and establish its independence were therefore in direct conflict . . . Images and memories from the past now became the ammunition in a national test of will between the children of Israel and the pharaoh and his charioteers . . .

. . . We can thus see the composition of the Exodus narrative from a striking new perspective. Just as the written form of the patriarchal narratives wove together the scattered traditions of origins in the service of a seventh century national revival in Judah, the fully elaborated story of conflict with Egypt—of the great powers of the God of Israel and his miraculous rescue of his people—served an even more immediate political and military end. The great saga of a new beginning and a second chance must have resonated in the consciousness of the seventh century readers, reminding them of their own difficulties and giving them hope for the future."[128]

New elements of the Exodus story would be added later, following incorporation into the Babylonian empire and the later Persian empire; but the essential elements of the first five books of the Torah were put together in seventh century Judah as a result of the needs of the ruling dynasty of the time, assisted by the priesthood of Jerusalem.

Other gods and goddesses

The development of the northern and southern states, at different times and under different conditions, were broadly similar from a socio-economic point of view and both had Yahwist cults, although with different observances and practices. Although the later southern scribes wrote Jerusalem and its temple into the Bible as the only legitimate place for sacrifice and worship, the northern cult had had its own temples and sanctuaries for many years prior to this. The Bible records that the first king of Israel, Rehoboam, set up shrines at Dan and Bethel in the north. The traditions of the northern prophets Elijah and Elisha were incorporated into the Bible, even though the lives and work ascribed to them showed no connection whatsoever to Jerusalem or a temple there. Centuries later, after the period of exile in Babylon,

---

[127] Finkelstein and Silberman, *The Bible Unearthed*, pp 44, 47
[128] Finkelstein and Silberman, *The Bible Unearthed*, p 70.

schismatic priests established a temple at Shechem, a former capital city of the northern state.[129]

From the surviving non-biblical evidence it is clear that for the early Israelites, in what developed as the northern and southern kingdoms, Yahweh may have been the 'chief' god but he was by no means the only god. Inscriptions dated to the late ninth/early eighth century BCE found at Kuntillet Ajrud, in the north west of Sinai, in what would have been the southern-most part of Canaan, include references to other gods. The inscriptions include the two phrases *"Yahweh of Samaria and his Asherah"* and *"Yahweh of Teman and his Asherah."* Samaria was the capital of the kingdom of Israel and Teman the equivalent in the kingdom of Edom. It is clear from this inscription that the fertility figure of Asherah was considered to be the female consort of Yahweh. As well as Yahweh and Asherah, the Canaanite gods Ba'al and El also appear in a poetic text.

In the early Israelite community, the only concrete evidence of religious or totemistic ritual is a figurine of a bull—identical to the old Canaanite bull deity *El*. There is no other evidence for religion observance at all. Later, from the time of the establishment of the monarchies there is more evidence of religious worship, such as numerous shrines, both public and private, with all the paraphernalia of sacrifice, as well as local temples. There are many (Asherah) fertility figures that have been found associated particularly with private dwellings. It is not clear whether El and Ba'al were traditional Canaanite gods worshipped by early Israelites or whether they were simply alternative epithets for Yahweh. A number of scholars believe that the figure of Ba'al was worshipped and incorporated into Yahwist tradition and that this former god only *later* evolved into the personification of an evil deity (Beelzebub).

In summary, hardly any biblical scholars today and virtually no archaeologists would subscribe to the idea that the early Israelite religion was monotheistic in any meaningful sense. The new Yahwism of Judah and the Torah, with its historical "authenticity" and newly created "traditions", was not the Yahwism of the *Apiru* and the proto-Israelites, but a product of a later period, by which time the cult had been usurped by a ruling elite far removed from the 'egalitarianism' of the previous period.

For a long time the Yahwists did not deny the existence of other gods—just that theirs was more powerful or more important. All of the new Iron Age kingdoms that came into existence in this period developed their own state religions as part of the bureaucracy and apparatus of government, and each had their own national god. Thus, the first Book of Kings refers to "Ashtoreth, the goddess of the Zidonians",

---

[129] This became the centre of what was effectively the Samaritan 'branch' of Judaism. Although the area was later conquered by the Maccabeans and many Samaritans were absorbed into a common Jewish culture, a tiny branch of separate 'Samaritan' Jews remained apart and still exists to this day. The different traditions of Samaritan Judaism are apparent in the New Testament story of the Good Samaritan, the implication being that, being 'good', he was an exception.

"Milcom the abomination of the Ammonites", "Chemosh, the abomination of Moab" and "Moloch, the abomination of the children of Ammon." Religion, after all, was the main vehicle of political power and when ancient documents mention national gods, it was with the explicit assumption that the god always favoured his or her own nation. The mid-ninth century Mesha stele, as we have shown, testifies to the existence of a powerful Israelite Omrid dynasty and, as was the fashion at that time, it refers to the war between the two nations as a struggle between the two gods: Chemosh of Moab and Yahweh of Israel. The victory over the Israelites was attributed to Chemosh in a literary style directly reminiscent of that used in the Bible when it credits Yahweh with similar victories of the Israelites. There was nothing essentially different about the Yahwist cult of Israel/Judah that in any way distinguished it from the similar national cults in other parts of the Near East.

But whereas other states and their gods have disappeared from the stage of history, never to return, the special strategic position that Judah came to achieve, as a client of a great imperial neighbour, allowed it to recover and revive, along with its cult. But in the final analysis the development of Yahwism as opposed, for example, to worship of Chomosh is due entirely to accidental factors of geography and history and not at all to spiritual causes or divine intervention.

The biblical text actually leaves many traces of the *generalised polytheism* that characterised both Israel and Judah in these early centuries. At one point, the prophet Jeremiah complains that there are "as many gods in Judah as there are cities".[130] There is no doubt that the significance of Yahweh was exaggerated by the later writers. The entire account of the two kingdoms of the north and south is written from the standpoint of a protracted struggle by the followers of Yahweh against an incorrigible tendency to worship other gods. But this is clearly the impression that later writers, supporters of the state-supported Yahwist cult, wanted to give about the history of Israel and Judah. In fact, besides temple worship, it had been a timeless tradition in Canaan to establish shrines and to make sacrifice in selected locations in the countryside—in the hills (the "high places"), in the woods (the "groves") and elsewhere. Writing from the perspective of two hundred years later, almost every king in the Bible is judged by whether or not he supported the shrines and "high places" or chose to have them removed in the cause of Yahweh. To take two instances from among many:

> "[Jehoahaz, king of Israel] . . . did that which was evil in the sight of the Lord, and followed the sins of Jeroboam, the son of Nebat, which made Israel to sin; he departed not therefrom. And the anger of the Lord was kindled against Israel . . ."[131]

---

[130]   Jeremiah, 11,13
[131]   2 Kings: 13, 2

> "Hezekiah the son of Ahaz began to reign . . . And he did that which was right in the sight of the Lord . . . He removed the high places, and brake the images, and cut down the groves . . ."[132]

There were occasional instances of kings described as righteous *but*, inexplicably, they still didn't quite do the business. Thus:

> "Amaziah, the son of Joash, king of Judah . . . did that which was right in the sight of the Lord; yet not like David his father . . . howbeit the high places were not taken away: as yet the people did sacrifice and burnt incense on the high places."[133]

Although it records many instances of the people being led by wicked kings and straying from the 'path of righteousness', the clear impression given in the biblical version of history, as it applies to the unified monarchy and to Israel and Judah, is one in which the *default* religious practice was worship of Yahweh under the auspices of the Jerusalem Temple. Yet the archaeology shows clearly that this 'golden age' of true fidelity to Yahweh was a late invention; what is described as the idolatry of sinful people was the normal way of life for the people of Judah and had been for generations.

The first version of the Deuteronomic History was written on the template of the Judahite tradition. But even the biblical account of the history of Judah occasionally gives the game away. Running as an unmistakeable thread through all the kings of Judah, despite some kings doing "that which was right in the eyes of the Lord" is a complete failure to remove the places of cultic worship in the "groves" and "high places" in the countryside. According to Susan Ackerman, investigating the Judahite cults after the conquest by Babylon, many of these cultic observances were probably no more than a popular form of Yahwism.

> "Most of the manifestations of popular religion which I have described are native to the west Semitic sphere and even to Israel, and they are indigenous in the practice of Yahwistic religion . . . sixth century Yahwism was characterised by a diversity which extends far beyond the parameters seemingly established by the biblical text. Indeed, it is only too obvious that there can be no one definition of what Yahwism was in the exilic period . . . the priestly/Deuteronomic/prophetic version of exilic Yahwism was only that: a version"[134]

---

[132] 2 Kings: 18, 1-4
[133] 2 Kings: 14, 1-4
[134] Susan Ackerman, *Under Every Green Tree: Popular Religion in Sixth Century Judah*, p 215, cited by Gottwald

Most scholars now argue, therefore, that the first definitive Deuteronomic History was composed as a *propaganda work* to sit alongside Josiah's religious reforms and his political programme to restore the empire of David. In the words of the authors of the History, the fall of the north had been God's punishment for straying from the path of righteousness. The creation of a unified Yahwist cult, which was centred on Jerusalem and authenticated by an ancient, unified history, was driven by the *economic, political and social interests of the Judahite ruling class*, which included as a subsidiary component its special caste of scribes and priests.

> "The radical centralisation attributed to Josiah entailed a centralising fiscal policy that would reduce the percentage of state revenues siphoned off by local and regional "tax collectors", stimulate business with increased pilgrim traffic, and generally prosper the economy of Jerusalem."[135]

There is not complete unanimity among scholars about the extent of the reforms of Josiah or his territorial expansion. Indeed, a number of scholars see the reported reforms as a fiction written much later and injected backwards into Judahite history. The only reasonably solid evidence of cultic reform is a suggestion of decline throughout the seventh century BCE in the use of anthropomorphic designs, suggesting a change in fashion or preference away from pictures of gods and astral imagery, to geometric patterns and calligraphy.

Likewise, there is little or no archaeological evidence for territorial expansion under Josiah, although Judah seems to have expanded slightly to the north, taking over the northern shrine in Bethel. Here again, Knauf is quite emphatic, that "from a purely archaeological point of view, it is evident that nobody destroyed the temple of Bethel between 734 and 520 BCE".[136] It is also noteworthy that outside of the biblical text itself, there is no surviving reference to Josiah, either in Egyptian or Babylonian writings.

Uehlinger, for example, poses the question as to whether there was any *cultic* reform during the period of Josiah at all. Pointing out that the system of religious *tithes* was in effect the equivalent of political system of taxation, he asks:

> "Was it not rather, an economically and politically motivated effort to centralise and consolidate the power of the Judahite state administration in Jerusalem, without any genuinely religious aim and purpose but merely related to religion in terms of cult-economy, undoubtedly a major preoccupation for an ancient Near Eastern state's policy and legitimacy?"[137]

However, notwithstanding the paucity of extra-biblical evidence, there is a consensus among scholars on the dating of at least a first draft of the Deuteronomic History to

---

[135] Gottwald, *The Politics of Ancient Israel*, p 83.
[136] Knauf *Good Kings and Bad Kings,* p 184.
[137] Uehlinger, *Good Kings and Bad Kings* p 281

this period. This early draft may have gestated over several decades but had reached something like completion towards the beginning of the sixth century BCE.

> "One of the most characteristic literary devices of the Deuteronomic History, betraying its seventh-century origins, is the phrase "to this day". It is used on dozens of occasions, scattered through the books of Deuteronomy, Joshua, Judges, Samuel and Kings, to point out ancient landmarks or explain unusual situations that could still be observed in the time of the compilation of the text."[138]

In summary, the Bible describes the seventh century and early sixth century BCE as a period of independence for Judah, although its status as a vassal state of Assyria is glossed over. The only period of relative independence is likely to have been during the years of the decline of the Assyrian empire at the end of the seventh century, although even in that short time, the evidence seems to show that from being a vassal of Assyria, Judah briefly became a vassal of Egypt.

We leave it to Warburton to summarise in a paragraph, an accurate description of the history of Israel and Judah, far removed from the account in the Bible:

> "The northern state of Israel did not differ significantly from the neighbouring societies with which it was allied in contests against the Assyrians. When the pagan state of Israel was eventually destroyed by the Assyrians, along with the other Aramean states, a vassal successor was established in the south, called Judah. Somehow this southern state claimed some form of independence, and established an historical link to the northern state by claiming a common political origin and a common religion. In fact, however, the Southern Kingdom was a creature of the Assyrians, with some very unique religious and social ideas. It had no independent history prior to the Assyrian conquests in the north. Its religion and customs can be recognised in the archaeology and the Old Testament narrative, but they do not antedate the Assyrians, and bear no relation to the customs of the northern state.
> The archaeological history of the independent state of Judah would imply that this was politically insignificant and that it lasted little more than a century, ruling little more than a small region around Jerusalem."[139]

At the end of the seventh century, the Assyrian empire was eventually overthrown and replaced by the Babylonians. The expansion of the new Babylonian empire into the territories of the vassal states of its predecessor brought it eventually to the gates of Jerusalem in 597 BCE. According to Gottwald, much of the contents of the Book of Jeremiah would have been written around this point. Faced with the

---

[138]   Finkelstein and Silberman, *David and Solomon*, p 193
[139]   Warburton, *Good Kings and Bad Kings*, p 332

overwhelming force of the Babylonian empire, the small Judahite kingdom was in a dilemma about whether to capitulate or to seek assistance from Egypt; this split in the ruling class is reflected in the works of Jeremiah:

"... this was not simply a narrow religious issue over who had the best foresight into coming events. Considerable socio-political information in the Book of Jeremiah reveals two opposed alignments of prophets, priests and political leaders crystallised around antagonistic political programs in the period 609-586. The kings and a majority of the bureaucrats, priests and prophets formed an 'autonomy' party that sought independence from Babylon with the aid of Egypt . . . a smaller group of court officials [including Jeremiah] . . . formed a 'coexistence' party which favoured continued submission to Babylonia or, once revolt had broken out, capitulation to the besieging enemy."[140]

The 'autonomy' party won the day but after installing a series of servile kings and facing a number of rebellions; eleven years later the Babylonians took the city after a siege, amid great slaughter and destruction. The Bible records that the incumbent king and large numbers of his family were deported, totalling up to ten thousand, depending on the account. The Great Temple was destroyed. According to the Book of Jeremiah, over seventy priests, officers and officials were executed and a second wave of deportations, of over eight hundred, took place; several years later there was a third wave of over seven hundred deportees.

Thus began the period of the great Exile for Judahite followers of Yahweh. The first draft of the texts of the Torah had been completed and the texts were taken with the Judahite ruling class and the priesthood into exile in Babylon, where they were subject to more far-reaching amendment, including the addition of the prophetic books of Jeremiah and Ezekiel. The second half of the Book of Isaiah (referred to as the Second Isaiah, although all of Isaiah is in one book in the Bible) was also written in exile. The new Deuteronomic History now had to take into account a theological explanation for the fact that God had allowed the destruction not only of the wicked northern kingdom, but also of God's temple in Jerusalem. Parts of Isaiah and Ezekiel describe how the Judahites lived in exile, both in the capital city of Babylon and in the countryside. The demise of Jerusalem, of course, was blamed on the sinfulness of the kings of Judah, Manasseh in particular.

---

[140] Gottwald, *The Hebrew Bible*, p 403

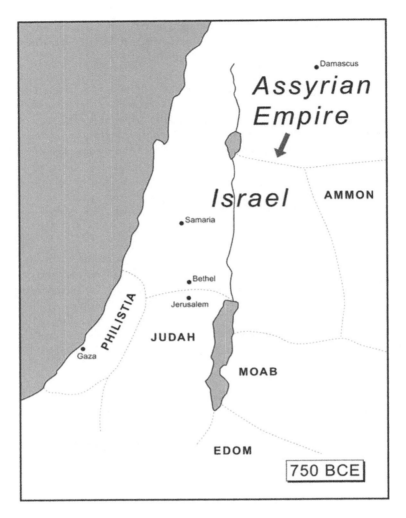

**MAP 2: The approximate disposition of kingdoms
in the area of ancient Canaan around 750 BCE**

A significant part of the Judahite population was assimilated into the Babylonian population. Even after the later release and return of the exiles (see next chapter) many descendents of the Judahites, although remaining attached to their former religion, chose to stay on in Babylon, thus beginning a centuries-long tradition of a large Jewish population in that part of the world. The beginning of the Persian era and the return of the exiles from Babylon—establishing the tradition of a new 'redemption' of the land of Israel—marked a new milestone in the development of Yahwism or what from now on would be more appropriately referred to as *Judaism*.

Chapter summary:

- The biblical references to the tribes of Israel reflects an early stage in Hebrew culture and an early primitive democracy

- Two separate kingdoms of Israel and Judah are attested by archaeological evidence, but there is no archaeological evidence for the great united kingdom of David and Solomon preceding them, or for the temple built by the latter in Jerusalem.

- The biblical books contain echoes the class struggle in the early kingdoms and the rise of an official religion with its priesthood.

- The relatively powerful Israelite kingdom of Omri is probably the model for later legends about the kingdom of Solomon. During the period of dominance of this kingdom Jerusalem was an insignificant hill town

- The conquest of Israel by the Assyrian Empire allowed the kingdom of Judah to develop as a vassal state of Assyria. It was in the kingdom of Judah—and as an expression of the interests of the Judahite elite—that the first versions of the Torah were compiled.

- Judah was eventually swallowed up by the Babylonian Empire, an event that led to the exile of Judahite priests and leaders.

- Most Israelites during this period were not monotheistic

Chapter 4

Exile and Return

We shall now look at the so-called 'Great Return' of the Hebrew people from Babylonian exile, which is recounted in the Bible and which, like the Exodus from Egypt, is an important element in Jewish tradition today. We shall show that the new Jewish state established by the returning exiles in fact represented a Persian puppet regime that was foisted on the people of Judah. We shall argue that it was the representatives of this new Jewish elite who completed the writing and editing of the early books of the Bible, including the Deuteronomic History. The Persian province of Judea was centred on the Temple with a bloated priestly caste which represented its own interests and those of the local and imperial ruling elite. Following the later Greek conquest, Judea was drawn into the economic and cultural orbit of the Greek-speaking Near East and this provided the setting of the Maccabean revolt, another important motif for modern Jewish political tradition. We shall argue, however, that the Maccabean revolt reflected not so much anti-Hellenism as the discontent of the mass of the population who were labouring under an excessive taxation regime.

. . . .

The next great milestone in the development of Judaism—and many scholars argue that it was the *single most important period*—came with the collapse of the Babylonian Empire and its replacement by the Persian Empire. Cyrus, the first great Persian king, is hailed in the Bible as a hero, the "anointed of the Lord", for his decision to "release" the Judahites and Israelites from their exile in Babylon. According to the biblical account, Cyrus not only decreed that the exiles be freed, but instructed that their temple should be rebuilt in Jerusalem.

The Bible account blesses Cyrus with motives he did not have, of course. Righteousness and morality played no part in his calculations. The new Persian masters of Judah were no different to their Assyrian and Babylonian predecessors in the ruthless exploitation of their subject peoples. It was simply that, like the previous empires, the Persians used population transfers as a standard part of their imperial policy.

"The transportation of gods and peoples under the guise of restoration was presented as the primary function of empire. The policy was reiterated in deportation texts under Cyrus' successors, Xerxes, Darius II and Artaxerxes. Policies of systematic deportation had begun as early as the ninth century

under the Assyrians. They were continued by the Babylonians and the Persians."[141]

The policy of population transfer also included the shipment of some peoples back to their point of origin, accompanied by imperial propaganda about 'liberation' and 'protecting' all the kings' peoples. As was the case elsewhere in the Empire, the new political realities facing the former exiles of Judah and Israel were to have a profound effect on their theology and religious practices.

> "In order for there to be a functioning Jewish community in Palestine, there had to be civil order and legitimate cult. It was the *Law*, supplemented by *Persian imperial administration* that provided the former, and it was the *sacrificial and ritual holiness system* centred on the Temple and expounded in the Law that provided the latter . . ."[142]

Under the Persian kings, several waves of settlers were transported from Babylon to the new province of Judea, in the Persian language, *Yehud*, from which the word *Jew* originates.[143] The biblical books of Ezra and Nehemiah and the 'later' prophets have integrated the histories of these waves of settlement into a single event, although they avoid their main purpose, which was *to establish a reliable client elite* to consolidate Persian imperial interests. What the biblical account offers is no more than a *theological apologia* for Persian rule. There are no fewer than *four* different versions of the decree of King Cyrus in the Bible: in Isaiah 44-45, 2 Chronicles 36, Ezra 1 and 1 Esdras 2. The biblical accounts are an expression in *theological* terms of the *political propaganda* of imperial Persia in pursuit of its policy in Judea.

> "The new Persian emperor, Cyrus, puts himself forward as the protector of the traditional religion throughout the empire. He is the liberator of those who had been enslaved by the Babylonians. Even Babylon itself is described as having opened its gates to his army and having welcomed his arrival. Not only the Bible's Yahweh but other gods appeared to Cyrus to give him instructions concerning their peoples. They ordered him . . . to restore people to their homelands, rebuild the homes (temples) of the gods, and re-establish the societies that the Babylonians had left in ruins. This is the language of propaganda, the language of deportation and population transference."[144]

It is not surprising that so many scholars date the completion of the Deuteronomic History and the early historic books of the Bible, like Samuel, Joshua and Kings to

---

[141] Thompson, *The Mythic Past*, p 191.
[142] Gottwald, *The Hebrew Bible*, p 461
[143] It is therefore legitimate, from this point on, to refer to the residents of Judah as 'Jews'.
[144] Thompson, *The Mythic Past*, p 212

this period. The whole rationale of these books is based on a theme that leads to the foundation of a new Israel, one that draws on the ancient history and learns from the mistakes of the old Israel. Indeed, the aspiration of a new Israel is one that keeps its momentum going for centuries, right up to and including the Christians. The entire theme of the Deuteronomic History, the books of Samuel, Joshua and Kings, leads to the redemption of Israel and the great Return.

The biblical history of old Israel includes a plethora of ultra-nationalistic outrages perpetrated by the Israelites, such as ethnic cleansing, the slaughter of prisoners of war and the mass murder of city populations. There are strictures in the Book of Numbers against marrying outside the Israelite people and even against inter-tribal marriages within the Israelite community. One story in the Book of Numbers, for example, recounts, almost approvingly, the murder of a man and a woman, merely because theirs was a 'mixed' marriage! The second Book of Chronicles even describes a covenant to kill all non-believers:

> "And they entered into a covenant to seek the Lord God of their fathers with all their heart and with all their soul
> That whosoever would not seek the Lord God of Israel should be put to death, whether small or great, whether man or woman."[145]

It would be difficult to find a social or political rationale for a scribe or priest writing this kind of 'history' in the earlier period of the Judahite kingdom. But it does make sense as a theological metaphor for the self-important Persian-sponsored elite, attempting to foist itself onto the reluctant population of Judea at the end of the sixth and throughout the fifth centuries BCE. Like the biblical books of the Persian-appointed officials, Ezra and Nehemiah, who demanded that the Israelites "put away" their "strange" wives, these histories were designed to emphasise that it was they, *the settlers newly returned from Babylon*, and not the indigenous "strangers", who were the true inheritors of ancient Israel.

> "It is in the return that Judah and Jerusalem become Israel. It is in the return that the 'God of Israel'—historically long established in Samaria—is given a home, in Jerusalem. It is in the return that the people of Judah came to understand themselves as the 'children of Israel' and as the 'new Israel'"[146]

The Persians appointed a committee, the *gerousia*, from leading nobles and heads of aristocratic families, to guard their mutual interests against those of the common people.

This body became more prominent in the later Hellenistic era and still existed in a different form during the Roman period.

---

[145] 2 Chronicles: 15, 12
[146] Thompson, *The Mythic Past,* p 195

But it was all very well Cyrus and his successors wishing to establish a puppet regime in Jerusalem. The problem was that Judea was not quite empty. Indeed the great theocratic propaganda drive was a necessary part of the Return precisely because of the opposition of the native population who had never been exiled in the first place.

A part of the priesthood in exile, perhaps the same group who updated the Deuteronomic History to take account of the destruction of Jerusalem, was now called upon to update the work again. As a means of asserting their interests as a part of the new ruling class in *Yehud*, and to promote a sense of national identity to the people of the former state of Judah, the priests revised the history one final time. Scholars have different views on what *proportions* of the History were written at what times, but there is a consensus that the period following exile saw the *final version* of the History take shape, even if it was based on an earlier template. The History was further supplemented by the Books of Chronicles and the Prophets, all of which served to create the *fiction* of Yahwism as the traditional faith of a previously 'unified' Israelite people.

> "Deuteronomy fits the context of an immigrant population, based around a temple, in conflict with some of the indigenous population as well as with Samaria, and encouraged to live and exercise their control by means of a written law, controlled by the priesthood . . ."[147]

By the end of the exile, Yahwism had completed its long march from being a *cult with revolutionary overtones* to one that was honed and refined to become the official state religion of the Persian-sponsored Jewish elite. The priesthood was not slow in asserting its own claims to special privileges; it is probable that the lengthy priestly elements of the books of Leviticus and Numbers were also reaching their final form around this time.

> "It is overwhelmingly clear that the style and emphases of these [priestly] stipulations represents a late exilic and early postexilic priestly community that was striving to establish the legitimacy of its leadership in a restored Judahite community."[148]

The one-time anti-monarchist and egalitarian cult was finally and completely usurped by the very same state forms to which it was originally opposed. To what degree the official adoption of Yahwism by various ("good") Israelite and Judahite kings was *retrospectively* written into the history and to what extent it had in actual fact been adopted earlier by some of these kings, it is impossible to say. Scholars are not agreed on it, although it has to be said that the entire history of the two early kingdoms, even as the Bible narrates it, is one long unremitting *failure* to impose a

---

[147]   Philip Davies, *Good Kings and Bad*, p 75
[148]   Gottwald, *The Hebrew Bible* p 207

uniform Yahwism on those 'sinful' nations. What is clear is that by the time it was imported into post-exilic Judah, the whole of the Deuteronomic History was in the process of being finally amended.

> "There is now a very strong trend to locate the emergence of exclusive monotheism in Persian age Judah. Older notions that monotheism began with Moses or with the prophets are now widely dismissed. Indeed, the very notion that the cult of Yahweh had a more or less stable homogeneous repertory of beliefs and practices over the centuries, which could be expanded when the time was ripe into the affirmation of Yahweh as the sole universal deity, is breaking down . . . in short, the pre-exilic cult of Yahweh was not as standardised as we formerly thought. It emerged only slowly in convergence with and differentiation from other cults to become the all-embracing monotheism of late biblical time. This means that one of the touchstones of most hypotheses about Israelite origins, namely, that a strong comprehensive Yahwistic cult unified the people from early times is thrown into grave doubt."[149]

This period probably saw the final redaction of the books that are named as the works of the earlier prophets, like Amos, Hosea, Isaiah and Jeremiah, supplemented by later prophets of the exilic and post-exilic periods.

The books of the prophets

Elements within the books of Amos, Hosea, Isaiah and Jeremiah, as we have shown, are a reflection of the social conflicts between the classes in Israel and Judah prior to their conquest by Assyria and Babylon, expressed in the only political language of the time, the language of religion. It is impossible to say whether or not the prophets named by these books were real people or personifications of popular political dissent, but even if they had been real and their ideas were transmitted orally for decades, their 'books' were not edited into their final form until well after the conquest of the two kingdoms. It may be that their final editing in the post-exilic period means that they reflect the class tensions in the period of final redaction rather than the earlier kingdoms. What is certain is that the passages that were written to explain the demise of Judah and Israel were later additions that were projected back to the earlier period as prophesies. Whatever periods the social commentaries represent, they have remained, interwoven with pious denunciations of errant kings and princes.

The prophets of the exile frequently refer to the imagined past unity of Israel and Judah. The Book of Ezekiel describes them as wayward 'sisters' reduced to whoredom, Samaria being the 'elder sister' of Judah. The greatest emphasis in the

---

149   Gottwald, *The Tribes of Yahweh*, p xli

collective redemption of the people is in the unity of the two states and therefore of the exiles:

> "I will make them one nation in the land upon the mountains of Israel; and one king shall be king to them all; and they shall no more be two nations, neither shall they be divided into two kingdoms any more at all."[150]

The mid-fourth century BCE was the period of the writing of the Book of Chronicles, which repeats much of the earlier material in the Torah as well as the rest of the Deuteronomic History in Samuel, Joshua and Kings, although not always with the same slant. Some sections in Chronicles are copied, word for word, from earlier books, while others appear to be in direct conflict with the narrative of the earlier books. But overall, it represents a drive to establish a continuous and unified Israelite tradition, albeit with precedence for the southern Yahwist tradition over the north. In the books of Chronicles:

> "All the critical or unflattering stories about David and Solomon have been intentionally and selectively omitted. Every story that could have shed negative light on David and Solomon is carefully excised."[151]

Gottwald likened this combined oral and early literary tradition to a river with small streams and sources gradually accumulating to larger and more developed texts, beginning in the monarchic period, then edited several times over, before their final form in Persian Judea. Both Ezra and Nehemiah were agents of the Persian king Artaxerxes, who we know ruled during the mid-fifth century BCE, so that would be the earliest possible date for their books to have been written. According to Gottwald, it was probably during the post-exilic period from 400 to 200 BCE, that the writings of the prophets were edited and rounded out, the Books of Chronicles written between 525 and 375 BCE and the Books of Daniel and Esther composed much later, about 165 BCE and 125 BCE respectively.

> ". . . the Book of Genesis, standing at the beginning of the Bible, did not reach its present form until after the Book of Deuteronomy through Kings had been composed during the late seventh and sixth centuries BCE . . . even when the core of a biblical book is correctly attributed to the named author, as for example Amos or Isaiah, numerous additions have been made by later hands, some by second, or third-generation disciples of the master . . . the final stage of the Hebrew Bible was reached over a span of postexilic time from the sixth to through the second centuries BCE."[152]

---

[150] Ezekiel: 37, 22.
[151] Finkelstein and Silberman, *David and Solomon*, p 223
[152] Gottwald, *The Hebrew Bible* p 14

The specific social function of *written* scripture is that it is a means of fixing oral tradition to a form and content that meets the needs of its authors, specifically in this case, the social and political interests of the client Jewish ruling class and the caste of the Temple priesthood. As far as the mass of the population was concerned, the Scripture was not written to be read, but to be *heard* as it was *read to them*, so the authors included dozens of hints that their interpretation of the past should be passed on, like the following.

> "So that you can recount to your sons and grandsons how I made fools of the Egyptians . . ."(Exod. 10, 2)
> "And when your children ask you, 'what does this ritual mean?' you will tell them . . ."(Exod. 12, 26
> "And when your son asks you in days to come, 'What does this mean?' you will tell him . . ."(Exod. 13, 14)
> "Teach your children and your children's children . . ." (Deut. 4, 9)
> "In times to come, when your children ask you, 'What is the meaning of these instructions, laws and customs . . . ?'" (Deut. 6, 20)
> "Question your father, let him explain to you, your elders, and let them tell . . ." (Deut. 32, 7)
> "When in the future, your children ask you, 'What do these stories mean for you?', you will tell them . . ." (Josh, 4, 6).
> "When in the future your children ask their fathers, 'What are these stones?', you will teach your children . . ." (Josh, 4, 21).

This is only a sample, with an even greater number of references to continuation of the transmission in the Book of Numbers.

The great Return of the Yahwist-worshipping elite, put in power by the Persians, did not go unchallenged by the local indigenous population and the struggle of the latter shows through even in the biblical accounts of the books of Ezra and Nehemiah. As it was in the case of the Assyrian deportations from Israel, the Bible exaggerates the numbers of Judahites who had been taken into exile in Babylon. By the time of the destruction of Jerusalem, Assyrian and then later Babylonian conquest of bits of Judahite territory had reduced the kingdom to a rump. Nevertheless, there is a lot of archaeological evidence to testify to the original destruction of Jerusalem by the conquering Babylonians in 586 BCE. Arrowheads, signs of burning, and so on, show that in that respect, at least, the biblical account seems genuine. Excavations in the area immediately around Jerusalem and in the city itself testify to widespread and systematic destruction.

> "The sack of Jerusalem created a demographic and cultural crisis: the archaeology indicates a total collapse. The number of inhabited sites fell two-thirds in the seventh and sixth centuries (from 116 to 41), the average size of the sites also fell by about two-thirds (from 4.4 hectares to 1.4), with a sudden collapse of the population by about 85-90 per cent.

Inhabited sites tended to be without walls or public buildings, production of high-status handicrafts ceased and the use of writing was rare. Only the central region of Benjamin escaped. With the fall of Jerusalem and other larger sites in the Shephelah, a region of impoverished villages was left, with a population of 10,000 to 20,000 persons."[153]

The immediate vicinity of the city, therefore, appears to have remained sparsely populated for decades afterwards. According to Finkelstein and Silberman, even after several decades, the population of the greater Jerusalem area was only forty per cent of the pre-exilic level. A few "scattered survivors" lived on the fringes of a ruined city. Many would have died in the conquest and in the privations that resulted from it, so that the total number of exiles may not have exceeded about twenty per cent of the original population, mostly the surviving population of Jerusalem, including the aristocracy, as well as city-based artisans, scribes and priests. But in fact, taking the whole of Judah into account, *the majority of the rural population must have remained behind*. In writing into the Books of Jeremiah and Lamentations a description of Jerusalem, and by implication the whole of Judah, as having been like "a desert", the later authors were reflecting the interests of the new settler elite who needed to justify their disregard of those who had been left behind.

It would appear that the returnees did not come in one single group, but in a number of waves, over a long period of time and they did not come back to an empty land, although archaeological evidence suggests that the population of Judah was not very great. Gottwald suggests a number barely reaching five figures:

"Estimates of the population of Persian Judah have been significantly downsized in recent years, throwing doubt on the nearly 50,000 returnees claimed in Ezra2/Nehemiah 7: 1-70. One recent estimate, based on an exhaustive review of the archaeological data, claims a population of about 13,000 prior to the mid-fifth century, increasing to about 20,000 thereafter. Estimates of the population of Jerusalem range from 1,500 to 4,500 at most. The vast majority of the settlements were small villages."[154]

The idea that *nearly all* of the Jews were exiled in Babylon and that *nearly all* of them returned with the reforms of Cyrus the Great is an important, if unspoken, element in the grand myth of the Jewish people. But other than the biblical account, there is no evidence for this. On the contrary, the archaeological evidence suggests that *the larger proportion of the original Judahite population had been left in situ*. Most of those who were forced into exile would have been from Jerusalem itself, including the ruling elite and the urban population. The returnees were not only a minority of the original population of Judah, they were, in all probability, a minority of the

---

[153]   Lester L Grabbe, *Good kings, bad kings*, p 9
[154]   Gottwald, *The Politics of Ancient Israel*, p 237.

exiles who had been transported to Babylon and Persia, not to mention those exiled to other Babylonian provinces.

The Persians' decision to establish a new state of *Yehud*—with former elements of the pre-exilic elite in positions of governance—was a measure calculated to strengthen their control of the region. Those elements of the Jewish ruling class and priesthood who supported the government of Persia *were effectively collaborating in the exploitation of the Jewish peasantry*. The first governor appointed was Zerubbabel, the author of two prophetic books in the Bible. The high priest appointed by him was another Joshua. According to the biblical account, these two worked together to rebuild Jerusalem and the Temple. But it is clear even from the biblical narrative that the Judahites who had remained—although their presence is never explicitly acknowledged—did not easily accept the new ruling elite foisted on them, or for that matter, the version of Yahwism which had been knocked into shape in Babylon over the last fifty years.[155] The Book of Ezra, for example, describes some of the *opposition* to the re-building of the Temple:

> "Then the people of the land weakened the hands of the people of Judah, and troubled them in the building, and hired counsellors against them, to frustrate their purpose"[156].

The biblical account describes a postponement in the building of new city walls, due to the opposition of local "kings", as a by-product of which, the construction of the Temple was also delayed. But if these public works had been authorised in the first place by the great Persian emperor (Artaxerxes), it is unlikely that he would have changed his mind so easily. Rather than the opposition of nearby kings, it is more likely to have been the *opposition of local people, the "people of the land"*, those paying the bill for the work through their taxes (the king's tribute), which was the main obstacle to the construction.

The Book of Haggai has another explicit theological defence of the Persian governorship of Zerubbabel—thus, "I take thee, O Zerubbabel, my servant, the son of Shealtiel, saith the Lord, and will make thee as a signet; for I have chosen thee, saith the Lord of hosts."[157]—but it, too, hints at the opposition of the population who argued that "the time is not come, the time that the Lord's house should be built."[158] Haggai alludes to the poverty of the masses:

---

[155] It is an interesting irony of history that the Bible (written, of course, by the 'victors') takes no account of the Judahite population who *had not been* exiled—just as modern-day Zionists have sought to 'redeem' Israel, ie populate Palestine, while taking no account of the Palestinians already living there.

[156] Ezra: 4, 4

[157] Haggai: 2, 23.

[158] Ibid: 1, 2

"Ye have sown much, and bring in little; ye eat, but ye have not enough; ye drink, but ye are not filled with drink; ye clothe you, but there is none warm; and he that earneth wages earneth wages to put it into a bag with holes."[159]

But this generalised want, to the prophet, is caused by a *spiritual* poverty that can only be remedied by the re-building of the Temple. The Book of Ezra is a much longer pious work, based on the same theme of the redemption of Israel, but even in this account, it is made clear that Ezra was sent by King Artaxerxes with powers to carry out Persian policy, with the threat of reprisal against any dissent within the local population.

"And thou, Ezra, after the wisdom of thy God, that is in thine hand, set magistrates and judges, which may judge all the people that are beyond the river . . . and whosoever will not do the law of thy God, and the law of the king, let judgment be executed speedily upon him, whether it be unto death, or to banishment, or to confiscation of goods, or to imprisonment."[160]

When the building work was resumed, the Bible relates, it was only with an *armed guard* provided for the workers.

"And it came to pass from that time forth, that the half of my servants wrought in the work, and the other half of them held both the spears, the shields, and the bows, and the habergeons . . ."[161]

The opposition of the majority of the people of Judea is understandable. Here was a new ruling elite, placed over them by their Persian overlords and with the force of the Persian army at their backs, taking the best land, houses, and property as was their 'right' as descendents of exiles. Forced to pay unwelcome taxes, many families were pushed into debts and bondage. The Book of Nehemiah echoes the impoverishment of the poorest sections of society:

"And there was a great cry of the people and of their wives against their brethren the Jews. For there were some that said, We our sons, and our daughters, are many; therefore we take up corn for them, that we may eat and live. Some also there were that said, we have mortgaged our lands, vineyards, and houses, that we might buy corn, because of the dearth. There were also that said, We have borrowed money for the king's tribute, and that upon our lands and vineyards. Yet now our flesh is as the flesh of

---

159   Ibid: 1, 6
160   Ezra: 7, 25-26
161   Nehemiah: 4: 16

our brethren, our children as their children: and lo, we bring into bondage our sons and our daughters to be servants and some of our daughters are brought into bondage already: neither is it in our power to redeem them, for other men have our lands and vineyards."[162]

The resentment would have been felt particularly in the rural areas. The new elite was based in Jerusalem and it was the rebuilding of the city itself that was costing so much blood, toil, tears and sweat for the outlying areas. So great was the opposition in the rural areas, that while the still poorly populated city was being rebuilt, it was locked at night against raids from the countryside. "Let not the gates of Jerusalem be opened until the sun be hot; and while they stand by, let them shut the doors, and bar them, and appoint watches of the inhabitants of Jerusalem, every one in his watch, and every one to be over his house."[163]

The process of the completion of the canonical Old Testament books, over many decades, was not a simple and one-sided process. Some sections, particularly in the books of the Prophets, reflected opposing class interests, and competing interests within layers of the ruling elite. Alongside the insistence of the Ezras and Nehemiahs that the temple be built and the priesthood restored to its rightful place, there are the frequent references to the plight of the poor and the rebukes directed at the ruling class. Nehemiah was one of the later governors sent by Artaxerxes—with "captains of the army and horsemen"—and in the book bearing his name he denounces those *earlier* governors who, unlike him, had been in the habit of exacting great profit from the people:

". . . the former governors that had been before me were chargeable unto the people, and had taken of them bread, and wine, beside forty shekels of silver; yea, even their servants bare rule over the people"[164]

Yet another implied criticism of previous governors is his reference to social unrest in the province:

"The remnant that are left of the captivity there in the province are in great affliction and reproach: the wall of Jerusalem also is broken down and the gates thereof are burned with fire."[165]

He was at pains to point out that he did not take the tribute that was due to him, "because the bondage was heavy upon this people". Moreover, he rebuked the Judean elite for their oppression of the poor:

---

[162] Nehemiah: 5, 1-5
[163] Nehemiah: 7, 3
[164] Nehemiah: 5, 15
[165] Nehemiah: 1, 3

"I rebuked the nobles, and the rulers, and said unto them, Ye exact usury, every one of his brother. And I set a great assembly by them.

And I said unto them, We after our ability have redeemed our brethren the Jews, which were sold unto the heathen; and will ye even sell your brethren? Or shall they be sold unto us? Then held they their peace, and found nothing to answer . . .

Restore, I pray unto you, to them, even this day, their lands, their vineyards, their olive-yards, and their houses, also the hundredth part of the money, and of the corn, the wine, and the oil, that ye exact of them."[166]

But the main factor in post-exilic Judea was the overriding need of the restored Judean elite to exercise its power and privilege and to cultivate an identity and a theological justification for its position.

". . . it was in the [Persian] conquerors' interests to cultivate a local Jewish elite. The leadership of the restored Judahite community, including Ezra and Nehemiah, were just such an elite . . . Decisions about holy books were thus not only decisions about religious matters but about who had controlling power in the life of the community . . ."[167]

A central plank, therefore, in the establishment of the new ruling class in *Yehud* was the drive to impose a Jerusalem-based Yahwist religion on a reluctant Judahite population. Some time in the middle of the fifth century BCE the prophet Ezra was appointed by the Persians as a priest-leader of the Jewish people. Among other things, the Bible tells us, he demanded the attendance of the people at community meetings, to be read "the Law", on pain of forfeiture of all goods. He also demanded the dissolution of all mixed marriages, to re-establish the purity of the nation. The population of Judah, who had intermarried with other nations during the period of the exile, were now expected to "put away" those wives who were not of the faith, along with any children of those marriages. "Separate yourselves from the people of the land, and from the strange wives."

". . . . therefore give not your daughters unto their sons, neither take their daughters unto your sons, nor seek their peace or their wealth for ever."[168]

It is extremely doubtful, to say the least, that this demand would have any support among the vast majority of the population. It is enough to imagine thousands of divorcees and their children wandering the countryside to realise how improbable it was. But the fact that the imperative of racial purity was given such prominence and enshrined in the Books of Ezra and Nehemiah is an indication of the intensity

---

[166]   Nehemiah: 5, 7 - 11
[167]   Gottwald, *The Hebrew Bible*, p 111
[168]   Ezra: 9, 12

of the drive to establish an official state religion—against what must have been the unorthodox cultic practices that still prevailed in the Judean countryside. It would have taken many decades before the ruling group in Jerusalem were able to enforce their brand of Judaism on the reluctant majority of the population and even then there was no consensus about what were canonical works of literature until the last century BCE.

Among other things, the Law so enthusiastically advanced by Ezra included the centrality of the Jerusalem Temple for all sacrifice and the funding of the priesthood.

> "Lacking the institution of kingship, the Temple now became the centre of identity of the people of Yehud. This was one of the most important turning points in Jewish history . . . Scholars have long noted that the Priestly source (P) in the Pentateuch is, in the main, post-exilic—it is related to the rise of the priests to prominence in the Temple community in Jerusalem . . ."[169]

The Book of Nehemiah numbers the priesthood in the Temple at two hundred and eighty-four, although this did not include other officials like gate-keepers, porters, scribes and singers. At the centre of the new vassal state, the Temple, therefore, was becoming a vast enterprise and central to the income, power and prestige of the ruling elite. *Yehud* was becoming something like a 'Temple-state'. Nehemiah also lists the tithe obligation loaded onto the populace and the many occasions upon which worshippers and pilgrims could be charged a fee by the priests of the Temple:

> "Also we made ordinances for us, to charge ourselves yearly with the third part of a shekel for the service of the house of our God
> For the showbread, and for the continual meat offering, and for the continual burnt offering, of the Sabbaths, of the new moons, for the set feasts, and for the holy things and for the sin offerings to make an atonement for Israel, and for all the work of the house of God . . .
> And to bring the first fruits of our ground, and the first fruits of all fruit of all trees, year by year, unto the house of the Lord . . .
> And that we should bring the first fruits of our dough, and our offerings, and the fruit of all manner of trees, of wine and of oil, unto the priests, to the chambers of the house of our God; and the tithes of our ground unto the Levites, that the same Levites might have the tithes in all the cities of our tillage . . ."[170]

The Temple became the principle focus of power in Jerusalem and, arguably, in the state surrounding it from the time of its establishment during the period of the Persian Jewish state until its destruction in the first century of the modern era.

---

[169]   Finkelstein and Silberman, *The Bible Unearthed*, p 310.
[170]   Nehemiah: ch 10.

". . . whoever succeeded in controlling the temple establishment in the restored Jewish community exercised significant political, economic and ideological power . . . as waves of deported Jews returned to Judah in the late sixth and fifth centuries, descendents of the various priestly groups that at one time or another had presided over the cult now contended for the plum of ecclesial leadership in the rebuilt temple . . . what is clear is that one group won out decisively over all the others" [171]

As much as the Judean ruling class assumed the mantle of "all Israel", in practice the petty temple-state of Judea was no bigger than the original state of Judah that had been conquered by the Babylonians. What had been Israel/Samaria to the north and Galilee further north still, was beyond its control. After the Persian Empire was established, in fact, a number of northern priests re-established their own temple in Samaria, also under the patronage of the Persian king. This Samaritan branch of Yahwism, later centred on a temple at Mount Gerizim, lasted until the conquest of the Jewish Hasmonean kings in the mid second century BCE, although it never attained anything like the prominence of the temple-city of Jerusalem. The predominance of the Jerusalem cult is reflected in what eventually became the Hebrew Bible.

"The Hebrew Bible no longer considers the northerners to be legitimate members of Israel . . . the vantage point from which the whole history is recounted is that of the colonial Judahite community" [172]

As an interesting aside, archaeological discoveries in modern times have shown that there were colonies of Jews outside Judea who continued in the old way, to worship Yahweh alongside other gods. Elephantine is an island in the River Nile and there were Jewish settlers there from perhaps the eighth century BCE. Among papyrus finds discovered there in 1890 were letters written in Aramaic from Elephantine to the officers of the Jerusalem Temple between 419 and 400 BCE. It seems that the Jewish temple in Elephantine was not only dedicated to Yahu (Yahweh), but also to Bethel (perhaps a remnant of the northern equivalent god, based in Samaria) and the Egyptian god, Anat.

The Hellenic period

The great empire of the Persians fell apart under the onslaught of the Graeco-Macedonian army of Alexander the Great, and Judea was duly conquered during Alexander's march from Syria into Egypt in 332 BCE. Upon his sudden and premature death, Alexander's enormous empire, stretching from North Africa to Afghanistan, broke into warring territories ruled by his former generals. For most of

---

[171]   Gottwald, *The Hebrew Bible*, p 461
[172]   Gottwald, *The politics of ancient Israel*, p 16

the third century BCE it was King Ptolemy and his successors, ruling from Egypt, who were the imperial masters of the Jews of Palestine and from about 200 BCE onwards it was the successors of Seleucus, who were based in Asia.

This was the Hellenic period in Judean history and it is reflected in the Bible in the books of 1 and 2 Maccabees. The books were written in reverse order, Book 2 shortly after the Maccabean revolt began, in 165 BCE and Book 1, more of a eulogy to the Hasmonean dynasty that followed the revolt, perhaps forty or fifty years later. The books of Maccabees do not appear in all copies of the Bible because although they are part of the official canon of Catholic, Coptic and Orthodox Christian publications, they are not in the Protestant or Jewish equivalents, where they are considered instead to be *apocryphal* works. They are considered by many modern historians as a useful source of genuine historical information, notwithstanding inaccuracies or exaggerations in some places. In her book *Apocalypse Against Empire*, Anathea Portier-Young cites a number of studies which suggest that the modern historian should treat the ancient historian of 1 Maccabees "with great respect". Non-biblical sources confirm so many episodes in 2 Maccabees that many other elements which are not similarly confirmed are nevertheless taken as reasonably reliable. This is particularly true of the period that immediately preceded the Maccabean revolt, one that drew only minimal attention from the later author of 1 Maccabees.

As Daniel Harrington has explained, it is difficult to understand the non-canonical status of Maccabees in the Jewish tradition, given that its revolutionary tradition has become the stuff of Jewish folk-lore, right up to and including the imagery and motifs of modern Israeli militias and armed forces.

"There has been, however, a puzzling ambivalence regarding the Maccabean revolt in the Jewish tradition. The feast of Hanukkah [celebrating the dedication of the Temple] has been celebrated through the years . . . More puzzling is the disappearance of the Hebrew original of 1 Maccabees from the canon of Hebrew Scriptures. These puzzlements lead scholars to suspect that at some point in the first century CE there was a Jewish reaction against the Maccabees and what they stood for, and a deliberate attempt to push them out of the sacred tradition of Judaism. Perhaps 'messianic' claims were being made about Judas Maccabeus or some other figure who traced his ancestry back to the Maccabean movement. Perhaps in the light of failed uprisings against the Romans by Jews claiming to follow the example of Judas and his brothers, the custodians of Judaism came to regard the Maccabees as too controversial and too dangerous."[173]

---

[173]   Daniel Harrington, *The Maccabean Revolt*, p 131

Ptolemies		
	Ptolemy I	305-285
	Ptolemy II	285-246
	Ptolemy III	246-221
	Ptolemy IV	221-204
	Ptolemy V	204-
Seleucids		
	Antiochus III	-187
	Seleucus IV	187-175
	Antiochus IV	175-164
	Antiochus V	164-162
Hasmoneans		
	Jonathan Maccabeus	153-142
	Simon Maccabeus	142-134
	John Hyrcanus	134-104
	Aristobulus	104-103
	Alexander Jannaeus	103-76
	Alexandra Salome (Queen)	76-67
	John Hyrcanus II (high priest only)	76-66
	Aristobulus II	66-63
	John Hyrcanus II (high priest only)	63-40
	Antigonus	40-37
Herodians		
	Antipater the Idumean (Governor of Judea)	60-43
	Herod (Governor of Galilee)	47-40
	Phasael (Governor of Jerusalem)	47-40
	Herod 'the Great' King of all Judea	37-4
	Herod Antipas (Ethnarch of Judea)	4 BCE-6 CE
	Herod II (Tetrarch of Batanaea)	4 BCE-34 CE
	Herod Philip II (Tetrarch of Ituraea and Trachonitis)	4 BCE-34 CE
	Herod Agrippa	
	• Tetrarch of Batanaea	37-41
	• Tetrarch of Galilee	40-41
	• King	41-44
	Herod Agrippa II	
	• Tetrarch of Chalcis	50-52
	• Tetrarch of Batanaea	50-100

Table showing rulers of Judea
from Alexander the Great to the Christian era

The Maccabean uprising

What, then, were the events and conditions in Judea which led to the Maccabean uprising? The Hellenic emperors established administrative structures which were designed to extract the maximum resources from the conquered territories. Created by conquest, these empires were maintained by military methods—armies, colonies, military expeditions, garrisons—all of which permitted the levying of tribute and service from the subjugated peoples. Gottwald has argued that there was little qualitative difference between the imperial regime of Persia and that of their Greek successors. The main object of the administration was the efficient collection of taxes and tribute. The Ptolemies were prepared to work with the already-existing political, administrative and religious structures.

> "Provided that the flow of taxes and goods was assured, considerable local autonomy was allowed. The old Persian system of a dual appointment of governor and high priest in Jerusalem seems to have been accommodated to Ptolemaic administrative practice by making the high priest titular head of Judah but appointing a civil officer who was the official representative of Judah to the Egyptian government . . . it appears that the tribute and tax burden on Judah was measurably heavier under the Ptolemies than it had been under the Persians . . ." [174]

Although it was left to their Judean proxies to raise tribute and taxes from the masses, the Ptolemies nevertheless maintained a strict oversight of the daily lives and government of Judea. An Egyptian military garrison was housed in the citadel (the *Akra*) in Jerusalem and it served as a visible daily reminder to the Judeans of the mighty power of the Ptolemaic empire. The garrison was itself a costly imposition on the people of Jerusalem and the surrounding area.

> "Soldiers stationed in Jerusalem would have required housing, service and food from the local population, displacing families from their homes and ancestral lands, enslaving local inhabitants and constituting a significant drain on the community's food supply."[175]

The burden of this provision, therefore, would have fallen overwhelmingly on the rural poor. Portier-Young cites another source (Hayes and Mandell) to the effect that "the practice of tax-farming led to an increased tax burden, generating ill-will among the general populace; it also created division and animosity between the wealthy families who competed for the privilege of collecting taxes."[176] Other

---

[174]   Gottwald, *The Hebrew Bible*, p 442
[175]   Portier-Young, *Apocalypse against Empire*, p 64
[176]   Portier-Young, *Apocalypse against Empire*, p 64

sources suggest that "probably the Graeco-Macedonian military settlers tried to make the Semitic peasants who worked their lots of land into their slaves".[177]

> "The size of the army and elephant corps Jerusalem provisioned can be estimated from the reports of the battle of Panion, fought 93 miles north of Jerusalem at the source of the Jordan River in 200 BCE . . . [Bazalel Bar-Kochva] estimates the size of the Seleucid army that fought at Panion at 'several tens of thousands'. He arrives at a more exact figure of more than 70,000 soldiers based on the description in Daniel 11:13 and figures for the earlier battle of Raphia. In addition to the soldiers, Antiochus III deployed a herd of 150 elephants." [178]

The account gives a general idea of the scale of the military economy under Hellenic rule and it meant a huge burden of taxation and tribute on the mass of the peasantry. Not surprisingly, from time to time there were movements of opposition or outright revolt. In common with other parts of the Hellenistic empires, the temples and religious sanctuaries were often the focus of opposition. Thus during the third Syrian war in 246-241, the Jerusalem high priest Onias II refused to pay the regular imperial tribute to Egypt.

> "This led to the intervention of the Tobiads from Transjordan, a Jewish landed family that had challenged Nehemiah's reconstruction programme in Judah and had more recently been installed by the Ptolemies as the head of a military colony of mixed peoples assigned to guard the desert frontier against the rising Nabatean Arabs."[179]

What made the burden of the Judean masses even greater was the misfortune of living in a border region which was disputed by two empires. Between 274 and 168 BCE, there were no fewer than *six wars* between the Seleucids and Ptolemaic kings, each one potentially devastating for Judea. Portier-Young has described this, in contrast to the two previous centuries of Persian rule, as an era of "almost ceaseless violence for Judeans." Jerusalem itself must have changed hands three or four times during these wars, causing incalculable damage and suffering to the population. In the rural areas around the city there would have been similar death, deprivation and suffering as villages, crops and thousands of lives were repeatedly destroyed.

There is no biblical account of the period from Persian rule to the period leading up to the Maccabean revolt, but it is possible to imagine, from the documents that have remained in the Ptolemaic and Seleucid archives, the unending exploitation of the mass of the population in which the ruling elite of Jerusalem played the part of client to one empire and then the other. There are, for example,

---

[177] Hengel, cited by Portier-Young, *Apocalypse against Empire*, p 64
[178] Portier-Young, *Apocalypse against Empire*, p 65
[179] Gottwald, *The Hebrew Bible*, p 442

preserved documents of the Seleucid regime that give a glimpse of the character of Seleucid rule, after the ousting of the Ptolemies in 200 BCE. The documents give a glimpse of the conditions imposed by the Seleucids but they were in all probability a restatement of the conditions that had pertained during the period of the Ptolemies. In one of these, a preserved decree of Antiochus III (223-187), the king offers the right of the people "to govern themselves in accordance with their ancestral laws". The self-government, of course, applied only to the Jewish elite and only provided they followed the policy interests of their imperial masters.

"Community leaders and cultic functionaries including members of the *gerousia* (a council of elders appointed by the imperial governor), the priests, the temple scribes and the temple singers, were given exemption from taxation—including the tax on the land's produce, the cattle tax, a crown tax and a tax on temple revenue."[180]

The exemption from tax represented a substantial privilege for the ruling urban elite and was intended to secure their support against, on the one hand, the ambitions of the rival Ptolemaic empire and, on the other, the discontent of the native population. It was the latter, of course, who bore the lion's share of the burden. Another preserved letter cites a taxation rate on agricultural produce of a "third of the grain and half of the fruit of the trees", a huge tribute by any standards.

Another surviving document deals with the specially privileged position of the temple. There is a high probability that the imperial decree in this area of policy was significantly influenced by the Jewish priesthood itself, since foreigners were not permitted within the Temple bounds. 'Unclean' animals were not to be reared anywhere within the city bounds or their meat and skins be brought into the city and Jews were permitted only to offer ancestral (ie traditional) sacrifices. This decree meant, therefore, that Jews were exempted from sacrifices to the gods of the Greeks on their special holidays and feast days.

However, the generous guarantees of the lavish priestly life and the concessions to the urban rich cut no ice with the majority of the population. Referring to the *programma,* a conciliatory decree of Antiochus IV (175-164), Portier-Young comments,

"Neither the splendour of the temple and its newly invigorated worship life nor the wealth of its treasury would suffice to ease all the hardships of a ravaged and divided people. In fact, the provisions outlined in Antiochus's *programma* for the safe-guarding of the purity of the temple cult, with attendant financial benefits for the priests themselves, may have *exacerbated* tensions and divisions among the people as a whole"[181]

---

[180]   Portier-Young, *Apocalypse against Empire,* p 56

[181]   Portier-Young, *Apocalypse against Empire,* p 72

For all their 'piety' and support for traditional Jewish culture, the whole bloated apparatus of the temple administration, including hundreds of priests and flunkeys, were a parasitic caste which served as an agent for the ruling empire. Many of the poorest and most deprived would have seen the situation for what it was. In any case, many of the imperial concessions granted to the ruling elite were short-lived. This was a period of great economic pressure on the Seleucid court since their victory over the Ptolemies had been brokered by the burgeoning Roman power and the Seleucids were obliged to make payments of crippling indemnities to Rome. Because the various local temples throughout the Seleucid Empire were centres of the local economy and often the administrators of local tax regimes, the Seleucids sought control over them as a means of diverting a greater part of the surplus in the direction of the imperial centre. A key component in this policy was the appointment of imperial administrators to exercise tight control of the assets, revenues and administration of the temples and sanctuaries throughout the empire.

Corresponding to this is another surviving document of the period: the so-called *Heliodorus stele*, dated to 178 BCE, the contents of which were only published in 2007. It was a document sent by Seleucus IV (187-175) to a state functionary, Heliodorus, and it indicates the intention of Seleucus to plunder the temple resources of Jerusalem and tighten the imperial control over the income of Jerusalem. According to Portier-Young, the decree of Seleucus:

> ". . . testifies to important shifts in regional and civic government, as first the fiscal administration of Jerusalem's temple and eventually the conduct of its worship came under the purview of Seleucid imperial control, violating an earlier agreement that protected the temple from foreign intruders and ultimately asserting power over Judean religious praxis." [182]

The stele is an important document for biblical scholars, because it broadly confirms the account in the second book of Maccabees that the court official Heliodorus was sent by the king to seize the treasury of the temple.

> "When Apollonius came to the kings, and had shewed him of the money whereof he was told, the king chose out Heliodorus his treasurer, and sent him with a commandment to bring him the foresaid money." [183]

The biblical account is hedged around with all manner of mystical and miraculous events, as Heliodorus is driven from the temple by terrifying horsemen and two young men, "notable in strength, excellent in beauty and comely in apparel". Leaving aside the hyperbole added later by the author of Maccabees, it is clear that

---

[182]   Ibid, p 80.

[183]   2 Macabbees: 3, 7

it was remembered as one of those key episodes that led to the later uprising of the population against the Seleucids.

Nor was the seizure of wealth from the temple a one-off confiscation; it seems from a surviving decree of Seleucus that the Judean people were to be expected to align their cultic practices and temple administration with the oversight of the empire, as was the case in other provinces. Antiochus IV Epiphanes (the latter part of the name means 'God manifest') succeeded Seleucus in 175 and he determined to pay the indemnities to Rome even earlier than they were due, in which enterprise he succeeded. In doing this, he raised levies by broadly continuing the same policies as Seleucus. In Judea, Antiochus began the practice of selling the office of high priest to the highest bidder among Hellenised Jews, first to Jason in 174 and then to his brother Menelaus, in 171. Rivalries between influential families linked to the priesthood had always been present, although largely below the surface. But increasingly these aristocratic clans, the Tobiads, Oniads and the Simonites, jockeyed for power to get their own share of privileges from the imperial table.

> "In a community whose elites imitated their Hellenistic overlords in their continued struggle for power, the new policy of imperial oversight of sanctuaries created new opportunities to negotiate privileges, purchase offices and propose reforms. These opportunities invited ambitious leaders to seek their own interests above those of the people they ostensibly served."[184]

Jason, who purchased the high priesthood that had been previously occupied by his brother, Onias III, is associated in 2 Maccabees with a policy of Hellenising Judean culture, including the renaming of Jerusalem as "Antioch-in-Jerusalem", as a formal recognition of its status as a Greek city-state, or *polis*, with its citizens to be known as "Antiochians of Jerusalem". There were also plans laid for the creation of a gymnasium in Jerusalem on the Greek pattern—at the same time a training ground for the sons of the ruling class, to continue the privileges of their fathers and a snub to the traditionalists in the city opposed to the expansion of Greek culture. "It cannot be doubted", Portier-Young has argued, "that Jason's reforms accelerated a cultural shift among the Jerusalem elites that had serious consequences for religious and civic life in Judea . . ."[185] But it is important to make the point that Jason's policies were not merely an ideological realignment; they carried with them real *material benefits* for the Hellenised upper echelons. The benefits of the high priesthood included the privilege of being able to enrol Jerusalemites as "citizens of Antioch", in other words as *first class citizens of the empire*. The high priest was clearly a door-keeper who was able to allow—at his own price, of course—access for friends and family to further privileges and patronage within the empire. The Book of Daniel, which was written around this time, makes reference to those Jews who

---

184   Portier-Young, *Apocalypse against Empire*, p 90
185   Portier-Young, *Apocalypse against Empire*, p 103

supported the Hellenisers: "them that forsake the holy covenant" (11,30), and those "such as do wickedly against the covenant shall he [ie Antiochus IV] corrupt by flatteries" (11, 32). The first book of Maccabees gives a similar account:

> "In those days went there out of Israel wicked men, who persuaded many, saying, let us go and make a covenant with the heathen . . . so this device pleased them well . . .
> Then certain of the people were so forward herein that they went to the king, who gave them licence to do after the ordinances of the heathen,
> Whereupon they built a place of exercise at Jerusalem according to the customs of the heathen:
> And made themselves uncircumcised, and forsook the holy covenant, and joined themselves to the heathen, and were sold to do mischief."[186]

Although the sharp contrast between Judean and Hellenic culture is an over-simplification introduced by the writer of Maccabees (which has been followed by scholars who have based their histories entirely upon it), it nevertheless provided *an ideological framework within which class struggle was expressed.*

On the one hand, the large majority of the Hellenisers in the Jewish community were from the ruling elite who benefitted from imperial patronage; it was in their direct interest to adopt the cultural practices of their imperial masters, the better to tap into the rich streams of privilege and rank available in the empire. It was the *material* pressure of the trade, commerce and economy of the Greek imperial culture which in the final analysis dictated development of Hellenism against the resistant ideology of ancestral Jewish traditions. The central role of *material* as opposed to *ideological* forces is further demonstrated in the fact that even with the later establishment of an independent Jewish monarchy, its participation in the Near Eastern trade and economy as a whole meant it was still impossible to hold back the increasing influence of Greek culture.

On the other hand, the mass of the urban and rural poor saw no benefits from imperial patronage and Hellenistic reforms and they were necessarily tied to the more traditional Jewish cultural framework. In particular it was the aspirations of the revolutionary peasants that were expressed in terms of the defence of the traditional forms of worship and the ancient temple regime. Moreover, the burden on the masses was becoming virtually unsustainable when, in 172 BCE, Meneleus took the high priesthood from his brother Jason, according to 2 Maccabees (4, 24), Meneleus outbid his brother by "three hundred talents of silver". As this was a recurring payment, Portier-Young points out, it

> ". . . was an increase in the annual tribute, a burden borne by the Judean people, not its high priestly leader. Meneleus's promise nearly doubled that tribute from 360 to 660 talents . . . this sum appears an enormous, indeed

---

[186] 1 Maccabees, 1, 11-15

impossible burden for the comparatively tiny Judea to bear. Antiochus did not foresee that Meneleus would be unable to raise the promised funds. Instead, he accepted his offer and transferred the high priesthood to Meneleus."[187]

Making the whole situation worse, between 170-168 BCE the Ptolemaic and Seleucid armies were again fighting—in the *sixth* 'Syrian' war. It ended with Roman diplomatic intervention, marking the beginning of Rome's reign as the Mediterranean super-power and its influence on the history of Judea and the Jewish people.

Friedrich Engels, paraphrasing the German philosopher Hegel, once explained that "accident demonstrates necessity". What this means in the fields of history and politics is that important historical changes like social revolutions are preceded by an accumulation of combustible socio-political 'kindling' and it is these that cause the inevitable, that is the "necessary" explosion. Whatever incident (or "accidental" factor) happens to trigger the event is entirely secondary.

The necessity lay in the fact that the period that led up Maccabean revolt was one of unremitting turmoil and upheaval. The general atmosphere of war, due to the two imperial armies fighting each other in the territories around Jerusalem, only exacerbated the seething discontent. The masses were on the point of revolt at their super-exploitation and what they perceived was a forced change in the traditional culture by a Hellenised ruling elite, submissively following their imperial masters. In fact, in describing this period as one of "utter peace", the Book of 2 Maccabbees could not be more wrong. Nevertheless, the biblical account probably preserves a number of key historical events and important insights into the social conditions and conflicts during the period of the revolt.

The 'accident' that demonstrated the 'necessity' came in 169 or 168 BCE. When the inevitable happened and the new high priest Meneleus was unable to pay the tribute he had promised, he resorted to looting the temple yet again. This was an act that led to the murder of a priest, Onias, who had tried to object. Antiochus IV then demanded that the tribute be collected by the commander of the military garrison in Jerusalem, a man named Sostratus. These developments resulted in riots and a force of 3000 troops was sent into Jerusalem only to be routed by the people of the city. This uprising in Jerusalem coincided with a revolt, launched from Transjordan by the ex-high priest, Jason, who opportunistically used the discontent in Jerusalem to seek a return to his former position as high priest, at the head of the queue for privileges.

Antiochus responded by murderously suppressing the revolt. He sent a force, according to 2 Maccabees, of 22,000, which occupied Jerusalem and massacred and enslaved thousands of its population, destroyed a part of the city walls and reinforced the Akra. According to the account in Maccabees, Antiochus . . .

---

[187]   Portier-Young, *Apocalypse against Empire*, p 121

". . . commanded his men of war not to spare such as they met and to slay such as went up upon the houses. Thus there was killing of young and old, making away of men, women and children, slaying of virgins and infants. And there were destroyed within the space of three whole days fourscore thousand, whereof forty thousand were slain in the conflict; and no fewer sold than slain."[188]

Antiochus's reprisals against the city have been likened by Portier-Young to the state terror of late twentieth century military dictatorships in Latin America, fighting a 'dirty war' against their own populations. From the now reinforced citadel, the Seleucid troops invaded homes, killed, pillaged and looted at will among the population of Jerusalem. Maccabees reports that in only three days, forty thousand people of all ages were slaughtered and as many again sold into slavery. Given the estimated population of Judea at the time, of about 40-50,000, this is clearly an exaggeration, (like almost all the numerical data in the Bible) but as Portier-Young comments, "we need not posit the historical accuracy of these numbers to recognise the impact of such a massacre."[189]

Some scholars have argued that the local temples in many other parts of the Persian and later Hellenic empires were often the focus of national identity and of revolt.

". . . at the centre of provincial subversion stood the local temples, revealed to have been far more vital than many have thought . . . it seems indeed that these indigenous sanctuaries knew how to preserve a high degree of autonomy through the ages; they fiercely defended their privileges under the Roman Empire, just as they had done against the Hellenistic kings"[190]

Despite the submissiveness of the temple bureaucracy, Antiochus IV Epiphanes may well have seen it as a potent symbol of Jewish identity and struggle. For tens of thousands, for millions if we include the Diaspora of Jews around the Near East, it was still the focus of worship and pilgrimage. Antiochus, on the basis of a vicious military-police regime in Jerusalem, began a programme of breaking the power of the Temple, by effectively outlawing all the traditional practices of Judaism. Temple sacrifice, Sabbath observance and circumcision were all forbidden.

"From the beginning of Antiochus's reign Judeans were already subject to tribute and garrison. Revoking the right to live according to their ancestral laws was continuous with the gradual erosion of freedoms in Judea and

---

[188] 2 Maccabees: 5, 12-14
[189] Portier-Young in *Apocalypse against Empire*, p 143
[190] Two authors cited by Portier-Young in *Apocalypse against Empire*, p 31

was intended as the last in a serious of measures aiming at the region's total subordination."[191]

The accounts in Maccabees relate the story of Eleazar, who was a scribe and elder, who was tortured rather than submit to eating pork. Another family were similarly mis-treated when they insisted on the Jewish right of circumcision. As perhaps the most significant token of imperial power, Antiochus announced his intention to dedicate the Jerusalem temple to the Greek god, Jupiter. All manner of profanities were allowed to desecrate the temple:

> ". . . the temple was filled with riot and revelling by the Gentiles, who dallied with harlots, and had to do with women within the circuit of the holy places, and besides that brought in things that were not lawful. The altar also was filled with profane things, which the law fobiddeth. Neither was it lawful [ie to the Seleucids] for a man to keep Sabbath days or ancient feasts or to profess himself at all to be a Jew."[192]

The biblical account reports that, in both Judea and Samaria, Antiochus instituted a more onerous tax regime, to raise finance and as a punitive action. It was at some point around this time (165 BCE) that open rebellion finally broke out in the countryside, led by a priest, Matthias, and his sons. Their use of guerrilla tactics and their support within the villages and communities meant that the Seleucids were unable to crush them. Matthias was killed and was succeeded by his son Judas—he became known as the "hammer" (*Maccabee* in Hebrew) and gave his name to the whole revolutionary movement. On four separate occasions over the next two years the Seleucids tried to crush the revolt but without success. But while the guerrilla movement could not be crushed, neither was it strong enough in its own right to take power in Judea, so that it was the support provided by a treaty with Rome that became the essential ingredient of the struggle of Judas. After the death of Judas, his brother Jonathan eventually succeeded in consolidating power in Jerusalem. Thus began the 'golden age' of an independent Jewish kingdom and the Hasmonean dynasty.

---

[191]   Portier-Young, p 189
[192]   2 Maccabees: 6, 4-6

Chapter 4 Time-line: the post-exilic period	
Dates (BCE)	**Events**
600	
	Exile in Babylon begins for a minority of Judahite population. Collapse of Babylon. **Persian king Cyrus** decrees a return to **Judea**
500	
	Ezra, Nehemiah are representatives of Persian imperial power (Final editing of the **Deuteronomic History**)
400	
	(Book of **Chronicles** written, based on earlier books.)
	Hellenic period: Alexander conquers Judea
300	**Ptolemaic** (Egyptian) rule of Judea begins
200	**Seleucid** (Persian) rule from 200 onwards. **Roman** influence begins.
	Maccabean Revolt leads to **Hasmonean** dynasty
100	(The Book of **Daniel** is written)
	Direct **rule from Rome** begins
0	

Chapter Summary:

- The 'Great Return' from Babylonian exile represented a Persian puppet regime foisted on the people of Judah and the new Jewish elite completed the writing and editing of the early books of the Bible, including the Deuteronomic History.

- The Persian province of Judea was centred on the Temple with a bloated priestly caste which represented its own interests and those of the local and imperial ruling elite.

- Following Greek conquest, Judea was drawn into the economic and cultural orbit of the Greek-speaking Near East.

- The Maccabean revolt and anti-Hellenism reflected the discontent of the mass of the population who were labouring under an excessive taxation regime.

Chapter 5

The Hasmonean dynasty and Rome

This chapter follows the class struggles within Jewish society in the last century of the old era (BCE) and the first period of the new (CE). The new Hasmonean kingdom that came out of the Maccabean revolt turned out to be as exploitative and oppressive as the Hellenic regimes which it had replaced and this dynasty was eventually eclipsed by Roman imperial rule. This period saw a great surge of messianic and apocalyptic writing which represented the *resistance literature* of the time, echoing the revolutionary sentiments of the population. It found its expression most typically in the works of the Essenes cult of Qumran, which were later discovered as the Dead Sea Scrolls.

For many decades the whole of Judea and the area we now know as Israel/ Palestine was seething with social upheaval, uprisings and rural banditry. There were numerous local leaders and 'messiahs' and this social ferment culminated in the great uprising against the Roman Empire in 66 CE. We shall argue that this was a *class* movement of rural and city poor, not only against Rome, but also against the local Jewish elite. This uprising was followed by later revolutions, all of which were brutally suppressed. The net result of a series of failed uprisings was the development of 'Rabbinic' Judaism, from the leadership of local rabbis and remnants of the temple priesthood and Pharisees. From this point on, Judaism was no longer based on the Jerusalem Temple but on local synagogues which functioned as meeting houses, places of education and worship and as social centres.

. . . .

Jonathan was the founder of the Hasmonean dynasty, effectively king, while at the same time assuming the position of high priest[193]. Hasmonean rule was only consolidated after a protracted period of guerrilla wars interspersed by repeated and feeble attempts by the Seleucids to regain control. The citadel in Jerusalem was held by Seleucid forces for a long period of time and proved to be a constant focus of opposition to the rebels, who apparently did not gain full control of it until twenty five years after the revolt had started. Although Judea now had a considerable degree of independence—far more than any Jewish state since the Israelite Omnid dynasty—this was premised on the much weakened position of the Seleucids and the (for the moment) benign patronage of the new master of the Near East, Rome.

---

[193]   It is the rededication of the 'profaned' Temple, in 164 BCE, which has been celebrated by Jews ever since as the Festival of Hanukkah.

Nevertheless, it was from this point that what had been a minor state, roughly the size of the former Judah, was able to expand by conquest to absorb Samaria and Galilee to the north and Moab and Edom (Idumea) to the south, almost like a mini-empire in its own right. It was under the influence of the Hasmoneans that the centralisation of the Temple cult of Jerusalem was completed. Prior to this period, the Samaritan temple at Mount Gerizim had continued as a rival but it was finally destroyed by the Hasmonean, John Hyrcanus, around 110 BCE. The Hasmoneans forcibly converted the population in these conquered areas, creating a much greater base for the faith than had ever existed in that part of the world before. Many modern Jews look back on this period as the period of Jewish independence *par excellence*. The whole of the territory of the Hasmonean kingdom has become established in Judaic tradition since that time as the 'Land of Israel' or *Eretz Israel*, a concept with great weight among Zionists today.

Despite it having been founded in revolution, an important element of which was the defence of traditional worship and culture, it was impossible, in the socio-economic milieu of the Near East, for the Hasmonean state to hold back the tide of Hellenisation. The Hasmoneans were drawn into the same spheres of trade, commerce and culture as their Seleucid predecessors and in effect, the Maccabean monarchy gradually morphed into a mini-Seleucid state. The dynasty developed increasingly along Hellenistic patterns, militarily and politically, as Greek mercenaries became a regular feature of state power. John Hyrcanus gave his sons Greek names and one of them, Aristobulus (104–103) even adopted the royal title *Philhellenist* as did his son and successor, Alexander Jannaeus. The state was Jewish in composition, but in its topmost layers as Hellenised as the previous Seleucid regime.

This period was the setting for the origin of the three great parties of later Jewish history, the Sadducees, the Pharisees and the Essenes. The Sadducees belonged to the upper layers of Jewish society, closest to the high priesthood and the wealthy landowning classes. For the greatest part of the Hellenic period, up to the revolution against Rome in 66 CE, it was the Sadducees who monopolised the high priesthood, despite the opposition of the Essenes and the Pharisees. The Sadducees disappeared after the destruction of the temple, in the aftermath of the revolution.

The Essenes were a group of pious Jews, numbering several thousand, according to Josephus, who were based almost entirely in the most down-trodden and poorest sections of society. They rejected the theology of the rich and powerful in Jerusalem and looked to the rise of a 'new Israel' and a messianic movement to redeem the people. They are most famously known for the settlement they had in Qumran, near the Dead Sea, and the scrolls which they hid in jars in caves near there, to be discovered two thousand years later. (See later section). But the Essenes did not all withdraw to the countryside and it would appear that they also worked and preached in the villages and countryside in Judea.

The literature of the Essenes is clearly different from the canonical literature of mainstream Judaism and little of it found its way into the Hebrew Bible. Their writing is littered with references to the 'Wicked Priest' and the 'Righteous Teacher' and although there is a fierce (and unresolved) debate among scholars as to the identity of these two, there is a plausible consensus that the former is the Hasmonean priest/king, Jonathan or one of his successors, and the latter an unknown, but to the Essenes, a better-qualified person for the high priesthood. The Essenes, it is thought, may have played a part in the revolt against Rome in 66 CE but afterwards they disappeared from history, except in so far as their traditions were partly echoed in tiny quasi-Christian sects in the first centuries of the modern era.

The largest party were the Pharisees. The Christian New Testament has given the Pharisees a poor press and the name is often used today as a by-word for self-righteousness and hypocrisy. Yet large numbers of literate and scripture-reading Jews, unaligned to the Essenes, but too lowly to be aligned with the Sadducees, would have been Pharisees. The historian Josephus considered himself a Pharisee, as did the Christian epistle-writer, Paul. The majority would have been pious Jews, close to the mass of the urban and rural poor, who advocated a greater degree of social equality and were opposed to the Hasmonean monarchy. Like the Essenes and the Sadducees, the Pharisees used their own interpretation of Holy Scripture to give authority to their views and their criticisms of the Hasmoneans, who they saw as the usurpers of the true traditions of the temple. The historian Josephus, when he recounts the events of the uprising of 66 CE, suggests that the Pharisees had much more popular support than the Sadducees:

> ". . . while the Sadducees are able to persuade none but the rich, and have not the populace obsequious to them . . . the Pharisees have the multitude on their side"[194]

The theological traditions of these three different politico-religious tendencies did not arise by accident but reflected their class orientation. The Sadducees, closest to the ruling elite and in most cases enjoying real wealth in the here and now put no great emphasis on the afterlife, whereas the Pharisees and Essenes were increasingly drawn into the framework of messianism and apocalypticism—with the promised of redemption in the next life—as befits those who were closest to the poorest sections of society.

The relative longevity of the Hasmonean dynasty is a reflection of some economic development and stability, although the benefits did not trickle down to the lowest parts of society. The territorial conquests of the Hasmoneans expanded the grip of the Jewish kings over a considerable area and created new opportunities for enrichment of the aristocracy and those in royal favour,

> ". . . but these benefits did not spread to the mass of the people whose conditions of life only worsened. Certain Pharisees demanded that Hyrcanus give up the high priesthood, no doubt with the intent of

---

[194]   Josephus, *The Antiquities of the Jews*, 13, 298.

denying him access to the lucrative temple economy and to the symbolic backing of the Jewish cult."[195]

The archaeological remains of tombs and preserved texts of the period show an increase in Greek names among Judeans, including the Hasmonean rulers themselves; the architecture and political culture of the Hasmoneans is thoroughly Hellenistic. Increasingly the state developed along typical Hellenistic lines. Excavations of buildings and tombs also show greater class differentiation, by the increased number of palaces and grand buildings over smaller more modest dwellings, and in the large numbers of tombs of the wealthy in Jerusalem. Conditions were returning precisely to those that created the Maccabean revolt and the rise of the Hasmoneans in the first place, and inevitably, at some points, revolt broke out.

> "During the reign of Alexander Jannaeus [103-76 BCE], the conflict flared into civil war that pitted a majority of the populace with the Pharisees against the king and his priestly and lay supporters. The internal political situation of Judah had shifted drastically in a few decades. Judas, the first Maccabee, had led a majority of Jews against a small but powerful group of Jewish Hellenisers and their Seleucid backers. In a turnabout, Alexander Jannaeus, a successor of the Maccabees, now led a small but powerful group of royal supporters in a desperate battle against the majority of countrymen who saw him as an embodiment of Hellenistic corruption and oppression."[196]

Alexander Jannaeus retained power, partly because the prospect of a Seleucid monarch was a worse alternative. His revenge was to crucify eight hundred rebel Pharisees and slaughter their families. Many other rebels melted away into the countryside, some, Gottwald suggests, to the Essene community in Qumran.

Messianic and Apocalyptic writing

The contrast between great wealth of the elite and the grinding poverty of the rural masses engendered an important new phase of apocalyptic writing, most of which did not find its way into the official canon of Jewish writings, and notably the writings based around the figure of an imaginary ancient prophet called Enoch. This was essentially a new genre in Jewish writing and it came to be closely linked to messianic writing at a later date, influencing both Jewish and Christian literature. Some of this scripture, composed as early the third and second centuries BCE, circulated among dissident Jews and was well represented in the Dead Sea Scrolls which originated with the of Essenes of Qumran.

---

195   Gottwald, *The Hebrew Bible*, p 448
196   Gottwald, *The Hebrew Bible*, p 448

One of the few pieces that did make it into the official Jewish canon was the biblical Book of Daniel, which was composed around this time. Although it was set in Babylon four centuries earlier, during the reign of King Nebuchadnezzar, there is an overwhelming consensus among scholars that it is a series of allegorical stories related to the issues of culture and religious identity during the Hellenic period. As a part of what scholars now refer to as *resistance literature*, it sought to persuade those who were flirting with an accommodation with the imperial culture to return instead to their traditional cultural and religious values. The Book of Daniel, Portier-Young suggests, although part of the resistance literature, had as its main thrust the idea *non-violent* opposition, ". . . by writing, proclaiming, and teaching an alternative vision of reality."[197]

The contests and conflicts in the first half of the book of Daniel relate to those issues that were the subject of great controversy in Jerusalem: observing the food laws, keeping the temple and denying the worship of idols and, not least, dealing with a king who thought himself above God.

The apocalyptic writing of the period was a reaction to the impasse faced by the mass of the population and articulated by scribes in the Essene/Pharisee tradition. As a literature of resistance, it included a range of theological/political ideas, some advocating violent struggle and others advocating non-violent resistance or a pious detachment from the society of the Hellenised Judeans. Portier-Young suggests that the non-violent dissidents who were the authors of Daniel were scribes and priests who were isolated from the privileged priests who managed the temple. By a continuous process of reading and re-reading of ancient scripture, by interpretation and re-interpretation, new traditions were created and many of these pointed in the direction of a future messiah who would relieve the suffering of the mass of the people. The Book of Daniel and other works introduced the idea of the coming "Kingdom of God" and a future redemption by a hero who would come "like a Son of Man"—both important theological notions taken up enthusiastically by Joshua (Jesus) cults two centuries later.

The Book of Enoch is a composite work of this genre, its earliest sections written perhaps as early as the third century BCE. The separate parts of the book are The Book of Watchers (1 Enoch 1-36), including the Apocalypse of Weeks, The Book of Parables of Enoch (1 Enoch 37-71), The Astronomical Book (1 Enoch 72-82), The Book of Dreams (1 Enoch 83-90) and The Epistle of Enoch (1 Enoch 91-108). Another book in this tradition is the Book of Jubilees, written around 100 BCE and known previously only from fragments and in sections cited in the works of early Christian writers.

These books have been known throughout modern history but they have always been put to one side as peculiar and well outside mainstream Jewish tradition. However, the discovery of large numbers of fragments among the Qumran scrolls has changed the view of many scholars about how common this literature was. The Qumran collection, for example, included fifteen complete scrolls of Jubilees

---

[197] Portier-Young, *Apocalypse against Empire*, p 277.

and many fragments of other copies. It is now thought that these works may have circulated widely in the Judean community, as a kind of counter-culture to the more orthodox works of literature that were later adopted as the official Hebrew Bible. The Qumran finds, in the words of one scholar, amount to "the re-discovery of Enochic Judaism", *almost as a different form of Judaism*, one closer to the aspirations and dissident moods of the poorest and most desperate sections of society. At the very least, the Qumran finds indicate a much greater fluidity in Judaism than had previously been thought to be the case.

> "The popularity of the early Enoch literature at Qumran and the high regard in which the writers of the later Enochic writings, *Jubilees* and the letter of Jude held the early Enochic literature testify to the influence of their teaching and writing."[198]

Portier-Young summarises the evidence for the considerable theological differences between official Judaism, as exemplified by the Pentateuch and Enochic Judaism, as follows:

> "(1) the absence of direct citation of Pentateuchal material; (2) the absence of explicit parallels to the Pentateuchal commandments; (3) a single reference to "covenant"; (4) the apparent dissociation between Sinai and the giving of the law; (5) the fact that Moses does not figure in the Astronomical Book, The Book of Watchers or the Apocalypse of Weeks, while the Book of Dreams does not identify Moses as lawgiver or covenant mediator; and (6) the elevated role and status of Enoch . . . The Enochic booklets claim an independent and direct authority grounded in the figure of Enoch and the revelations he has received and handed on . . . there are no explicit parallels to the Pentateuchal commandments in 1 Enoch."[199]

This is not the place for a theological study of the Enochic literature, although many scholars have dedicated time and energy to it. But clearly our picture of first century BCE Judaism has changed: rather than a single and more-or-less uniform stream of Judaic literature and culture, there now appears to be at least one contending stream in the form of the more subversive Enochic literature. These trends are not just *ideological* peculiarities, but represent different *social forces*—the official strand representing the temple administration and scribes and the unofficial strand representing dissent within the community. The *Book of Watchers*, for example, includes a section against the corrupt group of ruling priests, while *The Apocalypse of Weeks* calls upon its audience:

---

[198]   Portier-Young, *Apocalypse against Empire*, p 310
[199]   Portier-Young, *Apocalypse against Empire*, p 295-6

"to uproot the foundations of violence and the structure of deceit of their own day, and directed every act of resistance towards righteousness, justice, truth, and the order of life revealed by God. The Apocalypse also envisaged a future time when the 'righteous' would be given a sword to execute judgement on the 'wicked' in order to enact and establish justice."[200]

The writers of this resistance literature, Portier-Young suggests, would have been "activists", circulating like their literature, within the lower echelons of Judean society. History, of course, is written by the victors. But for the discoveries in Qumran, the real significance and authority of the Enochic literature would never have even been understood. Qumran has added even more complexity to an already complex picture of development which is far removed from the official history of the Hebrew Bible.

The Dead Sea Scrolls

Between 1947 and 1956, in eleven different caves, thousands of scrolls and fragments were found hidden in jars where they had been preserved in the warm dry climate for two thousand years. The conclusion of almost all scholars of the time, and still the view today, was that they were associated with the nearby Qumran community of the ascetic Essene sect which had been known from the writings of the Roman historian Pliny, the Alexandrian Jewish writer Philo and the Roman-Jewish historian Josephus.

Once the significance of the finds began to be realised and they were dated up to the era of the life of Jesus of Christian tradition, the analysis and translation of the fragments were taken under the control of a small group of archaeologists led by a Dominican priest, Roland de Vaux. His small team was composed of young and untried scholars, dominated by Catholics. It soon became clear that the team was extremely slow in translating any of the texts and when material was finally translated, the result did not find its way into the public domain, despite an obvious thirst for information in all academic and scholarly circles. Those on the outside were denied any access to the archive and a list of the full corpus of scrolls and fragments was kept from them. Objections were raised: comments began to be made, lectures delivered and eventually even books were written about the growing suspicions that the team were hiding something, perhaps something damaging to the traditional view of the origins of Christianity. The renowned biblical scholar Geza Vermes was one of those who condemned what was fast becoming "the academic scandal *par excellence* of the twentieth century".

"It should have been evident to anyone with a modicum of good sense that a group of seven editors, of whom only two, Starcky and Skehan, had already established a scholarly reputation, was insufficient to perform

---

[200] Portier-Young, *Apocalypse against Empire*, p 345.

such an enormous task on any level, let alone to produce the kind of 'last word' edition de Vaux appears to have contemplated. The second serious error committed by de Vaux was that he wholly relied on his personal, quasi-patriarchal authority, instead of setting up from the start a supervisory body empowered, if necessary, to sack those members of the team who might fail to fulfil their obligations promptly and to everyone's satisfaction."[201]

It was only in 1990, after the original team had controlled the research for *thirty-seven years* that this scandalous state of affairs was brought to an end. The Israeli authorities under whose auspices the research was being conducted agreed on a complete reorganisation of the investigating team, opening it up to many of the critics of de Vaux. A half-hearted attempt was made to introduce new restrictions, but faced with the pressure of international opinion—even to the point where it was raised in the Knesset (Israeli Parliament)—the Israeli government at last allowed unlimited academic access to the scrolls and they were soon published in full for the first time. Quite recently, the Israeli authorities have agreed to make all the scrolls available universally on line.

Despite a spirited defence of the role of the Vatican by some authors,[202] there are scholars who believe to this day that the near forty years of restrictions on access to the scrolls and their carefully managed publication by a small, secretive team actually did succeed in establishing a particular framework for how the academics and the world at large would judge the scrolls. Their view is that the de Vaux team had sought all along to distance the scrolls as far as possible from any connection with early Christianity and that as a result their basic paradigm has been followed ever since by most academics. We will examine later the ideas of one of these scholars, Robert Eisenman, who is in a minority in linking the scrolls directly to Christianity. Whether the tone was set by de Vaux or not, what is true is that the overwhelming majority of scholars today associate the Dead Sea Scrolls with an Essene community at Qumran and relate them to our understanding of the *earlier pre-Christian* period, from around 175 BCE to the end of the millennium, rather than the *later Christian* period between 0 and 68 CE.

The original dating of the scrolls, soon after their discovery, was done using the method of 'palaeography'—analysis of the style of writing—and this established that the writing dated approximately from the early-to-mid second century BCE to the first decades of the first century CE. In 1990, radiocarbon dating was applied to nine of the scrolls, using the most advanced techniques available at the time. These radiocarbon tests confirmed the conclusions of the palaeographers, although, as

---

[201] Geza Vermes, introduction to *The complete Dead Sea Scrolls in English,* p 5. It should be noted that even this 'complete' edition does not include every fragment. To the frustration of lay persons like the author, it leaves out small, 'insignificant' pieces and at least one other scholar finds these *do* have significance.

[202] See for example, *Jesus, Qumran and the Vatican,* by Otto Betz and Rainer Riesner.

Vermes has pointed out, "the manuscripts tested in 1990 did not include historically sensitive texts", leaving the door open once again for some suspicion of bending the facts to fit an Establishment view.

The view among the great majority of scholars is that the founding of the Essene community occurred sometime in the second century BCE and that it marked a split between the *Hasidim* (the 'pious'), led by a priest known in the Qumran literature as the "Righteous Teacher", and the "Wicked Priest", usually associated with Jonathan or another of the Hasmonean kings who were also high priests. It is thought that it may be a remnant of the Hasidim who founded the Qumran settlement, which survived until it was sacked around the time of the uprising against Rome in 68 CE. During its existence, the Qumran library housed many hundreds, if not thousands, of documents, many of them produced by its own scribes. Eventually, a substantial quantity of these were secreted in jars and hidden in the caves during the uprising, perhaps in fear of Roman legionaries destroying the whole collection.

Altogether, thousands of scrolls and fragments have now been discovered and translated. They are on papyrus and leather and one, the War Scroll, is embossed on copper. Most are written in Hebrew, with a small proportion in Aramaic and a smaller proportion still in Greek. Many fragments are so small as to be virtually insignificant; here and there they can be seen to correspond to a tiny section of other, previously well-known documents, like the books of the Torah. A claim that some small fragments in Greek represent bits of the New Testament is not substantiated. Other scrolls are more or less complete documents, and in some cases there are multiple copies. The most significant new documents to be discovered, which were not known previously, were the War Scroll, the Damascus Document and the Community Rule.

None of the works found at Qumran has a historical narrative equivalent to the Deuteronomic History or the books of Maccabees. The principal themes of the works are prophesies, messianic themes, rules of conduct for the pious, Qumran community rules and commentaries on well-known books, like Isaiah. The tone of most of the literature, however, is extremely important—and *it is stridently anti-Roman and apocalyptic*. The Qumran finds have reinforced the idea that Judaism at the end of the millennium was more fluid than had previously been thought. Although there were many separate scriptural books, there was clearly no agreed canon of Scripture which all Jews observed. It is clear that at this time, although there was a concept of holy 'Scripture', the idea of a Hebrew 'Bible' was at best a vague notion. Where there are multiple copies of the same scroll at Qumran they often have differences in wording from one copy to another. Rather than this being due simply to inaccurate copying, Vermes has characterised their approach to scripture as "scribal creative freedom."

> "If one had to single out the most revolutionary novelty furnished by Qumran . . . its contribution to our understanding of the genesis of Jewish literary composition could justifiably be our primary choice . . . diversity,

not uniformity reigned there and then . . . redactor-copyists felt free to improve the composition which they were reproducing"[203]

How those living at Qumran organised their lives is clear from the Community Rule document which paints a picture of a group of ascetic Jews, living largely in isolation from the rest of Judea, but considering themselves to be the 'true Israel'. In the Community Rule, they refer to themselves, among other epithets, as "the men of holiness" with strictly enforced rules for admission into the group and severe penalties, up to expulsion, for transgressions. In keeping with what they perceived as the ancient traditions of Judaism, their priesthood was divided into twelve, representing the tribes of Israel, something carried over into the Christian tradition of twelve disciples. Although a few remains of women have been found buried in nearby cemeteries, the Qumran community of somewhere between 150 and 200 members, was almost entirely male, strictly hierarchical, but with all property held in common.

> ". . . then shall he be inscribed among his brethren in the order of his rank for the Law, and for justice and for pure Meal; his property shall be merged and he shall offer his counsel and judgement to the Community . . . [204]"

Philo also commented at length on the character of the Essenic community, as well as a similar sect which he referred to as the *Theraputae*. Of the Essenes, he noted that:

> ". . . none of them wishes to have any property of his own, either a house, or a slave, or land, or herds, or anything else productive of wealth. But rather, by joining together everything without exception, they all have a common profit from it. The money which they acquire by various kinds of labour they entrust to an elected trustee, who received it and buys with it that which is necessary, providing them with abundant food and everything required for living."[205]

The Qumran congregation was not a place for the light-minded; one rule states sternly that "whosoever has guffawed foolishly shall do penance for thirty days." Apart from praying and reading scripture together, an important part of the daily ritual was a common meal, commenced by a priestly blessing of the food and drink, another practice continued by Christian congregations later in the form of the Eucharist. Exclusion from the common meal was considered to be a serious matter:

---

[203] Vermes, p 23

[204] These and other translated extracts from Vermes.

[205] Philo, *Hypothetica*, 11, 4

"If one of them has lied deliberately in matters of property, he shall be excluded from the Pure meal of the Congregation for one year and shall do penance with respect to one quarter of his food."

Other Qumran documents, including the Damascus Document and the Temple Scroll, for example, suggest an Essene life-style somewhat removed from the monastic existence at Qumran. Josephus suggested that there were as many as *four thousand Essenes* in Judea, and it may be that the Damascus Document and Temple Scroll referred to Essenes or Hasidim who either moved around or were settled in villages and towns in Judea. They would have followed the same strict religious codes with the difference that they lived, worked and were married with families, like other Jews in the general community. Although their brothers in the country at large would not be expected to give up all their property like those entering Qumran, there was a rigid contributory social fund in place, to assist those who fell on hard times like widows or orphans; this was equivalent to two days wages a month.

Vermes describes the Essenes' theological milieu as a "world of eschatological ferment". Convinced they were living in the 'last days' before God's judgement at the end of the world, one of the main preoccupations of the Qumran scribes was scouring the Scriptures, the prophets in particular, to find some explanations or prophesies that would cast light on the contemporary situation they faced in Judea.

A document given the title The Messianic Apocalypse is a good example for encapsulating the general theological colouration of the Qumran community in its preoccupation with apocalypse and messianism. Many of its themes can be seen to be expressed in words and language almost identical to those adopted in later Christian writings. It refers, for example, to "His Messiah" and the coming the new "Kingdom".

"For the Lord will consider the pious (*Hasidim*) and call the righteous by name.
Over the poor His spirit will hover and will renew the faithful with His power.
And He will glorify the pious on the throne of the eternal Kingdom.
He who liberates the captives, restores sight to the blind, straightens the bent
And forever I will cleave to the hopeful and in His mercy . . .
And the fruit . . . will not be delayed for anyone.
And the lord will accomplish glorious things which have never been . . .
For He will heal the wounded, and revive the dead and bring good news to the poor.
He will lead the uprooted and made the hungry rich . . .
The Life-giver will raise the dead of His people . . .
And we will thank and proclaim to you the righteousness of the Lord"[206]

---

[206] Vermes, *Complete* DSS, p 412

This writing borrows passages from the books of Isaiah and Psalms and is in fact so close to Christian terminology that Robert Eisenman, as we shall discuss later, has argued that it is not attributed by most scholars to the correct time frame and that it is actually *contemporary* with the period of early Christianity or proto-Christianity, as it might more accurately be described. But whether a Christian or pre-Christian date is attached to this document, it is nevertheless remarkable that material of this kind would be circulating in Judea at all. It has clearly gone far beyond traditional Judaism and is actively seeking a *new arrangement of society*, albeit in a language strange to modern readers, one of apocalypse and messianism. It is in every sense a piece of *resistance* literature.

Besides Qumrna, in the late 1960s the remains of two other communities of Essenes were found at Ein Feshkha, three kilometres further south and at En el-Ghuweir, on the shores of the Dead Sea, about twelve kilometres further south again, although these two sets of remains are not as extensive as those at Qumran. These indicate that Essenism was not peculiar only to one part of Judea. The whole of the Essene community, in the Qumran congregation and in the wider community, represented a counter-culture, a subversive opposition to the official Judaism of the Jerusalem Temple and priesthood. There is much in the literature which is in praise of poverty and the poor and same ideas found an echo in later Christian writings like "the poor shall inherit the earth", all of which was in keeping with the asceticism of the Essenes. It is evident from the Dead Sea Scrolls that numerous religious works were still being produced and circulated that did not end up in the official canon because they didn't reflect the social or religious outlook of the leading authorities.

Many fragments from the Qumran caves contain themes and language reminiscent of later Christian literature. For example, a piece referred to as the 'Testament of the Patriarchs' contains the following:

"He [the messiah] will atone for all the sons of his generation and will be sent to all the sons of his people. His word is like a word of heaven, and his teaching is according to the will of God. His eternal sun will shine, and his fire will spring forth to all the ends of the earth, and will shine over darkness. The darkness will pass away from the earth, and deep darkness from the dry land. They will utter many words against him and many [. . .]. They will invent stories about him, and will utter everything dishonourable against him. Evil will overturn his generation [because . . .] will be, and because lies and violence will (fill) his existence, and the people will go astray in his days and will become perplexed."[207]

And yet another fragment, in the same vein:

---

[207]   Vermes, *Complete* DSS, p 561. This DSS section is fragmentary

"... he will be great on earth ... and by his name he will be designated (or: designate himself) the son of God he will be proclaimed (or proclaim himself) and the son of the Most High they will call him ... Their (the people of God's) kingdom will be an eternal kingdom ..."[208]

Perhaps the document closest to the Christian era in terms of its palaeographic dating and its content is the commentary on the Book of Habakkuk, which latter was written during the period of Babylonian exile. The references in Habakkuk to the Babylonians are *re-interpreted* by the Essenes as prophesies that relate to the *contemporary* conquest by Rome (The "Kittim"). There are many references in Habakkuk to the "Wicked Priest"

"... when he ruled over Israel his heart became proud, and he forsook God and betrayed the precepts for the sake of riches. He robbed and amassed the riches of the men of violence who rebelled against God, and he took the wealth of the peoples, heaping sinful iniquity upon himself. And he lived in the ways of abomination amidst every unclean defilement ... this [section of Habakkuk] concerns the last Priests of Jerusalem, who shall amass money and wealth by plundering the peoples. But in the last days, their riches and booty shall be delivered into the hands of the army of the Kittim ...[209]"

It is easy to see how these themes could be taken up later by a variety of pre-Christian sects before there was any suggestion of a real person or historical character to fulfil the role of messiah. The whole milieu of Essenism at the turn of the millennium was drenched in the twin notions of the coming apocalypse and the hope for an anointed leader to lead the righteous to the new Israel and both of them were at the core of the Christian movement.

In contrast to the simplified and sanitised canon of modern Jewish and Christian scripture, the Qumran literature gives a glimpse of a hugely significant and revolutionary counter-culture, with its "activists" numbered in thousands and which permeated the whole of Judean society during this period. As we shall argue later, at the very least, it represents an important bridge between the older Jewish tradition and the messianic and apocalyptic sects that evolved into the later Christian tradition. Like all similar movements, it was a movement firmly rooted in the *material social conditions* of the day.

Uprising against Rome

From the time of the more or less complete Hellenisation of the Jewish state, around the beginning of the first century BCE, "civil war supplanted foreign war as a

---

[208] Vermes, *Complete* DSS, p 618.

[209] Vermes, *Complete* DSS, p 510

structural element in political life."[210] Strictly speaking, it was not so much civil war as wars of national liberation, and whereas under the four hundred years of Persian and Hellenistic rule there was only one significant uprising against the imperial masters, in the first two hundred years of Roman rule in Palestine there were no fewer than three. In 63 BCE the Roman general Pompey had made Judea a satellite of Rome. In the process of conquering Syria, and using the pretext of a civil war waged by two contenders for the Hasmonean throne, he had occupied Jerusalem and reportedly took treasures from the Temple, killing many of the local population who protested. The high priesthood established by the Hasmoneans continued for several decades, but the Romans later chose the Herodians, a royal family with links to Idumea (earlier known as Edom), as proxy rulers on their behalf.

Much of our information about this period comes from the writings of Flavius Josephus who, as an eye-witness and a participant in the Jewish revolt of 66 CE, is the main source and authority used by historians today. He was a representative par excellence of the ruling elite of Judea and although he was originally appointed as a military leader of the revolutionaries in Galilee, he went over to the Romans and subsequently became an apologist for their role in their suppression of the revolt. In his later life he was based in Rome, where he wrote the four books which remain with us today. They are: The Life of Flavius Josephus, The Antiquities of the Jews, The War of the Jews and Against Apion. The Antiquities and The War, in particular, recount in great detail the events leading up to and including the great revolt. The tone of his memoir was apologetic throughout; he may have remained faithful to his Jewish tradition but he wrote as an aristocrat, for a readership composed mainly of Roman aristocrats. His writing was intended

> ". . . not so much to justify his own tortuous progression as to try to show to his gentile readers, particularly those of *The Jewish War*, that the Jews of the richer class like himself were, despite the revolt, just like other aristocrats in the Greek East of the empire. Above all, he wanted to demonstrate that they should be entrusted again with the Jerusalem Temple."[211]

Marxists have made the point many times that a revolution is never a single event, but a *process*, sometimes lasting years, within which there are movements back and forward, as the revolutionary tide ebbs and flows. Josephus tracks all of these movements and even allowing for his recollections being refracted through the lens of the Judean aristocracy, they are still an invaluable historical resource. Reading between the lines of his upper-class prejudices, it is possible to see all the details of the great Judean revolution of the first century. We will have occasion to cite him many times.

---

[210]   Vidal-Naquet, *The Jews,* p 11.
[211]   Martin Goodman, *The Ruling Class of Judea,* p 6

Following the pattern of all the other great empires in the Near East, the Romans found it cheaper and more effective to rule through proxies, if it was at all possible.

> "The Romans . . . expected to find in each province a clearly defined aristocracy which, like their own, would be in control of war, law, religion and politics, and membership of which would be confined to the landed rich . . . the desire to preserve their property would keep such local leaders in favour of peace and therefore Rome, and their ownership of sufficient wealth would enable them to ensure regular payment of taxes from their own resources even if they came up against difficulties in collecting the required tribute from the rest of the population . . ."[212]

In an effort to cut across the squabbling within the remnant of the Hasmonean dynasty, the Romans put the Idumean aristocrat, Herod, on the throne in 37 BCE. Herod, according to Josephus, promptly made sure there were no other claimants to the throne by putting to the sword any remaining members of the Hasmonean royal family. His reign of more than thirty years was based on the most ruthless suppression of all opposition, even within his own family. Herod went through seven different high priests during his reign as he tightly controlled the income and financial management of the Temple. It is reported that even on his deathbed he ordered the murder of his own son and other potential rivals. As he lay dying, he ordered the mass killing of prisoners, so there would be mass grieving during the period of his own funeral. The bitter memory of Herod 'the Great' clearly outlasted the king himself and many decades later he was to play a starring role in the compilation of the Christian gospel stories about the birth of Jesus.

Herod's greatest, and perhaps only, notable achievement was the rebuilding of the Jerusalem Temple on a grand scale. It is the remnant of the base of the Herodian temple which remains in the city to this day as the Wailing Wall, which is still a focus for Jewish pilgrimage and prayer.

Herod's death, in 4 BCE, was followed by a decade of instability and eventually the emperor Augustus decided to make Judea a Roman province. There was widespread opposition to Roman rule, including riots. Josephus reports that the "whole nation" was in tumult. This coincided with the imposition of a census which was also vaguely remembered a century later when the writers of the Christian gospels were putting together a story of the birth of Jesus. But the census involved no mass migration of peoples to the towns of their birth: it was an attempt, with typical Roman efficiency, to assess the taxable capacity of the mass of the people and it was for that reason that it was bitterly opposed.

By far the greatest burden of tax and tribute was carried by the peasantry, hovering permanently between subsistence and penury. Poor harvests or drought would always threaten to throw them into debt from which they would not be likely to

---

[212]   Goodman, *The Ruling Class of Judaea*, p 35.

recover. The wealthy enriched themselves year on year, while the mass of the rural poor was ground further and further down.

> ". . . it was difficult to find work as a hired hand on the estates of the great landowners even at the busy times of the harvests, for a mass of permanent landless, some of them doubtless normally resident in the city of Jerusalem, competed for the work and the wages. Nor was it easy to supplement income by practicing a craft . . . short of limiting their children to a certain maximum, which . . . was ideologically odious, the heirs of such a farm might seem best served if they sold out to one of the many rich landowners eager to invest their city-won wealth in their property. The alternative was to borrow from the same rich men . . . deprived of land, such peasants had few options. Some presumably joined one of the great and flourishing communities of the Diaspora, [or chose to] turn to banditry or to seek employment in the cities."[213]

---

[213]   Goodman *The Ruling Class of Judaea*, pp 62-3

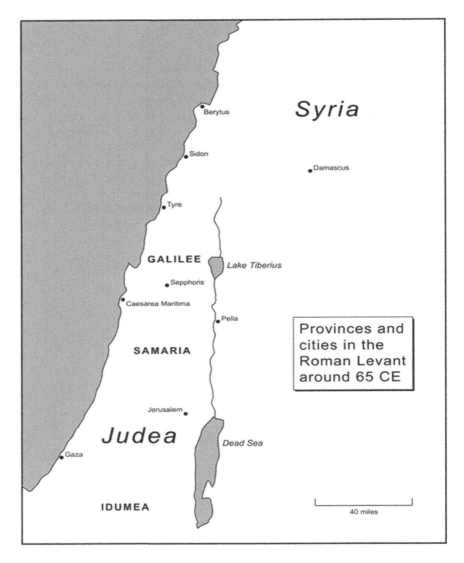

Map 3: The provinces of the Roman Levant prior to the Great Jewish Revolt

Banditry in the countryside

The majority of the peasants were indebted to some degree to the wealthy in Jerusalem. The rich made no attempt to build large country manors, although they were amassing great estates at the expense of the peasantry. They kept their moveable wealth and lived their opulent lifestyles in the city, along with the deeds of their properties and debtors. Many peasants were forced off the land by indebtedness and there was a constant stream of impoverished peasants seeking relief through work or charity in Jerusalem, adding to a large mass of undifferentiated city poor. Alternatively, for the younger and bolder, there was the option of joining one of the many groups of rural bandits. Josephus makes many references to the proliferation of banditry in the countryside. He refers to a band of brigands, in the mid-forties during the reign of Claudius, led by a leader called Eleazar who "had many years made his abode in the mountains." Around this time, he adds, "all Judea was overrun with robberies."[214]

Josephus referred by name to many leaders of the outlaw bands. In Galilee, for example, there was a Jesus, "the captain of those robbers . . ." as well as Eleazar, who was eventually captured by the Roman procurator, Felix.

> "This Felix took Eleazar the arch robber and many that were with him, alive, when *they had ravaged the country for twenty years* together, and sent them to Rome; but as to the number of robbers whom he caused to be crucified, and of whom who were caught among them, and those the brought to punishment, they were *a multitude not to be enumerated.*"[215]

It is inconceivable that banditry could continue on such a scale and for such a length of time, unless the outlaws had substantial support within the towns and villages from which most of them had recently sought refuge. Josephus, unable to understand what motivated desperate peasants, alluded to the robbers' "pretence" for the public welfare when in reality, he wrote, they were looking for "gain to themselves."

The biggest contributor to the debts of the peasantry was the impositions of taxation on the countryside.

> "The Jewish agricultural producers were now subject to a double taxation, probably amounting to well over 40 per cent of their production. There were other Roman taxes as well, which further added to the burden of the people, but the tribute was the major drain . . . coming as it did, immediately after a period of ostensible national independence under the Hasmoneans, Roman domination was regarded as wholly illegitimate. The tribute was seen as robbery. Indeed, it was called outright slavery by militant teachers such as Judas of Galilee, who organised active resistance to the census when the Romans took over direct administration of Judea in 6 CE."[216]

---

[214] AJ, 20, 124. Citations from the works of Josephus are abbreviated to WJ (*The War of the Jews*) or AJ (*The Antiquities of the Jews*), followed by the chapter and line number.

[215] WJ, 2, 253 (Italics added)

[216] Richard Horsley, *Bandits, Prophets and Messiahs*, p 56.

By the time that Festus became procurator of Judea in 58 CE, Josephus reports, "Judea was afflicted by the robbers, while all the villages were set on fire, and plundered by them". Sometimes the discontent of the masses was completely wrapped up in apocalyptic fervour and Josephus recounts how they would frequently come under the spell of self-appointed 'messiahs'. This corresponded to the widespread circulation of the kind of resistance literature that has come down to us in the Dead Sea Scrolls and the preaching by thousands of Essenes about the coming 'apocalypse' and the deliverance of the righteous by a 'messiah'. In the mid-forties, one such leader, Thadeus, took many of his followers into the desert, where they were met and killed by the forces of Festus:

> ". . . those that had been seduced by a certain imposter, who promised them deliverance and freedom from the miseries they were under, if they would but follow him as far as the wilderness. Accordingly, those forces that were sent destroyed both him that had deluded them and those that were his followers also."[217]

Josephus describes the way in which revolts spread like bush-fires from one part of the countryside to another:

> "Now, when these were quieted, it happened, as it does in a diseased body, that another part was subject to an inflammation; for a company of deceivers and robbers got together, and persuaded the Jews to revolt, and exhorted them to assert their liberty, inflicting death on those that continued in obedience to the Roman government, and saying, that such as willingly chose slavery ought to be forced from such their desired inclinations, for they parted themselves into different bodies, and lay in waiting up and down the country and plundered the houses of the great men, and slew the men themselves and set the villages on fire; and this till all Judea was filled with the effects of their madness. And thus the flame was every day more and more blown up till it came to a direct war."[218]

There are many more citations in Josephus about the brigandage in Judea than there is space to include here. Suffice to say, that at several points in his various accounts, he despaired that ". . . all Judea was overrun with robberies."[219] Richard Horsley, probably more than any other historian of ancient Judea, has put a strong focus on the popular movements of the time. His works, including *Bandits, Prophets and Messiahs* give a graphic illustration, much of it drawn from Josephus, of the vast scale of rural rebellion and its impact on Judean society.

---

[217]   AJ, 20, 188
[218]   WJ, 2, 264
[219]   AJ, 20, 124

"The Jewish revolt against Roman domination may be the most vivid and best-attested example from antiquity of a major peasant revolt preceded and partly led by brigands . . . The sudden increase of Jewish brigandage to epidemic proportions in the years just prior to 66 CE however, appears to have been a major factor leading to the outbreak and continuation of widespread peasant revolt."[220]

The greatest burdens on the masses of Judea were the taxes and tithes put on the peasantry in the countryside, but there were other taxes based on tolls and commerce, the rights for the collection of which were sold as franchises to rich families.

"Publicans [ie tax collectors] had to be rich to carry out their duties, for when the right to collect taxes was farmed out by auction the successful bidder guaranteed payment of a minimum amount in the expectation that he would earn more than his original bid through conscientious collection." [221]

It was not surprising that tax collectors were very unpopular, as was noted by the later writers of the Christian gospels. When, after the death of Herod, his son Archelaus was imposed upon by "the multitude" to "ease them of some of their annual payments" and to "release those that were put in prison by Herod, who were many and had been put there at several times" others, clamoured for a reduction in those taxes which were placed "on what was publicly sold and bought."[222] Even Josephus occasionally lets slip a comment about the "men of power oppressing the multitude and the multitude earnestly labouring to destroy the men of power"[223]

In describing the situation before the revolt, Josephus introduces his readers to the *sicarii*, who were named for the short swords they used and who he describes as "robbers" who had grown "numerous". It is highly unlikely, as he suggests (and has been adopted ever since by other historians) that the sicarii were a political party or movement, in their own right.[224] What is likely is that some of the outlaw bands resorted from time to time to assassinations of leading Jerusalemites in much the same way that modern terrorists have been known to murder politician opponents

---

[220] Richard Horsely, *Bandits, Prophets and Messiahs*, p 77

[221] Goodman, *The Ruling Class of Judaea*, p 131.

[222] Josephus, AJ, 17, 204.

[223] WJ, 7, 260

[224] It has been suggested by some biblical historians that the name of the treacherous disciple of Jesus, Judas *Iscariot*, is a derived from *sicarii* and that Judas, therefore, was one of those assassins. There is no evidence for that, or for the suggestion that the writers of the gospels intended any connection.

today. Josephus, from his vantage point as an outraged member of the ruling class, cannot understand that the sicarii and the brigands are the same revolutionaries.

> "[The sicarii] . . . mingled themselves among the multitude at their festivals, when they were come up in crowds from all parts to the city to worship God . . . and easily slew those that they had a mind to slay. They also came frequently upon the villages belonging to their enemies with their weapons and plundered them, and set them on fire."[225]

In fact, in denial at the appalling condition of the masses, and unable to understand the inner workings of a revolution, Josephus frequently blamed the whole uprising on the influence of false leaders, religious 'imposters' and 'charlatans'. Writing down his recollections in Rome many years later, it must have seemed to Josephus that the lower classes had gone mad. For this historian the whole sorry saga of the uprising had begun sixty earlier, with Judas Gamala, who led a revolt against Rome.

> "All sorts of misfortunes also sprang from these men and the nation was infected with this doctrine to an incredible degree; one violent war came upon us after another, and we lost our friends, who used to alleviate our pains; there were also very great robberies and murders of our principal men. This was done in the pretence indeed for the public welfare, but in reality for the hope of gain to themselves, whence arose seditions, and from them murders of men, which sometimes fell on those of their own people (by their madness of these men towards one another while their desire was that none of the adverse party might be left), and sometimes on their enemies; a famine also coming upon us, reduced us to the last degree of despair, as did also the taking and demolishing of cities; nay, the sedition at last increased so high that the very temple of God was burnt down . . ."[226]

Prophets and Messiahs

Josephus describes how, near the end of the revolt, when the Romans were already inside the walls of Jerusalem, a "false prophet" persuaded people to climb to the top of the Temple, "that there they should receive miraculous signs of their deliverance." He even gives a rationale for the support for these prophets: "a man that is in adversity does easily comply with such promises"! The people who climbed the Temple, of course, were killed.

Another 'false prophet' described by Josephus was an unnamed Egyptian:

---

[225]   AJ, 20, 187
[226]   AJ, 18, 6

". . . he was a cheat, and pretended to be a prophet also, and got together thirty thousand men that were deluded by him. These he led round about from the wilderness to the mount which was called the Mount of Olives, and was ready to break into Jerusalem by force from that place . . . but [procurator] Felix prevented his attempt, and met him with his Roman soldiers, while all the people assisted him in his attack upon them"[227]

Josephus gives an interesting account of one of these false prophets, also named Jesus, who preached for years in the vicinity of Jerusalem, before meeting his death during the siege.

"There was one Jesus b Ananus, a plebeian and a husbandman, who, for four years before the war began, and at a time when the city was in very great peace and prosperity, came to that feast whereon it is our custom for everyone to make tabernacles to God in the temple, began on a sudden to cry aloud . . . he went about by day and by night, in all the lanes of the city . . . our rulers supposing, as the case proved to be, that this was a sort of divine fury in the man, brought him to the Roman procurator; where he was whipped till his bones were laid bare, yet did he not make any supplication for himself, nor shed any tears, but turning his voice to the most lamentable tone possible, at every stroke of the whip his answer was, 'Woe, woe to Jerusalem!' . . . Albinus took him to be a madman, and dismissed him . . . he continued this ditty for seven years and five months, without growing hoarse or being tired therewith . . ."[228]

Christian purists will blanche at the thought of *their* Jesus being a madman who ranted unsuccessfully for years in Jerusalem before being killed (according to Josephus) by a stone fired from a Roman siege engine. But whatever its accuracy, this story is nevertheless an indication of the *messianic ferment* of the period and, with other vague memories recalled several decades later, may have provided a starting point for a Jesus character who was then transformed by the gospel-writers into something altogether different.

Apart from the possibility of employment in public works, the only help that kept the poor from complete starvation were the charitable organisations set up by the Jews themselves. This social support mechanism had no equivalent anywhere else in the Roman Empire, a factor, as we shall discuss later, of great significance in the following centuries when the communities of the Jewish and Christian Diaspora were thriving.

"Among Jews, by contrast, it was a religious duty of great moment to care for the destitute. This factor was perhaps one of the main social causes of

---

[227] WJ, 2, 261
[228] WJ, 6, 300

the cohesion of Jewish Diaspora communities, just as it was one of the attractions for converts to Christianity that the early Church inherited this care for its members from its Jewish origins . . . the result in Jerusalem was that the rich kept in their midst a host of shiftless poor sustained just above the breadline by private charity."[229]

Whereas King Herod had appointed relative nonentities to the high priesthood, after his death the Roman governor had appointed Ananus b Sethi, an aristocrat whose family was to dominate the post for sixty years, with all five of his sons holding the position one or more times. But it was an indication of the complete dead-end of Judean society that the ruling families squabbled among themselves for the division of the spoils, as a growing political vacuum coincided with the increasing desperation of the masses. An indication of the instability in the relations between the King and the Temple is seen by the fact that Agrippa II, appointed by Rome as tetrarch (one of a group of four rulers) from 50 CE onwards, deposed six high priests in the ten years leading up to the revolt. There were also tensions between different layers of the priesthood. Josephus recounts that the high priests—which would mean those of the aristocratic priestly clans—sent their servants to relieve the "poorer sort" of priests of their tithes, so much so that some of the latter "died for want". According to Josephus, the different aristocratic families who contended for the high priesthood used gangs of hired thugs to fight it out on the streets of Jerusalem.

> ". . . and now Jesus, the son of Gamaliel, became the successor of Jesus, the son of Damneus, in the high priesthood, which the king had taken from the other; on which account a sedition arose between the high priests, with regard to one another; for they got together bodies of the boldest sort of the people, and frequently came, from reproaches, to throwing stones at each other . . ."[230]

As well as the two high priests called Jesus, he names others like Ananias, Costobarus and Saulus who "did themselves get together a multitude of wicked wretches", who "used violence with the people", until eventually, "our city was greatly disordered, and that all things grew worse and worse among us." One of the strongest factions vying for office was the son of Ananus b Sethi, also called Ananus, who was high priest at the time of the revolt.

The whole countryside was on fire, but the key to the revolution was Jerusalem, which completely dominated the economy of Judea, in the words of Josephus, "as the head does over the body". Tens of thousands of pilgrims and visitors flocked to Jerusalem at all times of the year, but particularly at the time of religious festivals, and "at these feasts seditions are generally begun." Josephus suggests that nearly two

---

[229] Goodman, *The Ruling Class of Judaea*, p 65
[230] AJ, 20, 213

and three quarter millions were in the city during Passover in 66 CE, and even if this is an exaggeration, the numbers are likely to have been considerable.

> "The Temple attracted constant gifts both from Jewish pilgrims and from gentile visitors from outside Palestine, and Herod and his descendants lavished wealth created in other parts of their kingdom on this, their capital city . . . The city's inhabitants provided goods and services for the visitors, celebrating the great religious occasions of the year not only for their spiritual significance but also, as in pilgrimage centres today, for the custom that they brought."[231]

The Temple itself was a huge drain on the resources of the local population and pilgrims alike. According to an account of the second century BCE Hasmonean temple, there were as many as fifteen hundred priests, with hundreds on duty at any one time. From the numbers given by Josephus, the total of all the animal sacrifices must have amounted to hundreds of thousands of animals every year and that does not include smaller animals and birds, grain, oil, or wine.

> "Our modern conceptions of the Temple are altogether rather bloodless and undoubtedly too spiritual. An appropriate analogy is a slaughterhouse. Enormous amounts of animal blood spilled around the altar every day and splashed upon the priests as they worked."[232]

Large numbers of the Jerusalem population were still permanently on the edge of penury. An example of this was the crisis in 64 CE, when the work on the rebuilding of the Temple was finally completed and a crisis developed over the threatened lay-off of eighteen thousand workers who would no longer have a source of income. Some were quickly found labour in other state projects but a large under-class of unemployed and underemployed proletarians crowded into the city adding to the atmosphere of discontent.

> ". . . in AD 66 the unequal distribution of its [the economy's] benefits was perhaps then at its most blatant. The wealth of the Jerusalem rich has become fully apparent only in the last few years as archaeologists have unearthed in Jerusalem private houses of great size and luxurious appointments . . . one private mansion uncovered in the Jewish Quarter covers 600 square metres, and others are not much smaller. No expense was spared on the decoration of such houses, and Pompeian-style frescoes and fine mosaics abound."[233]

---

[231] Goodman, *The Ruling Class of Judaea*, p 52.
[232] Hanson and Oakman, *Palestine in the time of Jesus*, p 145
[233] Goodman, *The Ruling Class of Judaea*, p 55

All the classic social and political conditions were present for social revolution in Judea. In the countryside, the peasantry was in a state of open rebellion. In Jerusalem, even by the account of Josephus, the situation was getting worse and the ruling class had no policy, other than fighting amongst themselves to get the biggest share of the spoils. Inter-communal violence broke out in cities with a mixed Jewish/Gentile population, although it is not clear if this preceded or followed the outbreak of revolt in Jerusalem. There were massacres on both sides and Josephus reports that "all Caesarea was emptied of its Jewish inhabitants". Once the revolt was underway, Josephus reports, there were many more clashes in mixed cities and in many cases it was the Jewish population that suffered the most. He reports that in addition to the twenty thousand Jews killed in Caesarea, thirteen thousand were slain in Scythopolis and ten thousand in Damascus.

It would seem that it was the theft of treasure from the temple by the Roman governor, Florus, and the subsequent refusal of lower ranking priests, led by one Eleazar b Ananias, to offer the daily sacrifice in honour of the Roman emperor which triggered the wave of protests that finally led to open revolt.

Outbreak of Revolt

The refusal of the Temple to make any reference to the Romans or their emperor/gods had always been a source of contention: the Jews demonstrated a long-standing reluctance to have Temple rituals directly related to the emperors who were worshipped as gods in Roman temples. Riots had followed some years earlier when the Emperor Gaius Caligula had decided to put up a statue of himself in the Temple. That plan and the revolt it had provoked were somewhat diverted by the assassination of Caligula and his replacement by Claudius. But in 66 CE there was no such diversion. The rich and powerful in the city were terrified of the prospect of a revolt against Rome and they tried to persuade the dissident priests to recommence the sacrifices in honour of the emperor; when they were refused, this treacherous Jewish elite sent to Florus for assistance to crush the revolt. There were several days of bloody battles in the streets of Jerusalem for control of the city.

Revolution was unfolding across Judea and north into Samaria and Galilee. The fortress at Masada was taken by rebels and the Roman garrison massacred. One of the rebel leaders, Menahem, described by Josephus as leader of the sicarii, used the Roman armoury from Masada to provide arms to the revolutionaries in Jerusalem. Here, Josephus reports, the crowds set fire to the house of the chief priest and the palaces of the king Agrippa II and the queen, Berenice. After this, he reported, "they carried the fire to the place where the archives were deposited, and made haste to burn the contracts belonging to their creditors, and thereby dissolve their obligations for paying their debts."[234] The revolution was clearly gathering momentum, but writing his memoirs years later, Josephus could not see the burning

---

[234]   Josephus, *WJ*, 2, 426

of the debt contracts for the straight-forward revolutionary act it was, implying that it was done to "persuade" the poor to join the insurrection—not that the poor would have had a hand in the burning!

The Antonia fortress in Jerusalem fell to the insurrection. Josephus reports that he himself hid in the Temple in case he was taken to be part of the pro-Roman faction, as indeed he was. In September, some weeks after the revolution had started, the high priest, Ananias, was finally caught and put to death by the rebels. It was clear that there was no going back. Some signs of an ebb in the revolution were evident in the killing of the sicarii leader, Menahem, by the supporters of Eleazar b Ananias (the son of the murdered high priest) but the situation was still extremely precarious for the ruling class, ". . . no small fear seized upon us *when we saw the people in arms*, while we ourselves knew not what we should do."[235] There was no other option open to the ruling elite at this time, other than to *pretend* they were with the revolution, all the better to moderate, derail or betray it.

> ". . . *we pretended that we were of the same opinion with them*; but only advised them to be quiet for the present . . . *still hoping that Florus would not be long* ere he came, and that with great forces and so put and end to these seditious proceedings."[236]

Pity the poor representatives of the Judean ruling class caught up in all this! Their property was in jeopardy and they saw no way of avoiding the punishment of Rome coming down on their heads! ". . . every one of the moderate men . . . [in Jerusalem] were under great disturbance, as likely themselves to undergo punishment for the wickedness of the seditious."[237]

Troops sent by King Agrippa were forced out of Jerusalem and in a few days the remainder of the Roman garrison in the city was slain. The Roman governor, Cestus Gallus, now marched on the city with the Twelfth Legion, consisting of up to 40,000 seasoned veterans. The Romans destroyed and plundered cities all over Judea, cutting swathes of death and destruction along their path. Tens of thousands of Judeans were killed or taken into slavery and thousands more fled to the relative safety of the hills or into Jerusalem. As soon as the Romans arrived at the city gates the ruling class was already prepared to betray the people. Josephus reports that

> ". . . many of the principal men of the city were persuaded by Ananus, the son of Jonathan, and *invited Cestius into the city, and were about to open the gates for him*; but he overlooked this offer, partly out of his anger at the Jews and partly because he did not thoroughly believe they were in earnest; whence it was that he delayed in the matter so long, that the

---

[235] Josephus, *Life*, 21. (italics added)
[236] Josephus, *Life*, 21. (italics added)
[237] Josephus, WJ, 2, 455.

seditious perceived the treachery and threw Ananus and those of his party down from the wall"[238]

Once Cestius began his siege of the city, those Jerusalemites not with the "sedition" missed other opportunities to open the gates, "to admit Cestius as their benefactor." Cestius, we are told, was not aware of "how courageous the people were for him" and, not being prepared at this time for a long siege, he retired from the city, an action that was inexplicable to Josephus. Over the succeeding weeks, as the Roman army returned north, it was forced to endure a bloody harrying by Judean and Galilean guerrilla forces and eventually the Romans were forced to beat a hasty retreat after thousands of legionaries had been killed.

The retreat of Cestius was described by Josephus as a "calamity", after which many eminent citizens of Jerusalem left the city to find their own way to the Romans to surrender to them. Josephus, being sympathetic to their plight, hesitates to describe them as "rats", but he does point out that they "swam away from the city, as from a ship when it is going to sink." It is clear from the account of Josephus that his whole narrative is an attempt to dissociate the political views and actions of *his* class from those of the mob or from those of the "wicked ringleaders" who duped the mob into support for the revolution.

Following the retreat of Cestius, the Roman army for a while made no further effort to take Jerusalem or, for that matter, to suppress the generalised revolt. Because of the death of the emperor Claudius and the internecine conflicts over the succession, during which there were four emperors in a single year, no sizeable Roman army would return to Jerusalem for four years.

The countryside, meanwhile, exploded into revolt. One of the revolutionary leaders described by Josephus was Simon of Giora, "a young man", who allied himself with those who had seized the Masada fortress. This Simon, according to our historian,

". . . proclaimed liberty to those in slavery, and a reward for those already free, and got together a set of wicked men from all quarters. And as he had now a strong body of men about him, he overran the villages that lay in the mountainous country and when there were still more and more that came to him, he ventured to go down into the lower parts of the country, and since he was now become formidable to the cities, many of the men of power were corrupted by him, so that his army was no longer composed of slaves and robbers, but a great many of the populace were obedient to him as their king."[239]

---

238 Josephus, *WJ*, 2, 533
239 Josephus, *WJ*, 4, 508

Simon's forces numbered forty thousand according to Josephus; although most likely an exaggeration, he clearly had mass support in the countryside and he became one of the key revolutionary leaders in Jerusalem during the final siege of the city.

In Judea, the former ruling class was hanging on by its fingernails. Its representatives wheedled their way into leading positions in the revolution. Josephus himself, little more than nineteen years of age, was appointed as a 'commander' of the uprising in Galilee, although it is clear that he was not the first of the 'generals' to lead the Galilean revolutionaries. He was sent there only to moderate the movement and prevent 'excesses'; as he writes in his *Life*, ". . . they sent me and two others of the priests . . . in order to persuade the ill men there to lay down their arms."[240]

In Jerusalem, although the priests around Eleazar b Ananias had been the predominant faction, the more moderate leadership of Ananus asserted itself. The new government clearly saw itself as the harbinger of a new era as it minted its own coins indicating 'Year 1' and continued to issue coins for the next three years. It was to Ananus that Josephus looked as the commander-in-chief of the revolutionary army, although Ananus had played no part in the peasant wars in the countryside or in the street-fighting in the city. The leadership of Ananus, left to itself, would have led quickly to the collapse of the whole revolt, now effectively including the whole of Roman Palestine. The 'commanders' Ananus appointed, like Josephus himself, could not surrender to the Romans quickly enough, even though in the beginning of the year, revolutionary irregulars had been in control of large areas of Judea, Samaria and Galilee. As a result of the perfidity of the Jewish elite, the Romans quickly re-established themselves in key areas, including Galilee and the coastal cities. Throughout the whole period those eminent Jews who found it no longer possible even to pretend to support the revolution were going over the wall and throwing themselves on the mercy of the Romans.

Neil Faulkner, in his account of the revolt, *Apocalypse*, has compared this situation to the dual power situation that existed in the Russian capital Petrograd in the days before the October revolution, "where the government has formal authority but its ability to act is paralysed by a mass popular movement and where this movement contains within itself the potential to overturn the government and rule in its place."[241]

> "Dual power is rooted in class conflict: the rival political authorities—the actual and the potential governments, as it were—represent different and mutually antagonistic social forces. The second aristocratic government formed in late 66 CE was composed of property-owners propelled into

---

[240] *Life*, 29
[241] Faulkner, *Apocalypse, The Great Jewish Revolt against Rome, AD 66-73*, P 132.

opposition to Rome by an explosive insurrectionary movement of the Jewish people."[242]

The loss of the very populous region of Galilee to the Romans was a special blow to the rebels and with this military failure the revolutionaries in Jerusalem began to demand new leadership. At this point in his narrative Josephus begins to refer to the most militant of the rebels as "zealots", referring, of course, to their "madness". Two other revolutionary leaders came to the fore in the city: Eleazar b Simon and John of Gischala, the latter, with the support of two thousand peasant soldiers from Idumea, taking control of the Temple and exercising *de facto* control of the city for twelve months from the spring of 68.

> "The Zealots thus won influence first by imprisoning members of the ruling class who were not part of Ananus' provisional government but who had retained positions of authority from the procuratorial period. Chief among these was Antipas, a relative of the Herodian house, who had charge of the public treasury."[243]

In his own account of the dual power during the Russian Revolution, Trotsky makes the point that "a class deprived of power inevitably strives to some extent to swerve the [revolutionary] governmental course in its favour."[244] But although they were desperate to find a way to surrender to the Romans, the tide of the struggle was going against the old ruling elite. Open conflict broke out between the revolutionary forces, chiefly the zealots, and the counter-revolutionaries around the supporters of Ananus. The fighters of Eleazar b Simon and John of Gischala stormed the prisons and released thousands of prisoners who now swelled the ranks of the revolution and the peasant armies in the countryside. In his tearful description of the revolution, Josephus clearly alludes to the attraction of the revolution to the youth of the city:

> "These harangues of John's [John of Gischala] corrupted a great part of the young men . . . seditions arose everywhere, while those that were for innovations and were desirous of war, by their youth and boldness, were too hard for the aged and the prudent man"[245]

Quite understandably, the forces of the revolution denounced those Jerusalemites with links to the old regime and accused them of preparing to betray the city to the Romans. Josephus calls it a "lie" that "Ananus and his party, in order to secure their own dominion, had invited the Romans to come to them," but as Goodman points

---

242   Faulkner, *Apocalypse, The Great Jewish Revolt against Rome, AD 66-73*, P 133
243   Goodman, *The Ruling Class of Judea*, p 186.
244   Trotsky, *History of the Russian Revolution, Volume I*, p 202.
245   *WJ*, 4, 128

out: ". . . The accusation was plausible both because some of Ananus' coalition, including Josephus, had taken that route and also because successful treachery at this stage in the rebellion would indeed have confirmed Ananus' ability to control the population on Rome's behalf."[246]

The revolutionaries won the day and Ananus was killed, to be later eulogized by Josephus—"I cannot but imagine that virtue itself groaned"—for his efforts to control and limit the revolution. From the standpoint of the ruling class the measures of the revolutionary governments in France after 1789 and Russia after October 1917 were described as 'reigns of terror'. So it was with Josephus in his description of Jerusalem in 69 CE. "The terror that was upon the people was so great," Josephus wrote, "that no one had courage enough either to weep openly for the dead man that was related to him, or bury him". He went on to describe the "impudence" of the revolutionaries in asserting their own revolutionary justice through "fictitious tribunals and judiciaries." The revolutionary government of Jerusalem called seventy of the "principal men" of the city before the tribunals, "for a show" and accused them of betrayal to the Romans. As the zealots "grew more insolent . . . they made no longer any delay, nor took any deliberation in their enormous practices, but made use of the shortest methods for all their executions . . ."[247]. Although written from the point of view of a horrified representative of the Judean ruling class, these lines nevertheless are a real indication of the revolutionary character of the city population, after three years of war, slaughter and repeated betrayals by the Jewish elite.

Jerusalem sacked

Eventually, the Romans, having delayed their main offensive because of the internal struggles over the emperorship, began a march on Jerusalem with a substantial army under Vespasian, who, on becoming emperor himself, handed over command to his son Titus. Josephus narrates in great detail the ferocity and brutality of the Roman army as it devastated the towns and cities in Judea and Galilee. Tens of thousands of Jews were slaughtered, with no distinction made, Josephus regretfully points out, between those who had supported the revolt and those who had not.

In the Spring of 70 CE, for the first time in four years, the Romans reached the walls of Jerusalem. In the countryside, the most important leader of the peasant insurrection had been Simon b Gioras and his forces had long since retreated to the city where for the best part of the previous year they had been the biggest armed group. His forces, supported by the remaining Idumean troops, controlled the city while the forces of John of Gischala and Eleazar b Simon, controlled different parts of the Temple. The Roman historian Tacitus noted in his *Histories* that even as the Romans closed on Jerusalem, there were *three armies* in Jerusalem, all fighting one

---

[246]   Ibid, p 189.
[247]   *WJ*, 4, 334-356

another. In fact, the arrival of the Romans led to a truce between the revolutionary factions so they faced the siege as one.

After a long and bloody struggle, the Romans finally broke through into the city and it was sacked, its inhabitants slaughtered and the Temple razed to the ground. The remainder of the war consisted of a series of 'mopping up' operations, including the siege of the fortress at Masada, where, according to Josephus, those resisting the Romans committed mass suicide rather than surrender. Tens of thousands of Jews were crucified or enslaved and the entire economic infrastructure of Judea was devastated for a generation.

The memoirs of Josephus, written a long time afterwards and for a readership of Roman aristocrats, are positively fawning in the way they pay tribute to the 'generosity' and 'benevolence' of the imperial army in Judea. He comments on how Titus . . .

> ". . . pitied the people who were kept under by the seditious, and did often voluntarily delay the taking of the city, and allowed time to the siege, in order to let the authors have opportunity for repentance . . . and how often Titus, out of his desire to preserve the city and the temple, invited the seditious to come to terms of accommodation . . . how the Temple was burnt, against the consent of Caesar . . ."[248]

Whereas after the defeat of the revolutionary Paris Commune in 1871, Marx was on hand to pay tribute to the heroism of the Parisian workers who had "stormed heaven", after the great Jewish Revolt we have only the mealy-mouthed apologies of a spokesman of the Judean ruling class. Throughout all his narratives of the revolt Josephus pours a stream of invective on the leaders of the revolution. He regularly highlights the fact that there were many Jews who were 'responsible' and who supported the Roman rule, not that it did them any good in the repression afterwards. As for the rest, they were either duped by the revolutionary leaders or terrorised by them.

His accounts are an invaluable resource for any historian of the period, but it is abundantly clear that from his class standpoint, Josephus was organically incapable of understanding the inner mechanisms of a social revolution and the socio-political drivers behind it. Josephus was not able to make any connection between the upheavals in Palestine and the other revolutions taking place around the same time in other parts of the Roman Empire. Martin Goodman, whose work *The Ruling Class of Judaea*, we have quoted at length, unfortunately appears to share some of the vices of Josephus. Goodman, like Josephus, sees the whole revolt as a result of factional struggles within the ruling class. In fact the personal class backgrounds of this or that revolutionary leader are immaterial. What matters is what their movement represented in terms of its *class* support. Goodman points out that:

---

[248] JW, preface.

"Josephus describes Simon's proclamation of freedom for slaves and the abolition of debt not as part of a wider social programme but as a tactical move to win supporters for his aspirations to despotic power."[249]

But Josephus would, wouldn't he? Because our ancient historian was incapable of absorbing the fact that he was facing a *social* revolution, just like the ruling classes who faced revolutions even in modern times, like the French or the Russian. "Don't listen to the revolutionary leaders! They're only using you!" Goodman points to the lack of a clear revolutionary agrarian programme in an effort to minimise the significance of the social content of the revolution:

"In neither case [of Simon's proclamations, above] did such action indicate a policy for social reform or revolution. Simon showed no class solidarity with the peasants when it was to his advantage to instill terror into his opponents . . ." [250]

It is true, as Goodman has pointed out, that most of the political demands are couched in terms of religious fervour and often in a variety of forms of messianism. This is also evident in the frequent use of the title of a new Israel as opposed to new Judea on coins and inscriptions of this period, and the later uprising of 132 CE. But as Horsley writes, one is forced to ask,

". . . why so many hundreds, even thousands of Jewish peasants were prepared to abandon their homes to pursue some prophet into the wilderness, or to rise in rebellion against their Jewish and Roman overlords when the signal was given by some charismatic 'king', or to flee to the hills to join some brigand band. Peasants generally do not take such drastic action unless conditions have become such that they can no longer simply pursue the traditional patterns of life."[251]

Goodman is almost desperate to expunge the revolutionary content of the upheavals . . . as if the mass of the population could be mobilised to fight such a monumental war against Rome on the whim of a handful of leaders. He again echoes the sentiments of Josephus in ascribing the main motive of banditry in the countryside as the pursuit of profit.

"It seems to me preferable therefore to accept instead the motivation which is consistently ascribed by Josephus to all the Judaean leaders both

---

249 Goodman, *The Ruling Class of Judaea*, p 204.
250 Goodman, *The Ruling Class of Judaea*, p 204
251 Horsley, *Bandits, Prophets and Messiahs*, p 50.

before and during the revolt. The aim of those in power was more power. In Josephus' terminology, they were bent on tyranny."[252]

Goodman, in the end, accepts the view of Josephus that the social and class content of the revolution are immaterial. Most other historians, Goodman suggests, see it as a matter of "chance" that "social and class divisions are not explicitly mentioned by him [Josephus] as the causes of the civil strife". It is not "chance", of course. It is the *psychology of the political representatives of the ruling class* that prevents them from understanding the causes of revolution and which means that such causes are inevitably missing from their accounts. Richard Horsley is much nearer the mark in his view that the *fundamental conflict* in the revolt . . .

". . . was between the Roman, Herodian and high priestly rulers, on the one hand, and the Judean and Galilean villagers, whose produce supplied tribute for Caesar, taxes for Herod, and tithes and offerings for the priests and temple apparatus, on the other."[253]

Before the outbreak of the revolt, from Galilee in the north, to Idumea in the south, greater Judea was a boiling cauldron of discontent, resentment, bitterness and anger, albeit frequently expressed in the language of religious zeal and apocalyptic messianism. The classic conditions for social revolution were present in Judea and as a result the period from 66 to 70 CE was one of enormous social tension. However, it is almost a law of historical literature that commentators from the ruling class, when they relate the history of a revolution, *always minimise the importance of material class conditions as the driving force of the revolution.* Instead, they blame the revolution on agitators who dupe the masses and tyrants who terrorise them. Occasionally, as does Josephus, they admit to indecision or weakness on the part of the ruling class; but nowhere is there an acknowledgement, much less a description, of the seething discontent and boiling class hatred that is the real social force behind a revolution. Josephus is just such a historian, at all times playing down the real social and class content of the revolution. Goodman's summary, in an otherwise excellent book, is an indication that the same tendency is alive and well today.

Rabbinic Judaism

The destruction of Jerusalem and the Temple was an earth-shattering blow to the traditional culture and practice of Judaism. It is perhaps the most significant milestone marking the end of the foundation period of Judaism and the beginning of modern *rabbinic* Judaism. As long as the temple was in existence, at least since the Persian period, it had been the focus of Jewish religious practice and aspiration. Large numbers of pilgrims travelled regularly to Jerusalem and on feast days the

---

[252] Goodman, *The Ruling Class of Judaea*, p 207.
[253] Horsley, *Bandits, Prophets and Messiahs*, p xii

population of the city was swollen to huge proportions. Although it was not strictly needed from a financial point of view, across the whole of the already vast Jewish Diaspora, collections were made and sent to Jerusalem for the upkeep of the Temple. Even at a distance of hundreds of miles and across the length of the Mediterranean, the life of the Temple assumed a great significance in the day-to-day life of Jews. This state of affairs had now come to a bitter end with the destruction of the revolt. Increasingly, the life of Jewish communities revolved around the synagogues, not only as a focus of social organisation, but as a place of worship and religious ritual.

Synagogues are first attested historically in the third century BCE, but it appears that their earlier role was secular at least as much as it was religious. It was a place for meetings, teaching, a social centre and probably the main focus for the reading of scripture on the Sabbath.

> "The synagogue constituted . . . the principal centre and unit of Jewish communal organisation, this in much the same manner as the parish-system in late medieval England or France. The synagogue leadership, then, remained essentially lay 'rulers' of the Jewish *ethnos* in the empire, and the liaison between the people and the Roman authorities."[254]

Following its destruction, the Temple could no longer be the focus of Jewish religious practice and the synagogues increasingly took on the role of holy places themselves.

> "Virtually every synagogue (from the second century CE on) within and outside the Holy Land has as an architectural feature a niche front of the hall in which the scrolls of the Law probably were deposited . . . earliest rabbinic literature gives ample indication that regular readings of the Law on Sabbaths, festivals and perhaps during midweek took place in the antecedent non-rabbinic synagogues of the middle and late first century CE."[255]

The rabbis, formerly teachers of scripture, became leaders of service, effectively priests, as new liturgy, prayers and forms of service were developed in the late first and second centuries to replace the former focus on sacrifice and gifts to the Temple. Centres of rabbinical study, probably infused with refugee Pharisees from Judea, were established in cities like Caesarea and in other places outside Judea.

Messianic ideas were not immediately removed from the agenda, however. In 115 CE there were unsuccessful revolts against the Romans in Cyrene (modern-day Libya), Alexandria and Cyprus, leading to a large reduction of the Jewish population in those areas.

---

[254]   Lightstone, *The Commerce of the Sacred*, p 79
[255]   Lightstone, *The Commerce of the Sacred*, p 73

"A violent pogrom resulted in the decimation of the Jewish population of Alexandria. In the neighbouring Cyrenaica, another violent revolt broke out. Temples were damaged. Milestones near Cyrene point to roads destroyed by Jewish rebels. The revolt was put down savagely. Three thousand veterans were stationed in Cyrene to assist in the repopulation. In Cyprus, Salamis was devastated by the Jews. All Jews were banned from the island. Even those Jews sheltering or shipwrecked were to be put to death. Dio Cassius reports a death toll of 220,000 in Cyrene and 240,000 in Egypt. The historian, writing in 220 CE speaks of the exclusion of Jews from Cyprus as still in force."[256]

In 132-35 the Jews of Judea launched another desperate revolt, under the leadership of Bar Kochba. There is no detailed historical account of the Bar Kochba revolt in the manner of Josephus; it appears to have followed a similar pattern to the peasant uprising in 66-70 CE, although there is no evidence that the rebels ever took control of Jerusalem. The leader, Simeon bar Kosiba was nick-named "Kochba", the "Star", in clearly messianic overtones. Although not on the scale of the previous uprising, this revolt was nonetheless quite extensive.

"A large proportion of the Judean peasantry must have responded readily to Simeon's movement, undeterred by the rabbinic rejection of its messianic pretensions. For, in effect, Simeon and his followers enjoyed independent self-government for over three years while defending themselves against Roman re-conquest of Judea. They minted coins ascribed with 'Year 1 of the Liberation of Israel'"[257]

The end result was the same result as in 66-70; the peasant guerrilla army could not sustain itself indefinitely against the mighty military machine of Rome. The only reference to the revolt we have, by the Roman historian Cassius Dio, may exaggerate the destruction; but even so, it would indicate that the Jews suffered a retaliatory repression as bad, or even worse, than they had sixty-five years earlier.

"Fifty of their most important outposts and nine hundred and eighty-five of their most famous villages were razed to the ground. Five hundred and eighty thousand men were slain in the various raids and battles, and the number of those that perished by famine, disease and fire was past finding out. Thus nearly the whole of Judaea was made desolate."[258]

It was further reported that Jews were banned from living in Jerusalem, so it became entirely a Gentile and, later, a Christian city. The failed uprising of 132 CE

---

[256] Harding, *Early Christian Life and Thought in Social Context*, p 99
[257] Horsley, *Bandits, Prophets and Messiahs*, p 129.
[258] Cassius Dio, *Roman History*, 69, 14

finally put an end to the apocalyptic movements within mainstream Judaism and reinforced the movement towards a quietist rabbinic faith.

> ". . . this flourishing of messianic fervour was to be the last for a very long time. Leading rabbis concluded that the way of militant messianism was not the right one for Israel. It had proved destructive in 66-70 CE; it had done so in 115-7 CE, and now the third revolt had ended in complete disaster . . ."[259]

The foundations of Judaism, therefore, were framed by two long periods of enormous revolutionary upheaval: the extended revolt of the *Apiru* from the fourteenth century BCE and the revolutions of the Jews in the first two centuries of the modern era. Although Judaism had further to go in its transformation into what is recognizable as the faith today, all the main outlines had been established. Rabbinical Judaism was now the mainstream. Instead of sacrifices for the Temple, a sense of religious worth now came . . .

> ". . . through observance of the commandments which set Israel apart and made it a holy people; rules of purity, especially concerning food and drink, rules of sanctifying time and space, rules of sanctifying the human body and its natural functions, marital life, etc."[260]

The Rabbinical movement represented the development of a new leadership for the Jewish people; rabbis became the new "aristocracy of the Torah", so that when the Romans did eventually need to deal with representatives of the Jews in their midst, "appropriate candidates were ready at hand."[261] Rabbinical Judaism continued to be developed in the great Jewish Diaspora around the Roman Empire in the following centuries; it defined itself as much as anything in distinction to Judeo-Christians and Christianity up to and beyond the period when the latter became the official creed of the Roman Empire in the fourth century. New collections of writings of eminent rabbis, including biblical commentary, theological discussions and interpretations of the Law under the new conditions, led to the production of new revered works like the *Mishnah* and the *Talmud,* both of which are beyond the scope of this book.

---

[259]   Oskar Skarsaune, *Redemption and Resistance,* p 160.
[260]   Oskar Skarsaune, *Redemption and Resistance,* p 160.
[261]   Robert Goldenburg, *The Origins of Judaism,* p 138

Chapter 5: The Roman period and the Great Revolt		
Dates	**Events**	**Parties and literature**
150 BCE	**Hasmonean dynasty** established	**Essene** settlement at Qumran founded
	John Hyrcanus king Hasmonean dynasty increasingly weak	**Apocalypic** and **Messianic** resistance-literature throughout entire period
100	Aristobulus king	
50 BCE	**Direct Roman rule** established with puppet kings **Herod 'the Great'** becomes king	
—0—	4 BCE: Death of Herod	
	Banditry and social upheaval in all rural areas	
50 CE		
100	**66-70 Uprising against Rome**	Qumran community ends
	115 Jewish revolt in North Africa	**Rabbinic Judaism** begins to predominate
150	**132 Bar Kochba uprising**	

It has been estimated that in the first two or three centuries of the modern era, the Jewish population of the Roman Empire constituted as much as ten per cent of the total and twenty per cent in the territories of the eastern Mediterranean. The fortunes of the Jewish communities in this period and the reasons for their growth and development are essential factors in the growth of the Christian communities alongside them and therefore we will come back to them when we look at the social and political foundations of Christianity.

Chapter Summary:

- The Hasmonean dynasty that came out of the Maccabean Revolt was as exploitative and oppressive as the former Hellenic regimes.

- Messianic and apocalyptic writing represented the *resistance literature* of the time, echoing the revolutionary sentiments of the population. It found its expression most typically in the works of the Essenes cult of Qumran, later discovered as the Dead Sea Scrolls.

- For decades prior to the great uprising against Rome, the whole of Judea and Palestine was seething with social upheaval, uprisings and rural banditry. There were numerous local leaders and 'messiahs'.

- The uprising of 66 CE was a *class* movement of rural and city poor, not only against Rome but also against the local Jewish elite. This uprising was followed by later revolutions, all of which were brutally suppressed.

- Rabbinic Judaism arose out of the leadership of local rabbis and remnants of the temple priesthood and Pharisees. It was no longer based on the Jerusalem Temple but on local synagogues which functioned as meeting houses, places of education and worship and as social centres.

PART II

THE FOUNDATIONS
OF CHRISTIANITY

Chapter 6

Christian Tradition and the Evidence

Just as it was essential to begin an examination of the history of Judaism with the Torah and the traditional history, it is also necessary, in looking at the origins of Christianity, to examine Christian Scripture, the New Testament. We shall show in this chapter that the twenty-seven books of the New Testament are but a tiny fraction of the totality of Christian literature written in the first two centuries, much of which was the ideological expression of the class struggle of the Jewish peasants against Rome and the Jewish elite. The whole social milieu of Judea/Palestine at the turn of the millennium was virtually tailor-made for messianic sects and prophets and an upsurge of religious innovation and the new theologies, including early Christianity, reflected this. We shall show that although there are resources and writings dating from the first century, none of these, including the writings of the man who came to be known as St Paul, support what Christians believe to be the biography of Jesus.

. . . .

The classical description of the origins of Christianity is outlined in the 'New' Testament, a collection of gospels, epistles, books of 'acts' and apocalypses. The gospels of Matthew, Mark, Luke and John are usually assumed to be historical accounts of real events in the first thirty-five years of the first millennium: how Jesus was born of a virgin mother, how he performed miracles, preached alongside his disciples, how he was crucified for his preaching and how he returned from the dead after three days.

The four gospels outline the ministry of Jesus, which began in Galilee on the shores of Lake Tiberias and reached as far as Jerusalem many miles to the south. Much of his direct teaching is in the form of sayings, often enigmatic and open to a variety of interpretations, as well as exchanges with some or all of the twelve disciples he chose from among local fishermen and workers. The gospels also contain lessons and sayings in the form of stories and parables which are attributed to Jesus. One of the most famous episodes was the 'Sermon on the Mount' when Jesus was said to have preached to thousands. According to the New Testament he performed many miracles during the course of his ministry. The more familiar ones have become part of the common imagery of language, like feeding the five thousand with a few loaves and fishes, walking on water, turning water into wine, healing the sick and blind and raising the dead back to life.

Anticipating his own death at the hands of the Jewish leaders, Jesus invited his disciples to eat with him at the Jewish feast of Passover (Jesus and his disciples

147

were all Jews). This became known as the 'Last Supper' when Jesus dedicated his body and blood for the redemption of mankind and it is celebrated in the act of communion (eucharist) in Christian churches every Sunday, by eating wafers and drinking wine, which when blessed are assumed to represent the body and blood of Jesus[262]. During his ministry, Jesus had antagonised the Jewish elders by driving the money-lenders from the precincts of the Jerusalem Temple, by preaching on the Sabbath and by his claim to be the Messiah. Consequently, having been betrayed by his disciple Judas Iscariot, he was arrested and arraigned in front of the Roman prefect, Pontius Pilate. Pilate famously 'washed his hands' of the decision to condemn him to death and so Jesus was handed over to the Jewish leaders for a cruel and painful crucifixion. The gospels relate that Jesus was crucified between two common criminals and abused as he died on the cross.

After he died, his body was taken down and placed in a crypt, whereupon he rose again three days later and appeared in the presence of some of his disciples. The act of personal sacrifice and subsequent resurrection—for which all the miracles and ministry of Jesus were a mere preparation—are the two cornerstones upon which the Christian faith rests. The death of Jesus is seen as a *sacrificial redemption*, a payment for the sins of the world, after which the resurrection of Jesus promises eternal life: it is the victory of Jesus over death. The same redemption is available to all, but Christians would argue, only for those with faith in Jesus. Subsequent theological development raised Jesus from being merely the son of God to become a component part of a 'three-in-one' god, the so-called Trinity, consisting of the Father, the Son and the Holy Ghost (or Holy Spirit), each an equal aspect of the same, single God.

After the four gospels, the next most important part of the New Testament comprises the epistles (letters) of Paul, who, although not a contemporary of Jesus, was convinced by a vision of him to preach His message. Paul was a Pharisee from the city of Tarsus in the south of modern-day Turkey. He was previously named Saul, and had been an active opponent of Christianity, charged with hunting and persecuting Christians. But after he had a vision while 'on the road to Damascus'—another piece of imagery that has found its way into everyday language—he devoted his life to being an apostle of Jesus. During his ministry, Paul met and collaborated with some of the immediate disciples of Jesus, principally Peter, James and John, who were the leaders of the Jerusalem Church. Paul is credited with having been the main architect of the Church, in so far as he was the principal evangelist to the gentiles, the non-Jews, whereas Peter and the others preached mainly among Jews. Paul is believed to have founded many churches outside Jerusalem and his epistles are letters to these communities. His travels around the region and discussions with the other apostles are recounted in the Acts of the Apostles, which is taken to have been written after Paul's death by one of

---

[262] It is a fundamental tenet of Roman Catholic teaching that at this point the wafer and wine undergo "transubstantiation" and their "essence", if not their outward form, *actually become* the body and blood of Jesus.

his co-workers, the same author of the Gospel of Luke. Both Peter and Paul are traditionally believed to have been crucified in Rome, where Peter is also accorded the honour of being the first Catholic pope.

There are several other smaller books making up the total of twenty-seven in the New Testament, but probably the most important of the remainder is the Revelation of John, a book, as we shall see in due course, completely out of tune, in both style and content, with the others in the New Testament.

According to the official tradition, the growth of Christianity was due to a more or less uninterrupted campaign of evangelism and conversion, particularly among gentiles, as more and more people had their 'eyes opened' and saw the 'truth' of Christianity. It was the *moral superiority* of Christianity over the 'superstition' of polytheism that brought people flocking to the banner of Jesus. Despite three centuries of relentless harassment and persecution by the Roman authorities, leading to innumerable martyrs, the superior ideas of the Christians—and particularly the offer of life after death and the redemption of human sins by the death of Jesus—led to an increase of faith in Christianity. It became an unstoppable force and was eventually recognised by the Roman Emperor Constantine.

This, in outline, is the official glorification of Christianity. A glance at the appropriate section in any large book store or library will give an idea of the many tens of thousands of volumes that have been written about Jesus and Christianity over the centuries—a production line that shows no sign of slowing, as thousands more titles are hurled onto the shelves every year. But the overwhelming majority of this tidal wave of literature—books, reinterpretations and theological studies—are based on nothing more than a restatement or a re-packaging of what is already contained in the New Testament. Many of the fashionable books about the life of Jesus (and there are many): 'Jesus the Stoic', 'Jesus the rebel', 'Jesus the healer', 'Jesus the philosopher', 'Jesus the Jew', 'The Peoples' Jesus' and so on *ad infinitum*, are often no more than re-workings of the New Testament texts, interpreted to suit the slant of the author, but overwhelmingly accepting the Scripture as good coin. For these 'historians' the New Testament functions as a self-authenticating source.

To take just one random example from the many thousands that could be used, in his *New History of Early Christianity*, Charles Freeman suggests that "The first *known* public event in Jesus' life is his baptism by John the Baptist"[263], although this event is only "known" from the New Testament. There are many others who "know" it probably didn't happen. Another author, Etienne Trocmé, commenting on Paul's visit to Jerusalem, noted that "he went there to get to know Peter, with whom he stayed for two weeks. Doubtless Peter taught him certain features of the oral tradition about Jesus"[264]. Although Paul's epistles and Acts note his visit to Jerusalem, in all the literature on the subject, it is only Trocmé who is familiar with Paul's lodging arrangements—an easy-going and cavalier manufacture of facts that is typical of many historians. We will comment later on how much Paul was taught

[263] Freeman, *The New History of Early Christianity*, p 24 (italics added)
[264] Trocmé, *The Childhood of Christianity*, p 43

of the "oral tradition about Jesus", but it might be worth noting that in this one chapter alone Trocmé uses the word "doubtless" no fewer than ten times, showing the scale of his guesswork.

We now know that the twenty-seven books of the New Testament were only a small fraction of the total of Christian literature written in the first two centuries and there was no official canon (no 'New Testament', in other words) during this whole period. Many of those books that were given official recognition are now known to be forgeries or to be misattributed. All four gospels were written *anonymously* but that hasn't stopped Church leaders from ascribing the gospels to named individuals, including two of the disciples of Jesus. Many scholars today accept that not all the epistles attributed to Paul were written by him and of the thirteen in the New Testament, perhaps seven or eight are genuine. The others were added by later theologians who wanted to back up their arguments by using Paul's name as an authority. All of the New Testament epistles in the names of James, Peter and John are believed to be forgeries. It is also generally accepted now that the gospels were written in a different order to their appearance in the New Testament. The first to be produced was the shortest, the Gospel of Mark, followed by Matthew and Luke, who copied and embellished Mark, and these two were followed later by the Gospel of John[265]. Whoever authored the Gospel of Luke is also attributed with writing the Acts of the Apostles, which, as we shall see, deliberately skirted around the controversies among the early Christians and was written as an account close to the views of Paul. Scholars have postulated another hypothetical *lost* gospel, named 'Q', which was probably another source, besides Mark, for the authors of Luke and Matthew.

When it comes to dating the writing of the gospels, there is little or no hard evidence other than whether or not they were quoted by this or that Church father in the early decades of the Church. Most of the estimation of the dates is based on the writing style and little else, but bearing in mind that today we have, at best, the copies of copies of copies of gospels, much of the dating is dubious. Before the middle of the fifteenth century, no two surviving copies of a gospel were the same. The earliest current copy is no earlier than about 200 CE. Moreover, it is in the interests of Christian historians to project the writing of the gospels back as far as possible, to give authenticity to the works and to justify their own faith; within any range of dating, the earliest point is invariably adopted. It is largely as a result of centuries of Christian academic pressure that the accepted dates are for Mark, about 70 CE and for Matthew and Luke some time between 70 and 100 CE. There is less agreement on the dating of the Gospel of John, although most scholars put it later that Luke and Matthew. In fact, there is next to no concrete evidence for this consensus and the gospels may well have been written several decades *after* these dates.

---

[265]   For simplicity and in common with the accepted practice, we will continue to refer to the gospels as "Mark" or "Luke", etc, although the real authors are unknown.

The Gospel of Thomas, which was only discovered in the modern era, is believed to be at least as old as Mark and may have been partly used as a source for the four canonical gospels. This is a highly significant book in that *it contains no biographical references to the life or ministry of Jesus* and *no reference to his death and resurrection*, the central components of Christianity. Instead, it has over a hundred 'secret' sayings of Jesus, which simply reflect oral tradition and the common moral strictures of the time. The sayings nearly all begin with the expression, "Jesus said". Some of them are in the form on very short cameos which were amplified later into longer stories or parables in the better known gospels and it was probably used as a source in the composition of Mark, such as Saying 9[266]:

> "Jesus said, 'Now the sower went out, took a handful (of seeds), and scattered them, some fell on the road; the birds came and gathered them up. Others fell on rock, did not take root in the soil, and did not produce ears, and others fell on thorns; they choked the seeds and worms ate them. And others fell on the good soil and it produced good fruit: it bore sixty per measure and a hundred and twenty per measure."

This short piece clearly forms the basis of the much longer parable which appears in Mark in which it is given a biographical setting. Much of the Gospel of Thomas was more radical than the canonical gospels. One story (saying 64), about ungrateful rich men and merchants refusing an invitation to go to a dinner, ends with the sentence: "Businessmen and merchants [will] not enter the places of my father." Elsewhere, it comments:

> (54): "Jesus said, 'Blessed are the poor, for yours is the kingdom of heaven"
> (68): "Jesus said, 'Blessed are you when you are hated and persecuted. Wherever you have been persecuted they will find no place."
> (69): "Jesus said, 'Blessed are they who have been persecuted within themselves. It is they who have truly come to know the father. Blessed are the hungry, for the belly of him who desires will be filled."
> (95): "Jesus said, 'If you have money do not lend it at interest, but give [it] to one from whom you will not get it back".

But, like the other gospels, it still has (saying 100): 'Give Caesar what belongs to Caesar, give God what belongs to God, and give me what is mine'—which also found its way, in an expanded form, into the New Testament gospels.

Forgeries, fakes and misrepresentations

Bart D Ehrman, chair of the department of religious studies at the University of North Carolina, and a scholar who sees things from the point of view of a

---

[266] This and other sayings of the gospel of Thomas from Ehrman, *Lost Scriptures*.

Christian, has written a number of useful books outlining the many changes that have been made over the years to the books of the New Testament, as well as to the even greater number of books that didn't make it into the official canon. Of course, two thousand years ago books were copied by hand. The efforts of the copyists weren't helped by the fact that ancient Greek—the original language in which most of the New Testament was written—had no upper and lower case, no separation space between words and no punctuation marks. Not surprisingly, quite apart from the deliberate forgeries, of which there are many, accidental changes inevitably accumulated from one generation of text to the next, like the genetic mutations that accumulate on a long strand of DNA every time a chromosome is replicated.

But besides accidental changes, there were a lot of deliberate changes and outright forgeries. As late as the middle of the third century, the Church father Origen[267] complained about the multiple versions of scripture:

> "The differences among the manuscripts have become great, either through the negligence of some copyist or through the perverse audacity of others; they either neglect to check over what they have transcribed, or, in the process of checking, they make additions or deletions as they please."[268]

Origen has preserved in his own writing a quotation from Celsus, an opponent of Christianity, who mocked the Christian scriptures: "Some believers, as though from a drinking bout, go so far as to oppose themselves and alter the original text of the gospel three or four or several times over, and they change its character to enable them to deny difficulties in face of criticism."[269] Another pagan opponent, Porphyry, described the Christians as a "confused and vicious sect." Their evangelists, he wrote, "were fiction writers—not observers or eye-witnesses of the life of Jesus. Each of the four [gospel writers] contradicts the other in writing his account of the events of his suffering and crucifixion."[270]

As Ehrman implies, even in orthodox traditions it was almost considered the norm for copyists and scribes to alter texts here and there, to 'clarify' them. Notes that perhaps started off in the margins of earlier copies became part of the text of later versions, and so on. "It is enough to know," Ehrman adds, "that the changes were made, and that they were made widely, especially in the first two hundred years."[271] He suggests that taking into account versions in different languages and the citations of early Church fathers, there are as many varieties of the New Testament as there are words in the New Testament!

---

267   184/5–253/4 CE. See table with list of early Church fathers used in the text.
268   Quoted in Ehrman, *Misquoting Jesus*, p 52
269   Origen, *Against Celsus*, 2,27.
270   Porphyry: *Against the Christians*, 2, 12
271   Ehrman, *Misquoting Jesus*, p 57

"Scholars differ significantly in their estimates—some say there are 200,000 variants known, some say 300,000, some say 400,000 or more! We do not know for sure because despite impressive developments in computer technology, no one has ever been able to count them all."[272]

There are too many forgeries and late additions in the New Testament for us to repeat them all here. By textual analysis and by comparing modern texts to the most ancient texts available, it is possible to see single words added or changed to 'fine-tune' a meaning. Thus, from Matthew to Luke, "the poor" is changed to "the poor in spirit". The "anger" Jesus feels on being approached by the leper (in the earlier Mark, 1, 14) becomes "compassion" (in later versions of Mark, as well as Matthew and Luke). Sometimes, entire new sections have been inserted into the gospels, like at the end of the gospel of Mark where chapter 16, verse 9 to the end is all a later addition. The story of the "woman taken in adultery" in the Gospel of John is a later addition. Chapter 13 of Paul's first epistle to the Corinthians is a later addition. The prayer that Jesus uttered before his death on the cross, found in Luke (23, 334): "Father, forgive them; for they know not what they do". does not appear in any of the earlier versions of the gospel and is thought to be a later anti-Jewish addition. And so on, and so on.

There are twenty-seven books in the New Testament. Around nineteen of these are either anonymous and have authors' names *attributed* to them—which are guesses at best—or they are outright forgeries where the real author has deliberately used the name of someone else to give his views greater authority. Nineteen out of twenty-seven! Readers interested in the detail about the many amendments and additions to the New Testament should look at the books by Ehrman; we have to confine ourselves here only to those additions or amendments that have a clearly political agenda.

The presence of so many forgeries, misattributed writings and direct copying is accepted nowadays as a 'given' by the great majority of New Testament scholars and theologians, even in Christian academic circles. That doesn't make a lot of difference in the church services and Sunday schools, however. All around the world and every day, in tens of thousands of services, sermons, homilies, and religious instruction lessons, the New Testament is taken as if it were *wholly* correct, the unalterable Word of God, as some would put it. It is one thing for scholars in ivory towers to admit between themselves that so much of the New Testament is *fake*; but it is another thing entirely to share that knowledge with the rest of the flock!

External evidence

If we examine the historical evidence for the life and ministry of Jesus as they are described in the New Testament, we are at once struck by the fact that *there are no references whatsoever to the Christian Jesus in any non-Christian sources that would*

---

[272] Ehrman, *Misquoting Jesus*, p 89

be contemporary with him. Several episodes in the gospels record the presence of 'scribes', yet none of these supposed eye-witnesses has left us an account of any of the events surrounding the life of Jesus. Despite their vast collections of records, legal documents, histories, imperial announcements and decrees, there are no *contemporary* Roman authors who mention Jesus. Pliny the Elder (23-79 CE), Seneca the Younger (3 BCE-65 CE) and Valerius Maximus (20 BCE-50 CE) all travelled widely throughout the empire and left many manuscripts, altogether numbering hundreds of works . . . but not a Christian Jesus in sight.

In all the voluminous writings of Josephus there are only two references, but both of them are later additions by Christian scribes. In the first of these, in *The Antiquities of the Jews*, he describes Jesus as "a wise man" and "the Christ", both unlikely epithets to come from the pen of a man who considered himself a pious Jew and who even wrote a book, *Against Apion*, defending his faith. It is clear by reading around the inserted passage (it is included in its entirety in Appendix III) that it intrudes into the narrative and is a later addition by a Christian scribe, perhaps having started its life as a note in the margin of an earlier copy. The second reference is to the stoning of "the brother of Jesus, who was called Christ, whose name was James." This passage is absent in other copies of the works of Josephus that have been handed down and is also a later Christian insertion. It is notable that the early Church writer Origen uses Josephus as a source to prove the existence of John the Baptist, but (no doubt using an earlier more authentic edition of Josephus) does not use the same author to prove the existence of Jesus.

The Alexandrian Jew, Philo, as prolific a writer as Josephus and an even closer contemporary of Jesus, would have been expected to have noticed a movement of thousands behind a messiah able to work great miracles, particularly since as a pious Jew himself, he also followed affairs in Jerusalem very closely. But, again, Philo does not mention Jesus or the Christians. Christian scholars in the succeeding centuries were so sensitive, in fact, to the *deafening silence* of all contemporary Roman and Greek writers on Jesus that one of them resorted in the fourth century to forging an entire correspondence of fourteen letters between the apostle Paul and the Roman philosopher Seneca.[273] In these fictional letters Seneca, naturally, bowed to the great wisdom of Paul and was hugely impressed by the gospel of the Christians, as was his pupil, the emperor Nero.

Jewish writing, prolific during the first half of the first century, did not stop with the defeat of the revolt in 70 CE, but in the Talmud there are no references to the Christian Jesus until well into the second century, as a response to the gospels and even at this point they are very few. In his strangely mis-named book *Jesus in the Talmud*, Peter Schäfer laments an earlier published study by Johann Maier that had found no contemporary evidence of Jesus.

---

[273] See, for example, *Forged*, by Bart D Ehrman, p 90

"This is, in many respects, an amazing and disturbing book. It presents the most comprehensive, painstakingly erudite treatment of the subject so far. Maier has sifted through all the secondary literature, even if only remotely relevant, and showers the reader with excruciating details about who wrote what and when. More important, all the rabbinic sources that have ever been brought into connection with Jesus are analysed in every possible regards, with Maier taking great pains not just to discuss bits and pieces ripped out of context but to examine them always within the larger literary structure in which they are preserved . . . according to Maier, there is hardly any passage left in the rabbinic literature that can be justifiably used as evidence of the Jesus of the New Testament. The rabbis did not care about Jesus, they did not know anything reliable about him, and what they might have alluded to is legendary at best and rubbish at worst."[274]

Given this bombshell so early in his own book, one wonders how Schafer had the heart to complete another two hundred pages. But in the end his own conclusion matches ours—there is no reference in rabbinic literature that is even remotely *contemporary* and which therefore offers supporting evidence for the historical Jesus.

As an interesting aside, it is also notable that there is no reference in any ancient source to Nazareth, the supposed home town of Jesus and variously described in Christian literature as a city, a town, a village or even a hamlet. The town does not feature anywhere in all the books of the Hebrew Testament or in the non-canonical works of the period, although hundreds of other cities, towns and villages do get a mention. It is not mentioned in any of the authentic works of Paul or anywhere in the first century of Christian literature, that is, until the gospels were written. In the works of Josephus—bearing in mind that he was a commander of sorts in the rebel Jewish army in Galilee—there is no Nazareth to be found. In several places in his writings, Josephus gives surveys of the Galilee region, mentioning many towns and villages . . . but no Nazareth. The nearest reference to a town of that name is *Lake Gennesareth*, which appears in both the writings of Josephus and in the Gospel of Luke. From the description Josephus gives, this is clearly Lake Tiberias (or the Sea of Galilee) which borders on Galilee and in fact the area immediately adjacent to the lake, according to the author, is what gives *Lake Gennesareth* its name. For anyone looking for evidence of the real historical Jesus, this resounding silence needs some explanation, unless Nazareth is an invention. In the creation of the legend of Jesus, there is a plausible explanation for this supplementary piece of fiction, as we shall mention later.

But what is even more significant, in looking for the historical Jesus, is the deafening silence we find, not only in the Jewish literature of the period, some of which we will examine in due course, but also in the early Christian writings, notably in Paul. As we shall show, at the earliest stage in the development of

---

[274] Schäfer, *Jesus in the Talmud*, p 5

Christianity, *there was no real, historical Jesus character behind the movement*. Paul's genuine epistles, as opposed to those falsely attributed to him, (about half, let us recall, of those in the New Testament) are accepted by all scholars as the earliest documents in the New Testament. Yet although they make many references to a 'Jesus', and his personal sacrifice, they at no time mention events, incidents, times or places in the biography of an *historical* person. Paul wrote little enough about his own personal history, but what he did write is more than he wrote about Jesus.

At this point, the Christian scholar will object: 'what about 1 Corinthians, chapter 15'?

"For I delivered unto you first of all that which I also received, how that Christ died for our sins *according to the scriptures*;
And that he was buried, and rose again the third day *according to the scriptures*;
And that he was seen of Cephas, then of the twelve:
After that, he was seen of above five hundred brethren at once; of whom the greater part remain unto this present, but some are fallen asleep.
After that he was seen of James; then all of the apostles."[275]

But the clue is in the twice-repeated phrase, "according to the scriptures". This is clearly an insertion by a later Christian scribe, using the "scriptures"—the gospel accounts—as his guide. 1 Corinthians, in any case, is a much amended epistle, with liberal later additions—at least the whole of chapter 13 and chapter 14 verses 34-36 (contradicting an earlier view of the role of women in church in chapter 11). But even this crude amendment says nothing about the context and narrative of the life of Jesus.

The silence of Paul

Christian scholars have found Paul's omission of any biographical account of Jesus to be "strange" and "peculiar" but attach no great significance to it. We would argue, on the contrary, that *it is a fact of monumental importance*. Nowadays there is hardly a sermon preached or an article written by a Christian leader or priest that doesn't cite at least one example from the life and activity of Jesus: in Galilee, in Judea, in Samaria, on the shores of Lake Tiberias, in Jerusalem, or anywhere else. At almost every opportunity that presents itself, specific instances of the life and ministry of Jesus are held up as illustrations of good deeds of which Christians should take note. One would have thought that it would have been even more the case in Palestine, only a few years after the death of Jesus, when his disciples would have been buzzing with news and anecdotes of his life.

Let us consider what we are expected to believe about Paul. Here he was, writing voluminous correspondence to his churches about what did and did not

---

[275]   1 Corinthians, 15, 4-7 (italics added)

constitute the appropriate way of following the 'Lord'. Yet although he had been to Jerusalem several times, the earliest only seven years after the crucifixion, and had spent up to fifteen days discussing with key disciples of this Lord, Paul *does not appear to take note of any event, episode, parable, miracle or example from the life of Jesus which he can use in his letters!* He doesn't mention Mary, Joseph, Bethlehem, the three wise men, the three shepherds, Herod's slaughter of the innocents, Galilee, Nazareth, the Temptation by Satan, the 'Lord's Prayer', the Transfiguration, the Sermon on the Mount, walking on water, turning water into wine, healing the lame and blind, curing lepers, feeding the five thousand, Pontius Pilate, Judas Iscariot, Gethsemane, Calvary, and so on, and so on. Nothing.

Even in his epistle to the Galatians, when he was vigorously defending his right to be an apostle as much as the Christian leaders in Jerusalem, "which were apostles before me", Paul did not mention *why* the Jerusalem leaders were apostles "before" him. In fact, Paul could have claimed a 'higher' authority in that he was called by the Jesus who had 'risen' while the disciples only knew the 'earthly' Jesus. This would have been an appropriate point for Paul to have mentioned, for example, that the Jerusalem leaders had been in direct contact with Jesus or that they were his *immediate* disciples, walking and talking with him . . . but Paul made no such comments.

> "He bases not one of his most incisive polemical arguments against the adherents of the law on the ground that he had the historical Jesus on his side; but he gives his own detailed theological ideas without mentioning an historical Jesus, he gives a gospel of Christ, not the gospel which he had heard at first, second, or third hand concerning a human individual Jesus."[276]

Paul's epistles were not quick notes dashed off in a hurry. They were carefully constructed and purposefully argued; they were possibly meant to be delivered and read to assemblies of people. Luther Stirewalt, in *Paul, the Letter Writer*, is typical of a number of authors in drawing attention to Paul's great skill as a letter-writer and his likely training in rhetoric. In his letters, Stirewalt writes, "he incorporates personal history, biography, apology, defence. He also introduces excurses and illustrations and metaphors as they come to mind, and does it all in epistolary and/or rhetorical expressions as they fit his thoughts and mood."[277] The dispute with Corinth, for example:

> ". . . did not pit an untrained debater against sophistic Christian leaders in Corinth. Paul demonstrated substantial argumentative skills in his struggle against opponents . . . Paul overcame any oratorical limitations with

---

[276] Kalthoff, cited by Arthur Drews in *The Christ Myth.*
[277] Stirewalt, *Paul, The Letter Writer*, p 47.

157

epistolary argumentation which . . . could conquer the rhetorical devices of his adversaries."[278]

Yet other scholars have suggested that each of Paul's authentic epistles is actually a *composite,* a collection of several letters, brought together and edited *by Paul himself,* apparently a common practice among writers in antiquity.[279] Given these suggestions—and the first, if not the second is very likely to be true—there is all the more reason why Paul *would have* used imagery and metaphor from the life of Jesus to support his views, if such an exemplary biography had been available to draw upon. Having had close contact with the apostles in Jerusalem, only a few years after the supposed crucifixion, Paul would have found out about and used such a biography if it was known. It is simply not plausible to believe otherwise. We can reasonably assume that Peter was an historical person because Paul mentions his disagreements with him on several occasions. But the same cannot be said for Jesus—Paul does not mention anything about the life and works of this apparently great prophet, because for Paul such an *earthly* person had not existed.

It is important to make the point that the name Jesus is a Latinised version of the Hebrew name Joshua. The name Jesus has been used in this book up to this point, even naming Jewish revolutionary leaders called Jesus, but only as a concession to modern practice and as it has been translated in the books of Josephus. In fact, no-one in first century Palestine would have recognised the name Jesus. Many modern Christian writers practise a deliberate sleight of hand on this very simple point and the large majority of Christian theologians, when they write about the subject, project the *Latinised expression* back into ancient Greek and Hebrew texts, as if it had its *modern Christianised meaning* in first century Jerusalem. Indeed, most Christians today would not even know that the name didn't exist in ancient Judea.

This is important because Joshua was the name around which some of the new Jewish politico-religious sects focused, from the scriptural Joshua who in Hebrew legend led the Israelites in the conquest of the land of Canaan after the death of Moses. The basic root of the Hebrew name HO-SH-U-A is related to the word 'salvation' and it is easy to see how sects basing themselves on a messianic deliverance might attach themselves to the name of Joshua—a salvation sect being *by definition* a Joshua sect—but without it having any specific relationship to a contemporary prophet or even a particular person. Robert Eisenman, Professor of Middle East Religions and Director of the Institute for the Study of Judeo-Christian origins at California State University, points out in *The Dead Sea Scrolls and the First Christians,* that there is a phrase in one of the most important Dead Sea Scroll texts, the Damascus Document, as follows: "*His Name, until God shall reveal Salvation*", in which the last word is actually *Yesha,* or Joshua.[280] It is perhaps an important

---

278   Winter, *Philo and Paul among the Sophists,* p 237-9
279   Trobisch, *Paul's letter collection*
280   Eisenman, *The Dead Sea Scrolls,* p 367

example of the *generic* use of the name that meshes with the concept of 'salvation/ Joshua' adopted by messianic cults in a later period.

A messianic Joshua effectively meant a messianic salvation. If the name Joshua came to be attached to a sect, it was just as likely that it would evoke the tradition of the companion of Moses. Robert Kraft, another biblical scholar, after examining the question of the Messiah-Joshua traditions at the turn of the modern era, came to the conclusion that it was likely that "in one or more schools of pre-Christian Jewish eschatological speculation [ie concerning the end of the world], the idea had been entertained and developed that God's expected Messiah would fulfil or at least reflect the role of Moses' successor Joshua."

> "As to its origins, if indeed it had any *one* place of origin, the Northern Kingdom and particularly Samaria is the most likely candidate . . . the rudimentary Joshua messianology came to influence Greek as well as Semitic Judaism . . . when emerging Christianity, in the early stages of development, came into contact with this Joshua messianology, it applied and adopted it with respect of Joshua/Jesus of Nazareth . . . The clear-cut evidence is slim; but enough to suggest the possibility—I think it a clear *probability*—some section of pre-Christian Judaism (but apparently not the 'main line' Judaism that survived) had developed something like what I have called a second Joshua messianology . . ."[281]

Besides Joshua the successor to Moses, another Joshua was instrumental in the establishment of the state of Judea in the first period of the Persian Empire. The Book of Zechariah describes the high priest Joshua, along with the Persian governor Zerubbabel, as the two "anointed ones that stand by the Lord of the whole earth."[282] This Joshua, like his earlier namesake, was exalted for having supposedly delivered the Jews once again from captivity—the first time from the Egyptians and Canaanites and the second time from the Babylonians.

In relation to the epistles of Paul, therefore, there is a far greater probability that what Paul was writing about was a *generic Joshua/Jesus* character. Paul mentions the crucifixion and resurrection of Jesus, but he is dealing with a *generic motif* that was common in the theology of the Near East. He was not able to include any biographical information about this Jesus because no such biography had been written *or made up* by the time he wrote his epistles. Rather than accidentally neglecting to mention anything about a real, historical person, it is far more plausible that Paul's mention of a Jesus is a mistranslation or a mangling of the Hebrew word for salvation—ie Joshua—from its original roots in messianic Judaism. It was ultimately a derivative of earlier *Joshua* cults that existed among Jewish messianic groups, based on the generalised idea of 'salvation' and an allusion

---

[281]   Robert A. Kraft, *Was there a Messiah-Joshua tradition at the turn of the era? From, ccat.sas. upenn.edu* (italics added)

[282]   Zechariah, 4, 14

to a *generic* messiah-figure, sacrificed at some undefined point in the past. In *The Christ Myth*, written more than a hundred years ago, Arthur Drews suggests that a twist in the traditional Joshua theology—from a messiah *still to come*, to a messiah who had *already been*—led Paul to the creation of what became a new faith.[283]

> "Might it not also be, as the believers in Jesus asserted, that the Messiah was not still to be expected, and that only on the ground of human righteousness; but that rather he had already appeared and had already accomplished the righteousness attainable by the individual through his shameful death and his glorious resurrection? The moment in which this idea flashed through Paul's mind was the moment of the birth of Christianity as Paul's religion."[284]

The *Epistle to the Hebrews*, which was attributed to Paul only in the fourth century and which remains in the New Testament, is not now believed to be an authentic Pauline letter. This is hardly surprising, given that it has a distinctive style and content completely out of tune with his authentic letters. Yet the letter was known to Clement, the bishop of Rome at the end of the first century and is usually dated sometime soon after the genuine letters of Paul. Interestingly, like the genuine letters, it has no commentary at any point on the life or activity of a historical Jesus, who is nevertheless frequently referred to as a "high priest", moreover, a high priest of "Melchisedec", a figure prominent in the Qumran literature, again linking this messianic cult with the messianism of the Essenes. *Hebrews*, like Paul's letters, represented a current of Joshua-messianism that elevated the role of the messiah to be a sacrifice for the redemption of sins, *although at that time there was no real biographical person upon which it was based*. Like the letters of Paul, it represents an *intermediate* theology between the generalised messianism and Joshua cults of the Jewish community and the rounded-out biographies of Jesus that were invented decades later.

When it comes to the historicity of the Christian Jesus, the overwhelming majority of Christian scholars fall back on the New Testament as a *self-authenticating source*. Even Bart Ehrman, author of so many books about scriptural forgeries both within and outside the New Testament, is influenced by the cultural pull of two thousand years of Christianity:

> "One of the striking, and to many people, surprising facts about the first century is that we don't have any Roman records, of any kind, that attest to the existence of Jesus. We have no birth certificate, no references to his works or deeds, no accounts of his trial, no descriptions of his death—no

---

283 Lenin was in favour of the translation and circulation of this book of Arthur Drews, even though the latter's alternative to Christianity was not the "sole reality of matter" but some kind of Pantheistic religion "free of ecclesiasticastic guardianship"

284 Drews, *The Christ Myth*, p 189.

reference to him whatsoever in any way, shape or form. Jesus's name is not even mentioned in any Roman source of the first century."[285]

Then he expresses his "alarm" as follows: "This does not mean, as is now being claimed with alarming regularity, that Jesus never existed. He certainly existed, as virtually every competent scholar of antiquity, Christian or non-Christian, agrees, based on clear and certain evidence." This statement is certainly not true and his measure of "competence" seems to be based on whether or not a scholar *believes* Jesus existed. Like others of the same view, his belief may be perfectly genuine and sincerely-held, but it is not backed anywhere by evidence, especially of the "clear and certain" kind.

Social and political conditions

It is not possible or justifiable, therefore, to look for the origins of Christianity or to test the historicity of Jesus by using the New Testament as a source. It goes without saying that from a materialist point of view any explanation of the origins of the Church that relies on miracles, visions and divine intervention is a non-starter. A scientific view of historical development must begin with the social, political and economic background to the period in question.

One of the first and most important works that looked at the origins of Christianity from a materialist point of view was *Foundations of Christianity* written at the beginning of the last century by the German social-democrat Karl Kautsky. His view of history was not one that contented itself only with the consideration of historical *ideas*, but sought "to run down their causes, lying at the very base of society." Kautsky was scathing about the veracity of the gospels as a historical narrative of the life of Jesus and much of his critique is based on the idea that although there *may* have been a real historical character, it was not the one portrayed in the New Testament. If he existed at all, Kautsky suggested, it was as a *revolutionary leader* whose earthly political message was transformed beyond all recognition in the decades after his death. The transmission of folk memories, he points out, is particularly prone to distortion over the years:

> ". . . it is absolutely impossible for mere oral tradition faithfully to preserve the wording of a speech that was not set down at once, over a period of fifty years after its delivery . . . it can be proved that many of Jesus' statements do not come from him, but were in circulation before his day"[286]

We will have occasion to cite Kautsky many times later. As we shall argue, the basic outline of his analysis written a hundred years ago, that Christianity was a product

---

285   Ehrman, *Forged*, p 256
286   Kautsky, *Foundations of Christianity*, p 35

of *the material social conditions* in Palestine, is still valid in the light of newer evidence and more modern analysis of texts.

If the foundations of Christianity are not to be found in the New Testament narrative and the official histories of the Church, where, then, are they to be found? We should begin by looking at the conditions that existed in Palestine in the years identified by Christians as those covering the ministry of Jesus, from about 30 to 35 CE. As we have already shown, the first part of the first century was a period of enormous social and political upheaval. The majority of the population, overwhelmingly rural peasants, laboured under an intolerable burden of taxation, unredeemable debts and the threat of landlessness.

> "Herod the Great claimed 25-33 per cent of Palestinian grain within his realm and 50 per cent of fruit from trees. Direct taxation also included poll (head) tax in money. In addition, Herod imposed indirect taxation on transit trade and market exchanges . . . the temple establishment claimed 'taxes' in kind (sacrificial goods) and money (the half-shekel) on top of the rest . . ."[287]

The net result of the repressive exploitation of the peasantry was an increase in indebtedness and the growth of large-scale landholdings.

> "The firm enforcement of debt contracts through the courts led to the expansion of large estates under the control of the Judean oligarchy. After default on debt obligations, traditional village lands were added to these estates, while tenancy and landlessness increased to significant level in the period before the First Judean revolt. The elites, as increasingly big merchants with interests in local commerce and interurban trade, came to develop cash cropping on their estates. Rabbinic tradition could recall that three merchants could supply Jerusalem for ten years."[288]

We have already cited the works of Josephus which described in great detail the events that led up to the great revolt of 66 CE. In *The Antiquities of the Jews*, for example, he described the influence of those leaders who incited many people to revolt: "All sorts of misfortunes sprang from these men," he wrote, "and the nation was infected with this doctrine to an incredible degree; one violent war came upon us after another . . ."[289] In the years following the death of Herod, Josephus narrated that:

> "At this time there were great disturbances in the country, and that in many places; and the opportunity that now offered itself induced a great

---

[287]   Hanson and Oakman, *Palestine in the time of Jesus*, p 114.
[288]   Hanson and Oakman, *Palestine in the time of Jesus*, p 153.
[289]   *AJ*, 18, 6.

many to set up the kings; and indeed in Idumea two thousand of Herod's veteran soldiers got together and armed themselves, and fought against those of the kings' party; against whom Achiabus, the king's first cousin fought . . .

. . . in Sepphoris also, a city of Galilee, there was one Judas (the son of that arch robber Hezekias, who formerly overran the country and had been subdued by king Herod); this man got no small multitude together and broke open the place where the royal armour was laid up and armed those about him, and attacked those that were so earnest to gain the dominion.

In Perea also, Simon, one of the servants to the king, relying upon the handsome appearance and tallness of his body put a diadem upon his own head also; he also went about with a company of robbers that he had gotten together and burnt down the royal palace that was at Jericho, and many other costly edifices besides . . .

The royal palaces that were near Jordan, at Betharamptha, were also burnt down by some other of the seditious that came out of Perea."[290]

Beginning with the death of Herod in 4 BCE there had been armed uprisings in all parts of the country. After the near destruction of Sepphoris in Galilee during one of these uprisings, Herod's successor Antipas sought to rebuild the city. The cost of this would have been borne by the local population. Adding to the impositions on the population, he also embarked on the building of the new capital city of Tiberias, which he named after the Roman Emperor. These burdens added flames to the fires of revolution and at any time in this period revolutionary Joshua sects could have found a beginning and a ready echo among Jews throughout Palestine and the Diaspora. Philo mentions extensive pogroms in 38 CE and Josephus, as we have cited, alluded to a great deal of upheaval in the same period. A further small selection of commentaries from Josephus illustrates the turmoil of the period:

"Many [Jewish peasants] turned to banditry out of recklessness, and throughout the whole country there were raids, and among the more daring, revolts . . ." [291]

". . . the whole of Judea was infested with brigands . . ."[292]

"Felix [Roman governor, 52-58 CE] captured [revolutionary leader] Eleazar, who *for twenty years* had plundered the country, as well as many

---

[290]   *WJ*, 2, 55.
[291]   *Jewish Wars*, 2, 238
[292]   *Antiquities*, 20, 124.

of his associates, and sent them to Rome for trial. The number of brigands that he crucified . . . was enormous." [293]

". . . hostility and violent factionalism flared between the high priests on the one side and the priests and leaders of the Jerusalem masses on the other."[294]

One modern author has listed in a table all the episodes of banditry mentioned by Josephus and the count comes to at least sixteen, many of which amounted to extensive rebellions in their own right.[295] As we have described in the previous section, the boiling discontent erupted in a full-scale social revolution in 66 CE, which was ruthlessly suppressed by the Roman legions. However the Joshua cult came into being, it was born "in the shadow of what would stand as the most grievous violence against the Jewish people until Hitler's attempt at a Final Solution."[296]

It has to be said that reading the New Testament gospels, the Acts of the Apostles or the letters of Paul, *one would get no sense whatsoever of a society seething with discontent, upheaval, repression and revolution.* This upheaval is completely absent from the picture that comes out of the New Testament gospels and which claim to describe the life and ministry of Jesus. It is as if the narratives of the New Testament were located in an ethereal 'other' world divorced from the reality of first century Palestine. As indeed they were.

The material social conditions described by Josephus were almost tailor-made for the mushrooming of messianic sects and prophets. It was not that the masses were reacting to new theologies, but that *the new theologies reflected the condition of the masses.* The existence of the lower classes, as Kautsky explained, was becoming more and more wretched.

"The more miserable the latter became, the more ardently did they cherish the hope of *revolution* . . . The Messiah meant revolution, which of course came to be based more and more on superhuman powers, on miracles, as the actual alignment of forces gradually shifted to the disadvantage of the exploited and tormented masses. As the belief in the miracles and the faith in the miraculous power of the Messiah who was to come increased, the mass of the sufferings and sacrifices demanded by the struggle against oppression increased in the same measure, also the number of martyrs who succumbed in this conflict . . . Judaism owed the success of its propaganda

---

[293]   *Jewish Wars,* 2, 235. (Italics added)
[294]   *Antiquities,* 20, 180.
[295]   Hanson and Oakman, *Palestine in the time of Jesus,* p 91
[296]   Carroll, *Constantine's Sword,* p 78.

up to the time of the destruction of Jerusalem in large measure to the belief in the resurrection."[297]

It is now known for certain from the Dead Sea Scrolls, the literature retrieved from the Essene community at Qumran, that the upheavals noted by Josephus had a reflection in the messianic and apocalyptic writings of the time. The latest possible date for the existence of the Qumran community is about 68 CE when it was sacked by the Roman armies during the great revolt. But in the thirty year period before its destruction—in the years usually associated with the life of Jesus—the Qumran community would have been thriving and in active contact with Essene-like preachers in the communities around Palestine. These activists, numbering four thousand according to Josephus, promulgated a form of *political Judaism* that was far removed from the sanitised histories and narratives that have found their way into the official canon. It was in every sense of the word a *revolutionary literary* tradition.

So all-pervasive were the apocalyptic visions that even Josephus himself was affected by them, at one point reporting a vision, witnessed, he says, by many people in the days immediately before the uprising in Jerusalem:

". . . a certain prodigious and incredible phenomenon appeared: I suppose the account of it would seem to be a fable, were it not related by those that saw it, and were not the events that followed it of so considerable a nature as to deserve such signals; for, before sun-setting, chariots and troops of soldiers in their armour were seen running about among the clouds . . ."[298]

The literature of revolution

The resistance-literature of the Essenes and the other apocalyptic and messianic works circulating at the time were the *ideological expression* of the class struggle of the Jewish peasants against the Roman Empire and its client Jewish ruling class. The whole framework of the Qumran and other contemporary literature is *political* in nature, looking ahead to the destruction of the contemporary state and the rise of a new and glorious kingdom of righteousness, ushered in by a messiah. Most of this literature failed to find its way into the official canon of Jewish or Christian literature and is nowadays described as "Pseudepigrapha" ("false writing"), although it has been preserved in whole or in fragments mostly on the fringe of Christian tradition. Among the most important of this resistance literature, as we have previously mentioned, is *The Book of Enoch*, which is an amalgam of several works produced over many decades, the earliest of which may go back as far as the third century BCE. In keeping with other literature of the genre, the book of Enoch rails against the rich and powerful in the most uncompromising terms:

---

[297]   Kautsky, p 292.
[298]   WJ, 6, 297

". . . on the day of judgement, all the kings, the governors, the high officials and the landlords shall see and recognise him—how he sits on the throne of his glory . . . all the kings, the governors, the high officials and those who rule the earth shall fall down before him on their faces, and worship and raise their hopes in that Son of Man. They shall beg and plead for mercy at his feet"[299]

This was the character of a large part of the literature that circulated in the first thirty years of first century Palestine. Read aloud in prose or verse, it would have helped to galvanise a large part of the Jewish population in their opposition to the Jewish elite and the Roman state it served. It is a million miles removed from the milk and water homilies of the New Testament gospels. There is some doubt, to say the least, about the historical veracity of the "Sermon on the Mount" where Jesus was supposed to have quietly recited a large number of traditional sayings to an attentive crowd. But, on the other hand, it is far more plausible to imagine that the poorest Judeans and Galileans would have thronged from miles around to hear itinerant preachers shouting these lines:

"Those who amass gold and silver,
They shall quickly be destroyed.
Woe unto you oh rich people
For you have put your trust in your wealth
You shall ooze out of your riches . . .
In the days of your affluence, you committed oppression,
You have become ready for death, and for the day of darkness and day of great judgement . . .
Woe unto you who gain silver and gold by unjust means . . .
For your wealth will not endure
But it shall take off from you quickly . . .
And you shall be given over to a great curse . . .
For you men shall put on more jewellery than women and more multicoloured ornaments than a virgin
In sovereignty, in grandeur, and in authority, in silver, in gold, in clothing, in honour and in edibles
They shall be poured out like water . . .
Woe unto you who build your houses through the hard toil of others . . ."[300]

The vision of the great judgement is associated in Enochic literature with the coming of the Messiah, frequently referred to as "The Anointed One" or the "Son of

---

[299]   1 Enoch, chapter 62. These and other extracts from Enoch are taken from James H Charlesworth's *The Old Testament Pseudepigrapha*.

[300]   Extracts from 1 Enoch, chapters 94 to 99

Man", as the later authors of the gospels had Jesus describe himself. One particular passage from Enoch even presages the later Christian creed of the 'Trinity' in which the figure of God has three equal facets of Father, Son and Holy Spirit.

> "Son of Man was given a name, in the presence of the Lord of the Spirits, the Before-Time, even before the creation of the sun and the moon, before the creation of the stars; he was given a name in the presence of the Lord of the Spirits . . ."[301]

Scholars dispute the range of dates within which the Enochic literature was composed, but there is a consensus that this and similar literature was freely available at the time and that it circulated widely, particularly within the community of the Essenes and their adherents. The preservation of much of it for centuries as a 'fringe' element of Christian scripture was an indication of its significance in the evolution of that faith from within this milieu of Jewish sectarianism. The themes it contained—of the coming of a messiah, the establishment of a 'new' Jerusalem, the resurrection of the righteous, the judgement of sinners—were clearly linked to economic exploitation and political oppression. These were the literary flames that ignited the thoughts and activities of the many new Jewish sects that began to proliferate, *one of which evolved into Christianity.*

> ". . . it is clear that the Enochic concepts are found in various New Testament books, including the Gospels and Revelation. 1 Enoch played a significant role in the early Church; it was used by the authors of the Epistle of Barnabas, the Apocalypse of Peter, and a number of apologetic works. Many Church fathers, including Justin Martyr, Irenaeus, Origen, and Clement of Alexandria either know 1 Enoch or were inspired by it . . . but beginning in the fourth century, the book came to be regarded with disfavour . . ."[302]

Another work from the same period, again Jewish in origin but very popular among early Christians, is the *Apocryphon of Ezekiel,* which has only survived in fragmentary citations in the works of the early Church fathers. Among the usual themes of messiah and resurrection, it includes a parable on the "king and the wedding feast" which reappeared later in a modified form in the Gospels of Matthew and Luke. It is a reminder, as one scholar puts it:

> ". . . that inter-testamental Judaism was not nearly as monolithic in its theology nor as homogenous in its literary tradition as the rabbinic Judaism of a slightly later time. Moreover, the wide popularity of the Apocryphon of Ezekiel in early Christian sources witnesses a certain

---

[301]   1 Enoch, chapter 48.
[302]   Charlesworth, *The Old Testament Pseudepigrapha,* p 8

latitude in the concept of canon that became less common as the Church became less diversified in later centuries."[303]

An entire sub-genre of prophetic literature, under the general heading of the *Sibylline Chronicles* was written and redacted over many centuries and is grouped because it follows a general pattern: each chronicle is a reflection of current theological concerns in the form of an historical survey followed by apocalyptic and messianic prophecies. Many of these chronicles also circulated among Christians in the first centuries of the modern era and for a long time afterwards, although some of them originated in the same milieu of Jewish messianism. Book 5 of the Chronicles, written approximately during this period in Palestinian history, is almost unparalleled in its vitriolic animosity towards the emperor Nero and Rome in general:

"You will be among evil mortals, suffering evils,
But you will remain utterly desolate for all ages yet,
(it will exist, but it will remain utterly desolate forever), despising your soil, because you desired sorcery.
With you are found adulteries and illicit intercourse with boys,
Effeminate and unjust, evil city, ill-fated above all.
Alas, city of the Latin land, unclean in all things . . .
You have a murderous heart and impious spirit . . ."[304]

In the literature of the Essenes, a clear connection was made between the Hebrew idea of the Jubilee when the loan-pledged property of the farmer would be redeemed to him, with the forthcoming Apocalypse, almost as if the two had fused into a single event.

"The End of Days preached by messiahs and sectarians came to mean also the Jubilee of the peasant. Through this vision, the peasant could transcend the household and the village . . . So the Apocalypse was not just the hoped-for end of corruption and injustice; it was also a way of organising to achieve it, a way of turning a class of farmers and villagers into a revolutionary force for overturning the state and building heaven on earth. By the 60s CE, all the currents of anger and protest at the base of society—and hunger, social banditry, messianic movement, urban riots, sectarian agitation—were flowing in the same direction."[305]

A significant point that has to be made in relation to all this literature is that it was extremely widespread in first century Palestine and much of it was contemporary

---

[303] Charlesworth, *The Old Testament Pseudepigrapha*, p 489
[304] Charlesworth, *The Old Testament Pseudepigrapha*, p 397
[305] Faulkner, *Apocalypse*, p 119.

with the alleged life of Jesus of Nazareth. Yet despite the clearly apocalyptic and messianic message it contains—*the entire genre is lacking any specific references to a real, historical, Jesus-like figure.* That this literary tradition existed is not in question: it is attested by evidence that remains with us to this day. It is clear proof, two thousand years later, of a rich and complex theological melting pot which reflected the social and political ferment of the time and from which developed the particular messianic theology that was later simplified into the New Testament.

As late as 100 CE, when according to the orthodox view of Christianity, the new faith was already clearly established and differentiated from Judaism, Jewish messianic/apocalyptic writings were still being created with remarkable similarities to the themes and even specific phraseology of the New Testament. The *Fourth Book of Ezra* for example, has the following comparisons: "Many have been created, but few will be saved" (8, 3) compared to "For many are called but few are chosen" (Matthew 22, 14); "How long and when will these things be?" (4, 33) compared to ". . . but when shall these things be?" (Luke, 21, 7), and many others. According to Charlesworth, a few extracts from this old document are still used in some Christian liturgy today.

It is not an accident that Josephus mentions, in hundreds of places in his books, the errors of those he described as the "innovators", those people straying from the traditional customs and practice of Judaism as he saw it. But *it was precisely political and theological "innovation" that characterised Judaism at this point in its history.* Nor would the ferment within Judaism have been confined to Palestine, even if that was the crucible of Jewish oppression. We will discuss later the enormous scale of the Jewish diaspora and its organisation around synagogues throughout the Roman Empire. There can be no doubt that the sectarian struggles taking place in Palestinian Judaism will have had their reflection in all these Jewish communities abroad and this explains the rapid growth of the 'Christianised' sect from the second half of the first century. Following the defeat of the revolt and the destruction of the Qumran community, the former Essene activists would not have simply disappeared. Those who survived the repression would have continued to preach the same apocalyptic and messianic message, perhaps now with even greater urgency than ever before and scattered over a wider geographical area. The defeat and the destruction of the Temple would have brought the fulminations of the sectarians to a frenetic pitch and would have widened ever further the spectrum of different messianic sects and grouplets.

Messiahs and prophets

It is from within this raging sea of sectarianism that the biographical character of Jesus eventually emerged. There are many individuals whose activities would have qualified them for a permanent place in folk memory and all of these might have contributed something to the Jesus 'template' used by the first gospel writers. Josephus complained long and hard about those charismatic leaders who led these sectarian movements and who he accused of duping the common people. The only political language of the day was religion and almost all of the dissident movements of the poor of town and countryside were led by prophets and messiahs. As Horsley has summarised it,

> ". . . it is clear from the accounts of the Judean historian Josephus and other sources that the Judean and Galilean peasants produced several concrete movements led by a popularly acclaimed king or prophet. These concrete movements that assumed social forms distinctive to Israelite tradition, moreover, proved to be the driving forces of Judean history during the crises of late second-temple times."[306]

Throughout this whole period, Josephus reported, albeit with the jaundiced view of a representative of the Judean ruling class, that Galilee and Judea were infested by 'charlatans, 'false prophets' and 'messiahs' of all kinds.

> "These were such men as deceived and deluded the people under pretence of divine inspiration, but were for procuring innovations and changes of the government, and these prevailed with the multitude to act like madmen and went before them into the wilderness, as pretending that God would there show them the signals of liberty: but Felix thought this procedure was to be the beginning of a revolt; so he sent some horsemen and footmen, both armed, who destroyed a great number of them."[307]

Josephus described "an Egyptian false prophet" who duped tens of thousands of his countrymen:

> ". . . for he was a cheat, and pretended to be a prophet also, and got together thirty thousand men that were deluded by him; these he led round about from the wilderness to the mount which was called the Mount of Olives, and was ready to break into Jerusalem by force from that place . . . but Felix prevented his attempt and met him with his Roman soldiers, while all the people assisted him in his attack upon them."[308]

Elsewhere the historian recorded "that a certain magician, whose name was Theudas, persuaded a great part of the people to take their effects with them and follow him to the river Jordan; for he told them he was a prophet . . . [Florus] sent a troop of horsemen out against them; who, falling upon them unexpectedly, slew many of them and took many of them alive. They also took Theudas alive and cut off his head, and carried it to Jerusalem."[309].

---

[306] Horsley, *Bandits, Prophets and Messiahs*, p xiii.
[307] WJ, 2, 259
[308] WJ, 2, 261
[309] AJ, 20, 1.

Many decades later the New Testament authors recalled this uprising as well as the earlier revolt of Judas of Galilee, because they are referred to in the Acts of the Apostles (5, 36), although not in the correct chronological order. The fact that these movements were part of folk memory when Acts was written at the end of the first century, is an indication of the impact they must have made on the early proto-Christian sects at the time. The uprising led by the "Egyptian", was also remembered long afterwards and was referred to in Acts (21, 38) as a movement of four thousand people who were led into the wilderness.

There is also a tenuous link between the memory of the "Egyptian" and in the later account of Jesus as he is described in the Gospel of Matthew. Unlike in the other gospels, in Matthew's story, Mary and Joseph, acting on the advice of an angel, took the infant Jesus to Egypt to escape the wrath of King Herod. Jesus "was there until the death of Herod; that it might be fulfilled which was spoken of the Lord by the prophet, saying, Out of Egypt have I called my Son."[310]

Josephus, in describing the messianic fervour of these movements, also mentions the Star Prophecy which, he wrote, was the main driving force behind the uprising against Rome. The prophecy comes originally from the Book of Numbers (24, 17), "There shall come a star out of Jacob", and is mentioned in three places in the literature of the Dead Sea Scrolls. This again finds an echo in Christian literature (Matthew) in the star which guided the three wise men to the infant Jesus. Another of the more notable movements that resurfaced in the gospels was that of John "the Baptist". Josephus recounts that during the reign of Herod, which is before 4 BCE,

> ". . . when many others came in crowds about him, for they were greatly moved by hearing his words, Herod, who feared lest the great influence John had over the people might put it into his power and inclination to raise a rebellion (for they seemed ready to do anything he should advise), thought it best, by putting him to death, to prevent any mischief he might cause, and not bring himself into difficulties . . ."[311]

We also need to add that Joshua was a very common name. Josephus names *fourteen* altogether, including many notable leaders, at least two high priests, a false prophet and a leader of bandits. In the latter case, he is described as "the leader of a seditious tumult of mariners and poor people . . . [who] took with him certain Galileans and set the entire palace on fire . . ."[312]. This Joshua became the effective leader of Tiberias for a while during the period of the uprising. As well as being "a seditious person", Josephus notes that in terms of his religious views, he was "an innovator beyond everybody else". If one needs a single candidate who might qualify more than any other to contribute to the model for the Christians' Jesus, this is surely he,

---

[310] Matthew, 2, 15
[311] AJ, 18, 118.
[312] *Life*, 66

although the anti-hero of Josephus is clearly not the son of God portrayed in the New Testament.

This brief survey is an indication of the real Palestine of the period—a cauldron of revolution and counter-revolution—and it is here that we need to look for the real foundations of proto-Christianity, as some authors describe it, not in the New Testament. If the writings of Paul are correctly dated in the sixth decade of the first century, then there must have been Joshua sects in Jerusalem and around the Jewish diaspora in the years or decades prior to this, although, despite Christian suggestions to the effect, there is no evidence that Paul himself established the communities to which he addressed his epistles. It may be that messianic sects spread out from Palestine any time in the first half of the century, following particular periods of repression or failed revolts and supported by itinerant preachers like the Essenes. It was these revolutionary messianic cults of Judaism—in Palestine and across the Jewish Diaspora—that carried the politico-religious genes of what later became Christianity.

Chapter Summary:

- The twenty-seven books of the New Testament are a small fraction of the Christian literature written in the first two centuries.

- There are no references whatsoever to the Christian Jesus in any non-Christian sources that would be contemporary with him. Neither is there any reference to an historical Jesus in the earliest Christian writings, including the writings of Paul.

- The ideological expression of the class struggle of the Jewish peasants against the Rome and the Jewish elite was the resistance literature of the Essenes.

- The material social conditions were tailor-made for messianic sects and prophets and the upsurge of 'innovation' and new 'theologies' reflected this.

Chapter 7

The Early Christian communities

We shall continue to examine in this section the lack of evidence for the historical figure of Jesus. While the name Jesus would not have been known in ancient Judea, the name Joshua, linked to its *generic* Hebrew meaning of salvation, was the basis of early cults expecting an apocalyptic end of the world and messianic deliverance. Like the Essenes, these early Joshua cults had a primitive communist form of organisation and are probably the original Christian sects. We shall argue that the earliest Christian writings of the time show a clear absence of any biographical link with the biblical Jesus and what was written much later as a *retrospective* narrative was a pastiche of incomplete memories of different prophets, leaders and 'messiahs' of the time.

We shall argue that it was one branch of early Christianity—that around St Paul—which became modern Christianity; that this was a spin-off, bitterly opposed by its original Jerusalem congregation and at odds with the primitive communism, poverty and egalitarianism of the Joshua cult. It was this Church which came to write the official history of the early Christians so as to promote its own significance and which later created an elaborate organisation, with bishops, deacons and an elite bureaucracy, as it grew and developed.

. . . .

It is impossible to know with any certainty the details of how specific religious groups arose and developed, two thousand years after the fact. All we can say is that there was an abundance of raw material from which could emerge a story that was based on a prophet or messiah able to perform miraculous deeds, command popular support and who was executed by the Romans. Moreover, there is enough folk memory, scriptural tradition and salvation literature for precisely such a prophet to be linked with the name Joshua. In all likelihood, the real deeds of different messianic and rebel leaders merged and intermingled as the oral tradition shifted and changed over the succeeding decades. Some events are remembered in outline, some lost altogether, some exaggerated and some minimised: the stories thus evolved and assumed the forms most acceptable and agreeable to the listeners. Such is the nature of oral history.

The first Joshua cults based themselves on the coming apocalypse and messianic deliverance and they would have had an extremely close affinity with the Qumran community and the Essenes. In all likelihood, they were derived from them. As we have shown, the Essenic literary tradition, as it is revealed in the Dead Sea Scrolls, was based on the coming of the Kingdom and the new Israel/Jerusalem. One of the most important of the Essenic traditions, and one that survived the Jewish revolt in a variety of messianic cults, was the *primitive communism* of their community. Josephus, who claimed to have lived with the Essenes for a period, describes the tradition in some detail:

> "These men are despisers of riches, and so very communicative as raises our admiration. Nor is there any one to be found among them who hath more than another; for it is a law among them, that those who come to them must let what they have be common to the whole order . . . every one's possessions are intermingled with every other's possessions . . ."[313]

These comments of Josephus have since been confirmed by the Dead Sea Scrolls and the Community Rule document in particular. Although the Essenes are usually associated with their community at Qumran, Josephus related that they also lived within the general community and that they offered mutual support to one another. "Many of them dwell in every city; and if any of their sect comes from other places, what they have lies open for them, just as if it were their own."[314] Although most were known for their celibacy, Josephus describes "another order of Essenes" who were not celibate but had wives and children. The principle of mutual support and a communitarian spirit, therefore, went far beyond Qumran itself and must have had a considerable basis in the general community for Josephus to notice and remark on it.

In his commentaries on the Essenes, Philo also clearly implied that Qumran was not unique and he referred to similar groups of ascetics in Egypt, known as the *Therapeutae*. He too noted that the Essenes mixed freely among the population: "They dwell in many cities in Judea", he wrote, "and in many villages, and in great and populous communities."

> ". . . no one among them ventures at all to acquire any property whatsoever of his own, neither house, nor slave, nor farm, nor flocks and herds, nor anything of any sort which can be looked upon as the fountain of provision of riches, but they bring them together into the middle as a common stock and enjoy one common general benefit from it all . . ."[315]

Philo described how the members of the sect had a wide variety of skills, as shepherds, herdsmen, artisans, cultivators and handicraftsmen, and so on, but that all their work was done for the common good:

> ". . . each of these men who differ so widely in their respective employment, when they have received their wages give them up to one

---

[313] WJ, 2, 122
[314] WJ, 2, 124
[315] Philo, *Hypothetica*, 11.4

person who is appointed as the universal steward and general manager, and he, when he has received the money, immediately goes and purchases what is necessary and furnishes them with food and abundance, and all other things of which the life of mankind stands in need . . ."[316]

The accuracy of Philo's description can only be guessed at and it is not clear whether he was writing here about workers within the Jewish community at large, in the villages and towns, or those in places like Qumran. But he did make it clear that they were highly regarded among the Jewish people in general, "as worthy of so much honour."

The Essenes may have been the largest sect of its kind, or it may be a *generic* term for a particular kind of ascetic Jew who was a member of a communistic cult. In any case, it is clear from the literature that at this time there was a huge proliferation of sects and among these would have been the Joshua-sects. One or more of these developed the oral and later written traditions which eventually evolved into the New Testament narrative. The Acts of the Apostles mentions a meeting of Christians, soon after the crucifixion of Jesus, which numbered one hundred and twenty. Even if that is not an exaggeration, it indicates a very small group in the midst of probably dozens of other sects within an essentially Jewish milieu.

Kautsky made the very important point that whereas the details of speeches and events are not transmitted accurately in oral tradition, memories of the general outlines of *organisational* structures are more tenacious and not so easily distorted. He expressed his incredulity that so many scholars would deny the close personal contact between the earliest Christian communities and the Essenes.

> ". . . it is far more probable, that in that early state of the Christian congregation, in which it was as yet producing no literature, its organisation was under the influence of Essenian models. And this could only have been an influence in the sense of the actual carrying out of communism, and not in the sense of merely imagining an alleged communistic past, corresponding to no reality."[317]

Indeed remnants of the communist tradition of the early Christian communities did linger and eventually found a reflection in some places in the New Testament, notably those occasions when Jesus is reported have told rich listeners to give away all their wealth. The Acts of the Apostles, supposedly an account of the deeds of the disciples after the death of Jesus, suggests that primitive communism was indeed the normal mode of organisation of the earliest Christian communities:

---

[316] Philo, *Hypothetica*, 11.10
[317] Kautsky, p 338.

"And they *continued* steadfastly in the apostles' doctrine and fellowship, and in breaking of bread, and in prayers . . . and all that believed were together, and *had all things in common*; and *sold their possessions and goods, and parted them to all men, as every man had need* . . ."[318]

"And the multitude of them that believed were of one heart and of one soul: neither said any of them that ought of the things which he possessed was his own; but *they had all things common* . . . neither was there any among them that lacked: for as many as were possessors of land or houses sold them, and brought the prices of the things that were sold. And laid them down at the apostles' feet: and *distribution was made unto every man according to his need*."[319]

These little extracts in the New Testament are like literary fossils in an otherwise lifeless sediment, exposing for the modern reader what the real early Christian communities would have looked like. In the final analysis, it was the *material social and political conditions* in first century Palestine that created the rich mix of ingredients necessary for the evolution of a proto-Christian sect. These ingredients were: the well-developed literature of messianism and apocalypse, the Jewish Joshua cults, and the practical experience of the primitive communism of the Essenes.

The impression of ancient Palestine that is given by modern Christians and Jews is one of a generalised orthodoxy of either the one faith or the other. But that couldn't be further from the truth. As would be expected in what was arguably *the most disturbed period in the whole of Palestinian history*, there was a huge proliferation of sects and messianic currents. Even before the outbreak of the great Jewish Revolt, it is clear that the early Joshua cults had undergone some evolution, as they are reflected in the earliest Christian writings. Paul's theology was already several stages removed from its origins—his mission was exclusively outside of Palestine and he wrote in Greek—and his perception of Jesus had moved beyond that of the original Joshua cults. As we have argued, Paul had moved from a generic *salvation* Joshua to a *personalised*, but still generic Joshua. But he was nonetheless unable to recount any meaningful biographic detail in his letters, because *at that stage the biography hadn't been invented*. That is the meaning of Paul's failure to comment on the life of Jesus, not a quirk of his writing style or an accidental omission.

Kautsky's view

We will discuss the actual setting down of the gospel accounts later but, as we have already suggested, it is far more likely that the figure of Jesus that eventually emerged in the New Testament was an *amalgam* of memories of different leaders and messiahs, at different times: a *pastiche* of stories which was embellished over

---

[318] Acts, 2, 42 (italics added)
[319] Acts, 4, 32

the years and which, once written down, became an accepted view of real events. Interestingly, the view of Kautsky is that Jesus *probably did exist*. "If Jesus had been the product of the imagination of some congregation with an exaggerated messianic vision," he wrote, "such a congregation would never have thought of making a Galilean of him. We may therefore at least accept his Galilean origin, and with it his existence as extremely probable."[320] We cannot agree with the logic of Kautsky's argument here—Galilee was the focus of a huge degree of social unrest and according to Josephus had its fair share of false messiahs fomenting sedition. It is just as likely, therefore, that the origin of the fabled Jesus would focus here as anywhere else and this fact alone does not make his existence "extremely probable". No-one would argue today that Robin Hood's apparent attachment to Nottingham Forest is proof of his existence.

On one point we agree completely with Kautsky: the gospels are no historical source. "The hodge-podge of moral maxims and miraculous deeds which is offered by the Gospels as a report of these activities is so full of impossible and obviously fabricated material, and has so little that can be borne out by other evidence, that it cannot be used as a source."[321] According to Kautsky, the real life and activity of Jesus *as a revolutionary* was overlaid with fiction after his death.

> ". . . a crown of legends began to form about this character, into which pious spirits would weave whatever they wished their model to have spoken and done. But as Jesus began to be regarded more and more as a model for the entire sect, the more did each of the numerous contending groups, of which the sect had consisted from the start, attempt to assign to his personality precisely those ideas to which each group was most attached, in order then to be able to invoke this person as an authority. Thus the image of Jesus, as depicted in legends that were at first merely transmitted from mouth to mouth and later set down in writing, became more and more the image of a superhuman personality, the incarnation of all the ideals developed by the new sect, but it also necessarily became more and more full of contradictions, the various traits of the image no longer being compatible with each other."[322]

Kautsky puts forward the suggestion that the gospels may retain an echo of a real political event, an attempted *coup d'état*:

> ". . . the Christian tradition in its original form must have contained a report of a carefully planned *coup d'état* in which Jesus was captured, a *coup d'état* for which the time had seemed to be ripe after he had successfully driven the bankers and sellers out of the Temple. The later

---

[320]   Kautsky, p 395
[321]   Kautsky, p 395
[322]   Kautsky, p 38

editors did not dare to throw out this report, deeply rooted in tradition, in its entirety. They mutilated it by making the use of force appear to be an act undertaken by the apostles against the will of Jesus . . ."[323]

Here, Kautsky is alluding to the reports carried in Josephus, which we have already cited, of an unsuccessful insurrection led by a man known as "The Egyptian" who led his forces to the Mount of Olives from where he was going to break his way into Jerusalem. Although the uprising was crushed, Josephus makes no comment about the fate of "The Egyptian" other than the fact that he "ran away". Kautsky's suggestion of a *coup d'état* is supported, he argues, by the account in the Gospel of Luke of the arrest of Jesus. As he is captured, one of his disciples takes up a sword and strikes the servant of the high priest, cutting off his right ear. Notwithstanding the fact that the ear was made whole again by yet another miracle, Kautsky argues that this somewhat odd insertion represents an old fragment of what was a more realistic account of an insurrection. There is also a passage in Luke (22, 36), in which Jesus advises his disciples to take up swords: ". . . he that hath a purse, let him take it, and likewise his scrip: and he that hath no sword, let him sell his garment, and buy one", although on being told later that there were "two swords", he replies that "it is enough".

This idea of Kautsky's may indeed be true, but there is no way of knowing. That the revolt of the "Egyptian" was remembered by the author of Luke is clear, because the same author mentions the revolt in Acts. The main point, in any case, is that *it was the general political turmoil and insurrectionary atmosphere*—which was soon to lead to the revolt of 66 CE—which was also the mainspring of the early proto-Christian sects. The myths that came to surround the early days of the sect need not have been based on a single political leader or revolt, as much as an *idealised amalgam* of different leaders and revolts at different times. While the author of Luke and Acts had long since forgotten most of the details, the memory of a *generalised revolutionary milieu* will have remained.

Elsewhere, Kautsky suggests that the common meals and comradeship of the early Christians is something that existed before the crucifixion and it was an important rallying influence afterwards:

> "It was the organisation of the congregation that served as a bond to hold together Jesus' adherents after his death, and as a means of keeping alive the memory of their crucified champion, who according to the tradition had announced himself to be the Messiah."[324]

Once again, Kautsky's speculation is based on the existence of a particular *revolutionary* Jesus. His specific point may or may not be correct; we have no way of knowing. But the *general* implication in his argument is undoubtedly correct: the

---

[323] Kautsky p 366
[324] Kautsky, p 377.

Joshua or proto-Christian sect was held together during this period of enormous political and revolutionary upheaval, before and after the revolt of 66-70 CE, not by the Holy Spirit but by its comradeship, fellowship and the guiding principles of its primitive communism.

> "It was not the faith in the resurrection of the Crucified which created the Christian congregation and gave it its strength, but, on the contrary, it was the vigour and strength of the congregation that created the belief in the continued life of the Messiah . . . we must not overlook the fact that the entire messianic literature of the Jews was shot through with the thought that the future glory could be obtained only at the price of the suffering and death of the righteous, a thought which was a natural consequence of the trials and tribulations to which the Jews were then exposed.

The faith in the crucified Messiah gave every indication, therefore, of becoming simply one of the numerous variations of the messianic prophecy among the Jews of that day . . ."[325]

One of the sects that we know continued long after the Jewish revolt and which was based around a Joshua/Jesus figure, was the sect of the *Ebionites*, a name that comes from the Hebrew root word meaning 'the poor'. The epithet 'Christian' was first used, according to Acts and later Christians writings, in the city of Antioch early in the second century. When we, like most authors, refer to the earliest Christians, it is something of a misnomer, because the term did not exist at that time. The question that necessarily follows is—what did the followers of Joshua/Jesus *call themselves* in Jerusalem, where the movement started? A clue can be found in the writings of Paul. When he refers to the Jerusalem community, he calls them "the saints" or "the poor". This name probably did reflect the original sect in Jerusalem—one based on the revolutionary poor and dispossessed, one hoping and preaching for messianic salvation and the new Kingdom of God and, above all, one composed of pious Jews who saw themselves as being faithful to the traditions of the Hebrew Testament. It is this movement from which Paul's own Church had first evolved and from which it went off at a tangent. Today we know of the existence of the Ebionites only from the writings of their opponents in the hierarchy of what became the orthodox Church, but it would appear that this Jewish-Christian sect survived until at least the fourth century. Their name and Jewish orientation also suggest that they may have clung onto other primitive aspects of their primitive beliefs, like the common ownership of property.

It is this primitive and messianic form of Christianity which is reflected in all of its early literature. The portrayal of Jesus—or Joshua, as it most likely would have been represented—is the intermediate form already noted in the writings of Paul, one that *personalises* the concept of Joshua/salvation, but without any biographical

---

[325]   Kautsky, p 378.

or historical context applied to the person in question. Such is true, for example, of *The Apocalypse of Adam*, which was discovered among the Nag Hammadi finds in Egypt in 1945 and which we will examine later. The Apocalypse of Adam, according to the most authoritative translators of the Nag Hammadi collection, is a very early document, perhaps first century. Like much of early Christian literature, it makes references to a redeemer, a messiah-figure and even the idea of a virgin birth, but it nowhere makes any allusion to a real, historical messiah, living and preaching in Galilee, Judea, or anywhere else. The absence of specific references to the history of Jesus has led some scholars to even consider The Apocalypse of Adam as non-Christian, although, in fact, it is typical of all early Christian literature.

The Book of Revelation

The early and indisputably Christian literature included the *Revelation of John* which was held in such high regard by early Christians that it found its way into the official New Testament. *Revelation* is for us one of the most important works of the official canon, in that it is from a completely different tradition to the gospels. In its style, language and content it has very little in common with the Gospels of Mark, Matthew, Luke or John, or, if it comes to it, the Acts of the Apostles or the Epistles of Paul. *Revelation* comes directly from the apocalyptic and messianic traditions of revolutionary Judaism and it is one of the earliest written of all the New Testament books. Its internal content points to it having been written just prior to the sack of Jerusalem in 70 CE, while the revolution was in full swing. There is not a single positive statement in it about Rome or the Romans. Thinly disguising Rome as 'Babylon', the book pours venom and bile on the whole structure of the Empire and its 'whores'. As one author wrote, "Hardly ever can such a resounding, fulminating polemic have been written against a rule system as we have in this remarkable book."[326] Whereas even the gospels, which were written later, already express a certain accommodation with Rome—"render unto Caesar" and so on—the *Book of Revelation* is unrelenting in its demand for retribution and justice. It is a revolutionary text. But yet, again, although the messiah is introduced as the sacrificial "lamb" for the people—an allusion to the common practice of sacrifice at Passover—there is no mention in *Revelation* of a real Jesus, living and preaching in Palestine.

The author of *Revelation* addresses his writing specifically to messianic *Jews*, at one point writing, "I know the blasphemy of them which say they are Jews, and are not, but are the synagogue of Satan"[327]. The true relationship of *Revelation* to Christianity cannot be better described than it was by Engels, who wrote:

---

[326] Bousson, quoted by Wengst in *Pax Romana*, p 221.
[327] Revelation, 2, 9.

"Here it is therefore not a case of conscious Christians but of people who say they are Jews. Granted, their Judaism is a new stage of development of the earlier but for that very reason it is the only true one . . . That was how little our author was aware in the year 69 of the Christian era that he represented quite a new phase in the development of a religion which was to become one of the most revolutionary elements in the history of the human mind . . . We therefore see that the Christianity of that time, which was still unaware of itself, was as different as heaven from earth from the later dogmatically fixed universal religion of the Nicene Council . . ."[328]

Another work accepted as a very early document was the *Didache*. It was held in very high regard by early Christians and is frequently cited by Christian writers in the early centuries, although it did not find its way into the New Testament. The *Didache* has been traditionally given the sub-title "the Doctrine of the Twelve Apostles" although there is nothing whatsoever in the text that supports this naming: it is yet another example of a Church legend created out of nothing. The document is believed to be one of the very earliest Christian writings, Ehrman noting that although scholars tend to date the book around 100 or 120 CE, "it is probable . . . that the author compiled his account from several earlier sources."[329] It gives instructions as to how some ceremonies should be conducted—including baptism, the Eucharist (the sacred common meal), prayers, blessings and fasts. What is interesting in this book of liturgical instructions is that once again, it makes no reference to a living, historical Jesus from whom these prayers and practices may have originated. As in other writings from this period, there are only references in a *general* sense to the "Lord".

The *Letter of Barnabas*, purports to be written by a companion of Paul and is dated according to Ehrman at around 130 CE. Although it makes what appear to be two or three references to historical events—a crucifixion and suffering, Jesus being given vinegar and gall—they are notable precisely because of their scarcity. There is no reference in a very long document (as long as the gospel of Mark) to Nazareth, a ministry in Galilee, Judea and elsewhere, preaching to the twelve disciples, the miracles of Jesus, a trial in Jerusalem, and so on. It is as if there is no *full* biography yet, but the outline of a legend that was beginning to form.

Another work, the *Shepherd of Hermas* was the longest of all of the early Christian documents, longer than any book in the New Testament. Like the *Didache*, it was extremely popular for a long period of time and, according to Ehrman, was "on the margins of the canon". The document consists of a series of five visions with commandment', parables and symbolic discourses known as similitudes. Once again, while there are hundreds of references to the Lord, in this extremely long, early second century Christian tract, there are no references at all to Jesus. These omissions are always a puzzle to modern Christians:

---

[328] Engels, *On the history of early Christianity*, Die Neue Zeit, 1894.
[329] Ehrman, *Lost* Scriptures, p 212

"The theology of the Church must have been very elastic at a time when such a book could enjoy popularity and implicit, if not explicit, ecclesiastical sanction, for its Christology does not seem to square with any of the Christologies of the New Testament, or with those of contemporary theologians whose occasional documents have reached us."[330]

The works of Theophilus, bishop of Antioch are dated at some time in the late second century and they are quoted approvingly by the Church historian and biographer of Constantine, Eusebius. Yet in all the long extracts of the writings of Theophilus that remain, one would look in vain for any references at all to the historical Jesus, other than Joshua, the successor to Moses in the Old Testament. In his third book he presents a "chronology of the world" from Adam to the Emperor Marcus Aurelius, in which he fails to mention the birth, death or resurrection of Jesus. This is yet another example of very early Christian writing—the author frequently declares himself a Christian and there is a great deal of reference to a *generalised* resurrection—without any reference to an historical Jesus. Even if the majority of the text deals with Old Testament issues like the Creation and the Flood, it would not be unreasonable to expect some reference somewhere to the historical Jesus of Nazareth as the inspiration of the author's faith. Finally, we have already mentioned *The Gospel of Thomas* which was discovered for the first time as a complete copy at Nag Hammadi; this gospel reinforces this overall pattern. Even Christian scholars now accept that this is a genuine first century work, at least contemporary with the letters of Paul. Bart Ehrman suggests it is "one of the most sensational archaeological discovery of the twentieth century."[331] But once again, although it contains many sayings of Joshua—a written version of oral traditions circulating at the time—it nowhere makes reference to an actual *earthly* existence for him or any context in which the sayings might have been delivered to an audience.

In summary, it is clear that all the very early documents of the proto-Christian cults were derivative of the revolutionary traditions of messianic Judaism, but their development had not reached a state where they had a biographical saviour. Although they may mention the Lord or even a Joshua, none of these works—including the writings of Paul—*make reference to any actual historical events in the life of Jesus of Nazareth*. Paul's theology puts the crucifixion and resurrection at its centre, but this is to play on a theological motif, a device that was devoid of any real biographical reference point for such apparently world-shaking events.

The absence of the historical Jesus in early Christian literature is so much of a truism that it is almost possible to give an approximate date to a work simply by how and to what extent it refers to the life in a biographical sense. What is apparent is that the Joshua-sects followed a doctrine based on a *generalised messianic saviour/ Joshua*, perhaps with an understanding of martyrdom at some *indeterminate point* in the mythic past. It was only with the writing of the Gospel of Mark that a narrative

---

[330]   Graydon F Sneyder, *The Anchor Bible Dictionary,* v 3, p 1

[331]   Ehrman, *Lost Scriptures*, p 19

was finally created and then embellished by numerous other writers. Even after the completion of the four main gospels, there were many branches of the early Church, later to be denounced as heretics, who refused to acknowledge the stories of an earthly Jesus. It was not for nothing that the first Epistle of John, written some time after the gospels, admonished such non-believers: "And every spirit that confesseth not that Jesus Christ is come in the flesh is not of God."[332]

From the standpoint of a materialist, looking for real evidence of the historical Jesus, these considerations must weigh extremely heavily but, not surprisingly, it is barely noticed among Christian scholars and Church leaders. The fact that Jesus is missing from such a large corpus of early Christian literature and then he appears much later in four half-copied, half-contradictory accounts seems not to trouble them much. For some scholars, it is perfectly acceptable that there was a great variety of views in the earliest period of Christianity and they just *assume* that the traditions of Jesus were handed down orally and written later. For example, *The Beginnings of Christianity,* Welburn writes:

> "The diversity of points of view we encounter in the traditions of the apostles is no doubt partly due to the fact that they were *handed down orally over long periods of time* before getting committed to writing."[333]

This suggestion, that the biography of Jesus and accounts of his life and works were handed down orally for decades before being committed to writing, is a very common idea among Christian scholars. This is not surprising, since it is the only fig leaf they have. But this does not explain why it was, when Paul was writing extensive epistles, when there was a rich literary culture based in Palestine and elsewhere, when there were wall-to-wall scribes in the gospel stories, that the biography of Jesus was *left to some backwater of oral tradition for half a century* after his crucifixion. There is simply no plausible explanation as to why Christians would allow the real life of the single most important person in human history to be broken into scattered bits of oral tradition, transmitted by word of mouth and only committed to writing decades later.

The absence of a real historical messiah character within the early Joshua sects is not due to accidental omissions. Rather it is a clear indication that *the legend had not developed* to the point where it could find its way into Paul's epistles, or the *Didache*, or *Revelation*, or the *Shepherd of Hermas*, or any other early Christian literature. Another modern Christian author, Robin Scroggs, writing in *The People's Jesus*, suggests that the Hellenistic Church "placed no emphasis upon the life of Jesus and there is no evidence it had the slightest interest in Jesus as a wonder-worker." The writer asks, what happened to the real biographical Jesus?

---

[332]   1 John, 4, 3.
[333]   Welburn, *The Beginnings of Christianity*, p 52 (italics added)

"One can only speculate. The likelihood that seems to me at hand is the lack of interest in the earthly Jesus throughout the Hellenistic church. Just as it did not incorporate stories and sayings of the earthly Jesus, it seems to have felt that the earthly person, known by the simple name 'Jesus' was not adequate as a pointer to their faith in the resurrected and enthroned lord."[334]

One can indeed speculate, and turn this way and that, and suggest a "lack of interest". Whichever way one looks, there is no explanation for the absence of the historical character, as opposed to the generic salvation character, other than the fact that his biography *hadn't been invented* in the early days. The first Joshua sects had no need of a real person to carry their radical message of redemption and a new Kingdom.

The Dead Sea Scrolls

None of the Dead Sea Scrolls mention Jesus or John the Baptist and they are not usually associated *directly* with Christianity. But, nevertheless, as we have argued, they are an important background to the birth of Christianity in that they give a glimpse of the messianic fervour that gripped the revolutionary elements of Jewish society. Even in the earliest stages of the examination of the scrolls, in 1956, John Allegro noted that Christians could recognise familiar themes in the discovered documents:

". . . many of my Christian readers will have begun to feel the warmth of a familiar hearth. Here are the ideas of the New Covenant, the emphasis of justification by grace and a doctrine of perfection. We are indeed bordering very closely on to Christian soil and must accordingly begin to weave our threads of Qumran theology into the fabric of the New Testament to understand fully the considerable significance of the new material for the history of the Church."[335]

The consensus among scholars is that the Dead Sea Scrolls are very important in firmly establishing the depth and scope of the messianic and apocalyptic tradition, not as a mere fringe element, but as a *mainstream feature* of the Judaism of that period and in that sense they are important in understanding the development of Christianity. As we have mentioned, however, there is a lingering suspicion that the carefully managed translation and publication of the scrolls by a small and secretive team, biased towards a modern Christian viewpoint, did actually succeed in establishing a slanted framework for most of the academic assessment of the scrolls.

---

334 Scroggs, *The Peoples' Jesus*, p 69
335 Allegro, *The Mystery of the Dead Sea Scrolls revealed*, p 141

There is one scholar who *does* directly link the Dead Sea Scrolls with the story of Jesus. This is Robert Eisenman, who points out that the so-called commentaries (or *pesharim*) in the Dead Sea archive were found in *single* copies precisely because they were the most *up-to-date* writings of the Qumran community before its destruction. They must have reflected, therefore, the religious, social and political polemics in the first half of the first century, in other words, during the period that would have been covered by the ministry of Jesus. Eisenman scoffs at the idea that the Essenes, whose community continued up to 68 CE, would have stopped making contemporary commentaries on scripture at some time in the far distant past.

> "This is as absurd as thinking that nowadays a preacher would interpret Biblical scripture in terms of the events surrounding the lives of George Washington, Napoleon, or the Duke of Wellington . . . It is inconceivable that the community as a whole had nothing new to say or no new reactions while 150 years of the most vital and controversial history in Palestine passed before its eyes; that on the contrary it sat passively and piously by studying or penning texts relating to the period up to 63 BCE or before."[336]

The Qumran commentaries are based around books of the Hebrew Testament, but they are *re*-interpretations in the light of contemporary events. One of the most notable, as we have already mentioned, is the commentary on the *Book of Habakkuk*. According to Geza Vermes, "the palaeographic dating of the manuscript (30-1 BCE) has been confirmed by the radiocarbon tests (120-5 BCE)"[337]. But Eisenman disputes the palaeographic analysis, which involves a study of the style of writing and letter formation and setting it against the styles as they gradually evolved over the years. As Eisenman points out, it relies on comparisons that by their very nature may not be entirely accurate over the span of a few decades or even half a century. Imagine a young twenty-year old scribe, working alongside his eighty-year old mentor—they could have such very different styles of writing that palaeographic analysis might set them half a century apart, even though they are sitting next to one another. Radio-carbon dating, he argues, also gives too broad and inaccurate an estimate. Eisenman relies instead on what he calls "internal" evidence, in other words, what the *text itself* actually says. The *Habakkuk* commentary, for example, refers to the *Kittim* which many scholars take to be a code word for the Romans. According to Eisenman, reading the references to the *Kittim* make it clear that this commentary was written *during the revolt of 66 CE*, when it was facing imminent defeat.

---

[336] Eisenman, *The Dead Sea Scrolls and the First Christians*, p 81/82

[337] Vermes, *The Complete Dead Sea Scrolls.* p 509. Note, too, that carbon dating produces relatively broad margins of error and this is why the estimate is wider than the dating by palaeographic methods.

". . . the Kittim [who are] quick and valiant in war, causing many to perish. [All the world shall fall] under the domination of the Kittim . . . they shall march across the plain, smiting and plundering the cities of the earth . . . the commanders of the Kittim who despise the fortresses of the peoples and laugh at them in derision. To capture them, they encircle them with a mighty host, and out of fear and terror they deliver themselves into their hands. They destroy them because of the sins of their inhabitants . . . the last priests of Jerusalem, who shall amass money and wealth by plundering the peoples. But in the last days, their riches and booty shall be delivered into the hands of the army of the Kittim, for it is they who shall be the remnant of the peoples."[338]

This being the case, Eisenman argues, it means the *latest possible date* for the deposition of the Scrolls is 68 CE and therefore it opens up the possibility that other documents in the large collection may have been more recent than is usually conceded. Many of the Dead Sea Scroll documents, he argues, are couched in the extreme nationalistic, uncompromising and passionate language that typifies the period of the uprising against Rome and the years that led up to it. There are also clear allusions to religious concepts that eventually found their way into the New Testament theology of the messiah.

In many instances, where Geza Vermes in *The Complete Dead Sea Scrolls in English*, dates documents palaeographically as first century BCE, Eisenman and his co-worker Wise, date the same fragments, from their content, to a later period, about 50 CE. They cite, for example, a fragment from Cave 4, sometimes referred to as the *Testament of Levi* or the *Testament of Job*, as a late document. This document (in the Vermes version) refers to the messiah in the following terms: "He will atone for all the sons of his generation and will be sent to all the sons of his [people]. His word is like a word of heaven, and his teaching is according to the will of God."[339] Eisenman and Wise, on the other hand, include an additional translated fragment, ". . . Let not the nail touch him . . ."[340], which, they argue, appears to allude to crucifixion.

Some of the fragments found among the Scrolls are strangely labelled by Vermes, such as *Bless, my soul*, after its opening words, and this translator writes that they have "no sectarian features". On the other hand, Eisenman and Wise refer to these same fragments as the *Hymns of the Poor*, put them in a different order to Vermes, and link them to the *Ebionim*, the "Poor", which is the name the early Christians used for themselves. They note, as we have already mentioned, that when

338   Vermes, *The Complete Dead Sea Scrolls*. p 510

339   Vermes, *The Complete Dead Sea Scrolls in English*, p 561.

340   Eisenman and Wise, *The Dead Sea Scrolls Uncovered*, p 145

Paul refers to the Jerusalem community in his epistles, he sometimes calls them the "Poor", as in Galatians: "we should remember the poor . . ."[341]

> "As tradition proceeds, it becomes clear that the *Ebionim* (the so-called Ebionites) or 'the Poor' is the name by which the community descending from James' Jerusalem community in Palestine goes. In all likelihood, it descends from the one we are studying in these [Dead Sea Scroll] materials as well."[342]

In the *Hymns of the Poor*, we read, ". . . he has not despised the Meek, nor has he forgotten the distress of the Downtrodden . . . He opened his eyes to the Downtrodden . . . he did not abandon them in their great distress nor give them into the hands of violent ones . . ."[343] Eisenman and Wise refer to the fact that the Ebionites lasted a long time and in the early fourth century were referred to by Eusebius who was based in Caesarea, close to the original home of the sect:

> "He tells us in *Ecclesiastical History*, 3, 27 that they were 'called Ebionites by the ancients (ie a long time before his own era) because of the low and mean opinions they held about Christ'. By this statement he means that the Ebionites do not regard Jesus as divine . . . Knowing that Ebionites means 'Poor Men' in Hebrew, he jokingly contends that they received this epithet because of 'the poverty of intellect they exhibited', ie in following such a primitive Christology . . .
>
> He knows that they considered Christ born by 'natural' means, 'a plain and ordinary man, who was justified by his advances in Righteousness only . . . They also insisted on the complete observance of the Law, nor did they think one could be saved only by faith in Christ and a corresponding life'. Rather 'they evinced great zeal to observe the literal sense of the Law . . . They observed the Sabbath and other ceremonies just like Jews'. Paul they considered 'an *apostate from the Law*'"[344]

In other words, they argue, the Ebionites were the supporters of the Jerusalem cult leader, James and the same group maintained their tradition long afterwards. Moreover, they add, the use of "*Ebionim*" as a term of self-designation at Qumran was very widespread, and was particularly notable in the commentaries.

What are also very important for Eisenman and Wise are the many references in the Dead Sea literature to the "Righteous Teacher" and his two protagonists, "Wicked Priest" and the "Liar" or "Spouter" (of Lies). These characters feature

---

341 Galatians, 2, 10
342 Eisenman and Wise, *The Dead Sea Scrolls Uncovered*, p 233
343 Eisenman and Wise, *The Dead Sea Scrolls Uncovered*, p 240
344 Eisenman and Wise, *The Dead Sea Scrolls Uncovered*, p 234 (italics added)

particularly strongly in the *Habakkuk Commentary*. The "Righteous Teacher", according to Eisenman and Wise, was the leader of the proto-Christian or Ebionite community in Jerusalem, in other words, James "the Just". Although he is not named as such, they argue that other Christian legends about the life of James would correspond to the Qumran sources. The "Wicked Priest" was the high priest of the Jerusalem Temple, possibly Ananus, who was responsible for the death of James. This, for Eisenman, was the decisive turning point which triggered the scattering of James' community a few years before the outbreak of the great revolt. This was an event corresponding to the description in Acts of the Christian community fleeing Jerusalem after the crucifixion of Jesus.

The Spouter of Lies, who, according to the Commentary, "led many astray that he might build his city of vanity with blood and raise a congregation on deceit", can only be associated for Eisenman with the figure of Paul, who was establishing messianic Joshua communities that did not follow the laws and strictures of traditional Judaism. Paul is also identified in other Qumran literature as the "Seeker of smooth things", implying that he peddled an easy road to salvation.

Paul's differences with Jerusalem

That there were differences between Paul and the Jerusalem Church leaders, Peter and James, is not disputed at all by any modern Christian writers. The disputes are frequently referred to in Paul's epistles and in the Acts of the Apostles. Paul's essential view was that it was not necessary to follow the "Law" of Judaism, particularly circumcision and dietary observation, but that a "new covenant" had been established, which was based on "faith". Over and over again, he makes reference to this new arrangement and the importance of faith. The following is only a sample:

> ". . . if the uncircumcision keep the righteousness of the law, shall not his uncircumcision be counted for circumcision? . . . he is a Jew which is one inwardly; and circumcision is that of the heart . . ."[345]
> ". . . the promise that he should be the heir of the world, was not to Abraham or to his seed through the law, but through the righteousness of faith."[346]
> "Circumcision is nothing, and uncircumcision is nothing, but the keeping of the commandments of God."[347]
> ". . . if ye be circumcised, Christ shall profit you nothing."[348]

---

[345] Romans, 2, 26-29
[346] Romans, 3, 13
[347] 1 Corinthians, 7, 19
[348] Galatians, 5, 2. The word 'Christ' is the Greek term for 'messiah'

The Epistles and Acts also refer to Paul's clashes with the leaders in Jerusalem who disagreed with him and who held on to the traditional Jewish practices. Paul argued that he was given the mission of preaching to the gentiles, while the leaders in Jerusalem preached to the Jews—as an agreed division of labour: "the gospel of uncircumcision was committed unto me, as the gospel of the circumcision was unto Peter."[349] The rivalry was very intense and Paul records that when he met Peter, "I withstood him face to face, because he was to be blamed."[350] Acts reports that the leaders in Jerusalem at first "contended with" Paul when they heard of his conversion of gentiles. When, according to Christian tradition, they fled Jerusalem after the persecution of Stephen, as far afield as Phoenicia, Cyprus and Antioch, they preached "to none but unto the Jews only."[351] James had clearly been the main leader of the Jerusalem community as Acts implies when he decides to leave the gentiles to Paul: "*my decision*", he is made to say, ". . . is that we trouble not them".[352]

The Acts of the Apostles, written a long time after Paul's epistles, deliberately played down what were in reality deep splits. The original Joshua cult in Jerusalem was based among the poorest Jews and held onto a primitive communist outlook; what they saw being preached overseas by Paul and his co-workers was a more easy-going and gentile version of their beliefs. To them, it was 'Judaism-lite'. There is an episode described in Acts in which Paul is physically attacked outside the Jerusalem Temple by some described as Asian Jews. Hyam Maccoby in *The Myth Maker*, is quite clear that the Jews were stirred up by Jewish-Christians who were incensed at Paul's teaching to the gentiles against Jewish Law. "This is the man," they shouted, "that teacheth all men everywhere against the people, and the law and this place."[353] Paul barely escaped with his life. But with the exception of this episode, the author of Acts air-brushed over the dispute. In contrast, the earlier works of Paul pull fewer punches. He scoffed at the traditional dietary laws of the Jews:

> "For one believeth that he may eat all things; another, who is weak, eateth herbs. Let not him that eateth despise him that eateth not; and let not him which eateth not judge him that eateth . . . there is nothing unclean of itself; but to him that esteemeth any thing to be unclean, to him it is unclean . . . for the kingdom of God is not meat and drink . . . meat destroy not the work of God. All things indeed are pure."[354]

---

[349]   Galatians, 2, 7.
[350]   Galatians, 2, 11
[351]   Acts, 11, 19.
[352]   Acts, 15, 19 (italics added)
[353]   Acts, 21, 27
[354]   Romans, 14, 6-20

He wrote that he had "many adversaries" and warned his readers against being "beguiled" by false preachers who "preacheth another Jesus, whom we have not preached". There were some, he warned, who "would pervert the gospel of Jesus" and "if any man preach any other gospel unto you than that he have received, let him be accursed."

Remnants of this dispute appear elsewhere in the New Testament. The *Epistle of James* was not written by James at all, but many years later by a Christian who stood in the tradition of that Jerusalem leader. The emphasis in this epistle is on keeping the Law, doing good works and it is opposed to acting on faith alone. "What does it profit my brethren", it asks, "though a man say he hath faith, and have not works? Can faith save him . . . faith, if it hath not works, is dead, being alone . . . wilt thou know, O vain man, that faith without works is dead?"[355]

On the other side of the controversy, it was a supporter of the "vain man" (ie Paul) who wrote *the Epistle to the Hebrews* and which we have already mentioned, putting Paul's name to it. The emphasis in *Hebrews*, as in the Pauline ideology, is on "faith". *Hebrews* was written to convince practising Jews that "Jesus the high priest" has introduced a "new covenant" in which traditional Temple sacrifice has been superseded by "faith". In Chapter 11 it recounts the many times great figures from the Hebrew Bible, like Abraham, Noah and Isaac were empowered by faith. The expression "by faith" or "through faith" appears sixteen times in one chapter. Although the *Epistle to the Hebrews* is not by Paul, it shows, nevertheless, that there were other authors at approximately the same time who had the same point of view. It shows, therefore, that Paul represented a *trend of opinion* within the early Joshua cults which was moving away from the Torah and the Mosaic Law.

Another important work, the *Testament of Abraham* shows the extent to which at least one other strand of Jewish tradition opened up to embrace not just practising Jews, but also gentiles who were prepared to follow *in broad terms* the moral and ethical code of the Jews. This *Testament*, is dated approximately to the end of the first century CE, and according to Charlesworth, it:

". . . bears witness to the existence of a universalistic and generalised Judaism, in which "good works" consisted of such obvious virtues as charity and hospitality, coupled with avoidance of obvious moral sins—murder, adultery, robbery—and according to which all people, whether Jew or gentile, are judged according to how well they observe these ethical requirements. The Torah and the covenant of Israel seem to play no role . . ."[356]

It is clear from this that the Christians' description of Paul as the first 'apostle to the gentiles' is an oversimplification of the real state of affairs. On the whole, the references in the New Testament to this split in the Joshua cult, including the so-called Council

---

[355]   James, 2, 14
[356]   Charlesworth, *The Old Testament Pseudepigrapha*, p 877

of Jerusalem in which the two trends clashed, are relatively muted. But whereas the New Testament reports are largely written from a 'Pauline' perspective, glossing over the depth and bitterness of the dispute, the *Habakkuk Commentary*, according to Eisenman, was written from the Jamesian viewpoint and exposes an acrimonious and irreconcilable split. The *Commentary* doesn't mince words in its denunciations of Paul and his Church:

> "those who were unfaithful, together with the Liar, in that they [did] not [listen to the words received by] the Teacher of Righteousness from the mouth of God . . . the unfaithful of the New [Covenant] . . . have not believed in the Covenant of God . . . members of the council . . . were silent at the time of the chastisement of the Teacher of Righteousness and gave him no help against the Liar who flouted the Law in the midst of their whole [congregation] . . . those who observe the Law in the House of Judah . . . God will deliver from the House of Judgement because of their suffering and because of their faith in the Teacher of Righteousness . . ."

The Qumran documents that refer to Paul as the "Liar" are so vitriolic that it explains, Eisenman suggests, Paul's defensiveness in his epistles, including one in which he explicitly writes "I say the truth in Christ, I lie not".[357] It is not only Paul, however, who feels the lash of the pen of this author. The description of the "Wicked Priest" in the Temple could most certainly apply to the high priests in the period leading up to the revolt in 66 CE:

> "He robbed and amassed the riches of the men of violence who rebelled against God, and he took the wealth of the peoples, heaping sinful iniquity upon himself. And he lived in the ways of the abominations amidst every unclean defilement . . . the last priests of Jerusalem . . . shall amass money and wealth by plundering the peoples . . .

Eisenman argues that if the *Habakkuk Commentary* is dated prior to the period of the great revolt, then these references must represent real living people in the various currents and cults of Judaism *of that period*. The following extracts, all from the Qumran *Community Scroll*, are for Eisenman direct references to James and Paul:

> "He raised for them a Teacher of Righteousness . . . when the Scoffer arose who shed over Israel the waters of lies. He caused them to wander in pathless wilderness, laying low the everlasting heights, abolishing the ways of righteousness and removing the boundary with which the forefathers had marked out their inheritance . . . For they sought smooth things and

---

[357]   Romans, 9, 1

preferred illusions . . . they have spoken wrongly against the precepts of righteousness, and have despised the Covenant and the Pact—the New Covenant—which they made in the land of Damascus."

To support his argument, Eisenman cites Epiphanius (315-403 CE), one of the early Christian writers, saying that in Palestine, the followers of the Messiah were called *Jessaeans*, "by which, apart from his facile derivation of this term, he clearly intends *Essenes*", once again linking the original Palestinian followers of the Joshua cult to the revolutionary movement of primitive communism.

Eisenman's ideas are extremely plausible and they are certainly not incompatible with a materialist view of the rise of proto-Christianity, although it has to be said that they bring us no nearer to the legendary Jesus of the New Testament. The nearest Eisenman comes to identifying Jesus, is as a *Zaddik*, or a "pious" man, sometimes referred to as the "Just One", who, according to the Essenes, would have the rightful claim to the inheritance of the High Priesthood. But the most important point is that the general impression given is that there was an *unbridgeable gulf* between the Joshua/Messiah movement that developed originally in Palestine as a revolutionary communistic tradition and the movement that spun off it around the ideas of people like Paul:

"While the Palestinian one was zealot, nationalistic, engagé, xenophobic, and apocalyptic; the overseas one was cosmopolitan, antinomian, pacifistic—in a word, 'Paulinised'"[358]

The early Joshua cults were therefore split and it was the faction around Paul that developed churches among communities of Jews and gentiles around the Roman Empire, at the same time retaining most of the social features, if not the theology, of the original Joshua cult. The Jewish-Christians of Jerusalem evolved into the group who became the Ebionites, with more limited support but who lasted up to the fourth century. Remnants of their traditions may have had some influence centuries later in the development of new monotheistic currents in the Arabian Peninsula prior to the rise of Islam, as we discuss later. The orthodox history of the Church, however, as it is reflected in the New Testament, glosses over the bitterness of the split and in fact manufactured a reconciliation between Paul and Peter—on Paul's terms—and James was relegated to a minor role.

Western Christian tradition is much more heavily influenced by the Roman Catholic theological model rather than any other, but it is worth noting that those Churches which developed in the Near East, independently of Rome, and which acquired their own large bases of support, include many more features of the Mosiac (ie Jewish) tradition in their liturgy and practices. Thus, the Ethiopian and Eritrean Churches practise circumcision as a matter of course and in other Eastern Churches like the Coptic and Nestorian, it is also common.

---

[358] Eisenman and Wise, *The Dead Sea Scrolls Uncovered*, p 10.

Itinerants

After the leaders of the original Joshua cult were dispersed from Jerusalem and even more significantly after the destruction of Jerusalem by the Romans in 70 CE, the main centres of the developing cult were those based outside Palestine in the Jewish communities dispersed around the Eastern Mediterranean.

> "The Jewish Nazarenes never left the city at the time of the Jewish War; they stayed there and played their part, as loyal Jews, in the fight against Rome. When the Jews were broken by the Romans and their Temple destroyed in AD 70, the Jewish Christians shared in the horrors of the defeat, and the Jerusalem Nazarenes were dispersed to Caesarea and other cities, even as far as Alexandria in Egypt. Its power and influence as the Mother Church and centre of the Jesus movement was ended; and the Pauline Christian movement, which had up to AD 66 been struggling to survive against the strong disapproval of Jerusalem, now began to make great headway."[359]

These early communities of Christians were independent, self-organised and extremely varied congregations, supported by bands of itinerant preachers. These itinerants did not spend all their time on their knees: they were more like political activists and they were based principally and originally *within the Jewish communities*. Paul himself clearly fitted into this general category of property-less, wandering preachers. In his epistle to the Corinthians, he defended his right, against those who would "examine" (ie challenge) him, to do the same as Cephas (Peter) and live off the community, "forbearing" to labour for himself:

> "Am I not an apostle? Am I not free? Have I not seen Jesus Christ our Lord? Are not ye my work in the Lord? If I be not an apostle unto others, yet doubtless I am to you; for the seal of mine apostleship are ye in the Lord. Mine answer to them that do examine me is this, Have we not power to eat and to drink? Have we not power to lead about a sister, a wife, as well as other apostles and as the brethren on the Lord, and Cephas? Or I only, and Barnabas, have not we power to forbear working? . . . If we have sown unto you spiritual things, is it a great thing if we shall reap your carnal things?"[360]

Paul even complained to the Corinthians that he had not been paid by them but had been subsidised by *other* churches: "I robbed other churches, taking wages of them, to do you service . . . And when I was present with you, and wanted, I was chargeable to no man; for that which was lacking to me the brethren which

---

[359] Maccoby, *The Myth Maker, Paul and the Invention of Christianity,* p 174.
[360] Corinthians, 9, 1

came from Macedonia supplied: and in all things I have kept myself from being burdensome unto you . . ."[361]

Kautsky quotes at length from a piece of fiction by a Roman writer, Lucian, about 165 CE, in which he describes an imaginary Christian preacher, Peregrinus Proteus, who was something of a con-man and a fugitive after having committed murder:

> "At this time he also became acquainted with the admirable wisdom of the Christians by intercourse with their priests and scribes in Palestine. They soon appeared mere children in comparison with him; he became their prophet, the spokesman at their banquets, head of the synagogue, all in one person; he commented a number of writings and explained them to them, a number he wrote himself, in short, they took him for a god, made him their legislator and appointed him their head. Of course they still venerate that great man who was crucified in Palestine, for having introduced this new religion." After describing the supporters of this leader, as "old women, widows and orphans", he goes on: ". . . these sad wretches live in the conviction that they will be altogether immortal and live forever, wherefore they despise death and often seek it voluntarily. Furthermore . . . they esteem all things as equally unimportant, considering them common possessions, without having any good reason for this view. If they are visited by a clever imposter, capable of utilizing this situation, he will soon become very rich, because of his ability to hoodwink these simple folk" [362]

This satire of Lucian is interesting in several respects. Notwithstanding the fact that it is meant to ridicule Christians, the author must have based his caricature on something at least approaching real life and it is notable that he makes no distinction between the Christians and the *synagogue*. He also lays the greatest emphasis on the *most needy* layer of supporters (old women, widows and children), and he notes the *election* of leaders and at least a degree of lingering *communist* principles. In fact, this satire was probably composed just at the time when the Church was beginning to move towards *appointed*, rather than elected, bishops and Lucian's view may have been lagging behind events.

A contemporary of Lucian, and another opponent of the Christians, was Celsus. He too mocked the Christians for giving credence to any itinerant who happened along and who claimed to be seized by "prophetic ecstasy". Kautsky quotes Celsus as follows:

> ". . . others, roaming about as beggars, and visiting the cities and military camps, offer the same spectacle. Each of them has the words at the tip of his tongue and uses them instantly: 'I am God', or 'God's son', or

---

[361]   2 Corinthians, 11, 8-9.

[362]   Kautsky, 425.

'God's spirit'. 'I am come because the destruction of the world is already approaching, and you humans are going to destruction because of your unrighteousness. But I will save you and you will soon behold me coming again with heavenly power!' . . . these alleged prophets whom I have more than once heard with my own ears have admitted their weaknesses to me, after I convinced them, and confessed that they had themselves invented all their inscrutable words."[363]

One could be forgiven to thinking that Celsus had travelled forward two millennia in time and had watched evangelical TV channels. But leaving that aside and the accusations of charlatanism, it is interesting to note here that Celsus is accusing the Christians of preaching to the ranks of the Roman army, another likely fertile ground for conversion, given the insecurity and likely shortness of soldiers' lives.

We have already cited Paul, who insisted on his right to live off the congregation, paying for his physical needs in return for him providing for their spiritual needs. Paul alluded, even at this early stage—mid-first century—to a hierarchy among the itinerant preachers. "And God hath set some in the Church, first apostles, secondarily prophets, thirdly teachers, after that miracles, then gifts of healings," and he questions the authenticity of some: "Are all apostles? Are all prophets? Are all teachers? Are all workers of miracles?"[364]

It would appear, from early Christian literature, that the abundance of wandering preachers and prophets created some tensions between them and the local communities. The epistle of 2 Peter, not written by the disciple of that name, but by someone using his name at the beginning of the second century, nevertheless reflects complaints about false preachers at the time it was written. "But there were false prophets also among the people, even as there shall be false teachers among you, who privily shall bring in damnable heresies . . . and many shall follow their pernicious ways."[365]

The large number of warnings in the gospels about "false prophets" is an indication that at the time these works were written, in the late first or early second century, there were many itinerant apostles and teachers visiting Jewish and Jewish-Christian communities. To take one example, the author of the Gospel of Matthew has Jesus warn to "beware false prophets which come to you in sheep's clothing, but inwardly they are ravening wolves."[366] As we have pointed out, the early Christian document the *Didache*, doesn't deal in the slightest with the historical life of a Jesus but it does deal at some length with how Jewish-Christian communities should treat these itinerants, in effect offering communities advice in distinguishing genuine prophets and teachers from charlatans.

---

[363]   Kautsky, p 429.
[364]   1 Corinthians, 12, 28.
[365]   2 Peter, 2, 1
[366]   Matthew, 7, 15.

"Welcome anyone who comes and teaches you everything mentioned above. [The liturgy of baptisms, prayers and so on.] But if the teacher should himself turn away and teach something different, undermining these things, do not listen to him . . .
Let every apostle who comes to you be welcomed as the Lord. But he should not remain more than a day. If he must, he may stay one more. But if he stays three days, he is a false prophet . . . Not everyone who speaks in the Spirit is a prophet, but only one who conducts himself like the Lord. Thus the false prophet and the prophet will both be known by their conduct . . . Do not listen to anyone who says in the Spirit, "Give me money" (or something else) . . . If the one who comes is simply passing through, help him as much as you can. He should not stay with you more than two or three days, if need be. If he wants to remain with you, and is a tradesman, let him work and eat. If he does not have a trade—use your foresight to determine how he as a Christian may live among you without being idle."[367]

In these very early days it is clear that the Church retained important democratic elements of the original Joshua cult and that officials were *elected*. The Didache urges the community to "elect for yourselves bishops and deacons who are worthy of the Lord, gentle men who are not fond of money, who are true and approved. For these also conduct the ministry of the prophets and teachers among you."[368] The early literature of the Church shows how, from this jumble of itinerant preachers, teachers and prophets, *a full-time apparatus* began to develop, although originally its election was completely democratic. It would be inevitable, once a community in a particular place had a sizeable degree of support, that they would come to prefer their own respected leaders, as against itinerants, who were not always what they claimed to be.

Acts describes how "when the number of the disciples was multiplied" it was no longer possible for "the twelve" (presumably, the disciples), to be expected to "serve at table" and at the same time continue with their ministry. The congregation, therefore, were invited to elect seven *deacons* from among themselves. In the early Church, the deacons, both male and female, were elected from the assembly to manage the affairs of the community. Where the primitive communism of the early congregation was still the driving force, it was the *elected* deacons who administered the funds and organised the resources of the community. Where there were several communities—as would have been the case in large cities, for example—it became necessary to have another Church official to oversee the many deacons—this was the job of the *bishop*. It is interesting that whereas in the mid first century Paul was writing his epistles to *communities*, only forty or fifty years later the early Church leader Ignatius was writing his epistles to *bishops* at the head of communities.

---

367   *Didache*, 11
368   *Didache*, 15

"In the brotherhoods and societies of Asia Minor, the administrative and financial officials bore the title of *Epimeletes* or *Episkopos* (observer or overseer). The same name was also applied in the government of cities to certain administrative officials. Hatch, who traces this evolution in detail and describes it in a book, to which we owe much information on the subject, quotes the Roman jurist Charisius as follows: 'Episcopi (bishops) are those who supervise the bread and other purchasable things, serving for the daily sustenance of the city population' . . . the bishop, therefore, was an administrative official particularly concerned with the proper feeding of the population. It was natural to give the same title to the administrator of the Christian 'peoples' house'."[369]

The early bishops, like the deacons, were *elected* by the congregation. And inevitably, given the nature of the Church and the standing within the community of the person elected as bishop, the administrative leader of the Church became transformed into essentially the *spiritual* leader and his administrative duties were undertaken by his immediate servants. It was the bishops who more and more laid claim to authority in the Church. As Marx wrote many times, "conditions determine consciousness" and the ideology of the Church, increasingly determined by the writings and meetings of bishops, *began to reflect the changed economic and social position of the leadership*. It was natural to suppose, Kautsky wrote, that it was these men, "who represented the opportunistic revisionism in the Christian congregation, that they strove to attenuate the hatred against the rich man in the congregation, to weaken the teachings of the congregation to an extent that would cause the wealthy to feel more at home in it."[370]

The letter referred to as that of *1 Clement to the Corinthians*, written very late in the first century, is actually anonymous, but is allegedly written by the supposed third bishop of Rome. It was a long tract basically complaining about the Corinthian congregation having the temerity to depose their bishop and it was notable for the venom it reserved for those who did the overthrowing. Clement decried what he called a "detestable and unholy sedition", which was clearly "inflamed to a pitch of madness" by a few "headstrong and self-willed persons". He complained that the Corinthians' former reputation, that they "walked after the ordinances of God, submitting yourselves to your rulers", had been damaged and that the Church was overtaken by "jealousy and envy, strife and sedition, persecution and tumult, war and captivity". "So men were stirred up," he wrote, "the mean against the honourable, the ill reputed against the highly reputed, the foolish against the wise, the young against the elder." Worst of all, Clement complained, was that the displaced leaders had been *good people!* ". . . the greatest

---

[369] Kautsky, p 436
[370] Kautsky, p 439

and most righteous pillars of the Church." He went on to explain how dangerous it is to submit to rebellious views.

> "For we shall bring upon us no common harm, but rather great peril, if we surrender ourselves recklessly to the purposes of men who launch out into strife and seditions, so as to estrange us from that which is right."

Far better, he argued, to "be obedient unto God, rather than follow those who in arrogance and unruliness have set themselves up as leaders in abominable jealousy". Clement's view was that all members of the flock had to be content with their lot in life, their station as it were. For the first time in any Christian literature, this letter betrays a clear distinction between the laity and the priesthood: "Let each man be subject unto his neighbour, according as also he was appointed with his special grace." The positions of the Church bishops and deacons, he argued, had been passed down directly from the evangelisation of the original converts of the Apostles.

> "For unto the high priest his proper services have been assigned, and to the priests their proper office is appointed, and upon the Levites their proper ministrations are laid. The layman is bound by the layman's ordinances."

Those kicked out, in a nutshell, "we consider to be unjustly thrust out from their ministration." Clement complained that the sedition had already brought despair to a lot of people, "And your sedition still continueth".[371] His solution to the problem was that the sedition needed to be "rooted out quickly" and those who "laid the foundation for it" needed to submit themselves for their punishment and chastisement to the Church leaders.

The letter of Clement was expressed in the same political language that might be used by any spokesman for the imperial state and it is clear that the author—in stark contrast, for example, to the author of Revelation—had not only come to terms with Roman governance, but had come to embrace its political framework. "Let us forsake idle and vain thoughts;" the author wrote, "and let us conform to the glorious and venerable rule which hath been handed down to us". Clement, in other words, didn't question Roman rule at all. On the contrary, "he gives theological legitimacy to this rule . . . both Clement's perception of the conflict in Corinth and the aim that he seeks to achieve with his letter are indissolubly bound up with his Roman political perspective."[372]

We see in this epistle the dawn of the power of the bishops. As the epistle of Clement shows, by the beginning of the second century, new theological arguments were being advanced (and remain to this day) to the effect that bishops should be *appointed,* on the grounds that they follow a *line of succession* from the original apostles, and hence from Jesus himself. It is also interesting in that it was probably

---

[371]   1 Clement, translated by J B Lightfoot.

[372]   Wengst, *Pax Romana*, p 107/114

the first evidence of the Church of *Rome* using its wealth and prestige to throw its theological weight about and insisting on its advice being followed by another, smaller community. The primitive democracy of the early Church was already beginning to give way to a more rigid and hierarchical system of command and control.

As an aside, it is worth remarking that here again, in the epistle of 1 Clement, there are frequent references to Jesus Christ, his "sacrifice" and "blood", but *there are no specific historical references at all to his life and work*. This is all the more strange, considering that the author made so many references to the virtues and good works of many figures from the Old Testament—like Noah, Moses, Enoch, David, Lot and so on. This may again suggest that at the time of writing a narrative biography had not yet been worked out. It should be said that some Christians have tried to read bits of 1 Clement as if they were directly dependent on the gospels, like the phrase, "show mercy, that ye be shown mercy", but these references are dubious at best and are more likely to have been common sayings for many years. As we shall argue, the composition of the Gospels of Matthew, Luke and Acts, are set in the same historical period as the letter of 1 Clement and, like the letter itself, are a reflection of the growth of the power and significance of the bishops.

Chapter Summary:

- The first 'Joshua' cults were based on the expectation of apocalypse and messianic deliverance and, like the Essenes, they had a primitive communist form of organisation.

- The Dead Sea Scrolls are not directly linked to Christianity but give a glimpse of the messianic fervour within the revolutionary elements of Jewish society

- The biblical figure of Joshua/Jesus was an *amalgam* of incomplete memories of different prophets, leaders and 'messiahs' of the time.

- None of the earliest Christian works—including the writings of Paul—make reference to episodes, parables, miracles or examples from the life of a historical Jesus.

- Paul's Church, which became modern Christianity, was a spin-off from the original Jerusalem congregation and was completely at odds with the primitive communism, poverty and egalitarianism of the Joshua cult. The official history of the church, including the New Testament, glosses over the depth and bitterness of the split between Paul and the Jerusalem community.

- The early Christian communities were broadly democratic and had elected leaders, but as the congregations increased in size and number, a bureaucracy of bishops and deacons multiplied within it.

Chapter 8

The Gospels and the Church Bureaucracy

In this chapter, we will look more closely at when and why the New Testament gospels were written, showing that the order in which they appear in the Bible is not the order in which they were created. We shall argue that these allegedly biographical accounts of Jesus were written seventy to a hundred years after the events they purport to describe and that each successive biography was more elaborate than the previous one. The circulation of a biographical account of the life of Jesus was a reflection of the influence of Greek culture and religious tradition on what had been a primitive Christian cult and which had by now transformed its central Joshua figure, first into a real hero with a biographical narrative and eventually into a god. In fact, all of the theological and mythical motifs in the New Testament were anticipated in the Old Testament and in Greek myths: the messiah, virgin birth, redemption by sacrifice, 'love thy neighbour as thyself', resurrection and so on. But such an elaboration of the gospels was also a reflection of the material interests of a burgeoning Church hierarchy which used the elevation of the status of the disciples as a means, indirectly, of elevating themselves as bishops. Lastly, we shall argue that the Church did not grow as a result of any theological superiority, but directly from the social, political and economic crisis of Roman society.

. . . .

Although the gospels rely on old sayings like those in the early Gospel of Thomas and the even earlier Jewish Scripture, the whole style and form of the gospels is radically different to earlier Jewish messianic literature and much more in keeping with the Graeco-Roman style of writing. Despite being written in a later period, all four gospels and Acts retain faint echoes of *real* revolutionary events and the radical politico-religious movements from which the Christian communities had sprung many decades earlier.

How, then, did the gospels come to be written? The earliest surviving copies date from about 200 CE, although there is a clear consensus among Christian scholars about when the gospels were supposed to have been written.

"Most scholars think that Mark is our earliest surviving account of Jesus' life, written somewhere around 65 or 70 CE; that Matthew and Luke were produced ten or fifteen years later, possibly 80-85 CE; and that John was the last of the canonical accounts, written near the end of the first century, around 90 or 95 CE."[373]

These dates are ten to twenty years earlier than more sceptical scholars would accept and it goes without saying that that Christians have a vested interest in pushing the dates as far back as they can, to be as near as possible to the supposed time of the life of Jesus. It is for this reason that two of the gospels are attributed directly to his disciples, although the text would indicate that they were written anonymously.

If we examine for a moment the first narrative gospel to be written—that of Mark—we see that it shows only the vaguest appreciation of time-scales and sequences of events. There is no reference to the birth or childhood of Jesus and in chapter 1 verse 9 Jesus suddenly makes an appearance as he "came from Nazareth". Within a few more verses, out of the blue as it were, the start of his ministry begins with the words: "Jesus came to Galilee preaching the gospel." In the first day, if the text is read literally, Jesus recruited four disciples, taught in a synagogue, drove out an 'unclean spirit', cured a fever, and attained such fame that by the end of the day he was preaching to hundreds:

> "And at even, when the sun did set, they brought unto him all that were diseased, and them that were possessed with devils. And all the city was gathered together at the door. And he healed many that were sick of divers diseases, and cast out many devils; and suffered not the devils to speak, because they knew him."[374]

By chapter 3, his followers number in thousands, from as far away as Idumea, Tyre, Sidon and across the River Jordan. The author of Mark includes the famous incident of Jesus feeding the five thousand with only a few loaves and fishes. Yet the same miracle—this time feeding only four thousand—is repeated somewhat later.

Simply reading the Gospel as a piece, it is clear that *the text was not meant to be taken as a literal narrative*. The time-frames are clearly *a symbolic* representation, an *allegorical* description of how the good works and ministry of the Joshua character *might* have taken place. What it represents, as Kautsky puts it, is "the product of the evolution of legend". The later gospels of Luke, Matthew and John are embellishments of the first, with some bits directly copied and with additional sayings and stories not found in Mark. Elements of common mythological and magical themes were written into them, including the virgin birth, miracle cures and so on, many of which are copies from earlier stories in the Hebrew Scriptures or borrowed from other Near Eastern legends. (Many of the same miracles and visions were to reappear yet again in the legends that grew up around Mohammed, the Prophet of Islam).

---

[373]   Ehrman, *Lost Christianities*, p 20.
[374]   Mark, 1, 32-34.

"Just as Pharaoh heard of the predestined child's arrival and sought to kill him by killing all the infant males, so did Herod the Great with Jesus. And just as Moses' father refused to accept the general decision of divorce and received a heavenly message through Miriam announcing his child's destiny, so Joseph considered but rejected divorce from Mary [Miriam] upon receiving an angelic message announcing his child's destiny. Moses would 'save my people' from Egypt, but Jesus would 'save his people from their sins'"[375]

RG Price, in his book *Jesus, a very Jewish Myth*, uses two whole pages to tabulate two elements of the crucifixion scene in Matthew's Gospel, setting them alongside sections of Psalms 22 and 69, as well as parts of the Book of Isaiah. It has to be said that there is hardly a single element in the New Testament story, including the dying cry of Jesus, "My God, my God, why hast thou forsaken me?"[376], that hasn't come from the Old Testament. Likewise, Arnold Toynbee, in *A Study of History*, listed no fewer than eighty-seven points of comparison between a variety of Hellenistic saviour figures and Jesus. He noted twenty four similarities with the legend of Hercules alone. He concluded:

"This finding suggests that the legend of Herakles may be an important common source from which the story of Jesus on the one side and the stories of the pagan historical heroes on the other side may have derived some of their common features."[377]

It has also been suggested by some writers that the gospel writers plundered Mithraic legends wholesale to make up their own Jesus stories[378]. Long after the gospels were set down, Tertullian was to describe the adoption by the Mithras cult of similar practices to Christianity as the work of the Devil, conveniently missing out the fact that the Mithras cult *pre-dated* the writing of the gospels.

". . . the devil . . . by the mystic rites of his idols, vies even with the essential portions of the sacraments of God. He, too, baptises some that is, his own believers and faithful followers; he promises the putting away of sins by a layer (of his own); and if my memory still serves me, Mithras there, (in the kingdom of Satan) sets his marks on the forehead of his soldiers; celebrates also the oblation of bread, and introduces an image of a resurrection . . ."[379]

---

[375] Crossan, *Jesus, a revolutionary biography*, p 15.

[376] Psalm 22, 1

[377] Toynbee, *A Study of History*, p 475

[378] See Humphreys, *Jesus Never Existed*, pp110-111

[379] Tertullian, *The Prescription against heresies*, chapter 40

It is clear, therefore, that a variety of Jewish, Hellenistic and Near Eastern sources were used to make up and elaborate a biography to suit the needs of the growing Christian cult. For the story of the birth of Jesus, Matthew alone adds the story of the three kings attending the infant as well as King Herod's slaughter of the innocents, while Luke replaces the three kings with three shepherds, and adds an inn and a manger. The authors of these two gospel versions have composed full genealogies for Jesus, in the case of Matthew starting with Abraham and in the case of Luke starting as far back as Adam. The Gospel of John is different from the first three so-called synoptic gospels, in that it contains no parables and says little about the poor and the meek. It has often been labelled as Gnostic because of its more metaphysical and enigmatic imagery.

The twelve disciples is an allusion to the twelve tribes of Israel. The Hebrew Testament and Jewish Pseudepigrapha were all circulating widely in the early Christian communities and these provide many of the sayings and phrases that have found their way into the four gospels like "the meek shall inherit the earth" (Psalm 37) and "love thy neighbour as thyself" (Leviticus, chapter 19). *All of the theological and mythical motifs in the New Testament were anticipated in the Old: the messiah, virgin birth, redemption by sacrifice, resurrection.* Even the Sermon on the Mount is no more than a series of disconnected traditional sayings and aphorisms, the sermon scenario serving as a literary device to hold them together. Some of the sayings are enigmatic in the extreme and virtually devoid of any straightforward meaning. Modern theologians hold them up to the light, turn them this way and that, dissect them letter by letter and still cannot agree on what they mean. Phrases like, "if any man come to me, and hate not his father, and mother, and wife, and children, and brethren, and sisters, yea, and his own life also, he cannot be my disciple"[380], have generated acres of print and tons of books, and end up meaning . . . whatever the theologian wants them to mean.

Whilst Christians insist that the fundamental message of Christianity is peace on earth, they cannot account for Jesus saying, "Think not that I am come to send peace on earth; I came not to send peace but a sword. For I am come to set a man at variance against his father and the daughter against her mother and the daughter in law against her mother in law."[381] The answer, they will say, is that these are meant symbolically and not literally. Thus, the New Testament is taken *literally* when it pleases and *metaphorically* when it doesn't. Some Christian scholars cling almost desperately to the notion of a real, historical Jesus, even when they are obliged to acknowledge the *legendary* nature of much of the gospel narrative. Thus, John Dominic Crossan accepts that prophecy and history "interweave" and suggests that the first followers of Jesus:

---

[380]   Luke, 14, 26.
[381]   Matthew, 10, 34-35

". . . knew almost nothing whatsoever about the details of his crucifixion, death, or burial. What we have now in those detailed passion accounts is not *history remembered,* but *prophecy historicised.*"[382]

Crossan doesn't explain *why* his first followers "knew almost nothing" about the death and resurrection of Jesus, since they are the entire focus of their religious faith, but his acceptance of what is in effect, *history made up*, is very revealing.

An important straw to which many Christian historians cling is the tradition of sayings that were found in the Gospel of Thomas and which are implicit in the hypothetical gospel prototype called "Q" (from the German word, *Quelle*, meaning 'source'). But many of these sayings are no more than common-or-garden moral maxims that would have had an equivalent in any society. The fact that they pop up here and there in the writings of the early Church fathers does not show the influence of the gospels but simply that such proverbs were common. In his version of Q, Richard Valantasis creates one such saying from Matthew 16, 2 and Luke 12, 54. He has Jesus saying in the evening, "Fair weather, for the sky shines fiery red" and in the morning, "Today is winter, for the lowering sky shines fiery red."[383] In other words, where the rest of us thought that "Red sky at night, shepherd's delight . . ." etc was a common saying of farmers and peasants from the dawn of time, the rather laughable suggestion here is that it was a saying invented by Jesus . . . and if not invented by him, it is an admission that *everyday sayings* are put in his mouth.

Second century fiction

In his book, *Who Wrote the New Testament*, Burton Mack, professor of early Christianity at the School of Theology in Claremont, USA, provides a good account of how the myths arose and the written gospels followed. Strangely, for a book with the subtitle, *The Making of the Christian Myth*, the author finds it hard to tear himself away from the very myths he analyses. Thus, without backing it by a single piece of evidence (other than the New Testament), he suggests that the "Jesus movements started in Galilee during the 30s and 40s of the first century CE"[384]. Elsewhere, he repeats the same supposition, that most of the early Christians were "Galileans". Mack's entire book, in fact, is written within a framework which *presupposes* the existence and the ministry of Jesus. But it nevertheless describes quite effectively how, after his death, myths developed and blossomed into the legends that formed the gospel accounts.

"As the various systems of thought began to take shape in the several branches of the Jesus movement, the 'voice' and 'image' of Jesus changed

---

[382] Crossan, *Jesus, A Revolutionary Biography*, p 145. (italics in original)
[383] Valantasis, *The New Q*, p 33
[384] Mack, *Who wrote the New Testament*, p 43.

to match the shifts in the content of his 'teachings' . . . each group created Jesus, not in its own image exactly, but in the image appropriate for the founder of the school it had become or wanted to become . . ."[385]

Mack thinks—and we agree with him completely on this—that "the picture of Jesus portrayed in the New Testament gospels . . . did not occur until Mark wrote his story of Jesus." He goes on to discuss the early sayings source "Q", from which both Luke and Matthew are supposed to have taken much of their gospel material. It has to be born in mind that Q, is a *hypothetical construction* and, other than by a literary analysis of Luke and Matthew, there is no evidence of its existence. That hasn't stopped Christian scholars, including Mack, breaking Q down into still smaller pieces, called Q1, Q2 and Q3, each with its own characteristic content and date of writing. Looking for Christian sayings sources in the *historically verified* literature of Jewish messianists and in books like the Gospel of Thomas, with its 114 sayings, is one thing, but such detailed analysis of a *hypothetical* Q source is a forlorn exercise at best. This hasn't prevented scholars from publishing their own complete versions of Q.[386] Until fragments of a Q document are found with the original text, or some citation of the original text, it has no more reality than the strange universes created by theoretical physicists from mathematical constructs. For Mack to write that Q . . . "is the earliest written record we have from the Jesus movement", is stretching a *hypothetical* source rather too far into the realms of reality, much like his Jesus.

In the Gospel of Thomas (which did exist) and in Q (which is hypothetical), Mack notes that "there is no biographical interest in Jesus' life, whether in Galilee or in reference to a crucifixion and resurrection in Jerusalem."[387] Quite so, and, as we have pointed out, that is true of *all* early Christian writing, most significantly Paul. But this is not due, as Mack implies, to a lack of "interest"; it is due to the fact that the biography *hadn't been composed* by that time. It is Mack's hypothesis that there was a historical Jesus and it was the changes in the second half of the first century that "turned the Jesus movement into a cult of a god called Jesus Christ". But it is our view that there was no historical Jesus (except as a *generic* messiah figure) and that *the biography was created* to match the theology that was being developed by the movement. The biography was laced here and there with the memories of real historical events, but often inaccurately, as is inevitable with the transmission by oral tradition. Freeman quotes an example showing the limitations of personal memory, even in modern times:

"When the diaries kept daily by a selected group of British observers during the Second World War were compared to their own memories thirty years later, there was virtually no correspondence at all. 'Any relationship between the incident they had described in the diary and

---

[385]   Mack, *Who wrote the New Testament,* p 46.

[386]   See for example, *The New Q, a fresh translation with commentary,* by Richard Valantasis.

[387]   Mack, *Who wrote the New Testament,* p 61.

the story they told in 1975 was almost entirely coincidental. They got everything wrong: date, places, the sequence of events . . .'"[388]

If that is true in an overwhelmingly literate modern society, how much more true would it be of a society in which literacy was the preserve of a small minority? An extremely useful idea that Mack does add to the mix is that the myth of Jesus developed as a result of the shift of focus within the early Christian community, from the direct conversion of Jews in synagogues, which is evident in the journeys of Paul and in Acts, to the conversion of gentile god-fearers, who were attached to the synagogues, and other gentiles who may have had no previous contact at all with the synagogues. An increasing proportion of the new converts were, as the New Testament describes them, "Greeks", in contradistinction to "Jews". The Greek traditions that they brought into the Christian communities demanded new things of their prophets and preachers—for instance, that their messiah should have a real history with real deeds, like the Greek gods themselves. Above all, there was an expectation that he should be a god himself.

> "We see the myth developing just at that point where a Jesus movement was turning into a cult of the Christ. ['Christ' being the Greek rendition of 'Messiah'] The need to justify the inclusion of gentiles called forth a venture in mythmaking that shifted attention away from Jesus the teacher and his teachings to focus on his death as a dramatic event that established the movement's claim to be the people of God."[389]

What became, in Mack's expression, "mythmaking on the cosmic scale", elevated the idea of a Joshua-messiah—and lest we forget, in its original language, a "salvation-messiah"—into a living god, known henceforth as Jesus Christ. It was in exactly the same way that the expression 'Son of Man', originally an expression meaning mankind *in general* in early Jewish writing, evolved into the specific messiah figure of Christ as it came to be used in the New Testament. Paul's Jesus, who had been a *generic* figure, was transformed by Mark into a *real* person and transformed again by Luke, Matthew, Acts and especially John, into a living *god*. In Mark, there are only three occasions when Jesus claims that he is the son of God, but in Matthew the assertion appears thirty-one times and over a hundred times in John. The theological evolution was complete: from a generic term for *salvation*, to a *generic person*, to a *real man*, and eventually, as Jesus Christ, to a *god*. The biographical stories borrowed common motifs and themes from Greek, Roman, Persian and Egyptian mythology—a star prophesy, a virgin birth, miraculous signs, the twelve, resurrection and redemption—and became a history fit for a god. The first gospel writer was Mark, who wrote an allegorical biography fitting the concept of Jesus as it had developed.

---

[388] Freeman, *A New History of Early Christianity*, p 328
[389] Mack, *Who wrote the New Testament*, p. 86.

"Before Mark there was no such story of the life of Jesus. Neither the earlier Jesus movements nor the congregations of the Christ had imagined such a portrayal of Jesus' life. It was Mark's composition that gathered together the earlier traditions, used the recent history of Jerusalem to set the stage for Jesus' time, crafted the plot, spelled out the motivations, and so created the story of Jesus that was to become the gospel truth for Christianity. All the other narrative gospels would start with Mark. None would change his basic plot. And the plot would become the standard account of Christian origins for the traditional Christian imagination . . . Ever after Christians would imagine Mark's fiction as history . . ."[390]

Reading *Who Wrote the New Testament*, it is hard to see why Mack hangs on to a historical Jesus figure at all, because it is not necessary at all for the greater part of his analysis.

It is more than likely that the name of the town of Nazareth is also fictitious: as we have indicated, there is no reference to it in ancient sources, although every other city, town and village is mentioned. It is easy to see where the name might have arisen. It is an imaginary town written to correspond to the term *Nazirite* or *Nazarene*, which is not related in any way to a place, but to a way of life characterised by asceticism and a simple life-style. In the Old Testament, Samson, on account of his long hair was described as a *Nazirite*: "there hath not come a razor upon mine head; for I have been a Nazirite unto God, from my mother's womb"[391] The root of the word is also linked to the concept of separation, as a religious sectarian or a hermit might stand apart from the majority of people. In the Book of Numbers, for example, God instructs Moses to say to the Children of Israel:

"When either man or woman shall separate themselves to vow a vow of a *Nazirite*, to separate themselves unto the Lord: he shall separate himself from wine and strong drink, and shall drink no vinegar of wine, or vinegar of strong drink, neither shall he drink any liquor of grapes, nor eat moist grapes, or dried. All the days of his separation shall he eat nothing that is made of the vine tree, from the kernels even to the husk. All the days of the vow of his separation there shall be no razor come upon his head . . . And this is the law of the *Nazirite*, when the days of his separation are fulfilled."[392]

Nazirite, therefore, was a common term used to describe those itinerant preachers who lived frugal and ascetic lives, and many of the Essenes would have been so described. It would not be surprising if the members of the early Messianic Joshua cults, holding property in common and appealing chiefly to the poorest sections

---

[390] Mack, *Who wrote the New Testament,* p 152.
[391] Judges, 16, 17.
[392] Numbers, 6, 2-5/13

of society, were known, (as they are described at one point in the Acts of the Apostles) as "the sect of the Nazarenes"—because it fitted perfectly with their public image of asceticism and poverty. John the Baptist, as he is described in the New Testament—living on honey and insects in the wilderness and with a propensity for baptism—would certainly have fitted this label. Jewish first century writing in the *Talmud* continued to refer to Christians as *Nazari*, or something similar and the Arabic word for Christians has a similar root. It was from this that the *fictitious city* of *Nazareth* gets its origin. Nazareth exists as a town today, of course, but that is entirely due to the establishment of a Christian tradition based on the gospels.

There is another example of early Christians making a very similar mistake over the roots of a name. As we have said, the *Ebionites* were named, by the agreement of the overwhelming majority of modern scholars, from the word for "poor". Thus, the Ebionites were known as "The Poor". But that didn't stop the second century Christian writer Tertullian inventing a founder for the sect, whose name was "Ebion". "Nazareth" was no more a real place than "Ebion" was a real person.

Bishops and Deacons

The real drivers behind the development of the gospel myths were the *material interests* of the new leadership of the Church. The theology did not develop by accident—it reflected the Christian community *at a time when it was beginning to create its own hierarchy of leaders*—bishops and deacons—and it was accelerating away from the primitive communism and simple democracy of the original Jerusalem cult. What was new about the gospels and their accompanying book, Acts, was a clear shift from the fervent and *revolutionary* tone of much of the early Christian literature (Paul being the exception) towards a milk-and-water philosophy, albeit retaining fragments of the original zeal, which was more fitted to *coexistence within the established Roman state*. The gospels and Acts mark the shift in focus, towards a *more central role for the apostles* of Jesus and their inheritors, the leaders of the Church.

> "The 'historical' Jesus is not earlier but later than Paul; and as such he had always existed merely as an idea, as a pious fiction in the minds of members of the community. The New Testament with its four gospels is not previous to the Church, but the latter is antecedent to them; and the gospels are the derivatives, consequently forming a support for the propaganda of the Church, and being without any claim to historical significance."[393]

The author of the Gospel of Luke is generally thought to be the same as the author of the Acts of the Apostles. In the much earlier writings of Paul—and Eisenman would argue, in the Dead Sea Scrolls too—it is clear that there were bitter

---

[393] Drews, *The Christ Myth*, p 286.

ideological differences between him and the Jerusalem leaders, chiefly Peter and James. But in Acts, these differences are reconciled and Peter is now portrayed as being largely in agreement with Paul. This unification of the apostolic tradition was an essential part of the process of consolidation of the positions of bishops and other community leaders. At approximately the same time that Clement of Rome was suggesting that bishops should be appointed as a *line of succession* from the apostles—in the early first century—Acts was being written, as well as the gospels of Luke, Matthew and John, to emphasise the central role of the apostles of Jesus.

> "The idea behind much of the apostolic literature written around the turn of the second century was that disciples who had known Jesus personally formulated the instructions received from him and passed them on to the next generation of leaders. They needed texts. And so the writing of texts in the name of some disciple or apostle became standard practice."[394]

The bishops, Mack adds, "did not object to this literature, for they themselves were eventually graced with similar legends." Indeed they were. Not only was the apostolic tradition being firmly established, but there now began a long procession of "saints", eventually numbering in their thousands. A large proportion of these were to be bishops and popes who were almost automatically elevated to their super-human status in much the same way as Roman emperors were elevated to become deities, although admittedly in the former case it was usually a respectable time after their deaths.

Among the many texts written during this period were those mentioned which were falsely attributed to Peter: the *Gospel of Peter*, the *Preaching of Peter*, the *Acts of Peter* and the *Apocalypse of Peter*. Not one of them reflects the staunchly *Jewish*-Christianity of the Jerusalem leader who appears in the epistles of Paul in the mid-first century. None of these have found their way into the New Testament. These compositions were part of the literary drive to link Peter to what was fast becoming the mainstream Church, as distinct to its original Jerusalem tradition and, additionally, to associate Peter with the city of Rome, whose leaders were seeking to establish their pre-eminence among Christian communities.

Once the floodgates were opened, dozens of gospels were written, all claiming to be real narrative accounts of the life and activities of Jesus. The Church leaders gave free rein to their imaginations as they elaborated even further on the gospel accounts of Jesus. Eusebius quotes, for example, part of a work by the early second century Bishop Papias of Hierapolis in Asia Minor who wrote, "I shall not hesitate to append to the interpretations all that I ever learnt well from the presbyters . . . for I did not suppose that the information from books would help me so much as the word of a living and surviving voice." The "surviving voice" that Papias relies on, eighty or ninety years after the supposed event, is no more than oral folklore and fable, but he feels able to use this to freely supplement the legend of Jesus. At about

---

[394]   Mack, *Who wrote the New Testament,* p 202.

the same time, Justin Martyr wrote his own account of the crucifixion of Jesus, the passion narrative in which he incorporated elements of the gospels with added material from Psalm 22. This work, one scholar comments, "illustrates the living tendency to incorporate additional material into the basic Passion Narrative."[395] It only needs adding, of course, that the "living tendency to incorporate additional material" did not begin with the *completed* gospels, but that the gospels were themselves a part of that tendency.

In *Lost Scriptures* and its companion book, *Lost Christianities*, Bart Ehrman goes into all the details of the debates raging in the Church in the first two or three centuries and the many gospels, epistles and other writings that were produced but which failed to make it into the official canon. Ehrman lists sixteen additional gospels, six Acts, thirteen epistles and nine apocalypses and related literature, *none of which made it into the New Testament,* although some of these books circulated widely and were highly regarded by early Christians. Long after Mark, Matthew, Luke and John were committed to writing, and in some cases simultaneous to their writing, other legends were collecting around different versions and different gospels. As we shall mention in the following section, yet another version of the birth of Jesus surfaced in the Koran hundreds of years later. Some of these, like the gospels of Mary, Philip and the Gospel of Truth, do not contain any narrative description of the life of Jesus. As is the case with so much early Christian literature, the saviour exists out of normal time and space. But the majority of them are variations on the theme of the original Mark. The end of the first and the beginning of the second century was the heyday of the written legends of Jesus, only four of which have official sanction, despite the obvious copying from one to another and clear contradictions between them.

The *Gospel of the Nazareans* was a variety of the gospel of Matthew, suited to those Christians retaining Jewish laws and practices, close to the Ebionites. According to the early Christian father, Jerome, this variety of Matthew was considered by them to be *the* authentic version, although its 'pick n'mix' attitude to relaying the legends must have been typical of the time. A different *Gospel of the Ebionites* again shows a tradition of writing a gospel to suit needs, being a sort of pastiche of Mark, Matthew and Luke, with differences ironed out. An entirely new tradition—showing that the accumulation of folk-tales and oral tradition did not finish with the first three gospels—was the gospel according to the Hebrews. This book, written in the early second century, included new legends or reinterpretations of old ones. Like many non-canonical gospels, it no longer exists in totality and is only known through quotes of its detractors.

Another *Unknown Gospel* was discovered on a fragment of papyrus in 1935, and many scholars date this too as early as the canonical four. The surviving fragment includes four stories, some of which appear in Mark, Matthew or Luke and one of which has no parallel in the canon. The most recent of the new gospels

---

395   Marion Soards, *Jesus and the Oral Gospel Tradition*, p 347

to be discovered was only published in 1991; it was largely based on the canonical works, but added new prophecies and miracles not accounted for in the canon, again showing that the myth-making continued a century or more after the events they purport to describe.

One of the most amusing of the non-canonical gospels is the *Infancy Gospel of Thomas*, written supposedly by the brother of Jesus and not to be confused with the much earlier *Gospel of Thomas*. In his introduction to it, Ehrman mentions that "For modern readers it is difficult to decide whether such stories were meant as serious accounts of Jesus' early life or simply as speculative and entertaining stories of the youthful Son of God."[396]. But he misses the point here. *All* the gospels—not excluding Mark, Matthew, Luke and John—are "speculative and entertaining stories" that describe what *may* have happened, even if they aren't as amusing as the Infancy gospel. In the latter, Jesus appears to be a nasty, vicious little bully. It relates one occasion when Jesus was going through a village and "a child ran up and banged into his shoulder." Where an apology or a minor threat might have sufficed to most children, this did not satisfy the Lord. "Jesus was aggravated and said to him, 'You will go no further on your way'. And right away the child fell down and died."[397] Jesus used his super-powers to effect nice little miracles, like fashioning live sparrows out of clay (a story that reappeared a few hundred years later in the Koran and which Islamic tradition then attached to Mohammed), but it was his bullying of other children and adults that worried his parents. Things got so bad that Mary and Joseph didn't want to let him loose out of the house. Joseph ordered his mother not to let him past the door, we are told, "for those who anger him die."[398]

Not content with extravagant elaborations of the life of Jesus, the gospel writers went into some detail about the early life of his mother, Mary. According to the proto-Gospel of James, Mary's own birth, like that of Jesus, was also miraculous and the rest of her life was without sin at all.

Another second century fable, *The Acts of John*, has an amusing story about our apostle as he travelled around spreading the word of Jesus. He was staying one night at a hostel when he found his bed was infested with bugs. He addressed his tormentors, saying: "I say to you, you bugs, be considerate; leave your home for this night and go to rest in a place which is far away from the servants of God!" The lice, of course, kindly agreed and John had a good night's sleep. The bugs had stayed near the door and in the morning, John gave them leave to return to the bed so "the bugs hastened from the door to the bed, ran up the legs into the joints and disappeared."[399] We were not told whether or not these bugs would be rewarded for their considerate behaviour in the next life, but one would hope so.

Some of the later non-canonical writings clearly reflect the lingering controversies from the early Church over the direction it was taking. The *Letter*

---

[396]   Ehrman, *Lost Scriptures*, p 57.
[397]   *The Infancy Gospel of Thomas*, 4.
[398]   *The Infancy Gospel of Thomas*, 14
[399]   Ehrman, *Lost Scriptures*, p 97

of Peter to James and its *Reception*, for example, purport to be an epistle from the disciple of Jesus to James, "the lord and bishop of the holy church" and a description of the reception it got. The epistle contains a thinly disguised attacked on Paul, although he is only named as "the man who is my enemy". Scholars believe that the epistle is a work from within the Ebionite faction of early Christianity, opposing the Pauline traditions and arguing instead to uphold Jewish traditions and practices like circumcisions and dietary laws and it probably dates from the first half of the second century. Thus:

> ". . . some from among the Gentiles have rejected my lawful preaching and have preferred a lawless and absurd doctrine of the man who is my enemy. And indeed some have attempted whilst I am still alive, to distort my words by interpretations of many sorts, as if I taught the dissolution of the law". [400]

On reception of the letter, James is supposed to have assembled his elders to read it and noted that it had been passed on to "a good and religious candidate for the position of a teacher, a man who as one who has been *circumcised* is a believing Christian." Ehrman, says the document is "probably" from the third century, although he gives no evidence for that; in fact it might well be earlier, and associated in language, style and content with much of the so-called *pseudo-Clementine* literature which originated much earlier and which supported the general outlook of the Ebionite Church. Among the pseudo-Clementines are the *Homilies of Clement* in which Peter is again portrayed as the chief apostle and there is an attack on Paul, this time thinly disguised as the arch-heretic Simon Magus. Simon, it says:

> ". . . first and before me went to the Gentiles . . . I who came after him and followed him as the light follows the darkness, knowledge, ignorance and healing sickness. Thus, then, as the true prophet has said, a false gospel must first come from an impostor and only then, after the destruction of the holy place, can a true gospel be sent forth for the correction of the sects that are to come." [401]

New stories about Jesus continued to be created hundreds of years later within Muslim tradition, in which Jesus, or *Isa*, was seen as the last great prophet before Mohammed. Stories about a *Mahdi*—the coming of an Islamic saviour—were popular in mid-seventh century Arabian society and usually revolved around Jesus rather than Mohammed. This, as we shall argue later, is a reflection of the way that Christian myths were important constituents in the formation of Islamic tradition. According to the twelfth century chronicler, Ibn Asakir, Jesus was ranked above all other prophets. "In the end, his second coming as the *Mahdi* will conclude

---

[400]   Ehrman, *Lost Scriptures*, p 192
[401]   Ehrman, *Lost Scriptures*, p 197

the triumph of Islam over all religions and achieve ultimate peace on earth."[402] As a direct result of the Muslim defeats at the hands of the Christian crusaders, Ibn Asakir emphasised those traditions that portrayed Jesus as an austere ascetic, in contrast to the effete and pampered Muslim rulers who had allowed the 'killers of Jesus' (ie, the Christians) to defeat them. This is the description Ibn Asakir wrote of Jesus the ascetic:

> "Jesus son of Mary used to eat barley, walk on foot and did not ride donkeys. He did not live in a house, nor did he use lamps for light. He neither dressed in cotton nor touched women, nor used perfume. He never mixed his drink with anything, nor cooled it. He never greased or washed his hair or his beard. [When he slept] he never had anything between his skin and the ground [on which he lay] except his garment. He had no concern for lunch or dinner, and coveted nothing of the desires of this world. He used to consort with the weak, the chronically sick and the poor. Whenever food was offered him on [a platter], he would place it on the ground and he never ate meat. Of food he ate little, saying "[Even] this is too much for one who has to die and answer for his deeds."[403]

Most of this huge proliferation of legends, including theological arguments that ran counter to what was becoming an orthodox doctrine, was suppressed by the Church, at least in those areas which it controlled, and have only seen the light of day in modern times. Nevertheless, these stories circulated widely in the early Church and were so popular that many of them were treated as sacred scripture. There was no official Christian canon—no New Testament—for the first two hundred years of Christianity and a rather loose understanding for the next two hundred. Some of the old legends like the stories of the early childhood of Jesus (the less unsavoury ones) and the early life of Mary, still circulate in the Church today and because they fill a gap without directly conflicting with the canon they are taken as good coin. The Church, even today, will not stand in the way of a good fairy-story.

What was the social basis of the Church and why did it grow?

Why and how, then, did Christianity grow in three hundred years, from a relatively small sect to become so strong that it was recognised by the Roman Emperor? Christian scholarship is replete with the type of condescending superiority that puts their faith on a higher moral plain than paganism. "Its spiritual superiority over paganism", one writes, "was blindingly clear . . ."[404] This statement is pure

---

402   Suleiman A Mourad, *Ibn Asakir and Early Islamic History,* p 27
403   Cited by Suleiman A Mourad, *Ibn Asakir and Early Islamic History,* p 41
404   Veyne, *When our World became Christian,* p 15

self-righteousness, of course, and is necessarily devoid of any proof or evidence to back it up. We would argue that it was not the moral superiority of Christianity that drew converts, nor yet the activities of the Holy Spirit. The author of *A New History of Early Christianity* is at least a bit more honest: he is clearly stumped, when he writes, ". . . it is hard to say what drew people to Christianity"[405], although he gives a bit of a clue later. One thing is certain—it is the stuff of Hollywood epics to imagine that the mass of the population of the Roman Empire, ninety per cent of whom were illiterate, were converted to a new faith by the force of its theological or moral arguments.

It is the prevailing trend of opinion among Christian scholars to understand the spread of their faith from a purely *ideological* viewpoint. In *The Beginnings of Christianity*, for example, Andrew Welburn even suggests that the growth of monotheism was due a change in human psychological make-up. He approvingly cites another scholar whose view was that "the type of individual self-awareness we take for granted today *did not exist in ancient times*. Each man did not feel himself to have a centre of being within him . . ."[406] Deeply ingrained cultural habits may well affect the way that people view their relationship to the cosmos and to those around them, but there is no evidence for any change in the basic psychological capacities of human beings in the last few thousand years. Welburn continues:

> ". . . this radically new development of consciousness is of paramount importance for understanding the life of today. It is in ancient Israel that we see humanity beginning to tread the long road that leads to our modern sense of freedom and our demand for autonomy as spiritual agents in the world. It is also where we see the great barrier of guilt beginning to be erected, which it is part of the meaning and mission of Christianity to overcome."[407]

We cannot accept for a moment that millions of urban workers and illiterate peasants were somehow drawn into the Christian fold in order to be able to express their "autonomy as spiritual agents in the world". There may have been some religious attraction in the congregation that was not present in the synagogue or in the polytheism of Roman society, but we would suggest that this was a secondary factor, at best. To really understand the rise of Christianity from its roots in Palestine, it is necessary to look at the material conditions, the general *social milieu* in which it grew and the conditions of life for the masses in the Empire at that time. The evolution of the Church, Kautsky wrote, ". . . is easy to understand if we regard Christianity as the precipitation of certain class interests; but it cannot be understood if we consider Christianity merely as an ideological structure." [408]

---

405   Freeman, *A New History of Early Christianity*, p 130
406   Welburn, *The Beginning of Christianity*, p 64 (italics added)
407   Welburn, *The Beginning of Christianity*, p 66
408   Kautsky, p 415

More than a hundred years after it was written, the section of Kautsky's *Foundations* on the economic decline of Rome, still stands the test of time. Rome, he explained, was a *slave* state, resting on the labour of millions of the most wretched and impoverished in society. Slaves were imported in vast numbers from the outlying and newly-conquered parts of the Empire to work in the cities and on agricultural latifundia. A huge proportion of the total economic production of the empire was aimed solely at providing the ruling class with the wherewithal to live in the greatest possible splendour and opulence. Side by side with these two classes on opposite ends of the scale were:

> ". . . swarms of hundreds of thousands of freed citizens and freed slaves, also numerous impoverished remains of the peasantry, down-and-out tenants, wretched urban artisans and burden-carriers, as well as, finally, the *Lumpenproletariat* of the large cities, having the energy and self-reliance of the free citizens and yet having become economically superfluous in society, homeless, without any sense of security, depending absolutely on the crumbs which the great lords would throw to them of their own superfluity, moved either by generosity, or fear, or by the desire for peace."[409]

Roman society at the end of the republican period and the beginning of the imperial period, in the first four centuries of the modern era, was a society of "immense social oppositions, much class hatred and many class struggles, insurrections and civil wars, a boundless longing for a different, better life and the abolition of the existing order of society." As agricultural production declined and society stagnated, it was clear that slavery was leading society into a blind alley.

> "Society would have to be placed once more on the basis of peasant operation before it could begin a fresh ascent. But Roman civilization was incapable of even taking this step; for it had lost the necessary peasants . . . the ancient slave-owning economy was digging its own grave. In the form which it finally attained in the Roman Empire, this economy was based on war. Only ceaseless victorious wars, a continued subjection of new nations, and uninterrupted expansion of the imperial territory could furnish the immense quantities of cheap slave labour material which it needed . . . the disappearance of the free peasants meant the disappearance of soldiers for the Roman armies. It became necessary more and more to replace the number of soldiers liable to militia service by mercenary volunteers and professional soldiers . . . more and more numerous became the barbarian mercenaries in the Roman armies . . . there now begins an effort in the Roman empire to hold it together against the enemies threatening from without . . . Thus, in the first century of our era, the influx of cheap slaves

---

[409] Kautsky, p 71.

came to an abrupt stop. More and more it became necessary to *breed* slaves."[410]

During the period of the rise of Christianity, the Roman Empire was in inexorable economic decline with only brief periods of stability interrupting a general downward spiral. Moreover, the impact of economic decay was made worse by the effects of natural disasters like famine, as soil fertility declined, and by disease. Troops campaigning in the eastern provinces brought back to metropolitan Europe a new disease—smallpox—and in the next hundred years there were successive waves of epidemics throughout the empire. Between 251 and 266 CE disease was so rife in Italy that at one point Rome was losing as many as 5,000 lives in a single day. The combined effects of war, famine and disease were beginning to depopulate large parts of the countryside. Diocletian, emperor from 285 to 305 CE, was forced to promulgate laws to prevent agricultural workers from moving away or fleeing to the cities. Not coincidentally, this was also one of the few periods of official state-sponsored persecution of Christians, as Diocletian looked about for scapegoats for economic and social ruin.

It was the cities especially that experienced significant declines in their populations. Kautsky quotes the work of another author, Ludo M Hartman, on the depopulation of the cities:

". . . assume that the city of Rome in the time of Augustus had attained about 1,000,000 inhabitants, that it remained at about the same level during the first century of the Imperial period and then in the age of the Severi [Roman emperors] went down to about 600,000; after this the number continued to decrease rapidly."[411]

Agricultural slaves, by the nature of their social condition, were neglectful of both the land on which they were forced to work and the tools with which they worked, so they were not very productive. Their lives were mean, brutal and short and they had no stake in maintaining the productivity of soil or quality of their tools. Slavery inevitably led, therefore, to the impoverishment of the soil and a decline in agricultural productivity. While slavery remained a significant feature of life in the cities—in domestic service, in crafts and in administrative positions—the poor productivity of agricultural slavery meant that it became less significant in the countryside. Catherine Hezser, in her overview in *Jewish Slavery in Antiquity*, pointed to the changed demography of the slaves:

"In early second century CE Egypt, for example, the Alexandrian grandee would employ more than a hundred slaves in his country residences. In the third and fourth century domestic slavery seems to have continued,

---

[410]   Kautsky, p 75
[411]   Kautsky, p 76

whereas references [in Roman literature] to agricultural slaves are rare. With regard to the Roman empire at large, MacMullen estimates that in the rural regions and smaller towns slaves amounted to only a few percent at any point in the first four and a half centuries of the era, while in the middle-sized or larger cities the picture we have seems to accord with a figure approaching 25 per cent of the general population."[412]

Yet despite the declining productivity of a shrinking imperial population, the burdens of militarism increased, as the ruling class fought desperately to defend its power, prestige and influence and indeed its very existence. As Kautsky put it, "a constant process of social disintegration set in".

"The migration of nations, the inundation of the Roman Empire by hosts of rude Germans did not mean the untimely destruction of a flourishing, advanced civilisation, but merely the termination of a process of dissolution of a dying civilisation."[413]

With only a few years of relative tranquillity here and there, the late third century was a period of unremitting crisis and turmoil.

"After 268, almost every Greek city ceased to issue inscribed local coins . . . in the 260s and 270s, new public buildings in the cities ceased to be identifiable by inscriptions and signs of new private buildings elude the archaeologist . . . During these dark and troubled years "barbarian" invaders troubled many of the most famous places in the Empire: Antioch (c 253), Ephesus (262/3), Miletus (c. 263), Caesarea in Cappadocia (260), Athens (267/8) and Alexandria (270/1). Conspicuously, this list includes cities which are credited with the largest populations in the Empire . . . in the early 270s a civil war which was fierce even by Alexandria's standards caused havoc in that fine city . . . Of the bigger cities, only Rome and Carthage survived without attack. Even so, they were not safe. In the early 250s, a plague touched them both . . . Between the 250s and 280s, the Roman Imperial coinage was debased in a spectacular phase of inflation. The Emperors changed with bewildering speed, until Diocletian restored stable rule in 284."[414]

Conditions determine consciousness. The social, political and economic crisis within Roman society provided ample raw material for the growth of Christianity. But as we shall see, this was not so much due to ideological struggle and theological

---

[412]   Hezser, *Jewish Slavery in Antiquity*, p 124.

[413]   Kautsky, p 84

[414]   Fox, *Pagans and Christians*, p 572.

debate, so much as to the social and community structures that the Church provided and which were almost unique within the Roman world.

Chapter Summary:

- Mark was the first gospel to be written, as an allegorical story. Luke and Matthew copied from Mark. John's Gospel was last.

- The biographical accounts of Jesus were written seventy to a hundred years after the events they purport to describe and each successive biography was more elaborate than the previous one. Christian tradition always pushes the date of gospel writing as far back in time as possible.

- All of the theological and mythical motifs in the New Testament were anticipated in the Old: the messiah, virgin birth, redemption by sacrifice, 'love thy neighbour as thyself', resurrection and so on.

- The elaboration of the gospels reflected the need of the Church hierarchy to elevate the status of the disciples and therefore, indirectly, of themselves as direct followers in a line of apostles.

- Through the influence of Greek culture and religious tradition, the generic salvation-Joshua of the primitive Christian cult was elevated first to a biographical hero and then to a god.

- The Church grew as a result of the social, political and economic crisis of Roman society.

Chapter 9

'Judaism-Lite'

In this section, we return to the special significance of Jewish communities throughout the Roman Empire, in which Jews constituted around ten to twelve per cent of the total population. In particular, we will look at the communities which were organised around the synagogues, providing mutual aid, support and welfare, not only for Jews, but for a wide circle of what might be called semi-Jews: monotheists who observed only some Jewish customs and practices. This wide community of god-fearers formed the main reservoir of conversions first to Judaism and, at a later stage, to Christianity. What has often been neglected by historians of Christianity, and which is central to the argument advanced in this chapter, is the *social* role of the synagogue that was replicated and developed to a much higher level by the Church. This was not only the key factor in its growth, but was also central to the decision by the Emperor Constantine to formalise Christianity as the state religion. We shall also look at the various heresies and especially Gnostic Christianity, which was far more widespread than the official Church histories have accepted until recent times and the reasons why Gnosticism faded out within the Church as a whole.

. . . .

As we saw in the previous section, the raw material for the growth of Christianity was provided by the social, political and economic crisis within Roman society. But it was the Jewish Diaspora and its *social structures* that provided the scaffolding within which the Church took shape and a *template* upon which the early Christian communities could grow. The first Joshua sects that gave rise to Christianity were *Jewish* organisations. As we have mentioned, the polemic between Paul and the Jerusalem leadership was precisely that the latter insisted on converts submitting to circumcision and observing Jewish dietary laws, in other words that they *convert to Judaism*. In the Gospel of Matthew, Jesus is made to say to his disciples, "Go not into the way of the Gentiles, and into any city of the Samaritans enter ye not: But go rather to the lost sheep of the house of Israel."[415] As Kautsky correctly points out, this is a direct prohibition of evangelism among non-Jews. The description of Paul's evangelical activities in Acts has him travelling in many different cities and in almost every case, notwithstanding his self-imposed role as apostle to the gentiles, it was *to the synagogue* that he first goes to preach. Paul refers in Galatians and elsewhere

---

[415] Matthew, 10, 5

to his collections for "the poor", that is the Joshua sect in Jerusalem, which still considered itself to be *Jewish*. It is clear that by making such collections, Paul was establishing his own credentials and his right to carry on a mission among the *Jews* of the diaspora.

The orthodox histories of Christianity have air-brushed out its Jewish origins so much that in two thousand years of religious paintings and statues of Jesus there is hardly a trace of his jewishness. Christians today often need to be reminded that even in the New Testament story, Jesus lived his whole life as a Jew. The official histories have set the Church apart from Judaism almost from the very beginning. The impression is given that Christians actively proselytised in such a way that the Christian converts formed a distinct community, although it is acknowledged that there were lingering arguments about the observance of Jewish Law. According to the epistles of Paul and the Acts of the Apostles, the debates between Paul and the Jerusalem leaders James and Peter revolved around these very issues. To emphasise the separateness of the new Church from its Jewish past, great prominence is still given in Church history to the ministry of Paul and the special task he was supposedly given, of evangelising among the gentiles. There is a clear, if unspoken, implication that it was Paul and not the Jerusalem leadership, which built the Church and that it was built principally among non-Jews. The documentary evidence does show that the leaders of the Church increasingly distanced themselves *theologically* from their Jewish roots. As early as the end of the first century, in the *Didache*, Christians are enjoined to celebrate their fasts on days other than those used by the "hypocrites", that is the Jews: "Your fasting days should not be the same as those of the hypocrites. They fast on Mondays and Thursdays; you, however, must fast on Wednesdays and Fridays." As we have argued, at this early stage of separation of the one faith from the other, the creation of the Jesus myth was not central to the new religion. Klaus Wengst, a German professor of Hebrew-Christian studies, and a member of the German Evangelical Church, hit the nail on the head: "It seems to me that the development of the [Christian] community's own religious rites against those of Judaism was more important than Christology in the formulation of a separate identity."[416]

Through a long process of scribal clarifications, additions and amendments, the books of the New Testament, including the narrative of the life of Jesus, went through a metamorphosis. Even the immediate events around his crucifixion were changed from the original story, so that the responsibility for his execution lay less with the *Romans* and more with the *Jews*, until eventually the Jews were condemned *as a race* of "god-killers" by Christian leaders. Among the gospels and apocalypses that did not make it into the New Testament, there are some that are clearly written to implicate the Jews as opposed to the Romans in the death of Jesus. Thus, in the *Gospel of Peter*, written in the early second century,

---

[416] Klaus Wengst, *When did Christianity originate*, http://www.jcrelations.net

"Then the Jews, the elders, and the priests realised how much evil they had done to themselves and began beating their breasts, saying 'woe to us because of our sins. The judgement and the end of Jerusalem are near . . . the scribes, Pharisees and elders gathered together and heard all the people murmuring and beating their breasts, saying, 'if such great signs happened when he died, you can see how righteous he was!'"[417]

Origen, writing in the mid third century on the Roman sacking of Jerusalem in 70 CE, commented, "It was right that the city in which Jesus underwent such sufferings should be completely destroyed, and that the Jewish nation be overthrown."[418] The roots of modern anti-Semitism were well and truly laid down in the inflammatory and hateful writings of the Church fathers nearly two thousand years ago, all of whom have since been elevated to sainthood. Pontius Pilate, the Roman prefect who was supposed to have presided over the trial of Jesus, was a real historical character and, reading Josephus, his record is no less brutal than that of any other Roman commander in the years that led up to the Jewish uprising. Yet he was portrayed in Christian legends as an innocent bystander who washed his hands of the Jesus affair or, in some cases, even into a Christian convert. Some branches of the Christian Church still revere him today as a saint!

The attempt by the Church leadership to distance itself from its Jewish roots came to its logical conclusion with the complete abandonment of the Old Testament by the third century heretic, Marcion, probably the best known of the great heretics of the early Church. He not only abandoned the Hebrew god altogether, but he doctored the letters of Paul and the gospels to remove all traces of Judaism and published the very first entirely non-Jewish Christian canon. This was a step too far for Church leaders, who were fond of inferring all manner of prophesies of the coming Jesus from the writings of the Hebrew prophets and so Marcion was excommunicated from the Church.

However, whilst the Church leaders and the theologians were distancing themselves from the synagogue, the picture on the ground was much more complex. Despite the increasing theological divide between their spiritual leaders, not all the members of the two communities were completely separate. In significant parts of the Roman Empire, particularly in the east, the Christian community began its existence *as a part of the wider Jewish community* and appears to have remained so for an extended period of time. Indeed, the growth of the original Christian faction *within* as well as *alongside* Judaism cannot be understood except in the context of the great vibrancy and vitality of the Jewish community of the Diaspora. Although the writers and polemicists of Christianity and Judaism were marking out their theological differences and separate identities as early as the beginning of the second century—and this may have been reflected in many communities—there is

---

[417] Gospel of Peter, 25. 28
[418] Origen, *Against Celsus*, 4, 22.

considerable evidence that the followers of the two faiths led a close and sometimes symbiotic relationship for many decades afterwards.

The Jewish Diaspora

At this point we need to take a rather long diversion, to look at the nature and scale of the Jewish Diaspora throughout the Roman Empire and to consider its relationship with the Church. The Jewish population of the empire spread along the trade routes of the Mediterranean and established significant colonies in all the major ports and inland trading cities. The Diaspora was to provide the perfect substrate upon which Christianity could develop at a later stage and by the turn of the millennium it was enormous. It was not a product of the sacking of Jerusalem and the dispersal of the Jews after the revolt of 66 CE. Josephus makes reference to the Diaspora as having existed long before the revolt. Addressing remarks to the Jewish people themselves, he commented, "There are no people upon the habitable earth which have not some portion of you among them."[419] Elsewhere he noted that there were more than "eight thousand" Jews in Rome alone. The Alexandrian Jewish philosopher, Philo, boasted in his writings that on every Sabbath day there are "thousands" of synagogues open for teaching Jews and non-Jews alike. Philo may have exaggerated, but he put the number of Jews in Egypt alone at about one million. Putting words in the mouth of the Jewish king Agrippa, he described Jerusalem as the metropolis, not only of one country, Judea, "but also of many, by virtue of the colonies which it has sent out from time to time

> ". . . into the bordering districts of Egypt, Phoenicia, Syria in general, and especially that part of it which is called Coelo-Syria, and also with those more distant regions of Pamphyla, Cilicia, the greater part of Asia Minor as far as Bithynia, and the furthermost corners of Pontus. And in the same manner into Europe, into Thessaly, and Boeotia, and Macedonia and Aetolia, and Attica and Argos, and Corinth and all the most fertile and wealthiest districts of Peloponnesus. And not only are the continents full of Jewish colonies but also all the most celebrated islands are so too; such as Euboea and Cyprus and Crete. I say nothing of all the countries beyond the Euphrates, for all of them except a very small portion and Babylon and all the satrapies around which have any advantage whatever of soil or climate, have jews settled in them . . . it is not one city that would be benefitted by you, but ten thousand of them in every region of the habitable world, in Europe, in Asia and in Africa, on the continent, in the islands, on the coasts, and in the inland parts" [420]

---

[419]   WJ,

[420]   Philo, *On the Embassy to Gaius,* 281 - 284

"For no one country," Philo adds, ". . . can contain the whole Jewish nation, by reason of its populousness; on which account they frequent all the most prosperous and fertile countries of Europe and Asia." At one point, Philo was sent to Rome as a part of a mission on behalf of Alexandrian Jews—around 39-40 CE—to protest against the depredations of the Jews in Alexandria. Here, the Jews had occupied two out of the five districts of the city, with a few more scattered in the other three. But "they drove the Jews entirely out of four quarters, and crammed them all into a very small portion of one."[421]

On the same issue, Kautsky quotes a nineteenth century scholar of Christianity, Matthias Mommsen:

> "Alexandria . . . was almost as much a city of the Jews as of the Greeks; the Alexandrian Jews must have been at least equal to those of Jerusalem in number, wealth, intelligence and organisation. In the first imperial era it was estimated that there were a million Jews to eight million Egyptians, and their influence was probably greater than would be represented by this ration . . . they and they only, were permitted to form a community within the community as it were, and while other non-burgesses were ruled by the authorities of the burgess-body, they were permitted to a certain extent to govern themselves . . . . in Alexandria, of the five quarters of the city, two were inhabited chiefly by Jews"[422]

The Greek historian and geographer, Strabo, also commented that the Jewish race, "has already come into every city and it is difficult to find a single spot of the inhabited earth which has not received this nation and is not ruled (financially) by it."[423] Jewish presence within cities was tolerated by the state and they were accorded special privileges and legal rights not permitted to gentiles. They were relieved, for example, of any obligation to participate in the sacrificial rites at the festivals of the Graeco-Roman gods. The two religious currents were not always entirely separate, however:

> "As Judaism became affected by outside influences, and in turn influenced the surrounding society, various hybrid groups grew up side by side with the relatively orthodox elements. Such were the Judaising pagans: Julia Severa of Akmonia, benefactress of the synagogue and high priestess of the imperial religion; the Porphyrabaphoi of Hierapolis, who mixed practices of entirely Hellenic origin with the observance of the feasts of Passover and Pentecost; and the Hypsistarians, or Adorers of the Supreme God . . ."[424]

---

[421] Philo, *Flaccus*, 55.
[422] Kautsky, p 248.
[423] Quoted by Kautsky, p 254
[424] From www.jewishencycopedia.com

The Jews were an accepted part of Roman society. This is clear from Philo's later complaint about the policies of Emperor Gaius Caligula who appeared to be undermining the special position of the Jews. Philo wrote that under Caligula's great-grandfather, the great Augustus Caesar, the condition of the Jews in Rome had been much more favourable.

> "How then did he [Augustus] look upon the great division of Rome which is on the other side of the river Tiber, which he was well aware, was occupied and inhabited by the Jews? And they were mostly Roman citizens, having been emancipated . . . he knew that they had synagogues, and that they were in the habit of visiting them, and most especially on the sacred Sabbath days, when they publicly cultivate their national philosophy. He knew also that they were in the habit of contributing sacred sums of money from their first fruits and sending them to Jerusalem . . . but he never removed them from Rome, nor did he ever deprive them of their rights as Roman citizens . . . nor did he forbid their assembling for the interpretations of the law . . ."[425]

Philo's description may be somewhat idealised, and certainly did not persist, as subsequent emperors conducted or collaborated in pogroms against both Jews and Christians. But nonetheless, it gives an approximate picture of a very large and well-established Jewish community in Rome. The size of the Jewish community in Rome—at the heart of imperial power—was to become an important factor in the establishment of the Church of Rome as pre-eminent within the later Christian community, at least in the Western part of the Empire. It is interesting to note, too, that Augustus had turned a blind eye to the Jews' remittances of money to the Temple in Jerusalem.

> "So adamant was the diaspora Jew in forwarding monies to Jerusalem that here, as in other cases, Rome felt compelled to legally exempt Jews from standard policy. Rome forbade the export of large sums of money from one province to another, for obvious and sound economic reasons. Rome, nevertheless, looked the other way as regards payment of the half-shekel by diaspora Jewry to the Jerusalem Temple."[426]

The Roman writer Seneca at one point complained about the disproportionate influence of the Jews. "Meanwhile," he wrote, "the customs of this accursed race have gained such influence that they are now received throughout the world. The vanquished have given laws to their victors."[427] Based, among other things, on the Roman census of 48CE, there is an almost unanimous view among modern

---

[425] Philo, *On the Embassy to Gaius*, 155-157
[426] Lighthouse, p 63
[427] Quoted by Augustine, see Lighthouse, p 65.

historians that Judaism was spread widely throughout the Roman Empire—so widely, in fact, that Jews constituted around ten per cent of the overall population and up to twenty per cent in the eastern half of the Empire.

What is particularly significant for the growth of Christianity was that this Jewish community maintained itself by an active policy of proselytism and conversions. There was no impervious wall between the Jews and the gentiles around them. The barrier between the two was extremely porous and open to movement in both directions. It is also likely that long before the ministry of Paul the messianic sects that proliferated in the Jewish community in Palestine would have been reflected in similar trends and factions in the Jewish communities of the Diaspora. It was not in Jerusalem, according to Acts, but in Antioch that the followers of Jesus/Joshua were first referred to as Christians.

In later centuries, a Christianised Roman empire forbade the Jews any rights to convert non-Jews to their faith. But before Christianity became the state religion, many gentiles were attached to the synagogues and were converted to the Jewish faith. In fact, the first ever mention of a Jewish community in Rome, by Valerius Maximus, a Roman historian from the time of Tiberius, clearly implied an active policy of conversion. He wrote about a short-lived expulsion of Jews from Rome as early as 139 BCE for attempting, he says, to *pass on their religious practices to the Romans.* As Shlomo Sand argues, in his book, *The Invention of the Jewish People,* Jewish proselytism was conducted on a large scale and its history has been underestimated or deliberately suppressed. In the popular historical works and textbooks which shape public consciousness, Jewish proselytism has "all but vanished from the picture." There is a modern myth among Jewish people, he argues, that

> ". . . their 'nation' which must be the most ancient—wandered in exile for nearly two thousand years and yet, despite this prolonged stay among the gentiles, managed to avoid integration with, or assimilation into, them . . ."[428]

Many modern geneticists (particularly in Israel, where its scientists are world leaders in the field) have done extensive and exhaustive research to demonstrate by means of genetic markers that twenty-first century Jews are descended from a narrow group of Israelites excluded from Palestine two thousand years ago. The political purpose behind this science is to provide a basis for the Zionist model of a *biologically* separate Jewish nation which, in turn, is a means of justifying Israeli settlement policies in Palestine today. The genetic evidence does indeed appear to show that the Jewish people were never *fully* assimilated. But that is not the issue anyway, because humanity is not one vast melting pot, otherwise there would be no separate ethnic or racial groups at all. But what the genetic evidence does show is that there was a *significant degree of mixing* of Jews with local populations. In other

---

[428] Sands, *The Invention of the Jewish People,* p 16

words, the growth of the Jewish population in Rome, Alexandria, Antioch and in other cities in the four hundred years around the turn of the modern era was due more to *conversions* than to birth rates.

Philo even boasted about the growth of Judaism by conversion: "All men are being conquered by Judaism and admonished to virtue; barbarians, Hellenes, dwellers on continents and islands, the nations of the East and of the West, Europeans, Asiatics, the races of the earth." Josephus relates that under Nero, there was a pogrom against the Jews in Damascus, following an uprising by the Jews in that city. The good citizens of Damascus were prepared to slaughter all the Jews, "yet they did distrust their own wives, which were almost all of them addicted to the Jewish religion."[429] This support for Judaism among gentile women was echoed at a later stage by a similar attraction among women to Christianity. Jewish tradition relates that Nero's wife, Poppaea Sabina, converted to Judaism—a story echoed centuries later by Christian traditions that had emperors' wives and mothers converting to Christianity.

It is clear, therefore, that well before the mushrooming of Christianity, Jews constituted a considerable proportion of the population of the Empire and they formed active and proselytising communities.

> "The number of Jews in the Roman Empire is estimated at 6 or 7 million, or roughly 12 per cent of the total population, around 50 million. This substantial proportion cannot be explained by natural increase alone, even if the Jews were very prolific. The surplus must be attributed to conversion and it is likely that converted Jews outnumbered original Jews. It was during the Second Temple period (539-70 BCE) that the Jewish faith experienced its greatest expansion . . . Judaism was seen as a religion more sensitive to the needs of the poor and abused people. The antique world ignored compassion and charity . . ."[430]

Judaism spread eastwards towards modern-day Iran and India as well as along the coast of North Africa ". . . where Jews may have helped the Phoenicians found trading posts. The Phoenicians responded positively to Judaism because they tended to believe in only one god and circumcision was an established practice among them. They adopted many of the Jewish rituals, such as lighting candles for the Sabbath . . ."[431] In modern times there has even been a large population of Bantu-speaking Jews in Ethiopia, the Fallashas, and although its origins are disputed by scholars, it gives an idea of the full range of the Jewish dispersal.

---

[429] Josephus, *The Wars of the Jews*, 2, 560
[430] Corcos, *The Myth of the Jewish Race*, p 97
[431] Corcos, *The Myth of the Jewish Race*, p 100

The social role of the synagogue/church

What then, attracted the gentiles towards the Jewish communities and how did that impact later on the Christian Church? In his book *Against Apion*, which is a polemic in defence of his faith, Josephus boasted about the popularity of Jewish practices:

> ". . . the multitude of mankind itself have had a great inclination of a long time to follow our religious observances; for there is not any city of Grecians, nor any of the barbarians, nor any nation whatsoever, whither our custom of resting on the seventh day hath not come, and by which our fasts and lighting up lamps and many of our prohibitions as to our food, are not observed, *they also endeavour to imitate our mutual concord with one another, and the charitable distribution* of *our goods*, and our diligences in our trades."[432]

The attraction of the synagogue did not lie in the theological differences between monotheism and polytheism but to the *social attraction* of the community—its cohesion and mutual support mechanisms and its role as an intermediary in dealing with the Roman state. Other than the above citation, we learn practically nothing about synagogues from the writings of Josephus, but there is enough evidence to show that they were ubiquitous in Palestine and throughout the whole of the Diaspora. The synagogues were not only centres of worship, even after the destruction of the Temple. They were centres of teaching, scripture, healing (in the sense of driving out evil spirits), welfare, charitable support and public administration. They even functioned as hostels for visiting Jews and itinerant preachers.

> "Conversion to Judaism was more attractive to people of the lower class, who were socially not as integrated and who would gain by conversion and participating in the Jewish community's benefit system, which in comparison to the ancient context was very well developed . . . [The Jewish sympathisers were] . . . flexible in regards to the demands of non-Jewish society. They therefore remained well-meaning sympathisers towards the Jewish community; they sat, as it were, in the second row, adopting in some respects the Jewish way of life (which could, to be sure, happen with different levels of intensity), participating in synagogal life, especially, as far as possible in the Sabbath meeting, and in some cases supporting the community with money and bringing their influence to bear at the level of the municipal administration or the administration of the Roman province in cases of conflict or whenever it was in the interest of the Jewish community."[433]

---

[432]   Jospehus, *Against Apion*, 2, 282 (italics added)
[433]   Klaus Wengst, *When did Christianity originate*, http://www.jcrelations.net

"The synagogue", another author wrote, "offered the possibility of expression—and to a certain extent also resolution—of the increasing number of economic, social and specifically religious disputes."[434] There were organisations throughout the Roman Empire that catered for tradesmen, artisans and many other interest groups and many of these took on religious aspects by patronising particular gods and temples. Many also organised elements of mutual welfare and support. But in its consistency, inclusivity and efficiency *there was nothing to match the welfare organisations of the synagogues* and it was this feature of their organisations that was later adopted, continued and developed by the Christian churches and which led to their growth. The religious/ideological outlook of the synagogues may have been important to its fellow-travellers but it was essentially the *material* conditions of the latter—the social and economic pressures of every day life—that drew them into the periphery of Judaism and, at a later stage, into the Church. It was only as an incidental bonus that there was also the promise of eternal redemption in the coming of the Kingdom.

> "The synagogue of the later Hellenistic period, both literary, inscriptional and archaeological for which materials exist appears a multifunctional affair. Briefly put, the synagogue, at least in Asia Minor, Syria, Greece and Italy, constituted the principal centre and unit of Jewish communal organisation, this in much the same manner as the parish-system in late medieval England or France. The synagogue leadership, then, remained essentially lay 'rulers' of the Jewish *ethnos* in the empire, and the liaison between the people and the Roman authorities. [In this] largely politico-administrative character . . . lies the reason why the synagogue in some cases were afforded space by the Roman authorities within the latter's 'office-complexes' . . . Such a view of the synagogue explains as well the close integration between its administrative structure and the larger Jewish communities such as that of Rome . . . Synagogues were 'ruled' by an *archesynagoues* ('ruler of the community') often in conjunction with a *gerousia* ('senate') of elders. So too in a city like Rome all such parish units themselves came under the authority of a senate and its ruler (*archon*), in some locales (as in Alexandria) bearing the title *ethnarch* ('ruler of the *ethnos*') . . . the administrative structure of *archonetes* and *gerousia* would have constituted the legal government and administration of the Jews within their larger political settings . . ."[435]

This meant, in effect, that the synagogues acted as a local government *on behalf of the Roman authorities* among the Jewish communities, supervising law, fulfilling civic responsibilities and administering taxes.

---

[434] Momigliano, *On Pagans, Jews and Christians*, p 113.
[435] Lighthouse, p 79

". . . in their control of real estate, commercial and other material and property transactions, the rabbis governed the Jewish community as effective political authorities. Whatever beliefs or values they proposed to instil into the people, or realise in the collective life of the community, they effected not through moral persuasion or pretence of magic, but *through political power*. They could tell people what to do and force them to do it . . ."[436]

This role was later taken over with an even more developed level of organisation by the Church and was *the key factor* in the later decision by Constantine to formalise Christianity as the state religion. Had circumstances been otherwise, perhaps it may have been Judaism that was given the nod by Constantine in the early part of the fourth century.

It is important to emphasise that the important social role played by the synagogues was not restricted to circumcised Jews. There is abundant evidence in a lot of literature of large numbers of god-fearers in the periphery around the synagogue, even outnumbering the circumcised, full Jews. These god-fearers were monotheists and Yahwists of various kinds—including, at a later stage, supporters of the Joshua-cults—who were supportive of and attached to local synagogues, *without actually converting fully to Judaism*. There are even several references to these semi-Jews in the Acts of the Apostles and in the gospels. The early second century author of Acts is clearly recalling the *synagogic* origins of the early Church when he specifically described Cornelius not as "a Jew", but as "a just man, and one that feareth God" and his introduction into the narrative of Acts was to raise the issue of conversion among *this layer* of non-Jewish synagogue-goers. Acts even suggests that *Peter's* conversions were focused on this layer of Jewish sympathisers, because "in every nation he that feareth him, and worketh righteousness, is accepted by him."[437] Likewise, Paul was recorded as addressing Jews and god-fearers when he refers to his listeners as "Men and brethren, children of the stock of Abraham, and whosoever among you feareth God . . ."[438] Later, Acts refers to "Jews and devout persons" and the number of "devout Greeks" (ie god-fearers) who supported Paul is described as "a great multitude."

The reluctance to convert fully to Judaism was chiefly because of the requirement of circumcision and the strict dietary laws.

"The boundless zeal with which the Jews developed their Law had its influence on the population at large: and the Law thus became a significant factor in the formation of sects within Christianity . . . there were many otherwise orthodox Christians who displayed a notable sympathy for the

---

436   Neusner, p 25 (italics added)
437   Acts, 10, 35
438   Acts, 13, 26.

Law. The lower orders of the population seem to have been all too ready to embrace the idea that they should live and act by the Jewish Law."[439]

For many of these fellow travellers it was not only "zeal for the Law" which was so attractive about Judaism, although the reputation of Jewish courts for fairness and honesty carried well past the beginning of the era of the Christian empire. But it was fundamentally the mutual cohesion and support of the *community*. The Jewish community in the big cities were disproportionately linked to trade, commerce and business compared to the average in the population and this, too, may have offered a life-line in terms of employment and a livelihood rarely available elsewhere.

It may well be that some of the *children* of first generation god-fearers would have been converted to become full Jews—in other words, "I will not be circumcised, but my new-born son will be"—with added status and access to privileges. Thus, over time, the pool of god-fearers would have swollen the number of fully-practising Jews. But for some of those who were loath to be circumcised or to observe dietary laws, *the christianised faction of the synagogue offered an easier option*. For them, Christianity was 'Judaism-lite'. The god-fearers,

". . . formed broad peripheries around the Jewish community, took part in its ceremonies, attended the synagogues, but did not keep all the commandments . . . it was precisely in these grey areas, between troubled paganism and partial or full conversion to Judaism, that Christianity made headway. Carried by the momentum of proliferating Judaism and the flourishing varieties of religious syncretism, an open and more flexible belief system arose that skilfully adapted to those who accepted it."[440]

Jewish proselytism was particularly successful among women. Josephus notes in many places the number of prominent Roman women who, he claimed, were converts. According to Acts, although Paul came across a certain Timotheus, whose father was "Greek" but whose mother was a "jewess".

"The poet Martial, who came from Iberia, made fun of the women who observed the Sabbath. Epigraphic material from the Jewish catacombs names as many female converts as male. Especially notable is the inscription about Venuria Paulla, who was renamed Sarah after her conversion and became the 'mother' [ie patroness] of two synagogues. Fulvia (wife of Saturninus)—on whose account, according to Josephus, Jews were expelled in the year 19 CE—was a full convert. Pomponia Graecine, the wife of the famous commander Aulus Plautius, who conquered Britain, was put on trial and divorced by her husband because of her devotion to the Jewish (or possibly the Christian) faith. Poppaea

---

[439]   Lucas, *The conflict between Christianity and Judaism*, p 49.
[440]   Sand, *The Invention of the Jewish People*, p 172.

Sabina, the Emperor Nero's second wife, made no secret of her tendency to Judaism. These women and many other matrons spread the Jewish faith in Rome's upper classes. There is evidence that Judaism was also becoming popular among the lower urban classes, as well as among the soldiers and freed slaves."[441]

Christian proselytism

All of these niches for Jewish conversion, were subsequently monopolised by the Christians whose faith had all the advantages of Judaism and none of its disadvantages. Moreover, they were no longer relegated to the second row as they were in the synagogue, but could take their place in the front pews. Given also the Jewish community's ties to commerce, while the more affluent god-fearers stayed with the synagogue, the poorer god-fearers were more attracted to the Christians.

> "The spread of the idea of spiritual redemption through a Messiah with the attendant idea of political liberation from the foreign ruling power, during the period from the second century BCE to the first century CE must have given a great boost to the spread of Judaism . . . these uncircumcised Yahwists . . . were allowed into the synagogue, whether baptised Christians or not, participated in the liturgy on an ongoing basis, and practised with the Jewish community many of its more distinctive rites. That is to say, they seem to be more socially integrated into the organisation of the synagogue community of the uncircumcised than one might expect of some 'pagan' cult which 'borrowed' from Judaism"[442]

Wengst offers an amusing, if imaginary monologue that might have been heard in a synagogue at this time, the speaker complaining about the attractiveness of the Christian Church:

> "What is happening in our community robs me of my sleep. One has to fear that the Messianic fever—God forbid!—will spread further and further like an infectious disease. This talking about the Messiah, this getting worked up, does not remain hidden from Roman informants; that will make the province's administration suspicious and only get us in trouble. And think about it: a Jesus hanged by the Romans twenty years ago should be the Messiah! Simply ridiculous. And if so: where is the Messianic kingdom? What has actually changed? What is being brought into our community is simply senseless and harmful. Our Gentile friends, the God-fearers, especially tend to fall for it. And if one attempts to clarify relationships, they distance themselves from us and meet in their

---

[441]   Sand, *The Invention of the Jewish People*, p 171
[442]   Feldman, *Jew and Gentile in the Ancient World*, p 93.

private homes with all those that are messianically infected. There they give their donations that we used to receive. *The Messianic preachers offer them Judaism at a cheap admission charge.* This is neither fish nor fowl. Something like that can never be pleasing to the Holy One, Blessed be He. If they want to fully belong to us, they should convert to us, as it should be, with all the consequences. And in addition, our people stop being real Jews when they are with them in their homes. They stretch the point and don't watch where the stuff they eat is coming from". [443]

Although it was more likely that it was god-fearers and Jews who converted to Christianity, the proselytism was not a one-way street. The writings of the early Church fathers record instances of communities that were believed to have converted to Judaism from Christianity. A group known as the *Coelicolae* were thought by one (much later) writer to have been Jews who had originally been Christian. Another Christian leader, disputing this, wrote: "The Coelicolae were so to speak midway between Jews and Christians . . . They owned the God of Heaven and the sacraments of either Law, circumcision and baptism, whence a new baptism is to be attributed to them. In the end their superstition came closest to Mohammedanism."[444] The Coelicolae were thought to have similarities to yet another group known as the Hypsistarians who adopted Jewish dietary laws, the Sabbath and other Jewish liturgical practices, but rejected circumcision.

In the end, therefore, *it was social and political factors* that determined the growth of the two communities. It mattered little to agricultural labourers, poor city artisans or domestic slaves whether the Messiah was yet to come or whether He had been and gone: *it was the role of the community that mattered.* Above everything else, the Church, like all organised religions, was for the masses a question of social, political, family and cultural connections, the theology being entirely secondary. In so far as philosophical issues entered at all into the calculation of would-be converts, it lay in the hope of a messianic redemption at some point in the future, although, of course, the nearer the better. It is not a coincidence that the largest communities of Christians in the early period were in those cities where there was also significant numbers of Jews—Antioch, Alexandria and particularly Rome. As they increasingly differentiated themselves and separated out, the more Christianised congregations—ie the churches—assumed the same structures and organisational form as the synagogues they had copied and they therefore retained the same appeal to would-be converts.

Both faiths were actively converting new followers in the early centuries of the modern epoch, but the Christians out-converted the Jews until, once in command of the Roman state, they could legislate against their rivals and declare themselves winners for all time. But even then, despite their communities drawing apart, the affinity between the two congregations lingered for a long time and was a matter

---

[443]   Klaus Wengst, *When did Christianity originate*, http://www.jcrelations.net (italics added)

[444]   Quoted by Lucas in *The conflict between Christianity and Judaism*, p 22

of great regret to many of the leaders and theologians of both faiths for many years afterwards.

> "The evidence pertaining to Judaism in the Hellenistic diaspora indicates that the sociologies of the Early Gentile Church and the Synagogue were closely intertwined for the first three or four centuries of the Common Era. Put simply, uncircumcised Gentile Christians (probably among other uncircumcised parties) not only practiced Judaic rituals but also attended synagogues and celebrated with the formal Jewish community, attended at times Jewish law courts, went to Jewish charismatic Holy Men to be healed and exorcised, and did all this *qua* good Gentile Christians. On the other hand, there seems every indication that the Synagogue remained aware of this participation, did nothing to stop it, on the other hand, and made little or no attempt to lure these Christians into the formal Jewish community via proselytism, circumcision, on the other."[445]

Many of the writings of the early Church fathers confirm this. Conferences of bishops, right through to the fourth century, were concerned with what was referred to as the Judaising current within the Christian congregation.

> "In the Judaiser controversies of the second, third and even fourth centuries the leadership of the Church, much to its consternation, continued to witness the selected practice of Judaic rites by uncircumcised Gentile Christians. Such rites include observing Jewish Fasts, some type of Sabbath and festival observance, and at times, actual visits to the synagogue."[446]

Ignatius, in his *Epistle to the Magnesians*, dated to the first part of the second century, warned Christians against following Jewish customs and practices. "Do not be led astray by wrong views or outmoded tales," he wrote, ". . . For if we still go on observing Judaism, we admit we never received grace . . . It is monstrous to talk Jesus Christ and live like a Jew . . ."[447] In a further epistle to the Philadelphians, he returns to the same theme: "Now if anyone preaches Judaism to you, pay no attention to him. For it is better to hear about Christianity from one of the circumcision than Judaism from a Gentile [Christian]"[448]. As we have shown earlier, the early Christian document, the *Didache* makes a point of instructing Christians to observe their own specific feast-days in distinction to Jews.

In the long struggle for orthodoxy, those Jewish-Christians who were condemned as Judaisers by their opponents frequently hit back, giving as good as

---

[445] Lighthouse, p 88.
[446] Lighthouse, p 67.
[447] *Ignatius to the Magnesians*, 8-9.
[448] *Ignatius to the Philadelphians*, 6.

they got. The Coptic *Apocalypse of Peter*, a document dated from about the third century, condemns the orthodox strand of Christianity, with its officials and priests.

"There will be others of those who are outside our number who name themselves 'bishop' and also 'deacons,' as if they have received their authority from God. They submit to the judgement of the leaders. Those people are dry canals."[449]

As late as the fourth century, at the Church Council of Elvira, the articles agreed by the Council forbade marriage and adultery with Jews and condemned what must have been the common practice of having a Jewish cleric bless the harvest. Article 49 decreed that "Landlords are not to allow Jews to bless the crops they have received from God". At the Council of Nicaea in 325, the first since Constantine's conversion, it was announced that "all the brethren in the East who have hitherto followed the Jewish practice will henceforth observe the custom of the Romans". What was decreed in the council, however, did not always happen in practice. Decades later, sermons by the Christian writer John Chrysostom still complained about those members of his flock who regularly worshipped in local synagogues. "His flock, or many among them, saw nothing wrong with at once being Christian and at the same time participating in the synagogue liturgy"[450] In his *Homily against the Jews*, Chrysostom wrote:

". . . many who belong to us and say that they believe in our teaching attend their [the Jews'] festivals and even share in their celebrations and join in their fasts. It is this evil practice I now wish to drive from the church."[451]

These sermons and writings of Chrysostom were among the most anti-Jewish of any of the Church fathers and were not without purpose. It would hardly be necessary to condemn Christians worshipping in synagogues, observing the Passover, and so on, had it not been common practice in the first place. Even as late as the beginning of the fifth century, Jerome was complaining in his letter to Augustine about the influence of Jews on congregations of Christians.

"To this day there is a heresy among the Jews throughout the synagogues of the East, called the sect of the Minei, which is even now condemned by the Pharisees; these are commonly called Nazarenes, believe in Christ, the Son of God, born of the Virgin Mary, and say it is he who suffered under Pontius Pilate and rose again, in whom we also believe; but *while they wish to be both Christians and Jews they are neither one nor the other* . . . If we are

---

[449] *The Coptic Apocalypse of Peter*
[450] Lighthouse, p 40.
[451] See Lighthouse, p 88

absolutely obliged to receive the Jews with their Law, and *they are to be allowed to continue in the churches of Christ the usages which they practised in the synagogues* of Satan, I will declare my opinion that it is not they who will become Christians, but we whom they will turn into Jews."[452]

The evidence clearly shows, therefore, that the Church gained its converts initially among Jews and fellow-travellers of Jews, on the basis of the social and welfare structures that surrounded the Christian community. It was material rather than ideological factors that were more important. Drawing up a balance sheet of God against Mammon it was indeed Mammon that was the more significant factor in building the congregations.

But once the Church began to grow significantly, it was inevitable, given its hierarchical structure, that the voices crying for orthodoxy were raised louder and louder, not for the sake of theological clarity, but to underpin the power of the Church hierarchy.

The demands for orthodoxy

The epistle of 1 Clement, which we have already mentioned, is the first indication of the growing separation between bishops and lay Church members. As the Church expanded, the bureaucracy necessarily expanded with it. The Church apparatus became a huge self-perpetuating, administrative machine that eventually sat alongside and in many cases supplanted the official local government apparatus of the state. From having originally been the *elected servants* of the congregation, the bishops, with their elaborate supporting apparatus, became the *unelected rulers* of the Church, against whom the humble lay members were virtually powerless.

Whereas the early church was a collection of more or less independent and democratic organisations, the appointment of bishops and the move towards a hierarchical and permanent bureaucracy led to increasing demands for orthodoxy and clarity in theology. It was not in the interests of this increasingly rich and powerful bureaucracy that any church or its representative should be allowed to display different beliefs and practices. The bishops saw themselves as anointed in a direct *apostolic succession* and as a result only they could take decisions on what was to be considered official scripture and how that scripture was to be interpreted. They could brook no opposition that would undermine that claim. The whole apparatus of the Church rested on that claim of having a monopoly of sacred knowledge and any splits in the hierarchy would be noticed by the silent masses who filled the pews. Whereas the early Church had demonstrated a wide range of different beliefs—to a degree that would be inconceivable in any branch of the Christian Church today—the growing bureaucracy sought to consolidate its position through theological uniformity and unity in a catholic (meaning "universal") organisation.

---

[452] Cites by Lucas in *The Conflict between Christianity and Judaims*, p 51 (italics added)

Once established as the official imperial religion, the Church ruthlessly suppressed all those heresies that were opposed it. Libraries, books and their authors were burned in abundance so that the real picture of what the Church looked like in the first three centuries is only becoming clear now, with archaeological finds of books previously suppressed and known only by a few citations in the critiques of the Church fathers. Bart Ehrman refers to the trend which *became* the orthodox Church as proto-orthodox in the sense that there was no accepted New Testament canon before the end of the fourth century and because there were many arguments raging about what Christianity should mean.

An important development in the bureaucratisation of the Church was the growing predominance of the Church in Rome, the imperial capital city in the first three centuries. In the earliest writings of the Church fathers, there is almost equivalence in terms of status and authority in the bishoprics of the largest cities of the empire—Rome, Antioch and Alexandria, for example. But increasingly, it was Rome that claimed pre-eminence. There is no doubt that to a large extent, the theological struggles in the second and third centuries reflected the jealousies and rivalries of senior bishops in what was, in effect, a struggle for power and influence.

"Using the administrative skills of its leaders and its vast material resources, the church in Rome managed to exert influence over other Christian communities. Among other things, the Roman Christians promoted a hierarchical structure, insisting that each church should have a single bishop."[453]

The wealth of the Roman Church was greater than that of any other. Whilst the Church never pioneered the abolition of slavery at any time in its history, it is possible that the Roman church used some of its wealth for the manumission of slaves and the purchasing of freedom for prisoners and bankrupts. It would have been well placed to offer gifts and favours of holy relics or other paraphernalia to churches outside of Italy which supported its primacy. As Freeman writes in his *New History of the Early Christianity*, "There is yet no further evidence for the existence, let alone primacy of Peter in the Roman Church, but some time after 160 CE, a modest memorial was built over a grave in a cemetery on the Vatican that was revered as his resting place."[454] Paul, like Peter, was adopted by the Roman Church, although, once again, there is no evidence outside of the legend that he'd ever been in Rome. It was as a result of these two key adoptions and the legends of the crucifixion of both Paul and Peter in Rome that we now have St Peter's Square and St Paul's Basilica in the Vatican. The Church historian, Eusebius, refers to the Roman church sending contributions "to many churches in every city, sometimes alleviating the distress of those in need, sometimes providing for your brothers in the

---

[453]   Ehrman, *Lost Christianities,* p 175
[454]   Freeman, *A New History of Early Christianity,* p 115

[slave] mines . . ."[455] It was the *Roman* Church, therefore, whose proto-orthodoxy became *the* orthodoxy of the whole Church, at least until such time as the Church in Constantinople, the seat of the eastern part of a divided Roman Empire, came to assert its own authority and split away. In the end, the bureaucracies of the two great churches retained control over their own territories—the Roman Catholics to the west and the Greek Orthodox to the east.

Whereas Justin wrote in the mid second century rather vaguely about the recollections of the apostles, without any indication that there was an official list of gospels, only thirty years later the Christian writer Irenaeus had a very clear idea of which books should or should not be accepted by the Church. His justification for including only four of the many gospels current at the time was that the earth had four zones and four winds:

> ". . . it is not possible that the Gospels can be either more or fewer in number than they are. For, since there are four zones of the world in which we live, and four principal winds, while the Church is scattered throughout the world, and the pillar and ground of the Church is the Gospel . . . it is fitting that she should have four pillars."[456]

Those who were victorious in this struggle eliminated the vast bulk of the non-orthodox scripture so that much of it remained unknown until the present day. Not only that, but they also re-wrote the history of the Church to give the impression that the orthodox creed enjoyed a seamless development from the very beginning, with only a few unsuccessful heresies spoiling the party now and again. The writings of non-orthodox Christians were so efficiently suppressed that until recently it was only possible to know of them in the vaguest outline and that only through the occasional quotes in the Church fathers' diatribes against them. Modern discoveries, however, have given us new insights into the enormous debates and disputes that characterised the Church for the first three or four hundred years.

> "In some regions of ancient Christendom, what later came to be labelled 'heresy' was in fact the earliest and principal form of Christianity. In other regions, views later deemed heretical coexisted with views that came to be embraced by the church as a whole, with most believers not drawing hard and fast lines of demarcation between them. To this extend, 'orthodoxy', in the sense of a unified group advocating an apostolic doctrine accepted by the majority of Christians everywhere, simply did not exist in the second and third centuries."[457]

---

[455]   Ehrman, *Lost Christianities*, p 175
[456]   Irenaeus, *Against heresies*, 3, 11, 7
[457]   Ehrman, *Lost Chrisianities*, p 173.

Throughout the Near East and for the first three centuries, there was a great proliferation of cults and churches with theological, liturgical and organisational differences. Most of these have been lost in the near two thousand years since then, but echoes of the more significant heterodoxies remains with us. As we shall argue in the next section, a strand of Syriac Christianity probably had an important role in providing the early substrate for what later became the Koran.

One of the first large heresies the Church had to contend with was *Marcionism*, named after its founder Marcion. His attempt to draw a clear line between the new church and the synagogue resulted in him editing out all the vaguely pro-Jewish references in the gospels and the writings of Paul. As we have seen, he rejected the old Hebrew Bible altogether. The church leadership, however, still bases its scripture on the Hebrew Bible and, in fact used the prophesies of that literature to justify Christianity. A Christianised Old Testament, many elements of it re-interpreted as prophesies of the coming of Jesus, enormously enhanced the theological claims of the Church, especially with Jews and god-fearers around the synagogue who they would wish to convert. Marcion was excommunicated from the Church and was defeated in the end by the overwhelming power of the mainstream Church. Quite apart from the theology, however, his original rise to fame speaks volumes about the class character of the Church in the second century. Born in Asia Minor, the son of a wealthy ship-builder, Marcion moved to Rome as an extremely wealthy man. *It took no time at all for this man of substance to buy his way into the hierarchy of the Church*, after which he found that the only way to the top was to formulate his own ideas and start his own Church.

Another important heresy was *Montanism*, named after its founder Montanus, and based principally in North Africa. As much as anything, this heretical movement protested, even as early as the second century, against what it saw was the growing statism and bureaucracy of the Church, accompanied by moral laxity and worldliness. Montanus, had first began his prophetic activity some time in the middle of the second century and he and his followers claimed direct inspiration from the Holy Spirit, a claim that the Church could not tolerate. The Montanists, harking back to older Jewish messianistic traditions, resurrected prophetic revivalism, thereby threatening the peace and stability of the Church. Apart from anything else, two of the three main leaders of the Montanists were women, an unacceptable breach in the all-male theological orthodoxy being created by the church. "Montanism", the nineteenth century Church historian Edward Hatch wrote, "was theoretically in the right . . . [but] It was a beating of the wings of pietism against the iron bars of organisation. It was the first, though not the last, rebellion of the religious sentiment against official religion."[458]

"The church of the 170s and 180s had reached a sensitive, even prickly, stage in its development. It was emerging from the confusions of the Gnostic crisis and recovering from the harsh confrontation with Marcion,

---

[458]   Hatch, *The Organisation of the Early Church*, p 122.

but was still feeling after a clear consensus on the terms of its apostolic charter . . . The Montanists' renewal of prophecy suffered at the hands of a church preoccupied with closing the ranks, drawing clear lines of demarcation and safeguarding its heritage, an exercise in which apostolic was often synonymous with traditional. The condemnation of Montanism was a decisive point in the evolution of that kind of churchly Christianity which cherished office and order and had little room to 'welcome the charismata'."[459]

Nag Hammadi and the Gnostics

The most significant of all the great challenges that faced the Church was the spread of *gnostic* ideas, the significance of which has only become apparent with archaeological discoveries in the twentieth century. The finds at Nag Hammadi in Egypt in 1945 are in archaeological terms just as important as the Dead Sea Scrolls discovered only slightly later. But if the finds at Qumran were only important in providing a *backdrop* to the rise of Christianity, those at Nag Hammadi were immensely significant for an understanding of early Christianity itself. It appears that this stash of manuscripts was produced and then later buried some time late in the fourth century, probably by nearby monks in response to a move by the Church to suppress all heretical documents. The fact that they were hidden in jars strongly suggests that they were meant to be preserved for future use, perhaps when the theological climate in the Church had changed for the better.

The library consisted of twelve codices (books, as opposed to scrolls) as well as fragments of a thirteenth. Some titles were repeated, so altogether the collection included forty-five documents, many of which were completely unknown to modern scholars. Like the Dead Sea Scrolls, the Nag Hammadi library wasn't made available to scholars in general, this time because of the contending claims of different owners and custodians of the documents. The drive for personal prestige and profit from these priceless relics held back their publication for decades. By the mid-1970s they were finally published in total, the most authoritative translation being that of James M Robinson, Professor Emeritus of Religion at Claremont Graduate University USA.[460] In the opinion of many scholars, Ehrman suggests, the Nag Hammadi collection represents "the most significant manuscript discoveries of modern times."

Of the fifty-two treatises preserved among these books, six are duplicates, so that there are a total of forty-six separate titles. These include the Gospel of Philip as well as 'secret' revelations given to the disciples John and James. They also include mystical writings about the creation of the world and the divine realm as well as metaphysical speculations on the meaning of existence and salvation. They include

---

[459]   David F Wright, *Why Were the Montanists Condemned*, Themelios, September 1976

[460]   Robinson, *The Nag Hammadi Library, The definitive translation of the Gnostic Scriptures.*

polemical of attacks on the false and heretical views of other Christians, including those who would become mainstream Christianity.

Although written in Coptic and bound into books in the fourth century, they were translated from earlier Greek volumes that were in existence as early as the second century at the latest. Some of the works were previously known, but only from brief quotations in the critical works of early Church fathers, the original documents having been suppressed by the Church. The most important single document discovered was a complete copy of the Gospel of Thomas, which had only been known in short citations and some fragments prior to this and which we have already mentioned. But the collection also includes many gospels about Jesus which had never before been seen by modern scholars and which, if they were known about at all, were only known as fragments. These were now revealed and complete, for the first time in a millennium and a half.

The Nag Hammadi collection is particularly important for its illumination of the Gnostic form of Christianity, which has been known about for centuries, but as is now clear, with its significance considerably underestimated. One of the few unifying features of the Gnostic view of Christianity was the idea that a special understanding or *gnosis* of the Saviour is an essential part of redemption and the guarantee of ever-lasting life. Almost by definition, such an understanding was limited to only a few individuals, but was potentially available to all. True *gnosis*, and therefore salvation, was to be obtained by studying the scripture and by leading a righteous life, at which point many different brands of Gnosticism and righteousness came into play.

Gnostic scriptures were associated with wild and bizarre mythologies, some of which are barely recognisable as Christianity, but which were nevertheless compatible in that they sat as a background to the orthodox view. According to various Gnostic mythologies, there might be one god, several gods or hundreds, as well as demi-gods and many other metaphysical beings. The Nag Hammadi finds do not display one coherent brand of Gnosticism, but a bewildering array of Gnosticisms (plural). "There is scarcely any religious literature, written in any language at any time," Ehrman writes, "that can be more perplexing and deliberately obscure than some of the Gnostic writings of Christian antiquity. In fact, most of the time, *the English translation is clearer than the Coptic of the texts themselves.*"[461] (Emphasis added). Confusing issues even more, it appears that there were Jewish Gnostic traditions pre-dating the Christian ones.

As a post-script to the finds at Nag Hammadi, there was another find some thirty years later, about 200 kilometres north. What was unearthed was an ancient manuscript of *The Gospel of Judas*. This too has a gnostic flavour and appears to be a version of a work cited by the Christian writer Irenaeus, around 180 CE. The gist of this gospel is that Judas, in betraying Jesus, was actually carrying out his *instructions*, because he knew he was going to be crucified and needed to be

---

[461]   Ehrman, *The Lost Christianities*, p 115

certain of being arrested. It has no great theological significance, other than to those scholars who immerse themselves in such things, but it is yet again an indication of the wide variety of theologies that were available to Christians in the second and third centuries.

Given the wealth of Gnostic material that has now been unearthed, it is clear that at least in terms of *literary output* Gnosticism was a major trend in early Christianity and its true significance—along with its documentary output—has long been suppressed by the Church. The Nag Hammadi finds go a long way to explain why so many of the early Church fathers spilled so much ink in denouncing this particular brand of Christianity. But it begs the questions, why did Gnosticism flourish at all? What support did it have, and why was the heresy so easily defeated by the Church?

> ". . . the proto-orthodox leaders felt the pressure of these groups; otherwise, we would be hard-pressed to explain the massive expenditure of time and energy devoted to rooting out the Gnostic 'heretics', spurning their views, maligning their persons, destroying their writings, eliminating their influence . . . ."[462]

It is important to note that the supporters of Gnosticism for the most part did not set up separate churches like the Marcionites and nor were they based in a particular region like the Montanists. They were often organised within the main structures of the church. Their more esoteric philosophical meanderings may not have impacted to any great degree on the daily and weekly routine of the congregations and in fact may well have gone unnoticed by most of the community who were, in any case, illiterate. Then again, different texts have *elements* of Gnosticism in them: even in the New Testament as it has come down to us, documents like the Gospel of John and other texts have been labelled as "Gnostic". The mystical opening lines of the Gospel of John, "In the beginning was the Word, and the Word was with God, and the Word was God", has been compared to similar phrases in Gnostic writings. Likewise, in Matthew, the author has Jesus saying, "Because it is given unto you to know the mysteries of the kingdom of heaven, but to them it is not given . . ."[463] That is not to say that the authors of the gospels were gnostic, merely that the core of the idea of Gnosticism was present even at a relatively early stage in the development of Christian theology.

If the theologians of Gnosticism had any echo of support, it must have been linked to that other common theme in their writings—the idea that this world is an aberration, a mistaken creation or is in some way imperfect. Salvation, therefore, for the Gnostics, was not due in *this* world, but in the *next*. The idea that this material world has nothing to offer might well have found an echo among the most dispossessed in society.

---

[462]   Ehrman, *The Lost Christianities*, p 133
[463]   Matthew, 13, 11

"Do not be concerned from morning until evening and from evening until morning about what you will wear. Instead, all that the world has to offer, all the riches it can provide, should be rejected in order to escape this world: whoever finds the world and becomes rich let him renounce the world". [464]

For many, this life *is* a world of pain, suffering and misery in any case and there seems no hope but for the *next* life. It is not surprising, therefore, that at least this element of the gnostic view—which was, after all, no more than a deeply pessimistic variant of orthodox Christianity—found an echo. The Gnostics were, in a sense, *more fearless* and *more militant* in their denunciations of the world in which their flock were forced to live, a world that was inherently worthless and evil and a place from which to escape and be saved. For some of the community of Christians, this must have sounded like a very powerful and indeed overwhelming message. The documents of the Gnostics, Ehrman, points out, could even have an echo among Christians and followers of religious cults in the twenty-first century—because for many people we have a crisis-ridden society that just *doesn't make sense*. The Gnostics, he says,

> ". . . gave expression to what so many people over the course of history have known so well first hand—the starving, the diseased, the crippled, the oppressed, the deserted, the heartbroken. This world is miserable. And if there is any hope for deliverance, it will not come from within this world through worldly means, for example, by improving the welfare state, putting more teachers in the classroom, or devoting more national resources to the fight against terrorism."[465]

There was also an element in Gnosticism which opposed the rigid stratification of the Church between the laity and the clergy with an ever-growing hierarchy within the latter. The Gnostics followed a much more egalitarian practice that refused to acknowledge the hierarchy of the official church. Elaine Pagels in *The Gnostic Gospels*, quotes the comments of the Church father Tertullian, in a very revealing criticism of the gnostics,

> ". . . it is uncertain who is a catechumen [a 'prospective' church member], and who a believer: they all have access equally, they listen equally, they pray equally . . . their ordinations are carelessly administered, capricious and changeable. At one time they put novices in office; at another, persons bound by secular employment . . . Nowhere is promotion easier than in the camp of the rebels, where even the mere fact of being there is a foremost service. So today one man is bishop and tomorrow another;

---

[464] From *The Gospel of Thomas*.
[465] Ehrman, *The Lost Christianities*, p 114.

the person who is a deacon today, tomorrow is a reader; the one who is a priest today is a layman tomorrow; for even on the laity they impose the functions of priesthood!"[466]

It seems that without even a hint of irony, Tertullian, in the early third century, criticises fellow Christians for being "without authority" and "without discipline", in other words . . . for being like the original Church! Worst of all for some theologians in the orthodox Church, the Gnostics invited women to preach and treated them the same as men. Bishop Irenaeus, expressed his dismay at the number of "foolish women" who had been attracted to the Gnostics and even had the "cup handed to them" to officiate as priests. Tertullian put the Gnostics right on this question as well. A century and a half after the Church of Paul included women as members and preachers, he wrote:

> "It is not permitted for women to speak in the church, nor is it permitted for her to teach, nor to baptise, nor to offer [the Eucharist], nor to claim for herself a share in any masculine function—not to mention any priestly office."[467]

The rise of the bishops even grated on Tertullian himself eventually so that near the end of his life he broke away from the orthodox community, which he labelled as no more than a "number of bishops."

What militated against any mass support for the Gnostics in the long run were their very obscure and esoteric mythologies which would have had little appeal compared to the relatively simple theological models of the early orthodox Church, including simple doctrine, ritual and organisational form. In the final analysis, what factors determined which variant of Christianity gained the most support were not the fine theological arguments. They meant virtually nothing to the vast majority of the community. What mattered was what was happening on the ground and what support, mutuality and community welfare was available to those who were often on the brink of despair. It is one thing for a scribe or a well-off bishop to give vent to flights of fancy with his quill, but if his emphasis is always on some future salvation and there was no real, supportive community to sustain his flock, then neither his church nor its theology will persist.

> ". . . the religious perspectives and methods of Gnosticism did not lend themselves to mass religion. In this respect, it was no match for the highly effective system of organisation of the Catholic Church, which expressed a unified religious perspective based on the New Testament canon, offered a

---

[466] Pagels, *The Gnostic Gospels*, p 66-67
[467] Pagels, *The Gnostic Gospels*, p 81

creed requiring the initiate to confess the simplest essentials of faith, and celebrated rituals as simple and profound as baptism and the Eucharist."[468]

Almost as an afterthought, Pagels adds what is actually the most decisive factor. Equally important, she writes, ". . . are social and political structures that identify and unite people into a common affiliation." In the final analysis, what was decisive for the growth of the Church or any one of its factions was its social function and its material appeal to potential converts. In this respect, the official Church had no equal. "Even their pagan critics noticed," Pagels adds, "that Christians appealed to the destitute by alleviating two of their major anxieties: Christians provided food for the poor, and they buried the dead."[469]

Much of the theoretical debates on heresy centred on what modern theologians refer to as *Christology*, that is to say, the nature of Jesus. To what extent was the story of Jesus about a man, a god or a man-god or some other strange combination of the two? Was the human element of Jesus subsumed within the godly element or was it separate and equal to it? For some theologians, Mary was the mother of God; while for others—and notably the later Muslim theologians—the very idea of God having a mother (or a son) was a ridiculous notion. For some, Jesus lived and died a *man*; for others he was not, and so on. These obscure intellectual gymnastics had no significance at all to the vast majority of the Church congregation, over whose heads the debates floated like the proverbial clouds. But they were important as the *ideological livery* in the battles for prestige and influence between the rival Church patriarchs of Rome, Constantinople, Alexandria and Antioch. In due course each of these would preside over its own Church with its own sphere of power and influence: the Catholics in Rome and ultimately most of Western and Northern Europe, the Eastern Orthodox in Constantinople and Eastern Europe, the Copts in Alexandria and North Africa and the Nestorian Church in Antioch and east through Iran as far as China. It was the *political* significance of these power blocs rather than the theological nuances that was to have an impact in the later developments in the Near East and on the rise of Islam in particular.

Chapter Summary:

- Jews constituted around ten to twelve per cent of the population of the Empire. They organised around synagogues that provided mutual aid, support and welfare.

- Besides full Jews, the synagogues organised an even greater number of monotheistic god-fearers on their periphery and these were the main proselytes to the Joshua sect of Judaism, that is to Christianity.

---

468 Pagels *The Gnostic Gospels*, p 146
469 Pagels *The Gnostic Gospels*, p 151

- The *social* role of the synagogue was the main basis of conversion to Judaism and it was replicated and developed to a much higher level by the Church so that it became the key factor in Church growth.

- There were many varieties of Christianity within the early Church. But once established as the official imperial religion, the Church of Rome ruthlessly suppressed all those heresies that were different to it. Theological splits within the main bodies of the Church reflected the struggles for power and influence between the four main centres—Rome, Constantinople, Alexandria and Antioch.

- The theological debates between the Church and the Gnostics meant little to the vast majority of the community. Gnosticism failed, not only because of its esoteric doctrines, but because it was only the mainstream Church which offered support, mutuality and community welfare.

Chapter 10

The Class Basis of the Early Church

In this section we will examine how the structure and composition of early Church reflected contradictory class elements and that its main growth was based on an urban milieu, drawing in skilled and unskilled workers around its *inclusiveness* and sense of *community*. While the majority of its congregation were at the lower end of the social scale, as the Church increased in size, influence and power, its leading elements were increasingly integrated into the aristocracy of the Roman Empire. We shall also look briefly at the burgeoning movement of the monasteries, the growth of which was rooted in the social conditions of the time.

. . . .

However many different theologies there were, gnostic or otherwise, this should not mask the important social niche that the Joshua sects had filled from the very beginning—as class-based *mutual* organisations that appealed to the poorest layers in society. These were the real social roots of the Church and it was high above this down-to-earth foundation, in the theological clouds, that the Church leaders indulged in their theoretical debates. Only a tiny minority of society were literate and an even smaller minority bothered to wrestle with the finer points of Christology. But in so far as the theology did develop, it inevitably reflected the material and worldly interests of the leadership of the Church, as well as its burgeoning bureaucracy, leaving the laity far below it in the dirt. The drive for uniformity and orthodoxy in all things, not least in the theology, was predicated on privilege, power and position. As the Church hierarchy developed, so policy and theology developed in its interests and these interests increasingly coincided with those of the imperial ruling class.

In his critique of the work of Bruno Bauer, Friedrich Engels suggested that it was not enough to demonstrate the fictional character of the New Testament, because that brought us no nearer to explaining the growth of the Church.

> "A religion that brought the Roman world empire into subjection, and dominated by far the larger part of civilized humanity for 1,800 years, cannot be disposed of merely by declaring it to be nonsense gleaned together by frauds. One cannot dispose of it before one succeeds in explaining its origin and its development from the historical conditions under which it arose and reached its dominating position. This applies to Christianity. The question to be solved, then, is how it came about that the popular masses in the Roman Empire so far preferred

this nonsense—which was preached, into the bargain, by slaves and oppressed—to all other religions, that the ambitious Constantine finally saw in the adoption of this religion of nonsense the best means of exalting himself to the position of autocrat of the Roman world."[470]

What Engels means by the "historical conditions under which it arose" are the ongoing economic and political crises of the Roman Empire. These provided fertile soil for any religious sect that offered a sense of community, equality and security, especially one that offered the extra bonus of redemption in the next life. It was no coincidence that the period of the chronic decline of the Roman Empire was the classic period of the growth of Christianity. The mass of the population were increasingly alienated from the existing society and they aspired to something new. The Christian communities around the empire (and here and there, as we have argued, the Jewish communities) had an inclusive and egalitarian organisation which offered a degree of welfare and security and a hope of salvation in the world to come, if not in this one. Moreover, the Church was as well organised as the Roman state itself in the sense that its structures crossed national and international boundaries and boasted a universal creed that was underpinned by a growing corpus of literature.

Despite the occasional bouts of repression suffered by the Church, the social conditions that pertained in the Roman Empire during this whole period provided the most advantageous circumstances possible for the growth of a well-organised and increasingly well-connected political structure. Engels explained that it was in the midst of this general economic, political, intellectual, and moral decadence that Christianity appeared.

"In all previous religions, ritual had been the main thing. Only by taking part in the sacrifices and processions, and in the Orient by observing the most detailed diet and cleanliness precepts, could one show to what religion one belonged. Christianity knew no distinctive ceremonies, not even the sacrifices and processions of the classic world. By thus rejecting all national religions and their common ceremonies, and addressing itself to all peoples without distinction, it became the ***first possible world religion***. Judaism, too, with its new universal god, had made a start on the way to becoming a universal religion; but the children of Israel always remained an aristocracy among the believers and the circumcised, and Christianity itself had to get rid of the notion of the superiority of the Jewish Christians"[471]

Ernest Renan, the French nineteenth century theologian, thought he was scoffing at the likes of Engels and Bauer when he wrote "When you want to get a distinct idea of what the first Christian communities were, do not compare them to the parish congregations of our day; they were rather like local sections of the International Working Men's Association." But Engels agreed with this, adding that

---

[470]   Engels, *Bruno Bauer and the Early Christianity*, Sozialdemokrat, May 4, 1882

[471]   Engels, *Bruno Bauer and the Early Christianity*, in *Sozialdemokrat*, May 4, 1882.

Renan "did not know himself how much truth there was in the words." Christianity did indeed get hold of the masses. Engels wrote,

> ". . . exactly as modern socialism does, under the shape of a variety of sects, and still more of conflicting individual views clearer, some more confused, these latter the great majority—but all opposed to the ruling system, to 'the powers that be'."[472]

Kautsky in his work also noted that the majority of those who became Christian were drawn from the ranks of the lower classes.

> "It was a joke amongst the heathen that the Christians could only convert the simple-minded, only slaves, women and children; that they were rude, uneducated, and boorish; that the members of their communities were chiefly people of no account, artisans and old women. The Christians themselves did not dispute this . . . it is expressly attested by Christian writers that, even up to the middle of the third century, the new faith counted but few adherents among the higher classes . . ."[473]

After each of the three great rebellions of the Jews, from the first to the second century, the Roman Empire would have been flooded with newly captured Jewish slaves, among whom there would have been a proportion of Joshua followers and Judeo-Christians of various kinds. A proportion of these slaves, perhaps freed at a later point, or their children would have found their way to the security of the synagogues and the churches. Although the Church at no time developed a theological or moral justification for the condemnation of the institution of slavery—indeed it accepted the practice as part of the fabric of everyday life[474]—there are some suggestions here and there that Church funds may have been used to free slaves, or perhaps urban workers who had fallen on hard times and sold themselves into indenture. In a letter to Polycarp, Ignatius actually *admonished* community members for using Church funds to pay for the manumission of slaves, a criticism that might indicate it was a common practice.

The Christian leaders themselves acknowledged that the majority of their converts were from the poorest in society. However, as Kautsky suggests, it was not so much slaves as *freed proletarians*—and principally in the urban areas—who formed the main bulk of the poor of the Church. They would have had sufficient freedom of choice and movement to become involved voluntarily in the Christian communities, but they would have also "crowded out" the direct interests of the slaves themselves. Except in some communities like the Ebionites, there appears to have been no generalised attempt to free slaves and slavery was accepted as part and

---

[472] Engels, *Die Neue Zeit*, Vol 1, 1894-5
[473] Kautsky, p 324
[474] See Appendix

parcel of everyday life in Roman society. Nevertheless, to be counted among the righteous, in contrast to the lost souls outside the Church, would add enormously to the sense of self-worth of any slave or Roman citizen down on his luck.

The Church grew almost entirely within an urban milieu where it drew in both skilled and unskilled workers.

> "The vast majority of Christians were urban workers. Those artisans specifically mentioned on funerary inscriptions include linen weavers, traders, mat makers, mule keepers, stone cutters and tailors but there is a growing number of 'middle' class occupations: small landowners, bailiffs on the imperial estates and, at the higher end, the manager of the imperial dye factory at Tyre, a freed slave . . . this is overwhelmingly a Church of artisans with a minority of wealthy and more literate leaders."[475]

Funerary inscriptions would be far more likely to mark the graves of the well-to-do—what Freeman here calls "middle class"—rather than the more impoverished members of the congregation, so the real class composition of the community would have been skewed significantly towards the lower end in comparison to the archaeological record. Whilst there was a growing correspondence between the two aristocracies of the Roman state and the Church—which is an important development that we will return to—the upper echelons of Roman society are unlikely to have been a numerical majority or even a large minority in the Church congregation as a whole.

Writing in the mid-third century against the Celsus, a critic of Christianity, Origen quotes his opponent who dismisses the Church as a community of bumpkins: "In previous houses [churches] also we see wool-workers, cobblers, laundry-workers and the most illiterate and bucolic yokels, who would not dare to say anything at all in front of their elders and more intelligent masters . . ."[476] This is an interesting comment, not only for its description of city-based artisans as the main component of the Church, but it also alludes to the strict hierarchy, between the laity and their "masters", which was beginning to develop.

In *The First Urban Christians*, Wayne A Meeks develops this theme further, reinforcing the idea that it was *workers* rather than slaves or the outright destitute who were the mainstay of the Church. The first Christians were converts from Judaism or from among the fellow-travellers of Judaism, the god-fearers. Several studies of inscriptions and papyri show that the Jews' occupations were predominantly urban and artisan and the spread of Christian occupations matched that very closely. Meeks cites studies that mention a stone cutter, a maker of clay lamps, a painter, a seaman, a mint worker, a goldsmith, a coppersmith, a confectioner, a fowler, a greengrocer a dyer, carpenters, a bracelet-maker, a

---

[475] Freeman, *A New History of Early Christianity*, p 220.
[476] Origen, *Against Celsus*, 3, 56

sausage-maker and a moneychanger, as well as some impoverished farmers and slaves.[477]

That is not to say there are no references to slaves. In 1 Corinthians, chapter 7, Paul directly addresses a slave and suggesting that while freedom would be an opportunity it is not essential to be a Christian:

> "Were you a slave when called? Never mind. But if you can gain your freedom, avail yourself of the opportunity. For he who was called to the Lord as a slave is a freedman of the Lord."[478]

Paul's short epistle to Philemon is actually an appeal to the owner of a runaway slave to forgive the runaway who has become a Christian. It is quite clear, therefore, that there were slaves and slave owners in the Christian community. As an aside, in both of these (and in other) instances the Revised Standard Version of the Bible translates the key word, correctly, as "slave", whereas the Authorised King James Version uses the word "servant". This subtle change might be motivated by a desire on the part of some editors to gloss over the fact that the early Church *accepted slavery* as a simple fact of life and offered no theological or political justification for its abolition. The 'clarification' of the New Testament clearly did not end with the first few centuries of Christianity!

A significant factor in the growth of Christianity was its support within the imperial army. The daily life and activity of legionaries, mixing hardship and constant danger on the one side, with solidarity and comradeship on the other, made them a ready source of conversion. Their social position was analogous to that of skilled or semi-skilled workers in the cities and from that point of view, the Roman legion could be considered as being like a mobile town. By the time that the Church was given imperial sanction in the early fourth century, entire legions were reported to be composed mainly of Christians, and the introduction of Christianity to parts of the western empire was attributed to the presence of foreign garrisons.

There were few rivals to the growing Christian cult. The Mithras cult was perhaps the only one, for as well as being popular in the army, Mithraism had many similarities to Christianity, including a divine son born to a virgin, baptism, a symbolic shared meal, a sacrifice to conquer death and a resurrection. As Christianity gained a solid foothold within the Roman state, Mithraism was one of the first cults to be suppressed, with its shrines wrecked and temples destroyed.

Revision of the revolutionary message

But as the Church organisation became more established, its programme for the future gradually evolved, so that what came to be offered was no longer a social revolution, here on earth, but a *spiritual kingdom*—and that not even in the

---

[477]   Meeks, *The First Urban Christians*, p 39
[478]   1 Corinthians, 7, 20-22

foreseeable future. More importantly, as the class character of the Church ideology was transformed, the theology was changed to match. Some of these changes must have begun very early in the life of the Church because they are reflected even in the gospels. It is interesting to see how the New Testament reflects both the early egalitarian tendencies and the watered-down versions added later. For example, the Gospel of Luke has Jesus saying:

> "How hardly shall they that have riches enter into the kingdom of God! For it is easier for a camel to go through the eye of a needle, than for a rich man to enter into the kingdom of God."[479]

Similarly, in the Sermon on the Mount, Jesus is quoted as saying:

> "Blessed are the poor; for yours is the kingdom of God. Blessed are ye that hunger now, for ye shall be filled. Blessed are ye that weep now: for ye shall laugh . . . woe unto you that are rich! For ye have received your consolation. Woe unto ye that are full! For ye shall hunger. Woe unto ye that laugh now! For ye shall mourn and weep."[480]

The author of Matthew has Jesus making the same or similar statements about rich and poor:

> "If thou wilt be perfect, go and sell that thou hast, and give to the poor, and thou shalt have treasure in heaven: and come and follow me . . . Verily I say unto you, that a rich man shall hardly enter into the kingdom of heaven . . . it is easier for a camel to go through the eye of a needle, than for a rich man to enter into the kingdom of God."[481]

The New Testament epistle of James was written by someone in the middle of the second century. But even at this later stage, the hatred felt by the poorest Christians comes through:

> "Hath not God chosen the poor of this world, rich in faith and heirs of the kingdom which he hath promised to them that love him? But ye have despised the poor. Do not rich men oppress you, and drag you before the judgement seats. Do they not blaspheme that worthy name by the which ye are called? . . . Go to now, ye rich men, weep and howl for your miseries that shall come up on you. Your riches are corrupted, and your garments are moth-eaten. Your gold and silver is cankered; and the rust of them shall be a witness against you, and shall eat your flesh as it were fire. Ye have

---

[479]   Luke, 18, 24.

[480]   Luke, 6, 20.

[481]   Matthew, 19, 21-24

heaped treasure together for the last days. Behold the hire of the labourers who have reaped down your fields, which is of you kept back by fraud, crieth: and the cries of them which have reaped are entered into the ears of the Lord . . ."[482]

But by the time the Sermon of the Mount came to be written in the Gospel of Matthew, some of the class content has been changed to read, "Blessed are the poor *in spirit*: for theirs is the kingdom of heaven."[483] Unlike in Luke, there are no diatribes in Matthew against the rich with their "'cankered" silver and "moth-eaten" garments.

The Letter of Barnabas was one of the most important early documents of the Church. Some churches in fact included it as part of the New Testament. It is supposed to have been written by one of the companions of Paul, although clearly written later than his epistles, since it mentions the destruction of the Jerusalem Temple in 70 CE. There is the appeal to the poor and oppressed typical of much of the early Christian literature:

"Loosen every bond of injustice; unravel the strangle-hold of coercive agreements; send forth in forgiveness those who are downtrodden; tear up every unfair contract. Break your bread for the hungry, and provide clothing for anyone you see naked. Bring the homeless under your roof. And if you see anyone who has been humbled, do not despise him . . ."[484]

But in time, what had been for the early Joshua cults an outspoken revolutionary opposition to the Roman Empire was turned into servile acquiescence. Again, there are tendencies in this direction from a very early stage. Thus in his epistle to the Romans, Paul makes it clear that there is a duty on Christians: "Render therefore to all their dues: tribute to whom tribute is due, custom to whom custom, fear to whom fear, honour to whom honour."[485] Given his almost servile attitude to the Romans, there is little doubt that had he been in Jerusalem during the great revolt, Paul would have been in the same camp as Josephus, holding back and aiming to betray the revolution. The Gospel of Luke has Jesus say the now famous lines, "Render unto Caesar, therefore, the things which be Caesar's and unto God the things which be God's."[486] It is clear from the Gospel of Thomas, a very early work, that such sayings were common even in the early days of Christianity, but what was new was that they became completely *central* to the outlook of the gilded Church that developed in later centuries. By the time that we have the writings of the early

---

[482] James, 2, 5 and 5, 1
[483] Matthew, 5, 3
[484] *Letter of Barnabas*, 3, 3
[485] Romans, 13, 7
[486] Luke, 20, 25.

Church fathers they were full of praise for the *Pax Romana* under which the world lived.

Kautsky cites at great length some of the writing of John Chrysostom, a sainted Christian writer of the fourth century, who comments on the part of Acts which refers to the primitive communism of the early Christians. "If we should do this today," Chrysostom complains, "we should live much more happily", the clear implication being that by that time, *it was no being longer* done. Chrysostom muses long and hard about what it must have been like in the early days when the Church was far more principled than it later came to be.

> "Let us picture the thing to ourselves . . . if each man should give up all his money, his fields, his lands, his houses (not to mention the slaves, for we may assume that the first Christians had none, having most probably liberated them), I suppose a mass of about a million pounds of gold could be raised, perhaps even twice or thrice as much. For let us see, how many persons does our city (Constantinople) contain? How many Christians? Are there not fully one hundred thousand? . . . If this experiment [!] turned out so brilliantly successful in the case of three thousand or five thousand persons (the first Christians) and none of them suffered any lack, how much better must be the outcome in the case of so great a number as now? . . . For if in those days, when the number of the faithful was so small, only from three to five thousand, if at that time when the whole world was hostile to us, where we met with consolation nowhere, our predecessors set about the task so resolutely, how much more confidence should we have, now that there are faithful everywhere by the grace of God!"[487]

As a part of the changing class basis of the theology, the Church also altered the position of women in the Church. The genuine epistles of Paul and even the earlier gospels show that women had an important position in the early community. In the gospel narratives written at the end of the first century, women are frequently portrayed as the companions of Jesus and Mary Magdalene has an important role. In the authentic letters of Paul, there are several female Church members mentioned by name. It wasn't an accident that the detractors of the Church, like Celsus, were able to condemn the Church for being composed mostly of children, women and slaves. In 1 Galatians (3, 27), which is believed to be genuine, we find Paul writing: "There is neither Jew nor Greek, neither slave nor free; there is not male and female; for all of you are one in Jesus Christ."

But in 1 Timothy (2,11), written by a forger a century later, Paul is made to say the exact opposite, showing the change that was beginning to affect the Church: "Let the woman learn in silence with all subjection. But I suffer not a woman to teach, nor to usurp authority over the man, but to be in silence." It is not an

---

[487]   Kautsky, p 334

accident that the same second century epistle of "Paul" also upholds the role of the leaders and appears to hint that they have not always been monogamous: "A bishop, then, must be blameless; the husband of one wife, vigilant, sober . . . let the deacons be husbands of one wife."

The first epistle to the Corinthians is generally taken to be genuine, and there is an early passage (11,5), in which Paul writes, "But every woman that prayeth or prophesieth with her head uncovered dishonoured her head . . ."—suggesting, in other words that it was acceptable for women (with head covered) to pray and prophesy. Yet this passage is followed by another three chapters later (14, 34-35) which contradicts it: "Let your women keep silence in their churches; for it is not permitted unto them to speak; but they are commanded to be under obeisance as also saith the law. And if they will learn anything, let them ask their husbands at home; for it is a shame for women to speak in the church." In different early versions of 1 Corinthians, this misogynistic piece appears in different places. The obvious explanation that most scholars have arrived at to resolve this contradiction is that the anti-feminist piece was added a century later, perhaps by the same scribe or scribes who wrote the forgery known as the first epistle to Timothy.

Although it was described as a forgery by the church father Tertullian, who even named the forger and his motive for doing it, *The Acts of Paul* was another book that circulated widely in second century Christian communities. The forgery may have originated, like so much of the literature, in oral tradition and folk tales. One part of *The Acts of Paul*, known as *The Acts of Thecla* recounted the travels and ministry of a woman who had been an associate of Paul. Thecla's own preaching, the frequent scrapes she got into and the miraculous escapes must have had a special resonance among women in the congregation and as the leadership roles of women disappeared in the Church, it continued as something of a subversive document for centuries afterwards. There is no better illustration of the Church's diminution of the status of women than the manufactured legend of Mary Magdalene as a *prostitute*. Although she is nowhere described in the canonical gospels as such, to the Catholic Church she was a prostitute for nearly fourteen hundred years, from the declaration that she *was*, by Pope Gregory in 591, to the eventual admission that she *wasn't* by Pope John Paul II in 1969!

The delay of the Kingdom

The Joshua cults had made their initial appeals based on the imminent coming of the Kingdom in the sense of a *social revolution*. The supression of the revolutionary movements in 70 CE and 135 CE, therefore, must have shaken to the core the belief that many had in a messianic deliverance from Rome. But at least for some others, the day of judgement was still at hand, a belief maintained principally (but not exclusively) within the early Christian cults. The Book of Revelation, one of the earliest Christian books, is undoubtedly a product of this early post-revolt stage, when there was as yet no clear view of a real historicised Jesus character, but when the concept of the coming of the Kingdom and deliverance through a messiah still loomed large for its readers. Revelation, written even before the sacking of Jerusalem in 70 CE, was an important book for the early Christian communities, precisely because of its uncompromising apocalyptic tone and it was despite and not because of this that it was included in the official canon.

The epistles of Paul, the earliest writings to survive from any Christian leader gave the impression of the coming of the Kingdom *earlier* rather than *later*:

> "For the Lord himself shall descend from heaven with a shout, with the voice of the archangel, and with the trump of God: and the dead in Christ shall rise first: Then we which are alive and remain shall be caught up together with them in the clouds, to meet the Lord in the air: and so shall we ever be with the Lord.[488]

In his epistle to the Corinthians, Paul repeated the same message: "But this I say, brethren, the time has grown short . . . for the fashion of this world passeth away."[489] The gospels, written many decades after Paul's writings, also carry echoes of the early apocalyptic view. The first to be written, the Gospel of Mark, made reference to an imminent apocalypse even in the lifetime of the disciples. At various times, Jesus is made to say, ". . . The kingdom of God is at hand"[490], ". . . There be some of them that stand here, which shall not taste death, till they have seen the Kingdom of God come with power"[491] and ". . . this generation shall not pass, till all these things be done."[492]. The imminence is still reflected in Luke and Matthew: "This generation will not pass away until all be fulfilled . . ."[493] and ". . . when they persecute you in this city, flee ye to another; for verily I say unto you, Ye shall not have gone over the cities of Israel, till the Son of Man be come."[494]

But the imminence of the apocalypse was eventually brushed under the theological carpet and the redemption of the masses was postponed once and for all to the next life. The Kingdom of God was no longer an imminent revolution and was instead removed to the dim and distant future. In the meantime, the members of the congregation were enjoined to be pious, modest and respectful and to know their rightful place in the scheme of things.

The authors who came to dominate the written theology of the Church, who reduced the significance of women, postponed the Kingdom to an indefinite future date and, not least, looked out only for the "poor in spirit" rather than just the "poor" were the literate members of the community, the bishops and those with 'connections' to the ruling regime.

---

[488]   1 Thessalonians, 4, 16
[489]   1 Corinthians, 8, 29-31
[490]   Mark, 1, 14
[491]   Mark, 9, 1
[492]   Mark 13, 30
[493]   Luke, 21, 32
[494]   Matthew, 23

"It appears that the Christians copying the texts were the ones who wanted the texts—that is, they were copying the texts either for their own personal and/or communal use or they were making them for the sake of others in their community . . . some of these people—or most of them?—may have been the leaders of the communities. We have reason to think that the earliest Christian leaders were among the wealthiest members of the Church . . . Is it possible, then, that the Church leaders were responsible, at least a good bit of the time, for the copying of the Christian literature being read to the congregation?"[495]

The answer to this rhetorical question is a resounding 'Yes' . . . and more than "a good bit of the time." The gospels were written and later amended from time to time to become *the theological compass of the Church aristocracy*. Despite this, in what came to be the New Testament, there still remained some lingering echoes of the older Christian organisations that had been founded in primitive communism and had been based on the aspirations of the poor and oppressed.

"As the influence of the educated classes upon Christianity increases," Kautsky wrote, "Christianity departs more and more from communism".[496] From having been originally a community with *all wealth held in common*, the Church had gradually shifted its emphasis to the *giving of alms*. This was still, to be sure, a significant factor in the welfare and supportive functions of the Church: the sense of community provided within the congregation was unlike anything else in any other organisation in the Roman Empire. But it was nonetheless far removed from the original ethos. Instead of holding all things in common, the memory of fellowship was reduced to a common meal and even this was eventually ritualised to involve *symbolic* as opposed to real food. The early communism was retained only as *theoretical* obligation. The Christian writer, Tertullian, in the mid second century, described the organisational structure of the Church:

"Even if there does exist a sort of common fund, it is not made up of fees, as though we contracted for our worship. Each of us puts in a small amount one day a month, or whatever he pleases; and only if he pleases and if he is able, for there is no compulsion in the matter, everyone contributing of his own free will. These monies are, as it were, the deposits of piety. They are expended upon no banquets or drinking bouts or useless eating houses, but on feeding and burying poor people, on behalf of boys and girls who have neither parents nor money, in support of old folk, unable now to go about, as well as for people who are shipwrecked or who may be in the mines or exiled in islands or in prison, so long as their distress is for the sake of God's fellowship, and they themselves entitled to maintenance by their confession . . . we who feel ourselves united heart

---

495   Ehrman, *Jesus misquoted*, p 51.
496   Kautsky, p 337.

and soul, have no difficulties about community of goods, with us all is common, except our wives; the community ceases there, where alone others practise it."[497]

What Tertullian is describing is clearly not a society of primitive communism akin to the Essenes. It already had considerable class differentiation within its ranks. But it is a *welfare* organisation; the "confession of faith" offers an entitlement to *social insurance* that is simply not available anywhere else, with the exception of the Jewish synagogue. In a lecture given twenty years before Kautsky's book was published, the Christian historian Edward Hatch described the social role of the Church as follows:

". . . the Christian communities were unlike the other associations which surrounded them. Other associations were charitable: but whereas in them it was an accident, in the Christian associations it was of the essence . . . they brought into the European world that regard for the poor which had been for several centuries the burden of the Jewish hymns. They fused the Ebionism of Palestine with the practical organisations of Graeco-Roman civilisation . . . The Christian communities grew up, as we have seen, in the midst of poverty. They had a special message to the poor, and the poor naturally flowed into them. And the poverty in the midst of which they grew was intensified by the conditions of their existence. Some of their members were outcasts from their homes: others had been compelled by the stern rules of Christian discipline to abandon employments which that discipline forbad. In times of persecution the confessors in prison had to be fed: those whose property had been confiscated had to be supported: those who had been sold into captivity had to be ransomed. Above all there were the widows and orphans . . . Christianity was, and grew because it was, a great fraternity. The name 'brother', by which a Jew addressed his fellow-Jew, came to be the ordinary designation by which a Christian addressed his fellow-Christians."[498]

Kautsky probably does a disservice to the early guilds and clubs of artisans as well as to synagogue communities when he suggests that their charitable work was "accidental". On the contrary, they purposefully pursued such activities in the interests of their members. But nowhere were they as systematic, as extensive or as all-inclusive as the congregations of the Church. Even the great British historian Edward Gibbon places an emphasis on the social and charitable structures of the growing Church and the significance of alms.

---

[497]   Kautsky p 421
[498]   Hatch, *The Organisation of the Early Christian Churches,* p 36-42.

"According to the discretion of the bishop, it [alms] was distributed to support widows and orphans, the lame, the sick, and the aged of the community; to comfort strangers and pilgrims, and to alleviate the misfortunes of prisoners and captives . . . Such an institution, which paid less regard to the merit than to the distress of the object, very materially conduced to the progress of Christianity. The Pagans, who were actuated by a sense of humanity, while they derided the doctrines, acknowledged the benevolence of the new sect. The prospect of immediate relief and future protection allured into its hospitable bosom many of those unhappy persons whom the neglect of the world would have abandoned to the miseries of want, or sickness, and of old age."[499]

Kautsky argued that it was not the ideological structures that built the Church and that is confirmed by what Tertullian, Hatch and Gibbon are referring to here: that the strength of the Church lay in its social structures. *We would argue that the social role played by the Church was the fundamental reason for the growth of Christianity, not the promise of the redemption of sins.*

That is not to say that there would not have been resentment and even conflicts, as the growing differentiation between the alms-distributors and the alms-receivers became clear. The New Testament epistle of James, generally thought to be an early second century work, complains about the different treatment of rich and poor in Church:

"For if there comes unto your assembly a man with a gold ring, in goodly apparel, and there comes in also a poor man in vile raiment; and ye have respect to him that weareth the gay clothing, and say unto him, Sit thou here in a good place; and say to the poor, Stand thou there or sit here under my footstool; are ye not then partial in yourselves, and are become judges of evil thoughts? . . . Hath not God chosen the poor of this world rich in faith, and heirs of the kingdom which he hath promised to them that love him? But ye have despised the poor . . ."[500]

As the Church increased in size, influence and power, the leading elements of the bureaucracy were increasingly integrated into the aristocracy of the Roman Empire. The senatorial class, particularly in the western part of the Empire, were tremendously wealthy—they were rich landowners with great influence and power. The Church increasingly spoke to this class in a language that it would understand, preaching stability and loyalty to the state and removing any barriers, theological or otherwise, to possessing the same ostentatious wealth within the bosom of the Church. Christianity began to spread within the Roman aristocracy precisely because it posed no threat to their family wealth, prestige or influence. On the

---

[499]   Gibbon, *The Decline and Fall of the Roman Empire,* p 277
[500]   James, 2, 2

contrary, having a bishop or two in the extended family enhanced its social standing as charitable and righteous folk. Indeed, generosity to the poor was not so much seen as a benefit to the recipients as a shrewd investment in the afterlife. "Give to the poor", Augustine wrote, "and you shall have treasure in heaven. You shall not be without treasure, but what you are worried about on earth you shall possess secure in heaven. Send it on ahead then."

As the Church grew in prestige and the old imperial structures wobbled close to collapse in some parts of the empire, an ecclesiastic career became almost the default career of the sons of the aristocracy. Once the die was cast and Christianity received official sanction, the campaign of reassurances to the rich and wealthy went into overdrive.

> "As emperors and church leaders promulgated support for Christianity, as they strove to assure aristocrats that changing religion would not deny them social esteem nor undermine the aristocratic institutions upon which their social position rested, they also tried to make Christianity appealing to the aristocrats . . . As their sermons and letters show, church leaders in the late fourth century modulated the message of Christianity in ways that soothed certain aristocratic sensibilities . . . the discourse and sermons of Christian leaders came to incorporate not only the formal aspects of aristocratic status concerns but also the values and ideology of the late Roman Empire."[501]

This particular citation may be summarising the changes after Constantine, but the direction of travel of the Church had been established *long before*, reflecting the interests of the Church bureaucracy that had begun to coalesce around the bishops as early as the beginning of the second century. The theological and ideological outlook of the Church was constantly re-calibrated to match the interests of the Roman ruling class. By the fourth century, the bishops had become so wealthy that they were effectively the new princes of the ruling elite. Edward Gibbon makes the point that they were barely distinguishable from their pagan equivalents within the aristocracy as a whole.

> "Fraud, envy and malice prevailed in every congregation. The presbyters aspired to the Episcopal office, which every day became an object more worthy of their ambitions. The bishops, who contended with each other for ecclesiastical pre-eminence, appeared by their conduct to claim a secular and tyrannical power in the church; and the lively faith which still distinguished the Christians from the Gentiles was shown much less in their lives than in their controversial writings."[502]

---

[501] Salzman, *The Making of the Christian Aristocracy*, p 17
[502] Gibbon, *The Decline and Fall of the Roman Empire*, p 336.

Contradictory class forces

The Church is not the only example that history has provided of an organisation that reflects within itself contradictory class elements at one and the same time. The rise of the mass trade unions in Britain in the nineteenth century was a huge step forward for the working class, greeted with great acclaim by the pioneers of socialism, including Marx and Engels. But Marx and Engels also noted that once the trade unions reached a certain stage of development, there followed the rise of a labour aristocracy which, while providing a leadership to workers, also came to depend upon the unions' structure and finance for their livelihood. Rather than seeing the organisations of the working class as vehicles of struggle, to improve the condition of workers or to change society, the labour aristocracy came to see these organisations only as the source of their very lucrative salaries, which were well above those of the workers they purported to represented. Shortly before his death in 1894 Friedrich Engels wrote:

> "The history of primitive Christianity presents remarkable coincidences with the modern workers' movement. Like the latter, Christianity was originally a movement of the oppressed; it first appeared as a religion of slaves and freedmen, of the poor, the outcasts, of the peoples subjugated or dispersed by Rome. Both Christianity and Socialism preach an approaching redemption from servitude and misery; Christianity assigns this redemption to a future life in Heaven after death; Socialism would attain it in this world by a transformation of society."[503]

Kautsky used this citation and took the analogy of Engels one step further. "If Engels had pursued this subject", Kautsky wrote, "he would have discovered traces of similar transformations in the modern workers' movement."

> "Like Christianity, this [workers'] movement is obliged to create permanent organs in the course of its growth, a sort of professional bureaucracy in the party, as well as in the unions, without which it cannot function, which are a necessity for it, which must continue to grow, and obtain more and more important duties. This bureaucracy—which must be taken in the broad sense as including not only the administrative officials, but also editors and parliamentary delegates—will not this bureaucracy in the course of things become a new aristocracy? Will it not become an aristocracy dominating and exploiting the working masses and finally attaining the power to deal with the state authorities on equal terms, thus being tempted not to overthrow them but join them?"[504]

---

[503] Engels, *Die Neue Zeit*, September 1894, vol xiii, no 1.
[504] Karl Kautsky, *Foundations of Christianity*, p 463

Having posed the correct questions, Kautsky unfortunately ducks the answers, the parallel, he believes, not being "perfect". But in the words of Marx, "conditions determine consciousness" and as every worker knows, if one of their supposed representatives is able to wine and dine with the bosses of industry on equal terms, live at the same living standards and holiday on the same yachts, they can hardly see social and economic problems from a worker's point of view. They end up having more of a vested interest in their own status quo than in rocking the boat. The policy of the aristocrat of labour resolves itself into the emancipation of the working class, one by one, starting with themselves. As one historian put it, "the success of Christianity in late antiquity depended always on the balancing of the subversive and the bourgeois elements."[505]

Even in the very earliest communities of Christians, in the mid first century, there were some indications of stratification on class lines. The epistles of Paul, as we have already mentioned, testify to the existence of both slaves and slave owners in the Church. In his long letter admonishing the Corinthians for their backsliding, he refers to some members taking out lawsuits against others.[506] In the same letter, Paul refers to differences in the church—"when ye come together in the church, I hear that there be divisions among you . . ." Moreover, he continues, when the community comes together for a common meal the food is not in actual fact shared in common. "For in eating, everyone taketh before the other his own supper: and one is hungry, and another is drunken . . . if any man hunger, let him eat at home; that ye come not together unto condemnation."[507] This is interesting in that it shows that a genuine common meal was the expected norm for Paul, in keeping with the origins of the Church in primitive communism, but that some within the Corinthian community perceived themselves as being "condemned" for their poverty, perhaps in not taking sufficient food to the shared meal. In Corinth, it appears, the common meal no longer involved a genuine sharing of food.

In *The First Urban Christians*, Meeks makes reference to this divide between well-to-do Christians, in whose large and comfortable houses the congregation would have met, and the poorer members of the community. He cites another scholar, Theissen, who in turn uses some of the works of the Roman writer Pliny to show how it was not uncommon for a rich Roman to humiliate his poorer meal guest by putting food and wine of an inferior quality in front of him, while the host himself ate and drank only the finest.

> "If at the common meals of the Christian community, held in his [the rich man's] dining room, he moreover made distinctions in the food he provided for those of his own social level and those who were of lower rank, that would not have been at all out of the ordinary, even though

---

505   Averil Cameron, *Early Incomes in the Early Islamic State,* in *Elites Old and New in the Byzantine and Early Islamic Near East,* p 94

506   1 Corinthians, 6, 1-11

507   1 Corinthians, 11.

there were some voices in pagan society who protested the practice. It was precisely the humiliation of the have-nots to which Pliny and the satirists objected. Paul objects on quite different grounds, but Theissen has given good reason for seeking the roots of the denounced behaviour in the 'status-specific expectations' of a sharply stratified society."[508]

The composite document known as *The Acts of Peter and the Twelve Apostles* was one of those found with the Gnostic works at Nag Hammadi, but according to its translator, is not itself a Gnostic work. The editor of the work, according to James Robinson, was a second or third century Christian who "seems to be standing within the broad church and to be appealing for a return to apostolic practice on the part of the leaders."[509] The editor clearly stands in the tradition of the original Church, emphasising the class character of its appeal. It has Jesus commanding, for example,

> "To the poor of that city give what they need in order to live until I give them what is better . . . The rich men of the city, however, those who did not see fit even to acknowledge me, but who revelled in their wealth and pride—with such men as these therefore, do not dine in [their] houses, nor be friends with them, lest their partiality influence you. For many in the churches have shown partiality to the rich, because they also are sinful, and they give occasion for others to sin."

If there were signs of stratification on class lines in the early Church, how much more would that have been the case as the decades and centuries rolled by? From a very early point, therefore, the Church manifested contradictory features—the establishment of a community that offered material benefits to its flock and at the same time, the development of a layer of full-time leaders and bureaucrats who achieved great personal wealth and became increasingly tied into the machinery of the Roman Empire.

Notwithstanding this growing stratification, the Christian community was still more inclusive overall than any other voluntary association, club or society in Roman society. Moreover, as some additional compensation for the despair and insecurity faced by the most hard-pressed, Christianity at least seemed to offer some meaning to their lives and the promise of redemption in the next life.

> For the poor, the Church was an *international redeemer* as opposed to the Jewish God who was a *national redeemer*. The Christian creed "did not plan to throw off only the yoke of foreign rulers, but of *all* rulers, including those at home. They [the Christians] summoned to themselves only the

---

[508]   Meeks, *The First Urban Christians*, p 68

[509]   Robinson, *The Nag Hammadi Library, The definitive translation of the Gnostic Scripture*, p 289

weary and heavy-laden; the Day of Judgement was to be a day of revenge on all the rich and powerful. The passion that animated them was not race hatred but class hatred . . . a messianic hope that involved a redemption of the poor must necessarily have found a willing ear among the poor of all nations . . . the social content of the Gospel must have found ready acceptance in the proletarian strata of such 'god-fearing pagans'. It is they who transplanted it into other non-Jewish proletarian groups, which offered a favourable soil for the doctrine of the crucified Messiah."[510]

It would be wrong to completely ignore the significance of the Church, in Kautsky's words, as a religious "redeemer". For the overwhelming mass of the population, there were few reasons to be cheerful in the first few centuries of the Roman Empire and disease, starvation, war and poverty lurked around every corner. In the absence of any other hope, it would hardly be surprising if the meek should look for some meaning in their lives through the promise of redemption and eternal life in the hereafter. But the central factor in the growth of the Church was the fact that, as an organisation, it provided far more in material benefits than had ever been available in traditional civic and trade cults. Even long after the clergy were appointed, the Church retained a lingering veneer of democracy and, at least in words, parts of the gospels still criticised the rich and powerful.

To make it easier for newcomers to adopt the faith, particularly those who were not drawn in from the periphery of the synagogue, the Church adapted itself to local gods who were accommodated as saints and to local customs, including those pagan festivals from which we get Christmas. As the *New Catholic Encyclopaedia* records:

"The birth of Christ was assigned the date of the winter solstice (December 25 in the Julian calendar, January 6 in the Egyptian), because on this day, as the Sun began its return to northern skies, the pagan devotees of Mithras celebrated the Dies Natalis Solis Invicti (Birthday of the Invincible Sun). On December 25, 274, [Roman Emperor] Aurelian had proclaimed the Sun God the principal patron of the Empire and dedicated a temple to Him in the Campus Martius. Christmas originated at a time when the cult of the Sun was particularly strong in Rome."[511]

As the Church became increasingly successful and its role in the economic and civil governance of large communities became ever more extensive, it began to get supporters from the Roman middle and upper classes. As Kautsky explained,

"Origen, in the reign of Alexander Severus (222-235 CE) says that 'at the present day rich men and many high dignitaries, as well as delicate and

---

[510]   Kautsky, p 379/383
[511]   *New Catholic Encyclopedia,* volume III, p.656, 1967 ed

nobly born ladies, receive the Christian messengers of the word; that is to say Christianity then obtained successes of which it had not previously been able to boast . . . consequently, from the time of Commodus onwards, the spread of Christianity amongst the upper classes is variously and expressly attested, whereas the reverse is the case in regard to the preceding period . . ."[512]

It was somewhat of a paradox that the Church increasingly accommodated itself to the Roman Empire, even despite the occasional persecutions. In around 175 CE Bishop Melito of Sardes wrote to the Emperor praising successive Roman rulers and giving them credit for the success of Christianity: "Our way of thought first sprang up in a foreign land, but it flowered among your own peoples in the glorious reign of your ancestor Augustus . . . from the reign of Augustus the Empire has suffered no damage, on the contrary everything has gone splendidly and gloriously, and every prayer has been answered."[513]. For their part, the main preoccupation of the Roman leaders was civil order and the loyalty of the army—they couldn't care less about which gods their subjects followed or did not follow. The only expectation that was placed on all was their support for the state and the status quo.

> "Even such an elaborate attack on Christianity as that by Celsus includes an invitation to the Christians not to create difficulties for the Empire by refusing to serve in the army and in the imperial administration . . . Furthermore, the correspondence between Pliny and Trajan and the very texts of the Acts of the Christian Martyrs show that the Roman authorities did not find it easy to explain why they were persecuting the Christians."[514]

The leaders of the Church went out of their way to ingratiate themselves with the emperors. In fact, the unity and coherence of the Roman Empire was written into the theology of the Church in that it was attributed to being part of God's master-plan to spread Christianity. In the words of Origen, "God was preparing the nations for His teaching by submitting them all to one single Roman Emperor."

> "What is more remarkable is that Christian thinkers of the first three centuries should have built up a theology of history of this kind during persecutions, however intermittent, and while claiming religious obligations incompatible with the ordinary loyalties of the Roman state. The Christians built their interpretation of the Church while they were declared enemies of Rome."[515]

---

[512]   Kautsky, p 325
[513]   Quoted in Wengst, *Pax Romana*, p 172.
[514]   Momigliani, *On Pagans, Jews and Christians*, p 136.
[515]   Momigliani, *On Pagans, Jews and Christians*, p 152

Where Christians were persecuted, it was in most cases a locally-inspired assault and was invariably a result of their being made a scape-goat for natural calamities. It was considered a civic duty for all Romans to make the necessary sacrifices and observances to those gods revered in their own city, town or district, in order to guarantee a good harvest and deliverance from pestilence. Most times, it would be acceptable to turn a blind eye to what they called the "atheism" of the Christians—that is, their rejection of everyone else's gods. But on those occasions when there were natural disasters like epidemics or crop-failures, the wrath of the local population would fall on the local Christians or Jews who had been seen to neglect their civic duties. This is shown in the polemic against the opponents of Christianity, written by Tertullian in the early third century:

> "If the Tiber has overflowed its banks, if the Nile has remained in its bed, if the sky has been still, or the earth been in commotion, if death has made its devastations, or famine its afflictions, your cry immediately is, 'This is the fault of the Christians!'"[516]

The persecution of the Church was not without its effect, in terms of desertions from the community. One of the reasons for the popularity of the early Christian book, *The Shepherd of Hermas*, was precisely because the entire book was based on the problem of what to do with those who had fallen away from the Church. It argues that they should have a second chance if they embraced the faith again, although not a third one. The long list of Christian martyrs is highly exaggerated by Church historians—the historian Edward Gibbon puts the figure at fewer than two thousand over three centuries—and for the overwhelming majority of them there is little or no evidence. But, in any case, even the Church's own figures pale into insignificance in comparison to the bloody holocaust that was visited on heretics following the institution of Christianity as the official faith of the Empire.[517] On the whole, the Romans' persecution of the Church failed,

> ". . . partly because they were incompetently managed, partly because there were long periods of respite. In Gaul, for instance, the Christians were unmolested between 258 and 303 CE; and in fact the period of grace in this part was longer still as the ruler in 303 was Constantine Chlorus who was only half-hearted in carrying out the edicts of Diocletian. Christianity in Gaul, as in other near-frontier areas, was helped by the inactivity of government and by the invasions of the barbarians . . . one of the greatest strengths of Christianity was its social organisation. It was, from near its beginning, when it broke the early synagogue-link with the Temple, a universal religion whose missionaries developed their own local centres and persuaded their followers to maintain relations with one another. Here

---

[516] Tertullian, *Ad Nationes*, 1, 6, 7.
[517] The Inquisition, for example, was responsible for hundreds of thousands of deaths.

was a remarkable 'advance' on the isolated scattering that had seemed to be characteristic of many pagan cults"[518]

The last great repression against Christians was that of the emperor Diocletian, at the end of the third century. By this time Christianity probably had too great a hold in the state apparatus itself—notably the army—for the possibility of putting into effect any large-scale pogrom. Friedrich Engels, writing fifteen years before Kautsky, also referred to the revolutionary traditions of the early Christians. He makes a humorous comparison between German anti-Socialist laws and the anti-Christian laws of the emperor Diocletian. "Now almost sixteen hundred years ago," he wrote, "there was at work in the Roman Empire a dangerous revolutionary party . . . this revolutionary party, known under the name of Christians, also had a strong representation in the army; entire legions were composed of Christians."[519]

The monastic movement

The growth of the monastic movement was in part a reaction against what was seen as a growing secularisation of the Church, in the sense of its growing involvement in civic administration, and the merging of the Church aristocracy with the Roman aristocracy. Increasingly, the wealthier sections of the congregation and clergy were coming to reflect the pomp and wealth of the Roman aristocracy. Jerome, one of the most revered Catholic saints and an advocate of the monastic movement, railed against the ostentation being shown by some of the Church leaders. In a passage that could have been directed at the expensively dressed priests, bishops, cardinals and archbishops of the modern day, he wrote,

> "Such men think of nothing but their dress; they use perfumes freely, and see that there are no creases in their leather shoes. Their curling hair shows traces of the tongs; their fingers glisten with rings; they walk on tiptoe across a damp road, not to splash their feet. When you see men acting in that way, think of them rather as bridegrooms than as clergymen. If he sees a pillow that takes his fancy, or an elegant table-cover, or, indeed, any article of furniture, he praises it, looks admiringly at it, takes it into his hand, and, complaining that he has nothing of the kind, begs or rather extorts it from its owner."[520]

In his *Short history of Monks and Monasteries*, Alfred Wesley Wishart acknowledges that one of the factors that led to the growth of monasteries and its associated asceticism was the "worldliness" of the growing Church. Writing as a Christian himself, he comments that

---

[518]   Wardman, *Relgion and Statecraft among the Romans*, p 133.
[519]   Engels, introduction to *Class struggles in France, from 1848 to 1850, by Karl Marx*, 1895
[520]   Quoted in Wishart, *A Short History of Monks and Monasteries*, p 26

"It is a common tradition that in the first three centuries the practices and spirit of the Church were comparatively pure and elevated. Harnack[521] says, 'This tradition is false. The Church was already secularised [in the sense of being responsible for what we now call civil government—JP] to a great extent in the middle of the third century' . . . it was then that the great exodus of Christians from the villages and cities to the mountains and deserts began."[522]

Christian tradition is nowadays filled with ascetic saints who spent their lives living in caves, often with animals, living on five dates a day, living on the top of pillars, wearing nothing but sack-cloth and ashes, and so on. One would almost think there was a competition in self-denial, not to say self-torture, among these holy men. There must indeed have been a sense of revulsion against the growing wealth and political influence of the Church and its remoteness from its roots and this must have influenced many monks (and, to a lesser extent, nuns) who turned their backs on the regular church congregations. When, as a result of the influence of Eastern bishops and ascetics, the monasteries came to Rome, Wishart writes, "the lords of the Church were getting ready to sit upon the thrones of princes." Thus, it was the rejection of the materialism of the bishops that led inevitably to the rise of ascetic communities on a large scale. According to Wishart:

"Pachomius had fourteen hundred monks in his own monastery and seven thousand under his rule. Jerome says fifty thousand monks were sometimes assembled at Easter in the deserts of Nitria. It was not uncommon for an abbot to command five thousand monks. St Serapion boasted of ten thousand. Altogether, so we are told, there were in the fifth century more than one hundred thousand persons in the monasteries, three-fourths of whom were men."[523]

The figures quoted may well be exaggerated, of course, but there is no doubt that the relatively infrequent eastern monastic tradition had become far more widespread in the third and fourth centuries. But considering this growth from a purely ideological point of view is not an explanation, or it is at best half an explanation.

To give a more balanced explanation for the burgeoning of the monasteries it is necessary to point, again, to the social conditions of the time. As Kautsky explained so well, this period in the rise of the Church was one of generalised crisis and collapse of Roman society. Under such conditions, for landless and rootless peasants to move into religious communities was sometimes the best, or even the *only*, option available for their survival and general welfare. Given the choice of being a homeless

---

[521] Adolf Harnack, a nineteenth century Christian scholar.
[522] Wishart, *A Short history of Monks and Monasteries*, p 10.
[523] Wishart, *A Short history of Monks and Monasteries*, p 21. Those quoted are some of the early founders of monasticism.

beggar or participating in a community which produced its own food and shelter, however meagre, it is easy to see where most would go. Needless to say, many of these monks were only mildly interested in spending all their waking hours in work and prayer. Quiet contemplation and celibacy would have been alien to most of them. Instead, they often became, literally, the battle-fodder in the theological struggles of rival bishops and perpetrators of pogroms themselves.

"They swarmed down from the mountains like hungry wolves. They fought heretics, they fought bishops, they fought Roman authorities, they fought soldiers, and fought one another. Ignorant, fanatical and cruel, they incited riots, disturbed the public peace and shed the blood of foes . . . furious monks became the armed champions of Cyril, the Bishop of Alexandria. They insulted the [Roman] prefect, drove out the Jews and, to the everlasting disgrace of the monks, Cyril and the Church, they dragged the lovely Hypatia[524] from her lecture hall and slew her . . . The fighting monks crowded councils and forced decisions. They deposed hostile bishops or kept their favourites in power by murder and violence. Two black-cowled armies met in Constantinople and amid curses they fought with sticks and stones, a battle of creeds."[525]

The Church hierarchy attempted some half-hearted opposition to the spread of the monasteries. In 380 CE a council of bishops in Saragossa, Spain, even adopted a rule forbidding priests from wearing the habits of monks. The Church fathers all objected at one time or another to the disorderliness of the holy orders.

"Jerome, Ambrose, Augustine, and in fact almost every one of the Fathers tried to correct the growing disorders. We learn from them that many fled from society, not to become holy, but to escape slavery and famine: and that many were lazy and immoral . . ."[526]

But in the end, the compromise that was reached allowed the monasteries to develop under the hegemony of the Catholic Church. Indeed the monasteries not only absorbed the surplus labour of the town and countryside, but they took away from the general congregation any dissident ascetics who might be critical of the Church. As the Church became an increasingly powerful landowner, it was able to plant colonies, in the form of monasteries, in the countryside, helping to prepare the way for a new system of land ownership, feudalism, to replace the slave system. Monasteries were an answer to the Church's problem of efficient cultivation of those large tracts of land which now belonged to it. Battalions of monks drained

---

[524] Hypatia was a woman of Alexandria with extensive influence as an astronomer, philosopher and mathematician. But not a Christian.
[525] Wishart, *A Short history of Monks and Monasteries*, p 23
[526] Wishart, *A Short history of Monks and Monasteries*, p 42

swamps, cleared forests and turned inhospitable land into arable pasture that created a surplus. They even pioneered new agricultural tools and cultivation methods. Moreover, the surplus production they created meant trade and fairs where goods were exchanged and funds for the local bishop. For the next few hundred years the monastic movement played a key part in repopulating the countryside and in so doing they helped to create an agricultural surplus on which the cities and towns of feudal Europe depended. Wishart, writing about the period after Benedict had regularised the rules and ethos of the monasteries, writes:

> "The Benedictines rendered a great social service in reclaiming deserted regions and in clearing forests . . . Roman taxation and barbarian invasions had ruined the farmers, who left their lands and fled to swell the numbers of the homeless. The monk re-peopled these abandoned but once fertile fields, and carried civilisation still deeper into the forests. Many a monastery with its surrounding buildings became the nucleus of a modern city . . . they stimulated the peasantry to labour and taught them many useful lessons in agriculture . . ."[527]

The monasteries had all the appearances and asceticism of a communist community, but none of the content. The monks may have contributed uniformly to the general pool of skills and labour and they took out only such as was absolutely necessary for life. But instead of a democratic organisation, the monasteries were run in a strictly hierarchical fashion, on land owned outright by the Church and with leaders appointed by the Church. And it was the Church which benefitted from any surplus. By introducing and regularising the vows of "chastity, poverty and obedience", the Church ensured that its monastic property would belong to it in perpetuity, and meanwhile, the monks would do as they were told by the abbot, appointed by the bishop.

But even where vast tracts of unusable Church lands could not be developed by monasteries, the Church here and there offered leases that depended on the leaseholder making the land cultivable.

> "The beneficiaries of this development appear to have been the middling landowners of the provinces and those peasant freeholders who had sufficient wealth, and could obtain sufficient labour power, to take on new holdings and farm them."[528]

---

[527] Wishart, *A Short history of Monks and Monasteries*, p 51
[528] John Haldon *Early Incomes in the Early Islamic State*, in *Elites Old and New in the Byzantine and Early Islamic Near East*, p 202

Thus the establishment of the Roman Church, monasteries and all, became in the final analysis an important element in the dismantling of the old Roman slave state and the foundation of the new feudal economy.

Chapter Summary:

- The Church reflected within itself contradictory class elements at one and the same time.

- The Church grew within an urban milieu drawing in skilled and unskilled workers. A significant factor in the growth of Christianity was its support within the imperial army.

- As the Church increased in size, influence and power, the leading elements of the bureaucracy became extremely wealthy and were increasingly integrated into the aristocracy of the Roman Empire despite occasional pogroms and periods of repression.

- The reasons for the burgeoning of the monasteries lay in the social conditions of the time: with the collapse of Roman society the movement of landless and rootless peasants into religious communities were the best, or in some cases the *only*, option available for their survival and general welfare.

Chapter 11

The 'Conversion' of Constantine

In this final section on Christianity we will argue that by the fourth century CE, the self-perpetuating bureaucracy within the Church had become an important bulwark of the Roman class system. Moreover, in many areas of the Empire, the bishops and Church officials had become an unofficial or official civil service or local government on behalf of the Roman bureaucracy. At the same time, the Church had become the effective property of the bishops and archbishops. Constantine's alleged conversion was not a religious epiphany but a *political calculation* to prop up support for the Empire in a period of crisis. After Constantine's decision, the bishops were invited to undertake an even more direct role on behalf of the state and they were given powers appropriate to those responsibilities. Christianity was not victorious, therefore, as a revolutionary or even a radical movement, but as an overwhelmingly conservative prop for the Roman imperial elite. From the time of its official adoption as the official religion of the Roman Empire, right up to modern times, the Church of Rome has stood against progress in Science, in politics and in democratic rights. The Vatican today is essentially a *political* organisation, representing powerful conservative forces, socially, economically, financially, culturally and diplomatically.

. . . .

As we have suggested, by the early fourth century, in many localities, the Church was playing an important role as an auxiliary arm of the Roman state. It effectively attained the same kind of authority—but on a far greater scale—than had previously been held by the leaders of Judaism over the Jewish population. The rigid and self-perpetuating bureaucracy which had grown within the Church reflected the class divisions in society and had become an important bulwark of the class system. The sermons and homilies of the Church leaders, as well as their writing, reflected more and more the ideology and values of the aristocracy. The interests and concerns of the Roman upper class became the concerns of the bishops and archbishops.

Long before the so-called conversion of Constantine in the early fourth century, the Church was playing a key social and political role on behalf of the ruling class. Its trajectory of development had been established early in the second century as the bishops removed themselves from any accountability to their flock and became more and more powerful. By the end of the third century many officials of the Roman state were Christian bishops or eminent Church members and from these positions they played a key role in the management and organisation of local government.

271

After Constantine's rule, there was a huge increase in the number of Christians within the Empire, but even at the beginning of the fourth century they had already increased to such a significant degree that it was becoming difficult for the Church to be ignored. The proportion of Christians within the total population of the Empire at this point is estimated at about ten per cent, but taking into account the fact that there were still important regions where Christianity was virtually absent and that it was overwhelmingly an urban community, the social weight of the Church in all the most important cities of the Empire was disproportionally higher.

The growing confidence of the bishops was bolstered by their elaborate network of dioceses which was not so much a 'state within a state' as an 'empire within an empire'. In those parts of the Empire where the state apparatus was weak or in a condition of collapse, it was the Church which had stepped in to support its civic functions. By the time Constantine became Emperor, the Church was already a focus of so much power that it could potentially challenge the state itself. Diocletian's late persecution was triggered by what was perceived as a possible challenge.

> "Christians became more common in the army. In the Alexandrian persecutions under Decius we hear of a soldier who protested at the insults that were rained on the persecuted, as well as of a whole squad of men who protested audibly when 'a man accused of being a Christian was on the point of denying Christ' . . . it is clear from the events in the final persecutions that Diocletian's aim was (at first, at any rate) to purge the army and the imperial entourage of Christians. His purpose would only make sense if *there were a significant number of Christians in the imperial civil service and in the army*."[529]

In so far as it meant anything in a Roman Empire facing terminal decline, those running the Church *were* the local government in many areas. "These venerable institutions had gradually assimilated themselves to the manners and government of their respective countries."[530]

> "The Christians had been obliged to elect their own magistrates, *to raise and distribute a peculiar revenue*, and to *regulate the internal policy of the republic by a code of laws*, which were ratified by the consent of the people and the practice of three hundred years. When Constantine embraced the faith of the Christians, he seemed to contract a perpetual alliance with a *distinct and independent society*; and the privileges granted or confirmed by that emperor, or by his successors, were accepted, not as the

---

[529] Wardman, *Religion and statecraft among the Romans,* p 130 (italics added)
[530] Gibbon, *The Decline and Fall of the Roman Empire,* p 384

precarious favours of the court, but as the just and inalienable rights of the ecclesiastical order.

The Catholic Church was administered by the spiritual and legal jurisdiction of eighteen hundred bishops. Of whom one thousand were seated in the Greek and eight hundred in the Latin provinces of the empire."[531]

In other words, the bishops and Church officials collected taxes, distributed alms and supervised local legal cases and land disputes. Increasingly, they also assumed responsibilities for civic developments like the maintenance of roads and other public works. They were an unofficial civil service or local government on behalf of the Roman bureaucracy long before Emperor Constantine gave them imperial sanction. By the time Constantine legalised the Church,

"... he had seen the potential of the hierarchy as a governing class. They were as well organised as his own civil service, which they slowly replaced in the courts and in diplomacy. When in the year 330, the emperor took his entourage to Constantinople, on the site of the ancient Greek city of Byzantium, the bishops of Rome became more and more involved in civil affairs ... there was an inevitable growth in bureaucracy ..."[532]

The political and military crisis at the end of the third century was the turning point for the Roman Empire. Constantine calculated that under the leadership of its rigid hierarchy, Christianity was more likely to provide the Empire with coherent support and an ideological framework than the disconnected temples and sects of the traditional pantheon of the Graeco-Roman gods. Speaking in a lecture more than a hundred years ago, the Church historian Edwin Hatch commented:

"So closely did the ecclesiastical organisation follow civil organisation, and so firm was its hold upon society that in the France of the present day, with hardly an exception, there is a bishop wherever there was a Roman municipality and an archbishop wherever there was a provincial metropolis. As the municipal organisation became weak the ecclesiastical organisation became strong: Christianity was so enormous a factor in contemporary society, that the bishops gradually took the place of the Roman magistrates and exercised some of the civil jurisdiction which had belonged to him."[533]

By the fourth century, the Church had completed its transformation to become the effective property of the bishops and archbishops.

---

[531] Gibbon, *The Decline and Fall of the Roman Empire*, p 385 (italics added)

[532] Peter De Rosa, *Vicars of Christ*, p 40

[533] Hatch, *The Organisation of the Early Christian Church*, p 197

"This transformation found powerful support in, and was accelerated by, the state recognition of Christianity in the beginning of the fourth century. But, on the other hand, the recognition of the Catholic Church by the emperors was only a consequence of the progress made by the power of the bureaucracy and of the bishops' absolute power within the bureaucracy. As long as the Church was a democratic organisation, it was absolutely opposed to the imperial despotism in the Roman Empire. On the other hand, the bureaucracy of bishops, which absolutely ruled and exploited the people, was a very good instrument for imperial despotism . . . the emperors often presided in the councils of bishops, but in exchange they placed the state authority at the disposal of the bishops for carrying out the decisions of the councils and the excommunications."[534]

Whereas, in the pre-Constantine era, Church congregations were still meeting by and large in the houses of wealthy patrons, after his reign there were magnificent gilded cathedrals in many cities of the Empire. Bishops had worn no special dress, but now they emulated the proudest princes in their linen, jewels and expensive clothing, tip-toeing through puddles, as Jerome put it. Even the notion of fixed clerical salaries, "considered an outrage as late as 200 CE" [535] became the norm, and for the bishops, not inconsiderable.

Nowadays, Christian traditionalists propagate and kind of Hollywood-style myth about the conversion of Constantine, with visions of crosses and a divine intervention in a crucial battle. Most of this fable came from the pen of sycophantic biographers like Eusebius after the death of Constantine. These legends are nonsense, of course. For Constantine and his court advisers, theological considerations were secondary. What mattered was that the Church was capable of fulfilling a *social, political and economic* function on behalf of the Roman ruling class: no more and no less.

"It is less important to determine the kind of faith which moved the emperor personally than to estimate where he stands in relation to the social and political advance of Christianity, as it was to be shown in the number of its churches and the power of its bishops. The new cult (new to official life, that is) had already made an impact on society by its organisation which provided practical daily welfare and which had on the whole stayed intact through the persecution."[536]

Under the directions of Constantine, the bishops, especially those in the great metropolitan centres, were expected to use their considerable ecclesiastical skill and influence to exert power in the direct interest of the state. The Church became an

---

[534]   Kautsky, p 448.

[535]   Fox, *Pagans and Christians*, p 505

[536]   Wardman, *Religion and statecraft among the Romans,* p 138

agent of the state, to administer its regional government, while at the same time ensuring the loyalty or acquiescence of its subjects.

> "Alexander [bishop of Alexandria] supervised the city's only effective network of social services, arbitrated major disputes between Christians (and often between Gentiles), and was consulted by the civil authorities on a wide range of local issues. He managed the Church's burgeoning properties and finances, employed hordes of minor officials, builders, craftsmen, artists and labourers and supervised the affairs of several thousand priests, monks, and virgins dedicated to religious service. Perhaps most important, he played a vital mediating role between imperial authority and its subjects."[537]

The role played by the hierarchy of the Church became so important that it was eventually enshrined in Roman laws on the governance of cities, the bishops effectively supplanting the former nobles who had managed urban affairs. The Church became the prime avenue for ambition and advancement for the well-to-do. There may have been a few of the *hoi-polloi* who aimed for a Church career but they soon reached a glass ceiling. It got so bad that even some Church officials complained that the post of bishop was being changed into a hereditary position in some areas. 'Saint' Jerome even complained about the worldliness of the bishops:

> ". . . as though they were distributing the offices of an earthly service, they give posts to their kindred and relations; or they listen to the dictates of wealth. And, worse than all, they give promotion to the clergy who besmear them with flattery."

Writing in the context of the rise of Islam in the middle of the seventh century, the Israeli archaeologists Yeduda Nevo and Judith Koran, described the position of the bishops in the eastern part of the Byzantine Roman Empire:

> "During the 5th and especially 6th centuries . . . many functions of leadership and local administration were gradually transferred to the Monophysite church and specifically to the bishops. In [Emperor] Justinian's reign this process was largely completed: bishops not only exercised a legal jurisdiction paralleling civil magistrates, but had also taken over many duties formerly under civil jurisdiction, especially those concerned with the management of funds allocated for public works and for providing for the local population."[538]

---

[537] Rubenstein, *When Jesus became God,* p 51
[538] Yehuda Nevo and Judith Koran, *Crossroads to Islam,* p 58

This is a comment based on later centuries, but it illustrates a trend. It is important to make the observation that the wealth, power and prestige of the Church were made official and were thereby enormously increased by Constantine and his successors, but this line of development was established long before the beginning of the fourth century. It may well be that Constantine actually *mis*calculated, in the sense that he underestimated the power of the Church bureaucracy and the bishops. During two hundred years of development the Church bureaucracy accrued to itself considerable social and political clout.

> "Bishops . . . enjoyed economic power. The Church's right of inheritance and the imperial bequests both helped to swell the properties which came under Episcopal jurisdiction. Bishops were in control of considerable funds . . . The imperial generosity created—without perhaps intending to—a subsidized priestly class . . . men now began increasingly to make religion a way of life in which the offices were ends in themselves, not a quasi-political means to wholly political objectives."[539]

After Constantine, the role of the bishops, already considerable, was bolstered even more. Whereas at the beginning of the fourth century the Church was coming under the blows of Diocletian's persecution, Constantine invited the bishops to undertake a directing role on behalf of the state and were given powers appropriate to those responsibilities.

> "They were now important figures in their city communities at a time when other authority figures were under pressure . . . His church-building programme gave them control of local patronage. Some bishops were given grain supplies to hand out to the poor, responsibilities that fitted well with their traditional role as organisers of relief for their own congregations. They were granted legal powers that extended to the right to free slaves on the same grounds as other magistrates and to hear a wide range of cases"[540]

The Church managed and contained an increasing proportion of the poor and dispossessed and for that reason, not because of a spiritual awakening within the ruling class, it had been allowed to grow and develop. "The Christian church emerged 'as an organisation competing with the State itself . . . attractive to educated and influential persons'. The bishops of the Church formed the centre of large voluntary organisations, in politics, in charitable tasks, even in defending towns against attack"[541] The Church was allowed for the first time to hold property and quickly became fabulously wealthy.

---

[539]   Wardman, *Religion and statecraft among the Romans,* p 153.
[540]   Freeman, *A New History of Early Christianity,* p 228
[541]   Neusner (quoting Momigliano), p 20.

". . . hardly had the holding of property become possible before the Church became a kind of universal legatee. The merit of bequeathing property to the Church was preached with so much success that restraining enactments became necessary."[542]

When a number of churches in North Africa objected to the patronage of the Roman state—the so-called Donatists—Constantine played an active part in their suppression. He even re-imposed a short persecution, with the support of the mainstream Church, in the regions where the Donatists had support. Constantine was also instrumental in the convening of the council of bishops in one of his imperial residences, in what became known as the Council of Nicaea, in 325. The Emperor clearly wanted the Church to be a unified organisation; he had no time for what he saw as the petty theological squabbles between bishops and he foisted the Nicene Creed on the council as a supposed compromise. Although the Creed is still used today as the cornerstone of Christian belief, at the time it was anything but a solution to the squabbles, chief of which was the argument about whether Jesus and God were "of the same substance" (the Nicene view) or whether Jesus was a later creation of God's (the view of the Arians).

Constantine had convened the council of Nicaea to set the Church on a more consistent footing. Following its deliberations he effectively made the lower orders of priests his state officials. "The state now enforced Church discipline, treated heresy as a political crime, enforced decrees of Church councils through the state courts and administration."[543] The Church and the state increasingly blended together their functions and roles, just as the state penetrated the Church, the Church also penetrated the state.

"Christianity undertook to govern, shaped the public and political institutions of empires, and through popes and emperors alike defined the political history of the world for long centuries to come."[544]

Christian leaders today would blanche at the idea that their Church creed was a construction of the Roman state, rather than the inspiration of the Holy Ghost. But even Freeman, in his *New History of Early Christianity*, has to concede that "The imposition of the Nicene Creed was motivated as much by politics as theology."[545] In the final analysis, it was not theology that created the modern Christian Church; it was the political and social environment of the Church and the needs of the Roman state which created the theology.

Constantine, of course, was not the great Christian he is nowadays portrayed to be. At the same time that he was commissioning the establishment

---

542   Hatch, *The Organisation of the Early Christian Church*, p 149
543   Neusner, *Judaism and Christianity in the Age of Constantine*, p 15.
544   Neusner, p 17.
545   Freeman, *A New History of Early Christianity*, p 253

of new churches, he was still building and dedicating temples to Roman gods. In 326, he was implicated in a purge of the imperial family—so common among emperors—including the murder of an illegitimate son and his first wife. Nevertheless, he became effectively the head of the Church, dictating when the bishops would meet in conclave and what would be decided, although he wasn't even baptised until he was on his death bed—and we have only the word of Eusebius on that. After his death, in accordance with custom, the Senate duly decreed that he be placed among the ranks of the gods.

> "But Constantine's hopes of the Church as an institution were less readily met. It seems from his address to the bishops at Nicaea that he had envisaged a clear role for the episcopacy; it was to be parallel to his own function, described by himself in terms which have been much debated, as 'bishop of those outside'. Even before the Council of Nicaea the state had been disappointed in the cooperative activity of the Church. The end of the persecution and the beginning of imperial favour were not able to produce a unified organisation that would give the emperor the support for which he looked . . . it is fairly certain that he did not expect to have on his hands an insubordinate institution; no one who thought of pontiffs and augurs and Arval brethren, men in religious posts that had become more and more ceremonial over the centuries would have imagined that the chief priests of the new cult would prove so difficult. Undoubtedly Constantine expected the bishops to resolve their theological disputes and present the emperor with their unified support."[546]

The important role of the Church as a prop to the state can be gauged better by an examination of the attempt by his nephew Julian, hailed as the last pagan emperor, to roll back the reforms of his uncle. In his very short reign, Julian attempted in vain to re-establish some structures that would act as a social counter-weight to the Church. He made some attempts to bolster local city councils by favouring them with lands and wealth at the expense of the Church. But he also understood the role that the Church was playing in civil life and as an alternative he hoped to increase the power and prestige of the traditional pagan priesthood.

> "Julian's masterplan was no less than the creation of a religious infrastructure that would counter the Christian model at the grassroots level. He understood its success and appeal and knew the difficulties in going against what was a tight-knit organisation. 'Why have we not noticed that it is their benevolence towards strangers, their care for the graves of the dead and the pseudo-holiness of their lives that has done most to increase atheism [ie Christianity]?', he asked . . . with himself as head of the Church, he saw high priests as counterparts to the archbishops

---

[546]   Wardman, *Religion and Statecraft among the Romans,* p 145.

who in turn appointed and managed their own priests . . . he wanted the pagans to out-Christian the Christians."[547]

Julian, therefore, made strenuous attempts to upgrade the standing of pagan priests in civil life.

"As a supplement to the civic charitable ventures and as a counterbalance to Christian aid that was already in place, the [pagan] priests at a parish level were to help the old, the poor and the sick and provide charity . . . Julian wanted his priests to fulfill the same role that Constantine had assigned to Christians; pagan priests were to be agents of social change and also of social control. Not only did Christians have a thirty-year head start, pagans were handicapped in that they were not taken seriously . . ."[548]

But these counter-reforms were short-lived because Julian was to rule for only a short time and, in any case, the Church had too much of a head start. Julian was succeeded by Christian emperors who stopped his reforms dead in their tracks. The powers of the Church were quickly restored to the position they had been under Constantine and even enhanced.

After its consolidation as state religion, the political power and role of the Church were enormously increased. Ambrose, for example, was not only a bishop, but served as an ambassador to the court; Synesius, as bishop in Libya, ". . . helped to maintain law and order against invading tribesmen . . . as a local institution, the Church undertook and fulfilled many of the responsibilities which in the past had been carried out by private enterprise."[549] Besides their individual wealth, the number of bishops increased enormously in the post-Constantine period. By the mid-fifth century, it is estimated there were two thousand in the empire. Small towns that previously had no Christian community had newly-appointed bishops, often taking over pagan shrines and building churches on them. In the larger cities where there were multiple dioceses (originally each church had its own bishop) it was necessary to create a new higher layer of bishops and so archbishops became common.

"The church now offered a viable and prestigious career with many bishops being recruited directly from the civil service. Ambrose of Milan and Paulinius of Nola had both held governorships in Italy; the bishops of Cyzius, Eleusius had served in the imperial civil service . . . there were even cases of distinguished civil servants being 'awarded' a bishopric as an end-of-service post. Often the traditional roles of the elite were absorbed in the work of the bishop. Basil of Caesarea is found negotiating tax

---

[547] Murdoch, *The Last Pagan*, p 141

[548] Murdoch, *The Last Pagan*, p 142

[549] Wardman, *Religion and Statecraft among the Romans*, p 147.

exemptions for petitioners in much the same way a patron would have done in earlier days."[550]

The Church aristocracy

This gives a glimpse of the impact of imperial patronage and it says a lot about the wealth, power and prestige of a big city bishopric if it offers a better career than a governorship. What was particularly attractive about being a bishop was that once appointed they were virtually untouchable, even by the emperor himself.

"As bishops held their thrones for life, in contrast to governors who were often replaced after a year or two, promotion was slow and the death of a bishop might be the only moment when ambitious clerics could gain control of their local churches and their resources. Almost every election of which we have records was a violent one . . . the pretext was souls, but, in fact, it was desire for control, control of taxes and contributions . . ."[551]

Starting with Constantine and completed by the emperor Theodosius towards the end of the century, this lavish state patronage launched the Church on the path of becoming the strongest political force in the Empire.

"There is no knowing if the numbers of Christians would have continued to grow if they had been left to themselves but now the numbers expanded so fast that Eusebius complained of the hypocrisy of converts who had only joined because the going was good. Soon the Church's authority figures, the bishops, were recruits to the service of the state. Their social and legal status grew enormously as did their wealth. Vast churches, glittering with gold and mosaics, were to be found in the major cities of the empire. Although the Church continued to care for the poor, and was used by the state to do so, the transfer of resources to prestige building projects proved permanent . . . the role the emperors played in defining church doctrine was to prove enormously important . . ."[552]

Like his predecessor, the emperor Theodosius also intervened actively in church organisation and theology, announcing his own creed and insisting that only those who followed the Nicene Creed were acceptable as bishops. Henceforth, no bishop was allowed to meddle in the affairs of any church outside his own diocese. Those who continued to defy his creed,

---

[550]   Freeman, *A New History of Early Christianity*, p 262
[551]   Freeman, *A New History of Early Christianity*, p 266
[552]   Freeman, *A New History of Early Christianity*, p 225

". . . had to surrender their churches to those clergy who came within Theodosius' definition, lose any tax exemptions they had and they could not build replacement churches within the city walls. Any open protest was to be met with expulsion of the dissenters from the city."[553]

The fourth century was dominated by the struggle of the Church against the great Arian heresy, which held that Jesus was in a sense secondary to God, having been created by the latter. But behind the suppression of Arianism, and the invention of the Holy Trinity, lay the material interests of the Roman and Church aristocracy, the palaces, wealth and power of the one group indistinguishable from the other, as well as the often rival interests of other great archbishoprics, like Alexandria, Constantinople and Antioch.

"The problem for anyone, emperor, senior administrator or aristocratic landowner, who was concerned with upholding the hierarchical structure of the empire, was that the Jesus of the gospels was a rebel against the empire and had been executed by one of its provincial governors . . . There was an incentive to shift the emphasis from the gospels to the divine Jesus, as pre-existent to the Incarnation and of high status 'at the right hand of the Father'"[554]

The theology that was being developed sought to overcome the ambiguities in the original Nicene Creed but in the end, with a metaphorical shrug of the shoulders, the Church resolved the old contradictions by replacing them with a new one, the Trinity, only this time insisting that everyone accept it. As Kautsky put it so well:

"The fact of a god having begotten a son is nothing out of the way in polytheism; you simply have one god more to deal with. But to have God beget another god, and yet have God remain a unit—this is not so easy to explain. And the matter was not simplified by isolating the creative power emanating from the godhead in the form of a special Holy Ghost. The task now was to accommodate these three persons under a single conception that would embrace them all . . . therefore the Trinity became one of the mysteries that must simply be believed without being understood; a mystery that had to be believed for the very reason of its absurdity . . . it would be difficult to find any other religion so rich in contradictions and unreasonable assumptions as is the Christian, because hardly any other religion arose out of such strikingly different elements: Christianity was handed down by Judaism to the Romans, by proletarians to the world

[553] Freeman, *A New History of Early Christianity*, p 249
[554] Freeman, *A New History of Early Christianity*, p 252

rulers, by a communistic organisation to an organisation formed for the exploitation of all classes."[555]

The somewhat ludicrous theological disputes about the eternal nature of Jesus had little or no meaning to the vast majority of the membership of the Church, but the leadership nonetheless had one eye on their flock while this debate was going on and in the end they simply insisted that the contradiction of the Trinity be accepted. As inexplicable and illogical as it is, the Trinity is still referred to in the Catholic Church today as a "mystery of faith." Mystery indeed.

The *quid pro quo* for the Church's enormously enhanced wealth and power was that it offered a safety valve for the discontent of the city masses facing interminable economic and social insecurity. Other than its role in administering law, the main area for which the bishops provided a service to the state was in caring for the urban poor and dispossessed. The Church now had an official role in the provisioning of food for the large numbers of paupers in the cities. Because of its long established organisation, it was far more effective in doing this than the imperial state had been.

> "When Christians turned their focus on the poor, as they did with an intensity that had been lacking in pagan society, they found a mass of destitute 'shivering in their nakedness, lean by undernourishment' as one preacher put it. John Chrysostom estimated that 10 per cent of the population of Antioch lived in absolute poverty."[556]

The huge building projects undertaken in many large cities, brought about by imperial patronage and managed by the bishops, provided a means of passing the benefits of the patronage down the ladder to the urban working class. In Milan, Ambrose, who had become bishop of Milan (and eventually, of course, a saint) even before he was baptised as a Christian, was the greatest builder of them all. He had a whole series of basilicas built on the burial sites of alleged martyrs, a programme that employed thousands of stone masons, mosaic layers and many other craftsmen and labourers.

Besides seeing to the material interests of the artisan class and caring for widows and orphans, the Church raised the spiritual sights of the urban working class by providing its only opportunity to sit in the same building with landlords and bishops (if not the same pews) and even if there was limited hope in this world, they were at least offered the promise of equality with the rich in the next. The Christians offered a messiah and life after death, in contrast to the aloof and indifferent gods of Greece and Rome.

Christianity, in the end, was not victorious as a revolutionary or even as a radical movement. It had become an overwhelmingly conservative and reactionary force and a prop to the Roman regime: ". . . it not only did not eliminate the imperial power,

---

[555]   Kautsky, p 362
[556]   Freeman, *A New History of Early Christianity*, p 268

slavery, the poverty of the masses, and the concentration of wealth in a few hands, but perpetuated these conditions. The Christian *organisation*, the Church, attained victory by *surrendering* its original aims and defending their opposite."[557] For Marxists, dialectics is no more than the logic of change, the description of process. Using the dialectical language of Marx and Engels, in the historical development of the Church quantity had been transformed into quality. The accumulated quantity of regressive changes over more than two centuries had altered the Church so much that it had become qualitatively different to its founding community. But having been born in a slave society, by its new structure and outlook the Church was an anticipation of the feudal society that had been gestating within the body of the decaying slave-owning state. The Church didn't at any time campaign for emancipation, but in a society in which slavery as a social system was running out of steam, it offered a new arrangement for exploitation.

Once established as the unchallenged leadership of the Catholic Church, the office of the Pope became the most consistently powerful monarchy in Europe. Among the early popes, it was Gregory who enforced celibacy among the priesthood, so the property of the Church could not be claimed by the wives, families or mistresses of priests after their deaths.

> "This early pope and man of 'greatness' perhaps did more than anyone to erase the accumulated wisdom of the ancient world. Gregory ordered his bishops to desist from the 'wicked' labour of teaching grammar and Latin to lay people. Gregory even forbade lay people from reading the Bible and ordered the burning of the Palatine Apollo Library in order that its secular literature 'would not distract' from religious devotion . . . in an age of deprivation and poverty Gregory accumulated vast papal wealth and landed estates . . . the clergy were given regalia and 'privilegia' and with the connivance of secular authority, supplanted the imperial civil service . . . with the reforms of Pope Gregory, the Church became thoroughly secular in nature. Wealthy noblemen chose the pope, usually from among themselves, and illegitimate papal children were appointed cardinals. History's most successful criminal organisation was in business."[558]

Many of today's global community of more than a billion Catholics would object to their Church being labelled as a "criminal organisation" if they judged it by their local parish or diocese. The vast majority of the world's Catholics are sincere people who naturally feel an attachment to their cultural traditions and heritage, not to mention what they see as the good deeds done by Catholic schools, hospitals, hospices and other charitable organisations. Catholics can point to those priests and not a few bishops who have sacrificed much, including their lives, in the struggle for democracy, humanity and freedom. But the fact remains that the Church, *as*

---

557   Kautsky, p 461
558   Humphreys, *Jesus Never Existed*, p 391

an institution—and its hierarchy in particular—is a reactionary, self-perpetuating, *political* machine and has been so for nearly two thousand years. Its vast structure of four thousand bishops and four hundred thousand priests is organised in such a way as to perpetuate and support the self-interest of an unelected and unaccountable clique with enormous power and influence. It is a political, financial and diplomatic structure that is without parallel in Judaism, Islam or any other world religion.

Following the agreement made with the fascist leader Mussolini in 1929, the Pope was granted a unique "statehood" for his headquarters in the Vatican, a diplomatic absurdity that is nevertheless recognised by dozens of other states around the world. Although the Vatican has no permanent population, industry, transport, utility system, currency or any other of the distinguishing features of a true 'state', the Holy See is able to send its representatives to deliberate on committees of the United Nations, where it wields its vote and influence against even mildly progressive policies like the distribution of condoms to fight HIV/AIDS. What the Vatican does have, however, is an extremely wealthy bank, which has been implicated in financial scandals, linked with the Italian Mafia, Freemasons and all manner of political corruption on the right of the Italian political spectrum.

Throughout its history, the Church has been on the extreme right of the political spectrum, opposed to every single measure, in whatever country, that extended the right to vote, or extended women's or trade union rights. It is only a couple of hundred years since the Church was burning people for daring to translate the Bible from Latin into their local language. The Vatican has openly supported fascism in Spain, Italy and the Balkans and kept a deafening silence during the great Holocaust of the Nazis in central Europe. Even today, the Vatican refuses to open those parts of its vast secret archives that deal with its relationship with wartime Germany or with the assistance given to Nazis fleeing Europe for Latin America at the end of the war. The Church has handled its many recent scandals involving the abuse of tens of thousands of children in such a way that the interests of the victims and the pursuit of justice have come a poor second to the needs to maintain Church secrecy and reputation. Looking at the activity of the Church hierarchy and its financial and political activity over the centuries, it may not be too wide of the mark to describe it as "History's most successful criminal organisation".

The Church, therefore, has travelled a long journey. From having been at its inception a tiny revolutionary Jewish sect, in two thousand years it has become, at least in its dominant Roman Catholic form, arguably the world's most powerful political organisation. The Church is where it is, not because of the Holy Spirit or by the will of God but because it became, and remains to this day, a powerfully conservative political force, diplomatically, economically, financially, culturally and socially.

Chapter summary

- By the fourth century CE, the self-perpetuating bureaucracy within the Church had become an important bulwark of the class system.

- The Bishops and Church officials were an unofficial civil service or local government on behalf of the Roman bureaucracy. At the same time, the Church had become the effective property of the bishops and archbishops. After Constantine the bishops were invited to undertake a directing role on behalf of the state and were given powers appropriate to those responsibilities

- Constantine's conversion was not a religious epiphany but a political calculation to prop up support for the empire.

- Christianity was not victorious as a revolutionary or even as a radical movement, but as an overwhelmingly conservative prop for the Roman regime.

- Throughout history, the Church of Rome has always stood against progress in science, in politics and in democratic rights. The Vatican today is a powerful political organisation and represents a powerful conservative force, socially, economically, financially, culturally and diplomatically.

PART III

THE FOUNDATIONS OF ISLAM

Chapter 12

The traditional Story of the Prophet
and the Problem of Sources

In this opening chapter on Islam, we outline the traditional account of the life of Mohammed the Prophet of Islam, as well as the origin of the Koran. These are both unfamiliar subjects to most readers who were brought up in the Judeo-Christian tradition. We will recount what is the accepted story of Mohammed's life, set in early seventh century Mecca and Medina, whilse noting that, as was the case with the Christian Jesus, there is no contemporary or archaeological evidence to support any of the story. We will outline the significance of the Koran for Muslims and highlight the tremendous importance of later Islamic written tradition, collectively referred to as *hadith*, which supplements the Koran as the basis of the faith. The Koran itself contains little in the way of a narrative of events and its linkage with the life and work of the Prophet is entirely based on *hadith*, most of which was written no earlier than the ninth and tenth centuries. We shall also note the extent to which any scholarly works which have threatened to undermine the traditional Islamic history of have often faced repression in Muslim countries.

. . . .

Just as we have examined the foundations of Judaism and Christianity from the point of view of the social, economic and political movements that are the real drivers of historical change, we now turn to the origins of Islam. As in the case of the first two faiths, it is again necessary to summarise the traditional view of the historic roots of Islam and to examine the historical evidence for it. Although the traditional accounts vary in detail, there is a general consensus around which the overwhelming majority of Muslims would agree and this is the account outlined here.

The story revolves around the mid-seventh century CE and the city of Mecca, which was, according to Reza Aslan in *No God but God*, a "major population centre" at the time. Mecca sits in a barren stretch of land surrounded by hills in the west of present-day Saudi Arabia. It is fifty miles east of the Red Sea coast and is immediately adjacent to the so-called Empty Quarter, perhaps the largest continuous body of sand on Earth. This is one of the driest and most arid areas on the planet, where often years go by between showers of rain. In the centuries leading up to the arrival of Islam, Mecca was the location of a pagan sanctuary of considerable antiquity. Religious rituals revolved around the *Ka'ba*—a shrine that still exists and which is the focus of Islamic pilgrimage today. Muslims believe that the *Ka'ba* is associated with the ancient patriarch and founder of Judaism, Abraham, and his son Ishmael, or *Isma'il*. As well as being a centre for pilgrimage, Mecca was a "natural trading outpost between southern and northern Arabia" and the "financial centre of the *Hejaz*", which is the name given to the great hinterland of the Arabian Peninsula. As the city became increasingly prosperous in the sixth century, pagan idols of varying sizes and shapes proliferated around the *Ka'ba*. The traditional story has it that by the early seventh century as many as 360 statues and icons surrounded the *Ka'ba*, including representations of Jesus and the Virgin Mary.

This is where Mohammed was said to have been born in the year 570 CE. His father Abdullah died before he was born and his mother died when he was still a baby, so Mohammed was raised by his uncle, a member of the Quraysh, one of the leading families in Mecca, who Aslan describes as "a powerful and fabulously wealthy tribe". The Quraysh "acted as stewards of the trade that took place in and around Mecca, collecting a small fee for assuring the safety of the caravans . . . (and) managed to create a modest but lucrative trading zone in Mecca, one which relied almost entirely on the *Ka'ba's* pilgrimage cycle for its subsistence." [559]

Reza Aslan, introducing a social-liberal and more 'modern' interpretation to Islamic tradition, emphasises the class conflicts of the day.

> "The concentration of wealth in the hands of a few ruling families had not only altered the social and economic landscape of the city, it had effectively destroyed the tribal ethic. The sudden tide of personal wealth in Mecca had swept away tribal ideas of social egalitarianism. No longer was there any concern for the poor and marginalised . . ."[560]

In former times, the Meccans had followed a monotheistic religion based on the foundations laid by Abraham, a creed loosely associated with Christian and Jewish religious practices which were widespread in Arabia. By the time of Mohammed, these observances had lapsed and Meccans, like other Arabs, began to follow pagan gods and rituals. Hence there was a proliferation of statues and idols around the *Ka'ba*. Just as the young Mohammed objected to the ostentatious and selfish life-style of the Quraysh, he was similarly appalled by the lapse of Meccan society into paganism and idolatry. When he was to begin his preaching, one of the common themes he emphasised was that Meccans were required to *return to the old ways and observances* that prevailed before pagan practices became popular.

Although Mohammed's uncle was a member of the Quraysh, he belonged to a more modest branch of the tribe and therefore led a humbler life. Mohammed was said to have been employed in the leather trade as a young man where he met his first wife, Khadija, who was also his employer and was several years his senior. She was the first of what the traditions collectively put as a total of twenty wives.

---

559   Reza Aslan, *No God but God,* p 26
560   Reza Aslan *No God but God,* p 31

By the time he reached the age of forty, Mohammed was in the habit of taking himself off to Mount Hira for periods of quiet contemplation and it was here that he had his first revelation from God, through the mediation of the archangel Gabriel. The voice of Gabriel commanded Mohammed to "Recite!", and for this reason the Koran is known as the 'recitation'. Much of the Koran reads as if it were an instruction to the Prophet to 'say' this and 'say' that to those to whom he preached. The first visitation was said to have shocked the unsuspecting Mohammed so much that he went home in a daze. Khadija, unable to understand what had happened to her husband, went to seek the advice of her cousin, Waraqa, who was a Christian. "Waraqa was familiar enough with the Scriptures", Aslan writes, "to recognise Mohammed's experience for what it was . . . 'He is a prophet of the people', Waraqa assured his cousin."[561] Thus, according to tradition, the Prophet of Islam was given a very early endorsement by a Christian.

Many revelations were given to Mohammed over the next twenty-three years, in both Mecca and Medina, and usually through the mediation of Gabriel. According to some accounts, the recitations were occasionally combined with visits to heaven and meetings with the patriarchs of Jewish tradition, Abraham and Moses. From one such visit we learn that Moses was "a tall, dark, lively man with curled hair and a long nose", whereas Jesus was "neither tall nor short".[562] The recitations were all relayed by Mohammed to his family, friends and supporters, who either memorised them word for word or wrote them on pieces of bark or leaves. They were never written down by Mohammed, who was, in any case, illiterate; nor were they written down as a collection by anyone else in his lifetime.

The recitations of Mohammed were later collected by one of several of the caliphs who succeeded Mohammed after his death in 632. Depending on which specific tradition is accepted, the compilation was undertaken either by the caliph Abu Bakr, or Umar or Uthman, the last of these being the most popular candidate. The written revelations became the holy *Koran,* which remains for Muslims *the revealed word of God.* According to some of the traditions (for example, the fifteenth century *History of the Khalifahs* [563]) the Koran was memorised word for word even during the lifetime of the Prophet, by several different people. Whatever the precise origin, Muslims are agreed that since it was first written down, the Koran has remained unchanged, in its original Arabic, to this day. The traditional accounts record that there were many scribes associated with the history of early Islam, writing down treaties and agreements between tribes, the Constitution of Medina and so on. We will pass over for the moment the conundrum as to why, that being the case, the revelations of Mohammed were not *immediately* written down when it was clear that they *could* have been.

Throughout the centuries there have even been theological debates among Muslim scholars as to whether or not the Koran was 'created'—that is, through the

561   Reza Aslan *No God but God,* p 38
562   See Ibn Ishaq, *The Life of Mohammed,* p 59
563   As-Suyuti, *The History of the Kalifahs who took the right way,* reprinted by Ta-Ha, 1995

mediation of Mohammed—or whether it is 'uncreated' in the sense of *having always been in existence* since the beginning of time, locked, as it were, in the head of God. One of the most common aspects of Koranic tradition is the idea that the book is perfect in every sense, not only theologically but even that it is the highest possible expression of Arabic literary style and technique. The Koran is held is such high esteem that it is considered by many Muslims to be sinful to abuse the book in any way, for example by dropping it, discarding an old copy or even by holding it in the left hand.

Mohammed's early revelations imparted his mission to him—to bring Meccans and the Arab people in general back to *Al-lah,* which in Arabic means "the God". Mohammed's message included a requirement for complete "submission" to Allah and from the Arabic root for submission ("Islam") came the name "Muslim", *he who submits.* Although other Muslims would not agree with his slant, in his account, Reza Aslan chooses to highlight the socially radical or even revolutionary aspects of Mohammed's new religion. Mohammed was different to other, isolated, monotheists of Mecca, the so-called *hanifs,* who also preached a return to the old ways.

> "Mohammed was not just preaching 'the religion of Abraham', Mohammed was the *new* Abraham . . . Mohammed understood what the *hanifs* could not: the only way to bring about radical social and economic reform in Mecca was to overturn the religio-economic system on which the city was built; and the only way to do that was to attack the very source of the Quraysh's wealth and prestige—the *Ka'ba.*"[564]

Thus, Mohammed set about preaching against the paganism, idolatry and fetish worship in the *Ka'ba.* He demanded a change in the life-style of the Meccan well-to-do, a regularised system of alms and other support to help widows, orphans, the poor and the most down-trodden. He began to get support in his immediate family and it soon grew until it became a direct threat to the profiteering that surrounded the pagan pilgrimages and worship. Inevitably, this brought Mohammed into conflict with the wealthy Quraysh. The latter began to manoeuvre and scheme against Mohammed but it was when they finally plotted to have him killed that the Prophet found it necessary to migrate with his supporters to the city of Yathrib, 200 miles to the north, where he continued to receive revelations. Yathrib was subsequently known as the City of the Prophet, shortened to its modern name, *Medina.*

The migration to Medina, known as the *Hijra,* plays a very significant part in the tradition. It took place in the Year 622 of the Common Era, but that subsequently became 'Year Zero' in the Muslim calendar, which is usually denoted AH, the *Year of the Hijra.* The Muslims who moved to Medina with Mohammed were known as the *Muhajirun* and the residents of the city who welcomed the

---

[564]   Reza Aslan *No God but God,* p 44

Prophet and converted to his faith were known as the 'Helpers', the *Ansar*. Many of the traditional stories and anecdotes point to some subsequent differences and even rivalry between these two groups.

In Medina Mohammed established a community of Muslims, the *umma*, even going so far as to provide the *Medina Constitution* which outlined what was permitted under Islam and what was not. One of the main economic activities of the community in Medina seems to have been raiding the camel caravans belonging to the Quraysh as they stopped at Mecca on their journeys between the prosperous cities of Syria and Iraq in the north and those of Yemen in the south. Medina had a mixed population with a majority of the tribes being converts to Judaism. These tribes feuded with one another constantly, and in various combinations. Mohammed was invited to mediate between the tribes and was able to establish alliances, first with the non-Jewish tribes and then later the Jewish tribes and by carefully playing one off against the other, he gained strength. Some tribes were won over to Islam and by this means, as well as a few judicious political assassinations (also attested to in the traditions), he was able to increase the power of the *umma* at the expense of the non-Muslim tribes.

In their raiding of Meccan caravans, the Muslims were helped at various times by Arab or Jewish tribes. They were so successful that the Meccans sent a military force against Medina, but it was defeated by a much smaller Muslim force at the Battle of Badr. There were other, indecisive, battles but throughout the first ten years or so the Muslims went from strength to strength until they were powerful enough to return to Mecca as conquerors. In the name of Islam, Mohammed began a *jihad*, a holy war for the conquest of the whole of the Arabian Peninsula, unifying the Arab nation for the first time ever. "When the hosts of Arabia came flocking to his banner," Ameer Ali wrote in *A Short History of the Saracens,* "Mohammed felt that his work was accomplished."[565]

Mohammed died in 632, without an heir and without having named a successor. His closest supporters, described in tradition as the *Companions*, elected Abu Bakr as caliph but he lived only for a short time afterwards. Abu Bakr was succeeded by Umar, then Uthman and then Ali who was Mohammed's cousin and son-in-law, the last three all being murdered. (See table for a list of these and subsequent Umayyad caliphs).

---

[565]   Ameer Ali, *A Short History of the Saracens*, MacMillan, 1961

Time-line of the traditional account of Mohammed's life	
Dates (all CE)	**Key events**
570	Birth of Mohammed
610	Mohammed receives his first revelation at Mt Hira
622	Mohammed and his supporters move from Mecca to Medina (***Hijra***)
624	Battle of Badr (against Mecca)
630	Mohammed's conquest of Mecca
632	Death of Mohammed
632-4	Caliph Abu Bakr
634-44	Caliph Umar
644-56	Caliph Uthman
656-61	Caliph Ali. Beginning of divisions between supporters of Ali and Mu'awiya (Umayyads)

As an important aside, it should be noted that the traditional accounts of Mohammed's successors highlight the murders of Uthman and then Ali as the beginning of the Shia/Sunni split in the Muslim faith. The followers of Ali, who were suspected of having participated in the murder of his predecessor, became known as the *Shia*, from *Shi'at Ali* (the party of Ali) and other Muslims who considered themselves part of the mainstream tradition or *Sunna* of the Prophet, became known as *ah al Sunna,* or more simply, *Sunni.* The traditional story of the first civil war (*fitnah*) between Muslims relates that Ali's supporters were the more numerous but a group of *Kharijites*—'pious' Muslims—defected from him when they thought he prevaricated too much, fatally weakening him and allowing another rival, Mu'awiya, to take power.

The century-long dynasty of caliphs who succeeded Ali, starting with Mu'awiya, was known as the *Umayyad Dynasty,* from their family name. Friction and conflicts between the Umayyads and the followers of Ali (the *Alids*) continued for generations and Ali's sons and grandson were also killed. The site of the murder of Ali's son, at Karbala in modern Iraq, is an important site of pilgrimage for Shia Muslims today.

The four first successors of the Prophet: Abu Bakr, Umar, Uthman and Ali, are in most traditions described as the "rightly-guided" caliphs in the sense of having continued Mohammed's ideas and observances. This is to distinguish them from the succeeding caliphs of the Umayyad dynasty, who are not treated by tradition nearly as kindly. As we shall argue, there are reasons for this, chiefly the fact that the main elements of the tradition were only set down in writing during the period of the *Abbasid* dynasty which followed on from the Umayyads and which came to power following a revolution against the latter.

Following Mohammed's death, his successors continued the military expansion which had begun with the unification of Arabia, taking Islam to the territories of the former Roman (Byzantine) and Persian empires. According to one typical account:

> "Within a few years they founded the Islamic empire, subduing the greater part of the civilised world, their purpose being religious, their weapons piety, justice, and scrupulous observation of the Koran and the Tradition; their aim being the propagation of their religion, and their ultimate object the reward of the next world."[566]

According to tradition, the Koran is the only canonical book dating back to the time of the Prophet. Muslims believe that the Koran as it exists today represents the definitive text handed down from its original transcription by the first caliphs who had collected the revelations after the death of Mohammed. We will deal in more detail with the Koran later, but suffice to say at this stage that the book does not deal at all with the life of the Prophet and in fact rarely even mentions him by name. The overwhelming majority of the text consists of sayings that have no historical-biographical setting or social context relating to each 'revelation'. What has provided the *context* for the sayings has been the enormous weight of *supplementary tradition* that has been accumulated. These stories, interpretations and explanations, referred to as *hadith,* are invariably attributed to the Prophet or his Companions and for Muslims they are an absolutely essential means of understanding the Koran and without which the Koran would lose most of its significance. The *hadith* have been collected in the decades and centuries after Mohammed's death and constitute an enormous literary accumulation many times larger than the Koran itself. Each separate *hadith,* in order to be validated as a true record of the Prophet's words or actions, is associated with an authenticating chain of oral transmission, an *isnad,* from one named person to another, going all the way back to the Prophet or to one of his Companions.

The *hadith* have enormous significance in that they *interpret* sections of the Koran and give legal and religious judgements on issues and situations with which it does not deal. Thus, if the Prophet's opinion on this or that matter was said to be known and backed by a reliable chain of witnesses, this could be cited in a

---

[566] Jurji Zayadan, *History of Islamic civilisation,* p 57

judgement pertaining to contemporary issues. Because the total writings of the *hadith* far outweigh in volume the Koran itself, it is in these sources that there is the greatest scope for different interpretations and meanings in the Prophet's life and works. It would be hard to overestimate the significance of *hadith*. There is a truly enormous accumulation of tradition, most of it created long after the death of the Prophet, that relate to almost every single aspect of political, social and economic life, all of them linked in some fashion to a religious interpretation. There are traditions that put out-and-out racist comments in the mouth of Mohammed and others that have him speaking precisely against such views; there are traditions about how Mohammed combed his hair, how he dyed his beard, what he said about Bedouins, or didn't say about Bedouins, how he admonished others for what they might have said, and so on and so on.

In addition to *hadith*, and drawing directly from it, every verse and sentence in the Koran has been subject to *exegesis* at some time or other—by a careful and painstaking dissection of words and phrases to gain insights into the intended meaning. The particular meanings of verses have been interpreted and argued over—again by reference to a tradition going back to words spoken by the Prophet—creating yet more tradition. Not all interpretations are compatible with each other and many are in flat contradiction to others. Last but not least, over the centuries thousands of scholars have written *commentaries* from their exegesis—or *tafsirs*—which have also added even further to the huge corpus of theological works.

It is by using the Koran and setting it alongside the huge accumulation of *hadith* that Muslims understand the concept of *Sunna*, the correct 'Islamic' interpretation of Mohammed's life and doctrine. Another Arabic word, *Sira*, is used to describe the definitive description specifically of Mohammed's life and good works. Through *hadith*, almost every line in the Koran has been given a 'historical' context or setting by one or other of the Arab scholars, particularly from the ninth century onwards.

'Histories' that recycle the traditional account.

Despite differences in details, the traditional account described above represents for a broad consensus of Muslims what happened during and immediately after the life of the Prophet Mohammed. The important point to note is that although Muslims accept that the details of Islamic ritual, doctrine and institutions were worked out by scholars afterwards, *the emergence of Islam as a faith system is believed to correspond exactly with the life of Mohammed.* Although it is accepted that the Koran was only written after the death of the Prophet, it is considered to have been established only by the accumulation of his revelations and from no other source.

The Caliphs from the period of Mohammed's life (according to tradition) to the end of the Umayyad dynasty. Dates are approximate.

DATE (CE)	CALIPH	Sub-groups	Real events that form the basis of the traditional history
632-633 633-644 644-656 656-661	Mohammed . . . Abu-Bakr Umar Uthman Ali	Referred to in Islamic tradition as the **'rightly guided'** caliphs	622—ca 661 was a period of loose and unstable alliances in the first independent Arab state
661-680 680-683 683	**Mu'awiya** Yazid Mu'awiya II	**UMAYYADS:** These are also known as the *Sufyanids*	**Civil war** bringing 'strong man' Mu'awiya to power as *the first caliph attested by archaeological evidence.*
684-685 685-705 705-715 715-717 717-720 720-724 724-743 743-744 744 744 744-750	Marwan **Abd Al-Malik** Walid Sulayman Umar II Yazid II Hisham Walid II Yazid III Ibrahim Marwan II	These Umayyad caliphs are also known as the *Marwanids*, after the founding caliph	**Second civil war** bringing Marwan to power The **Dome of the Rock** built in Jerusalem Overthrown by revolution and the beginning of the *ABBASID dynasty.*

The belief that Islam was in its 'finished' form by the time of the Prophet's death has also led historians to view the Arab conquests of this period as 'Islamic' conquests and the subsequent empire that was established as an 'Islamic' empire. The Arabs did indeed achieve stunning military successes in a relatively short space of time and that is something that will be addressed in a later chapter[567]. The point to make is that traditional historians have put the conquests down to religious fervour. As

---

[567]   See chapter on 'The early seventh century and the origins of the Arab Empire'

Laura Vaglieri wrote, for example, in her contribution to *The Cambridge History of Islam,*

". . . the decisive factor in this [military] success was Islam, which was the coordinating element behind the efforts of the Bedouin, and instilled into the hearts of the warriors the belief that a war against the followers of another faith was a holy war."[568]

Another important element that needs to be noted is that the traditional story places the origin of Islam in a place *geographically isolated* or at least *peripheral* to the main branches of monotheism that were then current in that part of the ancient world, Judaism and Christianity. Although the traditional story has Mohammed interacting with Jewish tribes and some minor legends have the Prophet speaking with Christian teachers, it is a fundamental tenet of the faith that Islam grew in a milieu of paganism and polytheism, separate and apart from the other great monotheistic religions. Any 'debt' that it owes to the other great religious traditions is therefore minimised.

From the foregoing, it follows that the established view of Islam is that the religion existed only in Mecca and Medina *in its purest form* during the life of the Prophet. All observant Muslims today, of whatever sect or persuasion, will therefore project their own beliefs back to a starting point in the life of the Prophet Mohammed in the early seventh century and his life and activity is absolutely central to their faith. Mohammed's name is never mentioned in conversation by a pious Muslim without a blessing appended to it and it is a blasphemy of the highest order to attempt any figurative representation of the Prophet.

We have seen in relation to Judaism and Christianity that many historians take the traditional views of these two faiths, as they appear in the Hebrew Bible and the New Testament, as uncontested accounts of a real history. In exactly the same manner, most historians of Islam take the official accounts, as revealed in the *hadith*, as an authentic narrative of real events, notwithstanding the fact, as we shall show, that most of it was written centuries after the events described and that many of the stories are contradictory. Many, although not all, of these modern historians, both Muslim and non-Muslim, are happy to recycle even the finest details of the *hadith*, like verbatim accounts of speeches, as records of real events. To take an example of what is clearly *myth* elevated to *history*; this extract is taken from Ameer Ali's *Short History of the Saracens*:

"On his arrival at Mecca on 8th of *Zu'l-Hijja*, 7th March, and before completing all the rites of the pilgrimage, he [Mohammed] addressed the assembled multitude from the top of the *Jabal ul-Arafat* in words which yet live in the heart of all Muslims.

---

[568]   *The Cambridge History of Islam*, p 60

'Ye people! Listen to my words, for I know not whether another year will be vouchsafed to me after this year to find myself amongst you . . .'"[569]

Ameer Ali goes on to cite what purports to be a five or ten minute speech of Mohammed, word for word. This verbatim speech is only one of many quoted in his book, using sources written two hundred years after Mohammed. This re-heating of ninth century accounts of seventh century events as history is by no means unusual and is, in fact, the norm for most historians of Islam.

Another scholarly work by Wilferd Madelung, *The succession to Muhammed*,[570] fills a near 400-page book with the finest detail of the complex machinations and struggles for succession in the twenty years after the death of the Prophet. Madelung makes what he describes as a "judicious" use of resources to create a "reliable and accurate portrait of the period." No detail is left out. We are informed of the whereabouts of all the main characters, what they did and even what was said; everything almost, but what they wore—and even that in some cases!

There is not the slightest doubt that Madelung, as befits an Oxford scholar, was familiar with all the original Arabic sources and was able to translate them personally. In one section of his book, for example, on the death of Mohammed, he discusses different detailed accounts, all of which were written one hundred to one hundred and fifty years after the events described. He evaluates their authenticity according to how they chime with the likely motives and behaviour of Mohammed's wife and other family members. Yet Madelung appears to accept as good coin the personal characteristics that are attributed to the Prophet's wife even though *these too are part of the tradition written generations later*. Madelung, like many others, did not appear to accept that just because one set of traditions, replete with a massive amount of detail, happens to chime with another set of traditions, that, in itself, cannot be taken to authenticate either of them.

Even when historians have sought an interpretation of Islam based in social and political movements, as often as not they too recycle the tradition. Thus, a more recent historian, Julius Wellhausen, attempted to find social and economic causes behind the rise of Islam. Five years before Kautsky's *Foundations of Christianity*, he published *The Arab Kingdom and its Fall*, in which he described the establishment of the Arab empire from the time of Mohammed to the fall of the Umayyad dynasty in 750 CE. He presents an often bewildering succession of characters, events, stories, conflicts and battles over a hundred and fifty years, all of which are simply mined from the traditional accounts. If one were to take the traditional sources on face value, almost the entire history of the Arab peoples revolved around the personal attributes and ambitions of the main characters, kings, commanders and clan and tribal chiefs of the time. Wellhausen is one of those historians who even reproduces from time to time what are alleged to be the exact words and speeches used by various actors in this great drama.

---

[569]   Ameer Ali, *A Short History of the Saracens*, p 17
[570]   Wilferd Madelung, *The succession to Muhammed, A study of the early Caliphate*

But Wellhausen, at least, was one of the first to acknowledge that the question of sources is a serious problem. Like other historians, he has to use sources which were written a long time after the events they describe. The source material, he points out, is often contradictory. Just to take one important example, he comments on the Battle of Siffin in 657 CE, a supposed decisive encounter between Mu'awiya and Ali, rival pretenders to the Caliphate:

> "We have no clear picture of the course of the actual battle; it is described with just as great confusion as it was fought. We certainly find over and over again systematic accounts of the distribution, arrangement and leadership of the troops, but they do not agree with each other, and so have hardly any practical value for the real course of the battle. The description is a mass of one-sided traditions dealing with episodes, and the attempt of the editor to make a mosaic unity of it is a failure. There is a lack of inward connection; you cannot see the wood for the trees. *Every witness is inclined to regard the station of his own tribe as the centre-point,* and to ascribe the chief glory to the heroes of his tribe."[571]

It is notable in Wellhausen's book that the traditional accounts always give precise (although contradictory) numbers of horsemen and foot-soldiers involved in these battles. If the numbers were taken on face value one would have to believe the unlikely: that *millions* of Arabs fought and died in a succession of battles and skirmishes over the first century of the Arab empire. Unfortunately, the author doesn't draw the obvious conclusion—that these accounts are more than likely *made up* many decades and in some cases centuries later. Having then been passed on, at best as oral tradition, they were subject to exaggeration, change and further embellishment. It is not surprising that different stories exaggerate the role of different tribes—that was their purpose in being invented in the first place.

We have already seen that in his account, *No God but God,* Reza Aslan leans towards a social and political description . . . but it is still one based on the traditional accounts. What is even more surprising is that some scholars who stand in the tradition of Marxism also follow the same historical method. Thus, for example, the celebrated French writer, Maxime Rodinson, in his biography of Mohammed, faithfully stays with the stories as they occur in the *hadith*, although he draws out from it what he sees as the social, economic and political forces at work. It is equivalent to those 'modern' Christians who take the New Testament gospels as their starting point for a 'social' analysis of the life and times of Jesus, without ever questioning the authenticity of the gospels in the first place. In fact, as we shall see, there are serious doubts about the entire construction of the *hadith*, the overwhelming majority of which were written very late.

---

[571] Julius Wellhausen, *The Arab Kingdom and its Fall,* Curzon Press London, 1973 edition, p 80 (italics added)

The paucity of sources.

The problem with the traditional account of the life of Mohammed, whichever particular version is accepted, is that it depends on an Islamic tradition which has *no contemporary writings, inscriptions or other evidence to support it.* There is not even an equivalent to the Jewish historian Josephus, who wrote from personal experience about first century Judea. There is no-one similar to whom we can turn for a contemporary or near-contemporary account of social upheavals and class struggle in mid-seventh century Arabia. It was at the very earliest in the *eighth century* that Islamic scholars began to compile and sift the oral tradition and to invent new traditions. In the view of G R Hawting, senior lecturer in the History of the Near and Middle East at the London School of African and Oriental Studies, this means that oral tradition did not even start being written down until at least one hundred years after the events the tradition purports to describe:

> "It seems likely that it was not until the later part of the Umayyad period that traditions, religious or historical (and the distinction is not always clear), came to be committed to writing with any frequency." [572]

The early scholars mentioned by Hawting and others are *Ibn Ishaq* (who died around 761 CE), *Abu Mikhnaf* (d. 774) and *Awana* (d. 764). Making the task of historians even more difficult is the fact that the work of these ancients is now lost and is only known through later citations. In fact, there is no material now in existence that was written *prior to the ninth century.* Ibn Ishaq's work, for example, is found only in the later work of *Ibn Hisham* (d. 833), yet his work is an important source for historians. Patricia Crone, in *Slaves on Horses,* writes:

> "Ibn Ishaq is practically our only source for the life of Mohammed within the Islamic tradition. The work is late: written by . . . a great grandchild of the Prophet's generation, it gives us the view for which classical Islam has settled . . . and written by a member of the *ulema,* the scholars who by then had emerged as the classical bearers of the Islamic tradition."[573]

Moreover, Ibn Hisham, who collected the work of Ibn Ishaq, freely admitted to having edited the work of the earlier writer, thus rendering it even less reliable. In his own writing, according to Patricia Crone, Ibn Hisham admits that he

> ". . . omitted from his recension of Ibn Ishaq's *sira* everything without direct bearing on the Koran, *things which he felt to be repugnant* or which

---

[572]   G R Hawting. *The First Dynasty of Islam. The Umayyad Caliphate AD 661-750* 2nd edition., p 15

[573]   Patricia Crone. *Slaves on Horses* p 4

might cause offence, poems not attested elsewhere, as well as matters which a certain transmitter could not accept as trustworthy."[574]

The Constitution of Medina, for example, is supposed to have been based on the community established by Mohammed when the Muslims migrated there in 622. But what we know of it is based on the work of Ibn Ishaq, *via* Ibn Hisham, written, therefore, *two hundred years later*. Patricia Crone uses the metaphor of literary 'debris' and 'rubble' to describe the mix of oral traditions that have found their way into later collections centuries later. Referring to the Islamic *hadith* tradition, she writes:

". . . the basic trouble is that these *hadiths* are a layer deposited fairly late and that the layer underneath consists of rubble reorganised in minimal order. No scholar in his most extravagant fantasies would dream of reconstructing the Constitution of Medina from its debris in the *hadiths* about Ali; and yet scholars are doing precisely that when they reconstruct the origins of Islam from its debris in the Islamic tradition."[575]

Most of the written material that does survive, even at second or third hand, was written long after the fall of the Umayyad dynasty which had by then ruled an Arab empire for a century. These writings are not very complimentary to the Umayyad caliphs, which is not surprising given their gestation during the period of the Abbasid dynasty which had only replaced the Umayyads after a ferocious revolutionary struggle. Hawting again:

"A decisive role in the collection, transmission and reduction to writing of the material was played by scholars representative of the opposition to the Umayyads . . . the image of the Umayyads as leading opponents of the Prophet and Islam, and their late and opportunistic acceptance of the new religion, and the antiquity of the rivalry between them and the Banu Hashim [descendents of Hashim, the family of Mohammed], all seem possible creations, or at least elaborations, of political and religious feelings against the Umayyads which developed during the course of their caliphate." [576]

Patricia Crone adds:

"The tradition as we have it is the outcome of a clash between two rival claimants to religious authority at a time when Islam was still in

---

[574]   Patricia Crone. *Slaves on Horses*, p 6 (italics added)
[575]   Patricia Crone. *Slaves on Horses* p 8
[576]   Hawting, *The First Dynasty of Islam. The Umayyad Caliphate AD 661-750 2ⁿᵈ edition*, pp 16, 24

formation . . . in the later half of the Umayyad period *the doctrinal structures of Islam began to acquire stability* . . . the *ulema* now began *not just to collect, but also to sift and tidy up the tradition* . . . wherever one turns one finds compilers of different dates, origin and doctrinal persuasion presenting the same canon in different arrangements and selections . . . every compiler will have bits of the canon not found elsewhere."[577]

In her later book, *Roman, Provincial and Islamic Law*, Crone gives an additional list of sources, although no earlier than those mentioned above. She mentions *Ibn Hanbal* (d. 855), *Darimi* (d. 869), *Bukhari* (d. 870), *Muslim* (d. 875), *Ibn Maja* (d. 887), *Abdu Dawind* (d. 889), *Tirmidhi* (d. 892) and *Nasai* (d. 915). These ancient scholars often represented different 'schools' of doctrinal thoughts, reflecting the interests of different classes and layers in society. In collecting and compiling *hadith*—and those mentioned here each collected *thousands*—they had in mind the need to validate their own interpretation of Islam against others, often in bitter polemical disputes.

"It is clear . . . that hadith invoking the authority of the Prophet himself was proliferating in the second half of the eighth century—presumably in response to the escalating polemics between the schools . . . *the Prophet was everybody's authority and everybody ascribed opinions to him.*" [578]

It would appear from these citations of Crone and Hawting, therefore, that it was these religious scholars, the *ulema*, who *much later* provided the effective doctrinal foundation of modern Islam, not scribes who followed the Prophet around Mecca and Medina, or even scribes who acted under the instructions of Mohammed's immediate successors. Over many years the *ulema* as a social caste, wrote, revised and edited material within the swirl of oral history and contemporary politics. They created new traditions and filtered the old ones to suit their immediate political-religious *polemical* needs and by this means, over a period of centuries, they provided the basis of what finally came to resemble modern Islam.

Among the ninth century and early tenth century collections, those of *Ibn S'ad* (d. 845), *Baladhuri* (d. 892), *Al-Yakubi* (d. 897) and *Tabari* (d. 923) are perhaps the most often quoted by modern historians. These late sources, as usual, are *all based on the recycling of earlier material,* which itself may have been a secondary or tertiary source and which has since disappeared. The last in this list, Tabari, is perhaps the fullest and is most often quoted because his multi-volume history is available in English. It is important to note that this much-quoted author, whose work we will meet on many occasions, died nearly *three hundred years* after the events described as

---

[577] Patricia Crone. *Slaves on Horses*. Cambridge University Press, 1980, pp 6, 11 (italics added)

[578] Patricia Crone, *Roman, Provincial and Islamic Law*. Cambridge University Press, 1987, p 24 (italics added)

the life of Mohammed. The great majority of the fine details we read, for example in Reza Aslan's book, are based on writings three centuries after the events described. There is little, if any, real evidence of their veracity, other than the writing itself.

The traditional account, therefore, is not a seventh century history. The best that one could say about it, including the biography of Mohammed, is that *it is an account of what ninth century writers wanted to think was true of the seventh century.* However, as is the case with the accounts of alleged historical events in the Hebrew Bible, even if the detailed narratives of Islamic *hadith* are fictional, these very late accounts may faithfully reflect, at least in general terms, the social and economic conditions of their authors' times or earlier centuries. Stephen Humphreys, professor of Islamic studies at the University of California, writing in *Islamic History: a Framework for Inquiry*, concisely summed up the issue that historians confront in studying early Islam.

> "If our goal is to comprehend the way in which Muslims of the late 2nd/8th and 3rd/9th centuries understood the origins of their society, then we are very well off indeed. But if our aim is to find out 'what really happened,' in terms of reliably documented answers to modern questions about the earliest decades of Islamic society, then we are in trouble"[579].

What we have dealt with so far are the Islamic sources. We shall deal later, and in more detail, with the process by which the Koran and the *hadith* came into being. Suffice to say that those non-Muslim scholars who have analysed and evaluated the original sources in Arabic are no mere amateurs but are extremely learned and experienced scholars in their own right, with the added virtue that they have been able to approach their subject with greater objectivity than others might. We shall also deal later with non-Islamic evidence that casts some light on the seventh century and the early Arab Empire. There were documents, for example, written by Christian clerics of the Byzantine Empire, whose contemporary work is still extant today. The most notable of these is Theophanes, writing at the end of the eighth and beginning of the ninth centuries. The Chronicles of Theophanes cover the whole period of the rise of the Arab empire and Islam and it largely based on a prior document written in Syriac which was available to him.

Last but not least, there is an abundance of surviving archaeological evidence, including buildings, gravestones, rock and wall inscriptions, as well as papyri and coins which have been discovered and which we will discuss in due course. However, it is worth noting that even solid, *physical evidence*, of the kind that sits today in museums around the world, is not immune from misinterpretation. Volker Popp, in *The Hidden History of Islam*, discusses the dating of coins from the period of the early Arab Empire and is very critical of some of his colleagues in their manner of ascribing dates to coins. Fiddling the figures is not what one normally associates with archaeologists and historians, but Popp takes to task those of his fellows who

---

[579] Stephen Humphreys, *Islamic History: A Framework for Inquiry* p 69

choose to allow the traditional account of Islam to effectively override the evidence held in the palms of their hands. Referring to inscriptions on coins, he comments:

"If a date squares with the dates made known by the traditional Islamic literature of later centuries, then scholars consider it to be dating after the Hijra of the prophet of the Arabians; if it does not, then it is made to fit by adding twelve years and explaining it as following the Persian tradition."[580]

Popp is particularly scathing about using this supposed 'Persian' tradition to 'interpret' dates on Arabic coins. He criticises published lists of dated coins which, incredibly, "do not give the numbers found on the coins". In a further footnote, he denounces the practice of ignoring and misinterpreting dates actually stamped on the coins, in order to correspond to 'histories' written two hundred and fifty years after they were minted. Taking the example of the accepted date for the accession of the Caliph Abd Al-Malik, he comments:

"This dating to the year 52 of the Arabian era has been continually manipulated so that the result is the year 65 of the Hijra. This occurs according to the following method: (1) what Tabari [the tenth century historian] says and (2) what date Tabari gives. Then, one calculates a number X that must always be added to the number given on a set of coins, until one comes to a dating that is possible within the chronology supplied by Tabari. In this way, one finds that, in the literature of Islamic studies, the coins of Ibn Zubayr as *Amir-I mu'minin* are always dated according to the fictional 'Yazdgard [Persian] era' . . . However, as soon as Ibn Zubayr loses power and returns to Kirman as a pious Muslim, there is no longer any need for a corrective number X in dating his coins . . . Having become pious, Ibn Zubayr can do nothing other than to give up his pagan style of dating . . . this account is not credible, but it is accepted nonetheless."[581]

In fact, as we shall show, where there is *physical evidence* remaining from the seventh century, it is in flat contradiction with the traditional account of the rise of Islam and the life of the Prophet. Even where great efforts are made to 'amend' the facts, as in relation to Popp's coins, they invariably fall flat. For example, a website specifically dedicated to supporting the traditional view of Islamic history is www.islamic-awareness.org. It methodically lists historical 'evidence' in the form of inscriptions, coinage, papyri, gravestones, milestones and other physical artefacts that support the traditional view. It also has links to articles critical of revisionist historians, some of which we have already quoted.

---

580   Popp, *The hidden history of Islam*, p 38
581   Popp, *The hidden history of Islam*, p 111

Most of the artefacts referenced on this website are *self-dating* in that they include a date in their text, usually in Arabic but occasionally in Coptic or Greek. What is not in dispute is that Arabs numbered their years from 622 CE—many papyri and inscriptions carry the Arab date as well as an equivalent Christian date—but there is an explanation for this, which we shall discuss later when we come to the origins of the Arab Empire.

Although the website lists many fragments of papyri discovered in the first 'Islamic' century, it provides no new certainties to the traditional account of the origins of the Koran or Islam. Many of the papyri it mentions contain references to God or Allah but the earliest to mention Mohammed is dated 709-710 CE, with the phrase "Maamet is the Messenger of God". A Greek fragment dated 714 refers to Mohammed as "the Apostle of God". As we will later suggest, even these inscriptional references to 'Mohammed' are open to another interpretation. The authors of the website, are forced to concede that it is only after 74 AH (696 CE) that citations from the Koran begin to appear within papyri and inscriptions. It is not possible to judge, however, whether these fragments of writing were taken from a larger volume or whether the larger volume was itself a composition of fragments that were already in common circulation.

An inscription on a dam is dated by its reference to the Caliph Mu'awiya, "commander of the believers", to around 661-680 CE. Yet even though this inscription was found in Medina, the 'City of the Prophet', it makes no reference to Mohammed. Similarly, an inscription in Karbala in Iraq, dated to 684 CE, refers to "Allah the Merciful, the Compassionate" but has no reference to Mohammed. Another, also from Karbala and dated 684, has the phrase, "O Lord of Gabriel, Michael and Israfil" (other archangels of Judeo-Christian tradition) but no Mohammed. The website lists the earliest known Islamic textile, dated at 683-5 from the mention of the caliph Marwan, but again with no mention of Mohammed. And so it goes on, until finally, in 691, an inscription on a tomb refers to "Mohammed the Prophet" and to "the people of Islam".

In the entire list there is one *undated* inscription in Medina which bears the name of Mohammed and three of the first four caliphs after him: Abu Bakr, Umar and Ali. Scholars differ as to its age; some putting it late in the seventh century and at least one Muslim scholar puts it as early as 625. Another even suggests the inscription is in the handwriting of Umar himself, who "was known for his calligraphic skills", as if scoring an inscription into rock employed the same skill as writing with ink on parchment or papyri. This inscription does not even include the 'third' caliph, Uthman, but even ignoring that, it is hardly an authoritative confirmation of Islamic historical tradition.

Where inscriptions include citations "from the Koran" or elements that are "Koranic", we have the same problem: there are no early references to Mohammed. A parchment dated 710, for example, bears a pious invocation to God, in a "Koranic flavour", but makes no reference to Mohammed. It says, "lead us so we meet my Prophet and his Prophet in this world and the next". Interestingly, although it does not name the Prophet it invokes God as "Lord of Moses and Aaron", another allusion to Judeo-Christian tradition. The Koranic quotations are partial and inaccurate, so even the website refers to them as an "eclectic blend of words and phrases taken from different verses in the Koran". We would question whether these were in fact broken quotations from a much larger text (ie the Koran) or whether it is more likely that they were a part of a largely oral tradition of pious phrases, proverbs and sayings that were in common currency at the time.

As we shall argue, the traditional story of the life of Mohammed is not actually based on any contemporary historical evidence at all and is most probably entirely legendary. We shall argue, instead, that the evidence points to the evolution of Islam over at least two centuries from a version of monotheism closer to Judaism and Christianity than modern Islam. The historical fact of the rise of a huge Arab empire is not contested. But in its first decades, it was not an *Islamic* empire. Whatever may have been the role of an Arab leader called 'Mohammed', the religion that developed in his name did not exist in the mid-seventh century but arose from the class and ethnic conflicts within the Arab Empire and the stresses and strains of holding together the enormous conquests of the seventh century. It was not, we believe, divine revelation, but the social and political currents of the Near East that were the mainspring of Islam.

Repression faced by Islamic scholars

Most of the modern 'revisionist' historians are based in non-Muslim countries, largely because of the repression faced by Muslim scholars who might question the tradition in their own countries. Just as the Christian Church has shown great reluctance to examine the real historical and archaeological evidence of the early Christian era, so also many of the most influential scholars within the Muslim world have opposed the treatment of Islamic history as anything other than a matter of faith. For many Muslims, the Koran is the unerring word of Allah and in Islamic countries those few academics who have questioned the official histories or traditions have suffered intimidation, repression and in some cases, murder. Scattered throughout the last century there are many examples of writers and commentators paying very heavily for daring to challenge the traditional narrative.

Although the author Daniel Pipes approaches political issues as a right-wing commentator, his book, *The Rushdie Affair*, is nevertheless a useful resource in that it lists many occasions when scholarly work has been suppressed in the Islamic world. He refers, for example, to *Islam and the Principles of Government*, a book published in 1925 in Cairo, and written by Ali Abd ar-Raziq of *al-Azhar University*, in which it was argued that Islam, properly interpreted, should mean the separation of the state from religion. Abd ar-Raziq's ideas were condemned by other scholars in the university and he was stripped of his diploma, expelled from the university and barred from holding any religious office.

Also in the 1920s, Taha Hussein, a celebrated expert in Islamic and pre-Islamic poetry, published a book in which he questioned the historical accuracy of Koran interpretation. He came to the conclusion that much of the book was written long after the establishment of Islam, in order, *ex post facto*, to create a mythology that would give divine sanction to later legal and religious practices. Hussein was attacked at the time for 'apostasy', and he too was expelled from his university and forced to withdraw his book.

Following the revolutionary upheavals in Syria in the early 1960s, in which a significant part was played by the urban working class and poor, a section of the army officer corps and the Baathist Party were heavily influenced by the ideas of Marxism and socialism. Pipes quotes from an article in the Syrian army magazine *Jaysh ash-Sha'b* in April 1967, in which God and religion were condemned as "mummies which should be transferred to the museums of historic remains". This was too much for the more conservative sections of Syrian society, however and, following protest demonstrations, the Baathist regime was forced to condemn the article and send the author and magazine editor to jail to cool off for a time.

In 1969 a book was published in Lebanon by another radical professor, Sadiq al-Azm, in which there was a generalised criticism of the role of religion in the life of the Muslim masses. After publishing *A Critique of Religious Thought*, al-Azm, who was thought to be close to the PLO, was condemned by the Sunni establishment in Lebanon and had his book withdrawn. He was brought to trial in 1970 but managed to avoid going to jail as his detractors demanded.

Pipes also quotes the example of Mahmud Muhammed Taha, a Sudanese theologian who eventually paid with his life for his work. In an attempt to separate civil life from the religious sphere, he differentiated between the so-called 'Meccan' and 'Medinan' *suras*; but in 1968 he was found guilty of 'apostasy' by a *sharia* court in Khartoum. He was reprieved, although temporarily as it turns out, but his books were burned and following another trial in 1985, Taha, by then an old man of 76, was publicly hanged.

In June 1992, the liberal Egyptian writer Farag Foda was shot and killed by a group calling itself *al-Jama'at al-Illamiyyat*, in response to a *fatwa* that was issued by a group of teachers at *al-Azhar University* in Cairo. Dr Foda had been condemned for 'blasphemy' by his fellow academics because of his outspoken views in favour of the separation of religion from civil government. In his book, *The absent truth among those calling for a religious state*, Foda posed several questions to Islamic supporters of *sharia* law:

> "We face problems of great magnitude, so how can they be resolved by the application of *sharia law* since these problems did not exist in the early centuries of Islam? How could *sharia* for example, deal with the problems of housing, indebtedness, famine and unemployment?
>
> "We seem to be excessively interested and preoccupied with matters of worship; does that relieve us from our responsibility to get involved in the great scientific and technological advancements of our times? We are equally busy with *fatwas* that deal with such topics as marriage, how to relieve ourselves when we happen to be in the countryside and the like!
>
> "What are the benefits that come from the imposition of the *hijab* on Muslim women?
>
> "What good has come out of the practice of the so-called *prophetic healing* of the sick, as based on spurious hadiths when at the same time we witness

the astronomically growing number of the sick? And what about the latest charlatanry of those 'experts' who claim that healing may be found in flies' wings, as well as camels' urine?"[582]

Two years later the novelist Naguib Mahfouz, winner of the Nobel Prize for literature in 1988, was stabbed in an attempted assassination. He had become notorious for writing, among other works, the allegorical *Children of Gabalawi* (1959), a novel presenting 'heretical' conceptions of Allah and the Prophet Mohammed. Mahfouz had also condemned Ayatollah Komeini in Iran and had defended the novelist Salman Rushdie who had a *fatwa* declared against him by the Shia leader.

In 1995, Nasr Abu Zaid, an Egyptian professor of Arabic, was officially branded as an apostate for daring to examine the Koran as an *historical* rather than a *sacred* text. Being declared an apostate meant that his Muslim wife was obliged to divorce him. This resulted in Abu Zaid, who still considered himself a devout Muslim, fleeing to Holland in order to continue living with his wife. He would also have been aware that in orthodox Islamic law the traditional punishment for apostasy was death, just as he would have known about the fates of Foda and Mahfouz. Despite his persecution and exile, Zaid claims that some of his work still circulates in Egypt.

Another scholar who has been associated with an examination of the historicity of the Koran is the Algerian professor Mohammed Arkoun, who argued in *Lectures du Coran* (1982) that: "it is time [for Islam] to assume, along with all of the great cultural traditions, the modern risks of scientific knowledge." He suggested that "the problem of the divine authenticity of the Koran can serve to reactivate Islamic thought and engage it in the major debates of our age."[583] Arkoun argued for a re-evaluation of Muslim orthodoxy and a challenge 'from within' rather than leave a critical analysis to non-Muslims and others 'hostile' to Islam. Arkoun, based not surprisingly in Paris rather than Algiers, declared that the study of the Koran is a very sensitive business. "Millions and millions of people", he wrote, "refer to the Koran daily to explain their actions and to justify their aspirations. This scale of reference is much larger than it has ever been before."

One of the most extensive analyses of the Koran by a Muslim is *23 Years, a study of the prophetic career of Mohammed,* by the Iranian Ali Dashti, who was eventually executed for his views. His book was first published anonymously in Beirut and although written from the standpoint of a believer, it blows holes in much of the mythology surrounding the Koran and the supposed faultless life of the Prophet. Dashti was well-known through a long career in politics and writing on Islam and when the ayatollahs came to power in Iran it would have been known

---

[582] From www.news.faithfreedom.org '*Remembering the Assassination of Farag Foda*

[583] Quoted by Toby Lester, *What is the Koran, The Atlantic Monthly* January, 283 1999, pp 43-56

that he was a critic of the traditional view of the Koran. In 1981 he was arrested and badly beaten in prison. He eventually died in prison, an old man of eighty-four or eighty five years of age (the precise date is unknown). We will examine Dashti's views in more detail later.

Neither is the discouragement of scholarship confined to those countries where Muslims are in a majority. Writing in the *New Humanist*, Ibn Warraq gives the following example:

> "Very recently, Professor Josef van Ess, a scholar whose works are essential to the study of Islamic theology, cut short his research, fearing it would not meet the approval of Sunni Islam. Gunter Luling was hounded out of the profession by German universities because he proposed the radical thesis that at least a third of the Koran was originally a pre-Islamic, Christian hymnody, and thus had nothing to do with Mohammed."[584]

Edward Said, in his 1978 book *Orientalism* criticised western Arab experts who viewed Middle Eastern history from the standpoint of imperialist interests and policies. "The relationship between Occident and Orient," he wrote, "is a relationship of power, of domination, of varying degrees of a complex hegemony . . ."[585] and this has completely overshadowed the western view of 'the East' including the Muslim East. Said made a detailed analysis of the political and sociological studies of the Middle East and Islam in the nineteenth century and the first part of the twentieth and there was indeed a clear vein of haughty and condescending racism running through many of the earlier commentaries and histories on the Middle East. Consider, for example, these three gems from Theodor Noldeke's *Sketches from Eastern History*[586]:

> "Our general conclusion, then, is that the genius of the Semites is in many respects one-sided, and does not reach the level of some Indo-European nations, especially the Greeks; but it would be most unjust to deny their claim to one of the highest places among the races of mankind . . ." *It does not take a genius to guess which race stand "highest" in Noldeke's hierarchy.*

> ". . . Islam in its original form as a whole ranks far below primitive Christianity . . ." *Noldeke's faith in Christianity goes without saying.*

> ". . . in the dark continent, which offers no favourable soil for Christianity, the acceptance even of Islam means progress from the deepest savagery to a certain culture, however limited and limiting . . .". *The gist of the argument*

---

[584] *New Humanist*, Volume 116 Issue 4 Winter 2001
[585] *Orientalism*, Edward W Said, p 5
[586] *Sketches From Eastern History*, Theodor Noldeke, 1892, pp 20, 71 and 105

being that whilst Europeans have not adopted Islam, that faith is good enough for the 'savages' of the 'dark continent'.

Said quotes Noldeke as saying that the sum total of his work as an Orientalist was that it confirmed his "low opinion" of the Eastern peoples. It is hardly surprising that Muslims recoil in anger from such blatantly racist 'historical' traditions as those of Noldeke. Moreover, Noldeke has many modern-day equivalents, even if they are usually a little more subtle. But whereas Said's criticisms contained more than a grain of truth in relation to some of the scholarly circles of Western Europe and America, not to mention the yellow press, an overly liberal use of the term "Orientalism" has been used as a discouragement of *any* historical analysis of Islam and particularly if such analysis is by anyone not a Muslim. Edward Said, according to Ibn Warraq, has "intimidated feeble western academics" who have allowed the charge of 'Orientalism' to invalidate any criticism of Islamic tradition. Said's "pernicious influence", Ibn Warraq argues,

". . . is still felt in all departments of Islamic studies, where any critical discussion of Islam is ruled out *a priori*. For Said, Orientalists are involved in an evil conspiracy to denigrate Islam, to maintain its people in a state of permanent subjugation and are a threat to Islam's future . . . The unfortunate result is that academics can no longer do their work honestly. A scholar working on recently discovered Koranic manuscripts showed some of his startling conclusions to a distinguished colleague, a world expert on the Koran. The latter did not ask, "What is the evidence, what are your arguments, is it true?" The colleague simply warned him that his thesis was unacceptable because it would upset Muslims."[587]

An example of the venom directed at those seeking to revise the traditional Islamic history can be seen on the website www.scholarofthehouse.org in which one writer accuses those seeking a revision of Islamic tradition of being racist. "Revisionism," he writes, "like all forms of incipient or established bigotry, rests on several peculiar assumptions. Assumption number one is that Muslims invariably lie." Another assumption, it argues:

". . . is the one least confessed, but is unmistakable in methodology and conclusion. Muslims are a barbaric people; whatever good they might have produced, they must have conveniently borrowed from Judaism, Christianity or some other more civilized source. Whatever barbarism Muslims might have produced that, naturally, comes from the depth of

---

587   Ibn Warraq, *The Guardian*, November 10 2001

their hearts and souls, but whatever beauty they may have possessed they simply stole."[588]

On the same website there are a variety of satirical references, for instance, to "lying, cheating Muslims", supposedly to illustrate the intellectual grounds on which any western revisionism is based. This is far worse than Said's critique; it is a calculated attempt to dissuade or intimidate any non-Muslims from asking any questions on the historical validity of the traditional accounts. The author is saying, in effect, that Islam is 'off limits' to any non-Muslim historian, otherwise they risk being labelled as racist. The writer even compares the revision of traditional Islamic history to Holocaust denial, for the specific benefit of two Israeli revisionists who are criticised.

"Ibn Warraq", whose writing we have already cited, is in fact a pseudonym, the adoption of which is also described by the writer on www.scholarinthehouse.org as a form of bigotry, the "Ibn" prefix having been allegedly adopted because it was "cool" to have an Arabic name. Notwithstanding this slur, Ibn Warraq describes himself as a *former* Muslim and is the author of the book, *Why I am not a Muslim*[589]. Writing in *The Guardian*, he suggests that for too long Islam had been treated as a taboo subject, because of, among other things:

". . . political correctness leading to Islamic correctness; the fear of playing into the hands of racists or reactionaries to the detriment of the West's Muslim minorities; commercial or economic motives; feelings of post-colonial guilt (where the entire planet's problems are attributed to the West's wicked ways and intentions); plain physical fear; and intellectual terrorism of writers such as Edward Said."[590]

There is more than a hint here from Ibn Warraq of an *apologia* for the enormously damaging role played by imperialism in the history of the Islamic East and he unwittingly ends up lending support to what he seeks to criticise . . . Said's view of Orientalism. Koranic study, in a nutshell, carries a health warning. As R Stephen Humphreys put it:

"To historicize the Koran would in effect delegitimize the whole historical experience of the Muslim community . . . . The Koran is the charter for the community, the document that called it into existence. And ideally—though obviously not always in reality—Islamic history has been the effort to pursue and work out the commandments of the Koran in

---

[588] www.scholarinthehouse.org Sample Chapter from the Conference of the Books: The search for Beauty in Islam 'On Revising Bigotry'

[589] Ibn Warraq, *Why I am not a Muslim*. Prometheus, 2003.

[590] *The Guardian*, November 10, 2001

human life. If the Koran is a historical document, then the whole Islamic struggle of fourteen centuries is effectively meaningless." [591]

We would insist that Said's views, although they contain more than a grain of criticism when directed at the appropriate targets, *cannot be acceptable as a justification for the suppression of genuine studies of Islamic history and tradition.* Like the history of Judaism and Christianity, the history of Islam is a legitimate area of investigation and discussion, whether by Muslims or atheists, and the quality of the commentary should be judged on its own merits: by the evidence and arguments presented and by no other means.

Chapter summary

- The traditional account of the life of Mohammed and the origin of the Koran are set in early seventh century Mecca and Medina. There is no contemporary or archaeological evidence to support any of these stories.

- All of the accounts of Mohammed's life, the stories of the first four caliphs after Mohammed and the early part of the 'Islamic' conquests were written hundreds of years after the supposed events and are unsupported or contradicted by archaeological evidence.

- The Koran contains little narrative of events and its linkage with events in the life of Mohammed is based on writings of the ninth and tenth centuries. Besides the Koran, the total corpus of Islamic literature includes vast amounts of *hadith*—tradition that related back to the life of the Prophet, his Companions, the origins of the Koran and the early years of Islam.

- Scholarly work that in any way threatens to undermine traditional Islamic history or which questions the *hadith* has often faced repression in Muslim countries. Several historians and writers in the Near East have been killed for the views they have expressed.

---

[591]   *The Atlantic Monthly* January, 1998

Chapter 13

Critique of the Koranic Tradition

In this chapter, for the benefit of readers who have no knowledge of Islamic tradition, we will look in more detail at the Koran, including its structure, content and its relationship with figures in the Judeo-Christian Bible. We will note that the oldest copies of the Koran were not written in quite the same form as modern Arabic and that in the early period of Islam there were variants of the Koran and different interpretations of the text, so that what has become the definitive form of the modern Arabic Koran is relatively recent. We will argue that the Koran most probably has a *pre-Islamic* origin and is much older than most Islamic tradition, by a factor of centuries. We will look at the suggestion that the origins of the book lie in old Syriac Christian religious works, although its final form was arrived at in the Islamic era. For Muslims, every verse in the Koran has a context that places each revelation at some point in the life of Mohammed, either in Mecca or Medina. But we will note that these contexts were only fixed by scholars who wrote hundreds of years after the time accorded to the life of Mohammed. We will use extensively a critique of the Koran that was written by a Muslim who was later murdered for his work.

. . . .

From Koranic inscriptions on early buildings like the Dome of the Rock in Jerusalem and from other epigraphical remains, it is generally assumed that the Koran is an early work and that fact is taken by many Muslims as evidence of the chronological coincidence of the Koran and the Prophet of Islam. However, as we have already suggested, there is strong evidence that links the Koran with Arab Christian origins rather than any other and this is something that we will explore further. Because the overwhelming majority of those readers who come from a Christian-based culture are completely unfamiliar with the Koran, a short description is probably useful at this point.

The Koran differs considerably from the Old and New Testaments of the Bible. While the Bible consists of many separate books attributed (often falsely) to different authors, the Koran is composed of a single book made up of 114 chapters, known as *suras*, each of which is composed of verses which are generally longer than the verses in the Bible. The *suras* are numbered, but each one is also named after a particular feature or person which it contains (not necessarily prominently), like "The Cow", "Mary" or "The Towering Constellations." The earliest fragments of the Koran known to historians are dated approximately from the end of the seventh to the early eighth century. Not only do these fragments differ from one another in their structure, but there are no titles for the *suras* and the text differs from that of the modern Koran. It would appear that at this point—still the best part of a century after the traditional life of the Prophet—there was still no settled version of the book, although it may have begun to consolidate into a unified scripture. The aim of this section is to demonstrate that the Koran does indeed have a history, even if its details are disputed.

In contrast to most books of the Bible, there is little narrative in the Koran. Over the centuries, Islamic scholars have made judgements based on the content and what they perceive as the tone of each *sura*, to distinguish the so-called 'Meccan' from the 'Medinan' *suras,* as they were revealed to Mohammed in the earlier or the later phase of his prophethood. Despite this distinction, no attempt is made to arrange them chronologically; they are arranged in approximate size order, starting with the longest. The longer *suras* are about the same length as short biblical books—'The Cow' has 286 verses—and the shortest has only six short verses. What makes the Koran stand in such sharp contrast to the Old and New Testaments is that it has no overall plan or structure and it would gain or lose nothing from the rearrangement of its *suras* in reverse order, or for that matter, at random.

The only narratives that occur in the Koran are those that recycle stories from the Bible, like parts of the legends of Noah, Abraham, Moses and Jesus. Moses is mentioned 136 times, Jesus 24 times and his mother Mary 34 times, whereas there are only four specific references to Mohammed. The great majority of the text is composed of moral lessons that exhort pious behaviour and which focus on the need to follow the one true God. Believers, we are told in a thousand different ways (and occasionally in exactly the same repeated verses), will go to the Garden (heaven) after the Day of Judgment, whereas disbelievers will go to the Fire, or Hell. Those who do not come from an Islamic tradition and who come to the Koran for the first time will be surprised by the degree to which it depends on the religious themes of the Bible. It clearly draws on traditions that are exclusively Arabian, such as the references to prophets who do not feature in the Bible, like Hud, Salih, Shu'ayb, Luqman, and others. But despite this, and its context as a 'recitation', it is clearly addressed to people who are familiar with the Judeo-Christian tradition and not to polytheists or pagans. *Ninety per cent of the Koran could have been read to a seventh-century Jewish or Christian congregation without any objections.* On some occasions the Koran aligns itself with pious Jews and Christians, often called the "people of the Book", but in other cases it condemns them for having ignored or debased the teachings of their own prophets, notably Moses and Jesus.

"Fight those people of the Book who do not believe in God and the Last Day . . . the Jews said 'Ezra is the son of God' and the Christians said, 'The Messiah is the son of God' . . . How far astray have they been led!

They take their rabbis and their monks as lords, as well as Christ the son of Mary."[592]

Although the Koran accepts Jesus as the son of the virgin Mary, a large number of its verses contain direct polemics against those Christians who held that Jesus was the 'son' of God. "It would not befit God to have a child", the Koran says, "He is far above that"[593]. The 'Christology' of the Koran is therefore in close agreement with the Nestorian Church which was popular in the eastern, Persian, part of Arabia. It is also clear that in so far as the sayings of the Koran represent a Christian tradition, it is an *old* form of Christianity, much closer to the Ebionites of Jerusalem than to Pauline Christianity. The fact that the Koran contains a nativity story of the birth of Jesus quite different to those in the New Testament gospels is another indication of a different origin story, perhaps based on oral tales circulating in Eastern Christian communities, centuries before Islam.

Idolatry and the Koran

In his book on idolatry and the Koran, G R Hawting, Senior Lecturer in the History of the Near and Middle East at the School of African and Oriental Studies, London, suggests that the polemics within the Koran are not directed towards polytheists and idolaters in the sense that most people understand. The writers of the Koranic tradition—those who in succeeding centuries have provided biographical contexts for all the sayings in the Koran—have gone out of their way to create the impression that Islam was founded in the area of Mecca and Medina where the life of the Prophet was centred. The period before Islam, referred to as the time of ignorance, the *jahiliyya*, at least in this part of Arabia, is described as predominantly one of paganism, idolatry and polytheism, with Jews, Christians and the monotheist *hanif* as a minority. According to tradition, the Arabs of the *jahiliyya* were:

". . . a nation which had not previously been given a scripture or a prophet; sunk in ignorance in which it was unaware that there is a Lord and reckoning after death; on the wrong path and given to creating falsehoods; its people were enemies one to another and in mutual hatred; disobedient to God and lacking in fear of Him; worshipping idols and eating carrion and blood; allowing what should be prohibited, rejecting the right path and complacent in error . . . Thus it remained until God sent them this Prophet."[594]

---

[592] 9, 29
[593] 19, 35
[594] From a ninth century polemic against Christianity cited by G R Hawting, *The Idea of Idolatry and the Emergence of Islam*, p 99

In fact, if it has any validity at all, this picture was only true in the desert regions of Arabia, away from the main centres of population in Syria, Iraq and Yemen. In those parts of the region where the Koran originated and where Islam followed, it was not the case that polytheism was predominant. However, the fact that ninth and tenth century commentators interpreted these polemical passages in the Koran and 'explained' them as references to polytheism has meant that this has been accepted unquestioningly by historians ever since.

> "According to the traditional accounts Islam was not born in the same way [as other religions]—not as a result of disputes among monotheists but from a confrontation with real idolaters . . . Islam is presented as having arisen in a remote region which could be said to be on the periphery of the monotheistic world, if not quite outside it. None of this is impossible but it does seem remarkable and is a reason for suggesting that the traditional account might be questioned . . . *Islam should be understood as the result of an intra-monotheistic polemic*, in a process similar to that of the emergence of the other main divisions of monotheism."[595]

Hawting points out that the Christian reformers in northern Europe frequently referred to the Catholic Church as idolaters for their use of pictures of the virgin Mary and the saints and in the Koran the term is used in polemics with Christians who in their view falsely attribute a son to God. It was ever the case that low Church condemned high Church for its idolatry. In the same way, the Koran condemns unbelievers as idolaters even when it understands these opponents to believe in the one true God. The interpretation of the Koran as a polemic against polytheism in general is, according to Hawting, simply wrong. "The tradition interprets the Koran," he points out, and then "the Koran documents the tradition" in a classical circular proof. But in fact, ". . . the tradition often goes far beyond the text and elaborates it in ways that would not be obvious if they were merely derived from the Koran itself."[596]

Although he falls short of drawing an explicit conclusion, at least in this work, what Hawting is suggesting is that the Koran represents a polemic against the Trinitarian view of Christianity and the portrayal of Jesus as the son of God. The polemic against all forms of idolatry is a polemic against the *Christian* use of icons, pictures and the symbol of the cross itself, a view that fits in broadly with the development of Islam in the later part of the seventh century when the Arab Empire went from having pictures of its caliphs on coins—sometimes even with crosses—to completely non-representational religious symbols and Art in general. The view of Hawting also corresponds to the idea that Islam originated closer to the more heavily populated regions of Syria and Iraq, which were the heartlands of Arab Christianity, rather than in the relative backwater of the Arabian Peninsula. As we

---

[595] G R Hawting, *The Idea of Idolatry and the Emergence of Islam*, p 7 (italics added)
[596] G R Hawting, *The Idea of Idolatry and the Emergence of Islam*, p 23

shall argue later, it also corresponds precisely to the inscriptions on the Dome of the Rock, the first great centre of worship built by the Arab caliphs.

> "The area in which these key developments took place was not in Arabia but the wider Middle East and in particular Syria and Iraq. Whatever religious ideas the Arabs brought with them into the lands they conquered, it is likely that it was from the social, political and religious interaction of the Arabs and the peoples over whom they ruled that Islam as we know it was formed. Both Arabs and non-Arabs must have contributed to it but it is probable that it was the originally subject population that was the more instrumental."[597]

Many historians have tried to describe the origin of Islam from the point of view of the evolution of the modern faith from various monotheistic influences, but still within a largely polytheistic milieu and still based in western Arabia. Some 'Marxist' historians have even attempted to interpret the traditional conflict between Mohammed and the tribe of the Quraysh in Mecca in terms of a class struggle and the rise of a new revolutionary monotheism. But these interpretations are like colossi standing on chickens' legs—they all depend on a dubious and unwarranted interpretation of the Koran and an assumption, based on tradition established between the eighth and tenth centuries, that Mecca and then Medina were the starting points of Islam. This is something that now looks increasingly unlikely. If there was a revolutionary content in the polemics of the Koran, it was a reaction against the gilded Christianity of Syrian and Iraqi tradition and a drive for a purer and simpler religion with one true God and Jesus as no more than a prophet. This form of monotheism may have had its roots in the Arabian hinterland—we may never know—but it formed a key component in what later became Islam, with the traditions of Mohammed, Mecca and Medina bolted onto it a few centuries later.

The Arabic language holds a central place in Islamic observance. Converts to Islam, whatever their nationality, usually adopt an Arabic name and whatever their own native language, all Muslims pray and recite the Koran exclusively in Arabic. The Koran is often characterised by Muslims as a form of Arabic that is somehow perfect and has been unchanged since the time it was written, but this is not the case. The epigraphic evidence clearly shows that pre-Islamic and early Islamic Arabic did not have the diacritical points (the dots above and below Arabic script) which are characteristic of modern Arabic writing. These points adjust the text to refine the use and in some cases define the meaning of consonants, so whatever is taken as the precise meaning of a given phrase today may have been different in the past.

In fact, scholars have suggested that it is difficult *even for highly educated readers of Arabic* to understand parts of the Koran in the original. There are unexpected shifts in subject matter from verse to verse and it seems often to assume knowledge of past events and stories that have long since been lost even to the earliest Muslim

---

[597]   G R Hawting, *The Idea of Idolatry and the Emergence of Islam*, p 13

scholars. Sometimes the same story, such as an Old Testament narrative, is repeated in the Koran in a different or even a contradictory way. In that sense, it shows the typical features of a text that has *accumulated* from collected traditions, rather than having been written as a piece. As the German archaeologist Gerd-R Puin points out:

> "Every fifth sentence or so simply doesn't make sense. Many Muslims—and Orientalists—will tell you otherwise, of course, but the fact is that a fifth of the Koranic text is *just incomprehensible*. This is what has caused the traditional anxiety regarding translation. If the Koran is not comprehensible—if it can't even be understood in Arabic—then it's not translatable. People fear that. And since the Koran claims repeatedly to be clear but obviously is not—as even speakers of Arabic will tell you—there is a contradiction. Something else must be going on."[598]

The degree of confusion and syntactical anomalies in the Koran are, paradoxically, one of the best arguments for its age. Had it been created, like many of the general tenets of Islam, in the two or three centuries after the foundation of the Arab Empire, it is far less likely to have kept the abrupt breaks in sentences and tense and the style would have been far more in keeping with the style of the *hadith* which came afterwards. In its style, content and in its frequent incoherence, it is in marked contrast to the *hadith* traditions. That is not to say that the early form of the Koran couldn't have been subject to some changes and clarifications throughout the seventh century and afterwards because, as the physical evidence shows, the ordering of the *suras* was not the same in all early copies.

To the lay person, particularly to non-Muslims, the interpretations in the Koran can be a little baffling, to say the least. The English translation of *sura* 22:15, for example, says, "Anyone who thinks that God will not support him in this world and the next should stretch a rope up to the sky, climb all the way up to it, and see whether this strategy removes the cause of his anger."[599] Yet a footnote to the verse says that "another translation" of the first part is "stretch a rope up to the ceiling and hang himself". What is the humble reader to make of this? There is a world of difference between endeavouring to find something out by climbing a rope and . . . suicide by hanging! This startling contrast shows the considerable artistic licence that was used in translating what was obviously very unclear in the original. One wonders how believers can hold the view that God would have gone to the trouble of handing down revelations to his prophet but leave them to be collected in such a manner that even after the painstaking study of tens of thousands of scholars over hundreds of years, so much of the book is still undecipherable.

An explanation for the vagaries and contradictions in the Koran has been provided by Christoph Luxenberg in his book, *The Syro-Aramaic Reading of the*

---

[598]   Gerd-R Puin, *Atlantic Monthly, January 1998.*
[599]   Koran, *Oxford World Classics,* p 210

Koran. Luxenberg, a renowned scholar of the ancient Semitic languages, argues that the influence of Syriac—a branch of Aramaic and the language of the Christian Church in Syria, Palestine and much of Iraq—has been largely ignored by scholars up to now, yet it had a profound effect on the Koran. "The Arabic vocabulary of the Koran," he writes, "reaches back, in part at least, to the pre-Islamic usage of the Christian Arabs of Mesopotamia and Syria . . ." On the basis of his examination of those passages in the Koran that are particularly obscure, he comes to the conclusion that the book was probably written first "in *Garshuni* (or *Karshuni*), that is to say, Arabic written in Syriac letters."

> "Except for a few pre-Islamic 4th-6th century CE inscriptions stemming from northern Hejaz and Syria, the Koran is considered to be the first book ever written in Arabic script. The early form of the Arabic letters and the type of ligatures employed suggest that the Syro-Aramaic cursive script served as a model for the Arabic script. Both scripts have the following in common with the earlier Aramaic (and Hebrew) script: the writing runs from right to left; in principle the letters designate the consonants with only two letters serving to reproduce the semi-long and long vowels . . . The real problem in the early Arabic script, however, was in the consonants, only six of which are clearly distinguishable by their form, whereas the remaining 22, due to their formal similarities (usually in pairs), were only distinguishable from each other by the context."[600]

He goes on to explain that the consonants were distinguished from one another by "the much later innovation of pointing", that is, the introduction of diacritical dots above and below the cursive script which are so characteristic of modern Arabic. When this innovation was introduced, it not only *clarified* certain meanings but, perhaps based on oral or other tradition, fictional or otherwise, it actually *imparted* meanings by selecting one consonant rather than another. The first standardised modern Arabic Koran saw the light of day some time in the second half of the eighth century—by this time more than a century and a half since the supposed events of Mecca—and it is this standard that has been the basis of the overwhelming majority of Koranic commentary and interpretation ever since. By the time of the Islamic historian Tabari, in the tenth century, "the consonal text of the Koran already appears to have been fixed by the diacritical points introduced in the meantime . . ." Luxenberg, taking a historical step backwards, questions the criteria by which these points were introduced in the first place, and the extent to which the originators of the pointing really understood the original Christian Syriac writing.

> "It is characteristic of Western Koran research that it has never called into question the diacritical points that were subsequently added to the

---

[600]   Luxenberg, *The Syro-Aramaic Reading of the Koran*, p 30

Koran text and that in each case first determined the suggested letters in an original spelling in need of interpretation. Today the extant, still unpointed early Koranic manuscripts provide evidence that *these points are not authentic*. Nonetheless, the conviction has never been challenged that the later pointing was based on an assured oral tradition. A detailed philological analysis, however, will reveal that this is a historical error."[601]

According to Luxenberg, the Koran frequently combines grammatical forms of Arabic and Syro-Aramaic, which is hardly surprising since the Aramaic language group had dominated the region for the best part of a millennium and at the time of the origination of the Koran was the dominant language of the Near East. Indeed, when Arabic was only just becoming a written language for the first time, it would be more surprising if it *wasn't* influenced by Syro-Aramaic. He argues that the Koran may have been originally a *Christian lectionary*, that is to say, a collection of Christian sayings, based on Scripture, but specifically meant for *reading out* to a congregation. This, he argues, is the root meaning of the word, *Koran* or *Qur'an*. It was in this crucial period that the Arab Christians will have *spoken* Arabic but, in the absence of their own written script, *used Syro-Aramaic as the language of religious liturgy*, in services and worship. At the point when a written Arabic script began to develop, it did so under the influence of Syro-Aramaic. This is not a new idea. Luxenberg cites the nineteenth century scholar of Arabic, Theodor Noldeke:

> "During the entire dominance of Aramaic this language had at least a great influence on the vocabulary of Arabic. The more meticulous one's examination, the more one recognises how many Arabic words signifying concepts or objects of a certain culture have been borrowed from the Aramaeans . . . *the northern cultural influence* expressed in these borrowings contributed considerably to preparing the Arabs for their powerful intervention in world history."[602]

Another pioneer of Islamic history, Alphonse Mingana, noted that the Koranic form of personal names, like Solomon, Isaac, Ishmael, Jacob, Noah, Zachariah and Mary, all follow the Syriac pattern. Moreover, many of the *religious* terms in the Koran use the Syriac form, including words that are commonly (and exclusively) associated with Islam: words like *Allah* (God) and *kafir* (unbeliever). In the changing linguistic and cultural milieu of the Arab regions, the production of a simplified Christian *lectionary* in the new Arabic script would have been a very useful tool for the Church and such a development would be absolutely feasible. This early document would then have been the substrate upon which a specifically *Arab* monotheism could coalesce, a 'purer' Christianity that stood in sharp contrast to both Judaism and Christianity, although acknowledging the Scripture of both.

---

601   Luxenberg, *The Syro-Aramaic Reading of the Koran,* p 251 (italics added)
602   Luxenberg, *The Syro-Aramaic Reading of the Koran,* p 130 (italics added)

Luxenberg's thesis not only provides a solid basis for linking the Koran with the real world of Syria and Iraq during the dawn of Islam, but it specifically explains why so many sections of the Koran are, as the Muslim scholar Ali Dashti explains below, *incomprehensible* even to scholars of Arabic. Many of these incomprehensible parts, Luxenberg suggests, are due to the original mis-translation of the Syriac, including irreversibly fixing the diacritical points in the *wrong places*. The fact that the Koran is a translation may even be hinted at in many of its passages, of which the following are only a few examples:

". . . this revelation is in clear Arabic" (16,103)
". . . we have sent down the Koran to give judgement in the Arabic language" (13, 37)
"These are the verses of the Scripture that makes things clear—we have sent it down as an Arabic Koran so that you [people] may understand" (12,1)
". . . a Scripture whose verses are made distinct as a Koran in Arabic for people who understand . . ."(41,3)

It has been suggested that these and similar verses are simply an assertion of the Arabic character of the holy book. But one would have to wonder why, if the Koran was handed down in true Arabic in the first place, it needs to assert its Arabic identity over and over again. There are no equivalent passages in ancient copies of the Hebrew Bible or the New Testament, asserting their rendition in Hebrew or Greek. According the Luxenburg, the fourth verse quoted above, 41:3 should actually translate as, "A *scripture* that we have *translated* as an Arabic *lectionary* . . ." The mistranslation, according to this author, is only one of many that have accumulated over perhaps hundreds of years of history, until they were permanently fixed by the establishment of the tradition.

". . . notwithstanding the assertion in the Koran itself . . . that the Prophet had proclaimed the Koranic message in '*clear Arabic speech*', all Arabs, as well as all non-Arab commentators on the Koran have since time immemorial racked their brains over the interpretation of this language . . . one would not be far from the truth if one were to estimate the proportion of the Koran that is still considered unexplained today at about a quarter of the text. But the actual proportion is probably much higher insofar as it will be shown that a considerable number of passages that were thought to be certain have in reality been misunderstood, to say nothing of the imprecise rendering of numerous Koranic expressions."[603]

---

[603]   Luxenberg, *The Syro-Aramaic Reading of the Koran,* p 108

It is notable, as Fred Donner points out in *Muhammad and the Believers,* that the Koran includes over a thousand references to its adherents as "Believers", compared to fewer than seventy-five for "Muslims", which became the ubiquitous title for the pious only in later years.

A very detailed (and for the lay person almost indigestible) analysis of the traditional account of the Koran is contained in John Burton's book, *The Collection of the Qur'an.* In it he discusses the variants in the readings of the Koran and the contorted attempts by Islamic scholars to define those parts which had been, according to tradition, transmitted to Mohammed and then subsequently *deleted,* those parts that were not deleted but were *abrogated* in favour of later revelations and, finally, those parts that were variously translated by different authorities. It is clear that the entire industry of Koranic history, like the creation of *hadith* with which it is associated, is a product of ninth and tenth century debate around matters of law, the polemics of which demanded ever more authoritative backing. Burton comes to the conclusion, in the end, that the Islamic sources are unreliable as history:

> "It must now have become abundantly clear how little assistance is to be hoped for from the Muslim accounts of the history of the collection of the Qur'an texts. The reports are a mass of confusions, contradictions and inconsistencies. By their nature, they represent the product of a lengthy process of evolution, accretion and 'improvement'. They were framed in response to a wide variety of progressing needs."[604]

In his book, *In search of the Original Koran,* Mondher Sfar discusses at great length the enormous tradition that accumulated around the collection of the Koran itself. According to these (again . . . later) stories, there were different renditions of the Koran circulating in the early period of Arab monotheism. Tradition has it that not only did some of the Prophet's Companions amend the revelations but even Mohammed himself sometimes forgot some revelations and misremembered others. A new tradition therefore arose, according to which Mohammed met the angel Gabriel once a year to review what had been revealed and written down, something any worker will recognise as an annual performance management review. The idea of variant versions is in keeping with the suggestion by Luxenberg that the original work was an early translation into Arabic of simple Christian liturgies. The further definition of the text, for example by the addition of diacritical points and the stitching of different texts together, would create different meanings even within different dialects of Arabic. It was only upon the foundation of the Arab empire, with the administrative backing of a huge state machine, that a uniform copy of the Koran could be achieved. Even Sfar, himself a Muslim, concedes that

---

[604]   John Burton, *The Collection of the Qur'an,* p 225.

"... everything leads us to believe that the thesis of a written Uthmanian [ie from the Caliph Uthman] recension designed to serve as a reference document was forged at a time when Arabic writing was vocalised, that is to say, starting with the reign of the Umayyad caliph, Abd Al-Malik."[605]

The significance of the late seventh century caliph Abd Al-Malik we shall deal with later. But even as late as the mid-tenth century, Sfar notes, an Islamic scholar known as Ibn Shanabudh was publicly flogged in Baghdad for reading a version of the Koran different to the official one and a contemporary, Ibn Miqsham, was forced to publicly recant for using his own version of the holy book. Although in the early Umayyad period, there were apparently works that circulated discussing the different variants of the Koran,

"... practically all the works that flourished shortly before the end of the Umayyad dynasty dealing with the differences between the compendiums of the Koran have in fact disappeared. These were comparative studies of the state of the Koranic text as it was practised (especially orally) in the great regions of the Muslim Empire, Arabia, Syria and Iraq."[606]

Sfar comes to the conclusion that the story of the Caliph Uthman collecting the elements of revelation together into one book is a "fantastic reconstruction"

"... hiding a reality that people sought to erase from human memory: the Koran is multiple because *its text has a history* and thus presents *an evolution*, as well as variations over time. And this history was only possible because it was in the nature of the redaction of the text that would eventually become the Koran to take the routes of elaboration, composition, stylization and rectification. In short, it was the product of a historical elaboration and rectification (divine or human, it does not matter), and not a dictation carried out on the basis of a pre-existing text, definitive and ready to be published."[607]

Islamic scholars have devised a vast and complicated tradition of literature to account for variations, for missing elements of the Koran—witnessed and given authority by Companions, but somehow missed out of the text—and abrogations. But by far the simplest and most logical reason for variations and misunderstandings is that the Koran had a *pre-Islamic* origin and that it was passed down as a partial, inaccurate and incomplete translation into Arabic, that it was later added to, amended and subsequently clarified before it was finally canonised by the Arab Empire.

---

[605] Mondher Sfar, *In Search of the Original Koran*, p 75
[606] Mondher Sfar, *In Search of the Original Koran*, p 76
[607] Mondher Sfar, *In Search of the Original Koran*, p 77 (italics added)

The critique of Ali Dashti

Because of the often violent suppression of historical Koranic research in the Islamic world, it is not surprising that such investigation has been largely based in non-Muslim countries. But despite widespread discouragement and accusations of 'Orientalism', bigotry or racism, a genuine tradition of Koranic study has sometimes spluttered into life, even in the Middle East. One such example is the critique made by the Iranian, Ali Dashti. Like Reza Aslan, who we have already cited, Dashti was both a Muslim and a critic of the literalist interpretation of the book and the associated *hadith*. Like Aslan, Dashti cast doubt on the veracity of some of the stories in the official tradition.

He called his book, *23 Years, A study of the prophetic career of Mohammed*, after the years of the Prophet's ministry. It was first published in Beirut and translated into English in 1985. In it, he rejected the miraculous stories of Mohammed and supported instead an account based on a *person* he believed to have been a true historical character. "Muslims, as well as others, have disregarded the historical facts", he complained. "They have continually striven to turn this man into an imaginary superhuman being, a sort of God in human clothes, and have generally ignored the ample evidence of his humanity." [608] Up to the age of 40, Dashti argues, nothing is known about the life of Mohammed, yet by the third century after his death:

> "The great historian and Koran commentator Tabari in his exegesis of verse 21 of *sura* 2, could insert an unsubstantiated statement about the Prophet's birth which shows how prone the people were in those days to create and repeat impossible myths and how even a historian could not stick to history." [609]

Dashti quotes Tabari's legend about a rumour prior to Mohammed's birth, not unlike the New Testament story of the revelation given to Mary before the birth of Jesus. This rumour resulted, according to Tabari, in forty Meccan women calling their new-born sons Mohammed! Dashti mocks this idea by tartly pointing out that there were no birth registration statistics for the year 570 CE to support this daft idea. He then compared Tabari's story to that of another historian, Waqedi, who died around 823 CE. According to Waqedi, as soon as Mohammed came out of his mother's womb, he said 'God is great'; at one month, he crawled; at two months, he stood; at three months, he walked; at four months, he ran and at nine months he shot arrows. This, Dashti sneers, is yet another example of "myth-making and history-fabrication by Muslims." [610]

---

[608]   Dashti, *23 Years,* p 1
[609]   Dashti, *23 Years,* p 2
[610]   Dashti, *23 Years,* p 3

It should not be forgotten that Dashti considered himself a devout Muslim and he revered Mohammed as the Prophet of Allah and "an outstanding figure" whose greatness was "unquestionable". But after Mohammed's death, Dashti believed, "Popular imagination soon dehumanised him and endowed him with the qualities of a son of God . . ." He quotes at length one particular fable, popular in the sixteenth century, included in the *Tafsir ol-Jalalyn*, a book of commentaries written over a period of time by several authors. One particular commentary in the *tafsir* is based on a single verse from the Koran, verse 1 *sura* 17, comprising about twenty words and describing, allegorically, a visit to heaven by Mohammed. This twenty-word verse has been expanded in the commentary into a long and fabulous fairy-tale journey, during which the Prophet describes in his own words how he had conversations with the archangel Gabriel, visited each of the seven heavens and met Adam, Abraham and Moses.

About this same time Mohammed had had a revelation that he must pray fifty times every day and night, but on his way back from the heavens to earth he describes how Moses advised him to haggle with God. "Fifty prayers are too many", Moses advised him, "Ask the Lord to reduce them!" Eventually, Mohammed bargained God down to five times a day. It is not surprising that Dashti mocks this make-believe history. But even this mythical journey, he points out, "is pale beside the extravaganzas of Tabari's *tafsir* (Koran commentary) and the writings of Abu Bakr 'Atiq Nishapuri", which he likens to "folklore fables."

> "It is obvious the Prophet did not say such things and that these childish fables are figments of the imaginations of simple-minded people who conceived of the divine order as a replica of the court of their own king or ruler."[611]

As we have seen in previous sections, there are many books in existence today that describe themselves as "histories" and which quote long speeches by Mohammed or the Companions, word for word, as if the made-up myth was established fact. Even established 'scholars' have written biographies of the Prophet based on stories manufactured hundreds of years after the date of his death. By leaving out the more fabulous stories and only repeating the more plausible myths, such biographers seek to give their works an air of authority. Reza Aslan, for example, comments on the similarity of the stories about the births of the Old Testament King David, the New Testament Jesus and Mohammed, and writes, "It is not important whether the stories describing the childhood of David, Jesus and Mohammed are true."[612] But rejecting the most outlandish stories is not the issue. In reality *all* the facts about Mohammed's life were made up hundreds of years after the alleged events and, as we shall see, projected backwards to various authoritative figures to validate them.

---

[611]   Dashti, *23 Years*, p 7
[612]   Reza Aslan, *No God but God*, p21

For Dashti, it is "natural and normal that legends about great men should arise after their deaths . . . The greater the distance in time and space from the Prophet's death in 632 and from Medina, the more the Muslims let their imaginations run loose . . . [and] the more the mass of fiction grew, even though many of Islam's best scholars knew it to be incredible and considered it to be unworthy."[613]

A glimpse of the genuine roots of Islam is given in Dashti's comment on the monotheism prevalent in Arabia at that time. By the sixth century, he points out, "monotheism was not a novelty and was well understood in the Hejaz, particularly at Medina and in the north where Jewish and Christian tribes resided.[614]"According to tradition, the followers of the generalised Abramic monotheism in the region were known as *hanif* and the acknowledgement of their presence in the tradition is a reflection of the monotheism widespread among Arabs long before Islam. Dashti, as a Muslim, subscribed to the traditional view that Islam was founded *sui generis* ('of its own kind'), as it were, but nevertheless, his book clearly signals the close connection between his faith and Judeo-Christianity.

> "All the moral precepts of the Koran are self-evident and generally acknowledged. The stories in it are taken in identical or slightly modified forms from the lore of the Jews and Christians, whose rabbis and monks Mohammed had met and consulted on his journeys to Syria . . . *During the first thirteen years of the Prophet's mission at Mecca and the first year and a half of his mission at Medina, the Muslims prayed in the same direction as the Jews,* namely facing towards the 'Furthest Mosque' (ie the Temple site) at Jerusalem . . . In regard to polygamy, divorce, adultery, fornication, sodomy, and many other matters [food laws, fasting, circumcision—JP] the Koranic commandments are either modifications of Jewish laws or reforms of previous Arab practices."[615]

As we have suggested, the structure of the Koran has always presented problems for historians, with the *suras* arranged in approximate order of length, rather than chronologically and with many verses grammatically obscure. Not surprisingly, Dashti questions the traditional view of the Koran as the unerring word of Allah as dictated to his Messenger.

> "Among Muslim scholars of the early period, before bigotry and hyperbole prevailed, were some such as Ebrahim on-Nazzam who openly acknowledged that the arrangement and syntax of the Koran are not miraculous and that work of equal or greater value could be produced by other God-fearing persons . . . The Koran contains sentences which are incomplete and not fully intelligible without the aid of commentaries;

---

613   Dashti, *23 Years,* p8...62
614   Dashti, *23 Years,* p 14
615   Dashti, *23 Years,* pp 53-57 (italics added)

foreign words, unfamiliar Arabic words, and words used with other than the normal meaning; adjectives and verbs inflected without observance of the concords of gender and number; illogically and ungrammatically applied pronouns which sometimes have no referent; and predicates which in rhymed passages are often remote from the subjects."[616]

"The great and penetrating Arab thinker, Abu'l-o'Alo ol-Ma'arri," Dashti adds, "considered some of his own writings to be on a par with the Koran . . . To sum up; more than one hundred Koranic aberrations from the normal rules and structure of Arabic have been noted."[617] This comment, from Dashti the Muslim, on the grammatical and syntactical confusion in the Koran, is almost an exact echo of the comment from Gerd-R Puin which we cited above. Among western scholars unattached to the traditions of Islam, there is a growing acceptance of the idea that is at least hinted at in Dashti's critique, that the Koran and Islam as a whole *evolved* and *developed* over a period of time. As Gerd-R Puin, adds,

". . . the Koran is a kind of cocktail of texts that were not all understood even at the time of Muhammad. Many of them may even be a hundred years older than Islam itself. Even within the Islamic traditions there is a huge body of contradictory information, *including a significant Christian substrate*; one can derive a whole Islamic *anti-history* from them if one wants."[618]

Because there is no contextualisation for any of the sayings or revelations in the Koran it is only as a result of the deliberations of later scholars that different *suras* were attributed to the time Mohammed spent in either Mecca or Medina. One would be entitled to ask, if the Koran had indeed been written down from the scribblings of the Prophet's Companions after this death, why they didn't bother to write his revelations in the order in which they were given. Be that as it may, Dashti, in keeping with others who largely follow the traditional history, notes what he perceives as a change in the tone of the *suras* attributed to Mohammed's time in Medina, compared to those attributed to the earlier period in Mecca. Whereas the Meccan *suras* are characterised by theological issues and "human compassion", as Dashti puts it, the Medinan revelations are redolent of the rules, commands and regulations associated with authority, government and war.

Leaving aside the fact that the geographical attribution may be completely fictional (in other words, it is likely that *it was the different tone and subject material that was used to make the geographical attribution in the first place*) Dashti takes up the different meanings and implications of the two sets of *suras* and he points out that they give contradictory messages. In *Sura* 2, for example (attributed as the first

---

[616] Dashti, *23 Years,* p 48
[617] Dashti, *23 Years,* p 50
[618] Gerd-R Puin, *The Atlantic Monthly,* January 1998 (italics added)

Medinan *sura*), verse 257 states, "There is no compulsion in religion." Likewise, friendly relations are recommended towards other fellow monotheists, those with scripture—that is Jews and Christians—in many other Meccan or early Medinan *suras.*

Dashti cites those occasions when the Koran appears to be tolerant to other monotheists. For example, *Sura* 2 verse 62 says: "The believers, the Jews, the Christians and the Sabaeans—all who believe in God and the Last Day and who do good—will have their reward with their Lord. No fear for them, nor will they grieve." "On the other hand," Dashti writes, "in the 193rd verse, which perhaps came down when the Muslim community was stronger or on the occasion of some incident, use of force is enjoined: 'Fight them until there is no persecution and the religion is God's! And if they give up let there be no enmity except to evil-doers!'"[619]

Dashti, points out that *sura* 9 is attributed as being chronologically the last one and it contains "an unqualified and peremptory" call to the use of force: "Fight those People of the Book who do not [truly] believe in God and the Last Day! . . . Prophet, strive against the disbelievers and the hypocrites, and be tough with them! Hell is their final home . . . It is not fitting for the Prophet to ask forgiveness for the idolaters . . . you who believe, fight the disbelievers near you and let them find you standing firm."[620] "It is a remarkable and significant fact" Dashti suggests, "that the Meccan *suras* contain no mentions of holy war or fighting polytheists, whereas the Medinan *suras* are so full of verses on the subject that this obligation appears to be more heavily stressed than any other."[621] As Dashti explains, what is taken to be the Medinan period is characterised less by prophetic missionary work and more by the exigencies of government and war. In the latter case, Dashti points out, the period was marked by political assassinations by followers of Mohammed, as well as unprovoked attacks on peaceful tribes. Indeed, the traditional accounts describe the expulsion of non-Muslim tribes in a way that in modern terms would be equated with ethnic cleansing. It is easy to see how modern scholars can use the Koran to 'justify' their own attitudes to political and social questions and particularly to the question of political violence and *jihad*. More liberal and modernising Muslims will look to what are called the Meccan *suras* to underpin their views while the Taliban might define what is Islamic or un-Islamic by what are called the Medina *suras*. In his book, *The Great Theft*, Professor Khaled Abou El Fadl complains about Islam being expropriated by 'puritans' for their own purposes.[622]

---

[619] Dashti, *23 Years,* p 83. Note that Dashti's citations of the Koran are slightly different here and in other places to those in the *Oxford Classics* English translation used by this author (see Bibliography). The English translation is use for quotes and the verse numbers have been changed accordingly.

[620] *Sura* 9, verses 29, 73, 113, 123

[621] Dashti, *23 Years,* p 95

[622] Khaled Abou El Fadl, *The Great Theft,* p 96

"... the puritan orientation forces religious texts to validate the social and political frustrations and insecurities of its adherents. If the adherents of this orientation are angry at the West, for example, they read the religious text in such a way as to validate this hostility. Similarly, if the men of this orientation feel the need to compensate for feelings of powerlessness by dominating women, they read the text to validate the subjugation and disempowerment of women. In every situation, we find that the proverbial arm of the text is being bent and twisted to validate whatever the puritan orientation wishes to do. All along the puritans claim to be entirely literal and objective, and to faithfully implement what the texts demand without their personal interference. This claim is simply fraudulent and untrue because in every situation we find that the puritan reading of the text is entirely subjective."

Where the professor makes a mistake is in limiting this critique to the puritans. Interpretation of the Koran and the tradition "in every situation" in fact means what it says. In the final analysis, the characteristic features of any modern Islamic movement are not those based on this or that reading of the Koran or *hadith* because these can be found to validate *almost any* political position, but are the *social and class content* of the movement in question. It doesn't take a genius to guess where the pressure came from for Islamic scholars in Cairo to declare, in 1948, just when communist ideas were gaining a foothold among Egyptian workers, that "there is no communism in Islam."[623] The success or otherwise of religious currents are never determined by arguments between scholars about the correctness of an interpretation of scripture, but on the balance of forces in society.

As a Muslim, Dashti would have disagreed with the idea, but it is clear that the eclectic nature of the Koran, its contradictions and inconsistencies, are a reflection of its having been collected and edited *over a period of time* and from a *variety of sources*. The real chronology of the Koran is uncertain but the Christian substrate is probably its most important component while it also reflects the early *non-specific* monotheism of the Arabs, which was itself imported wholesale from Jewish tradition. The later attributions of sections of it to either Mecca or Medina are merely a rationalisation of the fact the *suras* of the Koran are often different in tone and reflect different traditions. The 'chronology' of the different *suras* is no more than a construct woven into the biography of Mohammed that was created much later and projected backwards in time.

The idea of the *evolution* of the Koran and the *evolution* of Islam would have been foreign to Dashti, but much of his criticism actually points in that direction. On the question of the pilgrimage to Mecca, an obligation for all Muslims at least once in their lifetime, he comments:

---

[623] Cited by Maxime Rodinson, *Islam and Capitalism,* p 55

"No thoughtful person . . . can discern any philosophical reason for pilgrimage (*hajj*) to Mecca and for the useless and meaningless rites which the pilgrims perform. The Prophet Mohammed's decision to set out on a visit to the Ka'ba in 628 is puzzling . . . the decision was surprising and so inconsistent with Islamic principles that many Muslims were upset. Several believers objected to the running between Safa and Marwa [part of the Mecca pilgrimage rites include running between these two hills near the Ka'ba—JP] because it had been a pagan Arab rite."[624]

The "puzzling" inconsistency is easily explained if it is assumed that the biography of Mohammed was being developed at the same time—in the eighth and ninth centuries—that the distinctly Arab version of monotheism was also being consolidated. It was only what later became modern Islam that developed a distinctly *Hejaz* flavouring, incorporating the semi-Bedouin traditions of the Arabs. The traditional history of Islam did not come to be centred on what in all probability was its *real* geographical birth-place, in the core regions of the Arab Empire, that is Syria and Iraq, but on Mecca. Its mythical 'history' was projected backwards and interwoven, somewhat imperfectly, with the incipient Koran and biography of the Prophet.

On the status of women in Islam, Dashti has a number of interesting points to make about what is and is not in the Koran. He lists all twenty wives or concubines of the Prophet mentioned in various parts of the tradition; he derides those traditions that polemicise about which sexual positions are deemed to be Islamic or un-Islamic and in general, he concludes that the status of women was very much second or third class in ancient Islamic society. There is a verse in the Koran, for example, that forbids Muslims from making monetary profit by hiring out their female slaves as concubines, the implication being, he suggests, that it was a common practice that required condemning. In further commentary, Dashti complains that although the Koran is taken to be the word of God, parts of it are clearly written in the third person, using "him" or "he". The Koran, contains many instances of confusion, he argues, between God and Mohammed, even in the same verse. In this and similar comments, Dashti is coming as near as possible to questioning the historical veracity of the Koran. He briefly touches on the old theological issue of free will, commenting that there are more than fifty Koranic verses which state that all the actions of humans are wholly dependent on God's will and guidance. How can it be, he asks, that God should guide many humans to do what is not right and then inflicts eternal and painful punishment on them for not being "guided aright"?

But it is on the question of the *abrogating* verses of the Koran that Dashti is at his most scathing. These are verses which are deemed to amend, correct or even contradict earlier revelations, the subject of the 'satanic verses' in Salman Rushdie's book of that name. Against the protests of those who cannot accept that God would

---

[624] Dashti, *23 Years,* p 93

'change his mind', the Koran, Dashti points out, even has an answering verse: "Whenever we abrogate a verse or order that it be forgotten, We bring a better one or a similar one. Do not you know that God is capable of everything?" Dashti asks, not unreasonably, that if God is capable of everything, "why did He not reveal the better verse first?" Dashti attributes the errors and confusion in the Koran to Mohammed being an ordinary, fallible, human being, but it is far more likely that the contradiction and confusion represents the piecemeal manner of the Koran's assembly from mistranslations of various earlier texts.

Although most Islamic tradition has the Koran collected by one of the first three caliphs to succeed Mohammed, there is one strand of the tradition that suggests it was memorised word for word during the life-time of the Prophet. The popular fifteenth century book on the caliphs, by Jalal ad-Din as-Suyuti, enthusiastically reprinted recently by Muslims in Britain, lists a number of Mohammed's Companions "who memorised all of the Koran"[625]. To any rational person, it would seem an absurdity that in the midst of wars, civil wars and social upheavals anyone would have the time or capacity to fully memorise such a large document, with all its half sentences and hidden meanings, least of all the main actors in the drama. In a comment that hints at a more likely origin of the Koran from different traditions, Dashti quotes the same fifteenth century scholar:

> "In Suyuti's *Etqan*, there is a chapter entitled 'passages in the Koran which were revealed at the suggestion of the Companions; among them were many which were revealed at the suggestion of Umar. According to Mojahed b. Jabr (an early traditionalist), Umar used to express an opinion, and then it was sent down in the Koran'. Umar himself is reported to have thought that three verses were revealed at his suggestion . . ."[626]

Dashti is extremely critical of the Islamic attachment to the lunar calendar which means that the annual cycle is out of synch with the universally recognised calendar of 365.24 days. In the Koran, he points out, "the old Arab use of the lunar year is seen as an inviolable law of nature." He ridicules the *Tafsir ol-Jalalayn* for the "absurd" comment that "the reason for the Moon's waxing and waning is to inform people of the right times for sowing, reaping, pilgrimage, fasting and break-fasting."

> "The Moon's phases are of course no help in agricultural timing, and the lunar months were prescribed for the timing of pilgrimage and fasting because the solar months had not come into general use in Arabia . . . The Creator of the Universe is certainly aware of these facts; He would therefore not have uttered words which would have put an effect in the place of its cause."[627]

---

[625] Jalal ad-Din as-Suyuti, *The History of the Khalifahs who took the right way*, p 22

[626] Dashti, *23 Years*, p 176

[627] Dashti, *23 Years*, p 164

Dashti paid with his life for comments such as these and for, in effect, questioning the myths, legends and metaphysics of the Koran. Yet to the end he considered himself a Muslim, and despite the "absurdities" which he noted, he could not bring himself to question the fundamental absurdity of the way the book has been interpreted and used. Nevertheless, his summary comments are worth quoting at length because they are a quite devastating answer to those who see the Koran as the unerring word of God.

> "The Koranic commandments and laws are not wholly clear and precise. Believers, therefore, had to find precedents in the Prophet's own conduct. For example, prayer is prescribed in the Koran, but the ritual and number of the daily prayers had to be determined by the Prophet's usual practice. It was this need which prompted the collection of reports or traditions about his custom (*sunna*) and his sayings and doings (*hadith*). The subsequent proliferation was such that by the 9th-10th century thousands of reports were in circulation and hundreds of inquirers were rushing around the Islamic countries to collect more reports. A class of professional traditionalists arose and acquired great respect in the Islamic world. They knew thousands of traditions by heart. One of them, Ebn'Oqda (d. 943) is credited with having known 250,000 together with each one's chain of transmitters . . . the vast bulk of the hadith compilations is in itself proof that not all of their contents can be authentic . . ."

> "It is an undeniable fact that the greater the lapse of time after the Prophet's death and the further the distance from the Hejaz, the more the number of miracles ascribed to him grew. Imaginations got to work and turned a man . . . into a being capable of existence only in the realm of fable."[628]

The critique of the Koran by Ali Dashti points in the direction of an objective view of Islamic history, even if the critic himself does not follow through with what is implied by his critique. Although it is written from a Muslim's point of view, it accords well with the hypothesis that Islam as we know it today originated *after* the establishment of the Arab Empire. A large part of the new empire was established in what had been the Persian Sassanid Empire. Once this region was consolidated into the Arab Empire and once Islam was established as the state religion, the "Iranians" as Dashti refers to them, (in reality the area covered by modern-day Iraq, Iran and further east) became "more Arab than the Arabs".

> "It was they [the Iranians] who systematised Arabic grammar and syntax . . . They outstripped the Arabs in Islamic zeal and poured scorn on their own former beliefs and customs. They not only extolled the Arab

---

[628]   Dashti, *23 Years,* p 206/7

nation and Arab heroes but even tried to prove that chivalry, generosity and leadership inhere in the Arabs alone. They describe Bedouin poems and trite aphorisms from pre-Islamic Arabia as pearls of wisdom and models of behaviour. They were content to be protégés of Arab tribes and lackeys of Arab *emirs* and glad to give their daughters in marriage to Arabs and to take Arab names for themselves.

"Iranian brains were soon at work in the fields of Islamic theology and law, hadith compilation, and Arabic literature. Approximately seventy per cent of the principal Arabic works on Islamic subjects were written by Iranians."[629]

Here the writer has inadvertently revealed a genuine trace of the real origins of Islam. The 'traditions' were written by scholars, hundreds of years after the attributed life of Mohammed, from made-up stories, oral tales and proverbs. The *hadith* were linked to particular legal and theological issues and were given authenticity by discovering suitable references to the past. Many of these early writings and traditions from Iran and Iraq were flavoured with opposition to the early Umayyad dynasty which had been based in Syria. Even the geographical setting that was written into the tradition was alluded to by Dashti. The "Iranians" to whom Dashti refers were effectively the religious clients of the Abbasid dynasty, with its capital in Baghdad but with a huge power base in Khurasan, in modern day Iran. It was during this dynasty, beginning in the middle of the eighth century, that the "Iranians" first began to write down and systematise the tradition. The 'Iranian' Arabs, like all exiles, harboured a nostalgic and romanticised attachment to what they saw as their former traditions. What this meant for them was a zealous attachment to Bedouin life, so they favoured, as the centre-stage of their story, the former pagan pilgrimage site at Mecca in the heart of the Arabian *Hejaz*. These traditions were largely compiled by Iraqis and Iranians, most of whom would never have experienced Bedouin life but who saw it as the epitome of the Arab character and who therefore embraced it as the focus of their adopted tradition. The whole story—the foundation of Islam set in a particular time and place—was projected backwards to the period before the great Arab conquests of the mid-seventh century and is still recycled as history today.

John of Damascus, a Christian who served as an administrator in the court of the Caliph in Damascus, writing around about Ishmaelite (Arab) heresies in the middle of the eighth century, complained that "a false prophet named Mohammed has appeared in their midst. This man, after having chanced upon the Old and New Testaments and likewise, it seems, having conversed with an Arian monk, devised his own heresy . . . he gave out that a certain book had been sent down to him from heaven"[630]. This description uses the usual Greek word for book rather than Koran.

---

[629]   Dashti, *23 Years,* p 207
[630]   From http://orthodoxinfo.com an orthodox Christian website.

It is clear that by this time—mid-eighth century—the tradition was beginning to accumulate, although it is noteworthy that this ancient author still attributed the contents of the Koran to the Bible and considered Islam as a heresy rather than as a different faith altogether.

The position we have today is that every single verse of the Koran has now been given a context by Islamic tradition—that is to say, a time and a place has been identified when the Prophet said such-and-such to so-and-so and the reason for him saying it. The circumstance of every revelation has been set down, as well as many other additional rulings by Mohammed on a whole variety of different issues and problems. Although the more difficult or obscure verses have given rise to contradictory or disputed meanings, most of the Koran has been contextualised so definitively over the succeeding centuries that later historians have taken this huge accumulation of tradition as *established fact*, although *it is nothing of the sort* and none of it appears in the Koran itself. The *hadith* that was written centuries after the crucial period of the mid-seventh century, include not only the circumstances of Koranic sayings but, as the central component of all the *hadith*, the biography of the Prophet himself.

Approximate time-line for Koranic history		
Dates (all CE)	Developments according to Islamic Tradition	? Likely history of the Koran ?
Up to 600		Syriac Christian Liturgical documents translated into Arabic to form early *substrate* of Koranic sayings
570-32	Life of Mohammed. Recitations committed to memory or small bits of parchment, bark, etc.	Addition of non-biblical Arabic traditions Combinations of oral traditions and sayings of Syriac origin
632-60	Collection of the 'recitations' by the successors of Mohammed and the destruction of false versions	Compilation of a holy 'book' with many variants *Suras* in no special order
690	'Koranic' inscriptions on the Dome of the Rock	Interpretation and clarification using diacritical points
700		Variants begin to be filtered out but many survive
800		Definitive version of Koran, *suras* put in 'canonical' order

Chapter summary

- The Koran does not deal in any sense with the life of Mohammed. It mentions biblical characters, including Moses and Jesus, much more often.

- The Koran has no chronological narrative and consists overwhelmingly of a series of sayings and religious strictures most of which would not have been out of place in a Christian or Jewish community.

- The Koran has a *pre-Islamic* origin, much older than its many commentaries and interpretations and parts of the oldest extant copies are unintelligible even to experts in ancient Arabic. Its origins lie almost certainly in Syriac Christian liturgical works that were passed down as partial, inaccurate and incomplete translations into Arabic. These were later added to, amended and subsequently 'clarified' before being finally 'canonised' under the auspices of the Arab Empire.

- The *suras* (chapters) of the Koran are not placed chronologically but in order of length beginning with the longest. There is no natural order in which they ought to be placed and early versions of the Koran ordered them differently.

- Modern Arabic is not identical to the ancient Arabic in which the oldest copies of the Koran were written. In the early period of Islam there were variants of the Koran and different interpretations of the text. The fixed and definitive form of the modern Arabic Koran is relatively recent.

- For modern Muslims, every verse in the Koran has a context that places its 'revelation' at some point in the life of Mohammed, either in Mecca or Medina. But these contexts were only fixed by scholars writing hundreds of years after the life of Mohammed.

Chapter 14

The Revisionist Scholarship

In this section we will look at the long tradition of revisionist scholarship, mostly among western academics, but nonetheless based on the original Arabic texts and *hadith*. We shall show that this scholarship has come to the clear consensus that most of the Islamic tradition was written in the eighth century or later, long after the reported life of Mohammed. Not only did the biography of Mohammed come to be written very late, but it appears that, in fact, Mecca was not the bustling city of Islamic tradition, but a small desert town with insignificant trade and that the traditions that link Islam to Mecca and Bedouin culture in general were also created very late. We shall show that this painstaking and detailed work done by many eminent scholars points inevitably to one general conclusion: that Islam as it has come to be understood in its modern sense did not exist in the first one hundred to one hundred and fifty years after the accepted time of Mohammed's death.

. . . .

For more than a century now, scholars of ancient Arabic, particularly those based outside the Islamic world, have challenged the traditional account of the rise of Islam. These are no mere amateurs, but extremely learned academics. Their work is based on the study of the oldest available Islamic writings and inscriptions and they have almost universally come to the conclusion that Islam, as it is understood today, is not a product of the seventh century as tradition has it, but is a much later creation. Before we examine the real origins of the Arab Empire and the Islamic faith, therefore, it is necessary to spend some time examining the work of some of these scholars and historians. As we shall see, there is now a considerable body of scholarly critique of the Islamic *hadith*, including detailed analysis of when, where and under what circumstances its accumulation took place, all of which comprises what has been described as the *revisionist* school of Islamic history.

Ignaz Goldziher

Two decades before Kautsky's book on Christianity, the Hungarian Islamist Ignaz Goldziher published a series of essays entitled *Muslim Studies* in which he looked at the history and character of Islam. He was extremely well read in Islamic tradition, being one of the few non-Muslims to have studied at Al-Azhar University in Cairo and the breadth of his expertise is still acknowledged today. What was clear from Goldziher's studies was that he did not simply accept *hadith* stories at face value but clearly linked their origins to the political and social circumstances in which they were created, generations after the events to which they are supposed to relate.

> ". . . it is easily seen that as spatial and temporal distance from the source grew, the danger also grew that people would devise ostensibly correct hadiths with chains of transmission reaching back to the highest authority of the Prophet and his Companions, and employ them to authenticate both theoretical doctrines and doctrines with a practical goal in view. It soon became evident that each point of view, each party, each proponent of a doctrine gave the form of hadith to his theses, and that consequently the most contradictory tenets had come to wear the garb of such documentation. *There is no school in the areas of ritual, theology, or jurisprudence, there is not even any party to political contention, that would lack a hadith or a whole family of hadiths in its favour,* exhibiting all the external signs of correct transmission."[631]

The work of Goldziher is in many ways the foundation stone upon which more modern historians have built, although with even more wide-ranging and radical conclusions.

Joseph Schacht

One of the most important works in the modern era was the ground-breaking study of Joseph Schacht, *The Origins of Muhammadan Jurisprudence*, a book still considered a classic work today. Schacht, a professor at Oxford University, demonstrated by reference to ancient legal disputes that the Koran was not used as the basis for Islamic law until well into the ninth century. "The great majority of traditions from the Prophet are documents not of the time to which they claim to belong," he writes, "but of the successive stages of development of doctrines *during the first centuries of Islam.*"[632] Schacht's work represented a complete overturn of what had been the accepted historians' view of Islamic *hadith*, *isnads* (chains of transmission) and the *sunna* traditions of the Prophet. By a painstaking analysis of precisely these legal and judicial traditions, Schacht demonstrates that *Islamic orthodoxy was derived over a long period of time* and much later than the supposed life of Mohammed and his Companions.

He focuses on one of the earliest Muslim jurists to develop and expound general Islamic legal theory, a scholar by name of Shafi'i, who died around 839 CE, over two hundred years after the date of Mohammed's death. It is important to emphasise that legal theory was not an esoteric discipline, remote from everyday life. On the contrary, the distribution of property and *property rights* were vital issues for the ruling class of the Arab Empire, from the caliph and his governors down,

---

631   Ignaz Goldziher, *Introduction to Islamic Theology and Law,* p 39 (italics added)
632   Joseph Schacht, *The Origins of Muhammadan Jurisprudence,* p 4 (italics added)

and were at the core of its *raison d'être*. For the first two centuries, the distribution of land, booty, taxes, tribute and slaves from the subject peoples to the ruling elite was a matter of far greater importance than fine theological arguments and it was in the development and refining of legal and property laws that Islamic doctrine was developed and elaborated.

Although it was two hundred years since the life of Mohammed, it was Shafi'i who was the first legal expert to insist that legal practice should be defined from those practices supposedly handed down by the Prophet. This was in distinction to earlier schools of legal thought who had relied on the living traditions, what may be called the 'custom and practice' of the Arab community. Schacht shows that Shafi'i's analyses and polemics with the other schools are very revealing about what practices had and had not been established up to that period. Legal scholars prior to Shafi'i were aware of traditions from Mohammed and his Companions but *they did not accord them any special status* and only interpreted them in the light of community tradition.

> "His [Shafi'i's] predecessors and contemporaries . . . while certainly already adducing traditions from the Prophet, use them on the same level as they use traditions from the Companions and his Successors, interpret them in the light of their own 'living' tradition and allow them to be superseded by it. Two generations before Shafi'i, reference to the traditions from Companions and Successors was the rule [and] . . . traditions from the Prophet himself the exception . . . it was left to Shafi'i to make the exception his principle. We shall have to conclude that generally and broadly speaking, *traditions from the Companions and Successors are earlier than those from the Prophet.*"[633]

Schacht demonstrates, in other words, that the traditions from the Prophet, having more authority that those of his mere Companions, *were made up later*, in order to cancel out or supersede the latter. Shafi'i and other Islamic scholars relied on the fact that traditions depended on alleged chains of transmission, the so-called *isnads*. To carry the necessary authority, each *isnad* had to be derived ultimately from a reliable source, preferably Mohammed or one of his Companions. The *isnad* had to have reliable witnesses and then be transmitted by an uninterrupted chain of reliable Muslims. The *isnads* took the form, ". . . The Caliph Umar told Ahmed b Talb, who told his nephew Zakir b Ahmed, who told . . .", and so on. Those *isnads* that passed muster were collected in the ninth century and form part of the huge corpus of orthodox tradition. But as many modern scholars and revisionist historians have noted, many of the great classical collections of tradition were only collected and saw the light of day *after Shafi'i's time*. "The first considerable body of legal traditions from the Prophet originated towards the middle of the second

---

[633] Joseph Schacht, *The Origins of Muhammadan Jurisprudence*, p 3 (italics added)

[Islamic] century, *in opposition to slightly earlier traditions* from Companions and other authorities and to the 'living tradition' of the ancient schools of law" [634]

Schacht's study of those *isnads* that were related to legal matters led him to the conclusion that they originated centuries after the Prophet and were extended back in time, in order to gain authority.

> ". . . the *isnads* show *a tendency to grow backwards and to claim higher and higher authority until they arrive at the Prophet*; the evidence of legal traditions carries us back to about the year 100 AH only; at that time Islamic legal thought started from late Umayyad administration and popular practice, which is still reflected in a number of traditions."[635]

Schacht in fact devotes an entire chapter of his book specifically to *isnads*, concluding that the majority of them, when they started, were fragmentary and incomplete but grew in time to become extensive and sophisticated chains. "Some of these *isnads* which the Muhammadan scholars esteem most highly," he writes, "are the result of widespread fabrications . . ."[636] Schacht realised that one of the best proofs that a legal tradition did not exist at a particular time was its *absence in a polemic*, when (had it existed) it would have been decisive and would therefore have been definitely cited by one party or the other as an essential component in the argument. Using this technique, Schacht was able to show how traditions were created over a period of time.

> ". . . every legal tradition from the Prophet, until the contrary is proved, must be taken not as an authentic or essentially authentic, even if slightly obscured, statement valid for his time or the time of the Companions, but as *the fictitious expression of a legal doctrine formulated at a later date*. Its date can be ascertained from its first appearance in legal discussion; from its relative position in the history of the problem with which it is concerned . . . the bulk of legal traditions from the Prophet known to Malik originated in the generation preceding him, that is, in the second quarter of the second century AH."[637]

The difficulties, in creating a consensus of what should be accepted as a genuine tradition, were illustrated by the enormous number of possible original sources. According to Shafi'i, upbraiding his Medinese opponents for their failure to demonstrate a consensus,

---

[634] Joseph Schacht, *The Origins of Muhammadan Jurisprudence*, p 4 (italics added)
[635] Joseph Schacht, *The Origins of Muhammadan Jurisprudence*, p 4 (italics added)
[636] Joseph Schacht, *The Origins of Muhammadan Jurisprudence*, p 161
[637] Joseph Schacht, *The Origins of Muhammadan Jurisprudence*, p 149 (italics added)

"There were in Medina some 30,000 Companions of the Prophet, if not more. Yet you are not able to relate the same opinions from perhaps as few as six, nay, you relate opinions from only one or two or three or four, who may disagree or agree, but they mostly disagree; where then, is the consensus?"[638]

This might come as a revelation even to Muslims today. Where the traditional story of Mohammed hints at his Companions as being the immediate entourage or the successors of the Prophet (perhaps a few *dozen* followers) Shafi'i, in the ninth century, cites a figure of *tens of thousands* whose personal knowledge of the Prophet is used to help define 'true Islam'. It is also notable in his polemics with the 'Medinese' school, that there is no trace anywhere in the mid-ninth century that Medina, the "City of the Prophet", was in any way the acknowledged home of the *sunna*. This was a claim only developed later as part of what Schacht called "a rising tide of traditions from the Prophet."

It is clear from Shaf'i's writings that the exclusivity of the Prophet-tradition and the Prophet-Companion-Successor hierarchy did not exist even by the end of the ninth century, more than two hundred years after the supposed life-time of Mohammed. Problems arose, of course, when two or more traditions 'from the Prophet' appeared to contradict each other. Shafi'i never considers that to be a real possibility and so elaborate contexts were devised in which Mohammed or his successors said such-and-such in one circumstance and something else in another circumstance. In this way, apparent contradictions were resolved, by, in effect, modifying or inventing new tradition.

Schacht makes the rather amusing point that there are even *traditions about traditions*. There can be fewer crassly made-up stories than the 'tradition' he quotes in which the Prophet declares from the pulpit, "Traditions from me will spread; those that agree with the Koran are really from me, but what is related from me and contradicts the Koran is not from me."[639] There is no escaping the conclusion that Schacht comes to. He describes what he calls a "mounting tide" of Prophet-traditions from approximately *the middle of the eighth century CE* and we will examine later the political and social origins for this occurring at precisely this point in Arab history.

In pushing the authentication of practice back towards the Prophet, the legal and religious scholars of the ninth and tenth centuries were also obliged to alter the chains of transmission or to show a somewhat arbitrary attitude towards them. Where a 'link' in the chain was thought to be unreliable, the *isnad* was sometimes discarded although the tradition itself was not. Sometimes traditions with *complete* chains were discarded if they were in conflict with a more acceptable tradition with an *incomplete* chain. Where doctrines were non-negotiable and therefore their

---

[638] Shafi, cited by Joseph Schacht, *The Origins of Muhammadan Jurisprudence*, p 83 (italics added)

[639] Joseph Schacht, *The Origins of Muhammadan Jurisprudence*, p 28

supporting traditions accepted, new *isnads* needed to be 'found' to authenticate them.

Thus, Schacht discovered that the bulk of the legal traditions relating to the Prophet originated in the early Abbasid period. They were *created* and put into circulation to reinforce the legal and property interests of the ruling elite and, in so doing, they consolidated the theological and liturgical doctrines of Islam, as well as the increasingly elaborate biography of the Prophet himself, two hundred years after the subject of the biography.

Summary of Schacht's work on Islamic Jurisprudence		
Dates	Key events	Progressive change in legal 'authority' over time
632 CE	(Traditional date for the death of Mohammed) The Umayyad dynasty	Legal authority mostly based on community *custom and practice* ↓
750 CE	The Abbasid revolution Shafi'i's polemics against schools of law who relied only on customary tradition for legal opinion. Shafi'i is the first jurist to insist, against the opposition of other legal schools, on the pre-eminence of traditions from the Prophet.	Legal authority mostly based on traditions of the *Successors* ↓ Legal authority mostly based on traditions of the *Companions* ↓
839 CE	Death of Shafi'i	Legal authority mostly based on traditions of the *Prophet*

This time-line broadly coincides with the researches of all the revisionist historians reviewed in this chapter, placing the development of Islamic tradition from the mid eighth century onwards, that is, from the beginning of the Abbasid dynasty.

The chronology worked out by Schacht from the original sources supports the idea of modern Islam evolving over a period of time. The earliest Islamic jurists—hundred years after the Arab Empire was established—first attempted to codify imperial law without reference to, and to a degree *against,* any prophetic tradition. The living tradition of the Arab community was, therefore, the primary element in the formation of imperial law. It was only later, in subsequent centuries, that reference was made to the traditions of the Companions and then, later still, to Mohammed. Moreover, the legal-judicial arguments were indissolubly linked to the theological-religious arguments; what is true of one is true of the other. The legal traditions did not stand in isolation from the theological polemics; they were essentially of a piece. The whole intellectual milieu of theology, law and Islamic philosophy was part of a single matrix and it was busy creating tens of thousands of *hadiths* to illuminate what the Prophet said, when he said it, to whom and for what reason. Most of what now is recycled today as the history of Mohammed and his life in Mecca and Medina, is based on the mountain of fiction written in this period and projected back to an earlier period.

From the eighth century onwards, but particularly from the end of the ninth, what we see is an enormous *filtering* process, using the Prophet, Companions and Successors as the outward form, whilst the content of laws and regulations were crystallizing out. The laws reflected the society in which they were set down (and in particular the material interests of the Arab ruling elite) but they were overlaid with the special form of Arab monotheism which defined itself more and more clearly by a manufactured tradition, including not only the life of the Prophet, but the early period of the wars of conquest up to and including the Umayyad dynasty.

John Wansbrough

Yet another slant on the history of the Koran has been provided by John Wansbrough, who was Professor of Semitic Studies at London's School of Oriental and African Studies. He used textual and linguistic analysis of early Islamic works to look at the exegetical tradition of the Koran which attempted to define the context or historical setting of many of the sayings in the Koran. Where, for example, a particular behaviour is mandated for Muslims, it was only much later scholars, in their exegesis, who added (from reliable sources, they would say) that the Koranic phrase was said by Mohammed at a certain time on a particular occasion. Not only were verses and phrases clarified, but additional theological conclusions were drawn from speeches and comments not contained in the Koran but reportedly made by the Prophet.

Wansbrough's argument, as his book title implies—*The Sectarian Milieu*—is that Islam only came to define itself as a specifically Arab form of monotheism through a protracted period of polemic with Christian and Jewish scholars. Those responsible for this defining process were the new social elite of religious scholars, the *ulema*, who emerged within Arab society during the period of the consolidation of the Empire. A layer of the *ulema* supported and were used by the Umayyad ruling class to give a more clearly *Arab* identity to what was becoming the state religion, but another layer reflected the lower classes, including non-Arab Muslims (clients) and slaves, and they clashed with the Umayyads. This group included those who sanctioned and participated in the mass revolutionary movement behind the overthrow of the Umayyads and who were retrospectively lumped together as a Shia tradition.

Wansbrough drew attention to the polemical character of much of the Koran, particularly focusing on Jewish tradition, with the clear implication that among large numbers of Arabs, Judaism and early Islam were significantly blurred together. Wansbrough argued that the firm establishment of a text for the Koran was part of a process of definition by which Islam differentiated itself from Judaism.

There is, for example, a passage in the Koran (2:142-7) which has some polemic about the *qibla*—the direction of prayer for Muslims. Wansbrough points out that this polemic also was given its alleged historic context in later exegesis by the identification and naming of the Jews involved in the debate with Mohammed. Strictly speaking, therefore, eighth and ninth century scholars weren't involved in 'exegesis' (ie interpretation) so much as the *creation* of historical context—what Wansbrough calls "historicisation"—of all the various passages in the Koran. He argues, not unreasonably, that exegesis of the established text more or less coincided with the crystallisation of the text itself. Most of the exegetical commentary on the Koran projects imagined events and historical facts backwards in time by up to two hundred years, to explain and give context to Koranic sayings. "The result", he writes, "was thus not history, but nostalgia."

Wansbrough selected two particular sources, the *Sira* of Ibn Ishaq, who died in 768 and the *Maghazi* of Waqidi (d 822) in order to contrast them and show the development of style and content over the relatively short time-span of two generations. In the *Sira* he says, ". . . history is itself generated by scriptural imagery or enhanced by scriptural references." The difference between Ibn Ishaq's and Waqidi's account of the *same events* is due, Wansbrough argues, to the fact that in the time between the two writers there was some consolidation of official canon. Waqidi's version of history covered the same alleged events as described by Ibn Ishaq, but often with more detail and sophistication. Once the basic story-line was established, in other words, the 'tale grew with the telling'. It was not unlike the elaboration of the Gospels of Luke and Matthew, based on the earlier and much shorter allegorical account of the life of Jesus in the Gospel of Mark. Other scholars of Islam, as we shall note, have commented on the way that historical accounts become elaborate with each passing century. The history produced by this accumulation of exegesis was precisely that which corresponded to the Arabs' identity of the new religion.

The drivers behind the elaboration and clarification of doctrine were, on the one hand, the theological polemics among Muslims themselves and between Muslims and Judeo-Christian sects. On the other hand, there were also legal and judicial disputes upon which scholars were obliged to take sides and to which we have already referred. In the latter case too, religion was the only available language of polemic, so the authority for decisions lay in the theology and tradition. In the clarification and definition of what was deemed to be orthodox practice the clerics would cite examples of previous practice—in other words seeking authority by projecting the contemporary arguments back a hundred or two hundred years to the Prophet or to one of the Companions or to another competent source.

"In the Middle East of late antiquity the only available medium of historical description was the language of salvation history. Every incident of *histoire evenementielle* ['event history'] was reported as the expression of a theodicy. [an act of 'God's grace']."[640]

"The illusion of antiquity, and hence of authority, is thus easily generated, and, like pseudepigraphy, consciously linked with key figures from the past. An example is the figure of Paul, whose 'apostolic authority' could be, and was, pressed into the service of diametrically opposed view of ecclesiastical organisation . . ."[641]

Different parts of the clerical elite reflected different strands and classes within society, so it was inevitable that they clashed over the *material* issues of the day—on property, tax liability, and the struggle for the rights of Muslims, non-Muslims and slaves. It is for this reason that the mass of traditional *detail* is often contradictory and confusing and is variously interpreted today according to the social composition and agenda of different groups of Muslims. Wansbrough's overall conclusion in *The Sectarian Milieu* follows the almost identical view set out by Schacht who wrote only a few decades earlier:

"Both the quantity and quality of source materials would seem to support the proposition that the elaboration of Islam was not contemporary with but *posterior* to the Arab occupation of the Fertile Crescent and beyond."[642]

"As witness to events," he argues, the source materials, ". . . are more than a little suspect. What they do not, and cannot, provide is an account of the 'Islamic' community during the 150 years or so between the first Arab conquests and the appearance, with the *Sira-Maghazi* narratives, of the earliest Islamic literature."[643] Wansbrough's analysis of the traditional sources suggests how what became the orthodox view of Islam succeeded within this milieu of debate and disagreement. All the political conflicts and struggles that took place would have been expressed in terms of doctrinal, religious disputes. It was those theological positions that were untenable in *the social and political milieu in which they were proposed* that fell by the wayside. The orthodox community, he suggests, "is simply the one which survived, its spokesmen that clerical elite whose position was least intransigent, its theology the neutralised precipitate of traditional polemic."

In summary, the inescapable conclusion from Wansbrough's analysis, although he doesn't put it in so many words himself, is that the entire Muslim tradition about the early history of the text of the Koran was manufactured.

---

640   Wansbrough *The Sectarian Milieu*, p 118
641   Wansbrough *The Sectarian Milieu*, p 125
642   Wansbrough *The Sectarian Milieu*, p 99 (italics added)
643   Wansbrough *The Sectarian Milieu*, p 119

Patricia Crone

We have already cited works by Patricia Crone, but, in another seminal work with Michael Cook, she took the analysis of Schacht and Wansbrough several steps further. Patricia Crone is a leading scholar of Islamic studies and has held fellowships at both Oxford and Cambridge Universities. Michael Cook has a similarly distinguished academic career and is currently professor of Near Eastern Studies at Princeton University. Through extensive analysis of traditional texts (the same Islamic source documents used by other Muslim and non-Muslim scholars) these two came to quite radical conclusions. Their work, like Joseph Schacht's has also been ground-breaking.

The title of their book, published in 1977, *Hagarism: The Making of the Islamic World*, was a reference to Hagar, the slave of the old Jewish patriarch Abraham. She had a son by Abraham, called Ishmail or Ismail, and both Jewish and Islamic legend cast him as the father of the Arab people. Crone and Cook, like most modern historians, are extremely suspicious of the traditions and, in their words, it was necessary to "step outside" of these sources. According to Crone and Cook, seventh century Syriac, Armenian and Hebrew sources did not describe the Arab conquests as Islamic, but instead depicted it as a quasi-Jewish messianic movement, heavily influenced by the Samaritan branch of Judaism. It was only much later, at the end of the seventh century, that the Arab conquerors shed the Judaic colouration, although retaining many of its overt features, like circumcision and dietary laws. The early Arab conquests, therefore, could be seen as the 'liberation' of Jerusalem from the Byzantine yoke. The doctrinal ideas of the Arab monotheists only developed into what is known as Islam after a long period of gestation, during which the Arab Prophet was created in the image of Moses and with a central locus in the Hejaz rather than Jerusalem. The fact that Syriac and Greek documents of the conquest period refer to the Arab community as *Magaritai*[644] or something similar, is taken by Crone and Cook as a distortion of *Hagarene* or *Hagarite*, meaning the descendents of Hagar.

> "The 'Mahgraye' may thus be seen as the Hagarene participants in a hijra to the Promised Land; in this pun lies the earliest identity of the faith which was in the fullness of time to become Islam."[645]

The ideas of Crone and Cook in *Hagarism* were not widely accepted, even by other revisionist scholars, although it was acknowledged as an extremely radical and fresh approach to historical research. In time, the authors themselves were to qualify their ideas and partly withdraw what had been originally put forward. But in later works

---

[644] The corresponding Arabic term being *Muhajirun*, those taking part in the *Hijra*, although it has taken on a wider meaning as an Islamic militant or fighter.

[645] Patricia Crone and Michael Cook, *Hagarism: the Making of the Islamic World*, p 9

Patricia Crone has continued to support the view of most modern scholars that the traditional account of Mohammed's life and the rise of Islam is a late creation.

In a later book by Patrician Crone and Martin Hinds, the authors point out that it was in the seventh century that the first known coins were struck identifying Mohammed as *rasul Allah*, (the messenger of God) and thereafter it became a common feature of coins. Crone and Hinds also point out that as late as 691 CE, "Muhammad and Jesus were both identified as messengers of God in the two long inscriptions on the octagonal arcade of the Dome of the Rock in Jerusalem."[646] It ought to be pointed out, however, as we will elaborate later, that other scholars interpret the word 'Mohammed' on these coins and on the Dome of the Rock, not as a proper name, but as an adjective meaning 'praiseworthy', so the *muhammad rasul Allah* would simply read "praised be the messenger of God".

Crone and Hinds refer to a long letter by the Caliph al-Walid II (743-744) which is one of the longest and most detailed letters of the period preserved in the chronicles of Tabari. The bulk of the letter is devoted, they argue, "to the supreme importance of obedience to God's caliphs", not to the prophets. Even though Tabari wrote two hundred years later, and, if anything, would have no wish to minimise the importance of the Prophet,

> "What is so striking about this letter is that caliphs are in no way subordinated to prophets (let alone to the Prophet). Prophets and caliphs alike are seen as God's agents, and both dutifully carry out the tasks assigned to them."[647]

This is an indication of an *intermediate* stage in which the Prophet Mohammed is acknowledged, but in which he has not yet reached the level of unparalleled esteem which was accorded to him in later centuries, something that is in agreement with Schacht's analysis of Shafi'i and the development of law. The view of Caliph al-Walid are echoed in similar views by his successor Yazid III, whose letters are also preserved by Tabari, the main point being, according to Crone and Hinds, "that *khalifat* and *rasul* were once seen as independent agents of God." These two authors, like Schacht, conclude that the later development of tradition and the further consolidation of Islam as a state religion meant a fundamental change in the outlook towards Mohammed. Although "parity" was the original starting point, "the last prophet had begun to acquire his capital 'P' at the cost of earlier prophets and subsequent caliphs alike . . ."[648]

In another parallel with earlier work by Joseph Schacht, Crone and Hinds looked at the references to *sunna* in the early literature. What they demonstrated was that although it was a required part of any polemic to invoke the established

---

[646] Patricia Crone and Martin Hinds, *God's Caliph*, p 25
[647] Patricia Crone and Martin Hinds, *God's Caliph*, p 27
[648] Patricia Crone and Martin Hinds, *God's Caliph*, p 29

sunna, the *sunna* 'of the Prophet' meant no more in the early days than the *sunna* 'of the caliph' or what was deemed to be traditional custom and practice. It was only in the later Umayyad period that the Prophet began to be invoked as a source of *sunna* tradition in his own right above that of other authorities.

> ". . . what the scholars took to be Prophetic *sunna* scarcely surfaced in the Umayyad period outside the circles of the scholars themselves. Practically no traditions, be they Prophetic or other, are cited in letters or speeches by Umayyad caliphs, governors or secretaries. None seem to be adduced by rebels. Scarcely any appear in theological epistles. Hardly any are cited in accounts about Umayyad judges being required to know the Koran, not tradition."[649]

Given the weight of evidence, Crone and Hinds, argue, ". . . we are entitled to conclude that *sunna* in the sense of concrete rules authenticated by *hadith*, scarcely surfaced before the Umayyads fell."[650]

Of course, as is the case with all political movements in this period, religious and traditional reference points invariably provide the ideological colouration of the message. But although the outward *form* of political and social movements invoked various authorities for what was deemed to be *sunna*, the real *content* of the polemical struggle were the *material interests* of the classes and social groups in question. Thus, Yazid III, who came to power after a coup in 744 CE, explained that his programme was to be 'on behalf of God and the *sunna* of the Prophet'.

> "Yazid III proceeded to state that he would engage in no building works, squander no money on wives and children, transfer no money from one province to another except in a limited way and with good reason, keep no troops in the field too long, destroy nobody's income by overtaxing *dhimmis* [non-Muslims] and thus forcing them to flee, and allow no mighty to oppress the weak; on the contrary, he would pay everybody's stipends and maintenance when they were due and treat remote provincials on a par with subjects close at hand . . . [651]

The works of those scholars we have cited so far all point to the same general conclusion. That conclusion is that even a careful examination of the *traditional source materials* shows that Islamic law, Koranic exegesis, religious practice and doctrine in general (not to mention the biography of the Prophet) are not products of their traditional seventh century setting, but are creations of the eighth and ninth centuries . . . at the earliest. What is clear is that the first century of 'traditional

---

[649]   Patricia Crone and Martin Hinds, *God's Caliph*, p 72
[650]   Patricia Crone and Martin Hinds, *God's Caliph*, p 80
[651]   Patricia Crone and Martin Hinds, *God's Caliph*, p 68

Islam' is not evidenced by any contemporary sources or even by the later Islamic sources.

Crone's critique of the Meccan origins of Islam

Islamic tradition goes to great lengths to create a geographical setting for the birth of Islam far removed from the centres of Christianity and Judaism but now even the official location for the origin of Islam—the holy city of Mecca—has been subjected to rigorous and quite revealing criticism by modern revisionist historians. The traditions relating to Mecca were created hundreds of years after the foundation of the Arab Empire and, like most of the narrative relating to early Islam, hardly stand up to scrutiny. Patricia Crone's most recent book, *Meccan Trade and the rise of Islam*, takes a fresh look at the historical evidence for Mecca having been the seat of the Islamic faith. Mecca, let us recall, is described in histories of Islam as having been a "natural trading outpost between southern and northern Arabia" and the "financial centre of the *Hejaz*". Other sources describe the city as having a *monopoly* of trade in certain commodities between India and East Africa to the South, and the Persian and Byzantine Empires to the North.

Crone makes the point in an earlier work that "not a single feature" of the Umayyad summer palaces ". . . has been traced to Mecca or for that matter anywhere else in the *Hejaz*"[652] In *Meccan Trade* she suggests that the claims that Mecca was a natural stopping point in desert travel are quite wrong: "barren places do not make natural halts wherever they may be located, and least of all when they are found a short distance from famously green environments"—a reference to the oasis of Taif, a few miles from Mecca. "Why should caravans have made a steep descent to the barren valley of Mecca when they could have stopped at Taif?"[653]

She scoffs at the very idea of a large-scale desert trade when sea routes were available to the east and west of the Arabian Peninsula. The Red Sea takes maritime traffic right up to within a hundred miles of the Mediterranean coast and the Persian Gulf takes trade up to the two great rivers of Iraq. Roman documentation, she points out, refer to *maritime* trade between Yemen and Egypt, and thence to Rome.

> "From the first century AD, not only the inhabitants of Mesopotamia, but also the Greeks and the Romans sailed directly to India, and soon also to Ceylon. The numismatic evidence indicates the trade to have been at its liveliest in the first two centuries AD. By the end of the third century AD, it had declined and though it was partially revived in the fourth, it petered out thereafter . . . by the sixth century, it was the Ethiopians who

---

[652]   Patricia Crone, *Roman, provincial and Islamic law,* p 121
[653]   Patricia Crone, *Meccan Trade,* p 6

conducted most of the eastern trade of the Byzantines, India and Ethiopia becoming increasingly confused in the sources."[654]

Where in all this, she asks, ". . . is there room for the commercial and political supremacy of Mecca, against the background of which Muhammad is usually said to have enacted his career?" Going into some detailed examinations of Roman and Greek sources, she comes to the conclusion that there was no Meccan trade in incense, spices or any other foreign luxury goods. It is a "fiction", she argues. It was quite remarkable that, for a city that was alleged to be a major trading centre in pre-Islamic times *there is a deafening silence about it* outside of the Islamic tradition. The city is not attested by any surviving literature, ". . . be it Greek, Latin, Syriac, Aramaic, Coptic or other literature composed outside Arabia."

> "It is the sixth century silence that is significant, and this silence cannot be attributed to the fact that the sources have been lost, though some clearly have. The fact is that the sources written after the conquests display not the faintest sign of *recognition* in their accounts of the new rulers of the Middle East or the city from which they came. Nowhere is it stated that Quraysh or the 'Arab kings' were the people who used to supply such-and-such regions with such-and-such goods . . . . and as for the city, it was long assumed to have been Yathrib [Medina]. Of Mecca there is no mention for a long time . . ."[655]

As to what was traded and with whom: having examined not only the external evidence but also the Islamic tradition, she found that many of the reports dealing with trade are contradictory or even mutually exclusive. In one case, she found *fifteen* different versions of the same story about a particular merchant trading with Damascus. Crone, therefore, came to the conclusion that the Meccans may have transported perfume from Yemen but as regards other goods, like textiles, leather, foodstuffs and livestock—most of these were already available in the Byzantine Empire. Oddly some traditions have Mecca importing such goods, while others refer to these being exported.

> ". . . we are now in a position to propose three negative points about the Meccan export trade. First it was not a transit trade. Second, it was not a trade of the kind that attracted the attention of the inhabitants of Egypt and the Fertile Crescent. Third, it was not a trade that presupposed control of any trade routes in Arabia."[656]

---

[654]   Patricia Crone, *Meccan Trade,* p 40
[655]   Patricial Crone, *Meccan Trade,* p 137 (italics in original)
[656]   Patricial Crone, *Meccan Trade,* pp 107, 133

If the Meccans traded at all, therefore, it was in relatively cheap goods, typical of a pastoral economy and these were traded locally. As Crone points out, Meccans would not have travelled across eight hundred miles of desert, "to sell coals to Newcastle." Although the book has Meccan trade at its core—with all the associated traditions of raiding and rivalry that stand alongside it—the general lessons of her study can be applied to the accumulation of *all tradition*, including the story of the life of the Prophet, and in that sense, Crone has added significantly to the revisionist understanding of Islam.

> "It is obvious that if one storyteller should happen to mention a raid, the next storyteller would know the date of this raid, while the third would know everything that an audience might wish to hear about it. This process is graphically illustrated in the sheer contrast of size between the works of Ibn Ishaq (died 767) and Waqidi (d 823), that of Waqidi being much larger for all that it covers only Muhammad's period in Medina . . . And if spurious information accumulated at this rate in the two generations between Ibn Ishaq and Waqidi, it is hard to avoid the conclusion that even more must have accumulated in the three generations between the Prophet and Ibn Ishaq . . . It is because the storyteller played such a crucial role in the formation of the tradition that there is so little historicity to it. As storyteller followed storyteller, the recollection of the past was reduced to a common stock of stories, themes, and motifs that could be combined and recombined in a profusion of apparently factual accounts . . . *they came to agree on the historicity of events that never took place . . .*"[657]

Suliman Bashear

The work of earlier scholars has been further underpinned by Suliman Bashear, a leading scholar at the University of Nablus in Palestine and another academic who has suffered for his views. He has written a number of articles and books touching on Koranic history and the growth of *hadith* traditions. Bashear examined the ample tradition of exegesis that was associated with one particular verse of the Koran (2, 114) which is taken to refer to objections by the Jews of Medina to the change of direction of prayer from Jerusalem to Mecca. In examining these traditions, Bashear went back to the original works of antiquity. He came broadly to the same conclusion as the western scholars we have already cited, that from the eighth century onwards, there was a dramatic shift in interpretation of this one verse—a shift that was specifically aimed at asserting the *Hejazi* (ie Meccan and Medinan) origins of Islam, as opposed to the *real* origins in Syria, Iraq and Iran. *Hadith* supporting an Arabian origin, therefore, only began circulating two hundred years after the traditional period of the life of the Prophet.

---

[657]   Patricial Crone, *Meccan Trade*, p 223-225 (italics added)

"The present enquiry has shown how precisely around this period (the mid-second century AH), elements of Hejazi orientation made their presence felt in the exegetical efforts to fit what became the canon of Muslim scripture into the new historical framework of Arabian Islam."[658]

Although writing as a Muslim, Bashear concluded that what he called the Arab 'polity'—the institutions of the Arab imperial state—only coincided with Islam as a finished religion in the eighth century. In other words, we have yet another corroboration that the *Arab* Empire became *Islamic* a century and a half after its foundation. He states clearly that the Islamic reverence for "certain locations in the Hejaz" only arose at the time of the Abbasids, in the eighth century.

". . . our attempt to date the relevant traditional material confirms on the whole the conclusions that Schacht arrived at from another field, specifically the tendency of *isnads* to grow backwards . . . our enquiry strongly leads to the conclusion that such issues were far from settled during the first half of the second century."[659]

He was somewhat shy of drawing the obvious conclusions but the clear implication of his work was that the arguments of Patricia Crone are correct: the Hejazi origins of Islam, including the entire saga of Mecca, Medina and the life of the Prophet, were manufactured and projected back two hundred years to consolidate a romanticised and fully 'Arabised' foundation to a state religion. In discussing the so-called 'conquest' of the early period of the empire, Bashear challenged the classical view of hordes of Arab Muslims pouring out of the Arabian Peninsula.

"The proposition that Arabia could have constituted the source of the vast material power required to effect such changes in world affairs within so short a span of time is, to say the least, a thesis calling for proof and substantiation . . . One may observe, for example, that in spite of all its twentieth-century oil wealth, Saudi Arabia still does not possess such material and spiritual might."[660]

As we have argued, the establishment of an *Arab* empire is not contestable, but the tradition of an 'Islamic' empire most certainly is. Bashear appears to come to more or less the same conclusions:

"That the Arabs politically benefitted from the collapse of the Persian and Byzantine imperial rule in the area and played a role in these developments is of course not to be denied. What cannot be accepted on face value

---

658   Bashear, *Quran 2:114 and Jerusalem*, p 238.

659   Bashear cited by Ibn Warraq, in *The Hidden History of Islam*, p 238

660   Bashear, *Arabs and Others in Early Islam*, p 113

is the assumption that such a role was part of a religious project of the Arabs right from the outset . . . the first/seventh century witnessed two parallel, albeit initially separate processes: the rise of the Arab polity on the one hand, and the beginnings of a religious movement that eventually crystallised into Islam."[661]

Bashear reinforces a view of the late development of Islam by looking at the history of those aspects of Koranic interpretation that deal with the relationship of Arabs with other nations. He notes, for example, that far from romanticizing the Bedouin with their pastoral desert lifestyle, the earliest interpretations of the Koran looked down on the Bedouin as an inferior class. Bashear refers to the faith being "eventually engulfed by other peoples and cultures" in the eighth century "fusion" of the Arab state and Islam. But it would be more accurate to say that the state, still dominated by an Arab elite, used Islam, as a distinct form of Arabian monotheism, rooted in an imaginary Arabian past, as a means of defining itself and distinguishing itself from the prior Byzantine and Persian cultures of subject peoples. Islam became the ideological expression *par-excellence* of the Arab ruling class.

The detailed work done on the traditional Islamic literature by Goldziher, Schacht, Wansbrough, Crone, Cook, Hinds, Bashear and others—all, let us recall, celebrated scholars in their field—points inevitably to one general conclusion, that *Islam as it has come to be understood in its modern sense did not exist in the first one hundred to one hundred and fifty years after the accepted time of Mohammed's death.* We might add that most of these scholars base their analysis on scriptural and epigraphic study of ancient sources, but their views are also well supported by archaeological evidence.

What is important for us (and it cannot be repeated too often) is that the traditions of the leading role of Mecca were written *centuries later* and, having been passed down from historian to historian, are largely today accepted in Muslim and non-Muslim circles alike as established 'facts', when they are nothing of the sort. Arab monotheism began as an amorphous and poorly defined strand of religious practice, more than likely in the north west of Arabia, where lingering Jewish tradition was stronger, rather than Mecca. It came to be woven into other strands which borrowed from Jewish and Christian traditions, and although it retained specifically *Arab* characteristics, little of this was derived from Bedouin culture and tradition. As we shall show, early Islam did not come into conflict with Christianity or Judaism, but on the contrary, co-existed with them, at times uneasily, while it borrowed much of its liturgical and ritualistic practices from them.

Chapter summary

- A long tradition of revisionist scholarship, based on the original Arabic texts and *hadith* has come to the conclusion that most of the tradition

---

[661] Bashear, *Arabs and Others in Early Islam*, p 116

was written in the eighth century or later, long after the reported life of Mohammed.

- Joseph Schacht and others demonstrated that references to the life of Mohammed as the highest authority in Islamic law became the norm only from the mid-eighth or ninth century onwards. Chains of transmission (*isnads*) that purported to authenticate the words or deeds of Mohammed down the centuries were mostly fabricated.

- Mecca was not a bustling city linked to international trade but a small desert town from which traders dealt in relatively cheap, local goods. The significance of the city of Mecca is not attested in any literature outside of the Islamic tradition before the eighth century and its central position in the foundation of Islam was probably a late fiction.

- The traditions that link Islam to Bedouin culture and the Hejaz were only started in the eighth century. This adds a further question mark, therefore, about the geographical origins of Islam in central Arabia.

- The detailed work done by many eminent scholars points inevitably to one general conclusion: that Islam as it has come to be understood in its modern sense did not exist in the first one hundred to one hundred and fifty years after the accepted time of Mohammed's death.

Chapter 15

The early seventh century

and the origins of the Arab Empire

In this chapter we will look at the social and political conditions that existed in the sixth and seventh centuries in that region of the Near East in which Islam was born. We will show that in the Arab world, including the Arabian Peninsula, *monotheism was the predominant faith* and there were long-standing traditions of Judaism and Christianity. Contrary to Islamic tradition, polytheism was not significant within the Arab populations.

We shall argue that the area of what is today Israel, Palestine, Syria and Iraq was the real strategic heart and the starting point of the Arab Empire, not the Arabian Peninsula, which was relatively undeveloped and with a small population. By the time of the beginning of the Arab Empire, Palestine, Syria and Iraq had been both *Arab* and *Christian* for centuries. We will outline how this core region of what was to become the Arab Empire was divided between the Byzantines and the Sassanid (Persian) Empires and how social upheaval, revolution and war preceded the establishment of the first independent Arab state.

We shall argue that the organised Islamic conquest of the core regions of Syria, Palestine and Iraq is largely a myth and that a specifically Arab tradition of monotheism, mostly originating in Judaism, was no more than one of several ingredients in the religious melting pot when the Arab Empire developed. We shall argue that the Arab era (beginning in 622 CE) is linked to the formation of the first independent Arab state and that the subsequent *Arab* Empire was not *Islamic* in the sense that would be recognised today. We will show, finally, that the first ruler of this Arab state to be attested by non-Islamic evidence is not Mohammed or one of the earlier traditional caliphs, but the Caliph Mu'awiya.

. . . .

As we have seen, the work of a large number of very eminent scholars, using original Islamic sources, have led us to the conclusion that the traditional accounts of the life of Mohammed and the origins of the Koran are unreliable as history. Although there is no dispute that the Arab Empire was founded in the early seventh century, most of the historical evidence points to the consolidation of the Islamic faith only from the eighth century onwards. Having established an approximate time frame, it is now necessary for us to identify the real historical drivers behind the foundation of Islam and to do that we need to examine the powerful social and political forces that were at work from the early seventh century onwards.

The key region to consider is not the poorly populated Arabian Peninsula, but Syria and Iraq. It is relatively easy, especially from the archaeological evidence, to suggest what did *not* happen here in this period, but it is far more difficult, given the paucity of solid historical evidence, to be certain about what really *did* happen. What seems to be the case is that by the beginning of the seventh century, there was an oral tradition linked to the components of what was to become a holy book which had evolved from the Syriac Christian traditions of Syria and Iraq, with an added leavening of specifically Arab monotheism.

What distinguished the Arab version of monotheism from its Christian and Judaic predecessors was a strong element of puritanism. It was a 'purer' piety which expressed a reaction against the great empires of the Byzantines and Persians which dominated the region. It was a response, in the same language of self-proclaimed piety we have seen in other traditions of *revolutionary religious movements*—the *Apiru*, the Essenes, the early Christian Ebionites and the revolutionary Anabaptists of seventeenth century Germany, to name but a few. In every one of these cases, the movement that sought a renewal and a purer form of the established religion was in the final analysis derived from a *social revolutionary movement* in a society riven with conflicts and contradictions.

What developed early in the seventh century was a distinct Arab version of monotheism, perhaps with a strong strand of egalitarianism, which then echoed down the ages as a core component within the Islamic tradition. This special brand of piety may have had its roots in the semi-nomadic and more isolated areas of Arabia, among Arabs with no stake in the wealth and exploitation that were characteristic of the Byzantine and Persian Empires. It would find an echo, too, among the most down-trodden in the more cosmopolitan hinterland of Syria and Iraq. But it would be making a fundamental error to simply draw a straight line from what started as a relatively minor element of Arab monotheism to the established religion that came to be known as Islam many generations later. It was only one aspect of Arab monotheism, moreover, one without form or a clear doctrinal base, and it would take many decades to become anything like the international religion we know today as Islam.

The Islamic faith did not come into existence with fully formed doctrines, riding on a whirlwind of conquest. The emergent Arab monotheism was at first ambivalent towards the other great monotheisms and stood alongside Christianity in particular in an uncomfortable accommodation, until the establishment of a mighty Arab empire provided the material base upon which it could develop, clarify and distinguish itself from its religious forebears. Our task is to identify the social, economic and political forces which shaped that early Arab monotheism and which later led to its evolution into modern Islam.

The long traditions of monotheism

Although later traditions came to centre Islam on the Arabian cities of the Hejaz, the first capital city of the Arab Empire was Damascus, not Medina, and its first great centre of worship was built in Jerusalem, not Mecca. It was this part of the Near East—what is today Israel, Palestine, Syria and Iraq—that was the real strategic heart and the starting point of the Arab Empire, not the economic and political backwater that was the Arabian Peninsula. As the sixth century was drawing to a close this key region was divided between two great empires, roughly along the line of the River Euphrates in Iraq. To the west, ruling modern-day Turkey, Palestine, Syria, western Iraq, Egypt and North Africa, was the old Roman Empire, referred to as the *Byzantines* from their capital in Constantinople (formerly Byzantium).[662] Ruling eastern Iraq, Iran and further east, as well as the area around the Gulf, was the Persian Sassanid Empire, named after its ruling dynasty. Both of these empires ruled parts of the Near East through *Arab client states*, the Ghassanids as vassals of the Byzantines and the Lakhmids as vassals of the Sassanids. It was the social upheaval within these two empires and the imperial wars between them that provided the backdrop to the expansion of an exclusively Arab monotheism and the establishment of a powerful *independent* Arab state early in the seventh century.

The two empires were based on the exploitation of the mass of the overwhelmingly rural population by an urban ruling elite which retained power by means of an extensive state bureaucracy and a large standing army. Later Islamic sources described a rigid social stratification within the Sassanid Empire:

"The priests appear at the top of the ladder. They are followed by the military estate. The third estate is that of the royal bureaucracy. Ultimately the commoners are enumerated, subdivided into peasants and artisans. It may be tempting to regard this picture as the reflection of an order imposed by a powerful monarchy, wielding effective means of control, supported by a strong priestly cast that bolsters its position with the sanction of divine blessing."[663]

---

[662] Modern historians refer to the 'Byzantines', as we shall continue to do, but they were regarded in this part of the world as the 'Romans' (*Rūm* in Arabic) even though they were predominantly Greek-speaking.

[663] Cited by Zeev Rubin in *Elites Old and New in the Byzantine and Early Islamic Near East*, p 241

**Map 4: The interface between the Byzantine
and Persian Empires around 600 CE**

But these empires did not rest on stable foundations and were not immune to social upheaval and class struggle. The histories of the Sassanid Empire, although as usual, written long after the events, describe a huge uprising in the early sixth century, led by Mazdak, a heretical Zoroastrian priest who claimed to be the Messiah. What was remarkable was that his uprising represented a mass movement of peasants, with a programme of primitive communism that continued to resonate centuries later. As late as the ninth century revolutionary uprisings against the Muslim caliphs were condemned by contemporary commentators as 'Mazdakite'. In words that echoed the sentiments of Josephus five hundred years earlier, when he described the revolt of the Judean masses, the Islamic historian Tabari gave vent to his fear and loathing at the revolutionary movement of Mazdak:

"Mazdak and his partisans . . . proclaimed 'God has established daily sustenance in the earth for His servants to divide out among themselves, with equal shares, but men have oppressed each other regarding it.' They further asserted that they were going to take from the rich for the poor and give to those possessing little out of the share of those possessing much, moreover, [they asserted that] . . . those who had an excessive amount of wealth, womenfolk and goods had no more right to them than anyone else. The lower ranks of society took advantage of this and seized the opportunity, they rallied to Mazdak and his partisans and banded together with them. The people [ie the higher levels of society] suffered from the activities of the Mazdakites and these last grew strong until they would burst in on a man in his own house and appropriate his dwelling, his womenfolk, and his possessions without the owner being able to stop them."[664]

Like Josephus, Tabari lamented the way that "vile people" took advantage of those who were basically "good".

"[Mazdak] . . . incited the lower classes against the upper classes. Through him all sorts of vile persons became mixed up with the best elements of society, criminals seeking to despoil them of their possessions found easy ways to do this, tyrannical persons had their paths to tyranny facilitated, and fornicators were able to indulge their lusts and get their hands on high-born women to whom they would never have been able to aspire. Universal calamity overwhelmed the people to an extent they had never before experienced."[665]

As late as the tenth century, Firdawsi, an Iranian poet, was still remonstrating with Mazdak and his followers in much the same vein, predicting all manner of social dislocation if their ideas were ever implemented:

"You have introduced a new religion to the world, whereby you proclaim women and property ought to be held in common . . . if all men were equal in the world, the priests would be indistinguishable from the lowly . . . in what manner would it then be possible to appoint rulers? When anyone dies, to whom should his estate and property belong, if the king should be of equal right with the menial worker? . . . it should not be

---

[664] Al-Tabari, V, 885-6
[665] Al-Tabari, V, 893

allowed that such an evil would ever take place in Iran! Are all to be lords? And who should be the treasure's guard? . . ."[666]

The revolt of Mazdak reflected the aspirations of the poorest and most downtrodden elements in society but it also represented a struggle for power, wealth and influence between the traditional ruling nobility of Persia and the young Persian King Kawad, who had cynically attempted to use the revolutionary impact of the peasantry to strike blows against the powerful aristocracy. But King Kawad had unwittingly unleashed a monster and inevitably the revolt took on a momentum and a logic of its own; so much so that the Mazdakite revolt was only crushed decades after it had begun, when the nobility were finally able to regain enough power to reverse the reforms and land distribution of the rebels. Sassanid society was in a state of prolonged crisis throughout the remainder of the sixth century, with the ruling class split among themselves and the poor in a semi-permanent state of revolt. The launch of an invasion of Byzantine territory in 606 CE was a last desperate throw of the dice for the Sassanid dynasty and after this military venture finally ran into the sand, the Persian Empire collapsed like a house of cards.

Lakhmids and Ghassanids

Up to the beginning of the seventh century, this rotten dynasty had ruled its south-western fringes, Iraq and the Gulf, through its Arab surrogates, the Lakhmids. The Lakhmid vassal kingdom, which dominated northern Arabia for nearly three centuries, was the first to boast a capital city overwhelmingly Arabic-speaking; this was Hira, on the Euphrates. It was in Hira that a written Arabic script was used for the first time, from where it spread west to the rest of the Arabic-speaking world. The Lakhmids were also predominantly Christian and there is documentary evidence that as early as 410 CE there was an Arab bishop of Hira. It is inconceivable that the generalised social upheaval throughout the Sassanid Empire for almost the whole of the preceding century would not have had a huge impact on the outlook of the Arab population in the Lakhmid region in the early seventh century. Moreover, there was an ongoing tension between the Arab part of the Sassanid Empire and the Persian/Iranian centre. In *The Lakhmids of Hira,* Zahran Yasmine, a Palestinian archaeologist, described the rivalry between Arabs and Persians and the affinity the Lakhmids felt for the Ghassanids who, as fellow Arabs, shared the same language, religion and tradition.

> "The Persians attempted in vain to prevent the Arabs from turning to Christianity, the religion of their enemies [the Byzantines], considered as betrayal. Hira was considered a Christian town and a centre of missionary Christianity in Arabia, but what the Persians feared most was conversion

---

[666] Cited by Zeev Rubin, in *Elites Old and New in the Byzantine and Early Islamic Near East,* p 253

in the ranks of the Lakhmid army. They could not countenance the idea of Lakhmid Christian armies fighting Ghassanid Christian armies, nor could they forget that a Christian soldier of Hira warned the Ghassanids of a forthcoming attack and another was vocally against the siege of Edessa, a Christian town conducted by Persians and Lakhmids."[667]

The crisis in the Lakhmid region was mirrored to the west in the Ghassanid state, settled by Arabs, particularly in the south, for many generations. The grandeur of the Byzantine court has even more references in Islamic historical tradition, because although the Persian Empire was later to collapse, the Byzantine Empire still stood and remained as a permanent military and economic rival of the new Arab state. Much of the later Muslim description of the Byzantine court accurately reflects the opulence of the Constantinople elite, although it has to be said that it was written precisely with the aim of creating an artificial contrast to its more modest Arab equivalent.

"Byzantine imperial dignity surrounded by rituals, processions, seclusion, rich court costumes, a highly developed court retinue, and beautiful objects made of gold, silver and precious gems was a far cry from the relatively simple ambience surrounding the leaders of the early Muslim community . . . the sumptuous Byzantine ceremonial, with the wealth it implied, was spurned by the Muslims, who accused the Byzantines of having amassed such wealth at the expense of the poor."[668]

Although Palestine, Syria and western Iraq were nominally a part of the Byzantine Empire, by the beginning of the sixth century the Byzantines had effectively withdrawn militarily, to allow the Ghassanid vassal state to rule in their place. The Ghassanids, too, were Christian. By the end of the sixth century, therefore, Syria and Palestine had been a part of the Roman Empire for more than six hundred years and was subject to the influence of Christianity during that whole time, for half of which it was the official imperial religion.

In their book *Crossroads to Islam*, Yehuda Nevo and Judith Koren confirm that the background to the Arab take-over was a Byzantine Empire that had long ceased to hold the southern provinces of Syria with its own troops and preferred instead to make payments to Ghassanid Arab tribes ('*foederati*') to police the areas on its behalf. By this means the Byzantines had the benefit of commercial links with the rich cities in these more populous northern parts of Syria but would not have had to pay for the expense of garrisons in the south. "In the sixth century [Byzantine emperor] Justinian finally abandoned the vestiges of the imperial army and transferred the total responsibility for defence to the Arab buffer state of Ghassan . . . leaving the

---

667 Yasmine Zahran, *The Lakhmids of Hira*, p 52
668 Nadia Maria El Cheik *Early Incomes in the Early Islamic State*, in *Elites Old and New in the Byzantine and Early Islamic Near East,*p 118

southern sector defended only by small federated tribes". Nevo and Koren cite evidence from a variety of sources to indicate that the 'imperial' army in this region became effectively an Arab army by the end of the sixth century. Not only were the federated tribes responsible for defence, but they also levied taxes, nominally at least, in the name of the emperor.

> ". . . the result of this situation was that the settled population became accustomed, already in the sixth century, to paying taxes to Arab tribesmen: the *foederati* who were the only imperial military forces left in the area".[669]

Like their Arab cousins in the Lakhmid regions, the Ghassanids had experienced social upheaval, civil war and revolution. At the beginning of the seventh century, Constantinople was shaken with a 'palace' coup by which the army chief Phocas overthrew the emperor Maurice. As in all such instances, this turmoil at the top was a reflection of crisis across the whole of society. Even at a time when the Byzantine state was subject to invasion from Persia, it was racked with civil war and social upheaval. The generalised chaos was exemplified by a revolt in Antioch, on the borders of present day Turkey and Syria, where an eighth century chronicler later described in purely *religious* terms what was, in effect, a *social* revolution of the rural masses (the "Jews") against largely urban ("Christian") landowners:

> "The Jews of Antioch, becoming disorderly, staged an uprising against the Christians and murdered Anastasius, the great patriarch of Antioch, whose genitals they put in his mouth. After this, they dragged him along the main street and *killed many landowners and burned them*. Phocas [was] . . . unable to stop the rising . . . Phocas was angry against the Christians and increased their taxes in Antioch, Laodicea and the rest of Syria and Mesopotamia."[670]

We have a situation, therefore, where the core region of what was to become the new Arab empire, in the former Lakhmid and Ghassanid Arab states (*which, let us recall, had already been predominantly Arab and Christian for centuries*) was shaken to its roots by revolution, social upheaval and war. Moreover, before, during and after the period immediately leading up to the beginning of the Arab Empire many charismatic revolutionary leaders were described as prophets of one kind or another. The Persian revolutionary Mazdak was not the first and by no means the last to wear the mantle. Even Islamic tradition counts at least three false prophets who were rivals to the Prophet Mohammed. As it was in Judea at the turn of the millennium, there were prophets under every stone.

---

[669] Yehuda D Nevo and Judith Koran, *Crossroad to Islam*, page 44

[670] Theophilus of Edessa, cited by Hoyland, Robert G (trans), *Theophilus of Edessa's Chronicle*, p 58 (italics added)

In the everyday life of Ghassanid and Lakhmid Arabs it is not clear what balance there was between, on the one hand, Aramaic (of which Syriac is one form) as the common written language of the whole region, and, on the other hand, Arabic which was more important as a spoken language. It has been suggested that until Arabic developed a written script, Arab Christians spoke Arabic in everyday life, but used Syriac in their Christian liturgy. As we have argued, it was probably from within this milieu that the Koranic tradition evolved, as written Arabic grew in significance. It was from this period that we find the oldest Arabic inscriptions anywhere in the Near East, *in a Christian Church*. The Church of St Sergius, near Aleppo in Syria, erected in 512 CE, bears the inscription in Arabic, 'This is a holy place'.

The Arabs' control of the region is further attested by the large collection of papyri discovered at Nessana in the Negev desert in modern-day Israel and dating from 460 to 630 CE. Whereas the earliest of the Nessana papyri used the Greek form for naming the scribes and copyists, those dated after 601 CE use Arabic. The period coinciding with the rise of the Arab empire is not shown in the Nessana papyri as a sudden and drastic change but one that took place gradually over a period of several decades until eventually the regulation of taxes came to be based in Damascus. What is also clear from the papyri is that the Christian Church continued for a long time to be responsible for the administration of the town.

It must not be forgotten that there was also a strong strand of Judaism within the Arab world, including the Arabian Peninsula, before Islam and possibly for centuries afterwards. A Jewish correspondent of the time even suggested that the armies of the early Arab Empire included Jews.

> "God it was who inspired the Ishmaelite kingdom to aid us. When they spread forth and captured the Land of the Hind from the hand of Edom, and reached Jerusalem, *there were Israelites among them*. They showed them the place of the Temple, and have dwelled with them to this day. They made it a condition that they preserve the place of the Temple from any abomination, and would pray at its gate, and none would gainsay them."[671]

A History of the Jews of Arabia, by Gordon Darnell Newby, examines in some detail both the Islamic and the Jewish traditions in this part of the world. "Judaism in Arabia, and in the Hejaz in particular, was a thriving and vital Diaspora culture," he writes. The Islamic tradition gives a nod in this direction by its references to Mohammed's struggle with the Jewish tribes in Medina. But in spite of this acknowledgement and the superficial similarities with Judaism—like circumcision and identical dietary laws—in general the Islamic tradition downplays the influence of Judaism. Talmudic tradition tells a story of "80,000 children who

---

[671] Testimony of Sebeos, cited by Shlomo Sand, *The Invention of the Jewish People,* p 181 (italics added)

were descendents of priests" fleeing "to the Ishmaelites" after the destruction of the Temple of Jerusalem by the Romans in 70 CE. Referring to Ibn Ishaq, the most well known biographer of Mohammed, Newby writes:

> "The story in Ibn Ishaq is full of legendary material and is part of the genealogical cycle that forms the introduction to the biography of Muhammad. Yet we know that when the Christian missionary Theophilus came to the Yemen in the middle of the fourth century, he found a great number of Jews. By the middle of the next century, the rulers of the Yemen are using monotheistic formulas that appear to be Jewish or based on Judaic ideas. The adoption of Judaism by the rulers of the Yemen does not necessarily mean that all of the native population was converted, but it does point to the cultural and political attractiveness of Judaism . . ."[672]

Even as late as the twelfth century, long after the supremacy of Islam in most of the Near East, there are reports of sizeable Jewish communities even in the heart of the Arabian Peninsula. Newby cites an Islamic source for a thriving Jewish community in the town of Khaybar, two hundred kilometres north of Medina:

> "Its people claimed to be descendents of the tribes of Reuben, Gad and half the tribe of Manasseh, who were carried as captives by King Shalmaneser of Assyria, and it is the descendants of these captives who built the large town, who now go to war against many kingdoms . . . Hubar (Khaybar) is a very large town with a community of 50,000 Jews, including many scholars and skilled warriors who are not afraid to go to war both against the northerners of Babylon and against the southerners of al-Yemen."[673]

Newby also cites the writings of travellers in later centuries, right up to the nineteenth, which testify to a significant Jewish presence, including Jewish *Bedouin*, in the Hejaz. "Both the persistence and number of reports," he adds, "leads one to conclude that the Jews of northern Arabia probably did survive in some form for a long period after the rise of Islam, but how long and to what extent is impossible to say at this time."[674]

Yemen, the southern-most and most populous part of the Arabian Peninsula, had a longstanding tradition of Christian and Jewish communities. For a period of time, a Jewish kingdom existed there. It is not possible to assess the degree to which Judaic custom and practice infiltrated the mass of the Arab population of southern Arabia, as opposed to the elite within the state, but there is no doubt that this historic Jewish state would have contributed to the reservoir of monotheistic

---

[672]   Gordon Darnell Newby, *A History of the Jews of Arabia*, p 38
[673]   Gordon Darnell Newby, *A History of the Jews of Arabia*, p 101
[674]   Gordon Darnell Newby, *A History of the Jews of Arabia*, p 104

traditions around which early Islam revolved. Although he does not acknowledge it in so many words, Newby clearly hints that it was not the theology but the *social and political situation* faced by ordinary Arabs that was the determining factor in deciding their faith: ". . . adoption of a particular Christological doctrine meant a declaration of loyalty to a religious ideal, a political party, a local language and an ideal of an autonomous region."[675] Although he refers here to the fourth century, the point is equally valid centuries earlier, or later.

Because of its long isolation from its origins in Judea, the Arabian form of Judaism had its own peculiar features which included a strong element of messianism. Even in much of the Islamic tradition, Jews are seen as having predicted the imminent coming of a prophet or a messiah and early Muslim sources relate the story of a Jewish self-proclaimed prophet, Ibn Sayyed, who lived at the same time as Mohammed and was effectively a rival for the ear of Jewish Arab tribes.

Overall, Newby produces such a well-researched historical survey of the influence of Judaism in Arabia as a whole that it is impossible to avoid the conclusion that the particular brand of Arab monotheism that was characterised by extreme piety and practices like circumcision and dietary laws was directly derived from Jewish influences. Indeed, in the highly charged religious polemics that followed the Arab take-over of the Sassanid state, many Nestorian Christians even referred to the Arab monotheists as the "new Jews".[676] This particular Arabian blend of quasi-Jewish monotheism, combined with the Arabian Christian traditions of the former Ghassanid and Lakhmid regions made up the main ingredients from which Islam developed.

As early as the fifth century, in the writings of Sozomen, a chronicler of the city of Gaza, the Christians clearly recognised many of the local Arabs as monotheists of some sort. Sozomen suggested that the Saracens were descended from Ishmael the son of Abraham and were as a result originally called Ishamaelites. According to Sozomen, because their mother Hagar was a slave, they sought to conceal the approbium of their origin and assumed the name of Saracens, as if they were descended from Sara, the wife of Abraham. Because of this origin, he wrote, they practiced circumcision like the Jews, refrained from the use of pork, and observed many other Jewish rites and customs. "Indeed there are some among them, even at the present day," he wrote, "who regulate their lives according to the Jewish precepts."[677] Sozomen goes on to describe how some among the Saracens were converted to Christianity. Sozomen, based in Gaza, clearly did not consider the Saracens to be wholly Christian, although it is not clear which people he was describing: the natives of greater Arabia, to the south, or the Arabs of Syria to the north east. Whatever group he is concerned with, it is a clear indication that

---

[675]   Gordon Darnell Newby, *A History of the Jews of Arabia*, p 36
[676]   Cited by Robinson in *Empire and Elites after the Muslim Conquest,* p 100
[677]   *The Ecclesiastical History of the Church*, p 309.

circumcision and Judaic food laws were in use long before the rise of Islam and that such practices were due to the influence of Judeo-Christianity.

What needs to be emphasised over and over again, is that at the beginning of the seventh century, which for the traditional account is the dawn of Islam, the Arabs in the key areas of Syria and Iraq were already overwhelmingly monotheistic. There may have been pockets of what, for the want of a better expression, may be described as paganism but monotheism was an organic part of the daily life of the majority of Syrian and Iraqi Arabs and this corresponds to what we have already described as the *monotheistic polemic* of the Koran. What is clear from the real historical record and which therefore needs to be emphasised, is that by the time of the arrival of Islam, monotheism in one form or another was dominant in the Arab world. It was within this swirl of contending monotheisms that polemical engagements arose as to which was the true faith: Judaism, Christianity (and which version of these?) or some other generic or Arab form and this *monotheistic sectarian milieu* was the seed-bed of Islam, not the divine revelations of an Arab prophet in the remote city of Mecca.

The wealth of *Christian* traditions (as part of early Arab culture) has been examined by Volker Popp in an essay in *The Hidden History of Islam*, in which he looks particularly at the evidence of coins minted in the early period of the Arab Empire. Popp emphasises the fact that both the Byzantines and the Persian Sassanids had promoted their own brand of Christianity in 'their' Arab areas. This meant, of course, that their competing military, strategic, and material interests were usually dressed up in the language of different Christologies and when, in the first decades of the seventh century, the two empires fought over Palestine, Syria and Iraq, they used mainly their own *Arab Christian* armies.

> "At the end of the sixth century, then, two Arabian dynasties were pitted against one another, with both serving as the representatives of foreign empires, taking the roles of regional rulers, and defending different Christian confessions . . . The war between the two great empires was essentially, in large part, a war of their representatives, led by their Arabian Christian vassals and their successors."[678]

The twenty-year war between the Persian and Byzantine Empires, that included the sacking of Jerusalem, the holiest city for all the varieties of monotheists, was devastating for the whole region. The chronicles of Theophilus of Edessa, written towards the end of the eighth century (although earlier than most Islamic historians) gives some insight into the upheavals caused by the war. Theophilus began his life in Edessa, a Ghassanid Arab city steeped in Syriac Christianity and ended up as a scribe in the Caliph's court in Baghdad, so he probably had some access to earlier sources. He described not only the invasion by Persia but also the devastation

---

[678]   Volker Popp, *The hidden history of Islam,* p 20

caused by the revolution and civil war between the supporters and opponents of the imperial pretender, Phocas.

> "The Persians crossed the Euphrates, subjected the whole of Syria and expelled the Romans from it . . . He killed and enslaved . . . There was no region that rose up against him which he did not devastate and destroy, killing its men and enslaving its populace. And while the Persians were thus ruining Roman territory, Phocas was outdoing them from within by his lack of clemency, killing the leaders of the Romans until his kingdom was bereft of powerful men."[679]

Not surprisingly when the rival Sassanid Empire began a large scale invasion, using their Arab Lakhmid forces, many towns and cities surrendered without resistance. In 614, after a siege, Jerusalem was taken. Within a few years the Persians had even pushed the Byzantines out of Egypt and their conquest is attested by coins minted there after 617, showing the Sassanid emperor, Chosroes II, in the form of a *Christian* ruler. Although the Persian armies did not penetrate very far south into the Arabian Peninsula, for more settled Arabs in the general region of Palestine and Syria this period must have been one of great social and economic upheaval. Theophilus describes in great detail the depredations of the former Byzantine area by the Sassanid armies.

> "The Persians took possession of all the lands of the Romans: Mesopotamia, Syria, Cilicia, Palestine, Egypt and the whole coast. They pillaged and took innumerable captives. They brought into Persia riches, prisoners and all manner of things . . . the power of speech is not capable of recounting the oppression, the exaction of taxes and tribute, the enslavement and slaughter that went on at that time as Khusrau behaved arrogantly due to the victory of the Persians . . ."[680]

The effects of the enormous suffering and dislocation in the former Ghassanid areas would inevitably have been felt by kinsmen and fellow Arabs in the areas to the south and even in the Lakhmid areas to the east. This was the real social backdrop to the rise of a new Arab state and the spread of the specifically Arab and ultra-pious brand of monotheism. The language of social and political conflicts was always the language of religion and the upheaval in this region could not have been without enormous religious significance. The later Islamic tradition relates that the Sassanid occupiers of Jerusalem allowed Jews the hope that they would be permitted to rebuild the Jewish Temple destroyed by the Romans five hundred years earlier, a promise dashed two decades later when the Byzantine Empire re-conquered Jerusalem and built a church on what would have been the temple site. When the

---

[679] Robert G Hoyland (trans), *Theophilus of Edessa's Chronicle*, p 58
[680] Robert G Hoyland (trans), *Theophilus of Edessa's Chronicle*, p 67

Arab empire itself was strong enough, several decades later, they, in turn, conquered the city and, under the caliph Abd Al-Malik, built the Dome of the Rock on the same site.

The first independent Arab state
and the legend of conquest

From within this furnace of revolution, war and conquest the significance of the year 622 emerges as the beginning of the Arab era, because it was in that year that the Byzantine Empire launched its military counter-offensive against the Sassanids with the result that the Persian Empire fell apart. It was the complete destruction of the Persian forces across the whole of Syria and Iraq that marked the beginning of the Arab era, not the migration of a prophet from one remote desert town to another. In the vacuum that resulted from the Sassanid collapse, Arab military units, aided perhaps by raiders from the Arabian Peninsula and Yemen in the south, were able to assume control of most of Syria and Iraq, effectively unifying the Arabs of both Ghassanid and Lakhmid traditions. Rejecting the client status of both of the previous Arab states, this loose federation of tribes approximated to *a new, independent state*, moreover one growing larger month by month by increasingly confident and sizeable raids into Iraq, Iran and south into Egypt.[681]

The new Arab Empire began its existence as a de-centralised and loosely organised state without any guiding religious impulse behind it. The Arab raiders and settlers included Christians and Jews as well as believers in the Arab monotheistic code. The faith of the latter contained an eclectic mixture of Christian and Judaic symbolism, but still, in its supreme piety, it was distinct from both mainstream religions as they were practised in Syria, Iraq and Iran. To begin with, it was happy to sit alongside them. More importantly, it was also quite different from the Islamic faith into which it would later evolve and was most certainly not the state religion at this stage.

The collapse of Sassanid and Byzantine control over this large area and the formation of an independent Arab state was therefore the occasion for the intrusion of a radical, dynamic and distinctly pious brand of monotheism into what had been essentially a Christian milieu. The creation of the new state was not a product of a holy war based on a new and fully-finished religion but a by-product of a scramble for plunder and loot. According to the traditional account the central part of the Islamic state (Syria and Iraq) was conquered from the southern Arabian peninsula by a unified Muslim army under the leadership of the early caliphs; it was only after the first four 'rightly-guided' caliphs that it was taken over by Mu'awiya, the first of the Umayyads. *But, in fact, the archaeological evidence for the traditional conquest narrative is completely absent.*

---

[681] The Persian set-back has left a faint echo in the Koran, in a verse (30, 2) written later as a 'prophesy': "the Byzantines have been defeated in a nearby land. They will reverse their defeat with a victory in a few years' time."

In *Crossroads to Islam*, Nevo and Koren examined the *physical* evidence of archaeological surveys and excavations for the seventh century and although their work was limited to the region of the Negev desert there are nevertheless significant findings. The Negev was effectively an interface between settled and nomadic regions—straddling the ill-defined border between the Ghassanid state and the Arabian hinterland to the south. This area would have been the crossing point for an Arab army moving between the *Hejaz* in the south to the villages and towns around Gaza and Petra, and eventually further north to Jerusalem and Damascus.

The work of Nevo and Koren has not only considerably fleshed out our general understanding of the Ghassanid state in the period before the Arab empire, but it has provided important insights into the years after its demise. Had the traditional story been correct, the remains of Negev towns and villages might be expected to reveal some clues about what would have been one of the first areas to be conquered from the south. In fact, these writers came to the conclusion that there can be no reconciliation between the archaeological evidence and the traditional accounts of the rise of the Islamic state through a conquest planned and organised from Arabia.

> ". . . the archaeological record shows . . . No destruction or abandonment of villages, no reduction in the settled or farmed areas, no diminishing of the population, accompanied the changeover from Byzantine to Arab rule. Both the physical remains (housing, household utensils, etc) and the literary descriptions of daily life show that the modestly comfortable standard of living achieved under Byzantine rule continued unchanged into the Umayyad period . . ."[682]

Nevo and Koren show that the whole of the eastern provinces of the Byzantine empire—the area including Gaza, Jerusalem and Damascus, known generally as Syria—was not so much taken by conquest as by *an effective politico-military withdrawal by the Byzantines.*

The archaeological evidence examined in the Negev by Nevo and Koren demonstrates that the establishment of the new Arab state meant a reversion to the *status quo ante*, as far as the majority of the population were concerned. The administration and government of the region were in the hands of Arab tribes linked to those elsewhere in Syria and Iraq but who remained on the payroll of the Byzantines for a number of years. Although the new regime was far more independent and ambitious—now prepared to conduct raids into Egypt and elsewhere in search of booty—the evidence shows that the majority of the settled Arab population were still Christians, whose Church effectively maintained local administration on behalf of the Arab elite.

The skirmishes that took place after the collapse of the Sassanid occupation were later conflated into large-scale military engagements and battles, but local

---

[682] Yehuda D Nevo and Judith Koran, *Crossroad to Islam*, page 91

sources written before the end of the early eighth century offer no evidence for a planned and large-scale invasion from the south,

> ". . . nor for any great battles which crushed the Byzantine army; nor do they mention any Caliph before Mu'awiya . . . The picture the contemporary literary sources provide is rather of raids of the familiar type; the raiders stayed because they found no military opposition . . . What took place was a series of raids and minor engagements which gave rise to stories among the Arab newcomers of How We Beat the Romans; these were later selected and embellished in late Umayyad and early Abbasid times to form an Official History of the Conquest."[683]

Similarly, the preserved writings of Sophronius, the Christian patriarch of Jerusalem, offer scant evidence of an Islamic invasion. His writings of the year 637 lament the depredations of the barbarians, but especially the "Saracens" in the area around Jerusalem. These, he writes, "have now unexpectedly risen up against us, and are carrying everything off as booty with cruel and savage intent and impious and godless daring."[684] This is not evidence of an organised invasion and describes a situation that could just as easily have come about from the disorganised raids of tribal leaders, warlords and petty kings in the anarchic post-Byzantine period. One thing that is clear is that Sophronius did not call the raiders Muslims and, in common with other Christian accounts of the period, made no reference to Mohammed, the Koran or Islam.

Chase Robinson's investigation of the Jazira region in northern Syria and the region around Mosul in northern Iraq, brought him to similar conclusions to Koren and Nevo. In *Empire and Elites after the Muslim Conquest, The Transformation of Northern Mesopotamia,* he bases his analysis on the relatively mundane records of administration and taxation in these regions. Although the records are very late, like all the Islamic histories, they are arguably more reliable than the fictionalised accounts of heroic deeds and battles. Where, after all, is the motivation for romanticising tax returns? Yet according to Robinson, they reveal significant patterns. He came to the conclusion that in the early days of the collapse of the Sassanid Empire, there was no question of this region of Mesopotamia being part of a unified and centralised Arab state. The new ruling elite collected tribute from the local population intermittently and haphazardly: there was no systematic policy of taxation. To cite Robinson, in the early so-called Islamic period, the Syro-Mesopotamian steppe region was more like a "theatre of tribal drama" than a "revenue-producing province of an empire." It was not until the period of the first civil war and the beginning of the Umayyad regime that anything like a centralised

---

[683] Koren and Nevo, Cited by Donner in *States, Resources and Armies, The Byzantine and Early Islamic Middle East*, p 345

[684] *Sophronius of Jerusalem and Seventh Century Heresy,* Pauline Allen (trans).

state structure began to make itself felt, particularly after the sweeping reforms of Abd Al-Malik.

> ". . . it is not until the 680s—at the earliest—that one can meaningfully speak of Islamic rule in the north. It was the decade from 685 to 695, rather than that of 635 to 645, that signals a break in Jaziran history. To varying degrees, the same thing could be said about other regions . . ."[685]

M A Shaban is another author who bases his history on a re-interpretation of the traditional sources, although he accepts the traditional myth that there was a large-scale invasion planned and organised in Medina. But even he is forced to accept that there is little evidence of any centralised authority in the early days of the empire:

> ". . . except for the broadest policy decisions for the regime as a whole, Medina exercise virtually no control over the newly conquered territories. *Central government as such did not exist* since such an institution demands a vast bureaucracy and Medina had none . . ."[686]

What really happened, therefore, was that the collapsing Sassanid Empire fell *piecemeal* into the hands of Arab clans, warlords and raiders, without there having been any overall plan, strategy or organisation. *There was no religiously motivated invasion behind this process,* only a short-term thirst for booty and an expectation of longer-term payment of tribute.

> "It is a well known fact that as the Empire of the Sassanids fell piece by piece into the hands of the Arabs, the latter maintained, with but few modifications, the system of administration which had long existed. Not only was the system itself preserved, but the language in which the records were kept continued in use; and where possible the officials who had worked for the Sassanids remained in office under the Arabs . . . In the Sawad [Syria], the agents who acted on behalf of the Arabs appear to have been a few surviving members of the old nobility, and principally the *dahqin,* or lords of the villages, large holders of land."[687]

The difficulty of using the traditional accounts to pick a way through the conquest legend is described by Hugh Kennedy who was trying to write a history of the Arab conquest. He reveals that in the traditional scenario, key events in the alleged

---

[685]   Chasse Robinson, *Empires and Elites after the Muslim Conquest, The Transformaiton of Northern Mesopotamia,* p 34

[686]   M A Shaban, *Islamic History,* p 55 (italics added)

[687]   Daniel C Dennett, *Conversion and Poll Tax in Early Islam,* p 14

conquest of Syria and Iraq are full of confusion and contradictions, even about key events like battles.

> "The narratives of the early Muslim conquests are replete with confusion and improbability, and are often impossible to accept at face value. Modern authors have tended to approach these in two ways: either to dismiss them as hopelessly inaccurate and not worth the attention of serious historians; or to cherry-pick them for incidental details, names, places, etc."[688]

Kennedy nevertheless soldiered on, relying principally on the works of Baladhuri who died about a hundred and fifty years after the first Arab state was founded and Tabari, who died about thirty years after Baladhuri. The vagueness, as he points out, is particularly noticeable in relation to the *earliest phase of the conquests,* when there were supposed to have been key battles in Syria and Iraq, for which the dates given in the traditional accounts range over three or four years. It is the stories of the early battles that have the strongest whiffs of outright fiction:

> "In general, the accounts of the first phases of the conquests, from the 630s to the 650s, are generally replete with the mythical and tropical elements, imagined speeches and dialogue and lists of names of participants. They are correspondingly short of details about topography and terrain, equipment and tactics."[689]

Most important of all, as Kennedy admits, *there is no archaeological evidence at all for the early conquests.* One would look in vain for evidence of a large-scale violent and destructive conquest: it is "archaeologically invisible."[690] The sites of the alleged great battles of Yarmuk in Syria and Qadisiya in Iraq have never been identified, despite centuries of searching and there are no ruined towns or burnt-out remains that fit into the scenario of a conquest at that time. The sum of the archaeological evidence from Syria points to a seamless transition. "Led by its cities, Syria-Palestine passed quietly and almost willingly without even the slightest whimper into a new and momentous age, the significance of which was neither recognised nor appreciated at the time."[691]

The conclusion to which we are inevitably drawn from the real, surviving evidence is that the incipient Arab empire was originally no more than a loose and confused series of alliances. These loose alignments of Arab tribal elites were the subject of fierce internal power struggles between a variety of leaders, one of whom may or may not have been called Mohammed. Chronologically, this long period of instability coincides with the setting for the traditional story of the life of Mohammed and it is likely,

---

[688]   Hugh Kennedy, *The Great Arab Conquests*, p 5
[689]   Hugh Kennedy, *The Great Arab Conquests*, p 27
[690]   Alan Walmsley, *Early Islamic Syria, an Archeological Assessment*, p 21
[691]   Alan Walmsley, *Early Islamic Syria, an Archeological Assessment*, p 47

therefore, that the traditional account is no more than a reflection of these real events. The details of the 'conquest' by an 'Islamic' army and the wars of conquest waged by Mohammed and his successors Abu Bakr, Umar, Uthman and Ali, are not recorded in any contemporary accounts or proven by any archaeological evidence. What may have been genuine rivalries between tribes and regions, most likely over their shares of the spoils of occupation, could have provided the foundation of the story of the Uthman-Ali rivalry, which is described as the origin of the Sunni/Shia split.

The traditional story of the first civil war between the supporters of Ali and Mu'awiya is no more than an echo of this unstable period before the Umayyads established complete control of the region from their power base in Syria, against rival Arab elites based in Kufa in Iraq. The rivalry between the 'east' and the 'west' was not based, as later Islamic histories would rationalise it, on the struggle for succession between the Companions of the Prophet, but on the different spheres of influence of what had been the original stamping grounds of the Ghassanid and the Lakhmid Arab elites. The first civil war, which established the semi-centralised state of Mu'awiya, also reflected the rivalry between the primitive 'democracy' of the tribal structures and the centralising tendencies of the incipient government. These conflicts were further antagonised by rivalries between the original Arab populations of Iraq and Syria and those Arab migrants and raiders who had moved to the new state to join in the plunder. The looters were falling out over shares of the booty and all these rivalries are reflected in Islamic histories of the civil wars and the so-called *ridda* wars which were against those Arab tribes who were said to have rejected Mohammed and looked instead to their own prophets and leaders.

It is not surprising that the accounts of the conquest and civil wars are so full of contradictions. Many different accounts were written or developed in oral tradition with the sole purpose of inflating the roles of this or that clan or tribal leader. Indeed, later claims to property and wealth depended on these tales. Thus, every skirmish became a major battle and every battle had a thousand decisive heroes who saved the day. So when the conquest stories were written down centuries later and they were left for historians to pick over a thousand years after that, the net result is either pure subjectivity (picking out what looks like a plausible story) or academic head-scratching.

Where the traditional account coincides with real history (at least in *broad* terms) is in the historical reality of the civil war that brought Mu'awiya to power as the first Umayyad caliph and *the first Arab leader attested by external (ie non-Islamic) historical evidence*. The traditional accounts of the first civil war (as a struggle for succession between the Prophet's nephew, Ali and Mu'awiya) are fabulous stories based on traces of real events: of Mu'awiya's emergence as the regional strong man, exerting his military authority over his rivals. It is important to note that there is some dispute about the dating of the first Umayyad Caliphs, the traditional date being 661 CE, but other scholars push the date further back nearer to 640. It took a second phase of civil war, leading to the caliphate of Marwan in 685, to completely consolidate Umayyad rule. Although most historians today use the Islamic narratives to describe the events of the first half of the seventh century, they blithely skip over the fact that they are using sources that were not contemporary to the events and which are wrong in much of the detail.

King Mu'awiya and the beginning of the Umayyad regime

The only certainty we really have, therefore, is that the first half of the seventh century saw a devastating war in this region between the Persian and Byzantine Empires, with the Persians gaining territory in the earlier phase and losing it again in the subsequent phase, at which point a new Arab state came into being. This new state included Lakhmid and Ghassanid Christians as well as newcomers from the south. For the first few decades of its existence it was an unstable and loose federation, torn by tribal feuds, with constant mutual raiding until eventually some measure of stability was achieved by the establishment of the first Umayyad 'king' Mu'awiya (see Table of Caliphs). For nearly forty years, the Arab forces were strong enough to fill the vacuum left by the Sassanid armies but too divided to form a significant centralised state, one even capable of minting coins, building monuments or leaving any other trace of itself in history.

Although Mu'awiya is the first caliph attested by archaeological evidence, the Arab state even during his reign still did not have the strong, centralised apparatus and bureaucracy it came to have under the reign of his eventual successor (after a further period of civil war), Abd Al-Malik. Mu-awiya's regime may have initiated what was in effect a hereditary monarchy, but it was still a very loose tributary state, much weaker in its central organisation than its successors. The following passage from the *Maronite Chronicle* was probably written after Mu'awiya's reign, but it reflects a real transformation from a loose federal arrangement to something more like a unified state:

> "Many Arabs gathered at Jerusalem and made Mu'awiya king . . . the emirs and many Arabs gathered and gave their allegiance to Mu'awiya. Then an order went out that he should be proclaimed king in all the villages and cities of his dominion and that they should make acclamation and invocations to him. He also minted gold and silver [coins] . . . Furthermore, Mu'awiya did not wear a crown like other kings in the world . . ."[692]

Rather than being a product of a centrally planned and organised conquest, therefore, the incipient Arab empire based in Syria and Iraq was the result of events that were much more haphazard, unplanned and accidental than the traditional accounts would have us believe. Its origin was anything but a religiously-inspired conquest of the Arab world, as the traditional histories describe it. Accepting that an Arab state came into being at this time, the questions that must be posed are: what

---

[692]   Cited by Jeremy Johns, *Archaeology and the History of Early Islam*, p 423 (italics added)

was the class character of the state and what religious outlook was predominant in its population and in its ruling class? As we have explained, there are no contemporary written accounts that we can use to answer these questions and all the traditional histories were written centuries later. But such evidence as does exist in the form of physical remains strongly points to the continuation of a generalised *Christian tradition*, not only alongside, but probably *still more important* than the Arab monotheistic tradition.

John of Penkaye, the Syrian monk who wrote towards the end of the seventh century, reflected the general view of Syriac Christian writers of the period in that he saw the upheavals of the Persian invasion and the later Arab state's domination as Acts of God, punishment for the sinfulness of the local people. It is interesting that this chronicler, writing at a time much closer to the real events than the majority of Islamic historians, gives a completely different picture of the emergence of the early Arab state compared to the traditional account.

> "When the kingdom of the Persians came to an end . . . the kingdom of the children of Hagar at once gained control over more or less the whole world . . . So the Lord, to punish the sons of Hagar for the ravages they had made, *gave them two leaders from the beginning of their kingdom* and divided them into two sections . . . but they were united until they had subjected the whole earth, but *when they returned to tranquility and rested from war, they fought one another.* Those in the West said: "superiority is due to us, and the king must be chosen from among us." Those of the East contradicted them and claimed that it was to them that this was due. As a result of this contention, they came to blows. *When they had settled the business according to their methods, the victory fell to the Westerners called Umayyads,* and this after a great slaughter that took place between them. *A man among them named Mu'awiya took the reins of government of the two empires:* Persian and Roman."[693]

The Islamic tradition, which does indeed describe civil war between different Arab leaders in the period before the Umayyad dynasty, and which is framed in religious terms, is an echo of these real events. This Syriac chronicler also hints at what may have been later conflated into the great Uthman-Ali rivalry in his reference to the 'men of the east' and those of 'the west'. Robinson's studies of the northern provinces of Syria and Iraq also indicate that there were rival collectors of taxes and tribute who were based in Kufa (in Iraq) and Syria. What is clear is that the incipient Arab state was racked by warlordism and petty conflicts—what Chase Robinson described as "a competitive and (sometimes) fractious milieu of local and imperial elites"—after the take-over of the rapidly collapsing Persian Empire. Mu'awiya, who was the first strong man to assert himself over the Arab armies as a whole, became

---

[693] John of Penkaye, www.tertullian.org (italics added)

the first caliph to be evidenced by sources outside the Islamic literature. It was only at this point that the traditional conquest story begins to correspond to real events because it was only after Mu'awiya's assumption of power that the Arab Empire began to expand its borders by the organised conquest and infiltration of regions beyond the old Sassanid Empire, in the Caucasus, eastwards towards Afghanistan and India and in the west as far as North Africa and Spain.

Following the accession of Mu'awiya, according to John of Penkaye, there was a period of peace and tranquillity and he cited the influence of the Arabs' leader, "Muhammad" for their tolerance towards Christians.

> ". . . they were so attached to the tradition of Muhammad, who was their leader, that they inflicted the death penalty on anyone who seemed not to obey his commands. Their troops went every year into distant countries and islands, raided and brought back captives from all the nations that are under heaven. From every man they required only the tribute, and left him free to hold any belief, and there were even *some Christians among them: some belonged to the heretics and others to us.* While Mu'awiya reigned there was such a great peace in the world as was never heard of . . ."[694]

Despite this mention of Mohammed, this account is but a pale reflection of the traditional story of the foundation of the Islamic community through Mohammed, Abu Bakr, Umar, Uthman and Ali, and it is clear that Christianity was not only tolerated but was *an accepted part of social life*. Indeed, *some of the occupying forces who were exacting tribute were themselves Christians.* The writings of John of Penkaye are a clear indication that the early days of the Arab empire were infused with more than just a little lingering Christianity. In fact, in bemoaning the sinfulness of the general population, the chronicler saw little difference between the sinners of different faiths:

> "Let's talk about the people; it is open to everyone to live like a sheep, in his own way. The law isn't for him, so he transgresses the law . . . What wickedness does not our perverse century bear! *There was no difference between pagan and Christian, the believer was not distinct from the Jew,* and did not differ from the deceiver"[695]

There is also recorded the comment by the Patriarch of the Church of the East, writing to a correspondent around the year 650:

> "As for the Arabs, to whom God has at this time given rule over the world, you know well how they act toward us. *Not only do they not oppose*

---

[694] John of Penkaye, www.tertullian.org (italics added)
[695] John of Penkaye, book 15. See www.tertullian.org (italics added)

Christianity, *but they praise our faith, honour the priests and saints of our Lord,* and give aid to the churches and monasteries"[696]

Wellhausen is one of those historians we have quoted who bases his history on the traditional accounts but he noted that the Christians and Arab monotheists (those he describes as Muslims) often shared places of worship. In Syria, he wrote:

"The Muslims there did not live apart in colonies founded especially for them, but together with the children of the land in the old towns of Damascus, Edessa, Qunnesrin, etc. They even sometimes went shares in the use of a place of worship, which then became half church and half mosque. The Christian traditions of Palestine and Syria . . . were also held in high esteem by the Muslims; Syria was for them, too, the Holy Land. Mu'awiya' had himself proclaimed Caliph in Jerusalem; afterwards he prayed at Golgotha and at the grave of St Mary." [697]

Here, Wellhausen's source for the story of Mu'awiya's praying at this Christian site is indirectly from a poet who lived in the Ghassanid region in the seventh century. It is worth commenting that when he describes buildings as "half church and half mosque", he is using the modern understanding of a mosque and projecting it back, without real justification, to a totally different arrangement in the past.

The thriving of Christianity in this period of early Islam is well testified in coins and inscriptional evidence. In the essay already cited, Volker Popp describes coins dated from 641 (year 20 of the Arab era) that have been found bearing the name Mu'awiya and which are believed to have been minted in Iran. These are the earliest dated coins of the Arab era and are minted in the traditional Sassanid style, with the name Mu'awiya in *Aramaic* rather than Arabic. Popp also cites the example of a building inscription in Palestine, erected during the reign of Mu'awiya, which is in Greek and which *bears the sign of the cross* at the beginning. In describing Mu'awiya, the inscription, uses the title *Abd Allah*, 'servant of God'. Volker Popp argues from this inscription and the marking of coins that this title was adopted by the Arab rulers to distinguish themselves from the Sassanids. It appears, he explains, on eight sets of coins from different mints in this period.

The region of the modern-day state of Jordan was part of ancient Syria and its archaeology shows that the number of Christian churches actually increased in the early period of the new Arab regime.

"The building boom, in the 6th and early 1st / 7th centuries, of churches seen in the cities and towns of Jordan did not change only the physical appearance of the towns but also contributed to the formulation of the

---

[696]   Cited by Sidney H Griffith, *The Journal of Syriac Studies*, Vol 3, No 1, January 2000 (italics added)

[697]   Julius Wellhausen, *The Arab Kingdom and its Fall*, p 133

city's Christian identity and in the Umayyad period this ecclesiastical 'civic structure' remained largely intact. Not only did churches continue to serve as houses of worship, but new churches were built and paved . . . what is remarkable in these churches is the continued use of Greek inscriptions with the indication of the Byzantine calendar year . . ."[698]

Archaeological digs have shown that in the area of modern Jordan there were over fifty churches in use right up to the mid-eighth century and eight new churches were built, complete with coloured mosaics and inscriptions in Greek. The Jordanian Ministry of Tourism puts this down to there being "little assimilation" between the "new Muslim rulers" and the local Christian communities. Far more likely, it is an indication that the Islamic conquest was no such thing. Even the man from the ministry is forced to admit that the "Arab immigrants" were "no more than a small fraction of the total population of the region and the countryside remained largely Christian and agriculturally prosperous." If the number of new immigrants was relatively slight throughout the Umayyad period, it was because the overwhelming majority of the population of Jordan *were already Arab as well as Christian* and little changed in their lives during the Umayyad dynasty except that they recovered from the privations of the Persian conquest and the unstable early decades of the new Arab state before the accession of Mu'awiya.

In his study of the early changes in northern Iraq and Syria, Chase Robinson came to the same conclusion: ". . . regardless of what jurists of the ninth and tenth centuries may have said, in the north (particularly Edessa and Tur Abdin) we have graphic evidence of continued church building . . . As far as the Christians were concerned, the evidence suggests that the controversy lay not in the legality of the church building under Islam, but rather in who had authority over the churches once built."[699]

In his essay reviewing the Christian tradition within the early Arab Empire Volker Popp noted that a Palestinian inscription from the period has a date that is recorded as the year 42 "following the Arabs". At that time, he argues, *the life of the Prophet was unknown* to the majority of Arabs and they were content to refer to their method of dating as the "Arab era." Popp also draws attention to a copper coin minted in Merv in Eastern Iran, dated to the Arabian Year 63, which also includes a cross, showing that the new Arab-dominated regime continued to mint coins based on the previous Sassanid model, rather than on an 'Islamic' model. Popp also suggests that Mu'awiya was represented by his eventual successor, Abd Al-Malik, as being comparable to Saul, the first king of the Hebrew Testament. Around the same time, Abd al-Malik issued some coins with a five-branched lamp stand similar to the *menorah*, the seven-branched lamp stands of traditional Judaism.

---

[698]   *The Umayyads. The Rise of Islamic Art*, Jordanian Ministry of Tourism, 2000, p 55.

[699]   Chase Robinson, *Empires and Elites after the Muslim Conquest, The Transformaiton of Northern Mesopotamia*, pp 13,14

"It is not without good cause that his [Mu'awiya's] successor, AbdAl-Malik, presented him as "Saul", in the sense of the Old Testament tradition, while presenting himself as a "new David", indeed, naming his own son *Sulayman* (Solomon)."[700]

<table>
<tr><td colspan="2" align="center">**Chapter 15 Time-line: The origins of the Arab Empire and later origins of Islam**</td></tr>
<tr><td align="center">**Dates**</td><td align="center">**Events**</td></tr>
<tr><td align="center">600</td><td>Palace coup in Constantinople, **upheaval in Byzantine Empire**. **Sassanid invasion** and devastation of Byzantine territories</td></tr>
<tr><td></td><td>**622 Byzantine counter-offensive** leads to collapse of Persian Empire. First independent Arab state. **The 'Arab era' begins** | Arab state consists of **loose federations** of Arab tribes, some Jewish, some Christian, some 'Arab' monotheists. Divided by **civil wars** until eventually a single 'strong man' takes power</td></tr>
<tr><td align="center">650</td><td>**Mu'awiya** crowned caliph and **Umayyad dynasty** inaugurates a unified state</td></tr>
<tr><td align="center">700</td><td>**Abd Al-Malik** becomes caliph. **Dome of the Rock built. Mohammed** now becomes central to the state religion. Sweeping new measures are introduced to further centralise state administration and taxes.</td></tr>
<tr><td align="center">750</td><td>**Abbasid revolution** and beginnings of most written tradition</td></tr>
</table>

The survival and even growth of the Christian community in the early period of the Arab empire was not due to tolerance on the part of the new elite. It was mainly due to it being the traditional religion of the majority of the Arab population in the core regions of the empire. Besides which, the apparatus of the Church was also the most efficient way of milking the local economy of taxes and tribute. As we have argued in previous sections, the growth of the Christian church was in no small part due to its social role in providing local government and a tax-raising structure on behalf of the Roman Empire, with the added bonus that the promise of a glorious afterlife helped to keep the masses in check. In the early period of the Arab Empire, therefore, the numerically small Arab elite had to rely on the Church to raise tribute for them.

"Byzantinists may argue about how clearly bishops' local authority was recognised by Constantinople, but that bishops and land owners were now

---

[700] Popp, *The hidden history of Islam*, p 36

wielding wide-ranging powers in the cities is anything but controversial . . . Edessa [in northern Syria] fits a regional pattern, for local (and early) hagiographies have Christians in charge of civil affairs in several towns in the north . . ."[701]

Chapter summary

- In the Arab world, including the Arabian Peninsula, *monotheism was the predominant faith* and there were long-standing traditions of Judaism and Christianity. Polytheism was not significant within the Arab populations.

- What is today Israel, Palestine, Syria and Iraq was the real strategic heart and the starting point of the Arab Empire, not the economic and political backwater of the Arabian Peninsula. By the time of the beginning of the Arab Empire, these parts of the world had been both *Arab* and *Christian* for centuries.

- Up to the beginning of the seventh century, the core region of what was to become the Arab Empire was divided between the Byzantines and the Sassanid (Persian) Empires. Social upheaval, revolution and war preceded the establishment of the first independent Arab state. An organised Islamic conquest of the core regions of Syria, Palestine and Iraq is largely a myth.

- A specifically Arab tradition of monotheism, mostly originating in Judaism, became an important ingredient in the melting pot when the Arab Empire developed. This Arab monotheism saw itself as more pious and 'purer' than its sister faiths.

- The dating of the Arab era (equivalent to 622 CE) is based on the date of the collapse of the Sassanid Empire and first independent Arab state. The subsequent *Arab* Empire was not an *Islamic* Empire.

- The early phase of the Arab state was characterised by a loose federation of tribes, broken by warlordism and clan rivalries, chiefly between eastern and western Arabs. It ended with the coronation of Mu'awiya, the first of the Umayyad caliphs and the first Arab king to be attested by non-Islamic sources.

---

[701]   Chase Robinson, *The Transformation of Northern Mesopotamia*, p 57

Chapter 16

Abd Al-Malik's centralised state

In this section we will deal at some length with the special role of the Caliph Abd Al-Malik, towards the end of the seventh century. He was the first to develop a centralised system of government, taxation and administration for the Arab Empire and his reign signalled the development of an Arabic and an Islamic identity. We shall show that as part of his religious reforms he built the Dome of the Rock as the first major place of worship, on the site of the Jewish Temple in Jerusalem, and that this construction was not a mosque. We shall show that it was only towards the end of the seventh century, during the reign of Abd Al-Malik, that the Prophet Mohammed began to be featured as the centre-piece of Islamic theology and that even this may have been originally based on a generic word meaning praiseworthy rather than a personal name. It was, therefore, the accession of Abd Al-Malik that gave a significant impulse to the development of modern Islam as a separate religion clearly distinguishable from Christianity. His caliphate marked a new departure in that it saw the first serious attempt to create a highly centralised imperial system which necessarily sought an ideological expression for the changes that were being implemented.

. . . .

Abd Al-Malik's father, Marwan[702], became caliph after a short civil war and the first necessity for him and his sons was military consolidation. The first Umayyad caliph, Mu'awiya, had gone a long way to unifying the empire, but the caliphate was by no means secure from all claimants. The second civil war (which is once again echoed in the traditional Muslim histories) reflected, like the first, the different interests of the eastern and western Arab elites. It was again the western Arabs, based in Damascus, who confirmed the pre-eminence of the Marwanid branch of the Umayyad family. They were quick to exact their revenge on the eastern Arabs; a thirteenth century chronicle records that the Marwanids appointed a new governor in Iraq who "destroyed without mercy, killing Arab leaders and looting their houses."

The state centralisation that was begun by Mu'awiya and continued by Marwan was carried through even more dramatically by the latter's son, Abd Al-Malik. It represented the replacement of a temporary elite of soldiers and tribesmen with a more settled and permanent, landowning Arab ruling class, working with and

---

[702]   Hence the caliphates of him and his sons are referred to as the 'Marwanids'.

alongside the old landowners. Where they did not actually *replace* the old local elite (and they relied in most cases on them to raise taxation on their behalf) the new Arab landowning class successfully merged with their predecessors. In some areas they only supplanted them over many generations.

It was not only in the east that the Marwanid branch of the Umayyads needed to consolidate. Revolt had to be suppressed also in the south, where an uprising had broken out in the Arabian Peninsula, based in Medina. The basis for the later elevation of this city and Mecca into having a central role in the foundation of Islam originated in the rivalry between Abd Al-Malik and an opponent, Ibn al-Zubayr, who was based here. According to the Chronicles of Theophanes, in 684, "The Arabs of Medina, troubled and aroused, made Abd Allah son of Zubayr their ruler . . . Abd Al-Malik . . . overpowered the rebels, killing Abd Allah, son of Zubayr."[703] This short account misses out the later tradition of a bitter siege of Mecca, including the near destruction of the Ka'ba, something that would have been impossible if the town had had the attachment to Islam that it came to have in later centuries.

The Islamic histories record that the Umayyad regime was beset by frequent revolts of the *Kharijites* and although the details may have been liberally edited or romanticised over the years, the centralising regime of the Marwanids elicited some opposition from those tribesmen and soldiers who were least favoured in land allocations, or who were otherwise disaffected from the burgeoning central power. Later historians have dressed up the Kharijites in the livery of Islamic piety and have linked all their revolts and activities in the civil wars to their supposed religious outlook. But it is questionable how much these tribal revolutionaries were a homogenous group in the first place and even more doubtful that they would have seen themselves as later historians saw them. They represented the last remnants of the marauding and raiding traditions of Arabian tribesmen but they also incorporated dissident Arab soldiers and peasants in general. They were the "Levellers" of Arab tradition and came to be involved in frequent and unsuccessful revolts after the Marwanid succession. Kharijism, Robinson argued, was "the Islamic form of that political and revolutionary edge of social action towards which banditry, given the appropriate conditions, can move."[704]

Despite their description by later historians as pious Muslims, the Kharijites may have even had Christians within their bands. Tabari, the Islamic historian with no particular reason to exaggerate the link between the two faiths, noted that the tax collectors and agents of the Umayyads were hated and he put the following words in the mouth of a local villager, when addressing Kharijite bandits hiding in the village church:

". . . these [Umayyad] people are tyrannical; they will not be spoken to, and they do not accept a plea. By God, if news reaches them that you are

---

[703]   Harry Turtledove, *The Chronicles of Theophanes*, p 59
[704]   Chase Robinson in *The Transformation of Northern Mesopotamia*, p 113

staying in our church, they will kill us when you leave (if you are so fated). We beseech you, stay near to [that is, not in] the village so that you do not create for them a grievance against us."[705]

This is a highly illuminating comment, not only because it has the piously Islamic Kharijites sheltering *in a church*, because it strongly suggests that these local bandits had support among local villagers who wanted them to stay "near".

The interests of Caliph Abd Al-Malik lay, of course, in a centralised empire as a *stable source of revenue* for the imperial centre and to that end he instituted important fiscal and administrative reforms that sought to regularise taxation and tribute across all of his territories. Prior to the caliphate of Abd Al-Malik there was no formal regime of taxation because there was no centralised state authority to administer it. The systems that existed varied enormously from region to region.[706] The *Zuqnin Chronicle*, an eighth century Syriac document, describes a census (*ta'dil*) carried out by Abd Al-Malik among the Syrians:

> ". . . Abd Al-Malik carried out a *ta'dil* on the Syrians [ie the Christian inhabitants of the north]. He issued a harsh order that everyone go to his region, village and father's house, so that everyone would register his name, his lineage [literally, 'whom he was the son of'], his crops and olive trees, his possessions, his children, and everything he owned. From this time, the *gizya* [head tax] began to be levied per capita; from this time, all the evils were visited upon the Christians . . . until this time, kings had taken tribute from the land, rather than from men. From this time the sons of Hagar began to inflict on the sons of Aram [Syria] servitude like the servitude of Egypt . . ."[707]

The regime of Abd Al-Malik introduced a programme of fiscal centralisation on a scale not seen before. In the region of Gaza in southern Syria, the Nessana papyri show the shift towards a tighter tax regime. Prior to his caliphate, the papyri record requisitions made upon the villages in the area of Gaza which were clearly *occasional* as opposed to *regular* demands of tribute. They had previously been paid in advance, in kind, in the form of grain and oil and were probably used to support the relatively small forces of Arab troops stationed in and around Gaza. In total, the amounts that were demanded of the Gaza villages were relatively slight and affordable. However, the situation changed after Abd Al-Malik became caliph. For the first time there is evidence in the papyri for a centralised administration of taxes and a register of households is evidence of a census made for taxation purposes. The two taxes that were imposed on the local people by the Egyptian province on behalf of the Arab empire, a land tax and a poll tax, were together far more onerous

---

[705] Tabari, II, 938
[706] See, for example *Conversion and Poll Tax in Early Islam,* by Daniel C Dennett.
[707] Cited by Chase Robinson in *The Transformation of Northern Mesopotamia*, p 45.

than the occasional requisitions under Mu'awiya. "So onerous were the new taxes," Jeremy Johns writes in *Archaeology and the History of Early Islam*, "that four or more villages, including Nessana, planned to send a joint delegation to the governor in Gaza to protest and to seek remission."[708]

The contrast between the reigns of the caliph Mu'awiya and Abd Al-Malik is evident in extensive testimony in Egyptian papyri as well and in the evidence of non-Muslim authors "who howl in protest at the administration and fiscal reforms instituted by Abd Al-Malik". The reign of Mu'awiya, was remembered in comparison, as a "golden age."[709] Not surprisingly, John of Penkaye, writing around this time, yearned for the good old days when Mu'awiya was caliph: the Syrian Christians had been treated more gently because what he called the "robber bands" of the Arabs had gone elsewhere for their plunder.

It was as a further means of legitimisation of his reign that Abd Al-Malik also initiated a programme of 'Arabising' and 'Islamicising' the empire. The Arabic language was declared to be the official language of the empire and all official documents, treaties, laws and trade agreements were written in Arabic. Like all ruling classes, the Arab elite sought to justify its existence, in this case by a dramatic and historic shift in the form and content of Arab monotheism so it could stand as a rival to the Christianity of the Byzantine Empire.

Much of the Jewish and Christian *written* tradition at this time was still in Hebrew, Greek and Syriac. It is inevitable, therefore, that those *Arabic* religious texts that were circulating at this time (including all the old translations from Syriac Christianity that formed the basis of 'Koranic' literature) would be given greater legitimacy as official religious guidance, as compared to rival Greek or Syriac texts. It was most likely in this period, therefore, that the first attempts were made to gather such traditions into a definitive collection, as an Arabic holy book. Some traditions suggest, in fact, that it was during the reign of Abd Al-Malik that the definitive Koran was collected and others destroyed. This timing for the gathering together of different components to create the Koran (the end of the seventh century) corresponds to the conclusions we have already cited of Mondher Sfar, in *In search of the Original Koran*. In the final assembly of what would more or less be the modern Koran, it would have also been necessary to add odd verses here and there, like the additional sections which make reference to false verses.

Suleiman Bashear, another of those whose work we have used, also links the assertion of Arabic as the official state language with newly-created traditions about the centrality of both the language and the culture of the Bedouin in Islamic history. From having been looked down upon like country bumpkins, the Bedouin more and more assumed the romantic mantle of ancient tradition. It was from this point, too, that traditions began to be created about Arabic being the language of Heaven and other languages (sometimes Greek, sometimes Pahlavi) being spoken

---

[708] Jeremy Johns, *Archaeology and the History of Early Islam*, p 422
[709] Jeremy Johns, *Archaeology and the History of Early Islam*, p 422

in Hell. Although it is recognised that the Koran includes borrowed words from Syriac and other languages, tradition from this time onwards affirmed Arabic as the one and only authentic language of the Koran, the language of God. Along with the assertion of an Arabian identity for the Koran and the Prophet, the ethnicity of God's chosen people was more and more clearly defined. Bashear refers to traditions developing at this time about everyone in Heaven being white so that even righteous black Muslims became white when they passed into Paradise.

> "The improvement in the position not only of Arabic, but also of the Arabs, was part of the process of fusion that resulted in the Arabisation of Islam and the Islamisation of the Arab polity. One dimension of this process is clearly reflected in traditions that rehabilitate the previous position of Bedouins, reconcile them with Islam and result in the emergence of an Arab ethnic entity related to its Bedouin roots."[710]

It was Abd Al-Malik who gave an impulse to the forging of an Islamic identity so it morphed from being a generic monotheism only vaguely different from its influential antecedents, into a new and free-standing system of belief in its own right. This change was not due to a dramatic attack of piety on the part of Abd Al-Malik but was driven by the direct material interests of the ruling elite he represented. It was as a public statement of the special *Arab* character of his faith that Abd Al-Malik built the first great centre of worship for the Arabs *in Jerusalem* on the site of the ancient Jewish Temple. It was as a gesture of the importance of this new Arab monotheism that Abd Al-Malik built the Dome of the Rock literally as a monumental rival to any of the great cathedrals or basilicas of which the Byzantines might boast.

> ". . . the very fact that the Arabs had built a sanctuary on the site of the Jewish Temple could be considered not only as an act comparable with the rebuilding of the Temple, a deed by which the most ancient holy place of the world and the symbol of the unity of Christendom was adopted by the new religion, but also as an event by which Islam could claim to be the successor of the other two monotheistic religions of the Near East."[711]

No mosque has been found to be earlier than this great cathedral of worship, despite a century and a half of archaeological research and it is notable that its overall octagonal shape bears no resemblance to later mosque designs. It was not a mosque. The design and site of construction in Jerusalem reflected the fact that Abd Al-Malik's brand of monotheism had by no means settled into what later became modern Islam. There are many Islamic traditions about an earlier abandoned

---

[710] Bashear, *Arabs and Others in Early Islam*, p 53
[711] Reinink, *Syriac Christianity under Late Sasanian and Early Islamic Rule*, IX, p 183

attempt by the caliph Umar to construct a temple on the same site. Theophilus writes,

> "At this time, while the Arabs were building the Temple of Solomon in Jerusalem, the construction collapsed. The Jews said 'if you do not take down the cross which is placed opposite the Temple on the Mount of Olives, the temple will not be built. As soon as they took down this cross, the construction stood firm . . ."[712]

These traditions are a form of historical gossip unfounded in fact, but interesting in the telling. Linking the Dome of the Rock with the Jews of Jerusalem, however tenuously, softens the embarrassment of the somewhat awkward historical fact that the early Muslims built their first place of worship on the site of the Jewish Temple.

The Dome of the Rock has important inscriptions which offer some of the earliest evidence of Arab religious views. For that reason, the inscriptions—one within the inner octagon of the building and the other around the outside—have been the subject of intense debate and discussion right up to modern times. That, in itself, is revealing, because their interpretation is not as clear cut and as simple as modern Muslim scholars would have us believe. Almost unanimously there is a consensus among non-Muslims that the inscription is not Islamic in the modern sense. The wording of the inscriptions is clearly *polemical*—an attempt by a specifically *Arab* monotheism (some would argue that it was still an Arab form of Christianity) to distinguish itself from those strands of Trinitarian Christianity with which it disagreed. Many parts of the inscriptions are similar to polemical parts of the Koran. In *The Hidden History of Islam*, Christoph Luxenburg, a scholar in ancient Semitic languages, who we have already cited, translates two sections of part of the Dome inscription as follows:

> "For (verily) the Messiah Jesus, son of Mary, (is) the messenger of God and his Word (Logos), (which) he has infused into Mary, along with his Spirit, / So, believe in God and his messengers, and do not say 'three'; / cease (doing that); (it would be) better for you. / For (verily) God is a unique God—may he be praised!—how could he then have a child! . . . O God, bless your messenger and servant Jesus, son of Mary!"[713]

At this early stage in the development of Arab monotheism the direction of prayer was not towards Mecca but, as it was with pious Jews and Christians, *towards Jerusalem*. There is a later rationalisation for switching to Mecca in the rather neat explanation that Mohammed ordered the change during his time in Medina. This story is a later fiction to explain away awkward facts, as was the tradition that the site was the spot from which Mohammed was taken up to heaven. Yet another

---

[712] Hoyland, Robert G (trans), *Theophilus of Edessa's Chronicle*, p 126
[713] Christopher Luxenburg, *The Hidden History of Islam,* p 128.

late Islamic tradition explains that Abd Al-Malik ordered Muslims to pray in the direction of Jerusalem because at that time the city of Mecca was occupied by his opponents and was therefore inaccessible, an explanation repeated by historian Julius Wellhausen. But the commissioning of an enormous temple that would take years to build and the abandonment of a central tenet of Islamic faith are hardly reasonable responses to Mecca's temporary inaccessibility. Besides which, even if it was not accessible to pilgrimage, one would assume that Mecca was still accessible to prayer. This story, too, looks like a later rationalisation to explain away the uncomfortable fact that the early Believers at prayer faced Jerusalem and not Mecca. It is also noteworthy that among the accusations made by later Islamic historians about the Umayyads, who "only converted to Islam at the last moment" (ie when Mohammed's victory was assured), was of trying to make Jerusalem the focus of the *hajj* pilgrimage in rivalry to the *Ka'ba* at Mecca.

Clearly, it was the resonance between Judeo-Christianity and the Arab monotheism of the early Arab Empire that explains why Jerusalem was the site of the first major temple of worship and why Jerusalem was the first direction of prayer long before Mecca was given that honour. It might also be added that although the links between early Islam and Judeo-Christian culture have been almost entirely papered over in the traditional *hadith*, the echo of those links resound throughout all the traditional stories in the huge number of Christians that figure in them. There are Christian slaves, servants, advisers, wives, court officials, generals and government ministers, all of whom have been accepted as pious people in their own right. What is explained away as an illustration of the tolerance of early Islam is, in fact, a reflection of the fact that what became Islam was steeped in Judeo-Christian tradition.

A close alignment between the early Islamic Believers and the Christian community certainly resonates with the complaint of John of Penkaye that "there was no difference between Christian and pagan". The Koran was at that time beginning to coalesce from earlier Christian Syriac mixed with Arabic texts. If there is one clear message that comes from these texts, it is that only the most pious would be saved at the End of Days and they would therefore have been the focus around which the Believers propagated their own Arab brand of monotheism. Fred Donner argues that many of the early Believers (he suggests that the word Muslim is inappropriate at this time) were in fact Jews and Christians.

> "At this early stage in the history of the Believers' movement, then, it seems that Jews or Christians who were sufficiently pious could, if they wished, have participated in it because they recognised God's oneness already. Or, to put it the other way round, some of the early Believers were Christians or Jews—although surely not all were."[714]

---

[714]   Fred Donner, *Muhammad and the Believers*, p 69

Moreover, the Christology of Arab monotheism is closely aligned with those Christian traditions that had developed in this region: where the Arab Christians had never accepted the so-called Nicaean Creed or the Trinitarian concept of the Byzantines. The Christology of the early Islamic Believers was based on the idea that although Jesus was a messiah, as he is described in the Koran, the interpretation of this title is closer to the idea of messenger or prophet than the son of God.

The Great Mosque of Damascus

Nancy Khalek is assistant professor of Religious Studies at Brown University. Her recent book, *Damascus after the Muslim Conquest,* attempts to steer a middle way between fact and fiction. She acknowledges the difficulty of using the traditional narrative because nearly all of it was written so much later than the events described.

> "Given the nature of the evidence, then, only a few are willing to admit that they want to find out 'what really happened' in the early days of Islamic history. Indeed, most have given up on such an enterprise . . . In Syria, the archaeological record demonstrates that it is virtually impossible, for example, to pinpoint when the region became anything that could be called 'Islamic'"[715]

It is some admission indeed, that a scholar should "give up" on trying to understand what happened in history, if that is what is implied here, but we will let that pass. Like all historians of Islam, Khalek is obliged to acknowledge the lateness—by at least two or three centuries—of the sources that deal with Damascus in the early Arab Empire:

> ". . . while not particularly interested in the past 'as it really was', this study is interested in how Syrians in the early Islamic period engaged with the past and in how they ended up with the versions of it they did. In part, this approach takes its cue from the nature of the material itself, which is not internally consistent and obviously reflects processes of redaction and choice . . . Islamic historiography is not a record of what happened so much as it is a record of what *different, multiple people* have said about what happened . . ."[716]

True to its word, the book is not "particularly interested in the past 'as it really was'". The clue is the unquestioning acceptance of the traditional account of the "conquest" of Syria by an "Islamic" army and the author taking as a given the

---

[715] Nancy Khalek, *Damascus after the Muslim Conquest*, pp 14,16
[716] Nancy Khalek, *Damascus after the Muslim Conquest*, p 22 (original italics)

origins of Islam in Mecca and Medina and the life of the Prophet, although all the proofs of these are also based on writings hundreds of years later.

The little problem of conflicting archaeological and other evidence is by-passed by what purports to be a "third way" between reliable historical evidence and fictional accounts. Khalek writes about a reassessment of traditional historical accounts and "the expansion of reality into new possibilities . . . because even problematic narratives serve not to undermine but potentially to enhance our understanding".[717] Dressed up in high-sounding phrases, what this really means is that although it is clear that nearly all the history of the period was written very much later, some of it might be true (a bit).

What can we say about ninth, tenth and eleventh-century histories of *seventh* century Damascus? All we can say is that they reflected what ninth, tenth and eleventh century historians *thought happened*, or what they thought *ought to have happened*. The large majority of the detailed accounts of events are, at the very least, suspect and they can provide no evidential base for the traditional narrative of a Syrian conquest from the Arabian city of Medina.

Khalek's book is useful however, in that it points in broad terms to the Christian character of seventh-century Syria and its capital in particular. She has no alternative, of course, since in the traditional accounts of ancient Syria, Christianity is *ubiquitous* and these accounts are supported by evidence still in existence today. So *in broad and general terms*, she cannot avoid the fact that the first "Islamic" capital was a *Christian city*. Our author is at a loss to understand why it was even the capital. "Taken alone, it is hard to conjure why Damascus should have been chosen as the capital of a Muslim ruling elite at the head of an expanding empire"[718]. The answer to this conundrum, of course, is that the *Arab* Empire began in Syria and Iraq, particularly the former, where Mu'Awiya was the local strong man, and in no sense was it Islamic at that point.

The most important admission that Khalek makes, although for her it remains forever secondary to the fictional Islamic character of the state, is *the overwhelmingly Christian character of the city of Damascus and Syria as a whole*. If we were to change in the following citation the words Muslim and Islamic to Arab (as would be more appropriate historically) it seems that Khalek even comes close, by accident as it were, to acknowledging the debt that the Koran owes to Christian Syriac writing:

"By way of monks' translations of literature into Syriac and Arabic, Christian religious culture permeated the early Islamic tradition in Syria . . . the linguistic disposition of the Christian community living under Muslim rule was the ready vehicle for the diffusion of religious culture. In the seventh and eighth centuries, first Syriac and then Arabic

---

717   Nancy Khalek, *Damascus after the Muslim Conquest*, p 23
718   Nancy Khalek, *Damascus after the Muslim Conquest*, p 89

texts delivered monastic and hagiographic ideals from Christian to Arab environments."[719]

Although, as we have argued, the *detail* of the later tradition can be taken with a pinch of salt, the overwhelming Christian influence in Damascus cannot be ignored. As we have explained, when the caliph Abd Al-Malik constructed the Dome of the Rock in Jerusalem, it was by no means an Islamic monument and it included polemical inscriptions directed against Trinitarian Christianity. Khalek's book deals with the traditions around the construction of the Great Mosque of Damascus, which, after the Dome of the Rock, was the *second* monumental place of worship to be constructed in the empire, not in Jerusalem this time but in the imperial capital. Yet this too was based on the site of a prior place of worship (what had been a Christian cathedral) and it incorporated into its structure the reliquery of the Christian saint, John the Baptist.

> "It is in my view unlikely," Khalek writes, "that the institution of John's cult in the new mosque was a policy of appeasement aimed at attracting Christian converts into the Islamic fold, by indicating openness to the well-established Christian cult of the saints. Rather, it was a move that acknowledged that veneration of the Baptist was an important part of the sacred landscape of Byzantine Damascus, while asserting both political and religious authority over that landscape."[720]

In fact, the two views are not mutually exclusive. The incorporation of the Baptist cult into the Damascus Mosque, by Abd Al-Malik's son Walid, is an indication that Islam at that stage *was not clearly defined* and in some respects, as a uniquely Arab brand of monotheism, was almost *quasi-Christian*. Both the Dome of the Rock and the Great Mosque of Damascus represent in their different ways, the *transition* of Arab monotheism from an ill-defined brand of pious observance into what we now know as Islam.

Supporting his arguments about the close links between the early Arab state and the Christian tradition, Volker Popp cites the example of a hoard of poorly-minted, square copper coins, currently residing in the Israel Museum in Jerusalem and the subject of a publication in 1947. On the obverse is the figure of a ruler, crowned with a cross and holding a cross in his hand and on the reverse there is another cross above the motto, *mohammed*. Popp argues that the use of the *mohammed* motto migrated from the Eastern-most parts of the Arabian Empire to the West and it coincided with the imperial policy of Abd Al-Malik to consolidate the Empire around a specifically *Arab* brand of monotheism in distinction to the monotheism of the Byzantine Christians and the Jewish Diaspora. Although influenced by both

---

[719] Nancy Khalek, *Damascus after the Muslim Conquest*, pp 54,55
[720] Nancy Khalek, *Damascus after the Muslim Conquest*, p 93

Judaism and Nestorian Christianity, in the final analysis the monotheism adopted by Abd Al-Malik was a new departure from both.

> ". . . His Mohammedanism derives much more from the Arabian understanding of Syrian theology. Further, this Arabian understanding of Syrian theology did not arise in the Nestorian imperial church of Iran; rather, as the tribal religion of the Mesopotamian and Iranian Arabs, it became a constitutive part of their ethnicity."[721]

The reign of Abd Al-Malik, therefore, was a watershed. It signalled a dramatic break with the past in that the regime began to consciously develop an Arabic and what became an 'Islamic' identity, not as ends in themselves, but as a part of the consolidation of a strong regime. *Islam was the ideological expression of the imperial elite which needed to consolidate its position militarily, economically, fiscally and administratively.* The Dome of the Rock reflected both the lingering affinities between the former Christianity of the region and the burgeoning Arab monotheism and this explains the polemical nature of its inscriptions. But its construction coincided with a number of important changes that began to take effect and which began to look and sound like modern Islam. Although the Dome of the Rock was clearly not a mosque, from the early eighth century onwards there was a sudden surge in the building of places of worship which *did* correspond to the design of modern mosques. The story of the cross on the Mount of Olives is only one of several similar traditions which apart from pre-empting the actual construction of the Dome of the Rock by many years, offers a rationalisation for the removal of crosses from churches which was another policy decreed by Abd Al-Malik.

> ". . . suppressing images emblematic of Christian/Byzantine rule (eg crosses), no less than building atop the Temple Mount, signals a new rhetoric of rule. In building and striking, the Marwanids thus began to lay imperial claims—permanent, justified, increasingly 'natural' claims—over subjects and lands, a project only completed by the Abbasids during the century that followed, when Arabs, now with several generations of settlement behind them, began to yield taxes themselves, and Muslim historians, now rubbing shoulders with Christian and Jewish elites in the cities of Iraq, reconstructed a past useful to the present."[722]

The removal of crosses, sacred pictures and icons corresponded to a drive against idolatry and a greater assertion of Arab monotheism. After some coins were issued with the image of standing caliphs, all subsequent coins were minted without any image or representation. As a result of the confident and aggressive shift in the religious outlook of the state, it was from this period on that Syriac Christian

---

[721] Volker Popp, *The hidden history of Islam,* p 57
[722] Chase Robinson, *The Transformation of Northern Mesopotamia,* p 167

literature shows a sudden and dramatic increase in apocalyptic writings. The Church now came under increased pressure, ideologically, but above all, fiscally. The main worry of Christian writers in this period was the danger that many of their flock would opt for voluntary apostasy, that is, conversion to the Arab brand of monotheism as a direct response to the tax disadvantage placed on Christians. One of the apocalyptic works of this period, the so-called *Pseudo-Methodius* was preoccupied with precisely such possibilities:

> ". . . what really made the author take up his pen to prophesy the imminent destruction of Arab power by the Christian [Byzantine] emperor was his fear of a subsequent period in which many of his co-religionists would plunge into a voluntary apostasy to Islam . . . greatly increased taxation of Christians created circumstances highly favourable to conversion to Islam."[723]

So many Christians began to adopt the Arab form of monotheism that in some cases their churches were simply converted to mosques, perhaps following a period of joint worship. From the point of view of the *social* role of the Church, there would be absolutely no change by its conversion into becoming a mosque. What had been its former role in the community, as a dispenser of alms, an organisation for burying the dead and a means of supporting the poor and destitute, remained unchanged, as if nothing had happened. The giving of alms and support for charity were, in fact, enshrined into the regular duties of a Muslim and, as with all such observances, justified by newly created tradition. An anonymous Syriac chronicler, writing no later than the year 775 CE, bemoaned the lack of faith of some of his fellow Christians with the following comments:

> "The gates were opened to them to [enter] Islam . . . . Without blows or tortures they slipped towards apostasy in great precipitancy; they formed groups of ten or twenty or thirty or a hundred or two hundred or three hundred without any sort of compulsion . . ., going down to Harran and becoming Moslems in the presence of [government] officials. A great crowd did so . . . from the districts of Edessa and of Harran and of Tella and of Resaina"[724]

There were already bitter historic rivalries between different branches of Christianity in the Near East and it would not have been difficult for some of the congregation to make the relatively short step from their former view of Jesus as merely a man to have him demoted to the last but one of God's holy prophets. Not that the theology

---

[723]   Reinink, *Syriac Christianity under Late Sasanian and Early Islamic Rule*, IX, p 181

[724]   From *Disputing with Islam in Syriac: The Case of the Monk of Bet Hale and a Muslim Emir,* by Sidney H Griffith, Hugoye: Journal of Syriac Studies, Vol 3, No 1, January 2000

was uppermost in the minds of the apostates. As we shall argue later, there were very considerable economic aspirations behind these mass conversions; there was little theology involved. But what was clear was that the local inhabitants were not converted *en masse* at the time of an Islamic conquest but several generations after the foundation of the Arab state when Islam began to clarify itself.

Although there appears to have been a growing awareness among Christian writers that Arab monotheism represented an entirely new departure from the previous faiths, some clung onto the idea that it was no more than a deviation from the past. *The Conversation between Yohannan and the Emir* is a Christian apologetic tract written early in the eighth century, whose author, one scholar suggests, ". . . is well aware of Islam being a religion different from Christianity, Judaism and Samaritanism; however, he takes great pains to prove that the faith of the new rulers is not a new religion, but rather a variant of the old Mosaic religion."[725]

The sudden upsurge in the use of the words Mohammed and Islam, the banning of crosses on churches and inscriptions, the forbidding of any representational imagery and the establishment of Arabic as the official language—these were all part of the ideological drive of Abd Al-Malik to give an identity to the Arab state. "Unlike the Byzantine emperor," Jeremy Johns writes, "who could draw on more than half a millennium's experience of bending material culture to the services of the state, Abd Al-Malik was a complete beginner."[726]

Mohammed makes an appearance

It is significant that it was only at the end of the seventh century, coinciding with the reign of Abd Al-Malik, that the Koran and the Prophet Mohammed were elevated to the positions they hold to this day. The court industry which produced a holy book in *Arabic* (from a Syriac template overlaid with specifically Arab mythology and lore and more recent verses) was part of a process of establishing the primacy of that language as the source of religious revelation and therefore political legitimacy. The production of a clearly defined Scripture to rival the books of the Jews and Christians would also have paralleled the production of *hadith* about a life of the Prophet, although the vast majority of the *hadith* belongs to the later Abbasid period.

Prior to the reign of Abd Al-Malik, Mohammed had been either absent or insignificant. The inscriptions that have been found from the first century of the Arab era are composed of a variety of pious phrases and references to God, *but make no mention of the Koran or Mohammed.* This would be unthinkable for the vast majority of scribes and writers of Islamic texts after the end of the century. Patricia Crone and Martin Hinds emphasise this point at some length:

---

[725]   Reinink, *Syriac Christianity under Late Sasanian and Early Islamic Rule*, XII, p 176
[726]   Jeremy Johns, *Archaeology and the History of Early Islam*, p 432

"It is a striking fact that such documentary evidence as survives from the Sufyanid period [the first Umayyad caliphs] makes no mention of the messenger of God at all. The papyri do not refer to him. The Arabic inscriptions of the Arab-Sassanian coins only invoke Allah, not his *rasul* [messenger]; and the Arab-Byzantine coins on which Muhammad appears as *rasul Allah*, previously dated to the Sufyanid period, have now been placed in that of the Marwanids. Even two surviving pre-Marwanid tombstones fail to mention the *rasul*, though both mention Allah, and the same is true of Mu'awiya's inscription at Ta'if. In the Sufyanid period, apparently, the *Prophet had no publicly acknowledged role.*"[727]

Fred Donner makes much the same point, that despite their piety, early inscriptions are striking for what they *don't* contain:

". . . missing are assertions of tribal chauvinism, expressions of rival political claims, overt expressions of an overt Islamic confessional identity, and statements of theological import beyond the very general assertion of God's unity. Moreover, th*ere are no references to Muhammad or to the sunna of the Prophet prior to 66 AH*"[728]

This reference to 66 AH is to the inscription on the Dome of the Rock, but as some have argued, this may not even be a reference to a named person, but to Jesus, as 'he who is praised'. Prior to Abd Al-Malik it was the *caliphate* that was central to Arab monotheism and it was only during this caliph's reign that Mohammed was declared the Messenger of God and the Prophet of the Arab people; it was only from this point on that he appears in all texts and inscriptions.

It goes without saying that a materialist view of history has no room for prophets with a direct line of communication with God. So where did the idea of the Prophet come from? Nevo and Koran take the view that Mohammed had been one of the early clan leaders or 'kings' in the tribal conflicts that followed the collapse of the Sassanid state, before a centralised Arab empire was consolidated. Robert G Hoyland, surveyed all the non-Islamic references of the period in his book, *Seeing Islam As Others Saw It: A Survey and Evaluation of Christian, Jewish and Zoroastrian Writings on Early Islam.* He takes the view that the writings of Thomas the Presbyter, a seventh century chronicler whose Syriac writings are still preserved in the British library of Syriac manuscripts, show the first recorded reference to Mohammed:

"In the year 945, indiction 7, on Friday 7 February (634 CE) at the ninth hour, there was a battle between the Romans and the Arabs of

---

[727] Crone and Hinds, *God's Caliph,* p 24 (italics added)
[728] Fred M Donner, *Narratives of Islamic Origins, The Beginnings of Islamic Historical Writing,* p 88 (italics added)

Muhammad (*tayyaye d-Mhmt*) in Palestine twelve miles east of Gaza. The Romans fled, leaving behind the patrician Bryrd whom the Arabs killed. Some 4000 poor villagers of Palestine were killed there, Christians, Jews and Samaritans. The Arabs ravaged the whole region."

Citing this same source, Fred Donner comments that

"This, at least, enables the historian to feel more confident that Muhammad is not completely a fiction of later pious imagination as some have implied; we know that someone named Muhammad did exist, and that he led some kind of movement."[729]

But this is precisely the kind of stretching of evidence that is typical of so many historians. The account of Thomas the Presbyter, even if perfectly accurate, puts the raid in question two years after Mohammed's death and well outside of his traditional raiding area—neither of which is contested within Islamic tradition. More to the point, the command of a raiding party does not imply leadership of a "movement", which has altogether different connotations. In fact, although it is possible that some lingering oral tradition linked this clan leader to the later life-story of the Prophet, there is otherwise no concrete link at all between the raid on Gaza and the elaborate and sophisticated "pious fiction" written centuries later. No more link, in fact, than Joshua, the leader of Galilean bandits, might have to the New Testament Jesus.

Christoph Luxenburg takes an altogether different view of the origins of Mohammed. We have already cited his work, *The Syro-Aramaic Reading of the Koran*, in which he emphasises the derivation of many of the words in the Koran from Syriac. Without going into his detailed argument about Arabic gerunds and grammatical minutiae, the gist of what he writes is that the meaning of the word *mohammed* is not a proper noun, a personal name, but derives from the adjective "praiseworthy", so its meaning was "one who should be praised". Referring to the inscription on the Dome of the Rock, the Islamic translation 'Mohammed is the servant of God and his messenger', becomes for Luxenburg '*praised be* the servant of God and his messenger'. He argues, like Popp, that the depiction of Jesus in the inscription as *Abd Allah*, the servant of God, goes back to early Christianity and has its roots many centuries before Islam. Although the inscription is directed at the People of the Book, which in Koranic terms means Jews and Christians, Luxenburg argues that in this case the intended audience are the Christians.

"By this teaching, Abd al-Malik defends his faith both in Christ as the 'servant of God' (*Abd Allah*) and also in the one God, over against the Trinitarian teaching of the followers of Nicaea. Abd al-Malik is defending hereby a pre-Nicaean Syrian Christianity, a version of Christianity that

---

[729]   Fred Donner, *Muhammad and the Believers,* p 53

one should not refer to generally as 'Jewish Christianity' but rather, more accurately, as 'Syrian-Arabian Christianity'."[730]

Not only was *Mohammad* not meant as a personal name in the inscription, Luxenburg writes, but the word *Islam* too was meant in its general sense of *submission* to the will of God, a conformity with the Scripture, rather than Islam as a religious faith.

". . . it is a historical error to see in this expression (*"islam"*) and in this context the beginning of "Islam" as we know it . . . However much the Koran may have existed partially before the rise of historical Islam—a possibility that the inscription on the Dome of the Rock suggests—it seems to have been a liturgical book of a Syrian-Arabian Christianity. Even if written Christian sources from the first half of the eighth century speak of a 'Mohammed' as the 'prophet of the Arabs', this phenomenon is to be explained as that this Arabian name for Christ was simply not current among Aramaic or Greek-speaking Christians. Therefore this metaphor, which would have sounded strange to them, must have seemed to be the name of a new prophet."[731]

In the discussion on the development of Christianity, we explained that the original name of Jesus, *Joshua*, meant salvation in Hebrew and this *generic* meaning contributed to the rise of the Joshua sects that pre-dated the development of modern Christianity. In a similar way, Popp has argued that what is now the *personal* name Mohammed, was used in early Arabic inscriptions, not in the personal, but in the *general* sense, as meaning *he who is praised*. It is Popp's contention, although by no means uncontested among other scholars, that the specifically Arab interpretation of Christianity recognised "*Jesus as the mohammed*" and that Jesus, in addition, was the person also accorded the title *AbdAllah* ('servant of God') from time to time.

Although he clearly accepts that Mohammed was a historical figure, Fred Donner, in *Narratives of Islamic Origins,* admits that there is no early evidence at all for his prominence within what he called "the community of Believers".

". . . around the 60s and 70s AH [ie at the end of the seventh century] . . . is when we first see evidence that Muslims began to point to the career of their Prophet, Muhammad, as the crucial beginning-point of their community . . ."[732]

The explanation for what Donner calls an "ahistorical" approach to the new faith is that "Believers were quite unconcerned with recording 'what actually happened' in

---

[730]   Christopher Luxenburg, *The Hidden History of Islam*, p 140
[731]   Christopher Luxenburg, *The Hidden History of Islam*, p 141
[732]   Fred Donner, *Narratives of Islamic Origins*, p 114

their community, because their interests as Believers were moral, not historical." We have heard this argument before, of course. Despite a proliferation of scribes and a great deal of literary activity in almost every other field, there is a glaring absence of any contemporary account of the life of Jesus and this too has been put down to a "lack of interest" on the part of the early Christian community: ". . . the Hellenistic church placed no emphasis upon the life of Jesus and there is no evidence it had the slightest interest in Jesus as a wonder-worker."[733]

We now have the same argument being applied to the biography of Mohammed. We are asked to believe that both communities—early Christians and early Muslims—were "ahistorical" and were so focused on their own piety that they were "not interested" in setting down a written account of the life of their respective prophets. Lives, let us remember, of world-shaking significance. This does not satisfactorily explain why the same aversion to biographical history seemed to rub off on all those other literate communities with whom they came into contact, not to mention a multiplicity of scribes and writers; and nor does it explain why the histories suddenly began to proliferate about a century later. Fred Donner, commenting on the school of literature that developed in Medina, the City of the Prophet, makes the point that "from the last quarter of the first century AH numerous learned Medinese specialised in relating accounts about the Prophet",[734] ignoring the fact that they didn't so much as lift a quill for seventy-five years. The absence of contemporary evidence for the historical Jesus and the identical absence of evidence for the historical Mohammed should be allowed to speak for themselves.

Whilst for Donner and other historians, the absence of Mohammed in early inscriptions and writings is an issue of no great importance, for us *it is enormously significant*, just like the absence of any biographical references to Jesus in the whole of the early Christian literary tradition. Rather than concocting unlikely explanations in the ahistoricity of the early Believers, or a lack of interest in biographical information, it is far more likely that the real reason for the lack of contemporary writing is the *obvious* one: that the biography didn't exist until almost a century afterwards because up to that point there had been no reason to make one up.

It cannot be definitively argued that there was no such historical person as Mohammed, as either a military/tribal or a religious leader, or possibly as both. What does seem clear from the evidence, however, is that the vast amounts of *hadith* surrounding the Prophet of Mecca, including his life and works and the foundation of the Koran, is almost entirely legendary.

Where we now see Mohammed occupying an absolutely central position in modern Islam, the evidence strongly suggests that was not the case for most of the first Islamic century. Even giving the caliphs the title of *khalifat rasul Allah*,

---

733   Robin Scroggs, *The People's Jesus*, p 68
734   Fred Donner, *Narratives of Islamic Origins*, p 219.

'successors of the messenger of God', was a later *retrospective* creation because it is clear from all the epigraphic evidence that the early caliphs only described themselves as *khalifat Allah*, equivalent to 'representatives' of God. The 'messenger' was not embedded into history at this early point. Indeed, the fluidity in the use of titles is evidenced by the fact that an Arabian silver coin, which Volker Popp argues was falsely attributed to the Khazars and dated to 766, still carried an inscription focused on Moses, reading *Musa rasul Allah*, meaning 'Moses the messenger of God.'

Although the sign of the cross eventually disappeared from all Arab coinage, this was not, Popp asserts, as a result of Islamic rejection or prohibition, as the traditional account has it, but as a result of the introduction of a new symbols. Eventually, the Islamic ethic, which still exists in modern times, of removing all 'idolatrous' and personal representations from Art, began to assert itself and crosses were removed from churches and figure-heads from coins. Nevertheless, the erasure of Christianity from within the body of the early Islamic milieu was a long process. Writing in *The Hidden History of Islam,* Karl-Heinz Ohlig also suggests that Syriac-Christianity was still "blossoming" as late as the eighth century, under Arabian rule.

> ". . . many cloisters and churches were built, and missions as far as China were undertaken. A good deal of literature is extant, including chronicles, saints' lives, cloister legends, and theological treatises. It is remarkable that Islam does not appear in this literature, except in John of Damascus, who speaks of the Christian heresy of the 'Ishmaelites' and knows a few *suras* . . . is it possible that a Christian population could be subjugated by an Islamic authority without this experience finding literary expression anywhere? In her recently published dissertation, Simone Rosenkranz did not bring to light a single source before the beginning of the ninth century which mentions Islam in conflicts between Jews and Christians; after this period, though, the situation changes."[735]

Whatever the precise meaning of the words Muhammad and Islam on the Dome of the Rock, it is quite clear that the reign of Abd Al-Malik represented an important turning point in the perception of both.

> ". . . It is remarkable . . . that *none of these early religious writings mentions either the Prophet Muhammad or his religion, Islam.* Thus, for example, the earliest tombstone of a Muslim, dated 31/651-2 from Egypt, makes no reference to the Prophet, an omission that almost never occurs after 72/691 . . . The problem is therefore how to account for the absence of Islam and the Prophet from the archaeological record . . . *All of the*

---

[735] Karl-Heinz Ohlig, *The hidden Origins of Islam*, p 395

> *earliest declarations of Islam are found on coins, documents, and monumental inscriptions produced under Abd Al-Malik and his successors.*"[736]

The Arab monotheism of the early Believers, therefore, was not Islam in the sense that it exists today and it was perceived as merely a more pious and stricter form of observance of God. In the Arab Empire that began to take shape after the collapse of the Sassanid Empire, Arab monotheism co-existed with Christianity which had been the dominant culture of the heartland of the new empire, Iraq and Syria. It was only with the caliphate of Abd Al-Malik that the identity and character of the Arab form of monotheism began to be clarified as a distinct faith different from that of his great rivals in Constantinople. For any elite to maintain itself in power, force of arms is never enough and every ruling class seeks an ideological justification for its privileges and position. That is precisely what Abd Al-Malik set about doing. In creating a more confident and assertive brand of Arab monotheism as its national ideology, the Arab ruling class was justifying its position at the top of society, to its national and international rivals, to its own people and, not least, to itself.

> "Abd al-Malik wanted to strengthen the Arabian empire from within by erecting an Arabian Church of the Arabian Empire. This Church was to be an imperial church in the Iranian sense, following the example of the Nestorian Church in Iran and its role as the Christian imperial church of Iran towards the end of the reign of the Sassanids."[737]

Last, but perhaps not least, it is worth noting that the only aspect of life in the early period of the Arab Empire for which we do have *definite evidence* is that of Art. But as Patricia Crone has eloquently pointed out, the early Art was in no way similar to the non-representational and non-figurative Art which Islamic doctrine demanded from the second century AH onwards, right through to the modern day. Looking at the early Art,

> ". . . we can actually *see*, as opposed to merely hope to see, what went into the formation of a highly distinctive Islamic mode of expression. And what is it that we see? Late antique sculpture, paintings in the nude, Greek allegories inscribed with Greek captions, Byzantine mosaics that would have won the admiration of spectators in Ravenna, to mention just some of the more startling surprises."[738]

The early Islamic Art reflected the early Arab Empire, mixing Byzantine, Sassanid and Christian traditions. There was none of the piety and simplicity of modern

---

[736] Jeremy Johns, *Archaeology and the History of Early Islam*, p 415 (italics added)
[737] Volker Popp, *The Hidden Origins of Islam*, p 57
[738] Patricia Crone, *Roman, Provincial and Islamic Law*, p. 17.

Islamic design: that would only come with the policies and campaigns of Abd Al-Malik.

Chapter summary

- Caliph Abd Al-Malik was the first to develop a centralised system of government, taxation and administration for the Arab Empire. The reign of Abd Al-Malik signalled a break with the past and a policy of developing an Arabic and an Islamic identity. The consolidation of Koranic literature into a single holy book coincides with the elevation of Arabic to become the imperial language.

- As part of his religious reforms, Abd Al-Malik built the Dome of the Rock as the first major place of worship on the site of the Jewish Temple in Jerusalem. It was not a mosque. At this time the direction of prayer for Arab monotheists was towards Jerusalem.

- Only towards the end of the seventh century, after having been absent throughout the whole preceding period, did the Prophet Mohammed begin to be written into inscriptions. For this reason, some scholars doubt the historical existence of Mohammed even as tribal leader and link the name Mohammed to the Arabic word for praised or praiseworthy.

Chapter 17

The Class Character of the Arab Empire

We shall show in this section that the establishment of the Arab Empire was not based on a religious campaign by Muslims spreading Islam, but on raids, incursions and occupations by Arab tribes to get booty, plunder, slaves, taxes and tribute. In the final analysis, the Arab Empire was based on the brutal exploitation of the populations under its control and although taxation arrangements varied across the Empire, in most cases it meant Arabs taxing non-Arabs. We shall look at how more fortunate subjects and prisoners of war became clients of Arab notables or tribes, adopting Arab customs, Arabic names and converting to the same religious practices of their patrons and that these clients increasingly demanded equal rights to Arabs as their numbers grew. We shall show that there were material advantages for a section of the subject peoples to convert to Arab monotheism but that such conversion was *actively resisted* by the caliphs, although later, as Islam became more clearly defined and the numbers of clients grew, opposition to conversion became impossible.

. . . .

The entire period we have outlined (the invasion of the Byzantine state by Persia, the collapse of the Sassanid Empire, the raiding and settlement by Arab tribes, the fusion of Ghassanid and Lakhmid Arab traditions and the eventual consolidation of a unified state) was one of great upheaval and instability. Civil wars, inter-tribal rivalries, ethnic and class conflicts characterised the early period of the Arab state. The Umayyad dynasty itself was born out of civil war, experienced another civil conflict in its twentieth year and was destined to collapse after a third civil war. These three great internecine wars do not even include the numerous minor wars and revolts of local and regional Arab rivals. All of these conflicts, whatever the ethnic, caste or class basis of each contending army, was fought in the name of true religion, at least according to later tradition. Yet, as we have seen, it was only from the end of the Umayyad caliphate, at the very end of the seventh century, that Islam really came into focus as anything like the religion we know today.

The Umayyad dynasty, beginning with Mu'awiya, was the most crucial period in the formation of what came to be Islam. The traditional Islamic history of the origins of the empire can be summed up in this comment from the *Cambridge History of Islam*:

"... the decisive factor in this [military] success was Islam, which was the co-ordinating element behind the efforts of the Bedouin, and instilled

402

into the hearts of the warriors the belief that a war against the followers of another faith was a holy war."[739]

As we have shown, the idea that Islam was fully defined at the time and that the conquest was planned and organised from Medina in the Arabian Peninsula is simply not borne out by the archaeological and other physical evidence. It was only the regime of Abd Al-Malik which created a centralised state for the first time, with a regular system of taxation, administration and governance and it was as *the ideological reflection of that centralising tendency* that Islam began to be clearly defined for the first time. G R Hawting, who we have already cited, summed up the role of the Umayyad caliphate as follows:

> "It seems clear that Islam as we know it is largely a result of the interaction between the Arabs and the peoples they conquered during the first two centuries or so of the Islamic era which began in 622. During the Umayyad period, therefore, the *spread* of Islam and the *development* of Islam were taking place at the same time" [740]

Just as it took a period of many decades before Arabic became adopted as the administrative language of the empire—and even then in the east of the empire and in parts of north Africa the native languages survived—so too it took more than a century after the establishment of an independent Arab state before the empire was truly an *Islamic* empire.

What then, was the *class* character of the new state that was forged by Abd Al-Malik at the end of the seventh century? How did the theology rounded out by ninth and tenth century Islamic scholars—or for that matter, the theology of modern Islam—square with what was happening on the ground in the late seventh century? It has to be said that identifying the real social forces at play is extremely difficult. The overwhelming majority of historians from the ninth century to the present day are at least visually impaired when it comes to real social forces and movements and in some cases they are *wholly* blind. As we have explained, most modern authors rely completely on the histories written two hundred years after the events they describe. They see the play of historical forces almost exclusively in terms of personal, clan or tribal rivalries, usually dressed in the garb of religious polemic. There is little acknowledgement of the opposing *material social interests* of the peasants, the city artisans or slaves on the one side and the ruling elites on the other. For those who look for the real drivers of historical and political movements, that is, in the social and economic interests of different layers of society, it is necessary to dig deep into the historical records to find the truth.

The first thing that has to be emphasised is that, contrary to the impression given by a whole swathe of historical writers, the formation of the Arab empire

---

[739]   Laura Veccia Vaglieri, *Cambridge History of Islam,* p 61.
[740]   GR Hawting, *The First Dynasty of Islam,* p 2 (italics added)

and its expansion into North Africa, Spain and East as far Afghanistan was not motivated by a "holy war". The early phases in the creation of the Arab Empire were characterised by uncoordinated raids and settlements in those areas previously held by the Sassanid and Byzantine empires. These were often in territories that had previously been settled by Arabs for centuries and it was only after the establishment of the centralised Umayyad state that these raids became *organised* invasions by massed armies beyond what had been the boundaries of Sassanid territory. But from the beginning, these expansions were motivated by the simple desire for *booty*. All of the contemporary accounts and even the Islamic sources agree that cities and whole regions were subject to looting on a massive scale. Not only was there a huge shift of gold and valuables back to the centres of the empire, but there was a massive displacement of slaves, many of whom ended up in Syria and Iraq. Islamic histories, both ancient and modern, place a great deal of emphasis on the alleged egalitarian and simple outlook of the Muslims. The later traditions described the leader of the Christian Church in the Byzantine Empire and the role of the Emperor himself in terms that they did not apply to the Muslims.

> ". . . The master of the See is the partner of the emperor: no one else is equal to the emperor and he is the only person in front of whom the emperor bows . . . money from the pious foundations for the upkeep of churches, monasteries, bishops and monks is the responsibility of the patriarch . . . (Al-Mansudi)
> . . . all over the Rūm [Roman, ie Byzantine, Empire] is a man called patriarch who is the Lord of religion. (Marvazi)"[741]

Tradition also has it that the Prophet even wrote to the Byzantine Emperor Heraclius about the superiority of the Muslim faith. Islamic sources, of course, narrate that Heraclius was himself convinced and was only held back from conversion because of the pressure of his court officials and generals. The conviction of Heraclius was similar to that of the philosopher Seneca (who on corresponding with St Paul admitted the superiority of Christianity) in that it is a fiction.

We are told by Islamic sources, writing centuries after the fact, that the new Arab elite based in Damascus rejected the opulence and grandeur of the Byzantine court and was distinguished by its humility and lack of ceremony. There may have been some truth contained in this description; the characteristic Arab monotheism that developed at the time of the imperial expansion may have marked out its leadership—superficially—as different to the Sassanid and Byzantine predecessors.

> ". . . compared to Sassanian society, there appears to have been a general levelling of elite structures in former Sassanian territories during the century following the conquest. But members of the conquered population

---

[741] Cited by Nadia Maria El Cheik in *Early Incomes in the Early Islamic State,* in *Elites Old and New in the Byzantine and Early Islamic Near East,* p 116

seem to have seen the change as something more than this, and expressed it in terms of the overturning of the social order ("slaves have become masters") both in Christian literature and in Zoroastrian apocalypses. Toward the end of the seventh century, the East Syrian John of Penkaye thought that the proper order of kings, priests, and ordinary people had become confused."[742]

It may well be, that having experienced a century of social and economic upheaval under the Sassanid dynasty, large sections of the Persian population, especially but not exclusively those in the former Lakhmid territories, actually welcomed the change of regime. The new Arab elite may have donned the mantles of egalitarianism and humility to contrast with the hubris and pomp of the Sassanids. *But in the final analysis, the new Arab state was an empire like any other and it based itself on the relentless and brutal economic exploitation of the populations under its control.*

Exploitation of the imperial population

What was in historical terms an extremely rapid conquest of Spain, North Africa and the easternmost provinces enormously enlarged the empire and established a state in which there was a clear distinction between the conquerors and conquered. As we have stated, the motive for conquest was not religion, but pillage. But once all the movable booty was taken, the Arab conquerors set about looting the land by taxing those who cultivated it. The primary aim of the occupation of territory and the consolidation of the Umayyad state was exploitation. Patricia Crone described the relationship of the Arab elite to the conquered peoples as "almost exclusively fiscal".

> ". . . The non-Arabs were rarely asked or forced to convert; *on the whole they were dissuaded.* They simply had to pay for the upkeep of those who had defeated them, preferably in a manner which emphasised their twin humiliation of non-Arab ethnicity and unbelief. Now the landed aristocracy of Iraq and the Iranian plateau on the whole could afford the price and bear the humiliation, shielding themselves on their estates. *But their peasants, for all that they might have borne the humiliation, could not afford the price,* and in the Arab, unlike the Hellenic, Middle East, it was thus the peasants who went to live in the cities."[743]

If the very top layers of Sassanid society had been swept away, that was not necessarily true of local landowners and notables. ". . . lower-level local elites and

---

[742]   Michael G Morony in *Elites Old and New in the Byzantine and Early Islamic Near East,* p 275

[743]   Patricia Crone, *Slaves on Horses,* p 54 (italics added)

village headmen and landlords managed to survive in many places, sometimes by joining the Muslims . . ."[744] In the Jazira region of northern Syria, the old local elites were largely left in place. ". . . insofar as Byzantine-era elites in Jaziran towns and cities anchored their privileges to the land, we should assume that they continued to do so in the Islamic period too. It was presumably military pragmatism that led the conquering Muslims to extend to the city elites of the Jazira a series of very generous offers . . . where the Muslim presence was so thin, autonomy was real."[745]

We have already cited Julius Wellhausen, whose writings more than a century ago used the traditional sources, chiefly Tabari. But as even his work shows, there are occasional glimpses in the traditional narratives of the underlying class and economic forces at work in the great historical events of the seventh and eighth centuries. Wellhausen from time to time uses these sources to refer to what he saw as the important class differences that existed in the newly-established empire. He too commented on the fact that the new rulers left the old class structures largely intact and on the minimal role played by Islam in the conquest. The state, he wrote, "was, in fact, a specifically Arab state, an Imperium of the Arabs over the conquered peoples."

Not only did the Arab state exploit the already-existing class divisions within the former Sassanid society, but these divisions became more exaggerated in time. Within a couple of generations, a class divide opened up between different layers of the Arab community itself, from the unequal distribution of booty, from the unequal payment of military stipends to the occupying forces, from the prior precedence in the Arab community, including nobility and status and from the different mercantile and trading interests of sections of the Arab elite.

During the Umayyad period, especially after the fiscal and administrative reforms of Abd Al-Malik, there began a gradual assimilation of those Arabs who had previously stood aside from the local populations as a parasitic military caste. Instead of playing out the role of occupying troops, many of them became part of a permanent landowning class while others became traders. Now, their class interests did not always coincide with those of the imperial elite whose only interest was taxing the land. In place of an army of occupation, Abd Al-Malik was obliged for the first time to develop a standing army separate from the majority of Arabs and non-Arabs.

Meanwhile, as the state consolidated itself, the Arab elite set about looting the local population as if there were no tomorrow, ably assisted by the local landowning class. The friends, family and associates of the Caliph were especially privileged and had their noses pushed deepest into the trough. Huge amounts of tribute were sent to Damascus and there was always enough for everyone.

---

[744]   Michael G Morony in *Elites Old and New in the Byzantine and Early Islamic Near East*, p 276

[745]   Chase Robinson, *Empires and Elites after the Muslim Conquest, The Transformaiton of Northern Mesopotamia*, p 32

"The distinction between public and private money was tenuous in practice, and governorships soon came to be regarded as a source of private enrichment for the incumbent, so that what was actually sent on to Damascus depended largely on the good-will of the governor."[746]

Extensive land grants (*qata'i*) were given by the Umayyad caliphs and their governors and these were a further source of enrichment for a pampered Arab elite. Both in the new cities that had been former garrison town, like Kufa, and in agricultural areas from which landowners had fled, these grants enriched the most privileged and consolidated an Arab elite as a ruling *class*, as distinct from an occupying army. These grants were occasionally linked to *development* where land was marshy or otherwise uncultivable. One of the aims the Arab leaders had in capturing large numbers of slaves was to use their forced labour in clearing marshes and digging canals for irrigation, especially in the lower reaches of the Tigris and Euphrates. Such was the vast scale of slavery in developing the land in this part of Iraq that in the ninth century there was an uprising and the rebellious slaves, including many from East Africa, were able to establish and hold their own independent state for nearly fifteen years. (See appendix)

The grants of agricultural land (sometimes called *day'a*) included the holdings of the previous rural landowners, including houses and whole villages, which could then be exploited by the new Arab owners as a source of income. According to the ninth century historian Baladhuri,

". . . all the tithe land in Syria comes from what was abandoned by its owners and given as *qata'i* to the Muslims, and they revived it: that is to say, it was dead land to which no one had any rights, and they revived it with the permission of the governors."[747]

Some reports even suggest that smallholders entrusted their lands to local Arab chiefs in return for protection from banditry, so that the former owners became sharecroppers. This, and the occupation of empty land, probably did reflect the somewhat chaotic situation in the early years of the Arab state and even though related nearly three hundred years later, such reports probably reflect in broad terms the real political instability of the early Arab empire.

Once large land-holdings were established, they provided a permanent revenue for the new owners.

"The development of the *qata'i* and the *day'a* as a main source of financial support for the elite had a profound impact on the political structure of the later Umayyad and early Abbasid period, producing as it did wealthy

---

[746]   Patricia Crone, *Slaves on Horses,* p 33

[747]   Al-Baladhuri, *Futuh,* 152, cited by Hugh Kennedy, *Early Incomes in the Early Islamic State,* in *Elites Old and New in the Byzantine and Early Islamic Near East,*p 23

individuals and families who were not dependent directly on the state or court for their incomes . . . there is clear evidence of a property-owning landed aristocracy who felt secure enough to invest money and energy in long-term development projects. The legal position of 'dead lands' made such investment particularly attractive. The ownership of great estates was vastly profitable . . . The caliph Hisham [early eighth century] is said to have reckoned that his property developments in the Jazira [northern Syria] brought in more revenue than the whole of the taxation of the empire."[748]

Many areas of land in urban areas, especially the new garrison cities, were parcelled into chunks of real estate and made available to the favourites of the caliph and his governors. Commenting on the divisions in Baghdad under the later Abbasids, Hugh Kennedy noted that the city:

". . . contained a large number of elite members of the new regime with very large disposable incomes. Below them was a professional class of secretaries and soldiers who formed a real salariat; they may not have been as wealthy as the elite, but they too needed to buy food and could indulge spending on non-essential items." [749]

As well as land granted as favours to family and friends, the caliphs retained huge areas as a source of income for the state and for disbursement to the direct family of the caliph. According to Nejatulla Siddiqi in *Islamic Public Economics,* by the time of the later Umayyads,

". . . the produce grown on state owned lands has become a regular source of revenue to the state. Later on rent from houses and shops built on government owned lands became an important source of income to the state. A new department known as the Registry of government investments was created during the period of Umayyad caliph Walid bin Abd Al-Malik. It was established to keep a record of rent earned from lands leased to others."[750]

Taxation arrangements varied from one province to another, but generally speaking there was a tax placed on cultivated *land,* payable by anyone who cultivated it, and a further *poll tax* paid only by non-Muslims. Since the conquering Arabs did not at first cultivate the land they had conquered, in most cases outside the core

---

[748] Hugh Kennedy, *Early Incomes in the Early Islamic State,* in *Elites Old and New in the Byzantine and Early Islamic Near East,* p 28
[749] Hugh Kennedy, *Early Incomes in the Early Islamic State,* in *Elites Old and New in the Byzantine and Early Islamic Near East,* p 15
[750] Nejatulla Siddiqi, *Islamic Public Economics,* p 49

regions of the empire the tax regime simply meant Arabs taxing non-Arabs. The Muslim rulers stayed in the cities or the newly established garrison cities that were created, like Kufa and Basra in Iraq. In the territories of the former Ghassanid and Lakhmid states, particularly in the south, this picture was less clear-cut because both exploiters and exploited were Arabs. But increasingly, as the state apparatus indentified itself more and more with its own brand of monotheism, it came to mean Believers taxing non-Believers. Because the state religion now began to approximate to modern Islam from the early eighth century onwards, from this point on it might be accurate to describe the situation as one of Muslims taxing non-Muslims.

By the time of the Caliphate of Umar II (717 CE), now almost a century after the collapse of the Sassanid state and the formation of the Arab state, the Arab landowners were an established ruling class.

> "All the Arab warriors in the [provincial capitals] were owners of estates as a matter of course, and owned not merely their house and farm but also estates in the villages round about . . . the eagerness for land did not stop even at the taxable tracts of land belonging to subdued peasants, for they frequently passed into the possession of Arab lords by purchase or less honourable means." [751]

Although, as Wellhausen points out, there are some suggestions in the traditions that the Arab conquerors were not allowed to own land and that captured estates were owned by the Arabs *in common*, in practice these supposed rules were no more than a later romance and if they existed at all, were never put into effect. The later Islamic tradition that the early conquerors were forbidden to settle on the lands is a later rationalisation of the uncoordinated and chaotic picture of the early Arab state, in which petty warlords and clan leaders chased after loot and plunder and didn't have the degree of organisation required to establish a solid state machine.

Whereas the Arabs were supposed to be free of both poll tax and land tax (not being landowners in their personal capacities) in practice it was only the poll tax from which they became exempt. Frequently, tribute was extracted from a town or village as a *collective* sum from the whole community. It was allocated and collected, as it had been under the previous imperial regime, by local notables or by Christian bishops.

The ruling Umayyad caliphs, along with their family members and governors, did not stint in spending money on their own luxuries and lavish life-styles. Despite the alleged egalitarianism of these Arab kings and the supposed refusal of the first Umayyad, Mu'awiya to even wear a crown, no expense was spared in buildings for the Umayyad wealthy. It was not only the Dome of the Rock which characterised this dynasty, but a whole range of grand buildings and monuments in many parts of

---

[751] Julius Wellhausen, *The Arab Kingdom and its Fall*, p 275

the empire, including summer palaces and mansions, the archaeological remains of which still exist today.

From the lower levels of the new elite, the demobbed Arab army was assimilated into the cities to fill out the ranks of the artisans and semi-proletarians with the more fortunate becoming a new mercantile and commercial class. ". . . the Marwanid period saw the formation of the so-called Muslim bourgeoisie. The ex-tribesmen became shopkeepers, craftsmen and merchants and the *Sharia* [law] which they wrote is accordingly marked by a high regard for mercantile activities which landed nobilities usually despise."[752]

Mawali, clients of the Arab rulers

In the Arab Empire there was a clear distinction drawn between the conquerors and the conquered peoples. In so far as it meant anything at this early stage, Islam was regarded as the exclusive property of the Arab ruling elite, even in those areas which had previously been Arab and Christian for centuries. The less fortunate among the conquered peoples were left in exactly the same position as they were previously or, worse, were enslaved by their Arab masters. More fortunate subjects and prisoners of war often managed to become clients (*mawali*) of Arab notables or tribes and in doing so adopted Arab customs, Arabic names and, not least, converted to the faith of their patrons.

> "Being adherents of an ethnic faith the Arabs were not always willing to share their God with gentile converts, and being conquerors they were usually unwilling to share their glory with defeated enemies—both problems to which clientage provided an apt solution. Clients were freely accepted without conversion, but . . . newcomers to the faith [were] attached to the person 'at whose hands' they had converted."[753]

From the very beginning, therefore, as long as there were tax advantages to be had as part of the advantage of becoming clients of the new elite, *there was economic pressure on the local population to convert*, to whatever were the religious practices of their rulers. In some areas, where Muslims had been exempt from land tax, conversion was an ever more inviting route to escape from taxes and so it became increasingly unviable for land-owning Arabs to be allowed exemption from tax. Had the exemption from land-tax been permitted to all converts it would simply have meant the state extracting less and less from a locality or else the burden would have had to fall on a shrinking proportion of the landowners, or both.

> "If the tribute were lessened in proportion to the amounts dropped through the conversion to Islam, then the exchequer bore the brunt; but

---

[752]   Patricia Crone, *Slaves on Horses,* p 51
[753]   Patricia Crone, *Slaves on Horses,* p 49

if it was further raised to its old amount by a lump sum, then the burden was increased for the community, which had become less able to pay the taxes because of the conversions. Neither was it a good thing when the new converts, as frequently and perhaps mostly happened, left land and community to their fate and migrated to the Arabian towns. This took labour away from the land, so that it was in danger of becoming partly barren. The influx into the towns, however, was unwelcome. In Kufa and Basra there were plenty of new Muslims or *mawali*, originally freed prisoners of war, mostly of Iranian extractions. They occupied a position half-way between the Arab lords and the non-Arab subjects and while they certainly paid neither land tax nor poll tax . . . (they) received no pension . . . Their position being neither one thing nor another, naturally did not content them; Islam made them alive to their claims, and they sought to obtain full equal rights." [754]

In the decades after the foundation of the Arab Empire, when there was a material advantage for a section of the subject peoples to become clients of the new rulers, many moved to the cities, including the Arab garrison towns, to provide services as commercial and trade intermediaries. In return, they were able to enjoy the tax advantage of being *mawali*. In the countryside, the position of the peasantry was largely unchanged. They still toiled under the burden of their former tax-collectors and landlords (where they hadn't fled) and they were now expected to generate additional revenue for the Arab rulers.

". . . by the end of the period, in spite of the initial attempts by the Arabs to keep themselves apart religiously and socially from their subjects, and in spite of the refusal by caliphs and governors to allow the non-Arabs to enjoy the advantages of acceptance of Islam, large numbers of the subject peoples had come to identify themselves as Muslims." [755]

Throughout the new empire, *mawali* converts were second-class Muslims without the same rights as Arabs. It was only Arabs who were allocated pensions and stipends that were disbursed from the public purse for military service. Nevertheless, the *mawali* did gain real material advantages in access to the Arab rulers and in preferential treatment on taxation and other rights. In time these rights only whetted the appetites for equal rights with their Arab masters, particularly in the name of the equality that was theoretically prescribed by Islam. Wellhausen described how the *mawali* demands for equal rights increased as their numbers increased and how they became more involved in social and commercial activity and in the state apparatus, including the imperial army. He relates the development of *mawalism* in the conquered Iranian provinces as follows:

---

[754] Julius Wellhausen, *The Arab Kingdom and its Fall*, p 277
[755] GR Hawting, *The First Dynasty of Islam*, p 8

"Islam at first attracted the Iranians not so much for itself as for the advantages it offered. They employed it as a means to get closer to the ruling class and participate in its privileges, and to arabianise themselves, and then assumed Arab names and were incorporated with an Arab tribe . . . military service in the event of war of that time and district offered the most favourable opportunity of joining Islam. Following the example of the distinguished Iranians, the Arab gentlemen took with them into the field a personal following of servants . . . but the *mawali* were not fully recognised by the Arabs. If they served in the army they fought on foot and not on horseback . . . they received a share of the spoil but not a regular pension . . ."[756]

Wellhausen uses the words of the Iraqi governor of Basra, around 680 CE, to describe the dramatic increase in the relative numbers of the *mawali*: ". . . on his first coming there (to Basra) there had been registered . . . 70,000 regular soldiers (Arabs) and 90,000 tradesmen (*mawali*); now there were 80,000 regulars and 150,000 tradesmen."[757]

Historian Suliman Bashear comments on the social position of *mawali* and their openness to revolutionary ideas during the period that Hajjaj was governor of Iraq. "Of some relevance", he comments, "is a unique report concerning the circumstances in which Hajjaj had to dismiss a dark-skinned *mawla*, Sa'id ibn Jubayr, from the position of judge of Kufa. From it we learn that the Kufans protested against his appointment to this post, saying that it did not suit a *mawla* and that only an Arab was fit for the position. Later, we are told, Sa'id joined the rebels under Ibn al-Ash'ath and when caught by Hajjaj was put to death."[758] Another comment cited by Bashear, from an old poet, was that *mawali* ran shops "in all the markets of Iraq" and that it was an occupation frowned upon by Arabs.

The class structure of the Umayyad regime is of crucial importance because it was during this period that Abd Al-Malik first announced the prophethood of Mohammed and when Islamic scholars began for the first time to collect the traditions, or, more likely, to *write* them. The tradition of the *Sunna* is taken in Islam to represent the words and life of Mohammed and his immediate Companions and this began to be written down for the first time. The *hadith* that began to accumulate from this period did not simply echo the interests of the Umayyad regime. On the contrary, much of it reflected opposition movements and for that reason and the fact that much of it was written after the fall of the dynasty, Muslim tradition is overwhelmingly hostile to the Umayyads. The Umayyads are accused of behaving more like kings than true successors of the Prophet and it was at this time that the egalitarian traditions, harking back to a romanticised view of an Arab Bedouin past, began to be written. Islam was developing in a climate of

---

[756] Julius Wellhausen, *The Arab Kingdom and its Fall,* p 495-6
[757] Julius Wellhausen, *The Arab Kingdom and its Fall,* p 402
[758] Suliman Bashear, *Arabs and Others in Early Islam,* p 36

opposition to the exploitation and wealth which characterised the Umayyad elite. The key point is that it was not Islam that determined the social relations of the Empire, but precisely the opposite. *It was the social mix and the class contradictions in Umayyad society that were reflected in the hadith.* In the writings of a growing caste of Islamic scholars and scribes from the end of the seventh century onwards, Islam in its modern form began to develop.

> ". . . it was under the Umayyads that there began to emerge that class of religious scholars which eventually became the leading authority within Sunni Islam and which is chiefly responsible for shaping the historical and religious tradition . . . [which] emerged largely in opposition to the Umayyad government . . . in the emergence of this class the most important region was Iraq and in Iraq Kufa was the leading centre . . ."[759]

The literary tradition of Kharijism and the revolts of the followers of Ali (that is, *Shia* Islam) may have drawn from earlier folk memories of inter-tribal and clan wars but they are essentially products of this dynasty and the opposition it fostered in all quarters of the Empire, particularly in the east, in Iraq and Iran. It would eventually be the revolutionary movements in the east that would lead to the overthrow of the Umayyad dynasty in the mid eighth century.

Not surprisingly, many of the legal arguments about land ownership and entitlement were couched in religious terms, as were all the political, legal and philosophical debates of the times. To a large degree, the development of Islamic tradition was as a reflection of the need to resolve difficulties over the ownership and granting of land, booty, inheritance and all the juridical complexities of a new ruling class with vast properties and wealth. The Islamic jurists who debated these issues sought to authenticate their own particular views by finding pious references to the practices and life of Mohammed and the contents of the Koran. As the work of Schacht demonstrated, it was in this context and starting in this political period that many of the traditions began to be written down and projected backwards in time, by more than a century, to the Companions or, for even greater authenticity, to the Prophet himself.

In Suliman Bashear's examination of different traditions relating to Arab relations with other peoples, it is clear that there were many streams of tradition, reflecting different classes and strata within Umayyad society. There was, for example, "a whole group of polemical traditions concerning the issue of whether or not slaves and *mawali* are permitted to lead the believers in prayer."[760] It is not just that these traditions and their *isnads* were created quite late, but *they reflected struggles over contemporary issues and different class interests*—over taxation, tribute, land-holding, property-rights and inheritance. Some early traditions, he points out, describe some of the Prophet's companions as *mawali* or even as slaves who were

---

759   GR Hawting, *The First Dynasty of Islam*, p 2
760   Bashear, *Arabs and Others in Early Islam*, p 55

rejected by the aristocratic Arabs. There is another tradition he describes in which the Prophet dreams of herding black sheep, which are then mixed with white sheep, and this story, which dated from no earlier than the turn of the first/seventh century was a clear reflection, in theological terms, of the interests of the slaves and *mawali* within society. *Hadith* thus developed within the very real social turmoil of the empire and they reflect, not a sacred recitation from an angel or the holy words of a prophet, but the *contradictory class interests* within contemporary society.

As was shown by the work of Schacht, different schools of jurisprudence disagreed at first on which authority was the more important—that of custom or that of the Prophet and Companions. It was only after fierce polemic over the issue that the latter (the authority of the Prophet and Companions) came to predominate. Once that was the case and once a particular practice or legal precedent was suggested or agreed by scholars, the best way to make sure it was treated *as if it had always been thus* was to trace it back to the Prophet or his Companions to give it its due authenticity.

> "No doubt the jurists did yeoman service in this, but *what had really been the outcome of a complicated process mediating between opposing claims* they afterwards regarded as the matter-of-course law which always had been valid . . . the Muslim jurists have everywhere a way of tracing back to their beginnings the things that have come about gradually and which have been brought about by gradually arising needs or tendencies and of sanctioning them by the precedent of the Prophet . . ."[761]

Suliman Bashear recounts some examples of the contradictory stories have been passed down about the life and sayings of the Prophet, including some written to reflect the direct interests of the ruling elite:

> "One of the most striking aspects of the corpus of *hadith* and the origins narratives in general (including those original narratives that were compiled into the standard Muslim biographies of Muhammad) is the degree to which they reflect the salient political issues of the first and second centuries AH . . . For example we find many *hadiths* in which the Prophet addresses the question of constitutional authority . . . Quite common are statements of the Prophet, like 'Whoever obeys me obeys God; and whoever disobeys me, disobeys God. Whoever obeys my *amir* [king], obeys me and whoever disobeys my *amir*, disobeys me . . . *Hear and obey the amir, even if your back is whipped and your property is taken*; hear and obey . . .'"[762]

---

[761] Julius Wellhausen, *The Arab Kingdom and its Fall*, p283 (italics added)

[762] Donner, Fred M, *Narratives of Islamic Origins* p 40 (Italics added)

Many of the traditions that were created around or linked to the life of the Prophet were those that related to taxation and liability to tax. Fred Donner also cites a study of Islamic *hadith* that shows that many "have their roots in mid-to-late first century AH disputes between Muslim proprietors and the Umayyad state over the ownership and tax status of conquered lands, particularly in Iraq and Egypt. The dispute took the form of accounts describing particular cities or districts as having been conquered by force or taken by treaty, which was taken as decisive in determining the tax status of the land."[763] It was therefore as a result of different *vested interests* that conquest stories were elaborated by one party or another in disputes. The drive by the Umayyads to centralise and regularise taxation and administration of the empire was itself a key factor in the efforts by the later Umayyads to collect together the stories of the conquest.

> "The Umayyads, who from the time of Abd Al-Malik on seem to have supervised an increasingly clear articulation of the Muslim community as a distinct monotheistic confession, *began to encourage the recounting and collection of reports* about how the conquests had been organised and how they had succeeded. Their purpose was to establish what we might call a *narrative weapon* to bolster their claims to hegemony over their vast non-Muslim populations, by relating conquests' apparently miraculous success."[764]

When all the separate arguments over tax status had been settled, what was left was in *content* an imperial taxation code, but in outward *form*, it was a *conquest narrative*, complete with missing chapters, repeated pages, contradictions and outright mysteries. The opposition to the Umayyads that pervades the official Islamic tradition is a reflection of the very real dissent and frequent revolts against the Damascus regime. Time and again, opposition arose as a result of the discontent of *mawali* who had their Islamic privileges removed, or permitted and removed again, at the whim of provincial governors eager to extract the greatest possible tribute for the exchequer. Those Arabs who were landowners were subject to the same capricious policy swings—one moment permitting exemptions then having them removed, only to have them reinstated again and so on. The fundamental contradiction between the class interests on the one hand of the parasitic ruling elite in the imperial and provincial capitals and on the other hand of the local *mawali* and Arab landowners asserted itself over and over again and ultimately it led to the enormous revolutionary movement that overthrew the Umayyads in 750CE.

---

763   Donner, Fred M, *Narratives of Islamic Origins* p 171 (Italics added)
764   Donner, Fred M, *Narratives of Islamic Origins* p 181 (Italics added)

The pressure to convert

Where locals agreed to adopt the faith and religious observances of their Arab masters as *mawali*, they were better off in terms of taxation but they were only entitled to limited land ownership, inheritance and other rights. There was no equality for the *mawali*: they were effectively second-class Muslims and inferior to the Arab elite. Throughout the whole of the Umayyad period, therefore, there was a growing contradiction between the needs of the ruling class to tax the non-Arab masses (often through the intermediary of the original, local nobility) and the increasing economic and social pressure of the masses to seek economic relief through conversion. The dilemma was a simple one: the fewer Muslims, the greater the tax revenue, the more Muslims, the less the revenue.

> "Put generally, the problem was that Muslims did not, or at least should not, pay certain taxes to which non-Muslims were, or should have been liable. This provided an incentive for non-Muslims to become Muslims, but the widespread acceptance of Islam then cause a decrease in the revenues of the government, so *the Umayyad rulers had a vested interest in preventing the conquered peoples from accepting Islam* or forcing them to continue paying those taxes from which they claimed exemption as Muslims . . . To prevent this decline in revenue, the government or the local notables, as the case may be, either tried to prevent conversion to Islam or took no account of it when collecting taxes . . ."[765]

But conversions did take place, and, as we have explained, the main preoccupation of the Christian apocalyptic writings of the period were the dangers of apostasy among the long-suffering Christian peasants, many of whom were tempted to convert for the economic benefits it would bring. But as conversions increased, the tax burden on those remaining non-Muslims increased proportionally. So much so, that there were large-scale movements of peasants from the land into the towns.[766] The response of the governor of Iraq, Hajjaj, is described by Hawting:

> "Al-Hajjaj, faced with a decline in the revenue from taxation, reacted by rounding up the *mawali* in the towns, driving them out and forcing them to pay their taxes, stamping their hands as a token of the tax having been paid . . . . The result was the hostility not only of the *mawali* who were treated in this way, but also of the religious opponents of the Umayyads

---

[765] GR Hawting, *The First Dynasty of Islam*, p 77-79 (italics added)

[766] It has been suggested that the land taxes at this time were a key factor in transforming the large Jewish agrarian population either into conversion or into becoming a largely urban and mercantile people.

who saw the policy as an attack on the principle of an Islam open to all and conferring equality of rights . . . [767]

Islamic tradition acknowledges the reluctance of the Arab elite to allow mass conversions, although in the case of the one righteous Umayyad Caliph, Umar II, it ascribes this reluctance to his advisers. When his governors pointed out to him that his conversion policies were bad for the treasury, "that people are converting in order to escape their taxes that they ought to be tested for circumcision, and so on, he replies that god sent Muhammad to preach, not to collect taxes or to circumcise."[768]

There is not a hint here of the modern myth that the empire of the Arabs was brought about in order to facilitate the mass conversion of the world population to Islam. *Jihad* 'in the name of Islam' was not the policy of the Arab ruling class at all. Although it eventually became an unstoppable movement, conversion was not seen originally by the Arab elite as desirable, beyond a narrow caste of *mawali* adopted for their own convenience by tribes and tribal leaders. In the reports of the uprisings that began to take place with increasing frequency, the traditional accounts play down the significance of the *mawali*. In the course of one revolt, Wellhausen quotes one of the traditions as follows:

> "[At Jamajim] . . . there were 100,000 Arab defenders entitled to pensions, and just as many *mawali* but they appear in the following of their Arab masters. It was customary for the latter to take their clients, if they had any, into the field with them, and make them fight on foot whilst they themselves were mounted—a similar arrangement to that existing between knights and servants in the Middle Ages, so the fact that the *mawali* took part in it does not give the struggle its character."[769]

But notwithstanding this scepticism about their role in the uprising, as we shall see, the struggles of the *mawali* and the non-*mawali* peasantry came to represent huge class contradictions within the Arab empire, moreover, contradictions that become more critical with each passing year. Wellhausen quotes one of the traditional sources, Tabari, who cited a complaint lodged to the Caliph Umar II by the *mawali* in the army of Khurasan. The *mawali* who, "although they fought with the Arabs against the heathen at a strength of 20,000 men, were still excluded from the pension and actually had to pay tribute."

It was not only the Iraqi and Persian *mawali* who were a well-spring of discontent. In North Africa, the Berbers had adopted Islam and were the main body of the Arab army that later invaded Spain. But despite their Islamic status, they were still expected to give tribute to their Arab masters and were not accorded the same share of war booty as were Arabs. The tribute paid by the Berbers to the Arabs after

---

[767]   GR Hawting, *The First Dynasty of Islam*, p 70
[768]   Patricia Crone and Martin Hinds, *God's Caliph*, p 79
[769]   Julius Wellhausen, *The Arab Kingdom and its Fall*, p246

their original conquest, according to Baladhuri, consisted in part of the handing over of a particular number of Berber children each year, the girls as concubines, the boys as house or farm slaves.

Many former slaves and *mawali* found food and a roof over their head by enlisting in the Arab armies so that *mawali* troops became increasingly significant in the skirmishes and civil wars of the Umayyad period, until they eventually predominated in the standing imperial army. The tribal system which had still been a feature of the organisation of the Arab ruling elite in the early period, was overwhelmed by the army of former slaves and *mawali*. ". . . by the end of the Umayyad and the beginning of the Abbasid period, the last vestiges of the tribe had disappeared from the entire army organisation."[770]

Even if they weren't paid, the promise of loot from new conquests drew many former slaves and *mawali* and not a few impoverished peasants into the army as unpaid volunteers. "Admission to the army transformed a tax-payer into a tax-recipient . . . provided they paid their taxes, however, the peasants were perfectly free to work out their fascination with the army as unpaid and/or irregular volunteers . . . no less that thirty thousand were said to have participated in Maslama's [705 CE] expedition to Constantinople."[771]

Tens, perhaps hundreds of thousands of former slaves and *mawali* adopted Arab names as well as Islam and were effectively Arabised. This was particularly true of those drawn into the army, so that the Arab Empire became more homogenous ethnically whilst it also became more differentiated in terms of social class. ". . . the masses who flocked to Islam in the century of Umayyad rule," Patricia Crone writes, "simply became Arab Muslims. The Arabs, in other words, uprooted their subjects by enslavement in the course of their conquests, and by taxation in the course of their administration."[772]

Not surprisingly, as Wellhausen wrote, the Umayyads based in Damascus were constantly on the alert to suppress opposition movements and rebellions. Increasingly we see new revolts rooted in the discontent of assimilated Arabs in alliance with *mawali*.

> "They [The Umayyads] were further menaced by the implacable hostility of Iraq which broke out intermittently in gigantic revolts against the hated Syrian tyranny; *but the greatest danger for them was a social movement,* directed not against them alone, but against the Arab government generally."[773]

On an ever increasing scale, local converts began to demand an important role in the politics of the new state. Even as early as the second civil war (683-692) a

---

[770] Patricia Crone, *Slaves on Horses,* p 38

[771] Patricia Crone, *Slaves on Horses,* p 53

[772] Patricia Crone, *Slaves on Horses,* p 54

[773] Julius Wellhausen, *The Arab Kingdom and its Fall,* p308 (italics added)

revolutionary movement based in Iraq had been the first recorded revolt in which *mawali* played a significant role in a revolutionary struggle against the Umayyads. Theophanes recorded that in 683, ". . . Mukhtar the liar rebelled and, styling himself a prophet, became master of Persia. The Arabs were thrown into turmoil."[774] This revolt, against what was taken to be Islam was a *messianic* movement, from which, for the first time, came the idea of the *Mahdi*, as an Islamic messiah-figure heralding the End of Time. Within the community of Believers there were some messianic expectations associated with the end of the first Arab century and this coincided with the revolutionary ferment leading up to the Abbasid revolution. Even during the agitation around the period of that uprising, according to Tabari, one of the revolutionary leaders, after making a rousing speech, announced:

> "So know that the authority is with us, and shall not depart from us until we surrender it to Jesus the son of Mary—God's benediction be on him—and praise be to God, Lord of the Universe, for that with which he had tried us and entrusted us."[775]

In a footnote the translator adds that one *hadith* suggests "there will be no Mahdi but Jesus", although this is only preserved in Sunni tradition.

The real issues that were sparking these revolutionary upheavals and civil wars in the late Umayyad period were not the petty rivalries or the honour of different tribes and clans and nor was it the preaching of new messiahs, numerous as they were. It was the contending material interests of different social classes, *that is, issues of land ownership, exploitation, taxation, and political rights.* Wellhausen, almost in passing, gives a hint of some of the revolutionary ferment during the period of opposition to the Caliph Abd Al-Malik in 701 CE. He begins, (in a footnote!), by quoting Baladhuri on the uprising in Iraq which was suppressed in that year. He recounts how the property of those Persian landowners who had fled was confiscated as crown land and given out to supporters of the caliph. But when Hajjaj was governor of Iraq, the local people burnt the old title deeds,

> ". . . and everyone took whatever he could lay hands on. So the estates were in danger not merely from the fact that the Caliphs gave away part of them. *There lurked among the people a general rage against the latifundia of the state, the rulers and the great men.* They attempted to destroy or obscure the historical titles upon which rested the right of possession which was offensive to them." [776]

This revolt was directly connected, according to Wellhausen, to a decision of the governor, Hajjaj, to re-impose the poll-tax on the *mawali*, despite their conversion

---

774 Harry Turtledove (trans) *The Chronicles of Theophanes,* p 59
775 Tabari, *History,* XXVII, p 157.
776 Julius Wellhausen, *The Arab Kingdom and its Fall,* p 291 (italics added)

and their position as clients to Arab patrons. As we have seen, after the suppression of the revolt, Hajjaj ordered that the rebel *mawali* should be scattered to the land and villages and prevented from returning to the cities of Basra and Kufa. Wellhausen quotes some Islamic traditions in which Hajjaj is made to declare to the *mawali*, "Ye are barbarians and foreigners; your place is your towns and villages!"

> "Hajjaj wrote to Basra and other towns that those *mawali* who had immigrated there from the country should go back to their villages. Then those who were expelled assembled in Basra, not knowing whither to go, and called in lamentation upon the name of the Prophet." [777]

This particular movement was repressed but revolts and rebellions in the countryside reached epidemic proportions in the following period. This "general rage" described by Wellhausen was the real historic impetus for what was the greatest of all the revolutionary movements of the early Arab Empire. It was not only the revolution that replaced the Umayyad by the Abbasid dynasty and which provided the social basis for Shia Islam, but it also provided the basis for the rounding out of Islamic religious culture in general. It was during the reign of the Abbasid caliphs that Islam was finally defined in the form in which it is fully recognisable today.

Chapter summary

- The establishment of the wider Arab empire was not based on a religious campaign by Muslims spreading Islam, but on raids, incursions and occupation for booty, plunder, slaves, taxes and tribute. The new Arab empire was based on the brutal exploitation of the populations under its control.

- Taxation arrangements varied but generally speaking there was a tax placed on cultivated *land* and a *poll tax*. In most cases this meant Arabs taxing non-Arabs.

- More fortunate natives and prisoners of war managed to become clients (*mawali*) of Arab notables or tribes, adopting Arab customs, Arabic names and converting to the same religious practices of their patrons. *Mawali* demands for equal rights with Arabs increased as their numbers increased.

- There was a material advantage for a section of the subject peoples to become *mawali* and to convert to Arab monotheism. Such conversion was resisted by the caliphs but as Islam became more clearly defined, opposition to conversion became impossible.

---

[777]   Julius Wellhausen, *The Arab Kingdom and its Fall*, p286

Chapter 18

Class Struggle, Civil War
and the Abbasid Revolution

This chapter deals with the single most important revolutionary movement in the first century of the Arab era: the Abbasid revolution which blew away the Umayyad dynasty in the middle of the eighth century. It was this revolution which provided the real impetus for Shi'ism as the major schism in Islam. As we shall show, the Abbasid revolution drew millions, including the most down-trodden, along in its wake. But having satisfied many of the demands of the *mawali*, the new Abbasid elite crushed the aspirations of the masses by a full-scale counter-revolution. It was under the Abbasids that the first great collections of *hadith* were written down, collected and edited for the first time. The great torrent of writing which began at this time finally codified the orthodox traditions of Islam, both Sunni and Shia, and it is only in the great literary traditions of the Abbasids, more than two hundred years after the supposed life of the Prophet, that it is possible to recognise Islam in more or less the form in which we see it today.

. . . .

The centralisation of the empire under Abd Al-Malik and the later Umayyads inevitably meant the consolidation and integration of many subjects and subject peoples. Many non-Arabs, including hundreds of thousands of former slaves, became clients of the rulers and thereby sought to gain favour by conversion to the monotheism of their masters. There were also many soldiers of the former occupying armies who had become settlers, assimilating into and helping to Arabise the local population. The economy of the Empire became more integrated than ever before and it developed a more unified system of coinage, taxation and tribute, all of which were administered by a developed state bureaucracy.

Despite the consolidation of the Empire, or more accurately as a bye-product of it, the entire later period of Umayyad rule (more or less half a century) had been wracked by revolutions, crises and civil war. Sections of the old ruling elite were opposed to the centralising tendencies of the state, preferring to simply loot the land, even at the expense of its long-term economic development, while the more far-sighted wanted to put in place a guaranteed system of taxation and exploitation. The civil conflicts reflected the rivalries of different sections of the ruling elite, fighting over the spoils of an empire established by their great grandfathers. But the social crisis also reflected deep-rooted class tensions between the overwhelmingly Arab elite and the mass of local peasants and city poor, many of whom had converted to Islam in the expectation of some economic advantage. It was in the east of the empire in particular, in Iran and Iraq, that these revolutionary movements reached their high water mark and where, as often as not, they were to wear the religious garb of *Shi'ite* opposition to the Umayyads.

Historians have described the Abbasids' revolutionary movement as yet another clan conspiracy, the deeds of a few individuals, who replaced one branch of the Prophet's extended family by another. The role of the masses and the *mawali as a social class* has been written out of the narrative. Clan and family conspiracies there may have been and, as we shall see, the revolution did replace one elite by another, but the revolution would have been impossible in the first place but for a genuine mass movement in the east that encompassed millions of the most down-trodden and impoverished layers of society. The simplified description of Shi'ism as being based on the claim for succession of the family of Mohammed's son-in-law, Ali, was a later rationalisation of the longstanding different political and economic rivalry between the Arabs of Syria and Iraq. But the real impetus for Shi'ism as a major schism in Islamic tradition lies not in a family dispute but in the revolutionary upheaval that was based in the eastern part of the empire in the middle of the eighth century. Wellhausen described in some detail the struggles of the Umayyad regime to centralise its system of government against the opposition of the Arab rulers in Iraq:

> "In Basra, as in Kufa, the simple task which had to be performed was the establishment of the *Sultan*, ie the State, the supremacy of the government. In Basra it was necessary to put an end to the despotism of the tribes and the clans, whose first principle, in all cases, was to take the side of their clansmen, and even of their criminals not merely against the other clans but also against the government."[778]

Kufa and Basra were not ancient sites, but artificial cities based on what had been garrison towns in the early period of the empire. Wellhausen, like most historians basing themselves on Islamic sources, exaggerates the Bedouin history of these settlers but noted that their only traditions were based on Arab armies, "confusedly mustered from different tribes . . . cast up thither through war and . . . settled as military colonies." Finding themselves under pressure to be a part of a great kingdom and, moreover, one based in Damascus, "it is not surprising that they did not all at once change from Bedouin into rational citizens of a state".

It is significant that it was these particular areas, Kufa especially, which became important centres for the development of Islamic ideas, much more so than Mecca or Medina and a large part of the growing tradition was in direct opposition to the Umayyads in faraway Damascus. In this former garrison town, an important part of Islamic tradition was created by the growing caste of religious scholars, the *ulema*, who were based there: a tradition that grew in opposition to the Syrian-based

---

[778]   Julius Wellhausen, *The Arab Kingdom and its Fall*, p 129

regime and which harked back to an imaginary and romantic Bedouin idyll. As Ali Dashti put it, "the Iranians", that is, those in the east of the Empire, "were more Arab than the Arabs."

Just as we saw that the old Hebrew Bible retained echoes of class conflicts within the old kingdoms of Judah and Israel, so too we can see in the legends about Ali and Shi'ism the outlines of class upheaval in the last decades of the Umayyad dynasty. Wellhausen points at some of these in his *Arab Kingdom*. Referring to Ali, he notes that ". . . besides Kufaites and other Arabs who shared his political views, there joined to him many non-Arabs who objected to paying the taxes." "Ali", Wellhausen adds, "justified those who refused to pay taxes by saying that the tax . . . ought to benefit the poor of its own land and not the treasury . . ."[779] As it was with all social and political movements of the day, revolts and opposition to the imperial elite were framed in religious language. But that did not alter the fact that the revolutionary ferment under the later Umayyads was a product of economic and class contradictions.

> "The Umayyads had to be constantly on the alert to keep down the opposition which rose up against them in the name of Allah and the religion. They were further menaced by the implacable hostility of Iraq which broke out intermittently in gigantic revolts against the hated Syrian tyranny; *but the greatest danger for them was a social movement, directed not against them alone, but against the Arab government generally* . . . the wall of separation between masters and servants was broken through by the fact that the latter accepted Islam more and more and did away with the Arab army towns . . . the *mawali* were clamouring at the gates and demanding equal rights with the Arabs. They had Islam on their side and were recruited by the revolution which based itself on Islam."[780]

Shia Islam became the unifying force of all those in Iran who were opposed to the Umayyads. There were many sects of Believers who saw no difference between Arab and Iranian or between master and servant, and in the end these coalesced into what became Shi'ism. "It regenerated the Iranians, gave them backbone, and put into their hands a weapon against their masters . . . It was the Arabs who first roused and organised the *mawali* . . . Revolutionary Islam set the idea of the theocracy against the existing organisation, and invited men to fight for God against the Umayyads and their officials, for law and justice against wrong and force."[781]. But whereas historians like Wellhausen portray Shi'ism as the "deciding factor" in the revolution, *it was the revolution that was the deciding factor in putting Shi'ism on the map.* The Shi'ite interpretation of early Islamic history was written during the gestation period and after the success of the Abbasid revolt, in the first and second centuries. This

[779]   Julius Wellhausen, *The Arab Kingdom and its Fall*, p 86, 87
[780]   Julius Wellhausen, *The Arab Kingdom and its Fall*, p 308 (italics added)
[781]   Julius Wellhausen, *The Arab Kingdom and its Fall*, p 497

interpretation was based on the caliphal claims of Ali and his family, interwoven with the traditional history that was developing and its historical authenticity projected right back to the time of the Prophet. Shi'ism did not create the Abbasid or earlier revolutions. On the contrary, it was the Abbasid revolution that launched the entire tradition of the family of Ali and theological Shi'ism, but only as a faint historical echo of itself.

This book is not the place for a theological discourse about the differences between modern Sunni and Shia Islam; suffice to say that Shia Islam is based around the special role and character of Ali and his family and the historic right that was denied to them in the succession to the Prophet. The key point is that the greater part of the corpus of legends surrounding Ali and his family was created at a much late date and projected back to the mid seventh century and woven into the life of Mohammed and his immediate successors.

Throughout the early decades of the eighth century, the Umayyad dynasty faced one revolt after another. The caliphs attempted to divert the growing opposition of the *mawali*, and discontent in general, into new campaigns of conquest, but they were not always successful. There was a new attempt to conquer Anatolia and Constantinople, the latest in a long line of such efforts, which ended in catastrophic failure. Years of military campaigns against the Khazars had brought little in the way of tangible rewards and there were new revolts breaking out regularly in the Caucasus region. "Most ominously", Khalid Blankinship writes in *The End of the Jihad State*, "the Muslim troops were beginning to get tired of the endless, profitless, desperate campaigning with its high losses."[782]

As a sign of the decay at the centre, in 730-32 CE there were a number of related military defeats, in India, the Caucasus, southern France and Anatolia, which dramatically altered the balance of forces within the Empire. But blind to its own internal contradictions, the caliphate literally soldiered on and attempted to fend off revolution at home by even more desperate attempts to plunder abroad.

> "Despite the striking success of some of its final efforts, [the Umayyad caliphate] . . . ended the period a hollow shell, ruined by the expenses its military excesses claimed in lives and wealth. When the very hour of victory had arrived on some fronts, the caliphate found itself unable to exploit it. Rather, it awaited only the *coup de grace* from a fresh opponent to send its whole structure crashing to earth."[783]

The Abbasid revolution was not one single event, although it culminated in the overthrow of the Umayyads in 750 CE. Prior to that point, there was a whole series of revolts reverberating from one province to another. One of these was the great Berber revolt in North West Africa that lasted nearly three years. Islamic tradition records the spread of Kharijite doctrines in that area and this must have been a

---

[782] Khalid Blankinship, *The End of the Jihad State*, p 128.
[783] Khalid Blankinship, *The End of the Jihad State*, p 168

reaction against the social and national oppression of the Berber people. According to Tabari, many years after the Islamic conquest of North Africa Berbers were still being taken as tribute slaves to Syria and Iraq, even though by then they had embraced Islam. This revolt was crushed, but only at great cost.

The main centres of revolution against the Umayyads were in the east and particularly in the Persian province of Khurasan and in the city of Merv. Here, according to Wellhausen, there were many revolts, all of them with the outward form of a religious movement. A revolt in about 735 CE was suppressed, but not before its leader, Harith, had ". . . incited the *mawali* by declaring he would bring to realisation the freedom from the subject-tax and the participation in the military pension which were their due and which had been promised them, and . . . the people of the villages gathered under his black standard . . ." Nor were the revolts based simply on Iranian opposition to Arab rule. The relatively small number of Arabs who had settled in Persia had become assimilated and even spoke the local language. It was *class issues* that drove the mass of Iranians into opposing the state. ". . . the leaders of the movement for the bestowing of equal rights upon the Iranians who had embraced Islam in the theocracy were again Arabs", Wellhausen notes, but their main following lay in the non-Arab population. As a result of *class* appeals, Harith's army "swelled tremendously."

> ". . . the conversion of the non-Arab subjects to Islam did not free them from their connection with their tax-paying community. The subject-tax was a tribute irrevocably fixed in its amount by the historical act of capitulation, and if the numerous converts had no longer contributed to it, then the rest would have had to pay for them with the result that it would have been no longer possible to raise the amount. The duty of contributing thus descended from fathers to sons as a burden assumed by them at the capitulation even though the latter afterwards embraced Islam. According to this practice the native authorities acted with the approval of the Arab government . . . the land tax was correspondingly re-modelled and collected from all landed proprietors in proportion to their property, no matter whether they were subjects or Muslims . . . ."[784]

The poll-tax continued to be levied only from non-Muslims, but it was less significant. Wellhausen adds in a footnote, that although Muslim and Iranian landowners were treated equally in law, "in point of fact the Iranians had really to pay far more because the landed property mostly belonged to them, especially to the *Dihqans*, [Persian nobility] who on their part fleeced the peasants."[785]

The final demise of the Umayyads came with a mass rising in Khurasan in form of a Shi'ite movement. Here, according to Wellhausen, was the added factor

---

[784]   Julius Wellhausen, *The Arab Kingdom and its Fall*, p 479-80
[785]   Julius Wellhausen, *The Arab Kingdom and its Fall*, p 481

of the national question and the continued exploitation of the peasantry by the landowners of the former Sassanid regime. In relation to Khurasan, he writes:

"The population, the language and the industry in this fairly extensive region was Iranian. In politics there was a great amount of division, which cannot only have set in since the fall of the Sassanid kingdom. Under the aristocracy of the *Dihqans* the ruling dynasties soared above the simple nobility, landed proprietors and bailiffs in the villages. Everywhere in the isolated districts and larger towns we find hereditary princes with their own peculiar titles."

In the period leading up to open revolt, Qutayba, the governor of the Khurasan attempted to channel popular discontent into campaigns of conquest and looting on the borders of the Empire, although the end result was to drive the war-weary Arabs and *mawali* into the same revolutionary camp.

"Although the wars of Qutayba brought a considerable amount of booty to Khurasan, it also deprived the countryside of its needed manpower. This situation created a war economy and inflation which in turn caused the price of grain to rise. The levies from Khurasan were the first to be hurt by this situation and they were also the first to complain. Eventually, both the Arabs and the mawali became tired of the successive campaigns and at the first opportunity, while they were actually on an expedition to Farghana, they cooperated to depose and murder Qutayba in order to return to their homes. This was a turning point in the history of the Arabs in Khurasan."[786]

Wellhausen uses Tabari for a lot of his account of the revolution and despite the latter's long chronological displacement from events and his tendency to see all historical change being driven by the whims and rivalries of individual personalities, there are clear echoes of the social unrest in his account of the revolution. Tabari describes how a series of revolts in the east meant that eventually the authority wielded by the regime in any locality "began to unravel." Revolutionary currents began to gather around the figure of Abu Muslim, "a weaver by trade" (according to Theophilus). "In one day," Tabari notes, "the people of sixty villages joined him."

"When Abu Muslim openly proclaimed revolution" Tabari reports, "people hastened to join him, and the people of Merv began to come to him." [787] He recounts that large numbers of runaway slaves came to him but Abu Muslim refused to enrol them. This is an interesting issue, even leaving aside the truth of the detail as to whether or not Abu Muslim allowed the runaway slaves to fight with him (and Tabari, writing during the later Abbasid dynasty would want to minimise the

[786]   M A Shaban, *Islamic History,* p 176
[787]   Tabari, *History,* Vol XXVII, p 75

role of slaves in the revolt), the very fact that runaway slaves were flocking to his banner is of enormous significance. Later Tabari reports another local leader rallying revolutionaries in eastern Iraq and western Iran, when "the slaves of the Kufans ran away to join him." Wellhausen recounts that in Kufa, the revolutionaries were "all *mawali*, of Iranian nationality and shopkeepers and artisans to trade. Arabs indeed may also have belonged to the party but they did not occupy any leading position." He goes on to quote, from an Arabic poem, the words of the Umayyad governor of Iraq, on the revolutionaries as follows:

> "They are a mob of men without religion and without consequence, no Arab of ours, for us to know, and no *mawali* of any standing. They have a religion which comes not from the Messenger of God nor is it to be found in the holy books; it amounts, in truth, to this, that the Arabs are to be killed."[788]

According to the limited account of Theophanes, written much closer chronologically than Tabari, "The Khorosanians . . . incited the slaves to rise against their masters, killing many in one night. Once armed with the weapons, horses and money of these men, they had a powerful position."[789] Although Wellhausen's historical approach is based almost completely on the traditional Islamic sources, he is forced to concede that ". . . it was not the Arabs *per se*, but the *ruling* Arabs that were to be fought against," notwithstanding the fact that this was done in the name of piety and that the Umayyads were condemned as "godless" who "did not recognise the equal rights of the other Muslims in the theocracy."[790]

The revolution gained such momentum that it eventually swept westwards towards Damascus, uprooting the Umayyad dynasty which had ruled the Arab Empire for a century. The Abbasid elite moved quickly to massacre all the former supporters and families of the Umayyads and anyone else who would have had any claim to the caliphate, but the momentum of the revolution could not stop there. It inevitably led to a far greater incorporation of the *mawali* as full participants into Islamic society. It was the changed circumstances of the *mawali* that were the most significant results of the Abbasid revolution. Islamic tradition has narrated—ubiquitously and to such a uniform degree that it cannot be doubted—that small numbers of privileged *mawali* had played important and leading roles within the Arab Empire from a very early date. Not only were they advisers and administrators at all levels, but many of the generals and provincial governors closest to the caliph were *mawali* or descended from *mawali*. By the end of the Umayyad period, *mawali* were already beginning to play a disproportionate role in the fields of Art, Literature, Science and Jurisprudence, all of which were intimately woven into and inter-connected to the world of theology: the Koran, the

---

[788] Julius Wellhausen, *The Arab Kingdom and its Fall*, p 534
[789] Theophanes, *Chronicles*, p 114
[790] Julius Wellhausen, *The Arab Kingdom and its Fall*, p 535

Sunna of the Prophet and the development of *hadith*. But *the overwhelming majority of the mawali were not privileged and pampered by the court*; they had been effectively excluded from political and economic power by the relatively small Arab elite.

The Abbasid revolution, therefore, pitted *mawali* against *mawali* and Arab against Arab on *class* lines. What provided greatest impetus to the revolution were not the national characteristics of the protagonists, but the *class contradictions*. It was the poorest sections of the *mawali* who were joined by an increasing number of assimilated Arabs, exploited as workers or agricultural labourers by the rich and powerful Arab and non-Arab elites. The *mawali* and dissident Arabs tapped into a rich vein of anger and discontent among the population at large, including peasants, city poor, slaves and freed slaves, to create a revolutionary movement great enough to overthrow the Umayyads. What resulted from the Abbasid revolution was not simply the replacement of one ruling class by a new one, but *the extension and broadening of the old ruling class* by the incorporation of a wider strata of Arabised local merchants, landowners and wealthy (and now including large numbers of *mawali*) who became the effective bulwark of the new dynasty. The family of the former Umayyad rulers may have been mercilessly hounded to extinction but many of the old landowners and economic elite were left *in situ*, while the new standing army of the Abbasids was made up of *mawali*, former slaves and loyal Arabs, blowing away the last shreds of tribal and clan affiliations.

The aspirations of the former slaves and the most down-trodden, those who had been the foot-soldiers of the revolution, were not to be realised. Indeed, having satisfied many of the demands of the *mawali*, the Abbasids responded to the demands of the lower orders by a full-scale counter-revolution. The hopes of the revolutionary former slaves were quickly drowned in blood as first the revolutionary leader Abu Muslim was murdered and then localised revolts in his support were viciously suppressed by the new Abbasid regime. In northern Iraq, following the Abbasid conquest, there were stories of atrocities in Mosul, including the rape of Arab women. The newly appointed Abbasid governor was reported to have ordered the execution of 4000 black African soldiers, all former slaves, who had been among the revolutionary forces, as a reprisal against those who had allegedly committed atrocities. That black ex-slaves, the so-called Zanj, should be among the Abbasid forces is itself a fact of great significance, but as one author pointed out, the ruling Arab elite was poisonously racist and there is a strong suggestion ". . . that the ethnicity of the rapists was nearly as significant as the fact itself."[791]

The Abbasids moved quickly to establish their regime and it soon became clear that they depended on many of the same sources of income as their Umayyad predecessors. In many cases they owned the same estates and exploited them in the same ways." [792] But for those at the very bottom there was little or no change and their hopes turned to ashes in their mouths. Zanj slaves continued to toil in the fields and quarries of Iraq and their continued exploitation inevitably meant

---

[791]   Chase Robinson in *The Transformation of Northern Mesopotamia*, p 136
[792]   Hugh Kennedy, *Early Incomes in the Early Islamic State, Elites Old and New,* p 13.

that from time to time there would be new explosions of revolt and rebellion. (See appendix on the Zanj slave revolt).

The murder of Abu Muslim, who had been the charismatic leader of the Abbasid uprising, triggered further revolts throughout Iran and as far afield as Azerbijan, where new revolutionary leaders arose. In her book *Slaves on Horses*, Patricia Crone notes that the Abbasid revolt was not the end of class struggle and social upheaval within the Empire:

> ". . . witness the frequency with which fiscal or administrative oppression acted as a trigger. The Coptic *jacqueries* in Egypt, very likely also Bundar's rising in Christian Lebanon, the *Kharijite* rebellions in Sistan, possibly also those in the Jazira, the massive peasant revolts under the leadership of syncretic prophets in Transoxania, Khurasan, the Jibal and Azerbaijan, and the Transoxanian revolt of Rafi b. Lyth; all these were in their very different ways attempts to shake off the heavy hands of the Abbasid governors."[793]

In another work, Patricia Crone also surveyed the huge number of revolts that reverberated around the Empire like the after-shocks that follow a major earthquake. This was particularly true in the Caucasus region. Despite, or because of, the murder of the Abu Muslim, many of the new revolts took on the colouration of Mazdakism, a rigorously egalitarian form of Islam.

> "When Abu Muslim was killed, a great many of his recruits walked out, not just of Abbasid service, but of Muslim society altogether, and it was their revolts which started the conflagration. In the 760s and 70s al-Muqanna' rebelled in Transoxania; between 778 and 798 you have revolts by the Red-clothed Khurramis in Jurjan; in 778 and 807-9, Khurrami rebelled in Fars and Jibal, and in 816 to 837 you have Babak's revolt in Azerbaijan."[794]

Small wonder that the later chroniclers of Islamic history, like Tabari, sought to minimise the role of slaves in the original Abbasid revolt; they were mostly the scribes of the new ruling elite and they were never so free from threats of new insurrections that they could afford to extol the revolutionary fervour of the masses.

Yet despite the ongoing series of revolts and dissent, the ruling class that was set in power under the Abbasids was broader-based, more confident and more firmly established than at any time during the whole century-long history of the Arab Empire. Across an empire that stretched over thousands of miles and millions of subjects, the ruling class was able to develop trade, commerce and the economy on an unprecedented scale. The Arab Empire, like the Roman Empire in a previous epoch, was almost a world market in its own right.

---

[793]   Patricia Crone, *Slaves on Horses*, p 71
[794]   Patricia Crone, *Babak's Revolt*

"With the Abbasid revolution of 750, the equality established between ethnic groups, the conversion, now assured, of the majority of the population to Islam, and the Arabisation of a large part of the Empire, all caused commercial activity to become widespread among every section of the population, at least to the extent that the natural conditions in which they lived made this possible. The extension of the Empire, embracing regions that formerly had been cut off from each other, afforded an immense field to this activity, bringing new and diverse commodities into a common circuit. Then began the classical period of the economic development of the Muslim Empire and first and foremost its commercial development. This may be seen as broadly continuing (even if there was some lessening of activity) right down to the fourteenth century, inclusive. The merchants of the Muslim empire . . . seized any and every opportunity for profit, and calculated their outlays, their encashments and their profits in money terms."[795]

As a pre-capitalist economic formation, the Muslim Empire was not a copy or a mirror of the feudal states that began to develop in Europe around the same time. It showed elements of land ownership and exploitation that were similar to classical European feudalism, but it also demonstrated wide variety from region to region with some places retaining significant remnants of slavery, some dominated by sharecropping and yet others by large latifundia or small 'independent' producers. More importantly, its most significant feature was the predominance of an urban mercantile ruling class (a "mainly commercial bourgeoisie" is how Rodinson describes it) and intra-imperial trade so well developed that regional industrial and agricultural specialisation were possible, creating further interdependence between regions and an integrated market.

The Abbasid revolution in many respects clarified class relations. It would no longer be a question of Muslims exploiting non-Muslims because within a measurable period of time the vast majority of the Empire became Muslim. What was clearer than ever before was that it was a matter of the haves and have-nots.

". . . the inequalities between those who had been lavishly endowed with landed property and the rest, and then between the rich and the poor in general, continued to grow. As a result of conversions there were [even] *Muslim slaves* . . . the situation was so much out of accord with the aspirations of the masses that revolutionary movements started regularly appearing in the Muslim world".[796]

Although scholars now began to introduce a strong strand of egalitarianism into the *hadith*, as much as anything to justify the position of the *mawali* upstarts against

---

[795] Maxime Rodinson, *Islam and Capitalism*, p 59
[796] Maxime Rodinson, *Islam and Capitalism*, p 103 (italics added)

the opposition of the old Arabian traditionalists, the equality between Muslims remained only on paper. As Rodinson puts it, "the ideologists do not govern; they merely expound God's opinion." A burgeoning class of merchants, traders and bankers ran rings around the *theoretical* Islamic strictures against usury, for example. Maxime Rodinson cites the example of books that circulated as early as the ninth century that dealt specifically with ruses (*hiyal* in Arabic) to get around the theological limitations of trading. One of the many simple ways of getting around the ban on interest, for example, goes something like this: Imagine Yusuf wants to borrow 100 dirhams from Ahmed. Ahmed sells Yusuf a book, for, say, 120 dirhams, payable *in a year's time*. Yusuf then sells the book back to Ahmed *immediately*, with cash, for 100 dirhams. Thus Ahmed still has his book, Yusuf trousers 100 dirhams but he then has an obligation to pay for the book he 'bought' for 120 dirhams . . . twelve months later. No usury in sight.

The final elaboration and clarification of 'historical' tradition

The Abbasid dynasty was no different to its predecessor in its fundamental role as exploiter of the mass of the population. Although, as a Muslim state, the regime was obliged to provide hospitals, welfare for the poor, public drinking fountains and other public works from its funds, these public charitable works were no more significant than they were in the Christian empire to the north and constituted a minor part of the overall operations of the state. ". . . few Muslim rulers have given up much of their lavish spending on luxury, prestige and war in order to enlarge their expenditure on welfare."[797] The overwhelming mass of the resources of the state were at the disposal of the ruling elite and the whole *raison d'être* of the state bureaucracy, army and administration was the continuation and extension of its privilege, position and power.

The Abbasid dynasty represented a new elite that was based on a wider spread of interests than simply its own family aristocracy as were the Umayyads. Its two main instruments of power were the standing army of *mawali* and an Islam made more orthodox than before. In the words of Ignaz Goldziher, "they wished to be not merely kings, but primarily princes of the church . . . now religion was not only a matter of interest to the state; it was the state's chief business." The new regime quickly shrugged off the Shi'ite complexion of the revolution which brought it to power and mainstream Sunni Islam was brought closer to the court and sponsored by the central government. It was under the Abbasids that the first great collections of *hadith* were assembled, edited and published for the first time. This is the prime reason why Islamic tradition is not kind the Umayyad dynasty. The official views of the Abbasid court were represented by what became *Sunni* Islam, while a current within Islamic scholarship, particularly based in Iran and eastern Iraq, the main bases of the Abbasid revolution, kept alive other traditions based around Ali, the

---

797   Maxime Rodinson, *Islam and Capitalism*, p 108

son-in-law of the Prophet, and this became Shia Islam. The Abbasids effectively completed what the Umayyads had only just started: creating a new Arab form of monotheism to rival the traditional monotheisms of Judaism and Christianity. By the end of the Abbasid dynasty, Islam was more or less in the form in which it is known today.

The new developers of Islamic correctness, in drawing such a poor image of the Umayyad caliphs, necessarily had to project the foundations of the faith back a long way and leap-frog over the Umayyads. It was necessary to negate many of the Umayyads' original religious practices, like centring the religion on Jerusalem. The Abbasid scholars and *ulema* ". . . successfully cast the Umayyads as worldly rulers indifferent or even inimical to Islam: time and again it is by their departure from supposedly patriarchal norms that the Umayyads condemn themselves."[798]

The Abbasid dynasty, based in its newly-found capital of Baghdad, saw the flowering of Arabic and Islamic culture on a scale not seen before. The *mawali* of subject nations went out of their way to 'Arabise' their own family histories and traditions. Paradoxically, the Abbasid dynasty has been described as an upsurge of *Persian* culture, intruding into *Arab* culture, yet this was the greatest period of growth for the Arabic language and literature, as well as for the development of Islamic histories based on the romance of Bedouin lore. Although the Abbasids saw a huge increase in Arabic literature, it was the former non-Arabs and the Persians in particular, who were the main proponents of this cultural revolution. Arabic culture thrived and the descendents of Arab colonists were assimilated on a scale never seen before. Goldziher notes that many of the non-Arab peoples, including Egyptians, Berbers and Persians adopted Arabic names and invented Arabian genealogies for themselves. And with the genealogies they invented exploits about their ancestors' role in the conquests and the spreading of Islam.

The flowering of Abbasid culture marks that historic period from the eighth century onwards which was established by the scholarly works of Goldziher, Schacht, Wansbrough, Crone and others as *the true point of origin of modern Islam*. It was in the period of Abbasid rule that the final great surge of writing began that was to codify and fully establish the orthodox tradition of Islam, by development of *hadith* and Islamic law. "With the rise of the new dynasty," Goldziher wrote, "the time had come, after scanty and modest beginnings, for Islamic Law to blossom and flourish." A truly huge corpus of literature now began to be produced and collected and at an accelerating pace. It was centred above all on law and property relations, but was increasingly taking as its authority a growing corpus of tradition that projected back in time towards Mohammed and his Companions.

"The bulk of our historical texts on early Islam are to be found in a body of compilations and digests composed roughly between 850 and 950

---

[798]   Patricia Crone and Martin Hinds, *God's Caliph*, p 23

CE . . . as it happens, our principal accounts of the life of Muhammad were all composed in their definitive form between 750 and 850 CE."[799]

What is generally taken to be the first authoritative account of the Prophet's life, written by Ibn Ishaq, was actually commissioned, according to tradition, by a member of the Abbasid court. As Ali Dashti pointed out in his book, with the accounts of the life of the prophet multiplying, so also did the minutiae surrounding it, fixing every verse of the Koran to a particular moment in the biography. The life of the Prophet was only one of the key elements in the formalisation and regularisation of modern Islam. Shi'ism was pushed to one side by mainstream scholars under the wing of the Abbasids, although Shia scholars in the east continued to develop their own traditions in tandem and in correspondence with the 'official' *Sunni* variety in the west.

> "The Abbasids rose to power by staging a revolution of Shi'ite colouring in Khurasan, from the start employing *mutakallims* [theologians] who as religious disputants and propagandists played an integral part in the Abbasid establishment, and they soon inherited the bureaucracy of Iraq. They thus possessed what resources were available for a syncretic handling of Islam."[800]

The first collections of *hadith* that had been started during the Umayyad period were overwhelmed by a veritable mountain of new *hadith* that now began to be produced. These dealt fundamentally with property, legal and judicial issues, in other words linked to the material political and economic situation that pertained in Abbasid society. But they were all part of the process of clarifying and systematising Koranic text as it related to the life and *Sunna* of the Prophet a century or two earlier. Corrections were necessarily made to the established Islamic traditions of the Umayyads. Some of the older *hadith*, like those stories which had put Arab racial superiority into the mouth of the Prophet, were never quite eliminated, but they were balanced by newly discovered accounts of more egalitarian statements that had been made by Mohammed. As scholars like Schacht have amply demonstrated, the newly-invented *hadith* was authenticated by *isnads*, chains of personal transmission, that extended ever further backwards until they got to the Companions or to Mohammed himself. [801]

---

[799]   R Stephen Humphrey, *Islamic History*, p 71

[800]   Patricia Crone, *Slaves on Horses*, p 64

[801]   Bernard Lewis, in *From Babel to Dragomans*, (p 110) cites an instance of hadith being created in the modern times: "A tradition published in the Jerusalem daily newspaper al-Nahar, on 15 December 1990, and described as 'currently in wide circulation', quotes the Prophet as predicting that 'the Greeeks and Franks will join with Egypt in the desert against a man named Sadim, and not one of them will return'. The allusion is clearly to the build-up of coalition forces leading up to the Gulf War."

The *sunna* of the Prophet (the totality of this life and works) became the touchstone of all legal, doctrinal and liturgical practice under the Abbasids. Just as in centuries gone by the political polemics between Jewish factions had revolved around "the way" and the "path" as metaphors for what was or wasn't "righteous" in the eyes of God, so the scholars and jurists of Islam debated over what was and wasn't correct *sunna*. Under the previous dynasty, ". . . the Umayyads saw caliphal practice as identical with that of the Prophet for the simple reason that they approved of their own acts, while their opponents conversely saw it as opposed to that of the Prophet for the simple reason that they disliked the Umayyad policies."[802] In the past, when some reference to the *sunna* was a required part of any rhetoric, it had been done without reference to any particular text or ruling. "Practically no traditions, be they Prophetic or other, are cited in letters or speeches by Umayyad caliphs, governors or secretaries. None seem to be adduced by rebels. Scarcely any appear in theological epistles. Hardly any are cited in accounts about Umayyad judges, judges being required to know the Qur'an, not tradition."[803] Now, beginning with the Abbasids, texts were proliferating and there was suddenly an abundance of authorities and precedents that could be cited in the scholarly polemics.

In legal matters, Patricia Crone points out, "there is no trace of the Prophetic tradition until about 770" and it was the lawyers in particular who created the stories about Mohammed simply to back up their own arguments in law. "Numerous Prophetic traditions can be shown to have originated as statements made by the lawyers themselves . . . it was the lawyers who determined what the Prophet said, not the other way round."[804] Bukhari is said to have accumulated as many as 600,000 traditions, of which he only accepted as authentic 7,000, or *just over one per cent*! Bukhari's dismissal of ninety-nine per cent of traditions as being inauthentic did not, of course, mean their circulation was thereby stopped. One only has to contrast surviving *hadiths* that are in flat contradiction to one another to see to what extent Bukhari was trying to swim against a tsunami. As Crone argues in relation to the hundreds of thousands of *hadiths* that survived, "the presumption must surely be that *no* hadith is authentic."

In the same way that Christianity was forced to adapt to local customs when it became the state religion, Islam, too, as it came to extend across almost the entire imperial population, was forced to adapt to and accept many local saints, customs and practices into its regular calendar and rituals. The two great festivals of Islam are *eid al-kabir*, celebrated during the annual pilgrimage and *eid al-fitr*, celebrated at the end of the Ramadan fast. "But to these should be added any number of local celebrations of pre-Islamic provenance such as the Persian New Year festival of *Nawruz* and the Egyptian celebration of spring, *Shamm al-Nasim*. The celebration of Nawruz was customarily accompanied by bonfires or fireworks . . ." Not to be outdone by the Christians who had by this time adopted the pagan mid-winter

[802]   Crone and Hinds, *God's Caliph*, p 64
[803]   Crone and Hinds, *God's Caliph*, p 72
[804]   Patricia Crone, *Roman, Provincial and Islamic Law*, p 32

festival as an appropriate birth-date for Jesus, by the end of the Abbasid era, Muslims scholars had discovered the birthday for their prophet (on 12 *Rabi' al-Awaal*) and they had adopted "numerous other saints days, celebrated with the music of tambourines and lutes, dancing and singing."[805] Within a couple of centuries, Islam had its lists of saints and hagiographies as extensive as anything coming out of the Catholic Church.

As Goldziher pointed out more than a century ago, every argument in law, theology and in doctrine, from whatever point of view, developed its own *hadith* in its favour and extended its authority back to the Prophet or his Companions. "Every attitude of mind in Islam," Goldziher points out, "found expression in Prophetic sayings made to order." All those aspects of Islamic worship and practice that were borrowed from other traditions were similarly supplied with justification from the past.

> "Whatever Islam produced on its own or borrowed from the outside was dressed up as hadith. In such form, alien, borrowed matter was assimilated until its origin was unrecognisable. Passages from the Old and New Testaments, rabbinic sayings, quotes from apocryphal gospels and even doctrines of Greek philosophers and maxims of Persian and Indian wisdom gained entrance into Islam disguised as utterances of the Prophet. Even the Lord's Prayer occurs in well-authenticated hadith form."[806]

The Abbasids now ruled over a great empire and they had need of a great history. Islam could not be portrayed as the end result of a vague and ill-defined Arab monotheism, itself a by-product of Arabian Judaism, which was then combined with some of the literary leavings of Syriac Christianity. The Abbasid Empire demanded its own unique and untarnished progeniture and for that it mined the idyllic traditions of the Hejaz and Bedouin life—things far enough removed from the experience of the majority of Muslims to be beyond question, but strongly-enough attached to romantic and poetic tradition to be attractive. Rather than Jerusalem and Damascus, therefore, the wellsprings of Islam were shifted to Mecca and Medina.

It is as a result of histories written long after, but reflecting the Abbasid revolution, that Shia Islam still carries the tinge of radicalism today, in comparison with the majority Sunni branch of Islam. Even though most of the accounts of the life and activities of Ali and his family were written centuries later and retrospectively injected into the historical narrative, the remnants of the radicalism and the egalitarian moods of the Abbasid revolution still resonate in the accounts. Shaban's "new interpretation" in *Islamic History* describes the connection between Ali and the common people, in the story of his great revolt against Mu'awiya:

---

[805]   Amira K Bennison, *The Great Caliphs,* p 99
[806]   Ignaz Goldziher, *Introduction to Islamic Theology and Law,* p 40

"Ali entered Basra and was publicly acclaimed. It was now that he gave an important indication of his policy, for he divided all the money he found in the public treasury equally among his supporters. This did not mean that he rejected the special prestige and position of the early Muslims [ie converts], but that he gave equal value to the great role played by the later Muslims . . ."[807]

The great majority of the tradition and *hadith* originated, as Crone and Hinds point out, with "private scholars", because there was no Islamic equivalent to the rigid organisational structure of the Church in the empire of Constantine four hundred years earlier. But the Abbasids nonetheless took steps to mould official doctrine to suit their needs. It is no coincidence that it was during the Abbasid period that there are the first recorded examples of the suppression of deviant Islamic views. It was in Baghdad that tradition records that a scholar was tried and publicly flogged for reading aloud from an aberrant version of the Koran and it was under the Abbasid caliph Umar that the Islamic inquisition took further steps to bring uniformity to the state religion.

"Shortly before his death in 833, [caliph] al-Ma'mun . . . set up an inquiry (*mihna*) to insist that scholars and officials publicly adhere to the doctrine of the createdness of the Qur'an. Although often described as an inquisition, the *mihna* was nothing like as severe as the Spanish equivalent and did not routinely lead to executions—only one is recorded and a few other scholars died in custody. During its 126-year course many hundreds of scholars were examined about their beliefs and the majority bowed to caliphal pressure but avoided giving a direct answer."[808]

It goes without saying that the Umayyads, the Alids (Shia Muslims), the Kharijites and the Abbasids are reflected in Islamic narrative history only in a distorted way, devoid of any real social content and reduced to matters of theology, as well as family and tribal rivalries. The official traditions and histories of the origins of Islam are not a faithful account of events as they really happened in the mid seventh century. They are a narrative written by theologians, jurists and scholars two or three centuries later, reflecting their own society and their own understanding of how things ought to have been and, indeed, how things must have been. The official history is like a collective mirror into which thousands of ninth and tenth century scholars peered, thinking they were seeing the past when they were simply reflecting themselves. In much the same way, Islamic scholars today will painstakingly search for some *hadith* or tiny element of Koranic interpretation to specifically reflect their own political or religious agenda, when in reality a mirror would do just as well.

---

[807] M A Shaban, *Islamic History*, p 74

[808] Amira K Bennison, *The Great Caliphs*, p 35

Chapter summary

- The real impetus for Shi'ism as a major schism in Islamic tradition lies in the revolutionary upheaval of the Abbasid revolt which was based primarily in the eastern part of the empire and which blew away the Umayyad dynasty in the middle of the eighth century.

- The Abbasid revolution swept millions along in its wake. But the aspirations of the former slaves and the most down-trodden were not to be realised. Having satisfied many of the demands of the *mawali*, the newly-installed Abbasid elite responded to the demands of the lower orders by a full-scale counter-revolution.

- Despite an ongoing series of revolts, the Abbasid ruling class was broader-based, more confident and more firmly established than at any time during the whole history of the Arab Empire.

- It was under the Abbasids that the first great collections of *hadith* were written down, collected and edited for the first time. The great torrent of writing which began at this time finally codified the orthodox traditions of Islam, both Sunni and Shia.

- It is only in the great literary traditions of the Abbasids, more than two hundred years after the supposed life of the Prophet, that it is possible to recognise Islam in more or less the form in which we see it today.

Appendix I

The Genesis Enigma

A book by Andrew Parker, *The Genesis Enigma*, puts forward the idea that the Book of Genesis can be considered to be a correct description of the origin of Earth because, in the light of modern scientific understanding, it outlines a sequence of events which is broadly accurate. "In this book," he writes,

> "I will be arguing that the latest understanding of how the world and all life on it came to develop and evolve, as demonstrated by solid evidence-based science, reflects exactly the order of events set out in Genesis." [809]

"Could it be," he enthuses, "that the creation story in Genesis was written as it was, complete with its seemingly odd order, because that is in fact the correct order of events at the beginning of the world?"

Parker gives a potted history of the development of life on Earth, from simple life forms 3900 million years ago to multi-celled organisms, fish, mammals and so on. After some overviews on aspects of modern scientific knowledge, he finally comes to the dramatic conclusion about the creation story:

> "*. . . this page of the Bible could, perhaps more than any other, represent God's hand in the Bible.* The true account of how we came to exist may have been handed to humans by God." [810]

In fact, there is no enigma. The book of Genesis simply lists the different elements of creation from the point of view of human knowledge as it would have been nearly three thousand years ago—strictly hierarchical and anthropocentric, with Man, of course, as the pinnacle. Despite Parker's enthusiasm for the idea and his comparison of the creation story to a scientific chronology, his theory only hangs together by completely ignoring some sections and mangling others in the Genesis story. The supposed "accurate" sequence and the premise upon which the whole book is based only works by picking and choosing what is cited from Genesis and what is not, and even then it gets key elements in the wrong order.

It might seem to be insulting the intelligence of the average twenty-first century reader to make these points, but *The Genesis Enigma* purports to be a serious book

---

[809]   Andrew Parker, *The Genesis Enigma*, p 10
[810]   Andrew Parker, *The Genesis Enigma*, p 399 (italics in the original)

and is no doubt read by serious people. The author is described as an Honorary Research Fellow of Green Templeton College at Oxford University, a Research Leader at the Natural History Museum and a professor at Shanghai Jiao Tong University. Yet it's not difficult to demolish the book's central case; a sixth-form student could do it. Take the creation of the Sun, for example. The author attributes the creation of our local star to the first day of creation, so he places it first in the sequence.

"And God said, Let there by light, and there was light." (Genesis, 1. 3)

"This", he writes, "must represent the creation of the solar system." Subsequent to this, God created Heaven and Earth on day two and then plants—grass, herbs and fruit trees—on day three. But then the author has to deal with the fact that on the fourth day God creates the Universe all over again!

"And God said let there be lights in the firmament of the heavens to divide the day from the night; and let them be for signs, and for seasons, and for days, and years; And let them be for lights in the firmament of the heaven to give light upon the earth; and it was so. And God made two great lights; the greater light to rule the day, and the lesser light to rule the night; he made the stars also. And God set them in the firmament of the heavens to give light upon the earth. And to rule over the day and over the night, and to divide the light from the darkness; and God saw that it was good. And in the evening and the morning were the fourth day." (Genesis, 1, 14-19)

Anticipating a challenge to this second creation of the Sun, Parker glibly responds that "this cannot be referring to that, although it appears to invoke the Sun again, somehow." His readers are being asked leave to out of consideration how the first three "days" were measured before "days" as such could in fact be gauged. Likewise, they have to leave aside the creation of flowering plants and grasses—in the "correct" sequence it is alleged—before day and night and the rest of the Milky Way galaxy or even, more locally, before seasons, tides and all the astronomical features that come from our orbiting around the Sun with our companion moon.

The only enigma attached to this book is how it ever came to be on bookshelves under popular science. It is proof that, for some publishers, academic titles make better qualifications than good sense. But what is significant about the book is that it is an example of how academics can sometimes attempt to shoe-horn modern scientific knowledge onto ancient myths. Stripped away from its camouflage of scientific facts and illustrations, the theory in the *Genesis Enigma* is a mangled and hideous caricature of scholarship, somewhere between the absurd and the comic. Yet it is meant to be a serious book. It is a warning to those who might look at a writer's academic credentials and professional attachments before evaluating what has been written.

Appendix II

Two separate Noah stories

Richard Friedman[811] has separated out the two biblical accounts of the Flood story, as they are shown here. The two columns can be read separately as two versions of the same story, each told in a slightly different way. The numbers of chapters and verses are given as they appear in the combined version in the Book of Genesis.

'Priestly' source

Genesis 6

9. These are the generations of Noah: Noah was a righteous man, perfect in his generations. Noah walked with God.

10. And Noah sired three sons: Shem, Ham and Japheth.

11. And the earth was corrupted before God, and the earth was filled with violence.

12. And God saw the earth, and here it was corrupted, for all flesh had corrupted its way on the earth.

13. And God said to Noah, "the end of all flesh has come before me, for the earth is filled with violence because of them, and here I am going to destroy them with the earth.

'J' source

Genesis 6

5. And Yahweh saw that the evil of humans was great in the earth, and all the inclination of the thoughts of their heart was only evil all the day.

6. And Yahweh regretted that he had made humans in the earth and he was grieved to his heart.

7. And Yahweh said, "I shall wipe out the humans which I have created from the face of the earth, from human to beast to creeping thing to bird of the heavens, for I regret that I have made them."

8. But Noah found favour in Yahweh's eyes.

---

[811]   Friedman, *Who Wrote the Bible?* p 54

14. Make yourself an ark of gopher wood, make rooms with the ark and pitch it outside and inside with pitch.

15. And this is how you shall make it: three hundred cubits the length of the ark, fifty cubits its width, and thirty cubits its height.

16. You shall make a window for the ark, and you shall finish it to a cubit from the top, and you shall make an entrance to the ark in its side. You shall make lower, second and third stories for it.

17. And here I am bringing the flood water over the earth to destroy all flesh in which is the breath of life from under the heavens. Everything which is on the land will die.

18. And I shall establish my covenant with you. And you shall come to the ark, you and your sons and your wife and your sons' wives with you.

19. And all of the living, of all flesh you shall bring two to the ark to keep alive with you, they shall be male and female.

20. Of the births according to their kind, and of the beast according to their kind and of all the creeping things of the earth according to their kind, two of each will come to you to keep alive.

Genesis 7

1. And Yahweh said to Noah, "Come, you and all your household to the ark, for I have seen you as righteous before me in this generation.

2. Of all the clean beasts, take yourself seven pairs, man and his woman; and of the beasts which are not clean, two, man and his woman.

3. Also of the birds of the heavens seven pairs, male and female, to keep alive seed on the face of the earth.

4. For in seven more days I shall rain on the earth forty days and forty nights, and I shall wipe out all the substance that I have made from upon the face of the earth"

5. And Noah did according to all that Yahweh had commanded him.

7. And Noah and his sons and his wife and his sons' wives with him came to the ark from before the waters of the flood.

10. And seven days later the waters of the flood were upon the earth.

12. And there was rain on the earth forty days and forty nights.

16 (part). And Yahweh closed it for him.

21. And you, take for yourself of all food which will be eaten and gather into you, and it will be for you and for them for food.

22. And Noah did according to all that God commanded him—so he did.

Genesis 7

6. And Noah was six hundred years old, and the flood was upon the earth.

8. Of the clean beasts and of the beasts which were not clean, and of the birds and of all those which creep upon the earth.

9. Two of each came to Noah to the ark, male and female as God had commanded to Noah.

11. In the six hundredth year of Noah's life, in the second month, in the seventeenth day of the month, on this day all the fountains of the great deep were broken up, and the windows of the heavens were opened.

13. In this very day, Noah and Shem, Ham and Japheth, the sons of Noah and Noah's wife and his sons' three wives with them came to the ark.

14. They and all the living things according to their kind, and all the beasts according to their kind, and all the creeping things that creep on the earth according to their kind and all the birds according to their kind and every winged bird.

17. And the flood was on the earth for forty days and forty nights, and the waters multiplied and raised the ark, and it was lifted from the earth.

18. And the waters grew strong and multiplied greatly on the earth, and the ark went on the surface of the waters.

19. And the waters grew very, very strong on the earth, and they covered all the high mountains that are under the heavens.

20. Fifteen cubits above, the waters grew stronger, and they covered the mountains.

22. Everything that had been breathing the spirit of life in its nostrils, everything that was on the dry ground, died.

23. And he wiped out all the substance that was on the face of the earth, from human to beast, to creeping thing, and to bird of the heavens, and they were wiped out from the earth, and only Noah and those who were with him in the ark were left.

Genesis 8

2. (part) And the rain was restrained from the heavens.

3. (part) And the waters receded from the earth continually.

15. And they came to Noah to the ark, two of each, of all flesh in which is the breath of life.

16. (part) And those which came were male and female, some of all flesh came, as God had commanded him.

21. And all flesh, those that creep on the earth, the birds, the beasts, and the wild animals, and all the swarming things that swarm on the earth, and all the humans expired.

24. And the waters grew strong on the earth a hundred fifty days.

Genesis 8

1. And God remembered Noah and all the living, and all the beasts that were with him in the ark, and God passed a wind over the earth, and the waters were decreased.

2. (part) And the fountains of the deep and the windows of the heavens were shut.

3. (part) And the waters were abated at the end of a hundred fifty days.

4. And the ark rested, in the seventh month, in the seventeenth day of the month, on the Mountain of Ararat.

6. And it was at the end of forty days, and Noah opened the window of the ark which he had made.

8. And he sent out a dove from him to see whether the waters had eased from the face of the earth.

9. And the dove did not find a resting place for its foot, and it returned to him to the ark, for waters were on the face of the earth and he put out his hand and took it and brought it back to him to the ark.

10. And he waited seven more days and he again sent out a dove from the ark.

11. And the dove came to him at evening time, and here was an olive leaf torn off in its mouth, and Noah knew that the waters had eased from the earth.

12. And he waited seven more days and he sent out a dove, and it did not return to him ever again.

13. (part) And Noah turned back the covering of the ark and looked, and here the face of the earth had dried.

20. And Noah built an altar to Yahweh, and he took some of each of the clean beasts and of each of the clean birds, and he offered sacrifices on the altar.

5. And the waters continued receding until the tenth month; in the tenth month, on the first day of the month, the tops of the mountains appeared.

7. And he sent out a raven, and it want back and forth until the waters dried up from the earth.

13. (part) And it was in the six hundred and first year, in the first month, on the first of the month, the waters dried from the earth.

14. And in the second month, on the twenty-seventh day of the month, the earth dried up.

15. And God spoke to Noah, saying

16. "Go out from the ark, you and your wife and your sons' wives with you.

17. All the living things that are with you, of all flesh, of the birds, and of the beasts, and of all the creeping things that creep on the earth, that go out with you, shall swarm in the earth and be fruitful, and multiply in the earth."

18. And Noah and his sons and his wife and his sons' wives went out.

19. All the living things, all the creeping things and all birds, all that creep on the earth, by their families, they went out of the ark.

21. And Yahweh smelled the pleasant smell, and Yahweh said to his heart, "I shall not again curse the ground on Man's account, for the inclination of the human heart is evil from their youth, and I shall not again strike all the living as I have done.

22. All the rest of the days on earth, seed and harvest, and cold and heat and summer and winter, and day and night shall not cease."

Appendix III

The Christian insertions into

The Antiquities of the Jews,

Book 18, by Josephus

As can be seen here, there is a natural continuity in reading directly from Chapter 2 to chapter 4. That continuity is broken by the intrusion of chapter 3, which is a later Christian insertion into the work of Josephus.

2. But Pilate undertook to bring a current of water to Jerusalem, and did it with the sacred money, and derived the origin of the stream from the distance of two hundred furlongs. However, the Jews were not pleased with what had been done about this water; and many ten thousands of the people got together, and made a clamour against him, and insisted that he should leave off that design. Some of them also used reproaches, and abused the man, as crowds of such people usually do. So he habited a great number of his soldiers in the habit, who carried daggers under their garments and sent them to a place where they might surround them. So he bade the Jews himself to go away; but they boldly cast reproaches upon him, he gave the soldiers that signal which had been beforehand agreed on; who laid upon them much greater blows than Pilate had commanded them and equally punished those that were tumultuous and those that were not, nor did they spare them in the least; and since the people were unarmed, and were caught by men prepared for what they were about, there were a great number of them slain by this means, and others of them ran away wounded; and thus an end was put to his sedition.

3. Now there was about his time Jesus, a wise man, if it be lawful to call him a man, for he was a doer of wonderful works—a teacher of such men as receive the truth with pleasure. He drew over to him both many of the Jews, and many of the Gentiles. He was the Christ; and when Pilate, at the suggestion of the principal men amongst us, had condemned him to the cross, those that loved him at the first did not forsake him, for he appeared to them alive again the third day, as the divine prophets had foretold these and then thousand other wonderful things concerning him and the tribe of Christians, so named from him, are not extinct at this day.

447

4. About the same time also another sad calamity put the Jews into disorder; and certain shameful practices happened about the temple of Isis that was at Rome. I will not first take notice of the wicked attempt about the temple of Isis and will then give an account of the Jewish affairs . . .

Another very short insertion, in book 20, concerns the stoning of "the brother of Jesus, who was called Christ, whose name was James." *This passage, which is again out of context with the general narrative, is absent in other copies of the works of Josephus which have been handed down and is clearly another later, Christian amendment.*

Appendix IV

Slavery in ancient Judaism, Christianity and Islam

Modern supporters of religion have argued that only religion can provide a moral compass for human behaviour. An obvious response to that argument is that all the major religions have changed their moral compass to match the prevailing morality of the times. Just to take one very important instance, in the ancient world, all of the writers of religious tracts and apologias—be they Jewish, Christian, Islamic or pagan—*took slavery for granted* as part and parcel of the fabric of society. Even if the writers did not all own slaves themselves, they were comfortable with their friends and associates owning slaves. The overwhelming majority of the written literature, with the possible exception of the tiny revolutionary messianic tracts on the fringes of mainstream religion, was aimed at literate, urban, slave-owning members of society.

Judaism

Throughout the Hebrew Scripture there are references to slaves and slavery as an integral element in society. The patriarch of Judaism, Abraham, fathered a child on Hagar, who was a maid of his wife Sarah. She was given by Sarah to Abraham "be his wife", but is described later in the text as a slave; in other words like most female slaves in the patriarchal household, she was available for sexual exploitation by her owner. It is made quite explicit in the Torah that slavery is acceptable and that the worth of a slave is less than that of other members of the household.[812]

> "You may buy male and female slaves from among the nations that are round about you. You may also buy from among the strangers who sojourn with you and their families that are with you, who have been born in your land; and they may be your property. You may bequeath them to your sons after you, to inherit as a possession for ever; you may make slaves of them,

---

[812]   These and other extracts in this Appendix are taken from the Revised Standard Version of the Bible because the Authorised King James Version often translates 'slave' as 'bondsman' or 'servant'. These latter two renderings represent a softening of the original meaning, a subtle hint that slavery was not accepted by early Christians, when in fact it was and the Church offered no theological or political justification for its abolition.

but over your brethren the people of Israel you shall not rule, one over another with harshness."[813]

"When you buy a Hebrew slave he shall serve six years; and in the seventh he shall go out free, for nothing . . .
If his master gives him a wife and she bears him sons or daughters, the wife and her children shall be her masters and he shall go out alone."[814]

In the latter case, the slave can only remain with his family if he agrees to serve his master "for ever." If a master savagely beats a slave, it is better that the poor victim lingers a while before he finally dies:

"When a man strikes his slave, male or female with a rod, and the slave dies under his hand, he shall be punished. But if the slave survives a day or two, he is not to be punished; for the slave is his money."[815]

Philo reflected Jewish attitudes to slavery, seeing it as a part of the normal ethos of society but one open to abuse and misuse. The view of Philo, along with all the Stoics and Christians, was that:

". . . the actual bodily enslavement was not considered so important and that the slaves were not urged to escape but rather to give in to their fate. To some extent, then, these teachings helped to maintain the status quo of slavery as an indisputable institution within ancient society."[816]

<u>Christianity</u>

When the early Christian writings began to see the light of day, there was no change in the attitude towards slavery as compared to the traditional view of Judaism. There are many references in the New Testament to slaves and as a social institution it is nowhere condemned. Paul's short epistle to Philemon is an appeal to the owner of a runaway slave to forgive the runaway who has become a Christian and who Paul was sending back to his owner. In his first epistle to the Corinthians, Paul directly addresses a slave and suggests that while freedom would be an opportunity, it is not essential to be a Christian:

---

[813]   Leviticus, 25, 45
[814]   Exodus, 21 2-4
[815]   Exodus, 21, 20
[816]   Catherine Hezser, *Jewish Slavery in Antiquity*, p 61

"Were you a slave when called? Never mind. But if you can gain your freedom, avail yourself of the opportunity. For he who was called to the Lord as a slave is a freedman of the Lord."[817]

It was common in Roman society for female slaves to be used as sexual objects by their owners and some interpretations of Paul's epistles have the evangelist condoning the practice. When, in 1 Colossians, he exhorts the men in the Christian community to demonstrate morality, he appears to suggest that they use a female slave—a "vessel" in some translations—as an alternative to prostitution.[818]

The second century forgers who wrote in the name of Paul, followed their mentor's view in urging slaves to accept their fate. The author of 1 Timothy wrote:

"Let all who are under the yoke of slavery regard their masters as worthy of all honour, so that the name of God and the teaching may not be defamed. Those who have believing masters should not be disrespectful on the ground that they are brethren; rather they must serve all the better since those who benefit by their service are believers and beloved."[819]

Likewise in the epistle to Titus:

"Bid slaves to be submissive to their masters and to give satisfaction in every respect; they are not to be refractory, nor to pilfer, but to show entire and true fidelity, so that in everything they may adorn the doctrine of God our Saviour."[820]

The first epistle to Peter, also a second century forgery, clearly condones the beating of slaves when they "do wrong" and even if slaves are beaten in error, there is no explicit condemnation of slavery or the master's cruelty. Instead, the text focuses on the need for the slave to suffer the abuse "patiently".

". . . one is approved if, mindful of God, he endures pain while suffering unjustly. For what credit is it, if when you do wrong and are beaten for it you take it patiently. But if when you do right and suffer for it you take it patiently, you have God's approval."[821]

The later writings of the Church fathers are also full of references to slavery and slaves and to an extent these Christians even used slave ownership as a status symbol, like any other Roman aristocrat.

---

817 1 Corinthians, 7, 20-22
818 See Glancy, *Slavery in Early Christianity,* p 60
819 1 Timothy, 6, 1
820 Titus, 2, 9
821 1 Peter, 2, 19

"John Chrysostom maintains that a priest who lacked a slave would 'bring shame on himself' and could not be respected properly within society. Augustine believed that even the poorest man might own a number of slaves. Rabbis similarly considered the ownership of at least one slave appropriate even for a poor person of high birth."[822]

The great Christian writer of antiquity, Saint Augustine, accepted as much as any of his contemporaries that slavery was part of the normal arrangement of society.

"In several letters written early in the fifth century, Augustine confronted some problems he perceived with the slave system. What he found disquieting was not the institution of slavery itself. Indeed, in these letters he explicitly acknowledged that scriptural tradition enjoined slaves to submit to their masters. What disturbed him was what he identified as a North African trend towards the enslavement of free persons . . . details supplied by Augustine contribute to a picture of the breakdown of social order often seen as characteristic of his period: fathers sold children into permanent slavery . . . worst of all, Augustine claimed, were the kidnappings that seemed to be happening on a massive scale. These kidnappings were so common, alleged Augustine, that they were reducing the populations of North Africa.[823]

The *Apostolic Traditions* of Hippolytus, written in Rome in the early third century, included qualifications for acceptance into a Christian community and it was clearly not worthy of comment that a slave required his master's permission to become Christian in the first place. Applicants to the congregation:

". . . must give full details of their marital status and occupation and *if they are slaves must confirm that they have the permission of their masters to attend instructions*. The slaves have to promise further that they will continue to please their masters if they are pagan."[824]

On the whole, therefore, Christian leaders did nothing to disturb the status quo.

"When Christian slaves in an Asian Church community began to propose that their freedom should be bought from community funds, Ignatius of Antioch advised firmly against the suggestion . . . Like the Stoics, these Christian leaders began from a principle of the equality of man, yet argued that worldly differences of status should continue undisturbed. The greatest slavery was man's slavery to his passions. As if to prove it,

---

[822]   Catherine Hezser, *Jewish Slavery in Antiquity*, p 123
[823]   Glancy, *Slavery in Early Christianity*, p 71
[824]   Freeman, *A New History of Early Christianity*, p 166 (italics added)

pagan slaves continue to show up in the ownership of Christians, even of bishops."[825]

Among the artifacts that have remained from the Roman period are the heavy metal slave collars that slaves were obliged to wear, to mark them out as someone else's property and as a disincentive to running away. A large number of them, particularly after the period of Constantine, are marked with inscriptions and Christian symbols. One famously has the inscription: "I am the slave of the archdeacon Felix. Hold me so that I do not flee."[826]

Islam

It is a common myth that Islam arose as a movement of the most downtrodden and oppressed and that as Islam expanded it facilitated the liberation of slaves throughout the former Byzantine and Persian empires. Nothing could be further from the truth; the early Muslims thought no more about the abolition of slavery than did the early Christians six hundred years earlier. "The Muslim teaching of the equality of all men in Islam remained a dead letter for a long time, never realised in the consciousness of Arabs and roundly denied in their day to day behaviour."[827]

Among the most important booty captured by the Arabs as they forged their new empire there were tens of thousands of slaves and all the major cities, including newly-established garrison cities, had slave markets. Even the traditional, orthodox accounts of the Arab conquests describe, for example, that the regular provision of slaves to the imperial court was often part of the tax paid by subject nations, such as the Berbers of North Africa.

> "The overwhelming majority of converts in the Sufyanid and very likely also the Marwanid periods were prisoners of war who had been enslaved and were subsequently manumitted. The number of prisoners of war which the Arabs took in the course of their conquest was staggering, and enslavement hit all social, ethnic and religious groups in the Middle East."[828]

Tens of thousands of slaves were repatriated to Syria and Iraq. Many of the great civil engineering projects undertaken by the Arabs, such as the draining of the marshes in southern Iraq, the building of dams and the digging of irrigation canals, were undertaken by slaves, not by the occupying armies or the local peasantry. As well as those slaves obtained by military conquest, there was a steady stream of slaves from Arab slave traders operating in East Africa.

---

[825] Fox, *Pagans and Christians,* p 296
[826] Glancy, *Slavery in Early Christianity,* p 9
[827] Goldziher, *Muslim Studies,* 1/98
[828] Patricia Crone, *Slaves on Horses,* p 50

In the late ninth century, southern Iraq and Persia were gripped by one of the greatest slave revolts of all time, far surpassing the Spartacus revolt of the Roman period. The revolt lasted fourteen years, from 869 to 883 and involved the East African slaves who had formerly worked in the salt marshes in the area of the Tigris delta. The uprising, which became known as the Zanj revolution, was joined by many black soldiers who had been conscripted into the Arab imperial army and even by some Bedouin regiments. The slaves, who considered themselves Muslims, set up their own kingdom, (including with their own slaves) with a newly-built capital city at Mokhtara in what is now southern Iraq. During the wars against the imperial armies, which were characterised by great brutality on both sides, the slave army at one point captured Basra and came to within seventy miles of the Abbasid capital Baghdad.

The English translation of Tabari's chronicles dedicates the best part of a whole volume to this slave uprising. But whereas in dealing with the life of Mohammed, Tabari is writing about a story based two hundred years before his own time, his account of the Zanj revolt was *contemporary* to him and can therefore be taken as a much more accurate reflection of real events. He makes it perfectly clear that the slaves involved were not Arabs but "black" slaves. These extracts from Tabari outline the early days of the revolt, under the leadership of a former slave with the name Ali:

> "Ali set out from [the castle al-Qurashi]. When he had reached the farthest end of the castle precinct, some slaves . . . met him as they were setting about their business. Ali ordered them to be seized along with their agent, who was placed in fetters. They numbered in all some fifty slaves. Ali next proceeded to a place where al-Sanai worked and there around five hundred slaves were seized . . . their agent was likewise bound with fetters and taken along as well . . . captured there another one hundred fifty slaves . . . eighty more slaves . . . Ali continued to operate in this fashion all day until he had amassed a large number of slaves.
>
> Assembling them together, Ali rose and addressed them, raising their spirits by promising to lead and command them and to give them possession of property . . . he continued efforts to gather blacks (*al-sudan*) to his camp right up to the time of prayer breaking the fast of Ramadan."[829]

The slave revolt clearly had a traumatic effect on Tabari himself. Like Josephus in his description of Judean revolutionaries, he frequently refers to the lower classes of society as "riff-raff" and bemoaned the terrible plight of the ruling elites as the slave revolt gained momentum and eventually the slave army occupied the city of Basra. At this point he wrote, "Not a day passed when a group of affluent persons was not stripped of their possessions and then put to death."[830]

---

[829] Tabari, Volume XXXVI, pp 36,37
[830] Tabari, Volume XXXVI, pp 133

This is not the place to give a detailed account of the Zanj revolt. Suffice to say that after managing to maintain an independent state-let for fifteen years, the revolt was eventually broken and slavery continued to be a feature of the Islamic Near East for centuries afterwards. There was an extensive and well-developed trade in slaves right across the Sahel region.

Although the horrors of the trans-Atlantic slave trade are fairly well documented, there is less literature on the Middle East slave routes and some historians have argued that in the sheer number of slaves taken out of Africa the two are comparable.[831] It was only in 1962 that slavery was formally abolished in Saudi Arabia, and, some would suggest, that abolition has remained only on paper.

Of course, none of the above is to suggest that being a Jew, a Christian or a Muslim imparts any special propensity to own slaves. But what history does show is that being a person of religion has not conferred on the believer any special obligation *not* to own slaves and that the morality of the early Jews, Christians and Muslims, in this regard at least, was no different to the prevailing morality of the time.

---

[831]　See, for example, *The Legacy of Arab-Islam in Africa,* by John Alembillah Zaumah

Postscript

This book is not intended to be a history of Judaism, Christianity or Islam. It is a contribution to understanding only the foundations of these three faiths. It may well be that in the light of new evidence or new archaeological discoveries, some of the arguments advanced here may turn out in the end to be incorrect or in need of modification. That is all well and good. But the fundamental contention is that when the three 'Abramic' religions were founded, at different times and in different circumstances, it was in each case *as a result of the material forces at work in society*. Leaving aside all supernatural causes, the origin of these religions can only lie in the economic, social and political circumstances of the time in which they were born.

Neither should the dominance of one or another of these religious systems over large geographical areas and for extended periods of time delude us into thinking that in each case they were the only religious strands of their type. The dominant orthodoxy we appear to see invariably grew from a very complex melting pot of religious ideas. What led to one or another particular doctrinal strand emerging as the mainstream was not its superior theology but the correspondence of its political and organisational form to a social and political need. The vast majority of Jews, Christians and Muslims down the ages did not choose but were born into their faith. Where conversion played any part at all, it was the social role of the communities of the faithful that was the attraction, rather than their philosophies.

Billions of people today still cling to Judaism, Christianity, Islam and, for that matter, other religions. But what is it that decides, say, that a girl born in Italy grows up a Catholic and a yet boy born in Iran grows up Muslim? One only needs to pose the question to see the answer. For ninety-nine per cent of people who express an attachment to a religious faith, their attachment is not in the slightest a matter of theology, but one of national, cultural, ethnic and family *identity*. Except for a tiny handful of professional scholars, religion is not at all a philosophical question, but is a political and a social one. To take a more concrete example, if there has been an increase of support for Islamic 'fundamentalism' in Europe—especially among youth—it has nothing to do with a new-found search for God but has everything to do with the wars in the Balkans, Iraq, Afghanistan and Palestine and, not least, with racism at home: in other words, with *political* questions.

These arguments have important implications for the twenty-first century, because, with the best will in the world, having atheists debate and argue with people of faith will not lead many of the latter to change their views. Such a dialogue might be stimulating and interesting, but it will not lead to the demise of religion. Neither can religion be abolished by legal decree. What will lead to the *withering away* of religion, as with all superstition, will be the elimination of our present society which is based on the national state and the private ownership of the means of production, distribution and exchange and its replacement by a planned society structured on democratic and rational lines. Such a revolutionary change will

457

lead humankind to undreamed-of opportunities and will lead to the overcoming of poverty and ignorance and, thereby, in the fullness of time, eliminating the *need* for religion.

Faced with economic uncertainty (and now endless austerity), political corruption, social breakdown, wars and permanent crises, the discontented mass of the world population have not yet seen an alternative to our present society. It is not surprising that in the absence of a serious alternative, religious and ethnic identity continue to form a significant part of the psychology of the mass of the population. But this situation will change under the hammer-blows of events. Ironically, among the multitudes who will wield the battering rams that will break down the old society, there will be hundreds of millions who are people of faith. As the magnificent movement in Egypt showed in early 2011, their religious affiliation will not prevent them moving on *class* lines to challenge the old order. Workers of all faiths and nationalities will walk side by side against the ruling representatives of their own faiths in the march to get rid of the old and usher in a new society.

Comments to: behindthemyths@live.com

Bibliography

Abou El Fadl, Khaled, *The Great Theft, wrestling Islam from the extremists,* Harper, San Francisco, 2007

Abrahamson, Ben and Katz, Joseph. *The Persian conquest of Jerusalem in 614CE compared with the Islamic conquest of 638CE.*

Ackerman, Susan, *Under Every Green Tree: Popular Religion in Sixth Century Judah,* Harvard Semitic monographs, 1992.

Ali, Ameer. *A Short history of the Saracens,* McMillan, 1961. First published in 1889.

Ali Al-Iman, Ahmad, *Variant Readings of the Qur'an,* The International Institute of Islamic Thought, London, 2006

Allegro, John, *The Mystery of the Dead Sea Scrolls revealed,* Penguin, 1956

Allen, Pauline (trans), *Sophronius of Jerusalem and Seventh Century Heresy,* Oxford Early Christian Texts, OUP, 2009.

Aslan, Reza. *No God but God,* Arrow Books, 2006.

As-Suyuti, Jalal ad-Din, *The History of the Khalifahs who took the right way,* late fifth century CE, reprinted by Ta-Ha Publishers, UK, 1995.

Azumah, John Alembillah, *The Legacy of Arab-Islam in Africa,* Oneworld publications, UK, 2001

Bashear, Suliman, *"Quran 2:114 and Jerusalem,* Bulletin of the School of Oriental and African studies, 1989.

Bashear, Suliman, *Arabs and Others in Early Islam,* Darwin Press, Princeton, USA, 1997

Bennison, Amira K, *The Great Caliphs, The Golden Age of the Abbasid Empire,* I B Tauris, 2009

Berkey, Jonathan P, *The Formation of Islam,* Cambridge University Press, 2003

Betz, Otto and Riesner, Rainer, *Jesus, Qumran and the Vatican,* SCM Press, 1993

Blankinship, Khalid Yahya, *The End of the Jihad State: The Reign on Hisham Ibn Abd Al-Malik and the Collapse of the Umayyads,* State University of New York Press, 1994

Bloom, Harold, *Jesus and Yahwah, the Names Divine,* Riverhead Book, USA, 2005

Bockmuchl, Markus and Paget, James Carleton (editors), *Redemption and Resistance,* T & T Clark, 2007.

Books LLC, *Jews: Israelites, Wandering Jew, Pharisees, Who is a Jew?, Y-chromosone Aaron, Genetic Studies on Jews, Jewish Ethnic Divisions,* Books LLC, USA, 2010

Bowersock, G W, *Roman Arabia,* Harvard University Press, 1983

Brown, Peter, *Authority and the Sacred, aspects of the Christianisation of the Roman World,* Cambridge University Press, 1995

Burton, John, *The Collection of the Qur'an,* Cambridge University Press, 1977

Carroll, James, *Constantine's Sword, The Church and the Jews,* Mariner, USA, 2001.

Celcus, *On the True Doctrine, A discourse against the Christians,* R Joseph Hoffman (trans), Oxford University Press, 1987

Charlesworth, James H, *The Old Testament Pseudepigrapha, volume one: Apocalyptic Literature and Testaments,* Hendrickson Publishers, USA, 2009.

Cook, Michael, *Muhammad,* Oxford University Press, 1983.

Corcos, Alain F, *The Myth of the Jewish Race,* Bethlehem Lehigh University Press, USA, 2005.

Crone, Patricia and Cook, Michael, *Hagarism: The making of the Islamic World,* Cambridge University Press, 1977.

Crone, Patricia. *Slaves on Horses.* Cambridge University Press, 1980.

Crone, Patricia and Hinds, Martin, *God's Caliph,* Cambridge University Press, 1986

Crone, Patricia, *Roman, Provincial and Islamic Law.* Cambridge University Press, 1987

Crone, Patricia, *Meccan Trade and the rise of Islam,* Georgias Press, USA, 1987

Crone, Patricia, *Babak's Revolt,* on-line essay, www.parstimes.com

Crossan, John Dominic, *Jesus, a Revolutionary Biography,* Harper Collins, 1995

Crossan, John Dominic, *The Birth of Christianity,* Harper San Francisco, 1999

Dashti, Ali. *23 Years, a study of the prophetic career of Mohammad.* George Allen & Unwin, 1985.

Dawkins, Richard, *The God Delusion,* 2006

Dennet, Danial C, *Conversion and Poll Tax in Early Islam,* Idarah-i Adabiyat-i Delli, Delhi, 1950.

De Rosa, Peter, *Vicars of Christ,* Poolbeg Press, Dublin, 1988

Dever, William. *Who were the early Israelites and Where did they come from?.* Eerdmans Publishing, 2003.

Donner, Fred M, *Narratives of Islamic Origins, The Beginnings of Islamic Historical Writing,* Darwin Press, Princeton, USA, 1998

Donner, Fred M, *States, Resources and Armies, The Byzantine and Early Islamic Near East,* (Ed Averial Cameron) Darwin Press, Princeton, USA, 2001

Donner, Fred M, *Muhammad and the Believers,* Belknap, Harvard University, 2010

Drews, Arthur, *The Christ Myth,* Oxford, 1998, first published in 1910

Dubnov, Simon. *History of the Jews, vol 1 from the beginning to the early Christian era,* Barnes, USA, 1967, (first written 1925-29)

Dunn, James D G, *Did the first Christians worship Jesus?,* SPCK, 2010

Ehrman, Bart D, *Lost Christianities,* Oxford University Press, 2003

Ehrman, Bart D, *Lost Scriptures,* Oxford University Press, 2003

Ehrman, Bart D, *Misquoting Jesus,* Harper, USA, 2005

Ehrman, Bart D, *Whose Word is it?,* Continuum, 2005

Ehrman, Bart D, *Forged,* Harper, 2011

Eisenman, Robert, *The Dead Sea Scrolls and the First Christians,* Element Books, 1996.

Eisenman, Robert and Wise, Michael, *The Dead Sea Scrolls Uncovered,* Penguin, 1992

El Fadl, Khaled Abou. *The Great Theft, wrestling Islam from the extremists.* Harper Collins, 2005.

Ellegard Alvar, *Jesus, one hundred years before Christ,* The Overlook Press, 1999,

Ellis E Earle, *The Making of the New Testament Documents,* Brill Academic Publishers, USA, 2002

Engels, Friedrich. *Anti-Dürhring,* 1878. Progress Publishers, Moscow, 1969,

Engels, Friedrich. *Socialism Utopian and Scientific.*

Engels, Friedrich. *The Origin of the Family, Private Property and the State,* Foreign Language Press, Beijing, 1978.

Fatima, Dr Rais, *Ghazal Under the Umayyds,* Kitab Bhavan, New Delhi, 1995

Faulkner, Neil, *Apocalypse, The Great Jewish Revolt Against Rome, AD 66-73,* Tempus, 2002.

Feldman, Louis H, *Jews and Gentile in the Ancient World,* Princeton University Press, USA, 1993

Finkelstein, Israel and Silberman, Neil Asher. *The Bible Unearthed.* Touchstone, 2001.

Finkelstein, Israel and Silberman, Neil Asher. *David and Solomon,* Free Press, 2006

Fox, Robin Lane, *Pagans and Christians,* Penguin, 1986

Freeman, Charles, *A New History of Early Christianity,* Yale University Press, 2009

Freyne, Sean, *Galilee, From Alexander the Great to Hadrian, 323BC to 135CE,* T & T Clark, Edinburgh, 2000 (first pub 1980)

Friedman, Richard Elliott, *Who wrote the Bible?,* Harper Collins, 1989

Gibbon, Edward, *The Decline and Fall of the Roman Empire,* Wordsworth Edition, UK, 1998

Glancy, Jennifer A, *Slavery in Early Christianity,* Fortress Press, USA, 2006

Goldenburg, Robert, *The Origins of Judaism,* Cambridge University Press, 2007

Goodblatt, David, *Elements of Ancient Jewish Nationalism,* Cambridge University Press, 2006

Goodman, Martin, *The Ruling Class of Judaea,* Cambridge University Press, 1987

Goldenberg, Robert. *The Origins of Judaism.* Cambridge University Press, 2007.

Goldziher, Ignaz, *Muslim Studies,* Transaction Publishers, USA, 2006, first published in German in 1889

Goldziher, Ignaz, *Introduction to Islamic Theology and Law,* Princeton University Press, 1981, first published in German in 1910.

Gottwald, Norman K, *The Tribes of Yahweh, A sociology of the Religion of Liberated Israel, 1250-1050,* Sheffield Academic Press, 1979

Gottwald, Norman K, *The Hebrew Bible: A socio-literary introduction,* Fortress Press, USA, 1985

Gottwald, Norman K, *The Politics of Ancient Israel.* Westminster John Knox Press, USA, 2001

Grabbe, Lester L (editor), *Good kings and bad kings,* T & T Clark, 2007.

Griffith, Sidney H, *Disputing with Islam in Syriac: The Case of the Monk of Bêt Hâleand a Muslim Emir,* The Journal of Syriac Studies, Vol 3, No 1, January 2000

Gross, Nachum (editor), *Economic History of the Jews,* Schocken Book, NY, 1975

Haldon, John and Conrad, Lawrence I (eds), *Elites Old and New in the Byzantine and Early Islamic Near East,* Darwin Press, Princeton, USA, 2004.

Hanson KC and Oakman, Douglas E, *Palestine in the time of Jesus,* Fortress Press, USA, 1998.

Harding, Mark, *Early Christian Life and Thought in Social Context, A reader,* T&T Clark International, 2003

Harrington, Daniel J, *The Maccabean Revolt, anatomy of a biblical revolution,* Wipf and Stock, USA, 2009.

Hatch, Edwin, *The Organisation of the Early Christian Churches,* lectures delivered to the University of Oxford, 1880, published by Bibliobazaar.

Haught, James A, *2000 Years of Disbelief,* Prometheus Books, USA, 1996

Hawting, G R. *The First Dynasty of Islam. The Umayyad Caliphate AD 661-750.* 1986.

Hawting, G R, *The Idea of Idolatry and the Emergence of Islam,* Cambridge University Press, 1999

Herrick, James A, *The Radical Rhetoric of the English Deists,* University of South Carolina Press, 1997

Herrin, Judith, *Byzantium,* Penguin, 2007

Hezser, Catherine, *Jewish Slavery in Antiquity,* Oxford University Press, 2005

Hoffmeier, James K, *The Archaeology of the Bible,* Lion Hudson, 2008.

Holt, P M, Lambton, Anne K S and Lewis Bernard, *The Cambridge History of Islam, volume 1A,* Cambridge University Press, 1970 edition.

Horsley, Richard A, *Bandits, Prophets and Messiahs,* Trinity Press, USA, 1985

Hoyland, Robert G (trans), *Theophilus of Edessa's Chronicle,* Liverpool University Press, 2011

Hoyland, Richard A, *Non-Muslim Conceptions of Islam, Seeing Islam as others Saw It,* SLAEI series number 4, Darwin Press, New York, 1995

Humphreys, Kenneth, *Jesus Never Existed,* Iconoclast Press, 2005.

Humphreys, R Stephen, *Islamic History, A Framework for Enquiry,* Princeton University Press, 1991.

Ibn Ishaq, *The Life of Mohammed,* (ed. Michael Edwardes), The Folio Society, 1964

Ibn Warraq, *The Guardian,* November 10, 2001.

Ibn Warraq (ed), *The Origins of the Koran, Classic Essays on Islam's Holy Book,* Premetheus, 1998

Ibn Warraq, *Why I am not a Muslim.* Prometheus, 2003

Ibn Warraq, *The Quest for the Historical Mohammad.*

Ibn Warraq, *Leaving Islam, apostates speak out.* Prometheus books, USA, 2003.

Kautsky, Karl, *Foundations of Christianity,* Orbach and Chambers, London, first published in Germany in 1908

Kennedy, Hugh, *The Great Arab Conquests,* Phoenix, UK, 2007

Khalek, Nancy, *Damascus after the Muslim Conquest,* Oxford University Press, 2011

Koester, Helmut, *Ancient Christian Gospels,* Trinity Press International, 1990

Koran, The, translated by M A S Abdel Haleem, Oxford World Classsics, 2004

Kraft, Robert J, *Was there a 'messiah-Joshua tradition at the turn of the era?* http://ccat.sas.upenn.edu.

Kroskey, Herbert, *The Lost Gospel,* National Geographic, USA, 2006.

Johns, Jeremy, *Archaeology and the History of Early Islam, Journal of the Economic and Social History of the Orient,* 46, 2003

Jordanian Ministry of Tourism, *The Umayyads, The Rise of Islamic Art,* 2000

Josephus, *The Complete Works*, Translated by William Whiston, Thomas Nelson publishers, USA, 1998 edition.

Leloup, Jean-Yves, *The Gospel of Mary Magdalene*, Inner Traditions, USA, 2002

Lemche, Niels Peter, *The Israelites in History and Tradition*, Westminster John Knox Press, USA, 1998

Leon, Abram. *The Jewish Question*. Pathfinder, USA, 1970 edition.

Lewis, Bernard, *From Babel to Dragomans*, Phoenix, 2004

Lewis, Bernard, *The Jews of Islam*, Princeton University Press, 1984

Lightstone, Jack N, *The Commerce of the Sacred*, Columbia University Press, 2006

Lindsay, James E (ed), *Ibn Asakir and Early Islamic History*, Darwin Press, Princeton, 2001

Lucas, Leopold, *The conflict between Christianity and Judaism*, Aris & Phillips, UK, originally published 1910.

Luxenberg, Christoph, *The Syro-Aramaic Reading of the Koran*, Schiler, 2000

Maccoby, Hyam, *The Myth Maker: Paul and the invention of Christianity*, Harper & Row, 1987

Mack, Burton L, *Who Wrote the New Testament: The making of the Christian Myth*, Harper One, 1995

Madelung, Wilferd. *The Succession to Muhammed, a study of the early caliphate.* Cambridge University Press, 1997.

Manji, Irshad, *The Trouble with Islam Today*, Mainstream Publishing, 2004

Margoliouth, David S, *The Early Development of Mohammedanism*, Simon Publications Inc, USA, 1913

Margolis, Max L and Marx, Alexander, *A History of the Jewish People*, George Routledge, London, 1927

Marx, Karl and Engels, Frederick *The German Ideology*, Lawrence & Wishart 2007 edition, p 47.

Meeks, Wayne A, *The First Urban Christians, The Social world of the Apostle Paul*, Yale University Press, 2003

Merrick, Jim. *Humanism: an introduction*. Rationalist Press Association, UK, 2003.

Momigliano, Arnaldo. *On Pagans, Jews and Christians*, Wesleyan University Press, 1985

Momigliano, Arnaldo, *Essays on Ancient and Modern Judaism*, University of Chicago Press, 1994

Moran, William L (editor and translator), *The Amarna Letters*, The John Hopkins University Press, 1992

Murdoch, Adrian, *The Last Pagan, Julian the Apostate*, Sutton Publishing, 2003

Neusner, Jacob, *Judaism and Christianity in the Age of Constantine*, University of Chicago Press, 1987

Nevo, Yehuda D and Koren, Judith. *Crossroads to Islam*. Prometheus, 2003.

Newby, Gordon Darnell, *A History of the Jews of Arabia*, University of South Carolina Press, 1988

Noldeke, Theodor. *Sketches From Eastern History*, First published in English by A & C Black, 1892.

Ohlig, Karl-Heinz and Puin, Gerd-R (editors), *The Hidden Origins of Islam,* Prometheus Books, USA, 2010

Pagels, Elaine, *The Gnostic Gospels*, Phoenix, 1979.

Parker, Andrew. *The Genesis Enigma*, Doubleday, 2009.

Patai, Raphael and Patai Jennifer, *The Myth of the Jewish Race*, Wayne State University, Detriot, 1975

Perlman, Alan M. *An Atheist Reads the Torah*. Trafford Publishing, 2008.

Philo, *Complete and unabridged Works*, translated by C D Yonge, Hendrickson Publishers, USA, 2008 edition.

Pipes, Daniel. *The Rushdie Affair: the novel, the ayatollah and the West*. Birch Lane Press, 1990.

Portier-Young, Anathea E, *Apocalypse Against Empire, theologies of resistance in Early Judaism,* Erdmans Publishing, 2011.

Price, R G, *Jesus—A very Jewish Myth,* www.rationalrevolution.net 2007

Redford, Donald B, *Egypt, Canaan and Israel in Ancient Times*, Princeton University Press, 1992.

Reinink, GJ, *Syriac Christianity under Late Sasanian and Early Islamic Rule*, Ashgate, 2005

Robinson, Chase F, *Empires and Elites after the Muslim Conquest, The Transformation of Northern Mesopotamia,* Cambridge University Press, 2000

Robinson, James M, *The Nag Hammadi Library, the definitive translation of the Gnostic Scriptures*, Harper San Francisco, USA, 1990

Rodinson, Maxime, *Islam and Capitalism,* Saqi Essentials, 1966

Rubenstein, Richard E, *When Jesus became God*, Harcourt, 1999

Said, Edward W, *Orientalism*. Penguin modern classics, first published by Routledge & Keegan Paul, 1978.

Salzman, Michele Renee, *The Making of a Christian Aristocracy*, Harvard University Press, 2004.

Sand, Shlomo, *The Invention of the Jewish People*, Verso, 2008

Sardar, Ziauddin, *Muhammad,* Hodder Education, London, 2012

Schacht, Joseph, *The Origins of Muhammadan Jurisprudence,* American Council of Learned Societies, first published by Oxford University Press, 1950

Schäfer, Peter, *Jesus in the Talmud,* Princeton University Press, 2007

Schuster, Simon. *The End of Faith*. Simon & Schuster, UK, 2006.

Scroggs, Robin, *The People's Jesus, Trajectories in Early Christianity*. Fortress Press, USA, 2011

Sfar, Mondher, *In Search of the Original Koran, The True History of the Revealed Text,* Prometheus Books, 2008.

Shaban, M A, *Islamic History, A New Interpretation,* Cambridge University Press, 1971

Shanks, Hershel; Dever, William; Halpern, Baruch; McCarter, P Kyle, *The Rise of Ancient Israel*, Biblical Archaeological Society, Washington DC, 1992

Sherwin-White, A N, *Roman Society and Roman Law in the New Testament*, Oxford University Press, 1963

Siddiqi, Dr Nejatullah, *Islamic Public Economics,* Idarah-i Adabiyat-i Delli, Delhi, 2001

Spencer, Robert, *Did Muhammad Exist?,* ISI Books, Deleware, USA, 2012

Stirewalt, M Luther Jnr, *Paul the letter writer,* Eerdmans, USA, 2003

Tabari, *The History of Al-Tabari,* (various trans), State University of New York Press.

Theophanes. See Turtledove, below.

Thompson, Thomas L, *The Mythic Past,* Basic Books, 1999

Thompson, Thomas L, *The Messiah Myth,* Pimlico, 2007

Toynbee, Arnold, *A Study of History,* Oxford University Press, 1939.

Trobisch, David, *Paul's letter collection,* Quiet Waters Publication, USA, 1994

Trocme, Etienne, *The Childhood of Christianity,* SCM Press, 1997

Trotsky, Leon, *History of the Russian Revolution,* Sphere Books edition, 1965.

Turtledove, Harry (editor and translator), *The Chronicles of Theophanes,* University of Pennsylvania Press, 1982

Valantasis, Richard, *The New Q, a fresh translation with commentary,* T & T Clark, 2005

Vermes, Geza (translater), *The complete Dead Sea Scrolls in English,* Penguin, third ed 1987.

Veyne, Paul, *When Our World Became Christian 312-394,* Polity Press, 2010.

Vidal-Naquet, Pierre, *The Jews,* Columbia University Press, 1991, first published 1991.

Walmsley, Alan, *Early Islamic Syria,an Archaeological Assessment,* Duckworth, 2007.

Wansbrough, Henry (ed), *Jesus and the Oral Gospel Tradition,* T & T Clark International, 2004.

Wansbrough, John. *The Sectarian Milieu. Content and Composition of Islamic Salvation History.* Prometheus books, 1986, originally published in 1978 by OUP.

Wardman, Alan, *Religion and Statecraft among the Romans,* Granada, 1982

Watt, W Montgomery, *Muhammad at Mecca,* Oxford University Press, 1953

Weaver, Walter P, *The Historical Jesus in the Twentieth Century, 1900-50,* Trinity Press International, USA, 1999

Welburn, Andrew, *The Beginnings of Christianity,* Floris Books, 1991.

Wellhausen, Julius. *The Arab Kingdom and its Fall.* Curzon Press, London. First published in Berlin, 1902.

Wengst, Klaus, *Pax Romana,* SCM Press, 1987

Wengst, Klaus, *When did Christianity originate,* http://www.jcrelations.net

Whelan, Estelle, *Forgotten Witness: evidence for the early Codification of the Qur'an.* Journal of the American Oriental Society, 1998, Volume 118.

Winter, Bruce W, *Philo and Paul among the Sophists,* Eerdmans, USA, 1997

Wishart, Alfred Wesley, *A Short History of Monks and Monasteries,* General books, 2010, originally published in 1900.

Zahran, Yasmine, *The Lakhmids of Hira,* Stacey International, UK, 2009,

Zayadan, Jurji. *History of Islamic Civilisation Umayyads and Abbasids,* pub by Kitab Bhavan, New Delhi, 1981.

Index